Music in
Latin American Culture

Music in Latin American Culture

Regional Traditions

John M. Schechter, *General Editor*
University of California, Santa Cruz

Contributors
Gage Averill
Larry Crook
William J. Gradante
Ercilia Moreno Chá
Raúl R. Romero
John M. Schechter
T. M. Scruggs
Daniel Sheehy

SCHIRMER BOOKS
An imprint of Macmillan Library Reference USA
New York

To our musician-friends and teachers in Latin America,
those who have guided and inspired us,
and whose story we are privileged to be telling

Except for Figures 6-1, 6-2, 6-3, 7-2, and 7-3, all maps used in this book, including the electronic versions of them, and all of the rights therein, are the property of The Moschovitis Group, Inc., the copyright holder.

SCHIRMER BOOKS
An imprint of Macmillan Library Reference USA
1633 Broadway
New York, NY 10019

Library of Congress Catalog Number: 99-13859

Printed in the United States of America

Printing number:
1   2   3   4   5   6   7   8   9   10

Library of Congress Cataloging-in-Publication Data
Music in Latin American Culture : regional traditions / John M.
   Schechter, general editor.
      p.   cm.
   Includes filmographies, discographies, and bibliographies.
   ISBN 0-02-864750-5
Music—Latin America—History and criticism.   I. Schechter,
John Mendell.
ML 199.M86   1999
780'.98   dc21

                                             99–13859
                                                CIP

This paper meets the requirements of ANSI/NISO Z39.48–1992 (Permanence of Paper).

Contents

6. *Music in the Southern Cone: Chile, Argentina, and Uruguay* **236**

Ercilia Moreno Chá

9. *Beyond Region: Transnational and Transcultural Traditions*   **424**
John M. Schechter

Preface

Music-making is a measure of the regard of one person for another, of one person for a group or community, of one person for a people. Making music enhances our status as human beings. The experience draws us closer to our fellow humans, makes us esteem our community and its traditions of genre, ritual, and instrument. This book consists of the stories of individual music-makings, narratives of the love—expressed through music-making—of father for son, of mother for daughter, of singer for community.

Song is the pure sentiment of a region, a prized flower. In the following chapters, writers who have dedicated years of their lives to studying the musics of a particular Latin American region help you comprehend the nature of those musical sentiments, to learn to savor the unique melodic and rhythmic fragrances of these blossoms emerging from sundry Latin American soils. It is the human interactions that generate these sentiments, that are the stuff of this book and are what make it distinctive.

American readers interested in Latin American music have had, until fairly recently, relatively few sources. While Latin American ethnomusicologists and historical musicologists have produced major authoritative works in the Spanish language, on specific regional musics and musical instruments of particular Latin American countries, substantial English-language works on the music of the entire region have been few. Important milestones have been Robert Stevenson's books on Mexican and Peruvian music, and Gerard Béhague's treatise on Latin American art music. Scholarly journals dedicated to Latin American music, published in the United States, have existed for barely twenty years. Since about 1980, American students of Latin American music have had at their disposal: articles in music encyclopedias on Latin American musical instruments, and on the folk and art music of individual Latin American countries, and of Latin America as a whole; individual chapters on select Latin American music cultures, in textbooks exploring a number of different world music cultures; monographs on Latin American art music, on specific Latin American composers, instruments, or music of a particular country, or on the music of specific Latin American cultures; and journal articles on particular Latin American musical genres, instruments, or music rituals. A recently published encyclopedia volume of *The Garland Encyclopedia of World Music* (1998) is dedicated to Latin America. With country articles written by the authors of *Music in Latin American Culture: Regional Traditions* and by many other scholars, this volume addresses the need for a major music reference work for the entire Latin American region.

Notwithstanding a gradually increasing number of publications dealing with Latin American musical expression, those of us who teach Latin American music to undergraduate students have felt the need for a single volume, usable in the classroom, that would address in clear, accessible language, yet *in some depth*, musical traditions of the major regions of South America, Central America, Mexico, and the Caribbean. The ethnomusicologists who composed the following chapters are equipped to recount the human interactions that reflect and generate these traditions, in the depth sought, with an added vibrancy deriving from their personal experiences living and making music in the regions about which they write.

We decided to model our reporting on the approach of *Worlds of Music: An Introduction to the Music of the World's Peoples* (third edition, 1996). My experience using all three editions of that volume over the years in undergraduate world music courses has revealed the benefits of a single source. The one source would contain abundant classroom-performable musical transcriptions, recorded selections that are discussed in the chapters, biographies and autobiographies of successful regional musicians or music-ritual practitioners, and elaboration of the construction and cultural function of one or more regional musical instruments. Moreover, the idea that depth should prevail over breadth—perhaps the clearest departure of *Worlds of Music* from the approach of many prior world-music survey texts—was one we felt should be preserved, as we sought to present focal Latin American musical traditions we knew well, through our own observation of, and participation in, these traditions.

Chapters 2 through 8 of this book, then, explore regional musics of Latin America. But rather than endeavoring to provide minimal detail on dozens of musical practices within his or her own region, each author offers a framework of necessary geographical and cultural information, then focuses on a small number of music cultures that he or she has studied firsthand in the field. Thus music rituals, instrument-manufacturing processes, and text-improvisational traditions all come alive through the author's own observations. Most importantly, a music region is not so much a block on a map as a large community of people with a common history, a common dialect, a common view toward their own traditions, and perhaps mixed views—often representing generational biases—toward newer musical expressions. Thus, each author introduces you to many individuals from the region, but especially to a close research associate (who used to be called an informant) within the culture, to reveal how, for example, a unique local Colombian band came into existence, or how a Chilean child who grew up singing with her mother came to become expert in the folk musics of her entire country, or how a Jalisco musician developed a successful career in the world of the Mexican *mariachi*.

Chapters 1 and 9 frame these close looks at individual musicians and distinct regions. Chapter 1 suggests that, although Latin American musical expressions share certain features found in all the world's musics, one can identify four themes that are of great consequence in Latin American societies, nuclei around which revolve hundreds of songs and chants from a variety of cultures and traditions. Likewise, Chapter 9 steps out of the smaller circles of the several Latin

American regions to trace broader music-cultural circumferences in Latin America—issues that transcend region, nation, and culture.

Thus, like a biology text with its multiple overlays representing different bodily systems, *Music in Latin American Culture: Regional Traditions* presents a multilayered look at Latin American music and music-making through several different focal planes: geographical breadth (microcultural, regional, and transnational), content (music ritual, music genre, music instrument, and song text), time span (historical and contemporary), and conceptual perspective (cultural and personal).

Music in Latin American Culture: Regional Traditions is designed for use in undergraduate courses in world music, ethnomusicology, Latin American music, Latin American studies, anthropology, folkloristics, and comparative literature. Individual chapters can be singled out (e.g., for a course on the culture and history of Mexico, or of Brazil, or of the Southern Cone). Inasmuch as this book's chapters have been carefully integrated with each other, however, the volume is best appreciated by being used in its entirety over the course of one semester, or perhaps two quarters. Listings of References, Additional Reading, Additional Listening, and/or Additional Viewing at the end of each chapter provide the instructor with materials to broaden the presentation on the particular region under study.

Acknowledgments

I would like to acknowledge the assistance of University of California, Santa Cruz, Arts Division Faculty Services staff members Jennifer Clinton and Cecile Cruz, in preparing numerous drafts and numerous "translations" from different computer program languages. I am grateful to Ercilia Moreno Chá, Gwynne Cropsey, Stephen Snyder, Lara Greene, and Lydia and Héctor Zapana for their comments on drafts of Chapter 1. I owe debts of gratitude to Jill Lectka, formerly acquisitions editor of Schirmer Books, who invited me to submit the proposal for this project, and to Schirmer/Macmillan editors Richard Carlin, Richard Kassel, and Brigitte Pelner for seeing the manuscript to and through production. We are grateful to Peter Kahn for his exacting English translation of Chapter 6. I would like to thank Jeff Todd Titon, general editor of *Worlds of Music: An Introduction to the Music of the World's Peoples,* third edition (Schirmer Books, 1996), for his support of this project in the proposal stage. I thank all of the individual chapter authors for their patience in meeting endless deadlines over a two-year period, and for responding graciously and generously to dozens of requests for outlines, drafts and revised drafts, translations, clarifications, lists, photographs, and more lists. Beyond strictly editorial communications, though, this was an enlightening collaborative endeavor, one that benefited from a continuous and active e-mail exchange of ideas, suggestions, and approaches. Thanks go to my colleagues in the Music Department at UC Santa Cruz for giving me the opportunity to teach, on several occasions, the undergraduate course "Music in Latin American Culture," for which this volume was designed.

Inasmuch as this book deals, ultimately, with individuals, I would like to thank all the individual students at UC Santa Cruz who have expressed for fifteen years their sincere interest in Latin American music and—through our *Taki ñan* and *Voces* ensembles—Latin American music-making. Without your curiosity and, in many cases, strong commitment, this project would never have surfaced. In reaching out with this book to our American university students as they confront the multifarious musics of Latin America, we feel it fitting to express our appreciation here to one person in particular, who, when we were his students, opened the eyes of many of us chapter-authors to the richness and diversity of Latin American musical expression: Gerard Béhague, scholar and mentor. Finally, this book is dedicated by all its authors to our research associates—our musician friends and teachers—in Latin America, who saw our interest, who encouraged us to listen, to try to understand, to study, to practice, and to participate, and who will expect their stories to be told properly. *Les agradecemos su paciencia, su buena voluntad, y su amistad.*

John M. Schechter
Santa Cruz, Calif.
December 29, 1998

CHAPTER ONE

Themes in Latin American Music Culture

John M. Schechter

❧

MUSIC AND MUSICS

Does it make sense to speak of Latin American music? Like any music in the world, a song from Colombia or Argentina will reveal aspects that are at once local, regional, and universal. Anthropologists and cultural musicologists repeatedly have addressed the question of commonalities in all musics. The lullaby, for example, is sung by mothers everywhere—making it probably the most common musical expression in the world. All peoples combine religious activity with music, dance with music, and songs with words (Nettl 1983:40). All members of the human family would probably agree that, as David McAllester has put it, "music transforms experience" (McAllester 1971:380). When you think back to the last time you rehearsed with friends, played in or attended a concert, danced, or simply listened to your favorite compact disc, you will admit that music seems to be "a special kind of time" (Wachsmann 1971:384). Our involvement with music transports us to a realm different from our nonmusical existence. Moreover, we as human beings *are* a musical species (Blacking 1977:21–22), as much as we are a talking, thinking, and working species: we need to be making music as much as we need to be communicating in other ways, nurturing, learning, and teaching.

The world's musics have culturally determined structures—patterns which, like language, involve redundant elements. But music is more than just form and redundancy: it is sensitive to its context (McLeod 1974:108). It is part and parcel of the place and event from which it springs; it echoes with the sentiment of the people who worked to make it—to compose it, to perform it.

Certainly, music-making is a special activity. Singing and playing music have great power; as Mark Slobin points out in his discussion of *"affinity groups,* charmed circles of like-minded music-makers drawn magnetically to a certain genre that creates strong expressive bonding" (1992:72), music has the transcendent power to link us in a special way with our fellow performers, those with whom we share a particular body of music through a common locale, heritage, or simple preference. Music, then, can be an emotional representation of our ties with the community, or our feelings of joy or sadness, or our political stance. Societies use music to communicate with their gods and spirits, to enculturate their infants and youngsters, to tell their history, and to lament their dead. These are some of the many elements that go into making music.

But there are other factors that go into creating *musics*. Particular societies in all times and places have grounded musical styles in the ways they think, in what they believe in, in how they organize their communities, and in what they regard as proper, important, or beautiful. Every established music has criteria for appropriate performance. All of these are regional and local factors. These are the elements we will explore as we try to understand what makes the musics of Latin America "Latin American."

The story of Latin America is unique. Native Americans, Iberians, Africans, and their descendants encountered one another's histories, beliefs, and prejudices, as well as ways of making and using music. In a way, the story of Latin America is told through music: strong feelings of nostalgia and affection, ballads of leaders and heroes, comments on current events and outcries against injustice, and communications with spirits, deities, or ancestors. These accounts interweave to create a fabric of identifiable themes in Latin American music culture.

The threads of this fabric are particular musical units: songs, chants, instrumentals. In the chapters that follow, you will hear these pieces and study them to see how certain kinds of music become emblematic of certain regions and subregions of Latin America. This first chapter examines song-texts, music-cultural aspects, and belief systems, pointing to important thematic patterns in the quilt of Latin American music.

NOSTALGIA

A dominant pattern in this thematic textile is the shape of nostalgia. Hundreds of different Latin American regions, nations, and communities express in song their vivid impressions of past times, their love of place, their frequent praise for the local—local landscapes, women, ways of life, musical instruments. A traditional Ecuadorian song published during the 1880s, "En sumag palacio" [In a beautiful palace] (Example 1–1), sung in the indigenous language of Quechua, has perhaps the woman-singer-composer working in her smoke-filled kitchen, expressing some concern (probably justified) that her son or daughter, now living in a "beautiful palace," not forget his/her humble roots—their mother's poor rural home; that as s/he now eats rich food, the original diet of toasted corn, a staple in rural Ecuador, must not be forgotten (Jiménez de la Espada 1883: XXXIII–XXXV) (Example 1–1, "En sumag palacio").

Ex. 1–1. "En sumag palacio"

En sumag palacio	In a beautiful palace
Cuxxnico (kushnijun)	(it is getting smoky)
Causajunguimi	You are living
Ñuka chaglla (chuglla) guasi	My poor tiny house
Cuxxnico (kushnijun)	(it is getting smoky)
Yuyaringuimi.	You will remember.
Sumag pan de huevo	Beautiful eggbread
Cuxxnico (kushnijun)	(it is getting smoky)
Micujunguimi	You are eating
Ñuka sara cancha (kamcha)	My toasted corn
Cuxnico (kushnijun)	(it is getting smoky)
Yuyaringuimi.	You will remember.

Migrating from one's homeland frequently provokes nostalgic thoughts of one's roots, one's home village, town, or province. For example, in the *chacareras* of Argentina we find many expressions of migrants to Buenos Aires from the rural provinces of the country. A powerful example is provided in the following stanzas from the *chacarera doble* (longer than the typical *chacarera*) "Añoranzas" [Nostalgias, longings], as sung by the ensemble Los Tucu-Tucu (Example 1–2).

Missing dearly one's ranch, one's trees, one's "beloved ground." An echo of this idea of migrants' fondness for their "beloved ground" can be heard in "Asa-branca" (White wing), a song by Brazilian accordionist-singer Luiz Gonzaga. For a discussion of the nostalgic character of this song, see Chapter 5.

On a cold night in December 1979 in the rural highlands outside Cotacachi, Ecuador (near Lake San Pablo and Lake Cuicocha), on the slopes of Mount Cotacachi, I heard the sounds of an *albazo,* a type of rhythmic dance music known throughout the country, coming from saxophones, accordion, and trumpet on a pick-up truck as it approached my house. Sure enough, it was the much-loved "Aires de mi tierra" [Songs of my land] (Example 1–3).

What makes this such a stirring evocation of the region of Imbabura, Ecuador? First, the verses allude to prominent aspects of the region's topography—magnificent mountains, one of which gave its name to the province, and beautiful lakes. Second, there is a reference to the *rondador,* a single-rank panpipe typical of Ecuador (the double-rank panpipe is used in the southern Andes of Peru and Bolivia). Third, there is an explicit reference to the town of Cotacachi, a village (and surroundings) considered by many Ecuadorians as a "music-box" for its abundance of music-making. Finally, there is the making-sacred of the musical relic in the concluding stanza: the emotion-laden songs of Cotacachi attain, in the singers' minds, an almost holy aura.

Ex. 1–2.   "Añoranzas"

Cuando salí de Santiago

When I left [the province or city of] Santiago [del Estero]

Todo el camino lloré
Lloré sin saber por qué,
Pero, sí, les aseguro
Que mi corazón es duro,
Pero aquel día aflojé.

I cried the whole way,
I cried without knowing why,
But, yes, I assure you all
That my heart is strong,
But on that day I let go.

Dejé mi suelo querido,
El rancho donde nací,
Donde tan feliz viví
Alegremente cantando,
De entonces vivo llorando,
Igualito que el crespín.

I left my beloved ground,
The ranch where I was born,
Where so happily I lived
Joyfully singing,
Since then I live weeping,
Like the *crespín* [a bird].

Los años ni la distancia
Jamás pudieron lograr
De mi memoria apartar
Y hacer que te eche al olvido;
¡Ay! Mi Santiago querido,
Yo añoro tu quebrachal.

Neither the years nor the distance
Ever were able successfully
To remove you from my memory
And cast you to oblivion;
Ay! My beloved Santiago,
I miss your *quebrachal* [large group of trees of very hard wood].

Mañana, cuando me muera,
Si alguien se acuerda de mí,
Paisano, le voy a pedir,
Si quieren darme la gloria,
Que toquen a mi memoria
La doble que canto aquí.
. . .

Tomorrow, when I die,
If anyone remembers me,
Paisano, I'm going to ask of you,
That if they wish to help me attain Heaven,
That they should play in my memory
This "tolling" that I sing right here.
. . .

Tal vez en el camposanto
No hay un lugar para mí,
Paisano, le voy a pedir,
Antes que llegue el momento,
Tírenme en el campo abierto,
Pero allí donde nací.

Perhaps in the cemetery
There is no place for me,
Paisano, I'm going to ask of you,
Before the moment arrives,
That they just toss me into an open field,
But that it be *there,* where I was born.

Held high on a pedestal of place, along with home and landscape, are a region's women and their beauty. In "Cuzqueñita," a Peruvian *wayno* from the Cuzco region, the women and the place are honored as one (Pagaza Galdo 1967:21) (Example 1–4).

Sometimes the region's women are combined into one, who is given a name and takes her role in a distilled love ballad, as with "María Antonia" in this Colom-

Ex. 1–3. "Aires de mi tierra"

Música nacida	Music born
De montes y lagos	Of mountains and lakes
Con la dulce magia	With the sweet magic
De los rondadores,	Of the *rondadores,*
Aires de mi tierra	Songs of my land
Ecos del recuerdo	Echoes of the recollection
Tesoro escondido	Hidden treasure
En mi Cotacachi,	In my Cotacachi,
Que recoge el sol	That the sun picks up
Y le vuelve a Dios	And restores to God
Con suspiración hecho bendición	With a longing made into a blessing
Para este Ecuador.	For this Ecuador.
. . .	. . .

bian *bambuco* sung by the famous duo of Garzón and Collazos (Example 1–5; see also Chapter 7).

At other moments the man's beloved is truly exalted, being considered his salvation, unforgettable, as in "Negrita," a *danza* by Garzón y Collazos (Example 1–6).

Similarly, the region's personified woman, with whom the singer is in love, may metaphorically provide him with sustenance to live, as in "Como el rocío," a *pasillo* (a type of waltz) from the African-Ecuadorian community of the Chota River Valley in the northern highlands (Example 1–7).

In addition to a region's home, landscape, and women, its musical instruments and its ways of life may contribute to the nostalgia configuration. "Arpita de mis canciones," another Ecuadorian *albazo*, underscores the presence and importance of the harp in music-making throughout the highland regions of that country: "Arpita de mis canciones, de mis delirios, vibrando allí en otro tiempo, se hizo pedazos" [Dear harp of my songs, of my wild times, vibrating so powerfully there in another time, it ended up in pieces]. Chapter 5 will reveal how the *pífano,* a transverse cane fife and a staple of Northeast-Brazilian Zabumba fife-and-drum

Ex. 1–4. "Cuzqueñita"

Cuzqueñita de mi vida	Dear Cuzco woman of my life
Linda morena	Pretty brunette
Todo mi encanto	Entirely delightful
Hermosa ñusta	Beautiful [Incaic] princess
La flor andina.	Andean flower.
. . .	. . .

Ex. 1–5.   "María Antonia"

María Antonia es la ventera	María Antonia is the seller,
Más linda que he conocido,	The prettiest [one] I've ever known,
Tiene una tienda de besos	She has a shop of kisses
Al otro lado del río.	At the other side of the river.
A donde voy todos los días	Where I go every day
Desde antes que salga el sol	From before sunrise
A comprarle a María Antonia	To buy from María Antonia
Todos sus besos de amor.	All her kisses of love.
. . .	. . .

bands, came to serve as a nostalgic symbol for the Pernambuco homeland, among Northeast-Brazilian migrants working in São Paulo. The Colombian *cumbia* "El alegre pescador" [The happy fisherman] paints a picture of the coastal ways of life that are the traditional backdrop for this African-Colombian-Panamanian musical genre (Example 1–8).

It is specific regional words—the Quechua terms *chuglla guasi, sara kamcha,* and *ñusta,* the Spanish terms *chinchorro y atarraya, quebrachal,* and *crespín*—as well as topographical features (mountains, lakes, rivers) and even musical instruments (harp) that point to the distinct regions from which these songs emanate. Their inclusion in these musical expressions in a context of nostalgia helps to generate the strong sense of affection the singer has for his region. Listening to these

Ex. 1–6.   "Negrita"

Negrita, tú viniste en la noche	Negrita, you came in the night
De mi amargo penar,	Of my bitter suffering,
Tú llegaste a mi vida	You arrived in my life
Y borraste la herida	And erased the wound
De mi pena letal.	Of my lethal grief.
. . .	. . .
Negrita, pasarán muchos días	Negrita, many days will go by,
Muchos años, quizás,	Many years, perhaps,
Y grabada en mi vida,	And engraved in my life,
Llevaré yo escondida tu sonrisa	Hidden, I will carry your immortal smile.
inmortal.	
Nadie puede tu imagen	No one can tear
De mi pecho arrancar,	Your image from my breast,
Adorada y cautiva, estarás en	Worshipped and captive, you will remain in
mi vida	my life
Hasta la eternidad.	Until eternity.

Ex. 1–7. "Como el rocío"

Te quiero con el alma
Te quiero con dulzura
Te juro por mi vida
Tuyo es mi corazón.

. . .

Te quiero con el alma,
Con mucho sentimiento
Que mi amor es tan fuerte
Que rompe mi alegría.

Yo soy como las flores
Y tú, como el agua
Eres como el rocío
Que das vida a mi vida.

I love you with my soul,
I love you with a special sweetness,
I swear on my life
My heart is yours.

. . .

I love you with my soul,
With great feeling,
My love is so strong
That it tears asunder my joy.

I am like the flowers
And you, like the water,
You are like the dew
That gives life to my life.

cumbias, waynos, pasillos, bambucos, and *albazos,* you get the feeling that the singers' home region is the very essence of their lives.

DESCRIPTIVE BALLADRY

Continuing to examine this thematic cloth of Latin American musics, we find another locally distinctive marking or design—that of descriptive balladry, storytelling focusing on local figures, human (heroes or scoundrels) or animal. Going back to the time of the Incas, who ruled the Andean regions of South America

Ex. 1–8. "El alegre pescador"

Subiendo la corriente
Con chinchorro y atarraya
La canoa de bahareque
Para llegar a la playa.

La luna espera sonriente
Con su mágico esplendor,
La llegada del valiente,
El alegre pescador.

El pescador . . . habla con la luna,
El pescador . . . habla con la playa,
El pescador . . . no tiene fortuna,
Sólo su atarraya.

. . .

Going up the current
With his hammock and net[s]
The homemade canoe
To arrive at the beach.

The moon awaits, smiling,
With its magic splendor,
The arrival of the brave one,
The happy fisherman.

The fisherman . . . converses with the moon,
The fisherman . . . converses with the beach,
The fisherman . . . has no wealth,
Only his net[s].

. . .

before their conquest by the Spaniards in the sixteenth century, Latin Americans have been careful to recount in detail the exploits of their leaders and heroes, even minutely detailing features of regional animals and birds. This balladic tendency encompasses both an indigenous heritage of aural tradition and an imported, Iberian heritage.

There were several forms of indigenous musical history-recounting activity recorded for the preconquest and sixteenth-century Americas. The Native Americans on the island of Hispaniola performed *areíto* song-dances, in which they recounted past events, notably the lives of their chiefs. Similarly, natives of the preconquest regions of today's Mexico (Aztec), Nicaragua-Honduras, Colombia (Chibcha), Paraguay, Peru (Inca), and North America (Kwakiutl) had varying forms of historical song-performance (Simmons 1960, Boas 1927). Among the Inca of Peru, this type of *cantar histórico* [historical chant] was an established tradition. Their *harahuicus*, or rhetorically gifted poets, sang verses on Inca history at the Incas' June solstice festival of *Inti Raymi* [Feast of the sun]. Moreover, upon the death of an *Inca* (the leader of the Inca empire), the *harahuicus* would learn the exploits of the late monarch and compose a historical song of praise, a song placing the events of his life in careful order. The bard would then chant this song to the new leader and his royal family, or to large gatherings of people from throughout the empire, so that all could be informed of what the previous Inca had accomplished (Schechter 1979:193–194).

The Iberians brought to this hemisphere the *romance* ballad form, which dates back to the fourteenth century in Spain. Multiple versions of sixteenth-century Spanish *romances,* such as "Blanca Flor y Filomena" (based on a Greek legend— see Chapter 6) can still be found today in Chile (Barros y Dannemann 1970:61–70). Chapter 6 describes how "Blanca Flor y Filomena" is sung today to the music of the Chilean *tonada.*

There have been other approaches to this ballad form, apart from preserving vintage examples from the Iberian peninsula. The Spanish epic poem "El Cid" (ca.1140 A.D.) described the exploits of Ruy Diaz de Bivar, an eleventh-century champion of Christianity against the Moors, in 3,735 lines of exact, picturesque detail. But Argentines, Mexicans, and Chileans have exalted the exploits of their own noteworthy figures in briefer accounts which nevertheless feature telling localisms, along with exploits. We find, for instance, several Robin Hood figures in Argentina and Mexico, local heroes who took from the rich to give to the poor. Heráclio Bernal is a major Robin Hood figure in the Mexican *corrido* ballad tradition (see McDowell 1972:208–214), and Joaquín Murieta is another. Murieta, who frequented California *por el año del cincuenta* [around 1850] describes his activities in the *corrido* "Joaquín Murieta" (Sonnichsen 1975:5) (Example 1–9).

As Ercilia Moreno Chá discusses in Chapter 6 of this book, Juan Bautista Bairoleto assumed the same role in twentieth-century La Pampa province, Argentina, as the fourth *décima* (ten-line stanza) of the ballad-like *milonga* sung to his memory describes: "Sacaste al que más tenía. Y con esa gran hombría al pobre

Ex. 1–9.   "Joaquín Murieta"

A los ricos avarientos	From the greedy rich
Yo les quité su dinero.	I took away their money.
Con los humildes y pobres	With the humble and poor
Yo me quité mi sombrero.	I took off my hat.
Ay, qué leyes tan injustas	Oh, what laws so unjust
Fué llamarme bandolero.	to call me a highwayman.

diste sustento." [You took from him who had the most. And with that great manliness you gave sustenance to the poor.]

Among the Texas-Mexican border *corridos,* unquestionably the most widely known—"the epitome of the Border *corrido*" (Paredes 1976:31)—is "Gregorio Cortez." Following a shootout in June 1901 likely based on miscommunication, Gregorio Cortez escaped, having shot the sheriff who moments earlier had shot Cortez's brother. Riding some four hundred miles and walking about a hundred more along the Río Grande, Cortez eluded the hundreds intent on his capture. The twenty to thirty quatrains of this *corrido* highlight the emotional core of the saga in stanzas such as those recounting his insistence on the right to self-defense, his escape from three hundred pursuers, and his final surrender (65–66) (Example 1–10).

Where the Argentine *milonga* "A Juan Bautista Bairoleto" includes references to the horses and storms of the *pampa* of that country, "Gregorio Cortez" situates its story by means of border phrases in which English and Spanish cohabit: *perros jaundes* [hound dogs], *sherifes* [sheriffs], *rinches cobardes* [cowardly Texas Rangers].

Ex. 1–10.   "Gregorio Cortez"

Decía Gregorio Cortez	Then said Gregorio Cortez
Con su alma muy encendida	With his soul aflame
—No siento haberlo matado	—I don't regret having killed him
La defensa es permitida.—	Self-defense is permitted.—
. . .	. . .
Se fue de Belmont al rancho	From Belmont he went to the ranch
Lo alcanzaron a rodear	Where they succeeded in surrounding him
Poquitos más de trescientos	Quite a few more than three hundred
Y allí les brincó el corral.	But he jumped out of their corral.
. . .	. . .
Cuando rodearon la casa	When they surrounded the house
Cortez se les presentó:	Cortez appeared before them:
—Por la buena sí me llevan	—You will take me if I'm willing
Porque de otro modo no.—	But not any other way.—

The hero/outlaw tradition—even the three hundred men pursuing the coura- geous protagonist—find an echo in "El aparecido" [The phantom], a 1967 song alluding to Ernesto "Che" Guevara, written and sung by Chilean composer and martyr Víctor Jara. Here, instead of an outlaw and a localized border setting of cultural conflict, there is a revolutionary figure being pursued in the broader con- text of international political strife. Whereas "Gregorio Cortez" has no chorus—it is a *romance corrido,* a *romance* run straight through with no refrain, based on the form existing in Andalusia at the time of the Conquest—"El aparecido" has a re- frain. The fleeing revolutionary is told to stay on the run, or he will be killed (Ex- ample 1–11).

Interestingly, whereas ballads (including Texas-Mexican border *corridos*) are often performed deadpan, without emotion in the singing, Víctor Jara sings the story of "El aparecido" with great emotional intensity, climaxing with the "Run, run, run!" refrain.

There are all kinds of heroes. Víctor Jara wrote another song in the biographi- cal/ballad tradition to praise the skill of an unknown Mapuche (Chilean Native American) woman weaver, "Angelita Huenumán." The irony is immediately obvi-

Ex. 1–11.   "El aparecido"

Abre sendas por los cerros	He opens pathways through the mountains,
Deja su huella en el viento,	He leaves his trace on the wind,
El águila le da el vuelo	The eagle gives him flight,
Y lo cobija el silencio.	And the silence blankets him.
Nunca se quejó del frío,	He never complained of the cold,
Nunca se quejó del sueño,	He never complained of lack of sleep,
El pobre siente su paso	The poor man senses his step
Y lo sigue como ciego.	And follows him like a blind man.
¡Córrele, córrele, correlá,	Run, run, run,
Por aquí, por allí, por allá!	Here, there, over there!
¡Córrele, córrele, correlá,	Run, run, run,
Córrele, que te van a matar!	Run, for they are going to kill you!
¡Córrele, córrele, correlá,	Run, run, run,
Córrele, que te van a matar!	Run, for they are going to kill you!
¡Córrele, córrele, correlá!	Run, run, run!
. . .	
Hijo de la rebeldía,	Offspring of rebelliousness,
Lo siguen veinte más veinte,	Twenty, and twenty more pursue him,
Porque él regala su vida	Because he donates his life
Ellos le quieren dar muerte.	They wish to give him death.
¡Córrele, córrele, correlá!	Run, run, run!
. . .	. . .

ous: we now have a carefully elaborated account not of a cultural icon like El Cid, Gregorio Cortez, or Che Guevara, but of an isolated private artisan. Jara's eight verses laud not the skills of avoiding pursuers, but rather the skills of a gifted weaver of blankets. "Her hands danc[ing] in the hemp, like the wings of a little bird, she weaves a flower so miraculously, that you can smell its perfume. Angelita, in your weaving, there is time and tears and sweat, there are the anonymous hands of my own creative people." Jara carefully shades the hues of this local picture, noting how "la sangre roja del copihue corre en sus venas, Huenumán" [the red blood of the *copihue*[1] tree runs in your veins, Señora Huenumán].

Finally, there are examples in which the ballad tradition serves not to praise at all but to condemn, to bring to the ear of the listening public despicable traits of notoriety. Such is the case with the recently composed Ecuadorian Quechua song, "Antonio Mocho" (Schechter 1991) (Example 1–12).

This highly distilled ballad, a type of *sanjuanito* (*cf.* Schechter 1996:447–465), was composed by Segundo ("Galo") Maigua of Ilumán, in the northern highlands of Ecuador. Galo Maigua is a well-known musician throughout his home province of Imbabura. I recorded this song with him and some colleagues in Ilumán on September 16, 1990. Galo Maigua explained to me that the subject of the song, Antonio Mocho, was a local character who had achieved notoriety for beating his wife, despite pleadings by the community that he stop. Regrettably, as Regina Harrison has documented, wife abuse is not uncommon in the Andes, as the theme frequently emerges in the Quechua women's songs she has studied (1989:127–134). Antonio, himself a guitarist, was once rehearsing with Galo Maigua. A dispute arose as to whose technique was superior; in the ensuing fight, Galo threatened Mocho with—*music.* He told Mocho that he would compose a song, so that everyone in Imbabura province would become aware of Mocho's abusive behavior. Galo succeeded in his musical vengeance: Antonio Mocho, who

Ex. 1–12.   "Antonio Mocho"

Antonio Mocho machashka yalijun,	Drunk, Antonio Mocho goes on ahead,
Antonio Mocho machashka yalijun.	Drunk, Antonio Mocho goes on ahead.
Rusa Milapaj ishtangupi machashka,	Drunk in Rusa Mila's tavern,
Rusa Milapaj ishtangupi machashka.	Drunk in Rusa Mila's tavern.
Warmita makangapaj rijushka,	He went in order to hit his wife,
Warmita makangapaj rijushka.	He went in order to hit his wife.
José Mono machashka jarkajun,	José Mono, drunk, is detaining him,
José Mono machashka jarkajun.	José Mono, drunk, is detaining him.
Alkaldi-kaldi nishkami fawajun,	The so-called "mayor" is jumping on him,
Alkaldi-kaldi nishkami fawajun.	The so-called "mayor" is jumping on him.

was still alive in 1990, could walk the streets of Imbabura and hear countless people singing of how he beat his wife.

We have seen, then, how storytelling—extolling local, regional, or international heroes, but also lauding the artistry of certain unknown local characters, or speaking to the despicable traits of others—has been and remains a significant block in the quilt that is Latin American expressive culture. There is a different, if related, submotif of the Latin American descriptive, storytelling tradition: tales involving local animals and birds. An Andean Quechua myth dating back to the seventeenth century praised animals associated with the highlands—condors, pumas, and falcons. A 1975 version of this same myth still finds praise for the condor and the puma (Harrison 1989:103, 105). A Quechua song that Regina Harrison recorded in southern Andean Ecuador in 1975 (Example 1–13) relates in detail the significant attributes of the several animals the principal speaker encounters in the story: turkey buzzard, sparrow hawk, and Andean deer (all high-Andean creatures), as well as the toad (a creature of both lowland and highland elevations) (ibid., 105–106) (Example 1–13).

Another Andean animal song focuses not on animals associated with abduction, such as the turkey buzzard, but rather on a beloved livestock member—the sheep. Notice, as you read the words to "Ñuka llama di mi vida" [My sheep (not

Ex. 1–13.

Ushkitulla	Little ol' turkey buzzard,
puka washalla	red back,
sañi cristalla	dark-colored breast,
sañi chakilla	dark-colored feet,
ichapashlla kansitu	by any chance did you
ñu wawita rikurkangi?	see my baby?
Mana mana amiguita.	No, no, my friend.
Mana rikushkanichu	No, I haven't seen
kambak wawitata.	your baby.
Gavilansituta tapuy,	Ask the sparrow hawk,
ichapashlla paysitu rikurka.	perhaps he saw the child.
Gavilansitulla	Little ol' sparrow hawk,
kuchillu pikulla	knifelike beak,
yurak washalla	white back,
sañi chaquilla	dark-colored feet,
ichapashlla kansitu	by any chance, did you
ñu wawitata rikurkangi?	see my baby?
Mana, mana amiguita,	No, no, my friend,
mana rikushkanichu	no, I haven't seen
kambak wawitata.	your baby.
. . .	. . .

Ex. 1–14. "Ñuka llama di mi vida"

Ñuka llamagu chingashka Nachu kaiguma shamupan, (repeat couplet) . . .	My lost sheep It comes here, doesn't it? . . .
Ñuka llama di mi vida Putu chupagu kaparka. (repeat couplet)	My sheep of my life It had a short tail.
Ñuka llama di mi vida Chimbulu sikigu kaparka. (repeat couplet)	My sheep of my life It had a rear with clover-shaped thorns.
Ñuka llama di mi vida Piruru kachugu kaparka. (repeat couplet)	My sheep of my life It had a twisted horn.
Ñuka llama di mi vida Chilpi rinrigu kaparka. (repeat couplet)	My sheep of my life It had a split ear.
Ñuka llama di mi vida Chilpi sillugu kaparka. (repeat couplet) . . .	My sheep of my life It had a split hoof. . . .

llama) of my life] (Example 1–14), that this song, which I recorded just four years after Harrison's "Turkey Buzzard" song, observes the same oral-traditional process—that of detailed physical description of a prominent local animal or bird. In fact, "Ñuka llama" even has the same theme as the turkey buzzard song—loss—but here it is loss of the focal animal itself, not the loss of a mother's baby. The singer's recitation of the sheep's various features, punctuated with the refrain of affection, "my sheep of my life," shows the degree of fondness felt in the Imbabura region for these critically important creatures, which are typically herded by the likewise beloved little children (Schechter 1982:410–411).

And finally, there's a song/story that seems to combine the great leader with the bird, a song that also illustrates the often substantial continuity of songs in Latin American oral tradition. Here are two versions of what was called "Atahualpa Huañui" in Ecuador in 1868 (Example 1–15). In 1979, the same song was called "Ruku kuskungu" (Mera 1868:14–16, Schechter 1982:432–433; English translations, Schechter 1982:566–567, and Harrison 1996:97–98).

Ex. 1–15.   **"Atahualpa Huañui/Ruku Kuskungu"**

"Ruku Kuskungu," recorded by J. Schechter in December 1979 at a Quechua child's wake outside Cotacachi

"Atahualpa Huañui" in Juan León Mera's *Ojeada histórico crítica sobre la poesía ecuatoriana*, 1868

Ruku kuskungu	The old owl	Rucu cuscungu	The old owl
Jawa pakaipi	In his nest above	Jatum pacaipi	In his large nest
Wañui wakaita	His death-wail	Huañui huacaihuan	With his death-wail
Wakajunmari	Is wailing, indeed.	Huacacurcami.	Was wailing.
Urpi wawapash	And the dove-child	Urpi huahuapas	And the tender dove, too
Janaj pachapi	In Heaven	Janac yurapi	Up in the tree
Wañui wakaita	Its death-wail	Llaqui llaquilla	Sad, sad
Wakajunmari	Is wailing, indeed.	Huacacurcami.	Was wailing.
Puma shunguwan	With a puma heart	Puyu puyulla	Like a cloud, a cloud
Atuj makiwan	With a wolf's paws	Uiracuchami	The white [Spanish] men
Llamata shina	Like a sheep	Curita nishpa,	Gold, saying,
Tukuchirkami.	They did him in.	Jundarircami.	They were filled up with.
Kurraljundailla	The corral just filled	Inca yayata	The Inca leader
Llamakunapa	With sheep	Japicuchishpa	They grabbed him
Illai illarni	None at all	Siripayashpa	Laying him out
Kidajurkami.	Remained.	Huañuchircami.	They killed him.
Achi taitaka	The godfather	**Puma shunguhuan**	With courage of a puma
Wakajunmari	Is crying, indeed	**Atuc maquihuan**	With force of a fox
Llaki llakilla	Very sad	**Llamata shina**	Like a sheep
Tiyajujunmari.	He is, indeed, certainly.	**Tucuchircami.**	They did him in.
		Runduc urmashpa	While the hail fell
		Illapantashpa	The lightning struck
		Inti yaicushpa	The sun set
		Tutayarcami.	It got dark.
		Amauta cuna	The wise elders
		Mancharicushpa	Being frightened
		Causac runahuan	The men, still alive
		Pamparircami.	Buried themselves.

Ex. 1–15. "Atahualpa Huañui/Ruku Kuskungu" (continued)

Imashinata	How
Mana llaquisha	Shall I not lament
Ñuca llactapi	Seeing my community
Shucta ricushpa.	Possessed by another?
Turi cunalla	Among brothers
Tandanacushun,	We unite
Yahuar pampapi	On the plain of blood
Huacanacushun.	We weep.
Inca yayalla,	Inca leader
Janac pachapi	In the site above [Heaven]
Ñuca llaquilla	My sadness
Ricungui yari.	Observe it, indeed.
Caita yuyashpa	Contemplating all this
Mana huañuni.	Yet I'll not die.
Shungu llugshishpa	My heart withered,
Causaricuni.	Yet I continue to live.

The dramatic reference in the nineteenth-century version of this song to the murder of the last Inca, Atahualpa, at the hands of the Spaniards ("The Inca leader, they grabbed him, laying him out, they killed him") has attracted the attention of many writers. Regina Harrison has carefully analyzed this version for literary aspects that reflect the possibilities of either a Quechua author (the poem's ample parallelisms) or an Iberian-Ecuadorian author (Christian aspects). For our discussion, we should emphasize the presence of several animals and birds within this mournful story. The owl, a harbinger of death in Quechua culture, and the dove, an Andean symbol of love, both mourn the Inca's death. The puma and the fox (wolf) are feared in the Andes for their force and brutal nature, as the turkey buzzard was famed as a creature of abduction (Harrison 1996:93–103).

It is interesting that the modern version *does not* retain the references to the "Inca leader," but it *does* preserve verses from the 1868 version, particularly the **"Puma shunguwan"** strophe (marked in boldface type). And the Cotacachi Quechua musicians added the last stanza in the 1979 version ("Achi taitaka . . ."), where they take the "wailing" theme of the original song and apply it to the deceased infant's godfather standing in the doorway of the deceased's home, lamenting not the death of the Inca leader, but the death of this man's own godchild. We can see how this one song, in its two different versions, both exemplifies our ballad thematic pattern and illustrates the workings of an indigenous oral tradition in Latin America.

COMMENTARY ON CURRENT EVENTS, AND OUTRAGE AT INJUSTICE

Latin Americans also express in song their consciousness of current events in general, and their outrage at perceived injustices in particular. Eduardo Carrasco Pirard, artistic director of the Chilean ensemble Quilapayún, commented that "there can be no important event in the history of the people of Latin America that is not reflected in a song" (1982:612). Certain genres or types of Latin American music are famous in this regard, for example, the Trinidadian calypso, the Mexico-Texas border *corrido,* and the *Nueva Canción* (New Song) movement, the latter of which will be discussed in depth in Chapter 9 of this book. But we also find a preoccupation with current political events in Peruvian protest songs, and in many other genres of Latin American music. Let us take a look at some examples of these musical-political expressions and the circumstances that produced them.

The dynamically multiethnic society that is Trinidad, with its successive immigrations by black Africans, Spaniards, French Caribbean creoles, East Indians, and British over the last three hundred years has produced a rich musical heritage in which the highly topical calypso carries elements of all these traditions. Calypsos are sung in the Trinidadian vernacular, which includes both English and French patois. A recent book on calypso defines it as "any song that after about 1898 was sung at Carnival time in Trinidad, either in the streets by revelers or in staged performances by semiprofessional and professional singers" (Hill 1993:3). Calypso songs, sung by celebrated artists such as Lord Executor (García) and Atilla (Raymond Quevedo), typically describe a particular incident. The calypso's economy of words, satire, wit, and strong rhythmic syncopation make the genre unique. Samuel Charters's collection of recordings, *The Real Calypso: 1927–1946* (Folkways RF 13, 1966), includes calypsos recorded in the 1930s and 1940s, with pieces commenting on Bing Crosby, the Mills Brothers, the first Louis-Schmeling fight, and United States imperialism. The United States built a naval base and airfield in Trinidad in 1941, and its soldiers frequented the Carnival tents. Calypso singers commented on these American soldiers, whose postwar pockets were loaded with dollars (Hill 1993:208, 218)—thus, Lord Invader's calypso, "Yankee Dollar," recorded in 1946 (Example 1–16).

We have already seen, with "Gregorio Cortez" and "Joaquín Murieta," how the Mexico-Texas *corridos* served to convey noteworthy news in the border region, with its cultural conflict between *mejicanos* and *anglos* in the nineteenth and twentieth centuries. But it was not only *mejicano* heroes who were recorded for posterity in *corridos.* In its roughly 150-year history, the border *corrido* also recorded many current events and commented on labor-migration trends, the changing images of woman (see Chapter 9), and even the death of John F. Kennedy. The "Corrido Pensilvanio" opens with the singer about to leave Texas and a life of picking cotton, heading north—not on a cattle drive, but bound for the new land of "Pensilvania." In the 1920s, the steel industry that developed in Bethlehem, Pennsylvania, began importing Mexican labor from Texas; these un-

Ex. 1–16. "Yankee Dollar"

I had a pretty baby who confessed she loved me,
And she's from respectable family,
And she said that she had a soldier
Who was treating her much better,
Uh huh, she don't want no native fella.

So she told me plainly,
She love Yankee money,
And she said, Lord Invader,
Money for to find rum and coca-cola,
Don't bother, if you know you ain't
Got the Yankee dollar.

I started to chide the lady,
I pleaded so impressively,
I showed her a lot of English money,
But she made me to understand
She don't want no Trinidadian,
He must be an American or either a Puerto Rican.

So she told me plainly,
She love Yankee money

. . .

witting workers were recruited via *enganches,* labor contracts which enrolled laborers for risky endeavors under false pretenses (Sonnichsen 1975:11) (Example 1–17).

In "El Lavaplatos," a *corrido* of the 1930s, the protagonist has a more variegated migratory career, evidently entailing greater suffering. The young man in "El Lavaplatos" dreams of leaving Mexico for Hollywood to become a movie star. He ends up working in railroad construction, picking vegetables on his knees, laboring in the cement industry, and washing dishes, only to return, much disillusioned, to his native Mexico (Sonnichsen 1975:9). This message of disillusionment with the promises of the United States is still relevant today.

We temper our initial surprise, perhaps, on discovering a series of *corridos* written in 1963 and 1964, after the tragic death of President John F. Kennedy, when we realize that he was "a symbol of a minority—Irish Catholic—making it in American society" (Dickey 1978:21). Dan Dickey, who made a study of this special, chronologically pointed series of *corridos,* comments that the composers of the Kennedy *corridos* highlighted certain themes of Kennedy's life and character, themes shared by the great majority of Mexican-Americans—that Kennedy was to be praised as a champion of equal rights for all, that he made clear gestures

Ex. 1–17.   "Corrido Pensilvanio"

El día 28 de abril	The 28th day of April
A las seis de la mañana	At six o'clock in the morning
Salimos en un enganche	We left under contract
Pa'l estado de Pensilvania.	For the state of Pennsylvania.
. . .	. . .
"Adiós, estado de Texas	"Goodbye, state of Texas
Con toda tu plantación.	With all your fields.
Ya me voy pa' Pensilvania	I'm going to Pennsylvania
Por no piscar algodón."	To keep from picking cotton."
. . .	. . .

to Mexican culture and to Mexican-Americans, and that he struggled and ultimately sacrificed his life for his ideals and for his people (48–53). Indeed, in
Dickey's view, Mexican-Americans "saw themselves in a shoulder-to-shoulder
struggle alongside with Kennedy . . . because of the cultural and religious bond
they felt with Kennedy" (53). Here are several verses of the Kennedy *corrido*
by José A. Morante who, like Kennedy, served with the American armed forces
during World War II. This was among the largest-selling of the seventeen
recorded Kennedy *corridos* (82–84) (Example 1–18).

This *corrido* observes several conventions of the classic Mexico-Texas border
variety—the use of eight-syllable stanzas, rhyming **a b c b;** the hero depicted as a
peaceful man; mention of the time and place of the event; and the use of formal
opening ("I sing of") and closing ("This is the terrible story") phrases (Dickey
1978:14, 38, 42).

The outrage expressed in song by the *corridista* composers of the Kennedy
corridos was echoed some six years later in Chile, when Víctor Jara (recall "El
aparecido") cried out in song ("Preguntas por Puerto Montt") against an attack
upon ninety-one unarmed Chilean peasant families in the port city of Puerto
Montt on March 9, 1969, an attack in which eight were killed and sixty injured.

Ex. 1–18.   José Morante's "Kennedy Corrido"

Como homenaje sincero	As a sincere homage
Canto su vida y su muerte	I sing of the life and the death
Del hombre que el mundo llora	Of a man for whom the world weeps
Porque fue un gran presidente.	Because he was a great president.
Kennedy tuvo la dicha	Kennedy had the good fortune
De demostrar su valor	Of showing his bravery
En la guerra que pasara	In the war which took place
El año cuarenta y dos.	In the year of forty-two.

Ex. 1–18.   José Morante's "Kennedy Corrido" (continued)

Fue comandante de un barco	He was the captain of a vessel
En las islas del Oriente;	In the islands of the East;
Nunca soñaba que un día	He never dreamed that one day
Podría ser el Presidente.	He would attain the presidency.
Anduvo por todo el mundo	He traveled all over the world
No hubo enemigo capaz	There was no enemy capable
De atentar contra su vida	Of making an attempt on the life
De este gigante de paz.	Of this giant of peace.
. . .	. . .
México le abrió sus brazos	Mexico opened its arms to him
Como a ninguno jamás	As it had never done for anyone before
Y Kennedy hizo justicia	And Kennedy did justice
Regresando el Chamizal.	By returning the Chamizal [a disputed border area].
. . .	. . .
El veintidós de noviembre	The twenty-second of November
No se me podrá olvidar	I cannot forget
Porque sin causa o razones	Because without cause or reasons
Su destino fue fatal.	His destiny was fatal.
En Dallas se le esperaba	The most important part
Lo grande de la ocasión;	Of the ceremonies awaited him in Dallas;
Nunca hubo presentimiento	There was no presentiment
De una horrorosa traición.	Of a horrifying treachery.
En su carro iban su esposa	In his car was his wife
Y el señor Gobernador;	And the honorable Governor;
Los dos iban saludando	Both were waving greetings
Cuando un balazo se oyó.	When a bullet was heard.
Alzó los brazos al cielo	He raised his arms to the sky
Sin saber que le pegó;	Without knowing what hit him;
Se oyó otra bala certera	Another well-aimed bullet was heard
Y el Presidente cayó.	And the President fell.
Su fiel esposa al momento	Instantly his faithful wife
Con su cuerpo lo cubrió	Covered him with her body
Y al señor Gobernador	And the other bullet
La otra bala le pegó.	Hit the honorable Governor.
Esta es la historia más negra	This is the terrible story
Que al mundo entero enlutó	That saddened the entire world
Cuando la vida de un grande	When the life of a great man
Un asesino truncó.	Was cut short by an assassin.

The artist's anger was undisguised; Jara spoke for those massacred and for their orphaned loved ones in impassioned verses triggered by the terrible event (Example 1–19).

Víctor Jara's outrage in this case was a response to a specific instance of unwarranted power. Peruvian musicians and artists have created protest songs and protest artworks to express outrage at fifteen years of violent internal strife in that country, beginning around 1981 (Isbell 1997). Caught between a body of determined, highland-based guerrillas adhering to a Maoist philosophy and Peruvian Civil Guard troops seeking to squelch the radicals, Peruvian highlanders were tortured and "disappeared" (dragged from their homes, often never to be seen again). From this cauldron of violence and counterviolence emerged many works of art. In the anguished song "Democracy and Liberty," composed in Quechua around 1992, a woman speaks of her "disappeared" husband, crying out that the promised "liberty" and "democracy" really arrive with imprisonment and death. In "Chinkaqkuna" [The disappeared ones], first sung and recorded in Ayacucho, Peru, the mother of a "disappeared" son searches high and low for him—she goes to various homes, to the office of the "Judicial Authority," to the soldiers' barracks, even to the dreaded "Infiernillo" [Little hell], a hilly area near Ayacucho where remains of "disappeared" and assassinated students were found. Billie Jean Isbell finds that these songs do not exhibit graphic images of the violence, but rather mention places like Infiernillo, known emblems for the violence. The listening audience knows, and they can imagine why this place is so significant (Isbell 1997).

Simultaneous with the composition of these songs, deterritorialized Peruvians (driven from their home territory and residing elsewhere) have created visual

Ex. 1–19.   "Preguntas por Puerto Montt"

Muy bien, voy a preguntar	Very well, I'm going to ask
Por ti, por ti, por aquel,	On behalf of you, you, that one,
Por ti que quedaste solo	For you who remained alone
Y él que murió sin saber,	And for him who died without knowing,
Y él que murió sin saber.	And for him who died without knowing.
Murió sin saber por qué	Died without knowing why
Le acribillaban el pecho	His chest was riddled
Luchando por el derecho	Fighting for the right
De un suelo para vivir.	To have a place to live.
¡Ay! ¡Qué ser más infeliz	Oh, what a "bastard" of a being
Él que mandó disparar	He who ordered to shoot
Sabiendo cómo evitar	Knowing how to avoid
Una matanza tan vil!	Such an evil massacre!
¡Puerto Montt, oh Puerto Montt!	Puerto Montt, oh Puerto Montt!
. . .	. . .

works in the form of *arpilleras* (quilts), *tablas* (tall rectangular pictures painted on wood and plaster), and *retablos* (series of pictures telling a story), fixing the scenes of violence in the mind's eye. The first *arpilleras* used to depict a terrible reality were created by Chilean women during the post-Allende dictatorship. One such Peruvian *arpillera,* created by an artist-member of the Santa Rosa Vaso de Leche [Santa Rosa glass of milk] program in a refugee settlement in Lima, depicts helicopters snatching victims away—they will later be "disappeared" in the mountains. A *tabla* entitled "The Cursed" depicts a woman being attacked and a man's head being stomped on while an overcrowded truck waits for prisoners to be taken away (Isbell 1997). A *retablo* by Severo Yaranga has one picture showing hooded guerrillas attacking peasants while the sun above cries blood; a second scene depicts guerrillas attacking a national guard post, with dead and wounded in evidence and women guerrillas being killed; a third picture shows a Peruvian Air Force helicopter and nurses picking up wounded antiterrorist soldiers, the scene witnessed by a television cameraman.

The song-texts we have examined so far have reflected the prominence of nostalgia and love of the locality, descriptive balladry highlighting noteworthy local figures and animals, concern with current events, and outrage at injustice and murder. Certainly non–Latin American cultures also prize their home villages, praise their heroes, and react in song against grievances and horrors. We argue that for Latin Americans these sensitivities are particularly acute—love of home territory, eloquent praise for heroes and depiction of critical fauna, and intolerance of what people perceive as government-sanctioned harassment and even violence.

COMMUNICATION WITH THE SUPERNATURAL

We find one more major, unique figure in our quilt of Latin American music culture: communications with the supernatural (sometimes called theurgy) or with figures from beyond present time—spirits, deities, or ancestors. We are not speaking so much here of religion. You will read in some detail of the *Semana Santa* [Holy week] ritual in Chapter 7. Rather, we are speaking more broadly, and cross-culturally, of musical expressions involving the supernatural. Here we encounter the native South American shaman, the Chilean woman singing a chant of paternal ancestors, the African-Brazilian initiate dancing in expectation of spirit possession, and the adults at a child's wake taking the "voice" of the deceased infant who is now considered an angel on the way to *Gloria.*

Societies approach the issue of healing in different ways. The biomedical tradition, practiced by doctors, is rooted in the study of pathogenic causes for illness, a study sustained by microbiology. The ethnomedical tradition, practiced by native healers or shamans, is grounded in the ways native practitioners cope with illness, drawing on regionally available resources. Native healers point to experience, knowledge of local plants, and ability to influence the relationship of the sick person with her/his environment and the cosmos (Bastien 1992:x–xi).

The practice of shamanism is thousands of years old, having come to this hemisphere from Central Asia and Siberia. In North or South Amerindian cultures, the male or female shaman shakes or strikes a musical implement while chanting, to assist in entering an ecstatic state. The essential function of the Latin American shaman is healing, though (s)he may have many other efficacies as well (*cf.* Eliade 1964:323–324 for a broad list of these functions). The shaman and her/his patients believe that most illnesses have a spiritual foundation, that they "involve either the flight of the soul or a magical object introduced into the body by spirits or sorcerers" (327) and thus require a shamanic cure. The shamanic cure, which is similar in many South American cultures, "includes fumigations with tobacco, songs, massage of the affected area of the body, identification of the cause of the illness by the aid of the helping spirits . . . and, finally, extraction of the pathogenic object by suction" (329). It is clear also that the shaman's music-induced, ecstatic trance state is part of the cure, for it is in this ecstatic state that the shaman discerns the cause of the illness and discovers how it might best be treated.

We will look briefly at shamans in Venezuela and Chile.[2] What makes shamanism particularly interesting to us as a phenomenon is that it ranges widely through Latin American Native America, and it is essentially musical—chant and rhythm. The shaman shakes or beats a musical instrument—a drum, rattle, bell, or gong—to aid in contacting the spirit world, using this regular percussive beating to make the transition, to travel back and forth, between the waking world and the world of the spirits (Eliade 1964:179; Needham 1967). The shaman sings of the journey between these two worlds, of the helpful and harmful spirits encountered on the journey, and possibly how (s)he has come to embody one or more of the powerful spirits, giving her/him enhanced curative powers (Whitten 1979). The shaman enters a trance state in which (s)he becomes the spirit(s), who sing through her/him.

The shaman, then, makes her/his own music (or is the "musicant" for her/his own trance-state [Rouget 1985:132]), undergoes a journey to the world of the spirits, exercises control over the spirits, may actually believe her/himself transformed into one, and enters trance voluntarily. Among the Warao rainforest canoe people of Venezuela, shamans are males; we will find female shamans among the Mapuche of Chile. Although hallucinogens are used by shamans in certain cultures to assist in entering trance, the Warao shamans do not employ them (Olsen 1996:17). The Warao have three types of shamans: *wisiratu, bahanarotu,* and *hoarotu.* All three types use music to transform themselves into beings able to maintain contact with the spirit world, in order to cure. The Warao shamans smoke ceremonial tobacco and typically use a gourd rattle; the latter instrument helps to provide the shaman with sufficient power with which to cure. A critical aspect of curing is to name the spirit essence believed to be at the root of the illness (38–39). Highest-ranking among the Warao shamanic specialists, the *wisiratu* shamans cure *hebu* illnesses—illnesses brought on when a *hebu* ancestor spirit places itself into, or takes the shape of, an object or animal to inflict illness.

In Dale Olsen's analysis of a curing ritual performance by a *wisiratu* shaman in 1972, he relates variations in the shaman's rattle tempo and sound quality to dif-

ferent moments in the shaman's transformation into the supernatural—his growing theurgical state of consciousness, or trance-state. As for the shaman's singing,
at certain points his voice is masked—the vocal cords are constricted, this caused
(the shamans believe) by the *wisiratu*'s spirit helpers in his throat and chest. In
addition to the presence of spirit helpers within his own body, the shaman has at
his disposal a group of guardian spirits who reside within the sacred rattle, in the
form of its quartz pebbles. These rattle spirits aid the shaman in communicating
with the supernatural world. During the course of the ritual, the *wisiratu* shaman
makes several attempts to name the illness-causing *hebu* (Olsen 1996:66, 159,
187–194). Finally, the *wisiratu*'s *hebu-mataro* rattle itself is symbolic for the
Warao: it is thought to be a head spirit, "with the handle, the calabash, the slits,
and the feathers on top representing the neck, the head, the mouth, and the hair
of the spirit." (Olsen 1980:377). Thus, in Warao shamanism we see an interaction
between the musical instrument and its specific use within the curing context, the
spirit-affected voice quality of the shaman-chanter, the spirits residing within the
rattle's pebbles, the symbolic structure of the musical instrument, and the stages
of the shaman's theurgic transformation. All of these elements contribute to the
powerful shaman's ability to exert control over the cosmic forces involved in his
overall therapeutic effort.

By contrast with the male Warao shamans, the shaman of the Chilean and Argentine Mapuche (or Araucanian) people is the female *machi*. Rather than the
calabash rattle, the *kultrún* is this shaman's instrument—a kettle-drum made of
wood or gourd, hollowed out like a deep dish and covered with hide membrane,
and played typically with a single stick. Isabel Aretz (1970) discusses and tran-
scribes a number of songs by Araucanian *machis,* and María Ester Grebe (1973)
analyzes the symbolic nature of the drumhead design of the *machi*'s *kultrún,* explaining how its typically four-part motifs represent the four cardinal points. As
with the Warao and other Amerindian shamans, the *machi* is the musicant for her
own trance-state. Grebe emphasizes the role of her mental concentration in this
process, the pendular movement of her body, and the regularity of her *kultrún*
rhythm (18). The musical transcription of the first segment of the chant of Hortensia Ancaye Llancao, a *machi* from Cautín province, Chile, reveals this extreme
regularity of rhythm, in this case that of the triplet, maintained with force on the
accompanying *kultrún* and clearly reflected in the vocal phrasing as well (Example 1–20, taken from the 1975 recording *Amerindian Ceremonial Music from
Chile*).

For the Mapuche there are two worlds—a natural world inhabited by people,
and a supernatural world in the heavens inhabited by gods. This latter world is divided into two regions, *wenu-mapu* and *anka-wenu*. The former is the home of
the tetralogical groups of gods and of auxiliary spirits and ancestors who grant life,
health, and prosperity to mortals. *Anka-wenu* is the abode of evil spirits who
cause disease. As a healer, the *machi* serves as intermediary between humankind
and the gods to restore the health of the ill person. The *machi* takes a central role
in brief, simple therapeutic rites for mild illnesses, and in extensive therapeutic
rites reserved for serious or chronic illnesses. In both cases the *machi* chants,

**Ex. 1–20.   First segment of the chant of Hortensia Ancaye Llancao.
Transcription by John M. Schechter.**

sim. (always *with* voice)
[continue]

Ex. 1–20.   First segment of the chant of Hortensia Ancaye Llancao.
   Transcription by John M. Schechter. (continued)

accompanying herself on the *kultrún* (Grebe 1973:29–30). Grebe's article includes several photographs of *machis* playing their kultrúns.[3]

How do we keep alive the memory of our ancestors? We do so by contemplating the slightly faded black-and-white, formal photographs of our grandparents on the living room wall or in a scrapbook, or perhaps by periodically visiting their grave. If the ancestral tradition is particularly strong, we might even follow in our grandparents' vocational footsteps—perhaps as craftspersons, winemakers, athletes, ritual specialists, or musicians. Argentine Mapuche women keep the ancestral connection alive in a particularly vivid, musical way—they chant *tayil,* a special music that links living Mapuche to their ancestors.

The Argentine Mapuche as a people have decided that a particular patrilineally shared soul (i.e., shared through the father's line) must be delivered, *performed.* They code that task into a map of visual imagery, a map which is then "executed" in musical action. The musical performance delivers the patrilineally shared soul to both living and ancestral members of this lineage. When Argentine Mapuche women perform *tayil,* they "pull the ancestors," an "act of fusing living and deceased members of a patrilineage in the performance of *tayil*-specific melodic contours and syllabic utterances" (Robertson 1979:397). These Mapuche use the term *kimpeñ* to refer to one's patrilineage, to one's ancestry in general, to one's patrilineally shared soul (401); the *kimpeñ* is the text of sung *tayil.* The Mapuche "think" via picture-words, visual impressions—they "see from afar." As a Mapuche woman prepares to "pull" *tayil,* she "sees it from afar" in her own head. In the course of her *tayil* performance, she moves back and forth between different kinds of reality. Since "pulling" *tayil* requires great concentration and substantial physical force, women "pull" *tayil* through clenched teeth. Moreover, "pulling" in this way, the women-singers clearly distinguish their sound from song—something that cannot attain the world of ancestral, past time. Thus, "pulling" *tayil* through clenched teeth assures the women "that the deities and ancestors being addressed will not confuse *tayil* with song" (407).

Different family groups associate their father's ancestry (and thus their shared soul, or *kimpeñ*) with different creatures or natural phenomena—sheep, water, or rock, for example. Accordingly, the sheep *tayil* will be distinguished from the water *tayil* and the rock *tayil* by a unique complex of melodic shapes and vocables (words or syllables with no currently widely understood meaning). Every *tayil* consists of four phrases called "tenses," which are each chanted once. These phrases or melodic movements correspond in the mind's eye of the *tayil* singer to movements among different domains—for example, from performer (singer) to listener, then from listener back into singer's field of action, then from present time into an idealized past time, then back from this cosmological past time into a "present-to-be" time, an as-yet-unvisualized present time. (See Carol Robertson's map of the four consecutive phrases, Figure 1–1.)

In any one *tayil* there is actually a single tone, identified by *tayil* specialists as *chempralitún,* that represents the bridging of the time barriers of present and past. In the case of *kurá* [rock] *tayil,* this time-bridging pitch is **E** (Example 1–21; Figure 1–1). The *tayil*-chanting Mapuche women, then, "see" the movement of

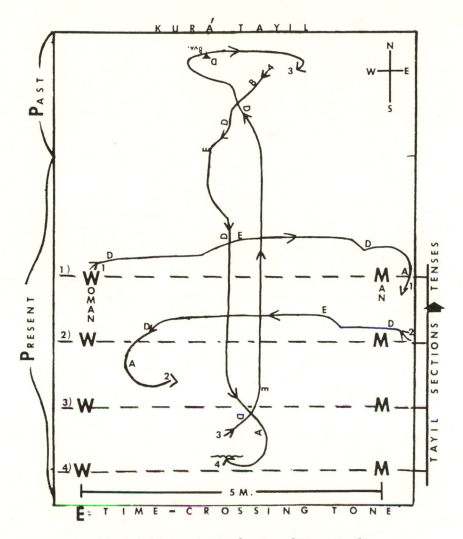

Fig. 1–1. Mnemonic visualization of "Kurá Tayil"

musical notes or melody in terms of relative distances between domains or spaces, rather than "hearing" them in particular musical intervals. Where the shamans "move" back and forth between the world of the patient and the world of the spirits, in the Mapuche domain of *tayil* there is a fluid form of transportation (or transformation) during the chanting of a *tayil*—back and forth to/from the chanter, the person whose *tayil* is being "pulled," the pertinent group of ancestors, and the arena of the overall performance event (Robertson 1979:410–411).

We have seen how Native American shamans in Venezuela and Chile, and *tayil*-singers in Argentina, in their activities of curing with the aid of spirits or of

Ex. 1–21. Musical transcription of "Kurá Tayil"

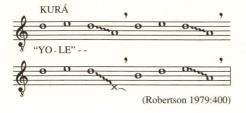

(Robertson 1979:400)

musically delivering a patrilineally shared soul to different hearers in different time-domains, transform themselves and their surroundings. With or without the self-accompaniment of musical instruments, these performers, confronting supernatural or ancestral realms, execute their transformed states of mind *themselves*, without the aid of other musicians. By contrast, in African-Brazilian spirit possession, dancing initiates do not journey to the realm of the spirits, but rather are "visit[ed] by" them; initiates enter an involuntary trance rather than a voluntary one, a trance-state into which they are "musicated" by *other* (drumming) musicians, not a trance-state for which they themselves are "musicants" (as the shamans are) (Rouget 1985:132).

African-Brazilian cults remain a strong symbol of the country as a whole. José Jorge de Carvalho, who has studied the Xangô cults of Recife, recently expressed the view that "undoubtedly, the main matrix of Afro-Brazilian identity is still the traditional cults of African origin, such as the *candomblé* of Bahia, the *shango* of Recife, the *tambor de mina* of São Luís, and the *batuque* of Porto Alegre" (1994:188). Let us examine *candomblé* to see how music effects a hoped-for transformation from dancer into god.

The term *candomblé* refers to Brazilian religious groups practicing West Africa–based religious rituals; the term is also used for the cult center itself or for the *xirê* ritual, in which dancing, drumming, and spirit possession take place (Béhague 1984:222, 237). The main figures in a *xirê* or *candomblé* ritual are the cult leader (male or female), the master drummer (who directs other members of the drumming ensemble), and the *iaôs* (initiates). The multiple deities, called *orishá* in the Yoruba-Ketu cults, each have attributes, and it is believed that each person in the cult is spiritually related to a specific deity and can represent that deity—for example, with specific types of dancing. In the transfer of gods from the West African homeland to Brazil (and to Cuba and Haiti), a syncretism (combination of different forms of belief or practice) occurred with Roman Catholic saints so that, for example, Oxossi, the hunting god in African-Brazilian cults, is syncretized with the Roman Catholic Saint George.

In this belief system derived from African practice, the involvement with the supernatural lies in the fact that the climax of the cult ritual is spirit possession—the manifestation of a god in the body of an initiate, a deity to whom the particular *iaô* has previously been initiated. Intense percussion music played on single-headed, conical *atabaque* drums in *candomblé* combined with responsorial (solo-group alternation) chanting (see Chapter 5, Recorded Selection 26, for an example of this type of chanting), is designed specifically to call the gods, to bring on spirit possession; the *iaô* knows the god is responding to her dancing when that male or female god takes possession of her. The spirit possession varies in form, according to the dancer's temperament and to the deity's attributes. Spirit possession is the moment everyone has been waiting for—the god has manifested itself, the dancer has now *become* that god; those present can now see, speak with, be advised by that god. Once the trance-state is achieved, the god is greeted and complimented, and the dancer is taken out and clothed in the garb befitting that deity, after which (s)he returns to dance to rhythms and chants reserved for it (Béhague 1977:9–10).

It is important to emphasize the role of music in this transformation into deity. Earlier and later scholars agree that the songs and drum rhythms used to call the gods are indispensable to the success of the ritual (Merriam 1956:55; Béhague 1975:72). There are at least twenty-five individual rhythmic themes, each specific to a particular *orishá,* each intended to trigger spirit possession by a dancing initiate *to* that *orishá.* Moreover, the acceleration and increasing volume of the music through the evening seem to help bring on possession. Speaking more broadly than merely for Brazilian *candomblé,* Rouget reminds us that possession in many cultures is generally accompanied by music, with music "almost always regarded as being more or less responsible for its onset" (1985:73, 80). *Candomblé* is discussed in detail in Chapter 5.

These, then, are some of the different ways Native Latin Americans and African-Americans have of communicating with beings from beyond this earthly realm—encountering the supernatural spirit-world by inducing your own trance-state, in order to heal; "pulling" a patrilineage chant to join together the world of the living with the world of the ancestors; serving as the vessel for the music-induced arrival of, and possession by, a god for whose character you have an affinity. It is probably fitting that we end with the encounter of the child, or actually "the child," with God. For hundreds of years in Latin American Roman Catholic cultures, families have believed that if a baptized infant passes away, the baby is at once transformed into an angel and prepares to enter Heaven, or *Gloria.* This is seen as a fortuitous circumstance, and the family celebrates the child's ascension with a festive wake, in which family and friends eat and drink and dance to their favorite local music. Dressed in its finest clothing, the child is typically displayed in an open casket for all to witness.

We see this same practice in Native American, African-American, and Iberian-American cultures going back to the eighteenth century in nearly all of Latin America. In countries such as Ecuador, Venezuela, and Chile, adults present at the *velorio del angelito* [infant wake] may take the part of the deceased and sing "farewell" verses to the waking family and friends. Fittingly, the verses are referred to as the *despedida del ángel* [farewell of the angel], and singers report that they perform these verses so that the child will go happily to Heaven. What you hear in verses such as "Farewell, my beloved parents, with all my little brothers and sisters, for I am now in Heaven, with the other little angels" (an example from Venezuelan folk tradition), or "My mother, . . . wet no more my little wings with your flattering weeping; you detain the entry into Heaven of your little white dove" (a composed *despedida* verse by New Song pioneer Violeta Parra), is the surviving adult singers effectively communicating with the supernatural, communicating with a being now believed to be an angel (Schechter 1994:55–56). Where the Warao shaman's "masked" voice reflects the presence of spirit helpers in his body, the *despedida* voices of the surviving adults at the *velorio del angelito* echo the voice of an angel, and the angel speaks to the surviving family through its *despedida*.

The vibrant quilt of Latin American music culture, as we perceive it, is now complete and spread before us. In one block explode the colors of a flower, fragrant with the beauty and essence of one's homeland. Next to it lies a square composed of bold and finely detailed strokes, outlining the figures of those we have greatly admired—or condemned. Across the fabric erupts an impressive mass depicting newsworthy events and gruesome tragedies. And in the upper corner, in rarefied space, sit images that suggest a meeting of our minds and psyches—through music—with those of other realms, other worlds. We now prepare to pull back this quilt and view the many layers of regional and subregional Latin American music cultures in the chapters that follow.

REFERENCES

Aretz, Isabel. 1970. Cantos araucanos de mujeres. *Revista Venezolana de Folklore,* 2a época, no. 3, Sept., pp. 73–104. Instituto Nacional de Cultura y Bellas Artes, Instituto de Folklore, Caracas, Venezuela.

Barros, Raquel and Manuel Dannemann. 1970. *El romancero chileno.* Santiago, Chile: Ediciones de la Universidad de Chile.

Bastien, Joseph W. 1992. *Drum and stethoscope: Integrating ethnomedicine and biomedicine in Bolivia.* Salt Lake City: Univ. of Utah Press.

Béhague, Gerard. 1975. Notes on regional and national trends in Afro-Brazilian cult music. In *Tradition and renewal: Essays on twentieth-century Latin American literature and culture,* ed. M. H. Forster, pp. 68–80. Urbana: Univ. of Illinois Press.

———. 1977. Some liturgical functions of Afro-Brazilian religious music in Salvador, Bahia. *The World of Music* XIX (3/4) (1977):4–23.

———. 1984. Patterns of *candomblé* music performance: An Afro-Brazilian religious setting. In *Performance practice: Ethnomusicological perspectives,* ed. G. Béhague, pp. 222–254. Westport, Conn.: Greenwood Press.

Blacking, John. 1977. Can musical universals be heard? *The World of Music* XIX/1–2 (1977):14–22.

Boas, Franz. 1927. *Primitive art.* Cambridge: Harvard Univ. Press.

Carrasco Pirard, Eduardo. 1982. The *nueva canción* in Latin America. *International Social Science Journal* 94 (vol. XXXIV, no. 4) (1982):599–623.

Carvalho, José Jorge de. 1994. Black music of all colors: The construction of black ethnicity in ritual and popular genres of Afro-Brazilian music. In *Music and black ethnicity: The Caribbean and South America,* ed. G. Béhague, pp. 187–206. Coral Gables, Fla.: Univ. of Miami North-South Center.

Dickey, Dan William. 1978. The Kennedy *corridos:* A study of the ballads of a Mexican American hero. *Mexican American Monographs,* no. 4. Austin: Center for Mexican American Studies, Univ. of Texas at Austin.

Eliade, Mircea. 1964. *Shamanism: Archaic techniques of ecstasy.* Translated from French by Willard R. Trask. Bollingen Series, no. LXXVI. Princeton: Princeton Univ. Press. (French edition 1951.)

Grebe, María Ester. 1973. El kultrún mapuche: Un microcosmo simbólico. *Revista Musical Chilena* 27(123–124) (1973):3–42.

Harrison, Regina. 1989. *Signs, songs, and memory in the Andes: Translating Quechua language and culture.* Austin: Univ. of Texas Press.

———. 1996. *Entre el tronar épico y el llanto elegíaco: Simbología indígena en la poesía Ecuatoriana de los siglos XIX–XX.* Quito, Ecuador: Abya-Yala, Universidad Andina Simón Bolívar.

Hill, Donald R. 1993. *Calypso calaloo: Early carnival music in Trinidad.* Gainesville: Univ. Press of Florida.

Isbell, Billie Jean. 1997. Validating experience in song and selling protest art as cultural commodities: Protest arts from Ayacucho, Peru. Paper presented at international symposium, The Quechua Expressive Art: Creativity, Analysis, and Performance, September 5, at Univ. of California, Santa Cruz.

Jiménez de la Espada, D. Marcos. 1883. Yaravíes quiteños. *Actas de la cuarta reunión, Congreso Internacional de Americanistas, Madrid 1881,* vol. 2, pp. I–LXXXII. Madrid, Spain: Imprenta de Fortanet.

Khe, Tran Van. 1977. Is the pentatonic universal? A few reflections on pentatonism. *The World of Music* XIX/1–2:76–84.

McAllester, David. 1971. Some thoughts on "universals" in world music. *Ethnomusicology* XV/3 (1971):379–380.

McDowell, John H. 1972. The Mexican corrido: Formula and theme in a ballad tradition. *Journal of American Folklore* 85:205–220.

McLeod, Norma. 1974. Ethnomusicological research and anthropology. *Annual Review of Anthropology* 3:99–115.

Mera, Juan León. 1868. *Ojeada histórico-crítica sobre la poesía ecuatoriana, desde su época más remota hasta nuestros días.* Quito, Ecuador: Imprenta de J. Pablo Sanz.

Merriam, Alan P. 1956. Songs of the Ketu cult of Bahia, Brazil. *African Music* 1:53–82.

Needham. Rodney. 1967. Percussion and transition. *Man* 2:606–614.

Nettl, Bruno. 1983. *The study of ethnomusicology: Twenty-nine issues and concepts.* Urbana: Univ. of Illinois Press.

Olsen, Dale A. 1980. Symbol and function in South American Indian music. In *Musics of many cultures: An introduction,* ed. Elizabeth May, pp. 363–385. Berkeley: Univ. of California Press.

———. 1996. *Music of the Warao of Venezuela: Song people of the rain forest.* Gainesville: Univ. Press of Florida.

Pagaza Galdo, Consuelo. 1967. *Cancionero andino sur.* Ministerio de Educación Pública, Escuela Nacional de Música y Danzas Folklóricas, Servicio Musicológico. Lima, Perú: Casa Mozart.

Paredes, Américo. 1976. *A Texas-Mexican* cancionero: *Folksongs of the Lower Border.* Urbana: Univ. of Illinois Press.

Robertson, Carol E. 1979. "Pulling the ancestors": Performance practice and praxis in Mapuche ordering. *Ethnomusicology* XXIII/3 (September):395–416.

Rouget, Gilbert. 1985. *Music and trance: A theory of the relations between music and possession.* Translated from French and revised by Brunhilde Biebuyck, in collaboration with author. Chicago/London: Univ. of Chicago Press.

Schechter, John M. 1976. Music of the Mapuche trutruka and the Mapuche nguillatún ceremony. Unpublished manuscript.

———. 1979. The Inca cantar histórico: A lexico-historical elaboration on two cultural themes. *Ethnomusicology* XXIII/2, (May):191–204.

———. 1982. Music in a northern Ecuadorian highland locus: Diatonic harp, genres, harpists, and their ritual junction in the Quechua child's wake. Ph.D. diss., Univ. of Texas at Austin.

———. 1991. Afro-Ecuadorian and Quichua compositional processes in Imbabura: The inspirations and innovations of Fabián Congo and Segundo Galo Maigua. Paper presented at Thirty-Sixth Annual Meeting of the Society for Ethnomusicology, October 11, at Palmer House Hotel, Chicago.

———. 1994. Divergent perspectives on the *velorio del angelito:* Ritual imagery, artistic condemnation, and ethnographic value. *Journal of Ritual Studies* VIII/2 (summer):43–84.

———. 1996. Latin America/Ecuador. Revised, expanded, and updated chap. 9 in *Worlds of music: An introduction to the music of the world's peoples,* pp. 428–494. 3d ed. Edited by Jeff Todd Titon. New York: Schirmer Books.

Simmons, Merle L. 1960. Pre-conquest narrative songs in Spanish America. *Journal of American Folklore* 73(287):103–111.

Slobin, Mark. 1992. Micromusics of the West: A comparative approach. *Ethnomusicology* 36/1 (winter):1–87.

Sonnichsen, Philip. 1975. Notes to recording *Una historia de la música de la frontera: Texas-Mexican border music,* vol. 2, *Corridos,* part 1, *1930–1934.* Edited by Chris Strachwitz. Folklyric Records LP 9004.

Wachsmann, Klaus. 1971. Universal perspectives in music. *Ethnomusicology* XV/3: 381–384.

Whitten, Norman E., Jr. with Julián Santi Vargas, María Aguinda Mamallacta, and William Belzner. 1979. Background notes, Notes on the recording. *Soul vine shaman.* Sacha Runa Research Foundation Occasional Paper No. 5.

RECORDINGS

Amerindian ceremonial music from Chile. Commentary by Manuel Dannemann. Recordings and photographs by Jochen Wenzel. Unesco Collection/Musical Sources: Pre-Columbian America XI–1, Philips LP 6586 026, 1975.

Cantan Garzón y Collazos. Industria Electro-Sonora, Medellín, Colombia, LP 12–104/IES–1 (pre-1970).

Cumbias, cumbias y solo cumbias. Almacenes Discos Bambuco, Bogotá, Colombia, Stereo LP DBS 5030 (pre-1970).

Los Tucu-Tucu. *Lo nuestro.* Polydor CD 529 887–2, Buenos Aires, Argentina, 1995.

Music of the Jívaro of Ecuador. Michael Harner, recordist and editor. Ethnic Folkways LP FE 4386, 1972.

Música etnográfica y folklórica del Ecuador. 2 LPs. Coordinación general, Carlos Alberto Coba Andrade. Grabaciones, José Peñín, Ronny Velásquez, y Carlos Alberto Coba Andrade. Cuadernillo [notes], Carlos Alberto Coba Andrade, con "presentación" escrita por Marcelo Valdospinos Rubio. Instituto Otavaleño de Antropología, Otavalo, Ecuador, 5748A, B, 5750A, B, 1990.

The Real Calypso: 1927–1946. Compiled and annotated by Samuel Charters. Folkways LP RBF 13, 1966.

Una historia de la música de la frontera: Texas-Mexican border music. Vol. 2, *Corridos*, part 1, *1930–1934.* Edited by Chris Strachwitz. Notes by Philip Sonnichsen. Folklyric Records LP 9004, 1975.

ENDNOTES

1. The Mapuche word for this tree is *copiu.* The red flower that it produces is the national flower of Chile.

2. For a discussion of a Quechua shamanic chant from the Ecuadorian lowlands, see John M. Schechter, "Latin America/Ecuador," in *Worlds of Music: An Introduction to the Music of the World's Peoples,* 3d ed., pp. 481–483, 1996.

3. You can hear chants by a Chilean Mapuche shaman on the LP *Amerindian Ceremonial Music from Chile* (1975); by Ecuadorian Jívaro (Shuar) shamans on the LPs *Music of the Jívaro of Ecuador* (1972) and *Música Etnográfica y Folklórica del Ecuador* (1990); by an Ecuadorian Lowland Quechua shaman on the LP *Soul Vine Shaman* (1979); and by Venezuelan Warao shamans on one of the three discs accompanying the text *Musics of Many Cultures: An Introduction* (1980), as well as on the CD accompanying Dale A. Olsen's book, *Music of the Warao of Venezuela: Song People of the Rain Forest* (1996).

CHAPTER TWO

Popular Mexican Musical Traditions

The *Mariachi* of West Mexico and the *Conjunto Jarocho* of Veracruz

DANIEL SHEEHY

In the yellow pages of the Mexico City telephone directory, there are four pages of "Orquestas, Conjuntos Musicales, y Coros" [Orchestras, music combos, and choirs]. Here are a few of the more prominent ads:

> Lo mejor de México con grupos profesionales: Conjuntos, Mariachis, Violines, Orquestas, Jarochos, Tríos, etc. [The best of Mexico with professional groups: combos, *mariachis,* violins, orchestras, *jarochos,* trios, etc.]
>
> Ambiente musicalísssimo [*sic*]: Música moderna, cumbia, rock, salsa, samba, danzón, cha-cha-chá, rumba, mambo, ranchera, y más [Musicalisssimo [*sic*] ambiance: Modern music, *cumbia,* rock, *salsa, samba, danzón, cha-cha-chá, rumba, mambo,* country, and more]
>
> Excelencia en música versátil para bailar, música hebrea, violines, concierto para piano, música para iglesia, trios, y mariachis [Excellence in versatile music for dancing, Hebrew music, violins, concert for piano, music for church, trios, and *mariachis*]
>
> Orquesta Clásica de México [Classical orchestra of Mexico]
>
> Conjuntos, Mariachi, estudiantinas, orquestas, violines, organistas, tríos, norteños, marimbas, show de Mickie, Jarochos, ballets [Small groups, *mariachi, estudiantinas,* orchestras, violins, organists, trios, northern-style groups, *marimbas,* Mickey (Mouse) shows, *jarochos,* folk ballets]

It doesn't take much more than a peek at the yellow pages to get a sense of the abundance of music in Mexico, or of the importance of music to social, commercial, religious, political, and cultural life. For many Mexicans, a baptism, *quince años* [fifteen years, a debutante celebration for a fifteen-year-old], wedding, birthday, festival, or even funeral is not complete without some kind of live music. *Discotecas* [record stores] abound in Mexican cities, each blasting the sounds of Mexican *música ranchera* [country music], *salsa* dance music (often called *música tropical* [tropical music]), or the latest North American rock 'n' roll to hit the streets. Also on the store's shelves are recordings representing dozens of other Mexican and foreign popular music styles, as well as styles associated with the Mexican regions. Music stores sell the latest electronic music equipment alongside folk harps and fat-bellied *mariachi guitarrón* basses. Along with soccer games, music-oriented variety shows such as *Siempre en domingo* [Always on Sunday] are the highlight of weekend television programming. The Mexican music and media industries are among the most powerful of their kind in Latin America, and take the latest popular music trends into all but the most remote corners of the country. Popular music groups from other Latin countries perform at concerts and dances in large theatres and auditoriums. Central city life is punctuated by itinerant musicians playing on sidewalks or buses, asking for donations. Speeches at political rallies are often preceded by brass bands or *mariachis* to attract an audience and to give a patriotic flavor. In this country where about 90 percent of the nearly 100 million inhabitants are at least nominally Catholic, choirs, *mariachis,* and other distinctly Mexican musical groups heighten many Catholic masses. Mothers sing lullabies to soothe their babies, and children sing game songs on the playground. In Mexico City as well as a few other large cities, a symphony orchestra might play a European classical music program of Mozart, Beethoven, and Brahms, or twentieth-century compositions of Mexican composers such as Manuel Ponce, Silvestre Revueltas, or Carlos Chávez. Mexico's many Indian groups continue to perform their traditional music for centuries-old ritual occasions.

It would take volumes to describe Mexico's musical life, and even then the work would never be finished, as new innovations and trends would emerge and new influences would leave their mark. To gain insight into some key factors that have shaped music that is distinctly Mexican, we can do a few things:

1. survey the panorama of several popular contemporary Mexican folk musics that emerged in particular regions but have become known throughout the country;

2. examine the sweeping social and economic changes of the twentieth century that have had a profound effect on Mexican musical life;

3. take a close look at two musical styles, the musicians who perform them, and a key musical instrument for each.

Let's begin with some social and musical history, take a brief "bird's-eye-view" of several popular folk musics, discuss how twentieth-century events have affected them, and then meet two musicians who play two of Mexico's most well-known styles of music—*mariachi* music and *música jarocha* from Veracruz.

ORIGINS OF TODAY'S MEXICAN REGIONAL MUSIC—THE FORMATIVE YEARS

When the Spanish *conquistador* [conqueror] Hernán Cortés landed near what is now the port city of Veracruz on Mexico's east coast in 1519 (see the map in Figure 2–1), he began a process of discovery of Mexico's Indian cultures that went on for centuries as Europeans and their descendants penetrated further and further into the territory that is now Mexico. Cortés and his Spanish comrades found dozens of Indian languages and a myriad of unfamiliar customs that were often difficult to understand and appreciate. Their main interest, of course, was conquering these societies and claiming land and riches for the Spanish motherland. The *conquistadores* encountered two major empires, the Aztec and Mayan, that had dominated other Indian groups in most of central and southern Mexico for centuries. As they deposed the Aztec emperor Moctezuma in 1521, they proceeded to ravage the temples, idols, social institutions, customs, and beliefs that might offer resistance. Several Spanish chroniclers wrote about the cultural, religious, and musical practices of the people they were conquering. Generally, they described a society of complex social organization with many cultural and architectural accomplishments that rivaled or surpassed those of Europe. The Aztec solar calendar, hieroglyphic writing, imposing temples atop massive pyramids, and a rich ritual life all impressed the Europeans. They also took special note of a

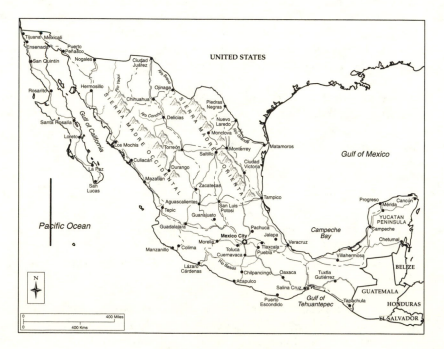

Fig. 2–1. Map of Mexico

musical life in which virtually all of Aztec society participated, where great value was placed on the specialized skills of highly trained musicians.

One of the earliest missionaries, a Franciscan cleric named Fray Toribio de Benavente (widely known as Motolinía) wrote the following observations around 1540, offering a vivid notion of this musical life among the Aztecs:

> One of the commonest occurrences in this country were the festivals of song and dance, which were organized not only for the delight of the inhabitants themselves, but more especially to honor their gods, whom they thought well pleased by such service. Because they took their festivals with extreme seriousness and set great store by them, it was the custom in each town for the nobility to maintain in their own houses singing masters, some of whom [not only sang the traditional songs, but] also composed new songs and dances. . . .
>
> Singing and dancing were nearly always prominent features in the public *fiestas* which occurred every twenty days. . . . The big *fiestas* were held outdoors in the plazas, but the less important ones either in the private patios of the nobility or indoors in the houses of the nobles. . . .
>
> The singers always decided what they were going to sing several days beforehand and practiced diligently on their songs. In the large towns (where there was always an abundance of good singers) those who were to participate in a particular *fiesta* got together for rehearsal well in advance, especially if it were a new song or dance to be performed, so that on the day of the *fiesta* all might go off with smoothness and propriety. (Stevenson 1952:20–21)

The *huéhuetl*, a large single-headed drum in the shape of a cylinder, and the *teponaztle*, a hollowed-out log with H-shaped slits that created two tongues which were struck with rubber-coated sticks, like a wood block, were considered sacred instruments whose predecessors were spiritual beings sentenced to presence on earth by the Aztecs' supreme deity, the Sun god. While the *huéhuetl* and *teponaztle* were considered to be semi-deities, other instruments were valued highly as well. In general, we know that music was an essential ingredient in the social/religious life of Mexico's Native American peoples before the arrival of the Spaniards.

While the Spaniards were busy discovering the Indians, Indian people were likewise discovering the trappings of European culture, some of which were new to them and others of which seemed familiar. The horse, the wheel, guns, and multistringed musical instruments were among the unfamiliar discoveries. A few Indian groups in what is now Mexico may have used a one-string bow to make music in early times, but anything like a guitar, violin, or harp was unprecedented. Indian musicians and artisans appropriated these instruments and in a remarkably short time became accomplished performers and instrument makers.

On the heels of the Spanish *conquistadores* came Catholic missionaries. The riches they sought were human souls, and they saw the musical inclinations of Indian people as fertile ground for planting the seeds of Christianity and as a gateway to the soul. They systematically taught the Indians the skills of performing and even composing Spanish church music. For their part, many Indians eagerly learned the new musical skills and religious practices—both offered striking similarities to their previous way of life. Throngs of Indian musicians were attracted to church music-making, this attraction attributed at the time by Bishop Sebastián Ramírez de Fuenleal to "the prestige they enjoyed among their fellow-Indians by virtue of their profession, and . . . to the privilege of exemption from taxation which they often enjoyed" (cited in Stevenson 1952:63, quoted from Henri Ternaux-Campans, *Voyages, relations et mémoires XVI*, 218, in Rafael Montejano y Aguíñiga, "La Conversión de los indios por medio de la música," *Schola Cantorum*, Sept. 1947, pp. 134–136). Similar benefits had been enjoyed in pre-Hispanic Indian life.

Furthermore, many aspects of the Catholic religion resembled Aztec precursors in certain ways, contributing to music's continued centrality in their religious worship. One striking example of this synthesis of Catholic and parallel indigenous ways is the acceptance of the Virgin of Guadalupe as the religious patroness of Mexico. In 1531 an Indian named Juan Diego reported seeing a dark-skinned apparition of the Virgin Mary on Tepeyac hill in what is now Mexico City. After expressing doubts early on, the Catholic church came to accept the apparition as valid, and the sanctified Virgin of Guadalupe was roundly accepted as a major Christian symbol of Mexico's Indian population. Today, the celebration of the Virgin of Guadalupe on December 12 is one of the most important religious events in Mexico, along with Easter and Christmas. On that day and during the weeks preceding, thousands of pilgrims, often led by musicians and ritual dancers, perform and worship in front of the Basilica of the Virgin of Guadalupe located at the foot of Tepeyac hill. It may be more than coincidence that the same hill had been the site of a shrine to Tonantzín, the Aztec virgin goddess of earth and corn, in precolonial times (Toor 1947:173).

The Spanish musical culture, flourishing in the midst of Spain's Golden Age in the sixteenth century (e.g., composers Victoria and Guerrero), came together with the highly developed and intensely practiced music of Mexico's indigenous peoples, laying the cultural foundation for a new musical culture that would place music as a central, highly regarded, and integrated part of Mexican life over the next five centuries.

Soon after the arrival of the Spanish in Mexico, millions of Indian people died of European diseases, against which they had little resistance, as well as from overwork and abuse. This decimation of the Native American populace reduced significantly the long-term impact of Indian cultures in the evolution of Mexican culture. At the same time, mainly in the sixteenth and seventeenth centuries, large numbers of Africans were brought to New Spain (the area corresponding to much of modern Mexico) as enslaved laborers. While they were not allowed to continue their African musical traditions in an overt fashion, they undoubtedly added their own musical mark to the music they performed, reflecting their roots in West and Central Africa. Official documents from Mexico's colonial period (1521–1810) include numerous references to Mexicans of African heritage enthusiastically performing in public events (Saldívar 1934:220). This practice was so extensive and so against Spanish custom that it occasionally attracted the censure of the Spanish authorities, as when the Viceroy himself declared in 1609 that "gatherings of Black men and women" in Mexico City that had caused "much disturbance" and "damage" could be held only in the public plaza from noon to six in the evening on *fiesta* days (cited in Saldívar 1934).

As people of European, Indian, and African descent intermixed racially during colonial times to create the new majority *mestizo* [mixed] population, so too did a new *mestizo* culture take shape. By the late 1700s there were clear signs of a Mexican identity distinct from that of Spain. These cultural differences were part of a general discontent with the continued Spanish control of Mexican life, and as the Mexican independence movement exploded in 1810, Mexican musical forms called *sones* and *jarabes* became associated with a new Mexican identity. In spite of this emerging national identity, it may be more accurate to say that many Mexican cultures had arisen, each identified more with a particular region than with a national whole. Writers in the newly independent country wrote of regional traditions such as those of Veracruz—for example, in 1844 José María Esteva wrote of the *jarocho* people of Veracruz that they "belong to a race [ethnic group] different from that of the Republic in general" (Esteva 1844b:62). He also wrote the following:

> What is a *jarocho?* Custom has led us to judge or to name in such a manner the rural people who live on the edges of Veracruz, as on the coast. . . . The true *jarochos* are not inclined to work in the country: the occupation of a farmer is arduous and monotonous for a burning and lazy soul, a quarrelsome spirit and friend of glory; because of this, the true *jarocho* prefers to dedicate himself to herding, slaughtering cattle, or horsebreaking, and almost never to being a sailor or a soldier, even though he would have an inclination for war or the sea. . . . The *jarocha* woman is normally gracious, kind with strangers. . . . Industrious and laborious, she spends most of the day in house chores. (Esteva 1844a:234)

By the beginning of the twentieth century, many regional cultures were widely recognized throughout Mexico, and the notion of regional distinctions was a fundamental tenet of national identity. At this point, we can address the question of where Mexican music came from. Up to the early twentieth century, it was for the most part the product of two processes: (1) the fabric of Spanish, Indian, and African musical threads that was woven together beginning in the early 1500s, which provided the foundation for new cultural creations; and (2) the rising of a new cultural mix during the colonial period and after. The factors facilitated the emergence of new styles of music that reflected the new consciousness of regional cultures. Music, like all aspects of culture, draws from the past, but it is always evolving in order to continue as a meaningful expression of cultural values, identities, and needs. Music evolved to reflect the new realities of regional Mexican life, and this is precisely why Mexican music is Mexican, and distinct from music of any other culture.

An overview of some of the more prominent regional musical traditions will help us better understand Mexican musical life in the past and in the present.

POPULAR MEXICAN REGIONAL FOLK MUSIC

The many local and regional styles and substyles of music in Mexico, let alone the many Indian music traditions, are too numerous to describe here. Some of these traditions—through recognition and dissemination by government, cultural, and educational programs and in popular media of recordings, radio, films, and television—have become widely known throughout the country. We will dwell on two of these, *música de mariachi* and *música jarocha,* later in this chapter. Some of the others include the following (most of which were listed in the Mexico City yellow pages, illustrating their professional status and broad popularity): *marimba* music from the southern states of Chiapas, Oaxaca, and Tabasco; accordion-driven *música norteña* from the arid north; *música huasteca* from the northeastern Huasteca region; from Yucatán, suave-sounding trios singing Colombian-derived *bambucos,* and instrumental groups playing fast-paced and more raucous music to accompany the Spanish-derived dance called *jarana;* and the various *banda* (brass band) traditions found throughout central and western Mexico and beyond.

While simplified versions of history can at times do injustice to more subtle details, for our brief discussion a few general comments about historical demographic trends will help us understand how the distinct regional traditions of Mexican music came about. Spanish colonialization of Mexico was most intense and most widespread in a wide swath stretching east to west from Veracruz on the Gulf of Mexico, through Mexico City and Guadalajara, to the Pacific coast. Most of the *mestizo* folk music in this region reflects the preeminence of the guitar (folk guitar types different from the "standard" six-string guitar—we will discuss two specific ones later on), violin, and diatonic harp (tuned to "white key" scales only, without chromatics) during colonial times. Other early Spanish contributions to Mexican music were a special kind of meter sometimes called *sesquiáltera* (more on this later), certain forms of sung verse, and specific genres of music. African people and their descendants in colonial times brought the vigor and basic rhythmic principles of their African musical heritage, as well as certain musical instruments. The heritage of Amerindian culture included a high degree of devotion to music-making, and music was essential in dance and ritual. The Yucatán peninsula was relatively isolated from the rest of Mexico until the twentieth century—no major highway connected it to central Mexico until the second half of the century—and consequently, the musical traditions there tend to be more distinct from those of the interior, reflecting the region's maritime connections to the Caribbean and northern South America. The dry, expansive northern third of Mexico was only sparsely populated during colonial times, and therefore the heritage of those times is not so marked in that region.

How did this history affect the specific regional musical styles mentioned above? Let us look at the *marimba,* a hardwood xylophone mounted over a wooden frame and struck with rubber-tipped mallets. The Mexican *marimba* is clearly of African origin. Xylophones have long been an important ingredient in many cultures in West and Central Africa. While it is unlikely that African slaves were permitted to bring any of their instruments with them to the New World, it is quite possible that escaped or freed slaves, or those more distanced from the watchful eyes of their overseers, were able to reconstruct instruments from memory. One striking similarity between the *marimba* of southern Mexico and African *marimbas* is the presence of gourd-resonating chambers beneath each slab of the instrument. Each of these resonators has a small hole covered with a thin membrane such as dried pig intestine or cigarette paper, and when the slab is struck by a mallet the air resonates, causing the membrane to make a buzzing sound. This ideal of a musical pitch accompanied by a sound modifier creating a buzzing sound ties the Mexican *marimba* to its African ancestors. The prominence of several types of *marimba* in Guatemala and Nicaragua is investigated at length in Chapter 3.

While the southern Mexican *marimba* betrays its African origins, the music it plays is commonly in a rhythmic meter that is very evocative of similar meters from the Spanish colonial heritage. In this meter, sometimes called *sesquiáltera* [changing sixes] in colonial times (though not by contemporary musicians), a 6/8 metrical feel alternates with a 3/4 emphasis. That is, a series of six pulses would sometimes divide by two, sometimes by three. The colonial *villancico,* a type of song particularly popular during the Christmas season, was often characterized by

Ill. 2–1. Three musicians (two playing the
**   *marimba* and one the drum set), serenade**
**   diners and passersby in the port city of**
**   Veracruz.**

this type of meter. You may approximate this shifting rhythm by counting the following series of six pulses of equal length and adding emphasis to the numbers in boldface:

Example 2–1 shows an excerpt from "La tortuga" [The tortoise], illustrating this meter:

Ex. 2–1.   Transcription of "La tortuga" excerpt

In these two musical phenomena, *marimba* and *sesquiáltera,* it is easy to imagine the African and Spanish contributions to a music that is nevertheless strongly identified with southern Mexico.

Sesquiáltera appears not only in Mexican folk music, but in the folk musics of many Latin American countries; examples include the Colombian *bambuco,* the Ecuadorian *albazo,* and the *cueca* of Bolivia and Chile.

Now let's turn our attention northward to the vast, arid region stretching across Mexico below its border with the United States, a region known as El Norte [The north]. While string instruments such as the violin, guitar, and string bass played an important role in the musical life of this region up to the early twentieth century, the music played was not so much the fast, *sesquiáltera*-syncopated *sones* rooted in Mexico's colonial period as it was the parlor dances and sentimental songs of a nineteenth-century flavor. Even though the independent Republic of Mexico was established in 1824, many Mexicans, particularly those of the growing middle class, looked to Europe for their musical models. European centers such as Paris were considered the fountainhead of contemporary cultural vogues. The waltz was one of Europe's most popular dance forms at this time. Strongly criticized in the moralizing Mexican press because it required dancers to dance *barriga a barriga* [stomach to stomach] rather than at a respectful distance, the waltz (perhaps *because* of this notoriety and changing social mores) quickly became a mainstay among Mexican social dances. In 1815, around the time the waltz was introduced to Mexico, a Spanish official wrote that the waltz was a "sinful and indecent dance . . . [that] transported to this kingdom the corrupt thought of disgusting France. . . . [Those who] defend and practice it are not only vulgar and libertine men, but also people of distinction and character. . . . [They] take their partner by the hand . . . [and] spin around insanely" (Saldívar 1934:179, quoted from *Archivo General de la Nación, Tomo 1457, Denuncia del Walz,* 1815).

The polka, also popular in Europe particularly during the latter years of the century, also had a major and even more enduring impact on *música norteña* [northern music], an impact reinforced by the arrival of Germans and other Central Europeans, for whom the polka had a special attachment, to northern Mexico in search of jobs in growing industries such as mining. The confluence of the polka's fast duple meter and the virtually universal popularity of singing in nineteenth-century *mestizo* music ushered in the special prominence of the *canción-polca* [song in polka meter] in northern Mexico.

Hitchhiking on the polka's popularity in the late nineteenth and early twentieth century came another European innovation—the button accordion. In the first decades of the 1900s, the accordion replaced the violin as the principal melody-making instrument in northern Mexico and southern Texas, and as the music became more professionalized, the notion of a typical *conjunto norteño* [northern musical group] emerged, with the fairly standard instrumentation of button accordion, *bajo sexto* (a twelve-stringed guitar with special tuning that can be used to play bass and chordal accompaniment), *tololoche* (a stand-up string bass with three strings), and occasionally a small *redoba* [woodblock] mounted around the waist in front of the body and played with two sticks.

In the regional *música norteña* we again see how the special historical and demographic circumstances of the region play out in helping shape a regional musical style. The accordion's favored role as lead instrument, the major association of nineteenth-century social dances such as the schottische, waltz, polka, and mazurka with *norteño* [northerner] identity, and the preeminence of the *canción-polca* all helped make this music culture distinct from any other. This came about through the region's relatively late settlement, a certain unity of geography and economic activity, the contributions of immigrant groups more influential in the north than in other regions, and other factors.

THE TWENTIETH CENTURY AND THE BLURRING OF REGIONALISM

To understand Mexican regional music at the end of the twentieth century, we must take into account the radical social and economic changes that occurred over most of that century and their impact on regional cultures and region-rooted musics. During the formative years of Mexican regional music, Mexico was primarily a rural, agricultural country. Different regions of the country to a great extent functioned autonomously, with limited contact among them. Firm control by an economic and intellectual elite further relegated the country's rural population to geographical stability and isolation.

The twentieth century brought sweeping social changes that swiftly eroded the bases of regionalism. The Mexican Revolution, first erupting in 1910, brought greater freedom and economic opportunity to working-class people. In the decades following the Revolution, intellectuals such as Dr. Atl, Rubén M. Campos, and Gabriel Saldívar championed the importance of Indian and rural *mestizo* cultures. Government educational programs promoted a broad knowledge of regional cultural expressions and created a select canon of songs and dances from different regions to be taught in all the nation's schools. A massive program of road-building reached communities that had been isolated for centuries. The rapid growth of the electronic media beginning in Mexico around 1930 invaded all but the most remote populations through radio, recordings, films, and television. A few regional musics gained a foothold in the media, but always at the cost of transforming themselves into professionalized commodities required to have broad appeal beyond their traditional regional audience. All the while, Mexico's population growth rapidly outpaced its capacity to keep people employed in small agricultural communities. By the end of the century, two-thirds of Mexicans would live in urban areas, separated from their rural, regional roots.

What happens to rural folk music in a late twentieth-century society marked by rampant population growth, migration from rural regions to urban centers (such as Mexico City, with a population of over 20 million, one of the world's most populous cities), the commercialization of culture, and government-backed canonization and dissemination of folklore? Is a pan-national "folk" music performed by professional musicians merely a style of music, or is it still a musical tradition connected to a distinct cultural community such as that of a region? What constitutes the musical culture of professionalized latter-day regional music? The twentieth century has raised many questions about our understanding of what "folk music" is and how older, rural regional attachments translate into an urban, media-dominated modern musical life.

The best place to find the answers to these questions about modern regional (or neoregional) music culture, as well as to understand how they first evolved, is to meet the practitioners themselves. Let's take a closer look at two of the most popular region-derived musics—*mariachi* music, originally from west Mexico, and *música jarocha* from eastern Mexico.

MÚSICA DE MARIACHI AND *MÚSICA JAROCHA*

MÚSICA DE MARIACHI

Until the early 1900s, the predecessors of *mariachi* were not widely known or clearly defined. People in rural areas relied for the most part on whatever musical resources they had available or whichever musicians happened to show up at a celebration, so instrumentation could vary from one ranch to the next, or from one event to the next. At the same time, there were certain similarities of musical style, repertoire, and instrumentation that linked neighboring peoples of a region and allowed them to be musically compatible. One of these regional musical cultures, sometimes referred to as *mariachi*, was found throughout a multistate area of western Mexico, centered in the states of Jalisco, Colima, Nayarit, Michoacán, and Guerrero (Jáuregui 1990:32).

The term *mariachi* has for decades been erroneously linked to the French word *mariage* [wedding], based on the false assumption that the small-stringed ensembles of the region were popular at weddings of the French during the years they occupied Mexico (1863–1867). This fanciful etymology has since been disproved, notably with the more recent discovery of a letter dated 1852 from a local priest named Cosme Santa Ana in Rosamorada in the western state of Nayarit, to his archbishop, in which he complained of the diversions called *mariachi* of music, drinking, and gambling on Holy Saturday, celebrations that offended the clergyman's sense of religious decorum. The good man of the cloth said he had reported his objections to the town mayor, but the mayor had responded by contributing money to hire more musicians for a *fandango* dance party that had lasted from Holy Saturday to the following Tuesday (quoted in Jáuregui 1990:15–16).

In other early written sources, the term *mariachi* has been used variously to refer to a wooden dance platform, to an occasion for musical celebration, or to a musician of the region. One of the most vivid descriptions of musical life in West Mexico in the late nineteenth century appears in Enrique Barrios de los Ríos's book *Paisajes de Occidente* (1908), in which he recounts a visit to the coastal region of Tepic. On a dance platform called a *mariache,* people danced "joyful *jarabes* to the sound of the harp, or of the violin and *vihuela,* or of the violin, snare drum, cymbals, and bass drum in a deafening quartet. . . . Up to four people at once dance on the [*mariache*], and the loud tapping of the clamorous *jarabe* resounds through the plaza and nearby streets. . . . The *mariaches* are surrounded by a pleasantly entertained crowd absorbed in that joyful and noisy dance" (Barrios de los Ríos 43–44). In the early 1900s, *mariachi* (or its variant, *mariache*) became more standardized and widespread as a term referring specifically to musicians identified with the greater Jalisco area and to the regional music they played.

While the specific instrumentation of a *mariachi* group varied in the years before 1940, it usually consisted exclusively of certain stringed instruments, all with roots in Mexico's Spanish colonial heritage. (There were also reports in the late 1800s of a drum called *mariachi* being included.) Basically, three musical functions needed to be covered: melody, chordal accompaniment, and bass. The melody was played by one or more violins and/or a large harp. One or other of the two five-stringed regional guitar types—the deep-bodied *guitarra de golpe* [struck guitar] and the curved-spined *vihuela*—provided a rhythmic chordal accompaniment. The bass was played on the low-pitched strings of the harp, or on a big guitar similar in shape to the *vihuela* known as a *guitarrón* [big guitar]. So, at one performance, there might have been an *arpa* and a *guitarra de golpe,* at another a *vihuela, guitarrón,* and two violins, and at yet another a violin, *arpa,* and *guitarra de golpe.* To some degree, these differences were localized, with certain local communities or musical groups preferring a particular choice of instruments.

The musicians were not highly specialized professionals, but rather individuals who had taken an interest in music, perhaps through growing up in a musical family. When they played for rural dances, religious ceremonies, or special celebrations such as birthdays, baptisms or weddings, they may have been paid for their services, but the occupation of full-time musician was not the norm. The public occasions for *mariachi* performance were joyous, as described in the report above by Barrios de los Ríos, and the vigorous dance pieces known as *sones* and *jarabes* were at the center of attention. The *son* was (and still is) an important Mexican musical form that drew from the culturally mixed colonial heritage and took on a new, distinctly Mexican musical identity. There are many regional styles of *son*, and many Mexican Indian groups have their own brand of *son*. The *jarabe* is closely linked to the *son* historically. At the end of the nineteenth century and afterward, it usually took the form of a medley of four or more *sones* and/or other melodies. Perhaps the most well-known *jarabe* is the "Jarabe tapatío," sometimes called "The Mexican Hat Dance" by English-speaking foreigners. *Tapatío* is an appellative referring to people from around the city of Guadalajara. It also should be noted that in addition to this repertoire for festive occasions, there also were instrumental devotional pieces called *minuetes* (no formal relation to the minuet) intended for religious events. Today, the *minuete* repertoire is all but forgotten.

Around the turn of the twentieth century, *mariachi* music was a local, isolated musical tradition, relatively unknown outside its home region. Little could people have known how swiftly and radically this would all change over the next fifty years. Here are some highlights of the *mariachi*'s ascent to national prominence. In 1907, an eight-piece *mariachi* ensemble and four folkloric dancers from Guadalajara presented a stage performance of their regional music and dance at the President's residence to mark the visit of the American Secretary of State, Elihu Root (Jáuregui 31, from the newspaper *El Imparcial*, Oct. 3, 1907).

This portended both the use of the *mariachi* as an "official" emblem of West Mexican and national culture and the major migration of musicians to Mexico City that would soon follow. In 1907, the first known phonograph recordings of *mariachi* music were made by a four-piece group, the Cuarteto Coculense [Quartet from Cocula, Jalisco], led by Justo Villa and comprised of *vihuela*, *guitarrón*, and two violins. The recording sessions took place in Mexico City and were released on both cylinders (a recording technology that predated phonograph records) and 78-rpm discs (Clark 1993:9). In 1920, the Mariachi Coculense led by Cirilo Marmolejo was invited by Dr. Luis Rodríguez to perform for a group of Mexico City's élite. The group stayed and became "the first *mariachi* to appear in a stage show in a legitimate theater in Mexico City [the famous Teatro Iris]; the first to appear in a 'sound' film [*Santa*, 1931] and, above all, the first to make 'electric' recordings, initiating the era of the dominance of the *mariachi* style in radio, film and especially on records, which has endured over fifty years" (Sonnichsen 1993:3). Marmolejo and his group, dubbed Mariachi Coculense, began performing regularly at the public plaza now known as Plaza Garibaldi in Mexico City where even today dozens of *mariachis* assemble daily.

The media played a major role in making the *mariachi* part of national musical life. As mentioned above, the first Mexican sound film, *Santa* (1931), featured *mariachi* music. An important genre of Mexican film developed similar to the Western, featuring "cowboy" actor/singers called *charros*. *Charro* singers such as Jorge Negrete and Pedro Infante achieved great notoriety in the late 1930s and 1940s by singing *música ranchera* [country music] to the accompaniment of *mariachi* groups. Such stars seldom had much personal connection to the grassroots culture of West Mexico, and most *música ranchera* was written by professional

Ill. 2–2. A mural memorializing *charro*-**style singers Pedro Infante (left) and Javier Solís at Mi Tenampa Bar, Garibaldi Plaza, Mexico City, a gathering place for** *mariachis* **since the 1920s.**

songwriters. Nevertheless, these idealized images of moviemakers had a powerful effect on popular tastes. Superstar actor/singers such as Negrete and Infante took on movie roles similar to those in American Westerns—pistol-toting horsemen-heroes who periodically broke into song, accompanied by a *mariachi* or other rural-rooted musical group.

The 1936 movie *Allá en el rancho grande* [Out there on the big ranch] was the first of these to have major impact (Clark 1992:5), and the title song of the same name became a mainstay of the national musical repertoire. These actors and others like them in the late 1930s to 1950s established the entertainment niche of the singing *charro* cowboy and brought *mariachi* music to national and international attention. The powerful radio station XEW in Mexico City began broadcasting in 1930, and *mariachi* music soon became one of the kinds of music it broadcast live throughout Mexico and beyond. Recordings of *mariachi* ensembles, either performing alone or accompanying a solo singer, rose in popularity. Massive migration to urban areas, Mexico City in particular, had begun, and *música ranchera* had a special appeal both to urban people who still identified with rural roots and to rural people.

As *mariachi* musicians became more professionalized, and as the music they played became more of a commercial commodity, new standards of musical instrumentation and performance style evolved. The most influential *mariachi* group in creating this style was Mariachi Vargas de Tecalitlán (named after the town of Tecalitlán, Jalisco). Gaspar Vargas had formed his group in 1898 and relocated it to Mexico City around 1944. By 1932, his son Silvestre Vargas had taken over as leader. Silvestre's insistence on strict discipline and professionalism earned the group a high reputation in the professional music world. Several years later, Mariachi Vargas performed regularly on national radio, and began performing in films in 1937, eventually appearing in almost 200 motion pictures (Clark 1992:3–5).

Another contribution of Mariachi Vargas to modern *mariachi* style was the addition and standardization of the trumpet. Trumpeter Miguel Martínez joined the group in 1941 (Clark 1992:6), and his mellifluous countermelodies to the vocal line and pronounced vibrato were widely imitated. A decade later, after a brief sojourn with another ensemble during which he added a second trumpeter, Martínez rejoined Mariachi Vargas, continuing as the group's only regular trumpet player. The ideal of two trumpets eventually caught on, though, and in the 1960s Mariachi Vargas added a permanent second trumpet. While Mariachi Vargas cannot claim the main credit for institutionalizing the use of two trumpets, its acceptance of this innovation solidified the trend, adding new possibilities for the dynamic alternation of melody instruments and for the striking volume of the brass instruments.

With the permanent inclusion of the trumpet, modern *mariachi* instrumentation was set. Two trumpets, three to six (sometimes more) violins, *guitarrón, vihuela,* and six-string guitar became the standard. The *guitarra de golpe,* the preferred instrument of Gaspar Vargas, all but disappeared from professional *mariachi* groups. While Mariachi Vargas continued to use the *arpa,* only a few other groups followed suit, most of them considering that instrument to be an

Ill. 2–3. A six-member *mariachi* comprised of two trumpets, two violins, *guitarrón*, and *vihuela* playing outside at Garibaldi Plaza.

added luxury for the sake of appearance and occasional flourishes. To be sure, many *mariachi* groups, for reasons of economy or lack of sufficient musicians, may be smaller in size, but nevertheless they emulate the sound and style of the larger groups.

MARIACHI REPERTOIRE AND THE SON JALISCIENSE

Mariachis perform a wide range of pieces, most being songs popularized by marquis-name solo singers. The *canción ranchera,* a song cast most often in a triple waltz meter or in slow and fast tempo versions of duple meter, claims the largest share of the repertoire of most groups, followed by the slow-paced, suave, and romantic *bolero.* Both of these song forms continue the long Mexican heritage of sentimental song. An added thread of tragic and/or embittered love themes delivered in an extroverted, emotional singing style typifies the *ranchera.* The more suave *bolero,* delivered in a more crooning fashion, is a "Mexicanized" version of a romantic song form that took shape in Cuba in the decades around the turn of the twentieth century. The *mariachi*-style *bolero* is a less syncopated derivative of its Cuban precursor, set in a standard rhythmic pattern, with the *guitarrón* playing a ONE, (REST), THREE, FOUR beat against a faster, constant flow of chords played by the *vihuela* and the guitar (below, and Example 2–2):

vihuela/guitar	x	x	x	x	x	x	x	x
guitarrón	x				x		x	

Other important kinds of music played by the *mariachi* are the *huapango* (in a syncopated *sesquiáltera* meter adapted from a traditional rhythm from the northeastern Huasteca region of Mexico and often including high falsetto vocal breaks evocative of that region's special singing style to add interest to the melody line) and instrumental dance pieces such as the polka, the *pasodoble* (a Spanish-derived one-step dance movement in a duple meter, a little slower than the polca), and the *danzón* (an instrumental dance piece of Cuban origin). The *danzón* and the *bolero* both reflect the far-reaching popularity of Cuban music earlier in the century.

While the *mariachi* has incorporated these and many other musical forms into their performances, nothing stirs yells of approval nor evokes grassroots sentiment in listeners like the *son.* "The *son* continues to be the backbone of *mariachi* music," in the words of *mariachi* musician Margarito Gutiérrez (interview, Mar. 2, 1997). The *son* typical of the *mariachi* is sometimes referred to as the *son jalisciense* [Jalisco-style *son*], though many of these *sones* are thought to be native to the neighboring state of Michoacán or another adjacent state, reflecting the previous shared

Ex. 2–2. Notation of *bolero* accompaniment

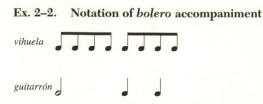

regional traits of *mariachi* culture. The *son* takes a range of structural shapes, though the most common is that of a strophic song (a song with a simple, repeated vocal melody, sung with different text for each repetition) with the song *estrofas* [strophes] separated by a musical interlude. Let us take a look at one of these *sones*, "Las abajeñas" [The lowland women], the Bajío or Lowland being a region of Jalisco in which *mariachi* tradition is strong. We will pay particular attention to a few characteristics that will enable us to contrast it with its historical relative, the *son jarocho* from eastern Mexico:

Ex. 2–3.   Text of "Las abajeñas"

Me gustan las abajeñas	I like the lowland women
Por altas y presumidas.	For being so tall and comely.
Se bañan y se componen	They bathe and fix themselves up
Y siempre descoloridas.	And always so fair-skinned.
Mariquita, mi alma	Little Maria, my dearest
Yo te lo decía	I was telling you
Que tarde o temprano, mi vida,	That sooner or later, my beloved,
Tú habías de ser mía.	You were to be mine.

The basic repeated structural unit of this *son jalisciense* is the sung *estrofa* (strophe) and the paired *intermedio,* or simply *música* [instrumental interlude]. Several repetitions of this section are preceded by a statement of the vocal melody and followed at the end of the rendition by a similar statement abruptly cut short and finalized by the common ending pattern:

Ex. 2–4.   Notation of *son* ending melodic pattern

The underlying driving rhythm is a more or less standard interlocking pattern supplied by the *vihuela*/guitar and *guitarrón:*

vihuela	x	x	x	x	x	x	x	x	x	x	x	x
guitarrón		x			x				x			x

The sung melody is in two parts, each part repeated one time in succession. During the second part of the strophe, the alternating I–V_7 chordal pattern is broken by a change to a I_7–IV–V_7–I–V_7–I pattern accompanying the second part. Then the instrumental interlude consists of a different melody and rhythmic emphasis, contrasting with the verse section. The ideal is to perform each strophe-interlude section the same way, without instrumental improvisation. As we will discover, this more fixed musical structure with no improvisation differs in significant ways from the structural principles of the *son jarocho*.

Ex. 2–5.   Transcription of a segment of "Las abajeñas"

Ex. 2–5.   Transcription of a segment of "Las abajeñas" (continued)

The *Mariachi Vihuela*

Now let's look more closely at the *vihuela*—its construction and how it is played. The *vihuela* is a five-stringed guitar. The details of its origins are not known, though the term *vihuela* during early colonial times referred to a type of guitar, usually one used more in the circle of the literate élite. The Mexican folk *vihuela* emerged in the same region as the *mariachi,* in western Mexico, and until the spread of the *mariachi*'s popularity the *vihuela* was not common to other regions. Folk guitars with five courses of strings are found throughout central Mexico, though, and the *vihuela* was, like virtually all of these guitars, probably a derivation of Spanish ancestral guitar types, molded over time to fit local technologies and to suit local tastes. Also, like most other Mexican regional guitars, the preferred wood for most of the body is the light, resonant cedar found in the lowlands of the central and southern regions. Unlike most of these other guitars, the top of the *vihuela*'s sound box is usually made of *tacote,* a resistant, but malleable, light-colored regional wood.

   Since most people know the sound of the "standard" Spanish six-stringed classical guitar, it might be helpful to compare the two instruments to describe the

Ill. 2–4. Renowned instrument maker Roberto Morales, in his shop in Guadalajara, showing the front of a *vihuela* he recently finished.

sound of the *vihuela*. Like the guitar, the *vihuela* is constructed in a rounded fig-ure-eight shape. Its overall length (about thirty-one inches) is shorter than that of the guitar (about forty inches). While its width (nearly twelve inches) is also nar-rower than that of the guitar (about fifteen inches), the back of its sound box is curved distinctly outward, making the sound box deeper than that of the guitar (about six inches and four inches deep, respectively). This is accomplished by joining two slats of cedar, each curved by heating and bending them and cut to fit the figure-eight base, resulting in a spine down the middle of the back. The exact size of the sound box varies, and some manufacturers will make different sizes ac-cording to the needs of their customers. Roberto Morales (see Illustrations 2–4 and 2–5), for example, offers three "standard" sizes of sound box. Some musicians prefer a larger, louder instrument for recording or for playing in a large group.

All five strings are nylon, whereas three of the "classical" guitar's strings are wound with metal; the tunings are similar to but different from the five highest-pitched strings of the guitar. The difference lies in the *vihuela*'s "re-entrant" tun-ing—that is, while the tuning of the guitar always rises in fourths or thirds from string to string, the second string of the *vihuela* falls a minor sixth from the third string instead of rising a major third. Thus, the tuning from the fifth string to the first is **A d g B e**. This re-entrant tuning, along with the use of five strings rather than six, means that the overall range of the *vihuela*'s open strings is confined to less than an octave. Also, the vibrating portion of the *vihuela* string is six inches

Ill. 2–5. Roberto Morales showing the curved spine of the *vihuela*'s sound box.

shorter than that of the guitar. Consequently, when the strings are plucked they do not vibrate as long, yielding a more percussive sound, and the deep sound box adds to the instrument's volume and resonance. The main point of this technical description is that the *vihuela*'s construction is appropriate to its most common musical role—to provide a clearly marked, percussive rhythmic and chordal framework for the rest of the ensemble.

The playing technique likewise reflects this accompanying role. The player holds the *vihuela* horizontally in front of the body, supported by a strap hanging around the neck and pressed against the rib cage. The left hand positions the fingers on the neck to produce the desired chords, and the right hand strikes the strings. The *vihuela* player never plucks individual strings to produce a melody. The strings are not simply struck, however; there is a repertoire of strokes and stroke combinations that is used to produce different rhythmic patterns. For example, the six-stroke rhythmic "building block" of the *son* (Recorded Selection 1) is produced by striking the strings downward two times, up once, down two times, and up once in an even, constant pulse. It might be expressed like this:

Ex. 2–6.   Illustration of the simple *vihuela* hand pattern

To produce the most basic twelve-stroke pattern of the *son* "Las abajeñas," the *vihuela* player would do the following:

Ex. 2–7.   Illustration of the twelve-stroke *vihuela* pattern

Notice the three rapid down-up-down "flourish" strokes—called a *redoble* [roll]—near the end (Recorded Selection 2).

To add even more "flavor" to the rhythm, the *vihuela* player might accent certain strokes to heighten the rhythmic pulse of the *guitarrón*. The more practiced, contemporary *mariachi* groups expect a high degree of coordination between the *vihuela*, guitar, and *guitarrón* to produce a rhythmically interesting, clearly accented, and tightly interlocked pattern. Together, the *vihuela*, guitar, and *guitarrón* are referred to as the *armonías* [harmony section or rhythm section].

These are some of the simplest and most basic patterns. Other types of strokes—rolling the fingers downward across the strings; stopping the strings while hitting them percussively; rapid combinations of open strokes, rolls, and stops—are used in certain other genres (the *huapango*, for example), adding considerable interest to the melodic accompaniment.

Ex. 2–8. Notation of *vihuela* and *guitarrón son* rhythm showing emphasis in *vihuela* strokes

As the *mariachi* became more professionalized, the demand for fine-sounding, accurately tuned, and attractive musical instruments grew. Roberto Morales, based in Guadalajara, is considered by most professional *mariachi* musicians to be the best contemporary maker of *vihuelas* and *guitarrones*. He was born in 1924 in the small town of Concepción de Buenos Aires, Jalisco, the son of a musician who played *arpa, guitarra de golpe,* and violin. After apprenticing in a carpenter's shop making coffins, he moved to Guadalajara in 1942:

> Here I opened my own little shop because I loved carpentry. . . . If it were possible, I would work in carpentry rather than with instruments, because I like it a lot. I love furniture and that type of thing, it fascinates me. And everything that I tried making came out very well. But then my father said, "No, son. That work is very difficult. Work with musical instruments. There is no one who makes instruments [well]. And those who do make instruments make really bad ones—bad-sounding and very badly constructed, very heavy. And your work, like the harps you have made, comes out well—magnificent. Keep it up, but do it like I tell you to do." He even helped me when a job came along. If something wasn't right—some piece of wood or something . . . he himself would look for the right wood [and say] "this is it." (Interview with Roberto Morales, Mar. 1, 1997)

Morales had made harps and a guitar previously, but in 1943 he began making *guitarrones, vihuelas,* or *guitarras de golpe* in his spare time. "[There was not such a demand for instruments] like there is now. There were only two or three instrument makers here in Guadalajara" (ibid.).

The father-son, musician-carpenter relationship paid off, as the reputation of his instruments spread:

> "In 1958 . . . don Gaspar Vargas, the father of Silvestre . . . ordered two *guitarras de golpe*. . . . The sound [of my instruments] more than anything else [attracted the customers]. In those times, we made the instruments without much decoration. The decoration was a design burnt into the wood, not inlaid like now. . . . But that man was attracted by the sound. . . . It had good resonance. . . . The members of Mariachi Vargas have been very clever people in the way of music. . . . Several times they came here. In 1965, the *guitarronero* came, the late Natividad Santiago. . . . I had three of four instruments already finished. He said, "Set this *guitarrón* aside for me." [I answered], "No, I think this one is better." [Santiago said], "I like that one. It sounds good. Put the strings on and I'll come for it tomorrow." . . . If it had some small problem, he would say, "Fix it for me here, it needs something here, this, this detail . . . ." And from 1966 up to now . . . many [of the best] groups would [order my instruments],

. . . and we are happy that all our clients like our work. (Interview with Roberto Morales, Mar. 1, 1997)

This close relationship between musician and instrument maker, spurred by the evolving musical expectations of the professional *mariachi* ensembles in the commercial music arena, led to a hand-in-hand refinement of both the instruments and the music they played.

Instrument making is part of a broader "material culture" including different sets of crafts skills surrounding *mariachi* life. As is the case through the experiences of Roberto Morales, the evolution and aesthetics of these crafts can expand our insights into the evolution and broader meaning of the *mariachi* and its music. The two other principal related crafts are those of the *traje de charro* [cowboy suit] and the *sombrero de charro* [cowboy hat]. The *charro* is not only important in Mexican life for its popular image, but there is a rich *charro* tradition involving the skills and implements of horse handling, the competitive, rodeo-like *jaripeo*, an international network of organized *lienzos de charro* [*charro* guilds], and traditional modes of dress. While the typical dress of the *mariachi* mirrors the look of the *charro* and *mariachis* are often referred to as *charros*, few *mariachis* in fact spend much time with horses. Perhaps their real link to equestrian *charros* is through the tailors and hat makers who make their clothes.

Both the suits and the hats of the *mariachi* closely parallel those of the *charro*. The *mariachi*'s *traje* [suit], though, tends to have *botonadura* [silver buttons] running down the entire length of the pants leg, reflecting the need to *lucir* [show off], while the horseman's *charro* tends to use only a few of these ornaments, so as not to interfere with horsemanship. In the deeply rooted *charro* tradition, there are several variations in hat shape, perhaps to imply that the owner is young, old, or wealthy. Modern *mariachi* musicians tend to know little of the subtleties of *charro* dress:

> The [real] *sombrero de charro* is serious, it is not very ostentatious, and in the movies, yes, it is ostentatious, because it gives life to the character who wears it. In this case, you can simply cite [the actor Emilio] "El Indio" Fernández, the person who came out with the *cocula* form, [called] *cocula Fernández*. It has two indentations in the crown and curved up in the front and in the back, but more so than the Jalisco-style hat. That is, it looks more *apanterarado* [tough-guy style] . . . so that the people would say, "Here comes that bad guy." In a word, he is really a man. . . . They were simple hats. Later . . . Antonio Aguilar, Luis Aguilar, and all those [singer/actors] . . . used more ostentatious hats, then with embroidery of silver and gold thread brought from France. . . . [Old-time horsemen *charros* were very detailed in the hats they wore.] The musician [however] tends to wear a hat the style of almost all the [popular] singers, the *cocula* form. It is very rare for one to wear a hat with four indentations, be it the Jalisco or San Luis style. It is rare for the musical group in the realm of entertainment to wear one of those kinds of hats because they really don't know the difference between something that is cowboy and something that is artistic. The *cocula* style is used by singers and by *mariachi* groups, by all those who believe that it is the true *charro* thing, because they want to associate themselves with being "real men," when in reality, "being a man" does not have to do with a hat. (Interview with Mario Romano, Nov. 29, 1997)

Ill. 2–6. Master *sombrero de charro* maker Mario Romano posing in front of his workshop with a Jalisco-style hat he made for a *mariachi* musician.

In short, the *sombreros* preferred by *mariachis* typically imitate the *cocula* image cultivated in the popular media, rather than coming from a direct knowledge of *charro* tradition.

PROFILE OF MARGARITO GUTIÉRREZ

Margarito Gutiérrez lives in a modest but lively home several blocks from Roberto Morales's instrument-making shop (Recorded Selection 3).

A third-generation *mariachi* musician, Gutiérrez was born in Ciudad Guzmán, Jalisco, in 1942. His grandfather, Hermenegildo Gutiérrez, was from around Ciudad Guzmán and passed on his musical talents to his son Matías, Margarito's father. Matías Gutiérrez was born around 1906 in the small town of Atemejac de Bruselas, Jalisco, near Ciudad Guzmán. He made music his career, and he even played for a time with Mariachi Vargas de Tecalitlán. Margarito described the instruments they played:

> [My father] played the violin. [My grandfather] played other instruments with my father, too. It would be the *guitarrón,* guitar, *guitarra de golpe,* and violin. . . . The *quinta [guitarra de golpe]* is like the *vihuela,* only with another tuning. The *guitarra de golpe* is a kind of *armonía* like the *vihuela,* but with another tuning and different fingerings from the *vihuela,* too. . . . The back is flat, like the guitar. (Interview with Margarito Gutiérrez, Mar. 2, 1997)

Ill. 2–7. (*Left to right*) Margarito Gutiérrez and his sons Guadalupe César and Rafael "Lalis" playing the *son jalisciense* "Las abajeñas" [The lowland women] on the violin, *vihuela*, and *guitarrón* in their home in Guadalajara.

Margarito was one of sixteen children, eight girls and eight boys. He learned music the way traditional rural musicians did—from his family:

> All of them [brothers and sisters] knew how to play, but not all of them dedicated themselves to [a musical career]. . . . One brother played *mariachi* music for a while, but not now. [The sisters] played, but not professionally, only at home. They learned two or three songs for house parties. This was because my father did not want them to play [professionally], because he was very particular, very strict. . . . But some of us learned. (Interview with Margarito Gutiérrez, Mar. 2, 1997)

He started playing the *vihuela* at the age of five. When he was sixteen, his father invited him to play with him in Tijuana:

> It was necessary to leave Ciudad Guzmán because there was not much work in that region. . . . Then my father decided, my father went off to Tijuana to look around for work. He left in 1955. He, Salvador, and [another] brother went. . . . Things went well for them. . . . They went, and then my father sent for us [in 1957]. . . . I started to play the *vihuela*. . . . I recall that I went to the September [Independence Day] *fiestas* in Tijuana, and I went out on September 13th. And by September 14th, my fingers were all bloodied and all that because my father wouldn't let me use a pick. . . . He wanted us to play the *vihuela* like it should be played [with the fingernails]. . . . [One played] from twelve noon until one or two in the morning. . . . Play, and play, and play, and play. We only had an hour off to eat during the day. . . . The work was good, very good. . . . [It was all *talón* playing, paid for each song by individual clients]. . . . [My father] had a big group . . . about eight members. . . . One thing about my father was that he always had a well uniformed group, with hats and good suits. . . . [The repertoire we played] you could say was traditional. . . . You know that the original aspect of the *mariachi* is the *sones*, frankly. Only *sones*, and *canciones rancheras* there. . . . I remember that in those times there still was no [more complicated arrangements of] classical music. It was because the musicians were not able to play well enough. Some yes, some no. And like I say, now everything is so evolved, one plays classical pieces, and like, *tangos*, and many kinds of music. (Interview with Margarito Gutiérrez, Mar. 2, 1997)

Gutiérrez remembers well the changes occasioned by the introduction of electrified musical groups in local *fiestas*, and the professional competition they posed for the all-acoustic *mariachi*:

> In those times [the mid 1960s], all the *fiestas* were good, because there weren't any problems [for the *mariachis*]. The problems came with the [electrified] *conjuntos* [groups] . . . it presents a problem, but on the other hand, everybody has the right to make a living. . . . The *conjuntos norteños*, the *bandas*, and those rock and roll groups . . . started to interfere a bit with the *mariachi*. . . . We went once [to a *fiesta* in Tecomán, Colima] in 1966 . . . we didn't play once because on every terrace there were [electrified] groups playing. . . . Well, who could play next to that [electrified sound] equipment? No. There was no way to alternate with them, to put ourselves up there. We didn't play one song. That same day we returned. (Interview with Margarito Gutiérrez, Mar. 2, 1997)

While *mariachi* musicians are glorified in the popular media and in government-sponsored displays of national heritage, at the same time they are often seen as somewhat undesirable, as low-class people or of dubious moral values:

> I don't know what the [general] opinion of the people is, but what I do know is that if [when I was young] . . . I wanted to have a girl for a girlfriend or something, well . . . if I met her as a regular person [it was all right], but if she found out I was a *mariachi,* it was like she said "no, no, no—never." . . . That is something of which I am very much aware, that here in Mexico is where we should be accorded a very good [prestigious] place for the simple fact that we represent the country. [But] no, that is not the case. (Interview with Margarito Gutiérrez, Mar. 2, 1997)

Following professional opportunities, Margarito returned to Guadalajara, switching to violin as his principal instrument. He then relocated to Mexico City from 1964 to 1969, where he was invited to join the respected *mariachi* Los Charros de Ameca, led by Román Palomar. There his professional skills expanded, as he was required to read music to play for recording sessions:

> I played the violin well, but, well, I knew nothing about [written music]. . . . But they thought, given how I played and how I sang, they thought I knew how to read [music]. . . . [A few days after I joined the group] they scheduled me at the Peerless Record Company for a recording session. . . . They gave you fifteen minutes to practice each new piece. . . . But no, "I don't know how to read music," [I said]. "How is it you don't know how to read music? You play so well and don't know how to read music?" In three months I learned how to read and then I went to record with them. I entered the *Escuela Libre de Música* [Free School of Music] and then I took private classes with my *compadre* Rafael Palomar. I learned the essentials. (Interview with Margarito Gutiérrez, Mar. 2, 1997)

So, are *mariachis* merely imitators of music and images served up by the popular media like films and recordings? Margarito acknowledges that films, for example, have had an important influence, but that *mariachis*—at least the better ones—are not mere imitators:

> The movies have influenced a great deal. . . . [but] there are no [mere] imitators, no. Now look, there is some of everything . . . there are ordinary groups [that cannot play difficult music]. . . . Right now in the present, what is happening is that the youth that is coming up in [*mariachi*] music has a lot of creativity. That is not happening through the movies. They are coming with other, more challenging ideas about the music, with a broader outlook. (Interview with Margarito Gutiérrez, Mar. 2, 1997)

In other ways, *mariachi* life is more than a professional craft, imitating popular models. The professional world of the *mariachi* is a world unto itself, an occupational community with oral traditions based on a shared way of life. The experiences and stories they hold in common, the mutual dedication to a style of music, the in-group networks of musicians and supporting craftspeople, all contribute to the strong ties felt among *mariachis,* and to a realm of creativity that expresses their way of life. One of the most lively and amusing expressions of this professional community is the oral tradition of *apodos* [nicknames]. Many musicians are known to most of their comrades only by their *apodos*. These names usually are inspired by some distinctive physical or character trait. Also, they are often merciless in their irreverence: La Escoba (the broom, for a tall man), El Cara de León (lion face), El Loco (the crazy man), La Perra (the bitch), La Hormiga (the ant), Santa Claus (Margarito's *apodo*, from his portly shape), El Cócono (the turkey), El Hot Dog (the musician's hand position on the violin looks like he is holding a hot dog), La Vaca (with a long, cow-like face), Jitomata (tomato, red-faced) are a few examples. These in-jokes are a constant source of both amusement and a sense of community among musicians.

Finally, as to whether there is a difference between professional *mariachi* musicians from Jalisco and those from elsewhere, Gutiérrez offered this opinion, given the thoroughly professional dimension of the music:

> Personally, I have known very good [*mariachi*] musicians, very good, even of other nationalities. . . . There are good musicians, and they carry on the tradition, but one thing is the tradition and another thing is the flavor. . . . The flavor of playing [*mariachi*] music is here in Jalisco, it's the flavor we give to the music of the *mariachi*. . . . If you analyze, you can see that one [person not from Jalisco] does not add the spiciness like this guy adds the spiciness to the [music] . . . and he [the former] is playing well. (Interview with Margarito Gutiérrez, Mar. 2, 1997)

So, a musician not from the region can be a perfectly good, respected musician among his fellow professionals, but musicians from the region maintain a special "flavor" that springs from their upbringing as members of that regional culture.

Apart from occasional *giras* [tours] (Recorded Selection 4), such as a recent four-month stay at a resort hotel in Cabo San Lucas, Baja California, playing for winter tourists, or *plantas,* regular daily or weekly performances at restaurants or nightclubs, Margarito Gutiérrez works mainly playing *chambas* [casual engagements]. On a typical day, the eleven members of his group assemble at the Plaza de los Mariachis in central Guadalajara shortly before midday. There, they wait for customers to arrive, with one or more of the members standing along the side of the street that runs next to the plaza, alert to the possible approaching client. As they wait, they pass the time socializing and trading stories with the dozens of other musicians waiting along with them and listening to the groups that prefer to play at the plaza itself, working *al talón* [on foot—roaming from table to table, playing for customers who pay an agreed amount for each song]. Margarito disdains working *al talón*, feeling that both the pay and the quality of work is better playing *chambas*.

During the busier hours, the street is lined with *mariachi* musicians, each dressed in his elegant *traje de charro*, waving to attract the attention of passing drivers who might want a *serenata* [a short serenade of six songs] for a loved one or a longer session of music for a party. As a car approaches a member of Margarito's group, he pokes his head in the car window, quickly pitching the quality of his fellow musicians, their uniforms, and their reasonable price. This client is looking for a *mariachi* to play for two hours at his new godson's baptismal celebration. They quickly agree on a price, the negotiator signals the other group

Ill. 2–8. A *mariachi* **ensemble working** *al talón*, **paid by the song, at the Plaza de los Mariachis in Guadalajara.**

members with a special whistle that they all recognize, and they all hustle into several taxicabs to follow the client to his party.

When they arrive, the partygoers are assembled around an interior patio, where the recently christened baby and his happy parents are the center of attention. The guests are clearly excited by the arrival of the *mariachi*. The client/godfather tells the father—who is now his *compadre*, a special relationship forged by taking on or offering the role of godfather—that the *mariachi* he has hired is ready to play. After tuning quickly, the group launches into "El son de la negra" [The *son* of the dark woman], one of the most tradition-charged pieces in the *mariachi* repertoire—the audience responds with outbursts of applause and *gritos* [yells]. Midway through the *son* a woman pulls a man into the middle of the crowd to dance a *zapateado,* a traditional step that goes along with the *son* rhythm. The audience asks for song after song and the *mariachi* obliges, not refusing a single request. It is a matter of professional pride for a *mariachi* that they be able to perform any but the rarest song in the total repertoire of literally thousands of pieces, and Margarito's group is no different.

When the godfather gives the sign, the group plays "Las mañanitas," the traditional congratulatory song typically sung at Mexican birthday parties, and all those assembled, from children to seniors, join in. As the two contracted hours come to a close, the godfather pays the *mariachi* its fee and the father invites the musicians to eat with them. The musicians gratefully accept the invitation, and when

Ill. 2–9. A *mariachi* musician negotiating with a prospective client on the street next to the Plaza de los Mariachis in Guadalajara.

they are finished they hail taxis to return them to Plaza de los Mariachis, where they will wait for the next client to come along. On any given day, business may vary from no work at all to eight or ten hours of music. Margarito's group, consisting of musicians who are generally older than the other groups, prefer to work in the day, and unless they are contracted to play late, they return to their homes at about eight or nine in the evening. As they leave the plaza more groups arrive and take their position along the street, looking for clients who will keep many of them busy until dawn.

Through the experiences of Margarito Gutiérrez, Roberto Morales, and Mario Romano we now know more about the answers to the questions posed earlier about the *mariachi,* and perhaps about those other regional musics that have survived transition in a radically urbanized Mexican society, with a media industry that has invented new images of its regional roots. The persistence of a distinctive West Mexican cultural region and the prominence of people in that region in the creation and performance of *mariachi* music help to maintain a close and real association with its region of origin. At the same time, a newer, more expansive "community" of professional *mariachi* musicians has grown around it, linked by ties to a common profession and a common lot in Mexican society. Professional *mariachi* ensembles are commonplace throughout Central America and the southwestern United States and may be found far beyond, from Chicago, New York, and Washington, D.C., to Canada, Colombia, Venezuela, Argentina, France, Italy, and many other countries. Much of *mariachi* culture is passed on aurally in the fashion of folk tradition, while for many it also implies a highly specialized degree of musical literacy and dependence on swiftly changing fashions of popular culture. The tradition is widely revered, while at the same time the lifestyle and perceived character of the professional *mariachi* musician is disdained by many. In sum, the modern *mariachi* tradition is multifaceted, with multiple layers of connections and meaning among the musicians. It is like a large river flowing in the same direction, but with many currents moving in slightly different variations.

MÚSICA JAROCHA OF VERACRUZ

Now let's turn to a musical tradition from the other side of Mexico, from the southern coastal plain of the state of Veracruz. While *música jarocha* [music of the *jarochos,* the people of this region] has not achieved the same popular notoriety as that of the *mariachi,* it shares much with its western relative. It emerged from similar circumstances in the colonial period, and then, faced with the same forces of change in the twentieth century—notably, a powerful, centralized media industry that commodified regional traditions, sweeping urbanization, and the growth of the middle class—it transformed itself, attaining a niche of its own in the popular consciousness.

The port city of Veracruz (located in the state of Veracruz) is often characterized in Mexican history as "the gateway to Spain"; it was the principal port through which the Spanish colonizers passed on their way to the interior. In more local terms, it was also the gateway to Africa and the Caribbean, as many African people were brought through as enslaved labor, and as African-Caribbean people and culture left their mark on local life through maritime activity. Today there is no major, separate, identifiable ethnic group of people of African heritage in Veracruz, but the prominence of African and African-Caribbean culture in the *mestizaje* [cultural blending] of the region distinguishes it from most other regions of Mexico.

As was the case with the *mariachi* tradition, before the twentieth century there was no "standard" regional musical group that marked the music of southern Veracruz. The musical heritage of the area, though, drew heavily from the same Spanish heritage of stringed instruments—in particular, the harp, folk guitar, and violin. Veracruz instrument makers left their own mark on these prototypes.

At the turn of the twentieth century, the principal instruments used in traditional music were the strummed guitar called *jarana,* a plucked guitar now known as *requinto jarocho,* a type of *arpa* [harp] constructed somewhat differently from that in West Mexico, and a violin. These instruments for the most part still exist, though some are quite rare.

The *jarana* comes in many sizes, from the small *mosquito* (twenty-one inches, with five strings) to the largest size (thirty-four inches, often known as *jarana tercera*) that approaches the length of the guitar. The *requinto jarocho,* also known as *rejona, jabalina* [wild boar, evoked by its sound], or *guitarra de son,* has four strings that are plucked by a four-inch pick carved from cowhorn or from a nylon comb. The modern *arpa jarocha* stands nearly five feet high and is played stand-

Ill. 2–10. (*Left to right*) *Jarocho* musicians Gonzalo Mata, José Gutiérrez, and Oliverio Lara, with their instruments the *arpa jarocha, requinto jarocho,* and *jarana jarocha,* respectively.

ing up. Its *caja* [sound box] is fashioned either from five individual slats pieced together or by bending a single piece of three-ply wood. There is a single sound hole in the rear of the sound box, and the pressure of the thirty-two to thirty-six strings bends the *tapa* [top covering] slightly outward (Sheehy 1979:85–86). The harpist usually plays a bass line with the left hand and arpeggiated melodies in the upper range with the right. The violin (quite rare today) is of the standard size and tuning.

Música jarocha in the first half of the twentieth century is not as well documented as *mariachi* music during that period, in large part because it was not nearly as prominent in the early recordings, radio programs, theatrical events, and movies as was the *mariachi*. This is not to say that it did not find a place in the popular media. In the 1940s, a harpist from Veracruz named Andrés Huesca achieved some notoriety in recordings and appearances in movies and live shows. His innovations, propelled by the popular media, had long-lasting repercussions on the *música jarocha* tradition. While the early *jarocho* harp generally was smaller than its western relative and was played sitting down, Huesca adopted the larger-sized harp of West Mexico and played it standing, perhaps feeling this form of presentation to be more appealing and masculine in a popular music setting. He, his brother Víctor Huesca, and others composed new pieces adapted to a *jarocho* musical style. The core of this style was the *son jarocho* [*jarocho*-style *son*], usually cast in a vigorous triple or duple meter. Professional songwriters, Lorenzo Barcelata and Lino Carrillo in particular, wrote new pieces called *sones* that had a *son* rhythm but were different in structure, vocal style, and character of the texts. Barcelata and others even copyrighted previously uncopyrighted traditional *sones*, claiming them and the royalties they generated as their own.

In the 1940s and later, other *jarocho* musicians migrated to Mexico City in search of professional opportunities for their musical talents. Following in the footsteps of Andrés Huesca, the two most celebrated of groups identified with traditional music from Veracruz were Los Costeños [The coastal ones] and later, Conjunto Medellín de Lino Chávez. Lino Chávez, a violinist in his youth, had migrated to Mexico City and played with Los Costeños. Chávez was encouraged by his comrades to take up the *requinto jarocho*, the instrument for which he would be best known the rest of his life. Chávez's group became the "Mariachi Vargas" of *música jarocha*, the nonpareil model for all other professionally aspiring *jarocho* musicians. The recordings by his Conjunto Medellín (named after a town in Veracruz) were distributed widely on the budget-priced RCA-Camden label and were heard throughout the country. Many other *conjuntos jarochos* [*jarocho* groups] made recordings, but none made as many or had the same impact.

The Conjunto Medellín set new norms for *música jarocha*. Their instrumentation—usually harp, *jarana*, *requinto jarocho*, and guitar—became the standard to which others adhered. The exclusion of the violin and the smaller sizes of *jarana* from the group undoubtedly hastened these instruments' way to obscurity. Chávez also shortened the length of the *son* performances and standardized a certain musical structure. Previously, a traditional *son* might be played continuously for as long as an hour or more, as musicians improvised new texts and lengthy instrumental interludes. Chávez's *son* recordings last around three minutes, the generally accepted length of most long-playing record selections at the time. The structure of the *son* as performed by the Conjunto Medellín was determined by the musicians. Typically, near the end of the *son*, the guitars would abruptly stop, leaving the harpist to play a solo to show off his skills. When the harpist signaled the end of his improvisation, the *requinto* would join in, foregrounded as he played his own solo improvisation. Then the *jarana* and guitar would be added, as the piece raced to a close. The style of *son* promoted by Lino Chávez was faster than its traditional predecessor and the tightly harmonized voices departed from the more individualistic tendencies of traditional *son* delivery, reflecting the three-part harmonies of popular music.

The *Son Jarocho*

The *son jarocho* is based on the same structural building block as the *son jalisciense:* the strophic song. The regional musical style imposed upon the strophic song form, though, transforms the Veracruz *son* structure into something quite different from the *son jalisciense*. There are two driving forces behind this difference: (1) a greater emphasis on improvisation, and (2) a distinct concept of *compás,* the underlying rhythmic/harmonic framework. In the context of *música jarocha, compás* refers to a relatively short, repeated section of rhythm and harmony that with few exceptions does not vary throughout the entire *son*. For example, in the *son jarocho* "La bamba," known to have existed in Veracruz since at least the early 1800s, the *compás* is the following, outlined by the strokes and harmonic changes of the *jarana:*

$$X \quad X \quad X \quad X \quad X \quad X \quad X \quad X \quad X \quad X \quad X \quad X \quad X \quad X \quad X \quad X$$
$$I \qquad\qquad IV \qquad\qquad V_7$$

This concept of a short, rhythmic pattern generating the underlying structure for the entire piece is strikingly similar to the cyclical rhythmic patterns of West and Central African music, the point of origin of most of the African peoples who populated this hemisphere, including Veracruz.

The vocal melody is superimposed over the *compás*. Unlike the *son jalisciense* in which the sung strophe typically follows a longer, multipart harmonic scheme (see "Las abajeñas"), the *son jarocho* does not, surrendering entirely to the short *compás*. Also in contrast to the *son jalisciense,* the instrumental interludes between strophes are traditionally of no fixed duration, allowing the musicians the freedom to improvise at length. It is difficult, given the chronological distance from its inception, to prove a direct cause-and-effect relationship between these African-like traits of the *son jarocho* and an African musical heritage, but the similarity, particularly when contrasted with the *son jalisciense,* is striking.

The *son jarocho* is also marked by alternation between singers, as in the *son* "Siquisirí," one of the most widely performed *sones jarochos*. The text might typically be presented as follows, with a *pregonero* [caller, lead singer] answered by one or more other singers, sometimes called the *coro* [chorus]:

pregonero

Muy buenas tardes, señores	Very good afternoon, sirs
Señoras y señoritas	Mesdames, misses
Señoras y señoritas	Mesdames, misses
Muy buenas tardes señores	Very good afternoon, sirs

others

A todas las florecitas	To all the little flowers
De rostros cautivadores	With captivating faces
Van las trovas más bonitas	Go the prettiest verses
De estos pobres cantadores	From these poor minstrels

pregonero

Ay que sí, que sí, que no	Oh yes, yes, no
De Veracruz a Alvarado	From Veracruz to Alvarado

others

Ay que sí, que sí, que no	Oh yes, yes, no

pregonero

Bien conozco la región	I know the region well

others

Ahora sí, mañana no	Now yes, tomorrow no

pregonero

Donde se come el pescado	Where they eat fish

others

Con la grande tú y con la chica yo	You with the big one, I with the small one

pregonero

Y muy sabroso el ostión	And the oysters are tasty
También se halla preparada	And also cooked there
La jaiba y el camarón	Are crab and shrimp

While the sung strophe takes many different forms, most involve some degree of repetition. This may be of indispensable help to the *pregonero,* who often is called upon to improvise verses for the audience. While the other singers repeat the first part of a stanza, the *pregonero* has the opportunity to think up several more lines to complete the poetic stanza. This improvisation is a vital part of *son jarocho* live performance, and many clients will hire *jarocho* musicians with the expectation that they are able to create clever *versos* [verses] fitting the occasion at hand. One tactic is to jest about the quirks of those present. For example, at a certain concert, José Gutiérrez (highlighted below) spotted a woman who had brought several children with her, and he sang the following *verso:*

Señora, es usted de educación	Madame, you are educated
Y mi mente me revela	And my mind reveals to me
Hoy que llega la ocasión	Today the occasion has arrived
Mi disciplina me anhela	My discipline inspires me
Carga niños de a montón	You have a lot of children
Parece maestra de escuela	You look like a schoolteacher

Attending the same performance was a man named Baldomero whom Gutiérrez knew to be a lawyer, and who became the subject of a *verso:*

Quizás por muchas razones	Perhaps for many reasons
Baldomero, con cuidado	Baldomero, careful
Ahora escúchenme, pregono	Now listen to me, I sing
Este verso improvisado	This improvised verse
Las leyes son acordeones	Laws are accordions
En manos de un licenciado	In the hands of a lawyer

While *versos* such as the former are invented whole-cloth for the occasion, many improvised texts such as the latter are mostly not improvised, but rather are in the singer's repertoire of relatively fixed *versos* that might be sung for common situations such as the presence of a lawyer. The singer simply inserts the name of the lawyer in question in an otherwise unchanging text, giving the strong impression of spontaneity that enlivens the audience. (For comparison, see Ercilia Moreno Chá's description of improvising *décimas* in the *payada de contrapunto* of Argentina/Uruguay [Chapter 6] and William Gradante's description of improvising *coplas de rajaleña* in Andean Colombia [Chapter 7].)

Another lively dimension of the *son jarocho* is dance. The *zapateado* with its emphasis on often complex, rhythmic footwork is central to *jarocho* dance. While formal dance troupes have fixed choreographies and certain *sones jarochos* may call for particular dance movements, the *jarocho* dance tradition, like the musical tradition, prizes improvisation. Dance may also play a musical role, as the percussive punctuations of the dancers' feet striking the *tarima* (a traditional dance platform raised off the ground to amplify the sound) adds a rhythmic thread to the sounds of the instruments and voices.

While in a more social, traditional setting, factors such as verse and dance improvisation can lengthen and shape the particular *son jarocho* performance, the typical overall form of the modern, "concert" *son jarocho* is an opening instrumental section followed by a series of strophes separated by instrumental interludes and ending with a final strophe. This final strophe often takes the form of a *despedida* [farewell], as in the case of this strophe from "La bamba":

Ay Cupido, te pido	Oh Cupid, I ask you
Ay Cupido, te pido	Oh Cupid, I ask you
De compasión	Out of compassion
Que se acabe La Bamba	That La Bamba come to an end
Que se acabe La Bamba	That La Bamba come to an end
Y venga otro son	And that another *son* begin
Ay arriba y arriba	Oh, up and up
Ay arriba y arriba	Oh, up and up
Y arriba iré	And up I will go
Yo no soy marinero	I am not a sailor
Yo no soy marinero	I am not a sailor
Por tí seré	For you I will be
Por tí seré	For you I will be
Por tí seré	For you I will be

THE *JARANA JAROCHA*

The term *jarana* derives from the same Spanish word meaning "merrymaking." In Mexico, it is the name of several regional types of guitar and of a folk dance from the Yucatán peninsula. So, we use the term *jarana jarocha* to describe the southern

Ill. 2–11. Isidoro Gutiérrez, father of José Gutiérrez, playing the *jarana* he made.

Veracruz brand of folk guitar, even though when talking among themselves, the musicians simply would call it the *jarana.*

In the older tradition, there were many different sizes of *jarana.* This variation in size came about for two principal reasons: (1) there was a musical preference, undoubtedly inherited from Spanish musical practice, for combining different sizes of the same instrument to create a well-blended ensemble over a wide pitch range, and (2) instrument makers made instruments according to their own preferences and to the tastes of their individual clients.

As mentioned above, with the transition of the *conjunto jarocho* to the urban popular music setting, virtually all sizes of *jarana* but one were excluded. The largest *jarana,* previously known as the *jarana tercera* [third *jarana*], became the principal accompanying instrument for the *arpa* and *requinto.* While the precise dimensions vary according to the preferences of the maker and the musician, the *jarana* is approximately thirty-four inches in length, nine inches at its widest point, and two and a half inches deep. The last dimension is considerably shallower than that of the *vihuela,* adding to a sharper, more percussive sound than the *vihuela* produces. The length of the vibrating portion of the strings is also relatively short—twenty-three inches—producing a more percussive sound of short duration compared to the guitar, fitting for the *jarana*'s rhythmic role in accompanying the *son.*

Similar to the *vihuela,* the *jarana* employs a re-entrant tuning, though the precise tuning is different. The *jarana jarocha* has ten strings, with four of them grouped together in pairs, resulting in five courses of strings, four double and two single. The re-entrant tuning occurs in the middle course, in which the two strings are tuned in octaves rather than to the same pitch:

$$F_\sharp F_\sharp \ BB \ E'E \ G_\sharp G_\sharp \ C'_\sharp C'_\sharp$$

Delineating the rhythmic and harmonic outline of the *compás,* the *jaranero* [*jarana* player] employs a range of possible hand patterns to add subtle variations in texture and emphasis to the rhythm. Some *jaraneros* use a large number of strumming patterns, others use only a few. In playing the *son jarocho,* there are two principal types of strum: a simple, sharp striking of all the strings simultaneously (Recorded Selection 5); and a *rasgueo* stroke in which the fingers sweep across the strings more slowly, creating a "roll" or "flourish" effect (Recorded Selection 6). There are many subtle differences in these strokes, depending on whether they are upward or downward, executed with the four fingers or with the thumb, and in particular combinations in sequence that create light unevenness in the rhythm. Striking the fingers into the strings, stopping them from vibrating while producing a percussive, "fingers-against-strings" sound may also be used. Two of the most common *maniqueos* [strokes] for a *son* in a *sesquiáltera* meter are shown in Example 2–9.

The *jarana* is strictly a rhythm and chordal instrument. It is not used for melody-making, unless perhaps the musician is doodling around or showing another musician how a particular melody goes.

Ex. 2–9. Two common *jarana maniqueos* [*jarana* strokes]

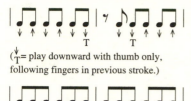

($\downarrow\!\!\atop T$= play downward with thumb only,
following fingers in previous stroke.)

PROFILE OF JOSÉ GUTIÉRREZ

José Gutiérrez (no relation to Margarito Gutiérrez) in many ways personifies the story of the modern *son jarocho* in its transition to an urban popular music setting (Recorded Selection 7). He was born in 1942, the same year as Margarito Gutiér-rez, on a ranch called La Costa de la Palma near the town of Alvarado in Ver-acruz. "I remember that more or less at the age of four or five, I started to *gorjear* [warble], as we say." His grandfather, Doroteo Ramos Palacios, played harp, as did an uncle and his grandfather. He believes his great-grandfather might have played harp, too.

Music was played for special occasions when people from nearby ranches like the one named Mosquiteros would get together for a dance:

> I remember when I was a young boy, I would take my guitar with my grandfather to where he would play, and I would fall asleep between his legs with my guitar in my hand. . . . I started playing the *mosquito* [a small *jarana*]. Back then, all my people had those small *jaranas*. There were no large ones, *jaranas terceras* as they were called. There were no *jaranas segundas* [slightly smaller] either. I remember that my grandfather and uncles would give their instruments names. One was called El Diablito [Little devil], for example.
>
> Actually, my grandfather had a group that played for dances. . . . They played *dan-zones*, waltzes, schottisches—*piezas* [composed pieces, not *sones*]. He knew how to play the *son jarocho*, too. . . . I remember we would play the *sones* with my grandfather playing violin. We didn't have a harp then.
>
> When I was still a young boy, I took a *jarana* and turned it into a *requinto jarocho*. I liked the way Güicho Delfín played, and he showed me how. We called it the *rejona*, or *requinto de cuatro cuerdas*. They called it the *jabalina* down around San Andrés Tuxtla. It was tuned the same way it is now. After a while I became one of the best *requinto* players around. There were only three in the region. (Interview with José Gutiérrez, Aug. 17, 1997)

Gutiérrez started to work as a professional musician in the tourist restaurants in Boca del Río, a fishing town next to the port of Veracruz. He returned to the ranch for a while, then:

> I went to Veracruz and played with Los Tigres de la Costa [The tigers of the coast]. It was 1961. We started to do programs on XCU, a radio station that is heard throughout

the Papaloapan River Basin [southern Veracruz] and all of Veracruz. . . . [The music] changed a lot because the style that we had there on the ranch is a style very distinct from the style [the Tigres played], but I already had an idea of the style that the Tigres de la Costa played because I learned from the records by Lino, Lino Chávez.

. . .

I played with them and with Los Pregoneros del Puerto. . . . I was invited to go play with the *ballet folklórico* of Silvia Lozano in Mexico City. So I went with them for a while, in 1966 or '67. We toured Europe and all over the United States. . . . I came back and played with a group in Acapulco. . . . Lino Chávez had been calling me to join his group. I went with him in 1971 and stayed with them until 1975; it was when he recorded "Fandango jarocho." I played *jarana* and sometimes I was the *pregonero*. . . . We recorded several records. We played in a restaurant [the Casino Veracruzano in Mexico City], where we worked every Friday . . . in a variety show. (Interviews with José Gutiérrez, Aug. 17, 1997 and Nov. 30, 1997)

Gutiérrez lived in the United States from 1975 to 1997, then moved back to Mexico to join the Ballet Folklórico de Amalia Hernández, where he performed weekly in the National Palace of Fine Arts in Mexico City, toured with the company, and played private parties with his musician comrades.

Regarding the change of musical style, Gutiérrez said:

It changed completely ever since the late Andrés Huesca started to play what was known as *música jarocha,* because he hardly recorded [what was really] *música jarocha,* very little. . . . He devoted himself more to playing *música ranchera* with Los Costeños and all that. But he did give a big boost to Veracruzan music because he transformed what was known as Veracruzan music, as did the late Veracruzan Agustín Lara. But they were Veracruzans who were not spreading the authentic music—that is, the folk tradition. Nevertheless they, as Veracruzans, were playing other things because they both were songwriters. . . . Lino was the one who made the change in the music happen . . . and later, well, we all copied from what was the *requinto* style and the finely decorated *jarana* and everything. . . . *Música jarocha* up to now has not evolved further. A lot of us do different arrangements, but it is the same [style]. After Lino, we played the same way. After Andrés Huesca, we played the same way. And the harpists, just like the *requinto* players, we play the same. (Interview with José Gutiérrez, Nov. 30, 1997)

Gutiérrez feels that there is no contemporary group equaling the quality of Conjunto Medellín. "There is a demand [for the music]. What happens is, we don't take the time to put together a really professional level group. . . . Before, there were [such groups]" (ibid.).

He also feels that music of the tradition is being lost. "[Young people] don't spend time learning it, like they used to. . . . The verses are being lost, and skill at improvising [the verses]. A lot of the richness of the tradition is being lost." But a healthy economic incentive augers well for the future existence of, at least, contemporary-style *música jarocha*. "We can make in one day more than, say, a college professor can make. And we don't have the education they have. Of course, we do know the music. . . . Groups like the Ballet Folklórico will carry the tradi-

Ill. 2–12. José Gutiérrez (far right) and fellow members of the Ballet Folklórico de Amalia Hernández performing on stage at Mexico City's Palace of Fine Arts.

tion on. . . . There are many good teachers who have many good students" (interview with José Gutiérrez, Aug. 17, 1997).

José Gutiérrez and his four-member *conjunto jarocho* play almost exclusively for either the *ballet folklórico* or *chambas*, hired by the hour. The *chamba* work is similar to that of Margarito Gutiérrez's *mariachi*, though most of their clients contact them through word-of-mouth. In Veracruz, however, professional *conjunto jarochos* most often work at the equivalent of *al talón*, playing for customers in restaurants and bars, charging by the song. His father Isidoro worked this way his entire professional career in the coastal town of Boca del Río, at the mouth of the Jamapa River just south of the port city of Veracruz.

During a six-month stay in Boca del Río in the late 1970s, I would accompany Isidoro and his comrades daily during their several-hour workday. Isidoro's house was located near the river, just one block from a half dozen open-air, fresh seafood restaurants. During most seasons of the year, the restaurants attract considerable crowds of tourists, mainly from Mexico City, who would begin to arrive about noon and disperse around four or five in the afternoon. The musicians would gather at Isidoro's place, where they had left their instruments the day before, each dressed in a multipocketed *guayabera* shirt and a traditional round-cupped, palm-fiber *jarocho* hat. After a bit of socializing, they would stroll off toward the restaurants, one with his harp and the others with their *jaranas*. Nearing the first restaurant, one musician would strum a few chords on his *jarana*, hoping to attract the attention of the diners. When a client called them over, one

Ill. 2–13. (*Left to right*) **Isidoro Gutiérrez, harpist (name unknown), and Emilio Córdoba gathered outside Isidoro's house in Boca del Río, Veracruz, before playing for tourists in nearby seafood restaurants.**

of the musicians would let him know the price of a song. Most of the customers were unfamiliar with the *jarocho* repertoire and simply would ask them to play one of their songs. Or those more in the know might ask for (improvised) *versos* or one of the dozen-or-so *sones jarochos* that have become known widely through the popular media—"La bamba," "Tilingo lingo," "Colás," or "María chuchena," for example. Still others would ask for popular *música ranchera* songs, and the musicians would have to decline, unless it was a classic such as "Cielito lindo," "Rancho grande," or the popular *bolero* "Veracruz."

When singing improvised *versos*, the musicians would usually play the *sones* "Jarabe loco" and "Siquisirí," generally favored by *jarochos* for this purpose. Isidoro was the principal *improvisador*. In casual conversation, he would try to glean a few facts about the customers—their names, line of work, home town, and so forth. Then, he would sing several *versos* for the occasion. To a man accompanied by a woman friend, he might sing:

Un verso le voy a hacer	I'm going to sing you a *verso*
Pero con mucha alegría.	Filled with happiness.
Félix, te doy a saber	Felix, I'm letting you know
Por medio de mi poesía	Through my poetry
Que Teresa no es la mujer	That Teresa is not the woman
Que trajiste el otro día.	You brought here the other day.

To a portly client drinking beer, he might dedicate this *verso:*

Traigo versos de a montón	I have lots of *versos*
Sacados de mi cabeza.	Pulled out of my head.
Hablo con satisfacción	I speak with satisfaction
Decirlo me da tristeza	To say it saddens me
Te estás poniendo panzón	You're getting a big belly
Por tanto chupar cerveza.	From drinking beer so much.

Nearly all of the improvised *versos* provoke an uproar of laughter and requests for more *versos* and other *sones*. After several *sones*, the client pays the musicians, and they move on to other tables and other restaurants along the river.

As the crowds would thin later in the afternoon, the group would walk back to Isidoro's house and split the day's earnings evenly among them. After a bit more socializing, they would deposit their instruments once again in Isidoro's house and return home, ending another workday.

Ill. 2–14. *Jarocho* **musicians Gilberto Valenzuela** *(jarana)*, **Ramón Hoz** *(arpa)*, **and Fortino Hoz (Spanish-style guitar) playing in Las Brisas Restaurant in Boca del Río.**

CONCLUSION

Margarito Gutiérrez and José Gutiérrez operate in multidimensional musical worlds. The musics they play continue to have strong ties to rural, regional cultures and identities. They both are deeply rooted in regional tradition. At the same time, they are fully professional and belong to new, additional cultural communities, those defined by the shared ambiance, goals, needs, and standards of the professional world in which they work. These new ties link them to other musicians who practice their style of music, both those from their region of origin and those from elsewhere. In this way, they are linked to tradition. At the same time, the subject matter of their profession—the musical repertoire—is influenced strongly by a commercial music industry driven by the quest for profit. In the minds of both, there is a give-and-take in this process; an important and beautiful part of the older tradition is sacrificed at the same time the remnants of the tradition in their evolved forms persevere, bolstered by the same economic incentive that ushered in change.

Both the genesis and the twentieth-century transformations of each of these music cultures underscore the close connections of music cultures to their evolving, broader ethnographic bases. The *son jalisciense* and the *son jarocho* emerged as part of the colonial *mestizaje* that drew from common roots, but at the same time reflected the cultural and historical distinctions that defined each regional way of life. In the tumultuous twentieth century, each music culture seems to be adapting to a rapidly changing modern society. As the Mexican population has become two-thirds urban, and as the media industry has imposed its profit-minded system in creating an idealized version of regional folk culture, both *música de mariachi* and *música jarocha* have been transformed by commercially successful innovators into widely accepted, popular forms of music. And as idealized notions of regional identity—as with the media-affirmed, stereotypical characters of Jalisco and Veracruz—have become defining components of nationality among the broad Mexican public, so have these regional musics become, by extension, part of a pan-Mexican musical life.

REFERENCES

Barrios de los Ríos, Enrique. 1908. *Paisajes de Oriente.* Sombrerete, Zacatecas, Mexico: Biblioteca Estarsiana.

Clark, Jonathan. 1992. Descriptive notes to CD *Mariachi Vargas de Tecalitlán: Their First Recordings 1937–1947.* Vol. 3 of *Mexico's Pioneer Mariachis.* El Cerrito, Calif.: Arhoolie Folklyric CD 7015.

———. 1993. Descriptive notes to CD *Mariachi Coculense de Cirilo Marmolejo: 1926–1936.* Vol. 1 of *Mexico's Pioneer Mariachis.* El Cerrito, Calif.: Arhoolie Folklyric CD 7011.

Directorio Telefónico, Sección Amarilla, Ciudad de México y Area Metropolitana. 1996/97 edition, pp. 2301–2306.

Esteva, José María. 1844a. Costumbres y trages [*sic*] nacionales: la jarochita. *El Museo Mexicano,* vol. III, pp. 234–235.

————. 1844b. Trages [*sic*] y costumbres nacionales: el jarocho. *El Museo Mexicano,* vol. IV, pp. 60–62.

Gutiérrez, José. 1997. Interview by author. Palacio de Bellas Artes, Mexico City, August 17.

————. 1997. Interview by author. Palacio de Bellas Artes, Mexico City, November 30.

Gutiérrez, Margarito. 1997. Interview by author. Gutiérrez home, Guadalajara, Jalisco, March 2.

Jáuregui, Jesús. 1990. *El mariachi: Símbolo musical de México.* Mexico City: Banpaís.

Morales, Roberto. 1997. Interview by author. Morales home, Guadalajara, Jalisco, March 1.

Romano, Mario. 1997. Interview by author. Sombreros Vargas hat-making shop, Mexico City, November 29.

Saldívar, Gabriel. 1934. *Historia de la música en México: Épocas precortesiana y colonial.* Mexico, D.F.: Secretaría de Educación Pública, Publicaciones del Departamento de Bellas Artes.

Sheehy, Daniel. 1979. The *son jarocho:* The history, style, and repertory of a changing Mexican musical tradition. Ph.D. diss., Univ. of California at Los Angeles.

Sonnichsen, Philip, with assistance from Hermes Rafael and Jim Nicolopulos. 1993. Descriptive notes to CD *Mariachi Coculense de Cirilo Marmolejo, 1926–1936.* Vol. 1 of *Mexico's Pioneer Mariachis.* El Cerrito, Calif.: Arhoolie Folklyric CD 7011.

Stevenson, Robert. 1952. *Music in Mexico: A Historical Survey.* New York: Thomas Y. Crowell Co.

Toor, Frances. 1947. *A treasury of Mexican Folkways.* New York: Crown Publishers, Inc.

CHAPTER THREE

Central America

Marimba and Other Musics of Guatemala and Nicaragua

T. M. SCRUGGS

INTRODUCTION

Look at a political map of the Americas, where each country is outlined or filled in with a different color. Besides the small island nations in the eastern Caribbean, you will notice a bunching together of smaller republics in Central America. Just as Simón Bolívar's dream during the independence struggle of a united Spanish-speaking South American republic fell apart, so the initial project of creating a single Central American republic in the 1820s collapsed, and several separate nation-states were consolidated. Culturally, these types of maps are deceptive—a single color for Brazil may correctly represent that this immense territory falls under one governmental administration, but it ignores the complexity of cultural and ethnic differences within Brazil's borders. For the seven Central American republics, the many political boundaries more accurately reflect the cultural makeup of the region. The distinctiveness of the people and the music of each Central American nation can be as notable as that between, for example, Mexicans and Colombians. The way a person speaks Spanish can immediately identify his nationality, especially to Central Americans. There are even greater ethnic differences within most of the current nation-states between the western and eastern parts of a country.

Nevertheless, there are many cultural and therefore musical commonalities that run through the region. Some of these commonalities predate the arrival of Europeans and Africans in the early 1500s. For example, most of the precontact population in the middle part of the isthmus arrived sometime after the eighth century in several waves of immigration from what is now central Mexico. While these groups maintained separate identities, they shared many cultural characteristics and were able to communicate among themselves in a common language, Nahuatl, which is still spoken in several native communities in central Mexico. The strongest linkages among Central Americans stem from the binding forces of Spanish colonialism. The long colonial experience replicated similar institutions, language, and cultural practices—including music—throughout the region. As in other parts of Latin America, the centuries-long process of *mestizaje*—the mixing of Amerindian and European peoples and cultures—produced a new group throughout the region: *mestizos,* also called *ladinos.* The formation of the *mestizo/ladino* population varied within Central America, with important musical consequences, as we shall see. For example, *mestizaje* was pronounced in Nicaragua, where over four-fifths of the large indigenous population was either killed outright by the Spaniards, died from the Europeans' new diseases, or were shipped as slaves to Peru. In Guatemala, despite horrendous treatment, the large Mayan communities fared much better and have always outnumbered mixed-race *ladinos.* As a result of these different histories, for several generations Spanish has been the sole language of over 90 percent of the population from Honduras and El Salvador to Nicaragua to Costa Rica, while more than half of Guatemala still speaks one of the Mayan languages. In similar fashion, there is a basic Spanish stylistic foundation in the music of the broad *mestizo/ladino* population along the isthmus. The commonalities of Central American *mestizo/ladino* culture provide the basis for a musical unity within the diversity that distinguishes each individual national culture.

This common Hispanic history does not really apply to one important part of the Central American musical map: the eastern coastal zone that borders the Caribbean. When Central Americans from the western part of the region travel for the first time to the eastern coast, they are often surprised at how distinctive it is from the majority national culture. In the 1980s, Nicaraguan friends told me they felt they had gone to a "foreign country." The reason for these reactions is that the Atlantic coast, as it is often (if somewhat incorrectly) labeled, has had a qualitatively different historical experience from that of the majority population on the Pacific coast. The Spanish never effectively controlled this part of Central America; most of the Atlantic coastal contact was actually with English traders. This relatively sparsely populated part of the isthmus has looked eastward, towards the Caribbean region, for its economic and cultural ties. Only recently have Atlantic coast communities become more integrated within the majority Spanish-speaking culture of their respective nations. Music played a key role in bringing about this move towards unification, as we will see towards the end of this chapter.

A SHARED INSTRUMENT: THE *MARIMBA*

If you travel in Central America there is one musical experience that you could easily encounter in almost all of the republics—hearing some kind of *marimba.* A *marimba* is any kind of xylophone with wooden keys, that is, a percussion instrument consisting of different-sized wooden keys arranged from large to small on top of a frame, which are struck with a mallet of some type. Almost all *marimbas* have individual resonance chambers under each key. It is safe to say that at any given time there is probably a *marimba* being played somewhere in Central America.

In the large city of Masaya, Nicaragua, a *marimba de arco* trio starts their first number at a private evening party. All the musicians perform sitting down. The *marimbero* [*marimba* player] has placed himself inside the hoop, or arc, attached to the *marimba,* and is flanked by family members playing a guitar and a small four-stringed *guitarilla.* The *marimba* has only twenty-two keys but its sound is *recio* [loud, strong]. The guests have to shout into each other's ears to be heard, and as the evening (and alcohol consumption) advances, they leave behind conversation and dance far into the night. At the same time, in an expensive tourist hotel in San José, Costa Rica's capital, seven musicians in coordinated outfits provide a dinner serenade on two large *marimbas.* The larger of the two instruments is over thirty feet long, and both have two rows of keys and elaborate carvings along their wooden frames.

At the Sunday market in Chichicastenango, a favorite tourist stop in northern Guatemala, a Mayan musician seats himself and props up his *marimba de tecomates*—a *marimba* with twenty-eight keys aligned in a single row, named for the *tecomates,* the gourds hanging underneath each key. He carried the instrument in from his Mayan village the day before and will return there later that Sunday. Throughout the morning he plays on a corner between the market and local shops. Wearing traditional Mayan dress, he plays to attract tips from the Guatemalan and foreign tourists passing by. Around sunset that same Sunday in Comayagua, the old capital of Honduras, musicians haul a duo of large two-row *marimbas* similar to the ones in Costa Rica up a stairway onto a porch overlooking the town's central plaza. Three musicians on the larger *marimba* and two on the smaller one then offer an accompaniment of waltzes, mazurkas, and other genteel forms to the couples that gather in the plaza. The sounds of the *marimbas* float across the plaza as the cool of the evening releases the perfume of the flowers lining the walkways: it is quite a romantic setting.

The *marimbas* you are most likely to hear in the United States and Europe are the large instruments with two rows of keys used in European classical music, in jazz, and now often in New-Age music. This type of instrument was developed in the last eighty years by modifying the Central American *marimba.* Where did the Central American *marimba* originate? This has been a vexing question and one that has generated some heated debate among Central Americans, especially Guatemalans.

Despite the fact that we don't know exactly when or precisely where, we do know that the *marimba* first appeared in several places in Latin America when captive Africans began to re-create different types of *marimbas* from various parts of the African continent. These early *marimbas* have now disappeared from several parts of Latin America where they once existed. For example, we know from descriptions and drawings that several African-Brazilian communities once played *marimbas*, but the use of the *marimba* there now has virtually vanished. Currently, *marimbas* are found in only two major regions: (1) southern Mexico and Central America, and (2) African-American communities along the Pacific coast in Colombia and Ecuador.[1] At present, there is a strong presence of *marimbas* in the southernmost Mexican states, especially Oaxaca and Chiapas. *Marimbas* continue to be found further south in Central America all the way to central Costa Rica, but they stop there—you have to leap over Panama to the western coast of Colombia to find them again.

The earliest surviving written reference to a *marimba* in Central America dates from 1680 in Guatemala (Juarros 1981:399), and it is reasonable to assume that *marimbas* must have been in use there for some time before that. The *marimbas* re-created by the small African population in Central America were soon adopted by indigenous communities and became one of their principal musical instruments. This adoption was so early and so thorough that for centuries the *marimba* has been associated with indigenous American culture in the region. (A similar association of the European-derived harp with Quechua culture appears in highland Peru.) This perception is aided by the fact that the number of Afro–Central Americans was so small that they mixed with the indigenous and *mestizo* population and eventually disappeared as a separate group. Further complicating the picture is the fact that most of the current Afro–Central American population in the eastern coastal area of the isthmus arrived in relatively recent migrations from English-speaking Caribbean islands, notably Jamaica. The fact that these blacks did not bring *marimbas* with them, and that the natives appear to have always had them, led to speculation that the *marimba* was originally Amerindian—specifically, Mayan.

Some nationalistic Guatemalans could not accept that the *marimba*, so popular as to be considered the national musical instrument, did not originate on Guatemalan soil. This attitude was also tinged with a healthy dose of racism that could not accept that people of African descent were the progenitors of their favorite instrument. A sometimes ferocious debate over this issue consumed many newspaper articles and even several books. One Guatemalan writer went so far as to forge a drawing in precontact Mayan style that purportedly showed a type of *marimba* being played. He claimed he had received it from Mayan priests who, coincidentally, had insisted on remaining anonymous (Armas Lara 1970). The debate on the *marimba*'s origin illustrates the important role that music, even just a musical instrument, can play in symbolizing ethnic and national identity and feelings.

This history of the *marimba* in Central America also highlights people's flexibility to use whatever musical resources are available for their own ends. The debate on the *marimba*'s origin could not have taken place if the process of musical-cultural adaptation of the *marimba* had not been so complete—that is, if Mayan and other Central American natives had not so thoroughly adopted the *marimba* as their own instrument. Maybe this process can be better appreciated if we look at a similar example in the United States: the adoption by whites of the banjo, an instrument that derived from West African instruments. The first generation of American banjo players were all African-American, yet one would be hard-pressed to find a stronger indicator of "whiteness" in contemporary North American music than the look and sound of a banjo. The ability of the indigenous peoples of Central America to make the African *marimba* their own parallels the adoption of the African-American banjo by the European-American population in the United States. Whatever the *marimba*'s earliest history, Central Americans and outsiders alike have always thought that the instrument was rooted in the indigenous population of the region.

THE *MARIMBA* IN GUATEMALA

In the last two centuries experiments by Central Americans and southern Mexicans have dramatically enlarged and changed the earliest forms of the *marimba*. The different sizes and types of *marimbas* eventually dispersed to one degree or another throughout most of Central America. Let's examine Guatemala, where all the various types are still currently used: the earlier forms of *marimba* are played in the countryside and larger, more recent types appear in towns and cities (see Chenoweth 1964 for additional information). These different kinds of *marimbas* are usually grouped into three basic kinds, known in Guatemala as the *marimba de tecomates*, the *marimba sencilla,* and the *marimba doble.*

MARIMBA DE TECOMATES

Listen to the recording of a *marimba de tecomates* (or *marimba con tecomates*), which means "*marimba* with gourds" (Recorded Selection 8 on the CD accompanying this book). Probably one of the first things that will impress you is the sound quality of the instrument. The buzzing sound, called *charleo,* is a characteristic of both African and Latin America *marimbas.* We will look more closely at how this sound is produced when we examine how the similar Nicaraguan *marimba de arco* is constructed. When Europeans and North Americans adapted the Central American *marimba* in the 1920s they eliminated this feature from the instrument. So you can immediately recognize a Latin American (and an African) *marimba* by the buzzing sound that comes with each note.

How would you describe the basic form of the music? Is it linear—that is, does it clearly move from one idea and progress to another and then another? Or is it more circular, revolving around repeated phrases and motives? The lower notes that form the bass line highlight how circular this piece is. When a particular phrase is used repeatedly in this manner it is called an *ostinato.* The bass *ostinato* is played by the player's left hand; his right hand plays the melody. Notice how the melody is also quite repetitive, but includes variations over time. Do you hear a single note in the melody, or more than one note simultaneously? In fact, there are usually two—the *marimba* player holds one mallet in his left hand, but has two in his right hand. The mallets are kept the same distance apart to produce the effect of a melody with parallel harmony in thirds—that is, the notes are three notes apart from each other. At times, the player's right hand rotates a bit and only a single note is very audible. Example 3–1 is a transcription that shows how

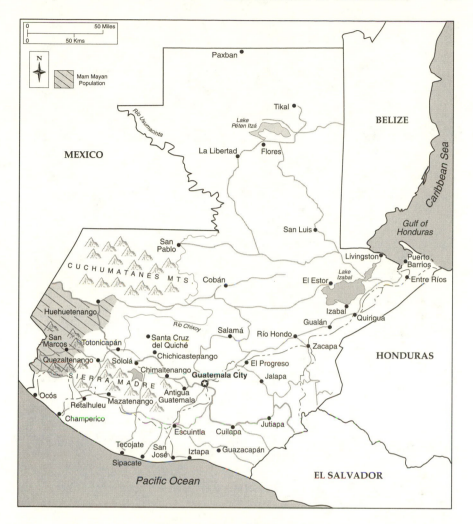

Fig. 3–1. Map of Guatemala

the two separate parts are produced by each of the *marimba* player's hands. At least for *marimba* music, centuries of Spanish musical acculturation have supplanted any distinct tuning system that the Mayans might have used previously. As you can hear, the notes all correspond to a standard Western tuning and the music clearly implies European tonal harmony.

This recording of a *marimba de tecomates* comes from a musician playing at the Sunday market in Chichicastenango described above (see Illustration 3–1).

This form of a *marimba de tecomates* has a hoop or arc of wood attached at each end of the frame, and a single musician sits inside the hoop to play the instrument. The *marimba* has twenty-eight keys of heavy, dense hardwood, and their weight usually obliges the *marimbista* (the preferred term for *marimba*

Ex. 3–1. Transcription of *marimba de tecomates,* recorded February 1990 in Chichicastenango, Guatemala

Ex. 3–1.   Transcription of *marimba de tecomates*, recorded February 1990 in Chichicastenango, Guatemala (continued)

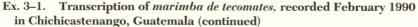

player in Guatemala) to prop up the front of the instrument with a small stick or place the keyboard across two boxes, as the musician in Illustration 3–1 did. The music played on the *marimba de tecomates* (and the dance it accompanies) is usually known by the generic title *son,* a common description throughout Hispanic America for a song or instrumental music type. In Chapter 2, Daniel Sheehy

Ill. 3–1. *Marimba de tecomates*, Chichicastenango, Guatemala, February, 1990.

discusses the Mexican *son jalisciense* and *son jarocho,* for example. Non-Mayans sometimes refer to all the types of *sones* as just "Mayan *son.*" Different types of *sones* are used in religious and secular contexts in Mayan Indian villages deep in the countryside, some accessible only by foot. The *marimba de tecomates* provides music at ritual functions, such as the blessing of the seed before planting. Often the *marimba* is accompanied by a small drum and vertical cane flute. Sometimes other instruments may play with a *marimba,* such as a folk harp or the oboe-like *chirimía.* As in this example, a Mayan *marimba de tecomates* player might occasionally come into town in hopes of earning some money, but the most common Mayan *marimba* in urban settings is the one known as the *marimba sencilla.*

MARIMBA SENCILLA

During the 1800s, Mayans and mixed-race *ladinos* living in towns developed what is now called the *marimba sencilla* in two stages. They first transformed the type of *marimba de tecomates* with an attached arc by adding more keys, so that several musicians could play on the same instrument. Contemporary *marimba sencillas* usually have four to five octaves (thirty-three to forty keys). The older hoop or arc had to be abandoned, and legs were attached to support the increased weight. This change emerged from a desire to perform the popular musical styles that circulated in more urban areas. With additional musicians, one player could play a bass line, one or two could fill in harmony in the middle range, and another one or two could play a melody line and improvise in the upper register.

Second, they changed the resonators that hang from the frame under the keys. Constructing a *marimba de tecomates* requires enough gourds—which grow on trees—of the right size to accommodate each of the keys. The longer keys need large-sized gourds to effectively amplify the low notes they produce. The *marimba* maker can fine-tune a *tecomate* by cutting off the top of the gourd a bit to size it, but he still needs a healthy supply of gourds of varying sizes with which to work. Gradual deforestation, increased demand for *marimbas,* and the greater number of resonators on each instrument all led to the construction of *cajones harmónicos* [harmonic boxes], rectangular wooden boxes fashioned to replace *tecomates.* Today, these *marimbas,* with one to five players on a single instrument, are very popular among both *ladinos* and the more urban Mayan population. *Marimba sencilla* groups can include various other instruments, from saxophones and other wind instruments to drums and small percussion instruments. You can find a wide selection of cassettes of *marimba sencilla* groups for sale in marketplaces and on sidewalk stands in towns and cities. Unfortunately for the musicians, these cassettes are usually unauthorized bootleg copies, but at least the musicians achieve some exposure from these sales.

Listen to the piece "T¨xe¨xpele.n (año nuevo)," performed by Marimba Indígena Flor Bataneca (Recorded Selection 9). This group consists of the three Mata brothers, members of the Mam group of Mayans, who are from a village near the northern city of Huehuetenango. This recording is from one of their cassettes, *Marimba Indígena* [Indigenous marimba], whose cover is shown in Illustration 3–2.

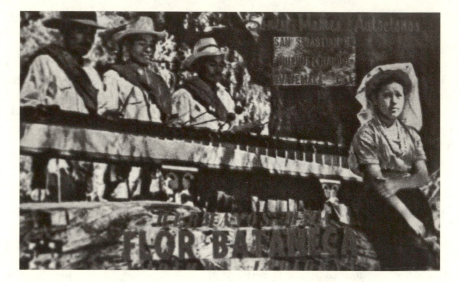

Ill. 3–2. Cover of the commercial cassette *Marimba Indígena,* **by the Hermanos Mata, a** *marimba sencilla* **group.**

What is similar to, and what is different from, the example of the *marimba de tecomates?* One thing that remains the same is the *charleo,* or buzzing sound, which is almost as strong as the *charleo* on the *marimba de tecomates* example. However, the strong circular organization of the music has changed and is more *linear*—that is, there are definite sections that are repeated in a particular order. Also, the pieces have a more defined length. In general, they hold to the conventions of most folk or popular songs. Many of these *marimba* pieces are instrumental versions of songs with lyrics. Note the division of the parts assigned to each player—bass line, middle chords, and top melody.

In Mayan Guatemala, this type of music is not just for listening, it is also dance music. The dance, also generically called *son,* is a couple dance in which the man and woman never touch. Their motions are calm and relaxed in appearance; their feet barely leave the ground, and the movement almost looks like a shuffle. This style of dance is common both in the countryside and among Mayans who have relocated to the cities. At parties among Mayans, either a live *marimba* group or *marimba* recordings commonly provide the music. Usually quieter *sones* are played at the beginning of a party, and later the music shifts to *cumbias* and other more energetic and broadly popular musical styles.

The word *sencilla* means plain, simple, or easy, and describes this *marimba* in comparison to the *marimba* we will look at next—the larger and more complex *marimba de doble teclado* [*marimba* with two rows of keys] or simply *marimba doble.* Even though there are usually more of them, the notes on a *marimba sencilla* offer the same basic pitch set as those on the *marimba de tecomates.* This tonal selection is diatonic: it offers seven notes to an octave, the basic equivalent of the white keys on a piano. On the *marimba doble*, a second row of keys is raised above the first and set back, imitating the position of black notes on a piano. This makes the *marimba doble* a chromatic instrument, capable of producing all of the twelve notes within a European equidivided octave.

Sometimes *marimbistas* have difficulty performing pieces on the *marimba sencilla* because the songs demand several notes that the instrument doesn't have—the music uses a chromatic pitch set, but the *marimba* is diatonic. For such occasions, *marimba sencilla* musicians (and players of other diatonic *marimbas*, such as the Nicaraguan *marimba de arco*) have two options. First, they can "fudge" the note by playing around it in ingenious ways that distract the listener's ear from noticing the slight modification to the melody to avoid a note the instrument doesn't have. Second, diatonic *marimba* musicians can set aside a small ball of beeswax, stuck on the *marimba*'s frame out of view of the audience. When a small amount of wax is attached to the underside of a key towards the end of the key, the pitch will rise slightly. The right amount of beeswax or other substance will produce a sound midway between the original pitch and the pitch of the adjacent key—this is the "missing" chromatic note that doesn't exist between the keys of the one-row *marimba sencilla*. Usually there is only one, or at most two, notes crucial to a chromatic melody that the diatonic *marimba sencilla* can't produce. The musicians on the upper register, who carry the melody, attach the beeswax at just the right moment—and then, of course, just as quickly have to remove it after the note is played.

MARIMBA DOBLE

It was just such challenges of playing chromatically based musics that led to the invention of the *marimba doble*, also called the *marimba cromática* or simply the *marimba grande* [large *marimba*]. Who made the first fully chromatic *marimba*? The answer depends on which side of the Mexico-Guatemala border you ask the question. Guatemalans maintain that Sebastián Hurtado of Quetzaltenango produced the first *marimba doble* in 1894; Mexicans in the southernmost state of Chiapas will tell you that Corazón Borraz Moreno made the first one in 1897. In both cases, the story of the instrument's invention turns on *marimba sencilla* musicians and *marimba* makers who strove to emulate the musical possibilities of a piano. For example, the story in Chiapas relates that Borraz Moreno constructed the first chromatic *marimba* based on a description from his uncle, who saw a piano for the first time in a neighboring town (Fernández López 1997:10).

Whichever *marimba* maker was actually first across the finish line, more important is the overall social context in which this invention took place. Towards the end of the nineteenth century, the relatively small middle classes were slowly expanding in southern Mexico and Central America. In these circles, the salon music of Europe was in vogue. This music consisted of European social dances, especially waltzes, and composers throughout Latin America produced a new, localized repertoire in these styles. Pianos began to be imported in quantity into Central America at this time. It was considered a mark of refinement for young, middle-class women to learn the piano, and their performances after dinner in living rooms and parlors were important occasions for this genteel music. The adaptation of the *marimba* to the musical potential of the piano moved this reper- toire into a wider social sphere for larger public performances and an audience from a wider class spectrum. It *creolized* the music once reserved for the piano— that is, it offered a new way to produce the same music on a thoroughly local in- strument, one that was—and is still to a great extent—identified with this part of the world only. Because of their ethnic chauvinism and class prejudice, economi- cally and socially dominant members of southern Mexican and Central American society had previously disdained the *marimba* for its association with lower classes, not to mention with the Amerindian population. The appearance of the *marimba doble* allowed for the popularity of *marimba* music to be cemented among the more economically powerful part of the population.[2] Following on the tremendous success of *marimba doble* ensembles in southern Mexico and Guatemala, the chromatic *marimba* soon became very popular in urban areas throughout Central America.

A *marimba doble* can be lavishly decorated with intricate wood carvings, often integrating the name of the group into the designs. As shown in Illustration 3–3, the resonators are in a tear-drop, rectangular shape and can be beautifully fin- ished. The lowest six to eight notes require a resonator so large that there is not enough room directly below those keys for the entire resonator to hang. The tops of the resonators are still placed just below the appropriate key, but they are so wide they have to stack outwards, and often the lowest resonator juts out past the frame. Unlike the *marimba de tecomates* and many *marimbas sencillas,* these in- struments are heavy and difficult to transport, and they can be quite expensive as well. *Marimbas dobles* are found in large cities of every Central American country except Panama and Belize. They all have the same basic characteristics except for one element that distinguishes a Guatemalan one from any other—in Guatemala,

Ill. 3–3. A Guatemalan *marimba doble*.

the upper row of keys (the equivalent of the black piano keys) is set directly above keys on the lower row. If you want to play a C♯, for example, you won't find it between a C and a D, but located directly above the C. This may seem like a small difference, but it takes some time to adjust to this arrangement. Pianists will quickly learn just how much the placement of black versus white keys has unconsciously oriented them to know where the notes are!

Listen to Recorded Selection 10, the piece "Atitlán," performed by the Marimba de Concierto (Concert Marimba) of Guatemala City. The *charleo* is still clearly evident, though a little more subdued than on the other *marimbas* we have heard so far. Especially noticeable are the bass notes. These *marimbas* are often played in pairs, as shown in the diagram in Figure 3–2.

The largest *marimba,* or *marimba grande,* usually has a range of six and one-half octaves (around sixty-eight keys) and accommodates four musicians. The second *marimba,* the *marimba cuache* [twin *marimba*] or *marimba tenor,* usually has a range of five octaves (around fifty keys). The three players on the *marimba cuache* duplicate all but the bass section of the *marimba grande.* The mallets, called *baquetas* in Guatemala, have different-sized heads of rubber for each player—the lower the notes (and therefore the larger the keys), the larger and softer the mallet heads are. The bass mallet heads are large, elastic balls of rubber as much as three inches in diameter, and the bass notes swell up in volume after being struck. In contrast, the small, hard mallet heads used on the upper notes produce a sharp sound that players work hard to soften for the flowing melodies of waltzes and other forms. Remember that notes on a *marimba* cannot be held; after the initial strike the sound dies away quickly. To give the impression of a sustained note or notes, *marimba* musicians have to roll an individual note (repeatedly strike the same note with a mallet in either hand) or do the same with two notes making up a harmonized melody. This can be a difficult technique to master, but it is a crucial one for the requirements of reproducing melodies originally designed for voice, or for a piano with its sustain pedal.

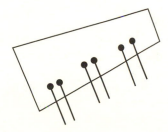

Marimba grande   **Marimba cuache (or tenor)**

Fig. 3–2. Configuration of a *marimba doble* ensemble

A common ensemble in Guatemala consists of a *marimba grande* and a *marimba cuache* together with a stand-up bass and trap drum set. However, practically every imaginable combination of instruments has been joined with one or more *marimbas* throughout Central America: saxophones, trumpets, and all types of percussion instruments. Earlier in the century these ensembles were extremely popular and were one of the prime sources for dance and popular music from southern Mexico to Costa Rica. Due to the wide variety of instrumentations, the classic ensemble of a *marimba grande, marimba cuache,* bass, and drums is known today as *marimba pura* [pure *marimba*].

In Guatemala the *marimba,* in its various sizes and types of construction, has long been considered the national musical instrument. Many Guatemalans feel an intense identification with it and its particular sound, even though they also listen to all kinds of music from elsewhere, including contemporary popular music from the United States. The *marimba pura* dropped in popularity during the 1950s and 1960s due to competition with electric instruments, inexpensive radios and record players, and the foreign media industry's promotion of Mexican pop and North American rock 'n' roll. There was some concern that a key symbol of Guatemalan identity would be subsumed by the onslaught of outside musics. In response, the military government then ruling the country decreed that all radio stations had to dedicate a certain amount of broadcast time to *marimba* music. At first there were some complaints when early morning radio shows were devoted exclusively to *marimba doble* groups. However, the law gradually had its desired effect and people began to call in and request *marimba* music. The Guatemalan public has since preserved a special place for *marimba,* despite the many commercial pressures against it. In fact, since the early 1990s a cultural renaissance of Mayan culture and pride has been slowly building. The most obvious manifestations of the Mayan majority asserting its ethnicity are political changes and a new appreciation of Mayan languages and dress, but the popularity and booming cassette market for Mayan *marimba* groups also serves as a clear indicator—and has been itself an important part—of this cultural movement.

THE *MARIMBA* IN NICARAGUA

As in most of Central America, dance bands based around large chromatic *marimbas dobles* were once quite popular in the major cities of western Nicaragua. However, unlike in Guatemala, Nicaraguan *marimba* music never received special protection from outside competition, and the last *marimba doble* groups were forced to disband in the 1970s. Nevertheless, one type of *marimba* still enjoys a high profile in the country: it is the relatively diminutive *marimba de arco* [arc *marimba*]. Nicaraguans consider this particular type of *marimba* the "Nicaraguan" *marimba.*

MAKING A *MARIMBA DE ARCO*

The *marimba de arco* is found throughout the densely populated low-lying plains and coastal hills of southern Nicaragua. *Marimba de arco* music revolves around the city of Masaya, and the best *marimba* makers come from this area.

Fig. 3–3. Map of Nicaragua, showing the locations of Masaya (Monimbó) and Bluefields

One way to conceptualize a *marimba de arco* is to take stock of the materials needed to construct one: rubber strips, twine, and nails, but most of all wood, of five different kinds. The first kind is the only one easy to obtain, as any type can be used to make the oblong frame that will hold the keys and the resonators. Unlike almost all other *marimbas*, the Nicaraguan *marimba de arco* adds a *tablilla*, a small piece of wood attached to the side of the frame. The *tablilla* will rest on top of the knees of the *marimbero* (the preferred name for a *marimba* player in Nicaragua) and keep the instrument supported.

The second kind of wood is really a thick, woody vine called *bejuco* that is bent to form the *arco* [arc or hoop]. This vine can be immense in size, over eight inches in diameter at its base. This obligates the *marimba* maker to climb far up the tree the *bejuco* grows around to cut off a piece where the diameter has diminished to about two inches. The *bejuco* is forced into an arc shape and then "cured" over flame, which will set it into a bent shape.

The third kind of wood is for the keys, the most important choice and the only wood that might vary from instrument to instrument. Only certain types of dense hardwoods are sonorous—that is, have the capacity to produce clear, ringing tones. Unfortunately, pressures for firewood from Nicaragua's expanding population have drastically reduced the stands of trees with sonorous wood; some types have become practically extinct in the last twenty years. When a *marimba* maker gets a good portion of sonorous hardwood he has it cut at a lumberyard into the basic shapes of the twenty-two keys on a *marimba de arco*. The best *marimba* makers then will cure these pieces, either by baking them in an outdoor oven or by laying them out in the hot tropical sun for several days. This process dries out the wood a bit and will bring out its clarity of sound. The *marimba* maker then chips away at the pieces to form the finished keys, carefully carving away wood from the middle of the underside of each key. Taking away wood from the bottom of the key—found in almost all *marimbas* everywhere—lowers the pitch. The lowest notes are cut away the most, which keeps them from having to be much longer and also provides for a brighter resonance (see Figure 3–4 and Illustration 3–4).

The Nicaraguan *marimba de arco* combines the traits of two of the principal types of Guatemalan *marimbas*: it maintains the arc found on the *marimba de tecomates* and it uses manufactured wooden resonators found on the *marimba sencilla*. Due to deforestation, *marimbas* have not been made with gourd res-

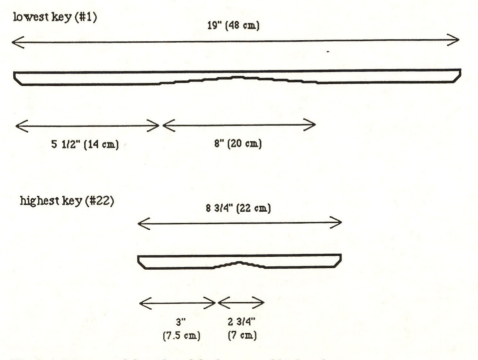

Fig. 3–4. Diagram of the sides of the lowest and highest keys on a Nicaraguan *marimba de arco*

Ill. 3–4. Carlos Palacios tunes a *marimba* key, raising its pitch by removing wood from the outside edge of its underside.

onators in Nicaragua for generations. Bamboo resonators were substituted, but musicians found that insects ate away the bamboo within a few years. Sometime early in the twentieth century Nicaraguan *marimba* makers switched to insect-resistant cedar wood. The straight tubular resonators imitate the shape of bamboo ones, a shape that distinguishes the Nicaraguan *marimba* from all other Central American types. Because of their shape they're usually called *tubos* [tubes]. At first glance it seems impossible for someone to have hollowed out the cylindrical resonators, especially the longer bass ones. On close examination, though, you can see a tell-tale hairline down both sides of the resonators where they have been glued together. The *marimba* maker first shapes the solid block of cedar into a smooth column shape, then he splits it with a *machete* and scrapes out each half. He glues the two halves back together and adjusts the finished *tubo* to the pitch of its respective key by cutting away some of the wood at its top.

The fifth type of wood is called *papamiel*, the stem of a flowering plant that grows two to three feet high in the Masaya region (especially on the hillsides of the extinct Apoyo volcano crater). It is a perfect weight and size for *bolillos* [mallets]. The hardest material to find is rubber for the mallet heads. Rubber trees have all but disappeared from the area within the last two generations. Some of my biggest contributions to the Nicaraguan *marimba* production came when I and several *marimba* makers—with their families along for the ride—made all-day trips to get bags of discarded rubberized cloth used in small raincoat factories.

Ill. 3–5. Carlos Palacios hollows out one of the two halves of a cylindrical cedar block that will form a *tubo,* a resonator tube.

When I saw the color of the raincoats I understood why some mallet heads had a bright yellow hue to them, and others were even pink.

The *marimba* makers lace the *tubos* to two strips of wood that hold them together as a set, and attach them into the frame with two removable metal pins. The hollow resonators are the only fragile part of the instrument and so they are made to be easily removable in case of repairs. To attach the keys, their nodal points must be found. This is the part of the key where the vibrations cancel each other out, a "dead space" where holes can be drilled that won't alter the pitch. You can imitate the same process *marimba* makers in Nicaragua and elsewhere follow on a concert *marimba*: spread some fine sand on a key, strike it, and observe the pattern formed by the ensuing vibrations. After drilling two holes on each end of a key, the maker positions them on top of strips of rubber cushioning and laces them to the frame.

This *marimba de arco* would sound very much like one used by an academic music department in North America. It's missing the last crucial step that provides the *charleo* sound. The *marimba* maker makes a small hole near the bottom of each *tubo* and builds up what looks like a small volcano out of black-colored beeswax. He places some kind of membrane over the open hole; the sticky wax will hold it in place for many weeks. Some Nicaraguans remember earlier *marimberos* using the thick webbing around spider eggs; in Guatemala *marimba* players have used plant leaves that can be peeled off in thin layers. The most common membrane is pig intestine that has been treated to take out the fat (see Illustration 3–6). After pounding and washing out the grease, dry, translucent, wafer-thin layers can be peeled off. When made taut across the hole, the result is the strong *charleo*, the same basic principle behind a kazoo. The technological advance of treated pig intestine retains the name *telilla* [spider's webbing].

The construction of a *marimba* is a complex and demanding process and requires years of experience to produce a well-made instrument. However, a concert *marimba* can be adapted to produce some of the same sound as a Central American *marimba* by adding the characteristic *charleo*. One possibility is placing thin wax paper across the bottom of the resonators. You can experiment to find more effective membranes—try spider-egg webbing!

PERFORMING MUSIC OF THE *MARIMBA DE ARCO* TRIO

The *marimba de arco* is never played solo but is accompanied by two stringed instruments. In performance, a guitar is positioned to the left of the *marimbero*, and on his right a *guitarilla*, a small four-stringed guitar. The stereo separation of Recorded Selection 11, "Aquella" [That woman], performed by the Martines Brothers, duplicates the sonic positioning the dancers hear as they perform directly in front of the trio: the guitar is on the right, the *guitarilla* on the left, and the register of the *marimba* moves from lowest notes on the right to highest notes on the left. The lower register of the guitar corresponds to the bass keys on the *marimba,* and likewise the *guitarilla* is positioned to combine with the treble keys. Sometimes the guitar is modified with one or two extra strings to bring out

Ill. 3–6. *Telilla* held by beeswax on a *marimba de arco* resonator tube.

the bass sound as much as possible. Both guitars are metal-stringed and only strummed, never plucked. The string players strum vigorously to match the loudness of the *marimba* and provide a strong rhythmic and harmonic foundation.

The *marimba* is responsible for all of the melody and a good deal of the rhythm as well. Nicaraguan *marimberos* like to point out that more skill is required of them than of their Central American counterparts. This is a somewhat specious claim, but they base it on the fact that the single *marimba de arco* player has to provide not only the melody and constantly changing harmonization of the melody, but also the bass line. To accomplish this, Nicaraguan *marimba* players essentially have to divide themselves in half: the left hand plays a separate, relatively constant bass pattern while the right hand carries the melody and changes hand position to provide different harmonizations of the melody.

A fundamental element of the principal repertoire for the *marimba de arco* is the rhythmic play of 3 against 2 within an overall 6/8 meter. Almost all of the music that accompanies the folk dance is in quick 6/8 meter, a meter that commonly can be divided either into two groups of three or three groups of two (see the discussion of *sesquiáltera* in Chapter 2). On the *marimba de arco* the bass line is based on a compound duple grouping of beats (six beats divided into two) and the melody on a simple triple grouping (six beats divided into three).

To get a sense of this rhythmic tension, a class can be divided in half and each group can clap, or individually anyone can use a pencil or pen and tap with each hand. (See also the *sesquiáltera* exercise in Chapter 2.) Start by establishing an underlying pulse in moderate tempo with both hands. Then tap the left hand with two beats per six-pulse group. Return to the basic pulse in each hand, then tap three beats per six-pulse group with the right hand. Now with both of these in your head, return to the basic pulse, begin the two-beat pattern in the left hand, and then add the three-beat pattern in the right hand. You can also begin with the simple triple and then add the compound duple. All of the repertoire of the folk dance that the *marimba de arco* trio accompanies is based on the ability to hold a basic two-against-three pattern around which the rest of the music is constructed. Now when you listen again to "Aquella," try following along by playing "air *marimba*": hold the two-note compound duple meter in the *marimba* player's left hand and imitate the melody's varying rhythmic patterns based around a simple triple meter in the right hand.

As shown in Figure 3–5, a finished *marimba de arco* provides a three-octave range. Nicaraguan *marimbas de arco* are usually pitched somewhere between C♯ and E. The first *marimba* I bought from Carlos Palacios (with the dimensions shown in Figure 3–5) is approximately in D one-third sharp. The pitch set of a *marimba de arco* shown has been transposed down to C for convenience. For those familiar with reading written Western musical notation, seeing what notes are available on the staff brings home the nature of a diatonic instrument. It is understandable why the entire repertoire for the folk dance (with the exception of only one part of one piece) is exclusively in a major key, because the diatonicism of the instrument lends itself to such a tonality.

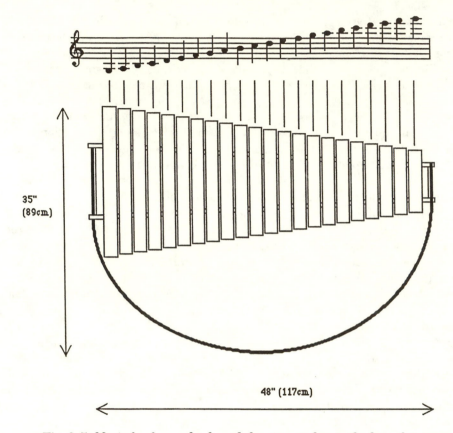

Fig. 3–5. *Marimba de arco* **keyboard showing pitches in the key of C**

"Aquella" is also a good example of the different positions the *marimbero* uses to hold the two mallets in his right hand. The piece starts with a fully open position of an octave that spans eight keys. This opening section ends with a descending line in sixths. The next section is recognizable from the new melody and higher register. In addition, the *marimbero* has now closed his hand to hold the mallets only three keys apart, producing harmonized thirds. For the next-to-last phrases in this section the *marimba* player only strikes a single key, so he needs to pull back the interior mallet and use the outside one, the one on his far right. These four positions are shown in Illustration 3–7. In European-derived classical music and jazz, *marimba* players have experimented with a variety of different hand positions. The hand position that has increasingly become standard is usually known as the Gary Burton method, named after the well-known jazz *marimba* and vibraphone player. However, this "new, innovative" style of playing is the same one shown in Illustration 3–7, the one *marimba* players in Nicaragua and Central America have probably used for centuries.

Ill. 3–7. Hand positions of a Nicaraguan *marimbero*.

Compared to many other *marimba* traditions, Nicaraguan *marimba* musicians strike the instrument with great force. The large and heavy mallets help them produce a sound that is *recio* [loud, strong]. This forceful playing, combined with the very long hours required for both traditional performances and private engagements, produces the tell-tale large callouses that every active *marimbero* has along the inside of his right index and middle fingers, the ones that bear the brunt of the mallets' pounding on the keys. When I did my research in Nicaragua, people often had a hard time believing that a foreigner was really learning the *marimba de arco*, an instrument played only by Indians and poor *campesinos* [peasants]. All I had to do was proudly show my (relatively small) callouses on my right index and middle fingers to dispel their disbelief.

Short samples of the most common strumming pattern of the guitar and *guitarilla* can be heard on Recorded Selection 12. Note how the guitar's basic rhythmic pattern is triple and the opposite accentuation of a waltz's three-beat pattern. Instead of a waltz's strong downbeat, or first beat, followed by two weaker accents, the guitar player deaccentuates the downbeat by stopping the strings and then stroking on open strings in the next two beats (see the transcription in Example 3–2). The guitar player stops the strings by striking them and then immediately dampening or stopping them with the same fingers. This technique (also used in the Mexican *sesquiáltera* strumming pattern) produces a sharp attack and a clearly audible sound, but one that is less strong than the open-string strummings of the last two beats. The guitar player's triple meter contrasts with the

Ex. 3–2.   Transcription of the typical rhythmic pattern of the guitar part and the bass line of a *marimba de arco* trio

compound duple meter of the *marimbero*'s bass line in his left hand, and in addition the off-beat accentuation of the guitar counterposes with the downbeat of the *marimba*'s bass line.

For most of the repertoire the *guitarilla* player strums in a fairly evenly accented pattern of six strokes; different pieces require slightly different accentuations. String players have various other strumming patterns and special breaks particular to specific pieces they must observe, but the string parts are clearly easier than the demanding *marimba de arco*. Often a *marimba* player is accompanied by younger male family members, especially sons of the *marimbero*, who are still learning the music. As *marimbero* Manuel Palacios, brother of Carlos Palacios (pictured in Illustration 3–5 and discussed below) put it, "You can play the *guitarilla* in your sleep."

THE *BAILE DE LA MARIMBA* IN SAINT'S DAY CELEBRATIONS

One of the principal performance opportunities for *marimba de arco* trios is the many occasions that revolve around the Catholic religious calendar; the most important of these are saint's day celebrations. Throughout Latin America, each town, even if it is quite small, has a patron saint, and the town stages what is often the largest event of the year on the day dedicated to the town's saint on the Catholic calendar. In southern Nicaragua, where most of the population resides, dances accompanied by *marimba de arco* trios are a central feature of these saint's day celebrations. The city of Masaya is exceptional: it has the largest number of dancers and its celebrations actually go on every weekend for over two months. However, in all the other smaller cities and towns the festivities center on the day of the saint, and then again on a reduced scale exactly a week afterwards (called the *octava* [eighth day]).

Preparations begin several weeks or even months before the event itself. A single individual or family generates a dance group, which will typically last for a three-year period. They are motivated by a *promesa,* a promise between themselves and the saint, in supplication or reward for the saint's intervention—e.g., for health or a good crop. (Compare this with the promise made in the Brazilian *novena de casa,* discussed in Chapter 5.) The musicians are contracted and the women begin to sew the costumes for that year. The generic name for these dances is simply the *baile de la marimba* [dance of the *marimba*]. People refer to the dances by the different costumes used—for example, *baile de los mexicanos* for northern-Mexico outfits, *baile de los húngaros* [Hungarians] for an imagined Gypsy costume, and so on. By far the most popular is the *baile de las inditas* [dance of the female Indians], and this is the costuming usually seen in processions on saint's days. People who wish to join the dance group to fulfill their *promesa* with the saint will cooperate with money for expenses—costumes, musicians, food, and drink. On weekends before the actual saint's day, the dancers meet with the musicians in the house of the sponsor and rehearse their dancing. Often children are included and they particularly need instruction on how to perform the dance properly.

The high point of the actual saint's day is the street procession of the image of the saint that resides in the main (or only) church. All the participants arrive in the latter part of the morning for a mass for the saint. The church is decorated in streamers of the saint's colors, and a brass *chichero* [brass band] provides music for the mass. When the mass concludes, the saint is hoisted onto a platform and, borne on several men's shoulders, leads the procession out of the church with the *chichero* band just behind. The church bells ring out and dozens of firecrackers explode: it is a joyous moment that ushers in the beginning of a day-long trek under a hot sun.[3] As the crowd spills out behind the plastic-cast image of the saint and perhaps other floats specially created for the day, the dancers try to form up behind their own *marimba de arco* trio. The women and men face each other in two lines down the street and try to hear their own *marimba* musicians over the din of the procession and *marimba* musicians playing for other dance groups (see Illustration 3–8). The dancers perform the dance steps while sidestepping to keep up with the forward motion of the procession. Even so, they inevitably slow down the procession for the roughly three-minute duration of a piece and everyone catches up when they finish. They will alternate dancing and walking with the procession for the many hours it takes for the saint to traverse the town. The dancers eat and drink along the way but never drop out of the procession—that is part of the *promesa*.

Accompanying dancers in a procession is probably the most difficult job a *marimba* player has. This is the only time he will be standing up to play the instrument. Two men carry the instrument from either end while the *marimbero* stands inside the *arco* [arc, hoop]. *Marimba* players face the perilous challenge of walking down a Nicaraguan street, especially the unpaved ones in villages and small towns, with the *marimba* keys hiding the potholes immediately in front of them, all the while concentrating on playing. It is a true test of the musician's ability. Heat from the midday sun can affect the tuning of the keys and the best players bring along a bit of beeswax to adjust their pitch, if necessary. Afternoon showers, common between May and November, can also wreak havoc with a *marimba*'s sound, not to mention sending the entire procession scurrying for shelter.

When the procession finally arrives back at the church in the afternoon, most of the faithful follow the image inside but the dancers usually perform several

Ill. 3–8. Procession with dancers and *marimba de arco* trio. The *guitarilla* is visible, but the guitar is partially hidden by the man carrying the bass end of the *marimba*.

numbers along the side of the church. Here the dancers can revert to the usual form that the dance takes, that of a couple dance. After dancing to several pieces, the groups take a welcome break and walk back to the house of their principal sponsor. After recuperating a bit, they will dance at the homes of the various sponsors and members of the group that reside within walking distance. The dancers are offered food and drink at each stop, though only the men accept alcoholic ones. The effect of this constant drinking on the males' dancing begins to show as the evening wears on.

When the group arrives at a house, the dancers typically proceed through to a back room or the backyard while the musicians seat themselves in a corner of the main room in the front. If the house is too small, everything is transferred to the packed earth immediately in front of the house. No sooner does the *marimba* player get seated than he usually hoists the *marimba de arco* onto his lap and hurriedly adjusts the *telilla* that inevitably has become loose or broken from being jostled in the walk from house to house. It is important that each note produce a full and vibrant *charleo*. The room rapidly presses full with expectant onlookers. The spectators crowd around an open circle in the middle of the room, often leaving the musicians stranded in a corner unable to view the dancing. The first pair of dancers enters and quietly tells the *marimbero* which one of the approximately three dozen traditional pieces they want played. If they are unable to actually see the dancers, the musicians wait to start when they guess the dancers are ready in the circle and the performance begins.

How can the dancers and the musicians perform without eye contact? The limited and relatively stable number of pieces in the repertoire allows the performers to accomplish this feat. The dancers have even become familiar with these particular musicians' interpretation of the same pieces everyone dances to. This is a remarkable statement on the codification and constancy of the repertoire reserved to accompany the *baile de la marimba*. The structure that characterizes these pieces also aids the dancers in following the music.

STRUCTURE OF THE DANCE AND MUSIC

The instrumental pieces in the folklore repertoire that accompanies the *baile de la marimba* are composed of discrete sections. (These different sections can be seen in the short video excerpts from one dance, the *baile de negras*, in Scruggs 1995.) The form of a piece is usually either **ABAB** or **ABABA,** though several pieces are more complicated and have several varying sections.

"Aquella" serves as a representative example of the folklore repertoire. Its form is **ABAB,** with different musical material and types of dance steps and choreography for each section. The piece begins with a dance-step style called *suelto* [loose, relaxed]. The dancers hold their upper body fairly erect and lightly alternate moving one foot in front of the other as they move around the open, circular area reserved for the dancers. In this **A** section the male and female dancers move around in circles and ovals, facing one another in a flirtation dance (see Figure 3–6).

The rhythmic activity of the music intensifies in the second, or **B**, section. The strings play with a sharper, more staccato attack. The *marimba*'s melody moves to a higher register and the melodic compass is reduced—there are fewer notes but more rhythmic drive. This increase of tension corresponds to the tighter movements and accentuated striking of the heel by the dancers called *zapateado* (from *zapato* [shoe]). This *zapateado* dance style has been adopted and adapted from the Spanish *zapateado,* most famous outside of Spain in *flamenco* dancing. (Daniel Sheehy also discusses the *zapateado* in the Mexican *son jarocho* dance— see Chapter 2.) The choreography of the dancers changes as well. When the **B** section begins they approach each other, making slow progress with the *zapateado* steps. When they get close, they turn to face the same direction. The male extends his arms outwards behind the female whose hands stay on her hips and they dance sideways, all the time "flirting" with each other. In reality, during the dances the couples' faces remain impassive: the dance is a serious *promesa,* and despite the festive nature of the occasion there is also a certain solemnity among the performers. The audience, especially in Masaya, carefully watches the dancers' execution of the steps and, when dancers begin the piece or a *zapateado* section for the first time, spontaneous, complimentary outbursts of applause often punctuate the music.

Even though in this example of "Aquella" the meter stays within a basic 6/8 meter in both sections, other pieces are further differentiated by dramatic

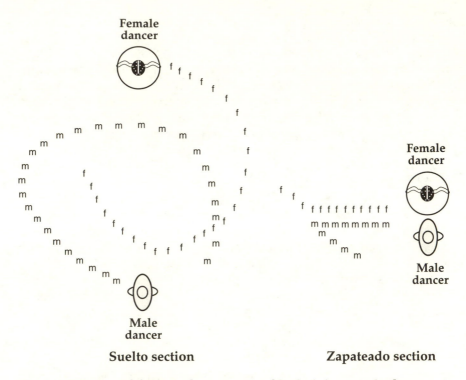

Female
dancer

Female
dancer

Male
dancer

Male
dancer

Suelto section   Zapateado section

Fig. 3–6. Diagram of the typical movements of *baile de la marimba* dancers in *suelto* and *zapateado* sections

changes between 6/8 and 3/4 meter. The meter in "El acuartillado" (no one is sure of the meaning of this title) alternates between 6/8 and 4/4, which requires a significant adjustment for both musicians and dancers.

Besides execution of dance steps and general bearing, precision in adjusting to the beginning of new sections is a mark of a good dancer. Fortunately, there are musical cues that help alert the dancers that one section is about to end and another to begin. The last musical phrase in a section fairly consistently ends with a descending melodic line down to the tonic, or principal note, which gives a sense of closure to the section. The *marimba* player's right hand almost always harmonizes this line in sixths, as happens in "Aquella" at the end of both sections **A** and **B**. The dancers probably know the piece by heart and are familiar with the interpretation of the *marimba de arco* trio contracted for that year, but even if they should lose their concentration during the performance this common descending phrase reminds them to anticipate a change to a new section.

PROFILE OF CARLOS PALACIOS RUÍZ

If you ask Nicaraguans to name a *marimba de arco* musician, the one—and probably only—answer they will give is "los Palacios" [the Palacios family]. The fame of this last name was originally established by the recordings of Elías, the oldest brother of his generation. Often accompanied by his younger siblings (including Carlos), he made several records in the 1970s—the only *marimba de arco* musician to have made multiple recordings. The name Palacios remains the one associated in the minds of the general public in large part because his three younger brothers also became excellent musicians, and each in turn has established his place in the music's history. (The quotations in this section are from several interviews conducted by Scruggs in Monimbó, Nicaragua, from 1987 to 1989.)

Most, though not all, *marimba* players learn within their families. The father of this generation of Palacios musicians was also a *marimbero,* who in turn learned from his uncles. Carlos remembers his father climbing up inside the house to

Ill. 3–9. Father gives his son the traditional "hands-on" instruction on the *marimba de arco* in Masaya.

retrieve spider-egg webbing for his *marimba;* this method for obtaining a membrane for the resonators is no longer used. Carlos was born in 1933; he was fifty-two years old when I first met him in 1985. He received little formal education. Like so many of his generation, he was forced to work to help support the family much of the time, and the school system did not extend to the poorest parts of the population. While most players begin playing by first learning the *guitarilla* and then the guitar, he started right out on the *marimba.* He also learned guitar and followed his father to parties and accompanied him for hours through the night. Eventually he was allowed to spell his father on the *marimba de arco* in the early morning hours towards the end of a party.

To support his family, Carlos's father needed to supplement his income from playing music with agricultural work. They lived in Pacaya, a small *comarca* [village] among the many scattered in the countryside in the Masaya region. This is one of the most populous areas of Nicaragua—one can walk along paths cut through lush vegetation and agricultural plots and continually find small *comarcas* that are often just several houses grouped together. The poor *campesinos* [peasants] in this part of the country have a notably higher percentage of indigenous blood than most residents of the larger towns and cities. However, the definition of an Indian is slippery in Nicaragua compared to, for example, Guatemala. There are few clear markers of indigenous identity left: by the late 1800s the Spanish had replaced the indigenous Mangue and Nahuatl languages, and distinctly indigenous clothing was disappearing. In fact, before they moved to Monimbó the Palacios family would more likely have been described as *campesinos* than as Indians. However, Monimbó is recognized as an indigenous community, and *monimboceños* (the local residents) take pride in their identity as *indios.* A key factor in maintaining an indigenous identity is the series of folk customs and celebrations that have made Monimbó famous throughout the Pacific coast. The best known of all these is the *baile de la marimba* [dance of the *marimba*], so when the Palacios family relocated to Monimbó they placed themselves in the epicenter of *marimba de arco* activity.

Out in the Masaya region it is not uncommon to find small shaker percussion instruments added to the basic *marimba de arco* trio, either *maracas* or a *guaya,* hollow metal containers filled with seeds. (The *guayo* of Cuba and the Dominican Republic is a scraper made of metal, gourd, or cowhorn.) Carlos recounted that when his musical family first moved to Monimbó from a small *comarca,* they began to accompany folk dance as they always had, with an ensemble that included a *maracas* player. They soon learned that people in Monimbó and Masaya consider such percussion an adulteration of the core sound of the tradition, and only suitable for some recreational music. They dropped the percussion from the group "because all of Masaya protested that one can't play with maracas—that's something for *trios* [a Mexican romantic, popular music style] . . . not for the indigenous *marimba.*" Just as the repertoire has remained remarkably stable over time, so the instrumentation and fundamental sound of the ensemble is carefully monitored by the community to maintain a continuity with the particular past practice identified with Monimbó.

Monimbó can either be considered a separate town that borders the larger *mestizo* city of Masaya, or the southernmost neighborhood of the city, depending upon one's point of view. The close proximity of the large *mestizo* city has allowed the generation of Elías and Carlos to live nearly full-time from their musical skills, a principal motivation for Carlos to relocate there. Married at sixteen, an average age for a poor *campesino,* he found that the early 1950s was a tough time to pursue his chosen profession of *marimba* musician. "The same year I began playing, the jukeboxes came in." Jukeboxes and portable sound systems were a sensation when they appeared among the poor *campesinos* and the community of Monimbó. Carlos Palacios remembers what he called his "bad luck" of trying to begin a career as a *marimbero* at this time, at the nadir of the popularity of the *marimba de arco.* "When the record players came all the *marimbas* plummeted to the ground, some took theirs apart, they burned them, because, who wanted to hire a *marimbero?* . . . When [the popularity of] *marimbas* went down, I took up my *machete"*—in other words, he returned to agricultural work for a time. Only gradually did the *marimba* recuperate its previous role of providing musical entertainment at parties and other social events. "For months I worked trying to overcome the jukeboxes." When Carlos started to gain some success, he claims "the other *marimba* musicians followed me."

Nicaraguans like to consider the *marimba de arco* a folk tradition in the purest sense, one not "tainted" with the constraints and influences of the media and the recording industry like electronically amplified popular music. However, Carlos Palacios effectively launched his career through radio. The local Radio Masaya, like many Central American radio stations until recently (and stations in the United States through the 1940s), relied heavily on live performances broadcast from their studios. While he performed live over the air for free, eventually the station allowed him to read small advertisements he had solicited in the city. The station would not pay him for his talents, so—via his music—he became something of a one-man advertising agency.

Carlos used the radio mainly to help gain name exposure among the *mestizo* population in Masaya. These *mestizos* looked for *marimba* trios for entertainment at parties and to accompany their own *baile de la marimba* groups. Since the early part of the century, *mestizos* in Masaya had begun to imitate the *baile de la marimba.* They copied the dance steps and the costuming, but no one outside of Monimbó or adjacent areas ever learned to play the *marimba de arco* with sufficient proficiency to be able to accompany the dance. Nor has any *mestizo* regularly played the guitar or *guitarilla* with a trio, though this scenario would be much more possible. As Carlos put it, "The dance moved downtown" but the music stayed in Monimbó and the neighboring *comarcas.* Why did *mestizos* in Masaya find themselves drawn to the dance but did not successfully attempt to play the music from which it is inseparable? No doubt one reason is the difficulty of the *marimba* repertoire, which makes *marimba de arco* performance a skill like that demanded of other trades. Participation in the tradition by the general populace in all parts of the country revolves around the dance and depends upon a specialized group to provide the music. However, the fact that not a single resident

in Masaya ever mastered the music indicates that this part of the tradition remained stigmatized as an *indio* practice, unlike all other aspects of the *baile de la
marimba*. Instead, for *mestizos* in Masaya and elsewhere, the presence of musicians from Monimbó, seated along the wall, playing the requested piece upon demand, serves as a touch of authenticity, a visual link with the roots of the
tradition.

In the 1960s Carlos's *marimba* trio became one of the most sought-after trios
in Masaya and Monimbó. When the first national folk dance troupe was formed in
Managua, they brought in Carlos as their musical leader. Although this troupe in
the capital city claimed to be a national folklore troupe, in fact all of the group's
dances were various types of *baile de la marimba* (such as the *inditas*, *húngaros*,
etc.). The dances actually varied only in costuming and Carlos provided all of the
musical accompaniment. The Managua troupe began to perform their version of
the *baile de la marimba* at schools and for more middle-class audiences wherever
they could throughout the Pacific coast. Carlos's trio traveled with the troupe to
several Central American countries where they represented Nicaragua in folklore
showcases. The insurrections against the Somoza dictatorship in the late 1970s
disrupted almost everything on the Pacific coast, but after the 1979 Sandinista tri-
umph Managua seemed to explode with new folklore troupes. Unfortunately for
Carlos and his brothers, touring now involved air travel to Europe and other parts
of the world. The Palacios brothers feared flying in airplanes and so had to relin-
quish their prestigious position as accompanists for the semiprofessional national
troupes.

At this point Carlos continued to perform as a *marimbero* leading his own trio.
Increasingly, however, he took the guitar part accompanying his younger brother
Manuel, who began to come into his own as a *marimba* musician. Carlos primarily
dedicated himself to manufacturing *marimbas* and established himself as one of
the top *marimba* makers in the country. During the Sandinista period in the
1980s many foreigners came both as tourists and as volunteers. This new clientele
and the heightened interest in folklore during this time brought in requests for
marimbas de arco beyond the needs of the local musicians. Carlos and his other
brother Juan hung a sign over their adjacent houses advertising *marimbas* and the
famous name of Palacios. Many *marimbas* with Carlos's name on them (actually
written by one of his daughters) have left Nicaragua for various countries. As a
matter of pride, Carlos always made a superior musical instrument worthy of the
best players in the country. But after several years he and other makers realized
that these new customers were more interested in the visual beauty of the
marimba de arco and were not aware of, or interested in, the finer aspects of the
instrument's actual musical qualities. Carlos started to make slightly inferior instruments for this new market. "These aren't made to accompany the dance,"
Carlos explained apologetically one day as we loaded several just-finished *marimbas* of this kind into my pick-up truck. He could tell that even without hearing the
marimbas I didn't think they were first-rate instruments. We took these *marimbas de arco* to Masaya's well-known open market, whereas usually the *marimbas*

Carlos manufactures are commissioned and sold directly to the musician. He felt a little sheepish as he said, "They're for tourists."

Carlos would rather concentrate on making quality individual instruments, but he cannot afford to ignore the demand from foreign visitors as well as the growing number of Nicaraguans who have relocated to the United States and want to take back souvenirs from their visits back to Nicaragua. Even this source of income has dwindled, as fewer tourists have come in the 1990s, and the "dollarization" of the economy has made the hardwoods for the keys extremely expensive. During the 1980s the Nicaraguan *córdoba* suffered hyperinflation, but the price of a quality *marimba de arco* remained stable at around sixty to seventy U.S. dollars. It took me almost a year to convince Carlos and his brothers that foreign tourists had the money to be treated differently. Considering the many days of labor it takes to make the fine instruments they produce, even when they finally began to charge foreigners 100 dollars their *marimbas de arco* were a steal. Four years later, in 1993, I returned with money from my university to purchase three *marimbas* and *guitarillas*. I looked forward to showering Carlos with several hundred dollars for each *marimba*. We laughed when I asked how much he charged for a *marimba* because we had talked so often before about a special "foreigner price" that the subject became a running joke in the family. Then, he shocked me when he announced straight-faced, "Now we are charging 500 dollars a *marimba*." The ruinous economy (for the majority of the population) has sent prices skyrocketing. The minimal controls against deforestation during the Sandinista government were being habitually ignored under the new government, and the stock of sonorous hardwoods was rapidly depleting. "No one can afford a *marimba* anymore," Carlos stated matter-of-factly. "Who can find *papamiel* [the plant used to make mallet sticks]? The old owners who were with Somoza have returned to the Apoyo Lagoon [where *papamiel* grows] and burned off and prohibited access to the hillsides." It was strange to think that a set of mallets now cost as much as an entire *marimba de arco* with mallets had cost only a few years before. Others involved in the music have fared worse. As the economy has steadily worsened through the 1990s, many *marimba* musicians have had to turn more and more to nonmusical jobs to supplement their income, and some have given up performing altogether.

Despite the economic hard times, the demand for a souvenir *marimba de arco* demonstrates what an important symbol this one instrument is for representing Nicaraguan identity. No other musical instrument can identify Nicaragua in such a unique way. When I visited again in 1996, Carlos and Juan Palacios were still able to sell some *marimbas de arco* but their families were increasingly dependent on the salaries their children brought in from nonmusical jobs. *Marimba de arco* music is still an indispensable part of musical life in western Nicaragua, carried on by a new generation of musicians from Monimbó and the surrounding area. However, no one in the younger Palacios generation has taken up music. It appears that Carlos's younger brother Manuel is the last of the Palacios "dynasty" of performing *marimba* musicians.

The Perseverance of a "Limited" Instrument

In the early 1900s, the new *marimba doble* spread from southern Mexico and Guatemala across national borders, as large chromatic *marimba* ensembles became a favored format for music in all of Central America. *Mestizo* musicians imported and copied the large *marimbas dobles* throughout the isthmus, including Nicaragua. Even though the dominance of the *marimba* in various sizes and ensemble formats has waned over the years, chromatic *marimbas dobles* are still found today throughout a common cultural area from Chiapas and Oaxaca in southern Mexico to as far south as San José, Costa Rica. In the last half of the twentieth century, the availability of inexpensive technologies for sound reproduction and the popularity of new musical styles from Cuba and the United States that did not translate well onto the instrument's wooden keys have successfully challenged the privileged position of the *marimba* as the vehicle with which to produce social dance music. Nevertheless, the *marimba doble* has tenaciously retained a presence throughout the region.

If you arrived in Nicaragua today, though, or anytime in the last twenty-five years, you would think that Nicaragua was an exception to the musical diffusion of the Guatemalan and Mexican chromatic *marimba doble* across Central America: it appears as if somehow the *marimba doble* skipped over Nicaragua on its way south to Costa Rica. I had been asking everyone I met in Nicaragua about *marimbas* for several months before someone casually mentioned that there once had been large *marimbas,* "ones that took several musicians to play." I found the few remaining chromatic *marimbas dobles* in Nicaragua relegated to schools or in storage. In either case, they are in poor condition and barely playable. I tracked down and became friends with Juan José Rodríguez, Nicaragua's last *marimba doble* maker. He died in 1989, and by that point he had long stopped making *marimbas.* The advent of transistor radios and rock 'n' roll displaced the large chromatic *marimba* ensembles as a primary source of popular dance music throughout Central America. In Nicaragua, these ensembles eventually disbanded and completely disappeared off the country's musical map by the 1970s.

By contrast, during this same time the Nicaraguan *marimba de arco* not only survived but enjoyed a slow increase in appreciation and popularity. Its indispensable role as accompaniment to folk dance brought it into national prominence when the once localized dances became promoted as national dances. These dances, and therefore the *marimba de arco,* especially flourished in the upsurge of interest in traditional folk culture during the first part of the Sandinista revolution in the early 1980s. The recuperation of pride in the Amerindian part of Nicaragua's makeup enhanced the profile of the *marimba de arco* as a cultural marker of Indian identity.

We should note that an association with Indian culture has also worked against the popularity of some *marimbas* in Central America. The violent repression against anything indigenous in El Salvador almost led to the disappearance of a Salvadoran variety of *marimba de arco.* In 1932 the army, on behalf of the large landowners who effectively controlled the country, unleashed what became known as *la matanza* [the massacre]. Anyone identifiably Indian was targeted and over

30,000 people were slaughtered. Out of fear, people of indigenous background began to use Spanish exclusively and drop their indigenous dress. *Marimbas* were burned or buried. Today, many Salvadorans think that there are no Indians in their country, but in fact many groups have managed to maintain their identity intact. The 1990s has seen a cautious revival of indigenous identity in El Salvador, parallel to the larger Mayan renaissance in Guatemala. In both social movements diatonic *marimbas* remain the primary instrument identified with Indians—in Guatemala the *marimba sencilla* and in El Salvador the *marimba de arco* in Izalco and other communities recuperating their indigenous identity. These more "limited" instruments have enjoyed an increase in popularity and importance in the last years of the century.

Imagine that you could travel back to several decades ago in Nicaragua. If you approached a *marimba doble* and a *marimba de arco* from the technical standpoint of each instrument's musical range and apparent musical potential, the large, chromatic *marimba doble* might appear as the obvious "instrument of the future" and Nicaragua's twenty-two-keyed, diatonic *marimba de arco* as destined to eventual extinction. Yet just the opposite has occurred. Despite musical limitations that make the diatonic instrument even less equipped than the chromatic *marimba doble* to compete in the arena of national popular music, the *marimba de arco* has become the most prominent—almost the only—type of *marimba* still used in Nicaragua because of its power as a marker of social identity. The public's identification of the *marimba de arco* with feelings of *nicaraguanidad* [Nicaraguan-ness] granted it a symbolic power that allowed it to persevere while larger *marimbas* were marginalized and overwhelmed by other musical competition. Such a history highlights that what is important about music is its meaning to humans—the significance music has for people, not its formal structure, complexity, or other factors. When one contemplates the world of electronic wizardry and gadgets contemporary musicians find themselves in, the continuing popularity of the *marimba de arco* and the disappearance of the *marimba doble* in Nicaragua is a sobering lesson that music is not a thing unto itself but derives its importance as a form of cultural expression.

THE *SON NICA*

The importance of *marimba de arco* music as a marker of Nicaraguan identity goes beyond the corpus of music actually produced on the instrument. The music of *marimba de arco* trios also served as the inspiration for an important type of popular song that most Spanish-speaking Nicaraguans still think of as the most representative, most traditional musical form in the nation—the *son nica*.

Actually, the *son nica* is a relatively recent invention by a single musician whose long life has extended into the 1990s. Camilo Zapata is from Chinandega, one of the several cities on the low-lying plains where the country's largest urban centers are located. When he attempted to launch his career as a musician in the late 1930s he felt frustrated by the strong popularity of Mexican and other foreign musics at the time. When we think of smaller, economically weaker countries in an unequal struggle with a large music industry based in a more powerful country, we usually think of the disproportionate control of corporations from the United States and Western Europe over Africa and Latin America. However, Mexico's music industry has had a tremendous impact in neighboring Central America and small, local music labels and recording studios have often found it hard to gain ground against such a much larger competitor. The Mexican film industry's golden era in the late 1930s and 1940s disseminated *ranchera* and *mariachi* music throughout Latin America with films that had almost as much singing by the main actors as dramatic action. The success of Mexican "subcultural imperialism" in Nicaragua can be measured by the local *mariachi* bands and Mexican-style trio ensembles that still gather today in a Managua plaza, waiting to be hired.

It was within this context of a strong presence of non-Nicaraguan music that Camilo Zapata deliberately set out to create a "new tradition," a musical style different enough from Mexican ones to be unmistakably *nica* [Nicaraguan]. When he surveyed folk music in western Nicaragua he found the most distinctive style to be that of the music of the *marimba de arco* trio. Even the visual look of the instrument set it apart from *marimbas* of other countries (remember that the *marimba de tecomates,* the only other *marimba* with an arc in frequent use, is relatively unknown outside of Guatemala). The importance of Nicaraguan *marimba de arco* music was enhanced by its accompaniment for the folk dance that participants in the folklore movement in Masaya had already begun to promote as Nicaragua's national dance. In the 1960s Camilo Zapata himself became involved in this process as the founder of the country's first semiprofessional folk dance troupe, one that exclusively featured varieties of the *baile de la marimba* (see Scruggs 1998).

Zapata borrowed selected stylistic features from the repertoire of the *marimba de arco* trio. The most obvious feature is the rhythm, adapted from the strumming pattern of the trio's guitar. The dampened downbeat followed by two fully strummed (and therefore accented) beats distinguishes the Nicaraguan *son* from any of the well-known *sones* from Mexico (see Example 3–2). In addition, Zapata's compositions are almost entirely in major keys, with very little use of minor chords. Such a preponderance of major tonality is a marked feature of the Nicaraguan *marimba*'s folk dance repertoire, but it is fairly unusual in Mexican and Latin American music. In addition, the melodic contour of *marimba de arco* pieces inspired the melodic shape of many of Zapata's songs. Finally, many *son nica* songs, especially those by Zapata, include a quick repetition of words in passages of compressed rhythmic activity. These sections imitate the *zapateado* sections in *marimba de arco* pieces that accompany rapid heel-to-floor dance movements in the folk dance. Zapata combined these musical traits with lyrics that referred to particularly Nicaraguan characters and situations, and used a vernacular Spanish that highlighted uniquely Nicaraguan vocabulary. All these characteristics marked his *sones nicas* as thoroughly Nicaraguan products. His songs of the 1940s and 1950s achieved an unprecedented level of acceptance throughout the southern plains and enjoyed a certain degree of exposure throughout the rest of western Nicaragua as well.

Although Camilo Zapata first thought of another name, he and others soon promoted his style as the *son nica.* The word *son* is used throughout Latin America as a generic label for a musical form (see Daniel Sheehy's discussion of *sones* in Chapter 2). In their discussions with me, Don Camilo and other pioneers of the *son nica* indicated that the use of the word *son* was a deliberate choice to pit the *son nica* against its immediate adversary, music from Mexico. In the view of the *son nica* pioneers, Nicaragua approximated the size of one of the cultural areas of Mexico, and therefore deserved its own *son* or stylistic form, much as the region around Jalisco has the *son jalisciense,* Veracruz the *son jarocho,* San Luis Potosí and its region the *son huasteco,* etc. The *son nica,* then, can be seen as a nationalist response to an instance of continental, if not yet global, circulation of style.

Several other singer/songwriters followed in his footsteps, cementing the place of the *son nica* as the most common song form in Nicaraguan popular music. The title of the *son nica* "Posol con leche" from around the early 1970s (Recorded Selection 13) refers to the consumption of traditional *posol* (made from corn) mixed with milk during the raucous celebrations for Managua's patron saint, Santo Domingo. This recording captures Otto de la Rocha and Jorge Isaac Carvalho, the two best-known *son nica* singer-songwriters of the time, at the height of their popularity. They are joined by Monimbó *marimbero* Alfonso Flores, known by his nickname Tun Tun (for being short and stout). Tun Tun remains the only Monimbó *marimba* player to learn and regularly perform on a small chromatic *marimba doble,* the instrument he uses on this recording (his own group interprets several pieces of popular music on the 1989 recording *Nicaragua . . . Presente!*). Carvalho plays electric guitar and his rhythmic strumming is easy to follow. Note how he uses two phrases, the first an exact replica of, and the second a slightly modified version of, the "reverse waltz" rhythmic pattern of a guitar in a *marimba de arco* trio (Example 3–2). On "Posol con leche" the group tries to re-create in the studio some of the unrestrained joy and infamous, sometimes violent, transgressive atmosphere of Managua's massive annual celebrations in early August.

NICARAGUAN CREOLE *PALO DE MAYO*

An Introduction to the Caribbean Coast of Central America

So far we have dealt only with the majority population on the Central American isthmus that has been impacted to varying degrees by Spanish culture. The more sparsely populated eastern parts of the countries bordering the Caribbean have a different geography and climate, and a very different human history. The indigenous peoples, most of whom are found in Honduras, Nicaragua, and Costa Rica, descend from a series of migrations that probably originated in South America and are not related to the Maya and other western and centrally located indigenous peoples. The eastern peoples had very little communication with the western part of the region before European contact, and even afterwards their primary cultural and economic relationship with the outside world has been with the greater Caribbean basin. When Spanish troops attempted to control the area they were frustrated by resistance from local peoples and competition from the English. The area is not rich in obvious natural resources, and the Spanish eventually abandoned their efforts to bring the eastern seaboard under the control of the colonial authority, which was based in Guatemala City and elsewhere inland. As a result, for centuries this area enjoyed more autonomy from direct European control, and until recently most outside influence has been from English-speaking traders and missionaries.

NICARAGUA'S "ATLANTIC" COAST

The eastern part of Nicaragua bordering the Caribbean Sea is usually referred to, somewhat inaccurately, as La Costa Atlántica [the Atlantic coast]. The major indigenous group there split into two factions after the English first established contact with them over four centuries ago. Those that shunned this contact, now called the Sumu (or Mayanga, estimated population 10,000), moved further up the rivers from the coast and have remained fairly isolated from events on the coast. There are no recordings or recent studies of their music. The other group, now known as the Miskitu (estimated population 120,000 in Nicaragua, 50,000 in Honduras), used their trading with the English to obtain weapons with which they established their dominance in the region.

We will not look at Miskitu music in depth, but we can compare excerpts from two versions of the same Miskitu song, "Syrpiki mayram" [Dear woman]. The first version is by an unidentified group of Miskitus recorded in Managua in the 1960s (Recorded Selection 14). The second (Recorded Selection 16) was made in the early 1980s by Creoles, a completely different set of inhabitants of the Atlantic coast. This Miskitu song is from the mainly secular type of music the Miskitu call *tun,* spelled *tiun* in Spanish but sounding like the English "tune," whence their word was borrowed. The Miskitu creatively folded into their own musical style ideas they took from their contact with the English over centuries, and missionaries and others in the last hundred years. For example, *tiuns* use basic European tonal harmony and the instruments are modified guitars, as indicated by their name *kitar* (from the English "guitar"). The lyrics in "Syrpiki mayram" address a woman who has left the singer, and call for her return. In the excerpt of the *tiun* "Syrpiki myram" (Recorded Selection 14) you can hear the two main singers accompanied by two *kitars.* You can hear how the lyrics fit the plaintive singing style and melody that starts with emphasized high pitches and then descends to the repeated lowest note that reiterates the phrase "syrpiki mayram." European and United States Moravian missionaries have used their economic power to destroy much of the Miskitu religion and religious music, the music that most closely conserved earlier Miskitu musical style. As a result, the generally nonreligious *tiun* that integrates many outside influences has been left as the principal genre of Miskitu music. The adoption into this musical genre of various non-Miskitu musical elements made it amenable to being adopted itself by an outside group, the Creoles, in the 1980s.

Besides a relatively small number of *mestizos* and European arrivals, several waves of African migration make up the other significant part of the eastern zone's nonindigenous population. Almost all African-Nicaraguans are Creoles, and some are descendants of the first Afro–Central Americans brought to work for English planters.[4] Some slaves escaped and several intermarried with Miskitus. These Afro-Nicaraguans developed a unique Creole English, similar in many respects to other varieties of Afro-Caribbean Creole English. In the end of the nineteenth century another influx of African-Americans joined the Creoles already settled in small villages and cities along the Nicaraguan and Costa Rican coast. This population was made up of laborers, principally from Jamaica, who came to work in the then-booming logging and mining industries. Their arrival further strengthened the existing Creole culture's connections with West Indian culture, including music.

Unlike the Spanish-speaking, Catholic Pacific coast population, Creoles are Protestant and their first language is Creole English (most also speak a good deal of Spanish). Creoles' cultural roots in the West Indies are also clearly evident in the most common musical form, usually referred to as *mento*. Many aspects of this form resemble the Jamaican type of folk music of the same name. Some general characteristics are common to these songs (which are also found among Costa Rican Creoles). They are in 4/4 meter and in a moderate tempo. The tonality is always major. The rhythmic accompaniment has syncopation but is not strongly polyrhythmic, like Afro-Cuban and some other Afro–Latin American musics. The singing uses an open vocal style and the singers follow a basic structure of alternating verse and chorus. The chorus section consists of single lines sung by the lead singer that are immediately repeated by backup singers in a call-and-response fashion (see also Larry Crook's discussion in Chapter 5 of Bahian carnival music in Brazil). The instrumentation reflects the Creoles' common cultural links with other parts of the English-speaking Caribbean—banjo, ass's jaw, washpan (wash-tub) bass, scraper, guitar, and more recently, accordion. The ass's jaw is the dried-out jaw bone of an ass or mule with the rear molars still embedded in their sockets. These can either produce a dry rattle when struck, or the player can scrape a thin stick across them.[5] The wash-tub bass is similar to those once found more commonly in the southern United States—a metal wash tub is turned upside down to serve as a resonator, and a single cord running from the tub's center is attached to a pole that the player moves back and forth to change the notes when he plucks it with his other hand. *Claves, bongos,* and *congas* are also occasionally added.

The recording of "Anancy oh" also includes a trap drum set (Recorded Selection 15). Listen carefully to the bass line. By pulling back on the pole, the washpan player controls the tension of the cord and on this recording brings out the three fundamental pitches of the song's chords. Even though this may be the only track on the accompanying compact disc with English lyrics, you may have a hard time following the Creole English of the singers. The musicians who perform it are from Bluefields, the largest city on the Atlantic coast; they came together in the early 1980s as the semiprofessional group Zinica (named after a hilltop,

Ex. 3–3.   Lyrics to "Anancy oh" as performed by Zinica

Lead singer	*Chorus*
Anancy Oh	Tingle eye [eye with a sparkle in it]
Anancy Oh	Tingle eye
Anancy Oh	Tingle eye
	You rub and a rub [dance]
	Tingle eye
I'm an old man girl	Tingle eye
I'm a fighting girl	Tingle eye
I'm a country girl	Tingle eye
I'm a black feet girl	Tingle eye . . .

considered a mountain in the flat Atlantic coast region). The chorus section consists of single lines, sung by the lead singer, to which the backup singers immediately respond in a basic call-and-response fashion. The beginning of this song illustrates the structural feature of initiating a song with the chorus section that will be repeated between verses throughout the song. Note the typical melodic contour of these songs where the singing starts on higher pitches and finishes with a descending line.

PALO DE MAYO FROM EAST TO WEST

During the spring there is a series of celebrations that include a version of maypole dancing, an adaptation of the English tradition. The name of this well-known custom was borrowed to label a new electrified interpretation of acoustic *mento*. Creoles are closely attuned to cultural developments in the English-speaking Caribbean. In the 1960s several creative musicians began to use electric guitars and bass with a standard trap drum set to interpret the *mento* repertoire. Young people in Bluefields transformed earlier couple dancing into a new, much more sensual version that emphasized pelvic movements and close body contact. These sensual aspects of the dance were further accentuated in the 1970s when stylistic elements of Trinidadian *soca* were integrated into the musical accompaniment. Older Creoles deplored the dances as lewd and lascivious. There's no doubt that the gyrating moves often include unmistakable sexual references; perhaps that accounts for its appeal among young Creoles (and later young *mestizos* as well). The electronically amplified music groups composed new songs, but the older *mento* repertoire remained a mainstay of these new bands. This use of a standing repertoire means that the bulk of the new dance music still conserves the lyrics, basic melodies, chordal patterns, and other musical elements held over from its acoustic predecessor. For example, as you can hear on the Creole version of "Syrpiki mayram" (Recorded Selection 16), much of the basic musical form of acoustic *mento* has not changed that much. However, the new style transforms *mento* by substantially increasing the tempo and substituting for the banjo, wash-tub bass, and accordion, a popular music instrumentation of trap drums, *timbales,* horn sections, and electric instruments, including electric bass, organ, and/or synthesizer. Instrumental solos are more pronounced and show that the musicians have been listening to a variety of popular musics from the Caribbean and the United States.

This music made a significant contribution to increasing the Pacific coast's appreciation of Atlantic coast peoples and culture. Under the Spanish-translated name of *palo de mayo* [maypole], the new dance and music made inroads with *mestizo* youth on the Pacific coast in the mid-1970s. With the success of the Sandinista revolution in 1979, *palo de mayo* exploded in popularity nationwide for several years as a symbol of politically and sexually liberated youth, the only time an Atlantic-coast style has gained national acceptance. The revolution held the promise of breaking with oppressive features of the previous dictatorship, including some of the restrictions on youth and women in particular. The sensuous dance attracted young *mestizos,* as did the rhythmic drive of the electrified Creole music. In addition, young *mestizos* were curious to learn about the eastern part of the country, which they were discovering for the first time. Even though practically no one understood the lyrics, Pacific coast residents were proud to embrace a potent music and dance whose origin was Afro-Nicaraguan and not—for a change—imported from abroad. *Palo de mayo* was the dance music of choice for most Nicaraguans on both coasts during the 1980s. Even *marimba de arco* trios included versions of *palo de mayo* at parties, though a hint of 6/8 rhythmic sensibility so prevalent in *marimba* music crept in—and when transferred to *marimba* and guitar, the music did lose something in the translation. The most popular band in the nation at that time was Dimensión Costeña [Coastal dimension], one of the many Creole groups that formed to satisfy the growing *mestizo* audience. Note how this band, like others, chose a Spanish name, a reflection of their target audience—Spanish speakers, who make up over 90 percent of the country's total population.

The popularity of Atlantic-coast *palo de mayo* on the western Pacific coast both reflected, and played a role in bringing about, a new stage in the development of a Nicaraguan national consciousness. *Palo de mayo* music and dance became the main point of contact between Creole culture and Spanish speakers on the Pacific coast. The Westerners' awareness of the peoples in the eastern region was furthered extended when several *palo de mayo* bands drew upon their familiarity with some Miskitu *tiuns* and recorded *palo de mayo* versions of them. The borrowings in *tiun* of various non-Miskitu influences allowed for its fairly easy overlay onto Creole *palo de mayo* musical form and style. Miskitus pass through the urban centers on the Atlantic coast (a few live in towns), and many Creoles can speak a bit of Miskitu. Creoles were looking for new material to record, once they began to exhaust the traditional *mento* repertoire, and they paid tribute to the other major group on the Atlantic coast by including several of their songs on their own albums. Grupo Gamma's version of "Syrpiki mayram" (Recorded Selection 16) became something of a national hit when it was released in the early 1980s. While Miskitu *tiuns* gained a very limited exposure through select cultural programs on television and radio, Miskitu music performed by Miskitu musicians was never popular with Spanish speakers. Instead, Miskitu music—that is, *tiuns*—received its greatest dissemination through the voices of Creole *palo de mayo* singers.

This music represented a special moment in Nicaraguan musical history: three leading ethnic groups of the nation were musically blended together within single songs. Recordings like "Syrpiki mayram" featured Creole musicians (together with some *mestizo* members in the band) in groups with Spanish names, performing Miskitu *tiun,* in Creole *palo de mayo* musical style, with Creole-accented Miskitu lyrics, all aimed at an overwhelmingly Spanish-speaking *mestizo* audience. These recordings represented the musical apex of a unifying trend in conceptions of what constituted the nation of "Nicaragua." We can use music as a key to help chart this process over time and understand its significance. The increased exposure and popularity of Creole and Miskitu music paralleled the rise in consciousness by western *mestizos* of eastern Atlantic coastal peoples, so the degree of the music's popularity also indicates a level of cultural awareness.

At the same time, a central point is that music itself can be used to play an important role in social transformation. In this case, it was one of the key resources that Nicaraguans utilized to help produce a new understanding of the many peoples and cultures that make up the nation-state of Nicaragua (for more on this topic see Scruggs, 1999). *Palo de mayo* remains popular in the western part of Nicaragua. Three of the ten songs on a recent album by today's most popular band, Macolla, are in *palo de mayo* style—one is an original song; one is a remake of a *mento/palo de mayo* song, masquerading under a different Spanish title with new Spanish lyrics; and one is the band's version of "Anancy oh." For the lyrics of this late-1990s interpretation of the old *mento* tune, Macolla dropped the verses and rewrote the chorus to be half English and half Spanish. They also added a short Spanish rap section in the middle of the song. There may not be Miskitu lyrics, and all the band members are *mestizos,* but Macolla's popularity demonstrates that Atlantic-coastal Creole music remains an important part of the popular music scene in Spanish-speaking western Nicaragua, a continuing cultural bridge between the two coasts of the country.

CONCLUSION

Although it is a relatively small part of the Americas in terms of geographical extension, Central America shares the fundamental tripolar cultural heritage of Latin America and the Caribbean—Amerindians, Europeans, and Africans. (Unlike parts of South America and the Caribbean, there has not been a significant Asian immigration.) This chapter briefly examined Mayan and Miskitu music. In both cases, the principal secular music shows an integration of several important features of European music, but it is used in a distinctly Mayan and Miskitu way. We would find a similar creative adaptation to outside cultural pressures among the Kuna in Panama. They have worked hard to maintain their own traditions, and as part of that strategy they have deliberately created dances just for display to tourists. In this chapter, the *marimba* was the point of departure for examining music of the majority *mestizo/ladino* mixed-race population. Even with such a focus, we did not get to address the various types of *marimbas* in Honduras and Costa Rica, not to mention the many other *mestizo/ladino* folk and popular musics in the region. To broaden our understanding of Afro–Central Americans, we could look at the large population of African descent in Panama, as well as the Garinagu (or Garifuna) in Belize, Guatemala, and Honduras, whose culture is a vibrant melding of various African and Caribbean (Arawak and Carib) cultures. The examples presented in this chapter introduce the musical landscape of the isthmus. All of the case studies presented here demonstrate that people make conscious decisions on how to use music in their lives, to define who they are and to further their own goals.

REFERENCES

Armas Lara, Marcial. 1970. *Origen de la marimba, su desenvolvimiento y otros instrumentos músicos.* Guatemala City: Tipografía Nacional.

Cáceres, Abraham. 1978. Preliminary comments on the marimba in the Americas. In *Discourse in ethnomusicology: Essays in honor of George List,* ed. C. Card, J. Hasse, R. L. Singer, and R. M. Stone, pp. 225–250. Bloomington: Indiana Univ. Press.

Chenoweth, Vida. 1964. *The marimbas of Guatemala.* Lexington: Univ. of Kentucky Press.

Fernández López, Ramiro. 1997. *Centenario de la Marimba Cromática (1897–1997).* Chiapas, Mexico: Comisión Editorial y Relaciones Públicas.

Juarros, Domingo. 1981. *Compendio de la historia de la ciudad de Guatemala.* Guatemala City: Editorial Piedra Santa.

Ritter, Jonathan Larry. 1998. La marimba esmeraldeña: Music and ethnicity on Ecuador's northern coast. M.A. thesis, Univ. of California at Los Angeles.

Scruggs, T. M. 1999. "Let's enjoy as Nicaraguans": The use of music in the construction of a Nicaraguan national consciousness. *Ethnomusicology* 43(2) (June).

———. 1998. Cultural capital, appropriate transformations and transfer by appropriation in western Nicaragua: *El baile de la marimba. Latin American Music Review* 19(1):1–30.

———. 1995. Nicaragua (4 video selections and liner notes). In *The JVC/Smithsonian Folkways Video Anthology of World Music and Dance of the Americas* VTMV–230, vol. 6, pp. 12–16.

Stuempfle, Stephen. 1995. *The steelband movement: The forging of a national art in Trinidad and Tobago.* Philadelphia: Univ. of Pennsylvania Press.

White, Thomas. 1978. The marimba in Esmeraldas [Ecuador]. *The Percussionist* (fall).

ADDITIONAL READING

Garfias, Robert. 1983. The marimba of Mexico and Central America. *Latin American Music Review* 4/2:203–208.

Kaptain, Laurence D. 1992. "The wood that sings": The marimba in Chiapas, Mexico. Everett, Penn.: Honey Rock.

Monsato Dardón, Carlos Hugo. 1982. Guatemala a través de su marimba. *Latin American Music Review* 3(1):60–72.

Muñoz Tábora, Jesús. 1997. *Organología del folklore hondureño.* Tegucigalpa, Honduras: Secretaría del Turismo y Cultura [1988].

Olsen, Dale A. and Daniel E. Sheehy, eds. 1998. *South America, Mexico Central America, and the Caribbean.* Vol. 2 of *The Garland encyclopedia of world music.* New York: Garland Reference Library of the Humanities, vol. 1193. (Entries for the Central American republics; includes two recordings from Nicaragua on accompanying CD.)

Salazar Salvatierra, Rodrigo. 1996. *Instrumentos musicales del folclor costarricense.* Cartago, Costa Rica: Editorial Tecnológica de Costa Rica. (First edition published 1992.)

Scruggs, T. M. 1991. Review of recordings *Patria: Music from Honduras and Nicaragua,* recording and notes by David Blair Stiffler (Lyrichord Records LLST 7364), and *Nicaragua . . . Presente!: Music from Nicaragua Libre,* compiled by John McCutcheon (Rounder Records 1989). *Latin American Music Review* (spring/summer) 12(1):84–96.

―――. 1999. Nicaraguan state cultural initiative and "the unseen made manifest." *Yearbook for Traditional Music* 30:53–73.

Vela, David. 1972. *Information on the marimba.* Edited and translated by Vida Chenoweth, 1957–58. Auckland, New Zealand: Institute Press.

Sadie, Stanley, ed. Forthcoming. *Revised new Grove dictionary of music and musicians.* (Entries for the Central American republics; also entries for individual Central American composers of European-derived classical music.) London: Macmillan Press, Ltd.

ADDITIONAL LISTENING

Recordings by various chromatic *marimba* groups from southern Mexico and Guatemala are often available in the United States.

Cardenal Argüello, Salvador, comp. *Nicaragua: Música y canto.* 7 CDs. Radio Güegüence/Alcaldía de Managua, 1992. (Originally released as an LP set by Banco de America, 1977.)

Marimba Yajalón. *¡Chiapas!* Heart of Wood Project 002, 1994.

McCutcheon, John, comp. *Nicaragua . . . Presente!: Music from Nicaragua Libre.* Rounder Records 4020/1, 1989.

Modern Maya: The Indian music of Chiapas, Mexico. Ethnic Folkways FE 4377. (Available on cassette through Smithsonian-Folkways.)

Scruggs, T. M., comp. *Nicaraguan folk music from Masaya.* Flying Fish Records 474, 1988. (Available on cassette through Rounder Records.)

Creole Music

Recordings of Nicaraguan Creole music are difficult to find. Recordings of Costa Rican Creoles are more accessible in the United States—their calypsos are similar to acoustic Nicaraguan *palo de mayo.*

Calypsos: Afro-Limonese music of Costa Rica. Lyrichord 7412, 1988.

Gavitt, Mr. [Ferguson Gavitt, Walter]. *Calypsos of Costa Rica.* Folkway Records, FTS 31309, 1982. (Available through Smithsonian-Folkways.)

ENDNOTES

1. See Cáceres 1978, White 1978, and Ritter 1998 for descriptions of the Colombian-Ecuadorian Pacific littoral *marimba* tradition.

2. See Stuempfle 1995 for an analogous development for the Trinidadian steelband.

3. The setting-off of firecrackers marks important ritual moments in processional ceremonies—such as saint's days and Corpus Christi—in many sites in Latin America. See, e.g., Evon Z. Vogt, "On the Symbolic Meaning of Percussion in Zinacanteco Ritual," *Journal of Anthropological Research* 33(3) (fall 1977):231–244.

4. Also on Nicaragua's Atlantic coast is a very small community of Garinagu, or Garifuna, once known as Black Caribs, that several generations ago migrated south from the main Garinagu population in Honduras, Guatemala, and Belize.

5. This same instrument, termed *quijada* in Spanish, is also used by Colombians and by Peruvians of African descent. See William Gradante's discussion of the Colombian Andean *rajaleña* ensemble, in Chapter 7.

CHAPTER FOUR

Caribbean Musics

Haiti and Trinidad
and Tobago

GAGE AVERILL

❧

INTRODUCTION

GEOGRAPHY

The Caribbean Sea lies nestled between North and South America, bounded by
the Atlantic Ocean to the east, the Gulf of Mexico and Florida to the north, and
Central America to the west. Arrayed in an arc starting with Cuba (below the
southern tip of Florida) all the way to Trinidad and Tobago (just north of the
Venezuelan coast) is a string of islands formed by volcanic eruption and coral ac-
cretion called the Antilles or the West Indies. The Antilles were the first part of
the Western Hemisphere explored by Christopher Columbus (who is believed to
have landed on one of the smaller islands of the Bahamas). At the time, these islands were home to a few distinct groups of Amerindians, most of whom belonged to the Taino and Arawak language families.

A narrow definition of the Caribbean region might include only the Antilles or
the West Indies, and indeed in this chapter we will look at music cultures specific
to the islands themselves. However, the Caribbean as a cultural region is far
larger than the Antilles. The littoral or northern coastal region of South America,
the eastern coast of Central America, and even the New Orleans region of the
United States bear a cultural similarity and share with the Antilles a history of
colonialization, sugar cultivation, slavery, and access to the sea that argues for inclusion in a Caribbean cultural region. More recently, in an effort to boost regional trade and hemispheric relations, the United States has popularized the
term Caribbean Basin, an even more expansive notion that includes all of the
nation-states bordering on the Caribbean Sea.

Fig. 4–1. Map of Cuba

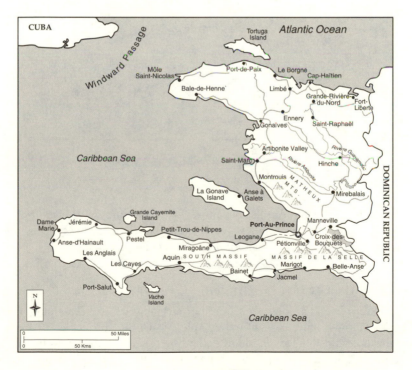

Fig. 4–2. Map of Haiti

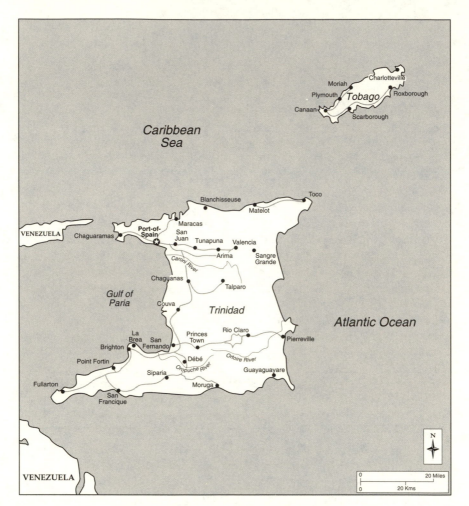

Fig. 4–3. Map of Trinidad and Tobago

Globally speaking, the Antilles occupy a relatively minor land mass. For example, Cuba—largest of the Antilles—is smaller than the state of Florida, and Jamaica is merely the size of the Florida Everglades. In light of this, why is it important to study the expressive culture of this region?

WHY STUDY THE MUSIC OF THE CARIBBEAN?

First, the Caribbean has long been an important geographical crossroads, producing a population of stunning cultural complexity. Under the impact of European colonialization and the slave trade, the Caribbean, already home to hundreds of thousands of indigenous people, was the meeting place of peoples from hundreds of distinct groups from Africa as well as many nationalities and regions from Europe, a demographic mix complicated further by the arrival of Chinese, Arabs, and East Indians in the nineteenth century. Languages spoken in the Caribbean include French, Spanish, English, Creole and Patois, Papiamento, Dutch, Saramaccan, Garifuna (Black Carib), Hindi, Urdu, and many others. In addition, many African languages have been conserved by speech communities, especially for ritual occasions. In the Caribbean, music cultures from at least four continents were hybridized (fused) and creolized (made part of the vibrant new culture of the Caribbean) under conditions of European political domination and cultural hegemony.

Second, many models for understanding the results of long-term contact between cultures were developed to account for the processes witnessed in the Caribbean. Terms such as transculturation, hybridity, syncretism, and creolization all have a special link to Caribbean intellectual history. Caribbean authors, scholars, artists, statesmen, and activists have been in the vanguard of global movements to reconceive identity, nationalism, ethnicity, and identity politics in the postcolonial environment. Caribbean music and dance reflect this ferment over identity and actively contribute to the formation of complex, multiple, and emergent identities in the region.

Third, the Caribbean has been responsible for some of the world's most celebrated music and dance genres, forms that have traveled the globe and helped to define popular music as we know it. Cuban *son*, *rumba*, *mambo*, and *salsa* developed worldwide markets, as did Trinidadian calypso and steel band, Jamaican *ska* and *reggae*, and Dominican *merengue*. Over the years, *reggae* has been embraced by indigenous tribal youth in Papua New Guinea, *salsa* played by orchestras in Japan, Cuban *rumba* played by the leading West African orchestras of the 1960s, steel bands formed in Switzerland and Sweden . . . put simply, this small corner of the world has launched a dizzying array of musical forms and sounds into orbit around the world.

I would argue that it is especially important for North Americans to understand the culture of the Caribbean because of the long-term geopolitical and demographic importance of the region to North America, especially the United States. The United States has claimed the Caribbean as part of its sphere of interest and influence from the time of the Monroe Doctrine until the present; in the twentieth century this was intensified because of the strategic importance of the Panama Canal to worldwide shipping. In addition, like many other industrial nations of the North, the United States has been a major destination of Caribbean migrants who have left the region due to economic stresses or political turmoil. As immigrants, as minorities within the host states, and as transnational populations with ongoing links to their homelands, these sizable Caribbean populations have helped to reshape the cultural landscape of the United States, Canada, France, Britain, and wherever else they have settled.

Finally, it is impossible to ignore the many representations of the Caribbean based on cultural stereotypes and touristic fantasies; this is how many people around the world know the Caribbean. Steel bands are used in commercials portraying friendly, laid-back natives ready to welcome intrepid tourists to an unspoiled paradise of virgin beaches, tropical breezes, and cool rum drinks. Hot-blooded, erotic Latin women are portrayed dancing *conga* in a permanent Carnival of abandon. Most of these images bear a "Made in the U.S.A." label, nurtured by Hollywood and Madison Avenue to foster the notion that there is still somewhere where one can "get away from it all." Although there are many beautiful beaches in the Caribbean, and although tourism is a major industry in most of the islands, it is important to understand that the tourist industry presents a one-sided and superficial vision of life in the region, relegating the messy details of daily life, as well as the survival struggles of millions of inhabitants, to the "backstage" areas. In a particularly ironic example, the songs of Bob Marley and the Wailers are now used to promote Jamaican tourism, overlooking the fact that *reggae* and Rastafarianism were born in the struggle for dignity and the fight against poverty, oppression, racism, and neocolonialism. Marley was, if anything, fiercely opposed to the notion of Jamaica as a feel-good, service-oriented, economically dependent tourist trap.

History

Columbus "discovered" a region with perhaps a half million or more indigenous Caribbean people, one group of which (the Caribs) gave this region its name. Borrowed by Shakespeare for the name of the primitive creature that lived on Prospero's island in *The Tempest*, Caliban, the Carib name also gave birth to the European word "cannibal." The Caribs had waged an ongoing conflict for territory with their Arawak predecessors in the islands; both groups had migrated from the mainland of what is now Venezuela, the Arawaks starting about 300 C.E. and the Caribs possibly around 1,000 C.E. Columbus landed on a small island in the Bahamas but formed his first colony, Navidad, on Hispaniola (also known as Saint Domingue or Santo Domingo). Navidad was destroyed by Arawak raiders, but Columbus founded more settlements on subsequent journeys and eventually carved four viceroyalties out of the Americas for the Spanish courts.

The *encomienda* system granted Spanish settlers the right to parcels of land and to own groups of natives. Most of the indigenous peoples, however, died in subsequent decades from disease and starvation and from overwork in the Spanish gold mines. For example, on the island of Puerto Rico there were approximately 30,000 natives in 1509; by 1514, only 3,000 remained. Twenty years later, nearly all had been wiped out. A widespread belief that the natives were unsuited to hard labor led to an increase in importation of slaves from the coasts of Africa. One of the horrifying ironies of this new trade in chattel slavery is that it was originally portrayed as a humanitarian act to protect Native Americans from forced labor.

The colonies were run on a mercantilist system backed by "Exclusive Acts," in which the various European monarchies created monopolies on maritime trade with their own colonies to extract taxes on the goods shipped. Attacks on legal shipping by buccaneers, filibusters, and privateers, some with "letters of marque" (permitting raids against ships of other crowns), were efforts to break or to redistribute these monopolies. Following their failure to mine sufficient amounts of gold, the colonists promoted tobacco farming, but the success of the Dutch with their Brazilian and Surinamese sugar plantations convinced many in the Caribbean to switch to sugar cane cultivation. Large-scale plantations were run by the local or absentee European "plantocracy."

Sugar required massive amounts of back-breaking labor, and planters turned to African slaves to fill the void. Sugar thus determined the fate of the region and the fate of many of the twenty million Africans brought to the hemisphere in what was arguably the largest forced migration in human history. The so-called Slave Coast stretched 3,200 miles from Senegambia to Angola; the vagaries of transatlantic winds and currents favored a "triangle trade" connecting the African coastline to the Caribbean and then to Europe. The Middle Passage of that triangle (the shipping of slaves to the Americas) resulted in an enormous loss of life; for Europeans, however, it made fortunes and drove the machinery of European capital accumulations and expansion. At its peak, the trade brought over 100,000 Africans each year to the Western Hemisphere.

A social structure evolved that included three legal categories—free, enslaved, and freed (*affranchi*). These categories corresponded loosely (but not entirely) to phenotype or race (white, black, and *mulatto* [mixed]) and to origin (Europe, Africa, and Creole [born in the colony, not necessarily *mulatto* but culturally mixed]). It was a social structure based not on the separation of these groups but on an extraordinary intimacy and dependence among them, and this is part of the reason that Creole culture was so vibrantly hybridized. Slaves not only worked the fields and the docks but also learned and plied trades, took care of households, raised European children, grew and cooked food, built houses and roads, and of course played much music for the Europeans.

The first major, successful challenge to the slaveholding and colonial system was the Haitian revolution, which evicted the French from Saint Domingue in 1804 and ended slavery on the island. Haiti became the first "black" republic and the second republic of any kind in the Western Hemisphere after the United States. The Haitian slave and anticolonial revolt spread a wave of panic among the colonists throughout the Caribbean. At about the same time, an antislavery movement was winning over the British citizenry, pressuring Parliament and the crown for "amelioration" of slavery. The British authorities responded by outlawing the transportation of slaves and passed laws banning the trade in 1809, eventually doing away with slavery altogether in the British colonies between 1834 and 1838. Efforts by the ruling classes to keep former slaves working on the plantations after emancipation were largely unsuccessful; most abandoned the plantations to till private plots of land. The plantations then recruited indentured laborers from Indonesia, India, China, Ireland, and Africa.

In 1898, the United States intervened in the Cuban rebellion against Spain, waged war on Spain, accumulated Spanish colonial possessions as spoils of war, and became a colonial power in the process (occupying Cuba, Puerto Rico, and the Philippines). In the following three decades, the Caribbean (gateway to the Panama Canal) was brought inexorably into the American sphere of influence, especially during a period in the 1910s and 1920s that saw the occupation by the United States of Haiti and the Dominican Republic.

Cuba achieved independence in 1902, joining Haiti and the Dominican Republic. Most of the rest of the Caribbean had to wait for nationhood until the great wave of decolonization that followed World War II (especially in the late 1950s and early 1960s). There are exceptions, however. Puerto Rico remains a Commonwealth territory of the United States, Britain still holds possessions such as the Turks and Caicos and Montserrat, and Martinique and Guadeloupe became fully integrated Overseas Departments of France. The governments of the Caribbean include a number of parliamentary democracies, but they have also included classic dictatorships (Trujillo in the Dominican Republic, the Duvaliers in Haiti) and a socialist revolutionary state (Cuba).

The Caribbean has endured a difficult transition to independence and development. Plagued by a reliance on single-crop agriculture (subject to wide fluctuations in price and demand) and on a seasonal tourist industry, the Antilles have struggled to define paths to development and self-determination. Class relations in many countries soured after independence as local elites strengthened their control over the nascent state and over local industries, and as the poor found themselves in danger of becoming a permanent underclass. Class conflicts often took on racial overtones as darker-skinned citizens saw their progress impeded by the residual prejudices of lighter-skinned elites, turning to black power movements to address these obstacles.

CULTURAL COMMONALITY

European colonialism left a powerful cultural imprint on the entire Caribbean region. Remnants of eighteenth-century European figure dances such as the *quadrille*, lancers, reel, jig, and *contredanse* are found throughout the islands. The functions of these dances may have changed dramatically, as in the reel performed in Tobago for an ancestor possession ceremony known as a *jumbie* [spirit] dance.[1] The *bèlè* [from the French *bel air*] is a Creolized version of the *contredanse* in Trinidad, Martinique, and Grenada (among others) that is still often performed in fancy dress (i.e., Colonial-era *affranchi* outfits). The Cuban *contradanza, danza,* and later *danzón* were descended from the *contredanse* brought to Cuba by planters and their slaves who migrated from Saint Domingue in the period surrounding the Haitian revolution. In Cuba, Haitian descendants still preserve some of the *contredanses* in a ceremony known as Tumba Francesa [French drum]. In Illustration 4–1, a couple in rural Haiti executes steps in a figure dance called a *kontradans* [*contredanse*] to the calls of a *mèt dans* [dance master, dance caller] and the sound of a small *fif* (flute) and percussion ensemble. The dance is held *anba tonèl* [under the thatched arbor].

Many of the final figures of figure dances (usually danced in couples) survive as the national expressions of various Caribbean islands, including the Haitian *méringue*, the *merengue* of the Dominican Republic, and the Martiniquan *béguine*. Each of these was transformed in the hands of performers of African descent, and thus they represent superb examples of cultural Creolization. Subsequent European dance crazes such as the polka, waltz, schottische, and mazurka are also found in the Caribbean. The Europeans also bequeathed a number of im-

Ill. 4–1. A *kontradans* in rural Haiti, held *anba tonèl* [under the arbor].
Photo by Gage Averill, Artibonite Valley, 1988.

portant literary and song forms to the Caribbean in the form of Spanish *décimas* (see Chapter 6), French *romances,* British ballads, and European children's songs and lullabies.

People of African descent have kept alive forms of African religions (covertly at first, and often syncretized to some degree with Christianity) in the form of Vodou (Haiti), Santería (Cuba), Shango (Trinidad), and Myal and Kumina (Jamaica), among others. These religions feature drumming and dancing in praise of African ancestors and deities and even possession of the devotees by the same deities (see the discussion of Vodou later in this chapter).

Protestant revivals in the Caribbean resulted in a number of nonestablishment churches including Jamaican Pukkumina and Zion Revival, as well as the Spiritual Baptists of Trinidad. These churches incorporate neo-African religious practices (ancestral spirit possession, dancing, and clapping), charismatic Christian practices of the "gifts of the spirit" such as speaking in tongues, singing of Protestant hymns and spirituals sometimes in overlapping call-and-response style, and rhythmic chanting and breathing used to help induce trance-like states.

Festival and processional traditions throughout the Caribbean blend European festive forms (especially Carnival or Mardi Gras and mummers' parades) with African secret society dances and masquerades. John Canoe or *jonkonnu* is celebrated in the Bahamas, in Jamaica, and among the Garifuna (the so-called Black Caribs; see Chapter 3) of Honduras and Belize, where it is known as *wanáragua* in addition to John Canoe. *Jonkonnu*-like figures, called *boum-boums,* parade in St. Lucia during Christmas and New Years Day, attired in dried banana leaves with masks and conical leaf caps. Their dance is based on a vigorous rolling of the hips similar to that found in Haitian *rara* or Trinidadian *winin'*.[2] Perhaps no event in the Caribbean is as well known as Carnival in Trinidad and Tobago, but Carnival is also a feature of cultural life in Haiti, Cuba, Martinique, Guadeloupe, Antigua, and elsewhere. In each of these locales, this medieval French celebration has become a phantasmagoric celebration of Afro-Caribbean cultural creativity. This chapter will treat two festive traditions: Haitian *rara* and Trinidadian Carnival.

This spirit of creativity is perhaps nowhere better demonstrated than in Caribbean popular and commercial musics. Beginning with the syncretic genres at the turn of the century—Martiniquan *béguine,* Cuban *son* and *danzón,* Trinidadian calypso, Haitian *méringue,* Dominican *merengue,* and Puerto Rican *plena,* among others—the particular constellation of peoples and conditions in the Caribbean has produced a rapidly evolving series of hybrid popular genres that include *salsa, soca, chutney-soca,* cadence-lypso, *mambo, cha-cha-chá, songo,* ska, rock steady, *reggae, zouk,* raggamuffin, and so on.

These innovations in the sounds of popular culture have responded to changes in identity, politics, and ideology. Nationalist sentiment has led to the founding of a number of folkloric troupes. The Conjunto Folklórico of Cuba, the Troupe Folklorique Nationale d'Haiti, the Ballet Folklórico of the Dominican Republic, the National Dance Theatre Company of Jamaica, and Martiniquan groups such as Créolita have produced stylized versions of national dances and musics for theatrical performance. Many of the Caribbean's most prominent musicologists and ethnologists have served as founders and directors of these troupes, which must be considered as a part of the contemporary musical landscape of the Caribbean, though their repertory consists of preserved or reconstructed versions of genres that often no longer find popular expression. With the rise of political movements based in the advocacy of black rights and identity (négritude, pan-Africanism, Black Power, etc.), many Caribbean genres—including those that were thoroughly syncretic or hybrid in nature—have undergone a process of re-Africanization. In the postcolonial Caribbean, urban popular musics have progressively cut the umbilical cords that tied them to Euro-American popular musics and have explored the realm of difference that links them to Afro-Caribbean traditional musics as well as to African popular or commercial musics.

Work songs, lullabies, improvised poetic contest songs, topical songs, sea shanteys, stick fight music, and small rustic ensembles all find expression throughout the Caribbean. In the end, however, this short section on commonalities that tie together cultures in the Caribbean can only begin to hint at the rich interconnections that cross the divisions of geography, language and nation-state.

RUMBA: AFRO-CUBAN DRUMMING, DANCE, AND SONG—A SUBSIDIARY MUSIC CULTURE

It was entirely by chance that I wandered into my first *rumba* in Matanzas, Cuba, a hilly and scenic city on the northern coast, in December 1976. Walking along a narrow sidewalk, I heard a commotion and poked my head inside a gate, only to find myself invited to a teachers' college end-of-semester party. While the group exchanged gifts of clothing and sweets, a few of them wandered over to some of the instruments (*congas* and other drums, sticks, and bamboo) lying in the corner. The *conga* drums and *claves* struck up a *rumba guaguancó* and a shy couple tried out some dance moves while the students urged them on with a few choruses. This was not, I would later learn, a high-quality *rumba* (in terms of its percussion, vocals, or dance), but its informality and group participation reflect the essence of the genre. In following years, I spent as much time as possible in the kitchens and living rooms of *rumberos* in the United States, trying my hand at the drums, dance, and chorus.

The word *rumba* comes from a Spanish word for party. There are many forms and varieties of *rumba*. Some of the elements of *rumba* percussion were present in an earlier dance popular among Cubans of Kongo descent called *yuka*. After the turn of the century, perambulating *coro y clave* [chorus and *clave*] groups mixed Iberian songs with Afro-Cuban percussion. Over the years, *rumba* went from a marginal form associated with the lowest classes, especially urban blacks, to something of a national symbol with many varieties in popular culture and in elite entertainments. Robin Moore notes the appearance of cabaret versions of *rumbas* in *zarzuelas* [light operas] and as interludes in the *teatro vernáculo* [vernacular theatre, akin to vaudeville].[3] These *rumbas* later headlined touristified cabaret shows like those at the Tropicana Club, featuring performers in stylized costumes (kerchiefs and ruffled sleeves for men, flowing skirts for women).

But it is the informal "party" *rumba*—played on percussion with singing and dance—that has made the greatest resurgence in the late twentieth century. Although *rumba* is generally considered to be an Afro-Cuban cultural expression (because it originated among black Cubans), its musical influences are broader, representing a creative fusion of elements and aesthetics from both Europe and Africa in a new form unique to Cuba, and—some would say—quintessentially Cuban.

There are three types of traditional or noncommercial *rumba* in common use today: *guaguancó, yambú,* and *colombia. Yambú* is generally slower-paced, sparser in its percussion, and danced by a couple as a stylized rendition of courtship. *Guaguancó* has a more intricate and dense percussive texture, is quicker and more lively, and is danced by one couple at a time without physical contact. The male exhibition *rumba,* called *colombia,* is quick and blends rhythmic stresses in 4/4 and 12/8 for a heightened rhythmic tension. Its songs and choruses are generally shorter and less complex, sometimes borrowing from Afro-Cuban *lucumí* [Yoruba] sacred songs. The *colombia* is inextricably linked to Matanzas, the center of its performance for many decades.

MUSIC AND DANCE IN *RUMBA*

Rumba songs explore a wide variety of themes, including (1) love and desire, (2) sociability and camaraderie, (3) rejection, persecution, and unfaithful lovers, (4) *rumba* itself, (5) local or national pride, and (6) philosophical discourses on topics such as how to survive in the face of adversity. *Rumberos*—those who play, sing, and dance *rumba*—typically believe that *rumba* lyrics, rhythmic play, choreography, and even vocal style capture the essence of a Cuban worldview. The vocal quality of the lead singer in *rumba* that is most prized is called the *voz de gallo* [rooster voice]—high-pitched, with a nasal timbre.

In olden days, *rumba* drummers often played on *cajones* [wooden boxes] used to ship salted fish to and from Cuban ports. When the *cajones* are used today, it is most often to accompany the old and stately form of *rumba* called *yambú* (see Illustration 4–2). The use of *tumbadoras* or *congas* [cowhide-covered barrel drums] has been far more common for many decades. The number of *conga* drums can vary (typically three for *guaguancó,* two or three for *yambú* and *colombia*). In each, one or more drums will play highly-patterned roles, articulating the basic percussion pattern or *ostinato* called a *tumbao,* while another drum (usually the smallest in size and highest in pitch) solos. The name for the small drum, *requinto* or *quinto,* is the same name applied to the higher-register lead string instrument in some Latin American string ensembles, and derives from a Spanish word meaning "to tighten a cord."

In *rumba guaguancó,* the *tumbao* is formed by the open tones of the medium-sized *conga* (which goes by the name of *segundo* [second], also known as *tres golpes* [three strokes], *tres por dos* [three for two], *seis por ocho* [six for eight] or simply *conga*) and the low-pitched *tumba* or *tumbadoras.* The player of the *tum-*

**Ill. 4–2. Three *cajones* played in a *rumba yambú* arrayed around a set of
conga drums. The percussionists, members of Los Muñequitos de
Matanzas, also include a *shekere* player and a *guagua* player (*rear*). Photo
by Gage Averill, Matanzas, Cuba, 1995.**

badoras emphasizes the last beat of every four-beat measure by hitting an open,
resonant tone. This is called the *ponche* [punch]) beat and it is a feature in almost
all Afro-Cuban musics. In *rumba,* it "converses" with the one or two open tones
played on the *segundo* drum. See Example 4–1 for a skeletal transcription of a
rumba guaguancó in Matanzas style. The open tones tell only part of the story,
however. Equally important are the many filler strokes on each drum, sometimes
collectively called *guapería* [prettiness, fluff]. These strokes are not the struc-
turally critical conversational tones, but they provide a complex and subtle environment of strokes that sets a good performance of *rumba* apart from a crude
performance. However, in trying to play and hear the "conversation" for the first
time, you may want to concentrate only on the open tones on the congas and the
strokes of the *claves* and *palitos* (see below).

Rumba is usually accompanied by one or more time-line (fixed-rhythm) patterns sounded on wooden sticks. The best-known and most important of these
patterns is played on two concussion sticks known as *claves.* The rhythmic pattern
itself is known as *clave* (singular). The *clave* represents an underlying asymmetric
pattern within the two-measure cycle of *rumba,* one half of which is more syncopated (the three-stroke side) and the other half of which lines up with the basic
four-pulse meter (the two-stroke side). In a good *rumba,* all the musical elements
(*tumbao,* solo drum improvisation, vocals, dancing, etc.) coordinate with this *clave*
pattern, and this interaction helps to generate rhythmic complexity, variety, and

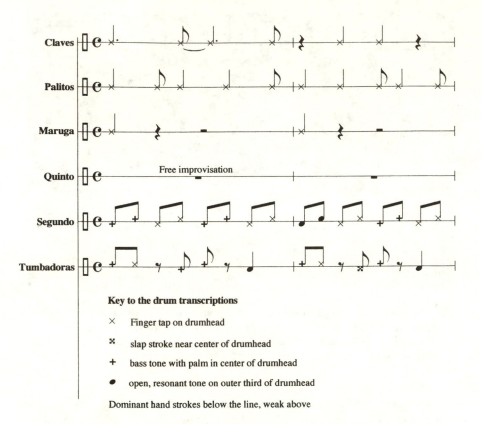

Ex. 4–1. *Rumba guaguancó* [Matanzas-style *rumba*], skeletal percussion. Open, sonorous tones on the drumheads are shown beneath the lines as noteheads. The slap on the *tumbadoras* (optional but common in Matanzas) is shown as a heavier X above the line. Filler strokes (taps and center thuds) are represented by notes (X) on the lines. The basic "conversation" can be seen in the interaction of open tones on the *tumbadoras* and *segundo*.

tension. The *claves* may be complemented by thinner percussion sticks played against a *conga* drum, on a bamboo tube, or against a chair or other object. These are known as *catá, guagua, cáscara* [shell], *paila,* and *palitos.* The *palitos* pattern is usually a more filled-in version of the *clave* (as in Example 4–1), and it follows the same principle of two-sided asymmetry. Other percussion instruments may be added to the mix (for example, a *maruga* metal rattle), but the combination of *conga* drums and sticks creates the core *tumbao.*

A *rumbero* will be able to recognize the difference in playing styles from one neighborhood to the next. In performance, all of the *conga* players vary their parts, respond to each other's variations, and push and pull against the underlying pulse to create drama, tension, humor, or other moods or commentary. This kind of performance mastery is attained after decades of listening, participating, and trial-and-error. In the hands of master *rumberos,* very few of the stylistic components that I have outlined above need to be present. The musicians can "imagine" *clave* and solo on any number of drums "around" the *tumbao,* never giving voice to the *tumbao* proper. This more profound version of *rumba* will be incomprehensible to all but experienced *rumberos.*

The dancing in a *guaguancó* is a pantomime on the theme of male-female flirtation and sexuality (sometimes described in terms of the dance of a rooster and hen). It is performed by a couple who dance apart using patterned footwork and a repertoire of conventional gestures and poses (see Illustration 4–3). The male dances his desire for his partner with the eventual goal of executing the symbolic gesture of copulation, the *vacunao* (vaccination), through a pelvic thrust in the woman's direction or sometimes by the touch of a hand or scarf. The female dancer, using movements called *botaos* can evade the choreographic attentions of her partner and deny him the *vacunao.* In a *yambú,* the male never executes the *vacunao* and the courtship tends to be more stylized and less aggressive. An excellent example of a street *rumba guaguancó* in Havana crops up in the final scene to the video *¿Qué se toca en Cuba?* (1985).

The performance of a *rumba* song generally takes shape over three contrasting sections. This three-part sectional structure involves changes in the singing, dancing, and drumming (see Figure 4–4).

Ill. 4–3. Two members of Los Muñequitos de Matanzas dancing
***rumba guaguancó.* Note the aggressive posture of the male**
dancer, and the evasive body language of the female dancer.
Matanzas, Cuba. Photo by Gage Averill, 1995.

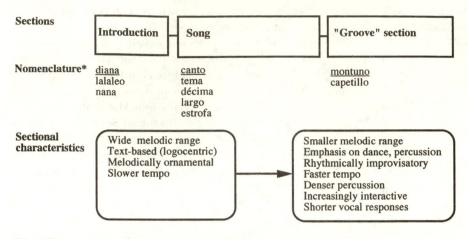

*Note: The most common sectional labels are underlined.

Fig. 4–4. *Rumba* **formal structure. The three-part structure of** *rumba* **has been widely influential in many genres of Cuban music. This figure includes a schematic diagram of** *rumba* **structure, variant names for each section, and a rough sketch of changes in style from the beginning to the end.**

The first section is called *la diana* [the opening of the day, reveille], *lalale* (which imitates the sound of the introductory syllables), or *nana*. It explores the pitches of the melodic mode with a florid melody of Iberian derivation using vocables. It may be sung solo by the *sonero,* or it may incorporate harmonies or responsorial lines from a secondary vocalist.

The main song section of the *rumba* is usually based on one of many popular Spanish poetic forms, including the ten-line *décima* (see Chapter 6) and/or the medieval four-line *romance.* This song section is called by many names—*canto* [song], *tema* [theme], *décima, largo* [from the musical term for slow or solemn passages], or *estrofa* [strophe]. This section affords the *sonero* the freedom to explore the lyrical content and theme of the *rumba.*

The third and final section of a *rumba* features call-and-response vocals between the lead singer—whose improvised lead lines are called *inspiración*—and the rest of the group, who sing the *estribillo* [refrain] or *coro* [chorus]. This "groove" section is called the *capetillo* or *montuno* [from the hills], and it features free-improvisatory *quinto* drum soloing in "conversation" with the dancers. Its tempo is usually a little faster than the rest of the song and the choruses are shorter, overlapping, and interactive. Many have remarked that the structure of a *rumba* parallels a transition from more European forms to more African forms— i.e., from long, elaborate melodies to shorter call-and-response patterns, and from melodic ornamentation to rhythmic improvisation. The basic *rumba* structure of introduction-song-*montuno* is used widely in Cuban popular music.

Havana and Matanzas, both port cities, were known as centers of *rumba* performance, and there are many varieties and stylistic differences associated with each city. Although the Havana style of playing *guaguancó* was perhaps better known around the world, it has been the Matanzas style that has traveled most widely in recent decades with the performances and tours of Los Muñequitos de Matanzas and Afro-Cuba de Matanzas, among other professional *rumba* ensembles. The lyrics in Example 4–2 are from a *rumba yambú* in Matanzas style, from the performance of Los Muñequitos de Matanzas (Recorded Selection 17). The lyrics make mention of Palo (a Kongo-derived secret society and religion that is much feared by outsiders), and they criticize a man for vanity and for not exercising sufficient respect for his elders.

Ex. 4–2.   Lyrics to "Congo yambumba"

Diana

Aña ña vele vela la la la
Aña vela vela vela volo volo vele vele va . . .

Inspiración

(1) Yo m'enteré	I discovered
Que tú anda(s) diciendo	That you're going around saying
Que ere(s) un Palo	That you're a Palo
Mi amigo Julián	Julián my friend
[Repeat first four lines]	
Tú debiera(s) decir,	You should be saying,
"Si no fuera por papá"	"If it weren't for *papá*"
[Repeat last two lines]	
(2) Ahora veo	Now I see
Que todo lo tuyo	That everything about you
Es un vano puro	Is pure vanity
Mi amigo Julián	Julián my friend
[Repeat first four lines]	
Tú debiera(s) decir,	You should be saying,
"Si no fuera por papá"	"If it weren't for *papá*"
[Repeat last two lines]	

Estribillo	*Refrain*
Congo Yambumba me llamo yo	They call me Congo Yambumba
Yo soy el terror	I'm the terror

Estribillo (2)	*Refrain (2)*
Ay-ay-ay-ay	Lead: Ay-Ay-Ay-Ay
Yo soy el terror	Group: I'm the terror

REPERCUSSIONS OF *RUMBA*

In *The Latin Tinge,* John Storm Roberts pointed out that what passed for *rumba* for decades in the United States was, by-and-large, any Cuban big band *son* [a form of Cuban popular dance music].[4] This confusion grew out of the first performance of Don Azpiazú's Havana Casino Orchestra in New York City in 1930, when the group premiered a stylized *rumba* dance as well as a *son* arrangement of a *pregón* [street-seller's song] called "El manicero" [The peanut vendor], which became a major hit. Henceforth, American journalists, bandleaders, and the public used the label "rhumba" (with the Anglicized spelling) for a range of popular Cuban dance musics. Despite this confusion, *rumba*—as a percussion, song, and dance event—has had a powerful impact on Cuban dance music. Many great performers of Latin music, like the early Havana *sonero* Ignacio Piñero, vocalist Beny Moré, and percussionist/composer Chano Pozo were ardent *rumberos.* In addition, in the period when *salsa* was developing as a New York–based Latin music (based on Cuban forms), *rumba* was the popular music for informal, street-corner jamming through which so many Latin percussionists developed their "chops." *Rumba* has helped to establish the structuring role of *clave* and *tumbao,* the conversational and interactional art of drumming, the three-part song structure, and a particular vocal timbre as core elements in Cuban (and indeed Latin) music. With the explosion of worldwide interest in the Matanzas style, with the ongoing exploration of *rumba* in contemporary *songó* music coming out of Havana, and with the export of *rumba* to Cuban and Latin neighborhoods in the United States and throughout the world, there is every reason to believe that *rumba*—as an artistic and a social practice—is more vital than ever.

HAITI AND TRINIDAD AND TOBAGO

We now turn from the Spanish-speaking Caribbean to focus on the French/Creole–speaking and English-speaking Caribbean. There are, of course, reasons other than language to focus on Haiti and on Trinidad and Tobago (not the least of which is that my own research and performance activities have been dominated by these music cultures).

Haiti is the Caribbean nation with the strongest cultural inheritance from Africa. Having obtained its independence in a fierce struggle against the French, Haiti has inspired antislavery and anticolonial struggles around the world. Paradoxically, the flight of colonists from the rebellion at the end of the eighteenth century helped to spread Haitian Creole culture throughout the Caribbean and spurred the development of Cuban *danzón,* African-American jazz, and Trinidadian calypso, among other musics. As a predominantly agricultural society of persistent (even deepening) poverty and a low level of infrastructural development, Haiti is nevertheless home to a rich and vibrant culture.

A Carib Indian stronghold, Trinidad was visited by Columbus on his third voyage, whereupon he named it Trinidad, for its three prominent mountains. There was no real settlement until 1592, when the Spaniards set up cocoa plantations (which would fail within two hundred years due to a blight). Few people lived there until 1783, when the Spanish crown issued a decree allowing non-Spanish Roman Catholics to immigrate. French-speaking colonists moved to Trinidad, especially after the French Revolution of 1789, when revolutionaries took over France's colonies in the Caribbean. As a result, the language of the Trinidadian masses before the twentieth century was French Creole. After Napoleon came to power, Britain went to war against France, forming alliances with various European countries to drive out Napoleon's armies from French-occupied territories in much of Europe. Then, when Spain joined the war on France's side, the British had an excuse to take Trinidad, still a Spanish colony. The British arrived in 1797 and occupied Trinidad, beginning a long eclipse of the power of the French plantocracy and of the pervasiveness of Creole popular culture. When the British took over in 1797, two-thirds of the population consisted of enslaved Africans and African descendants; of the remaining third, two-thirds was made up of free Africans and "coloreds." Thus, the population was largely of African descent until the nineteenth-century arrival of South Asians, who now constitute over 40 percent of the population. Although British culture was dominant for the first half of the twentieth century, Trinidad and Tobago share an older Creole culture with Haiti. What's more, Trinidad's Carnival is the Caribbean's most spectacular cultural event, and the island has produced a number of musics of global significance.

HAITIAN VODOU: THE FÈT DAOME AT MISTIK SOUVENANS

Serving the Spirits

Although there are no reliable statistics on religious affiliation in Haiti, it is widely believed that a majority of Haitians believe in and/or practice some aspect of the Afro-Haitian religion known as Vodou, even if in conjunction with another religious tradition such as Roman Catholicism. The religion is not often called Vodou in rural Haiti; rather, it is usually spoken of as "serving the *lwa* [spirits]," and while Vodou may be more popular in the countryside and among Haiti's lower classes, it is by no means restricted to these social sectors. Vodou encourages a reverence for ancestral spirits and for a variety of African deities that came with slaves to the Americas.[5] Adherents to Vodou believe that the spirits manifest themselves in ceremonies by possessing their devotees.[6] Food, drink, music, burning candles, material objects, and animal blood are all offered up to the spirits to maintain the bonds of respect and obligation that nurture both the material and spiritual realms. Music, which emanates from the ceremony and travels to Ginen (from Guinée, thought to represent an African spiritual homeland), is a point of contact with the spirits and is able to call them, to encourage them to possess their servants, to entertain them, to anger, and to dismiss them. The music is perceived by participants as a symbol of the cultural ties to Africa and to specific African nationalities, and is thus an exercise in cultural memory. And yet the religion is not strictly African by any means, having absorbed and transformed many Christian, European spiritist, Masonic, and even Islamic elements over the years. The spirits are often represented in their parallel identities as Christian saints, and *prèt savann* [bush priests] officiate certain Vodou ceremonies and often lead the singing of Catholic hymns and the recitation of Catholic prayers.

The great majority of Vodou rituals in Haiti are carried out in the privacy of homes using small altars and family shrines. Larger extended-family habitations (called *lakou* [literally, courtyard]) may have a building designated as a *peristil* [covered area for Vodou rituals and dances] with an attached *ounfò* [spirit house, a smaller room for worship, with an altar].

Most Haitian Vodou ceremonies can be thought of as belonging to one of two branches of Vodou—Rada or Petwo. Rada ceremonies and beliefs are more directly descended from West African prototypes, especially from religions of the Ewe and Fon peoples of the former kingdom of Dahomey (now largely in the lower latitudes of Togo and Benin) and of the Yoruba peoples of Nigeria. Rada ceremonies are considered "cooler" and less militaristic than Petwo. Petwo is heavily influenced by cultural influences from the Kongo region of Central Africa; it took shape in the revolutionary period of the late eighteenth century and retains its fiery militancy. Vodou still maintains its patriotic and military associations nearly two centuries after the Haitian revolution which it helped to mobilize. Many of the *lwa* in Haiti belong to one or the other branch, and many temples will serve only one branch or will keep the drums and other ritual media of Rada well away from those of Petwo. Petwo drums, played in sets of two, are carved and barrel-shaped, usually painted, with cowhide drumheads laced to the body. Rada drums, following the Ewe style, are goblet-shaped (sometimes with carved feet), are played in sets of three, and have goatskin drumheads attached to the body with pegs. Despite their different ethnic origins, both Petwo and Rada rites in Vodou show influences from many different African nations. For example, in Rada songs and dances, those of the Ibo (Igbo), Kongo, Mina (Akan-speaking people of the Ghana region), Mahi, Nago (Yoruba), and Daome (Fon-Ewe) peoples are all represented. They are best understood as multination rites that helped to join descendants of many African nations (with many languages, religions, deities, etc.) into unified religious congregations. Due to the relatively isolated nature of rural Haiti and the many multiethnic contributions to Vodou, and also because of its marginal status in Haiti for most of its history, Haitian Vodou has developed many regional varieties and permutations. Rather than attempting to discuss Vodou in the abstract, I believe it will be more illuminating to examine a specific ceremony.

The Temple at Souvenance

The dusty coastal city of Gonaïves is known as the "cradle of the revolution" for its long history as a hotbed of political activism, stretching back to the days of the Haitian independence and the antislavery struggle. It sits on the northernmost rim of the lush breadbasket of Haiti, the Artibonite Valley, home to the river of the same name. About ten kilometers west of the city, surrounded by fields of eggplant and millet, is the village of Souvenance, home to a large extended-family habitation at which is found the Tanp Mistik [Mystic temple] of Souvenance. For one week each year, it attracts hundreds of "servants" of the African *lwa* [spirits, deities] from all over the region and even some from elsewhere in Haiti or from the Haitian communities overseas. The week-long ritual is the Fèt Daome [Ceremony for Dahomey], coinciding with Easter. In Illustration 4–4, we see a group of initiates at the temple taking a break before a *manje lwa* [feast for the spirits], which is an important component in the ritual events. The description below is based on a series of four research visits to the *lakou* in the late 1980s in order to document this and another major ritual at the *lakou*. One of these visits was timed to coincide with the Fèt Daome.[7]

The temple at Souvenance is one of at least seven major *peristils* in the Artibonite region that are neither Rada nor Petwo but that retain links to specific African nations—in the case of Souvenance, to Daome (Ewe-Fon). Although the system of slavery often worked to eradicate ethnic identification among the slaves, it was sometimes possible for people belonging to the same African nation to congregate and hold festivities—especially in areas of dense sugar cultivation, where large slave populations sharing the same language and ancestry lived in close proximity, and where the colonial power structure either facilitated such gatherings or was ineffectual in preventing them.

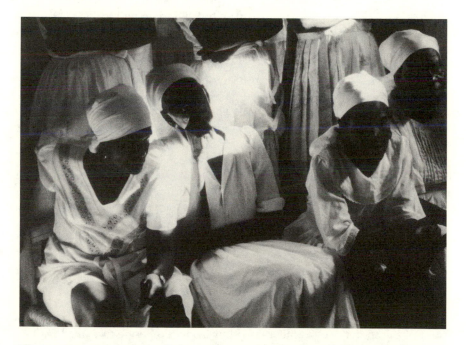

Ill. 4–4. *Ounsis* take a break from the ceremony in the room used for the *manje lwa* [feast for the spirits] at Lakou Souvenance. Photo by Gage Averill, 1988.

The Vodou Battery

The percussion at Souvenance consists of three drums, *tchatcha* [rattle], and *ogan* [metal timekeeper].[8] The drums are constructed like typical Rada drums of the Ewe variety but featuring cowhide rather than goatskin drumheads. The skins are fastened with pegs (*kòn* or *zoban*) and the bodies of the drums, carved from a single log, taper to a narrow base (Illustration 4–5). The largest of the drums—the mother drum—is called the *ountò* [spirit invocation] and is held at an angle by a seated assistant, so that the master drummer can play it with a single *bagèt* [stick] while standing up. The other two drums are played while seated. The lowest of the three is not the *ountò* (which would be more common in Haiti) but rather the *katabou,* on which the drummer plays a sustaining and highly repetitive pattern with two sticks. This same pattern is used in most of the Souvenance rhythms, and consists simply of open tones on the second and third beats of each tripletted main pulse (the pulse is accorded a dotted quarter-note in the transcription below). The smallest and highest-pitched drum is the *gwonde,* played with a curved (*agida*) and straight stick. The *gwonde* plays a more repetitive part than the *ountò* but it nevertheless responds with its own variations to those of the *ountò.*

The drums are "put to sleep" in a closet for most of the year and awakened for the Fèt Daome in April. The so-called "time-line" pattern is played on the *ogan* and is consistent for most of the rhythms played at Souvenance. In fact, it is a variant of a well-known and widely distributed time-line pattern in West Africa and throughout the African diaspora, sometimes called the "West African standard pattern." An example of a short selection of drumming from a *chasè* rhythm, one of the principal beats at Lakou Souvenance, appears in Example 4–3. The *ountò* and *gwonde* parts are a two-cycle sample from a single section; in practice, they will vary widely over the length of a performance. A cycle is defined as a complete statement of the *ogan* pattern. This follows the general outlines of Yih 1995 (274) except for choice of transcription system and bell pattern, which, on my own recordings, is a variant of the one transcribed by Yih.

Vodou drumming at Souvenance can be considered "typical" of Haitian Vodou drumming, first of all in its use of a size- and pitch-graded ensemble of drums, along with instruments of other sonorities (bell and rattle). In addition, the percussion instruments interlock their simpler individual parts in a dense resultant pattern that serves as an accompaniment to sacred dances and song cycles. The "mother" drum has the greatest latitude to vary the conversation, inserting breaks (*kase*) in the rhythm and introducing new rhythms altogether.[9]

Ceremonial Structure

The Fèt Daome begins on the Saturday eve of Easter Sunday. The *sèvitè* [priest, servant of the spirits] blesses initiates within the *ounfò* beside two small *sogbadje* [altars] at which offerings are made to the *lwa.* The *sèvitè* blows a *foula* [spray of rum] in the four cardinal directions and begins the first part of the week's musical segments, a song cycle in the privacy of the *ounfò,* called the *seremoni* (itself com-

Ill. 4–5. The three Daome drums used at Lakou Souvenance for the Fèt Daome, played outdoors for the *lwa* Ayizan. The lead drummer stands, striking the *ountò* with a single stick. Photo by Gage Averill, Lakou Souvenance, Haiti, 1988.

Ex. 4–3.   *Chasè* rhythm.

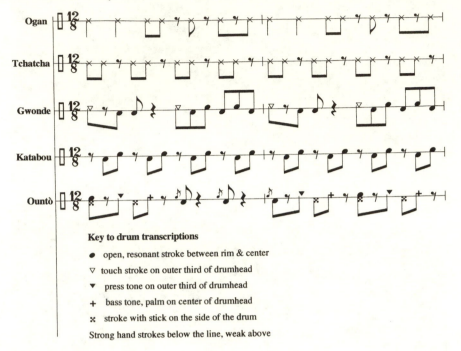

Key to drum transcriptions

● open, resonant stroke between rim & center

▽ touch stroke on outer third of drumhead

▼ press tone on outer third of drumhead

+ bass tone, palm on center of drumhead

✕ stroke with stick on the side of the drum

Strong hand strokes below the line, weak above

mencing with the *noble,* which serves as a greeting and a means of honoring the *lwa*). The songs of the *seremoni* in the inner temple are accompanied only by the priest's *tchatcha* [rattle], and they are sung in call-and-response fashion between the songleader *(larenn)* and the congregation *(ounsi).* During the *seremoni,* many of the *ounsi* are possessed by the *lwa*.

In Vodou, it is believed that the *lwa* can enter into a ceremony by "riding the horse" of the initiate, and that in the process a portion of the soul (the *ti bon anj*) of the horse is displaced temporarily by the visiting deity. In this way, Haitian *ounsis* have direct contact with their gods, greeting the spirits and inquiring after them. In contrast to Vodou ceremonies throughout most of Haiti, the *lwa* who come to Souvenance do not speak (and thus do not counsel the congregation or foretell future events)—instead, they mutely receive the greetings and questions of those assembled. They are also not given special implements or costumes identified with the possessing *lwa* as they are in some Haitian temples; instead, they may be tied around the waist with a cloth handkerchief *(foula),* and they may be turned first counterclockwise and then clockwise.

After the *noble* come two cycles of *seremoni* songs devoted to the two camps or battalions of deities at Souvenance: the *chasè* (named after the colonial military's light infantry divisions) and the *grennadyè* (named for the artillery divisions). Each camp has its own *chèf* [chief, director] and its own songs and rhythms.

Ex. 4–4.   Lyrics to "Danbala Wèdo nou solid o"

Danbala Wèdo, nou solid o

E anye nou solid o

E anye o solid o, eya Danbala

Danbala Wèdo, nou solid o.

Danbala Wèdo, we are solid [strong, united], oh

We are solid, oh

Oh, solid, oh, Danbala

Danbala Wèdo, we are solid, oh.

Throughout the week, the songs played follow this same pattern—a cycle for the *chasè* and a cycle for the *grennadyè*. This system of camps is peculiar to Souvenance. The following song from the *chasè* cycle is addressed to Danbala Wèdo (Recorded Selection 18), the Haitian equivalent of the West African god Dangbe Ayido Hwedo, a rainbow serpent god. In Haiti, Danbala is said to guard waterfalls and to symbolize rebirth. The song seems to affirm that the *ounsi* are present and strong *(solid)*, but Vodou songs are often pointedly ambivalent, switching person, using untranslatable syllables in a mystical language *(langaj),* and drawing on deep pools of spiritual knowledge to which only initiates or priests have access. Thus, it is often a mistake to accept an obvious denotative meaning of a song text.

When the ceremony has been sufficiently "heated" in the *ounfò,* the priest and the congregation (many still in a state of possession) file into the *peristil* to begin the night's *dans* [ceremonial dance], led by the *sèvitè* and his assistants. The three drummers and the *ogan* [iron beater] player begin the Daome rhythm to open the ceremony. They follow this with *chasè* and *grennadyè* beats, both of which are in a 12/8 rhythm (see the transcription of the *chasè* rhythm in Example 4–3). The songs they sing include "Kebyesou, badji-m anwo, badji-m anba" (Example 4–5; Recorded Selection 19) from the *chasè* section, addressed to Kebyesou, the deity of thunder and lightning (who himself comes from the Fon-Ewe sky deity Hevioso). Try singing this song with a rattle accompaniment as shown in Example 4–3, and

Ex. 4–5.   "Kebyesou, badji-m anwo, badji-m anba"

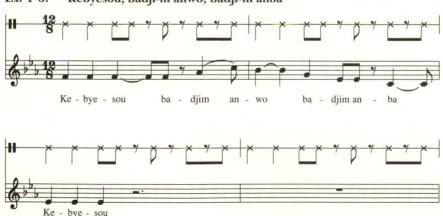

feel free to have someone who knows musical notation help with the melody and rattle rhythm. Once you have learned to sing the song following the notation provided in Example 4–5, you can attempt to combine it with a simple version of the *chasè* rhythm. Note that the vocal rhythm closely follows that of the *ogan* [bell]; this is certainly not always the case, and it is even common in Vodou for the percussion to be in a 12/8 framework while the vocals are in 4/4. David Yih and Elizabeth McAlister have noted that this song is found in the nearby temple of Soukri (devoted to Kongo rites), and that the song is to be interpreted as a reference to the existence of three sister temples in the region (Badjo, Soukri, and Souvenance), so that "if one is destroyed, there is still another."[10]

After the two song cycles, the drummers play a binary rhythm called Kongo Daome to *ranvwaye* [send away] the spirits. The entire group then moves to an enclosure elsewhere on the *lakou* for the *lwa* Parenn (Legba), a trickster deity who opens ceremonies and spiritual pathways.[11] Music is played while the *ounsi* form a procession, in this case by moving the bench for the drummers every few minutes or so all the way to the Parenn shrine. After songs for Parenn at this site, the group reverses the direction of their movement and returns to the *peristil* to conclude the dance for the evening.

The ceremony begins anew on Easter morning, with a cycle of *seremoni* songs in the *ounfò*. Again the group moves out into the *peristil*, but on this morning, the group begins chanting "anye, anye o" and rhythmically gesturing with the index finger, indicating that a sacrifice is underway. Two goats held aloft have been ritually prepared, and those among the *ounsi* who are in trance and who have attained a sufficient degree of spiritual mastery are allowed to come into contact with the blood, to *pran san* [take blood] as part of the offering to the spirits. Over the rest of Sunday and Monday, the group processes to a number of sacred sites on the grounds, such as (1) a space enclosed by low walls where they honor Ayizan, guardian of the marketplace and public spaces, with the sacrifice of a chicken; (2) a tree for a bull sacrifice to Ogun, god of warfare and iron, at which wooden swords are passed out for all to dip in the blood of the bull; (3) a pond where Danbala Wèdo plunges his "horses" into the muddy water; and (4) various large *gran mapou* trees in the fields that serve as repositories for the *lwa* Lisagbadji. Singing and drumming accompany the congregation wherever they go.

On Tuesday, the *lakou* holds an Asotò ceremony for the *asotò* drum and for the spirit of the same name that resides in the drum. The *asotò* is the largest drum in Haiti; the Souvenance versions are about six feet tall, and two of these are placed in the center of the *peristil*. A special rhythm is played on the three-drum battery and the congregation members, each holding a drumstick, circle

Ex. 4–6. Lyrics to "Kebyesou, badji-m anwo, badji-m anba"

Kebyesou	Kebyesou
Badji-m anwo	My temple is up above
Badji-m anba	My temple is down below
Kebyesou	Kebyesou

around the drums in a counterclockwise direction. A signal played by the three-drum battery directs the dancers to advance toward the drums and strike the heads; they then retreat, spin in place, and reverse the direction of their circumambulation of the two *asotò* drums. The practice of circling and striking the drums comes to Haiti from Dahomey, where it is performed on *sato* drums, the apparent predecessors of the Haitian *asotò*. This ritual is not performed much in Haiti anymore, but where it is, it is closely linked to the Daome nation and to rituals for the deceased.

On the following day, there is a *manje lwa* [food for the spirits], a ceremonial meal at which a number of the animals prepared for the blood sacrifice are cooked and consumed. A children's ceremony, a communion, and ritually-purifying leaf baths occur on subsequent days.

The Fèt Daome, like most Vodou rituals, represents a great sacrifice of time and resources in one of the poorest countries on earth, but it is believed to help insure the proper relationship of human beings to the spirit world, and thus to contribute to human health, prosperity, and survival. Vodou rituals bring human beings into a direct encounter with divinity, nurture a sense of community and solidarity, and profoundly shape the worldviews of those who serve the spirits.

HAITIAN *RARA:* MUSIC OF SPIRIT, POWER, AND CELEBRATION

On the Road with Rara Bands

Rara (Recorded Selection 20) is a genre of music, but it is also a season, an event, a procession, a band, and perhaps even a frame of mind. To introduce the reader to *rara* experientially, I want to sketch some early encounters with *rara*.

After my first *sòti* [outing] with a *rara* band named Corvée [work brigade] Band, south of the Artibonite Valley in 1988, I encountered many groups in the city which had come out for Carnival. Traditionally, however, the end of Carnival marks not only the start of Lent in Haiti but also the start of *rara* season. One night in March of 1991, I wandered off late at night in search of *rara* bands from Belair and Lower Delmas (neighborhoods near downtown Port-au-Prince) called Djab [devil] and San Andre.[12] The streets were deserted except for the *rara* bands because of the dangers created by the attacks from *zenglendos,* armed bandits that had been terrorizing the city. In the *rara*, at least, there was safety in numbers. The *rara* San Andre was snaking its way up the narrow street. The *kolonèl* [colonel] of the band snapped his whip and gave a shrill blast on his whistle to hold the group back. He turned toward a group standing on the porch of a small house at the side of the street and advanced. Three *majo jòns* (from *majeur jongleur* [baton twirlers with the rank of major]) came forward dancing in low, crouched positions and twirling their metal batons over their heads. They joined the batons in a cross and passed it over the bodies of their potential benefactors on the porch while the musicians played a slow, haunting *ochan* [salute]. The residents honored in this way donated money to the band (the ritual is called *peyisoti* [pay to make them leave]), after which the musicians picked up the tempo and broke into a spirited *rabòday* rhythm, and the *kolonèl* led the band down the dark streets, kicking up great clouds of dust.

Later in the week, I went out with a *rara* called Briyant Solèy [shining sun] which originated in a *lakou* in Carrefour du Fort near Léogane. This *rara* had not been operating for twenty-some years, after conflicts with other groups caused it to fall apart, but the group was reorganizing under the leadership of the elder member of the Similien family, who was also a Vodou *oungan* [priest]. The band had a secret society president, Nanpwen Moun [there is no person], as its *kolonèl*. Some of Briyant's songs deal with the difficult history of the group and with the desire to put conflicts behind them. Their *sanba* [song leader] had just written a few songs for this *rara*, including the following:

Ex. 4–7.   Lyrics to "Pawòl-sa-a m pa gen dwa bliye l" and "Men briyant wayo"

"Pawòl-sa-a m pa gen dwa bliye l"

Pawòl-sa-a m pa gen dwa bliye l	I don't have the right to forget this proverb:
"Jan m bon, se konsa m mouri"	"How you live is how you die"
Yo pran lan Briyant	They came into the heart of Briyant
Sere l anba dlo	And drove it under the water
Se sa m pa vle	This is just what I want to avoid
Yo ban mwen kou-a	They gave me a hard blow
Kou-a fè mwen mal o	This blow made me ill
Malgre sa-a, m anvi lape	Despite this, I still want peace

"Men briyant wayo"

Men Briyant, wayo	Here's Brilliant, oh
Nou pa lan goumen mesyè	We're not going to get into fights, sir
Nou pa lan goumen mesyè	We're not going to get into fights, sir
Met liyon nan lape o adye	Let's find unity in peace
Met liyon nan lape, Kay Similien	Let's find unity in peace, House of Similien
Nou pral nan rara o	We'll go out in the *rara*
Djab la rive, o	The devils are here, oh

Briyant Solèy allied with a large *rara* band called Ti-Malice. On one of the first nights of the final week of *rara* (Easter Week), all of the bands wanting to pay respects to Ti-Malice came by their headquarters and played *ochans*. Ti-Malice had a long-standing competition with two other groups in the region, and most of the bands in the Léogane region sided publicly with one of the three groups. Bands did their best to plan routes through the countryside and along the highway that would enable them to avoid their rivals, but this wasn't always successful. In addition to the fights that sometimes break out, groups will sometimes leave *zanm kongo* [Kongo "arms," malevolent powders or small packets of power-objects] for their rivals in the street, the goal of which is to cause the other group to *kraze* [break up or fall apart] or to *gaye* [become confused, lost]. To avoid this, the bands take a number of precautions that include ritual bathing and massage with *benyen fèy* [leaf preparations] and drinking *siwomyèl* [honey syrup]. They salute Mèt Kalfou [guardian of crossroads] at crossroads, which are considered places of special power and danger, and they hold ceremonies at the cemeteries for the deities called the Gedes (who mediate humorously and obscenely between the worlds of the living and the dead). They "put their instruments to sleep" in the *ounfò* [temple] to gather force and then "baptize" them at the start of *rara* season or during the Gede [feast of the dead] at the beginning of November. These ceremonial acts are designed to give the band the necessary physical and spiritual strength to keep the *rara* together and on the move. Thus, while to the casual spectator a *rara* seems to be given over to an exuberant and rowdy celebration—the apparent goal being to *lage kò-w* [let go of one's body], a *rara* is also deeply connected to its social and cultural milieu and is considered a form of sacred activity and obligation.[13]

The Meanings of Rara

Beginning with Lent and continuing until the day after Easter, *rara* season dates back to the colonial era and seems to derive its timing from an old French ritual of a second Carnival held to commemorate the end of Lent, called the Carnaval Carême. A *rara* procession makes for an extraordinary spectacle. At night, the bands are illuminated by kerosene lanterns carried on the heads of a few marchers. In some areas, vendors may accompany the bands selling candy, *fresko* [shaved ice with flavored syrups], and *kleren* [cheap sugar cane liquor]. At houses along the route, contributions are often made to the band in the form of cash or refreshments, including *siwomyèl*, a sweet honey syrup that is said to give the band the stamina to parade through the night. Celebrants move at a slow pace through the streets, usually with a shuffle motion of the feet, a roll of the hips called *gouyad* (from sacred funerary dances called *banda*), and sometimes with the arms spread wide or in the air. While on the road (even on the main highway), bands will stop traffic to collect a tax to be deposited in the skirts of the *rèn* [queens] or in a basket that they carry.

A respected elder often serves as *mèt* [master, owner] of the band and pledges to a *lwa* to sponsor the band for a certain number of years. Security and control of the band's route fall to the *kòlonèl*, who carries a whip and a whistle for this purpose. In *rara*, as in some Vodou rituals, the whip chases away malevolent spirits and purifies the space through which the group passes. The *kòlonèl* stops the band periodically, keeping the group together, and protecting it from other bands and from destructive magic. Marching in front of the bands, the *pòt drapo* or flag carriers display the emblems of the group. The band's *majo jòns* wear distinctive and colorful costumes—modeled in part on fanciful reconstructions of European court dress and in part on imagined Indian garb of the pre-Columbian period, all infused with Vodou symbolism. The *majo jòns* costumes include conical hats in the Artibonite (elsewhere, baseball caps are common), sequined vests adorned with symbols of the Vodou *lwa*, a sequined "apron" hanging below the waist, colorful scarves at the waist, sunglasses, tall stockings, and tennis sneakers (Illustration 4–6). The *majo jòns* are the principal spiritual symbols of the bands. In some areas, they are "reborn" from under white sheets at the start of Easter weekend. They execute difficult passes or twirls of the baton in tribute to patrons of the group and have their own rhythm *(mazoun)* with its delicate dance steps that stem from Renaissance French court dances. In Illustration 4–7 we see a *kolonèl* dancing in front of a Gonaïves *rara* band, followed by a *pòt drapo* (center), various *majo jòn* (right), and *rèns* [queens] (left).

Bands begin the season by practicing at whatever serves as their headquarters, where they *balanse rara* [heat the *rara* and raise its spiritual power]. Next they *fè egzesis* [engage in exercises] and *sòti* [take the band out on short skirmishes], often starting and stopping and changing direction to fool *lwa* who have been sent against the band by their enemies. On Sundays throughout Lent, the groups practice in this way, building toward the week preceding Easter when they step up their activity. The bands are en route each night from Thursday through Easter Sunday, often stopping only with the dawn.

Rara bands are highly sensitive to geographical issues. Their military structures may be partly a residue of their association with secret societies, which protected

Ill. 4–6. Three *majo jòns* with the *rara* Modèle d'Haïti. Photo by Elizabeth McAlister, Léogane, Haiti, 1991. Used by permission.

**Ill. 4–7. Gonaïves-area *rara* with *kolonèl*, *pòt drapo*, *rèn*, and *majo jòn*.
Photo by Jeffrey W. Bates, 1997. Used by permission**

peasant enclaves both before and after the Haitian independence struggle. *Rara* bands seek to project their power and that of their sponsors and patron saints into the streets, especially those streets or roads that form a natural geographical territory or home base. One *mèt* provided insight into the multiple meanings of *rara:*

> It came out of Africa and came to Haiti. Haitians passed it down in the *kòve* [work brigade]. When they worked in the brigade, they were making *rara.* There is an expression: "To arrive at something in life, you have to take a route."[14] It's on the route that you walk. If you sit down, understand, you'll never be anything. When you walk, you arrive at the crossroads. After you arrive at the crossroads, you enter into the cemetery. That's the last place you arrive. There's nothing for you after that. It's a system for joy, too. . . . It applies directly to the system of Vodou. [A *rara* participant] is showing you that he has something for himself—that he needs to get by. He has an energy that he has lost, he has to go in the *rara* to find it. He works all week long, even Saturday and Sunday. In *rara,* he shakes his body free, to take back what he's lost.[15]

In this perspective, *rara* is a release from day-to-day cares, a popular demonstration against oppression, an expression of Vodou, a system of justice, and a philosophy of life that touches on issues of work, discipline, order, collective protection, joy, and African identity.

Rara *Music*

Music accompanies *rara* throughout its ritual season. The music keeps spirits and energy high, unifies the group, provides a beat for marching and dancing, honors the saints, and projects the power of the *rara* band to all those within earshot. Songs are composed each year by a *sanba* and are often about recent community (also regional or national) events or about individuals who have committed an act worthy of censure. Among the most popular forms of *rara* song is thus the *chan pwen* [sung point], a song often directed against an unnamed target. The political, topical, and sometimes obscene lyrics of the *chan pwen* use double-entendre and metaphor to signify on the event, person, or rival *rara* band. Honorific songs, called *ochans*, may be sung for local dignitaries, allied bands, ancestors, or *lwa*. They are typically slow and stately, and show residual traces of European military drumming and harmonic structure.

The accompanying ensemble features three or more single-note bamboo trumpets of varying lengths, called *vaksins* or *banbou*. A closed node at one end of a bamboo tube is pierced to form a mouthpiece through which the tube is blown; the other end is open. Notes from different *vaksin* are interlocked, or hocketed, in short, repeating melodic-rhythmic patterns (*ostinati*, to use a Western musicological term).

The *vaksin* player sometimes also strikes the length of bamboo with a stick. The time-line played on a piece of iron (sometimes the same pattern tapped on the side of the *vaksin*) is called a *kata*, from a Ki-Kongo word meaning "to cut."[16] Flared trumpets made of hammered tin called *kònè* (from "coronet") may duplicate, substitute for, or add other parts to the *vaksin ostinato*. They may also

Ill. 4–8. *Vaksin* ensemble of the *rara* Ti-Malice. Photo by Elizabeth McAlister, Léogane, Haiti, 1991. Used by permission.

Ill. 4–9. Jean "Fanfan" Louis *(vaksin)* and Frisnel Lexius *(manman tanbou)* of the band Brillant Soleil. Photo by Elizabeth McAlister, Léogane, Haiti, 1991. Used by permission.

Ex. 4–8. **"Bann Sanpwèl la nan Lari-O"** (*kata, tchatcha* and *vaksins*)

"hum" along with the vocal melody contributing a haunting buzz to the song, akin to the sound of a kazoo. There are typical *vaksin ostinati* that are widespread in Haiti, but groups are free to orchestrate their own patterns. Intervallic relations of an approximate tritone are part of a widespread aesthetic present in the construction of these cyclical units, as are one or more intervals of a semitone. The pattern played by the *vaksin* forms a "ground" for the vocal melody. Using the short *ostinato* of three to five tones and the dense percussion, the musicians create a solid musical groove to motivate the ensemble for days on the road and to resist the effects of conflict, weariness, and magic potions.

Rara drummers play a one-headed, hand-beaten drum called the *manman tanbou* [mother drum], identical to those used in Petwo ceremonies in Vodou. This drum, however, is carried around the neck with a cord and is thus called a *tanbou a liny* [drum with cord] (see Illustration 4–9.) Other instruments used in *rara* include a *kès* [double-headed, stick-beaten frame drum], *graj* [metal scraper], *tchatcha (maracas),* an *ogan* or *fè* [iron beater], and various kinds of rattles made from sheets of tin, such as the *tchansi* [can filled with seed rattles]. In the last three decades, large horn sections featuring trumpet, saxophones, and trombones have

Ex. 4–9. Vocal to "Bann Sanpwèl la nan Lari-O"

Ex. 4–10. **Lyrics to "Bann Sanpwèl la nan Lari-O"**

Bann Sanpwèl-la nan lari-a   The Sanpwel band is in the streets
Bann Sanpwèl-la nan lari-a   The Sanpwel band is in the streets
Sa ma bay yo, tande   What will I give them, you hear?
                                          (alternate translation: What I have for
                                              them, Listen!)

(Translation, Elizabeth McAlister)

become commonplace, at least in regions within an hour's drive of the capital, Port-au-Prince. Example 4–8 is a transcription of some elements (*kata, tchatcha,* and *vaksins*) from the recording of the *rara* "Bann Sanpwèl la nan Lari-O."[17] The *vaksin* (or *banbou*) ostinato varies throughout the performance as instruments drop in and out and as they vary their parts, so this figure represents a "snapshot" of two cycles. Each pitch level articulated by the *vaksins* and *konès* would have to be produced by a different instrument.

The song, represented in Example 4–9, is likewise subject to continuous melodic and lyrical variation in performance. Note that *rara* tonality can support juxtapositions of pitches in the song melody and *vaksin* accompaniment that would be considered quite dissonant in most Euro-American musics. The words are set forth in Example 4–10.

You can approximate the *vaksin* sound with PVC plastic pipe or even cardboard tubes. A plastic or other cover over one end simulates the node of the bamboo, into which you can bore an oval hole large enough for the lips to vibrate (as though playing a trumpet). Practice will produce a sustained and identifiable pitch, the resonant pitch of the tube. Experiment with lengths to get an approximation of the intervallic relationships. Then practice coming in at the right time so that you supply the proper notes for the *ostinato*. Once you have this down, try tapping the *kata* on the tube with a stick. One or more players may just want to tap out quarter or eighth notes as well. You can build up from there, add an iron, an improvised *vaksin* rhythm on one tube, vocals, and even movement. Remember that pitch relationships in *rara* are not expected to be precise; it's more important to sustain a solid groove and to make the music hot.[18]

Rara, *Politics, and Popular Music*

The power of *rara* bands is regularly harnessed for political ends in Haiti (completely apart from *rara*'s ritual season), when bands play in protest or in praise of political figures. *Rara* bands are regular features of political demonstrations as well as street parties, sponsored by political leaders, called *koudyay*. The sounds and songs of *rara* have also been the inspiration for urban, popular musicians who have composed and recorded songs in a *rara* vein.

During the American occupation of Haiti (1915–1934) black middle-class artists and intellectuals formulated an ideology that became known as *indigènisme* [indigenism], later *noirisme* [black-ism], to advance the idea that Haiti's culture was more African than European, that the lighter-skinned élite had forsaken the masses by imitating Europe, and that peasant culture should be studied and integrated for a truly national art.[19] *Rara* became a link to an African past and a badge of cultural authenticity. Influenced by this idea, a group called Jazz des Jeunes pioneered a fusion of Cuban dance band orchestrations with local Haitian rhythms and songs—especially those connected to Vodou—in the postwar years, calling this fusion "Vodou-jazz." The group's composer, Antalcides Murat, borrowed a popular *rara* song to arrange the first big-band version of *rara*, using the *vaksins* along with the jazz-band instruments. The words (Example 4–11), in the tradition of *chan pwen*, talk about people who gossip and slander behind people's backs. When sung by Jazz des Jeunes, this was interpreted as a veiled reference to the opponents of the president at the time, Dr. François "Papa Doc" Duvalier. Papa Doc, who ran the country from 1957 to 1971, was a proponent of *noirisme* and a leading figure in the movement, and his candidacy for president was supported by most of the groups and individuals associated with Vodou-jazz.

Rara continued to be evoked by various social movements in opposition to, as well as in support of, Duvalier. Leftist cultural activists in what later became known as the *kilti libete* [freedom culture] movement used the image of a *rara* as a symbol of socialist models of collectivization and organization. The groups were attempting to make use of traditional music and culture in the struggle for socialism, and thus to undermine its association with Duvalier's dictatorship.

In the late 1980s, a countercultural music movement dedicated to Haitian Vodou and *rara* became commercially successful in the country and abroad. This movement was inspired in part by Jamaican Rastafarianism and looked to *rara* as an indigenous African expression, a music of resistance to Euro-American cultural and political dominance and, importantly, as a spiritual vehicle and vision. Called *mizik rasin* [roots music], this was really the first urban, middle-class movement to use Vodou and *rara* not primarily as a means of education or as folklore but as a spiritual and philosophic practice and lifestyle; the musicians attended ceremonies in Vodou temples to apprentice in Vodou drumming (see Illustration 4–10.)

The first widely disseminated *mizik rasin* movement song was called "Vaksine" [vaccinate]; it was written for a UNESCO-sponsored vaccination campaign and

Ex. 4–11.   Lyrics to "Kote moun yo"

Kote moun yo woy	Where are the people
Mwen pa we moun yo e	I don't see the people
Mwen pa we moun yo e	I don't see the people
Kote moun kap pale moun ma	Where are the people bad-mouthing others
Pa we moun kap pale moun mal	I don't see those who are bad-mouthing others
Ban m "devan byen deye mal" o	They're nice to your face, but nasty behind[20]

**Ill. 4–10. The *mizik rasin* [roots music] band Foula, with *rara* instruments.
Photo by Steve Winter, Port-au-Prince, Haiti, 1989. Used by permission.**

was played throughout the country on the radio as a jingle. It was soon sung by *rara* bands all over the island. The leading band in this movement, Boukman Eksperyans (named after an early slave leader in Haiti), achieved international fame with a *rara* song for Carnival 1990 called "Kè-m pa sote" [You don't scare me; literally, my heart doesn't jump] that criticized the military regime running Haiti and helped to topple the government. One roots band, Ram, used some of the lyrics of the earlier *rara* song "Kote Moun Yo" at Carnival 1992 as a protest against the exile of Haiti's elected president, Jean-Bertrand Aristide.[21] These popular artists drew on the power of *rara* songs as social critique. Increasingly, the combination of African-based spirituality, Third-World liberation politics, and a vibrant dance groove attracted adherents for a *rara*-based music in a market for global popular musics that was increasingly being called "worldbeat."

PROFILE OF MANNO CHARLEMAGNE, A HAITIAN MOVEMENT TROUBADOUR

At the time of this writing, Manno Charlemagne is serving as mayor of Haiti's capital, Port-au-Prince, and heading up a political party of his own, but for many years he was known as one of Haiti's most uncompromising movement artist-activists and a relentless critic of Haiti's dictatorship and élite class. Since his earliest years, he has been, in his own words, "submerged in the political question." His story offers a glimpse into the struggles of musicians working for social justice under conditions of dictatorship, into the myriad ways that music is utilized by political movements; his life also offers insight into the contradictions facing those who enter directly into the political fray.

Born in 1948, Manno Charlemagne was raised among the lumpenproletariat in Port-au-Prince and Carrefour, a run-down commercial strip famous for its nightclubs and prostitution along Route 2, west of Port-au-Prince. This environment helped to cultivate Manno's sensitivity to political and social injustice, as well as his expressive abilities.

> I can say I was born in a family where people sing. I was raised by my aunt, not my mother. And both of them are singers. I didn't know who my father was until I was thirty-seven years old, and it turns out that when I knew my father's family, they're all musicians, too. And I feel I had some psychological problems because of not knowing my father, some "child problems." If you listen to my songs, you can feel it. You see, I was raised in a *lakou*. A *lakou* in the Haitian countryside means several houses that connect to each other, because they all might work the land of some big landowner. Slavery continues after so-called independence. Toussaint L'Ouverture, Dessalines, they all gave lands to their relatives; they kept all the colonial structures. Anyway, I lived in an "urban *lakou*" in Port-au-Prince. That means you have the Abel family, the Odé family, the Charlemagne family, etc. When Odé had a problem with my mother, I could hear them arguing. I could hear the obscene words they used. And I also learned from the workers, streetworkers, those macho guys who came from the countryside to Port-au-Prince. They are the ones who built the roads in Haiti. When they are digging they are singing songs, obscene songs. So I was a specialist in dirty songs. I was the one who brought those songs to my school, helping rich kids who were raised behind high walls to know what was happening outside. I was their teacher. I was also singing church songs. I went to Catholic schools, I was raised by the priests, so you might hear that Gregorian thing when I'm singing. Eight years old, learning things from Jesus, from my school, and from the street. I always prefer the street.[22] . . .
>
> [My music has been political] since I was young; just sitting around in the neighborhood put me in some very subversive company. When I was eight years old, I saw the overthrow of [Haitian General Paul] Magloire [president, 1950–1956]—people fleeing bullets would come and hide in my yard. I come from the lumpenproletariat, right in the center of Port-au-Prince. And I spent my adolescence in Carrefour and the other "popular" zones. I would walk around and see guys making homemade bombs. Sometimes they would give me those bombs. I was nine, ten years old. They'd call me over and say, "Hey Manno, walk slow and give this to that man over there." I didn't know what it was for, but it made me feel important. You know, a man from the area asks you to help him and you're just a kid, that's really cool. I went to jail for the first time in 1963. I was fifteen years old. They said it was *brigandaj*, you know, stealing. But I was arrested because I tried to break up a fight—just one guy abusing another guy. And it turns out one of them was a Makout. He was a guard from the [National] Palace, which means Makout Palace. It's the same thing now. And I was arrested, beaten, freed.

Mizik Angaje

Manno began singing and playing the guitar at age sixteen, and in 1968, at age twenty, he formed a neighborhood *mini-djaz* [small commercial dance band] called Les Remarquables. They played Haitian *konpa*, a dance and music patterned on the *merengue* style of the Cibao region of the Dominican Republic. His second group, Les Trouvères [The troubadours], played more guitar-and-vocal music, like the old-time Cuban troubadours. Charlemagne next teamed up with singer Marco Jeanty; they began to play their *angaje* [engaged, politically-committed] songs in Carrefour and later in the capital city. Charlemagne began to express a deep anguish about the poverty and degradation he saw around him. In May of 1978, the duo came to the city for a session on Radio Haïti-Inter, and they succeeded in impressing many in the capital's music community. They released an album entitled *Manno et Marco* and began to receive radio play.

Their song lyrics, written primarily by Charlemagne, sang the lives of Haiti's poor and unemployed. In "Pouki" [Why], they ask, "Why doesn't life separate things equally, fifty-fifty? / Why does the shark bring such destruction / Large tooth-marks on the back of little fish?"[23]

Songs like this one that challenged the status quo in Haiti irritated the president-for-life, Jean-Claude Duvalier. In a crackdown on artistic and media freedoms in 1981, radio stations were ransacked, musical recordings by political artists were removed from stores, and newspapers critical of the régime were confiscated. Almost all of the better-known progressive artists, including Manno Charlemagne, left Haiti. Charlemagne slipped out from a performance at a cinema in Carrefour and fled the country. He ended up in Boston, where he released a series of albums including *Konviksyon* [Conviction] (1984) and *Fini les colonies* [The end of the colonies] (1985), reflecting Manno's increased awareness of his role as a movement singer. Manno was convinced that foreign powers and international organizations worked consistently to the detriment of Haiti, in collusion with Haiti's corrupt local élite. One of his more didactic titles was "Leta, laboujwazi, lepep" [The state, the bourgeoisie, the people]: "The state never serves people who are barely clothed / Or the poor who are dying, who cannot enjoy life."

Leading up to 1985, the dictatorship encountered growing dissent and eventually rebellion, and the Duvalier family and many of their ministers were forced to leave the country on February 7, 1986. Manno Charlemagne was among the thousands of Haitian exiles flocking back to Haiti in the months after, and soon after his return, he joined with Vodou drummers and singers from a particular temple to form the Koral Konbit Kalfou [literally, Chorale of the crossroads work brigade] to blend political and Vodou-roots music for the popular struggle. The references to Vodou were many in Charlemagne's songs of this period, but in contrast to some roots music groups, Charlemagne was far more concerned with the religion's political or revolutionary potential:

> Vodou can be a religion, a way of life for people, but it can also be a cultural arm. That's how I use it. I'm not going to discuss the religious part. I'm not going to say it doesn't exist. But I use, in a good way, the militant part of Vodou, and I use it for good. I call it "cultural resources."

One of the songs the group performed was a revised version of a song from 1974, "Ayiti pa fore" (Haiti is not a forest), with new verses chastising Michèle

Ill. 4–11. Manno Charlemagne performing at Miami's Tap Tap Restaurant. Photo by Peter Eves, 1995. Used by permission.

Ex. 4–12.   Lyrics to "Ayiti pa fore"

Lè w fè sa ma pè w	When you do that I'm so scared of you
Paske w se makout	Just because you're a Makout
Ou konprann ou ka kraponnen mwen	You think that you can fool me
Ou rale wouzi w	You take out your Uzi machine gun
Mwen rilax sou w!	But I relax back at you!
Ou rale baton gayak la	You take out your wood club
Mwen pi koul sou w!	But I'm even calmer in the face of it!
Tone kraze m Michèl Benèt	God damn it, Michele Bennet (the dictator's wife),
I am sorry for you	I am sorry for you [mocking, in English]
Se nan videyo wa gade pèp ayisyen	Only on video can you watch the Haitian people
Ou voye papa w a achte twa bonm	You send your father to buy three bombs
Pou vin bonbade lajenès an Ayiti	To come and bombard the youth in Haiti
Ki deklere ke dechoukaj la poko fini	Who declare that the uprooting isn't over yet
Konsèy Gouvenman chaje tonton makout	If the Council is full of Tontons Makoute.[24]

Duvalier, the president's wife (called by her maiden name Bennet), the Tonton Makout (Duvalier's feared secret police), and the governing council that took over after the dictator fled (Example 4–12).

The song argues that struggle was far from over. Manno was fighting to maintain the intensity and focus of the popular struggle and to forestall any relaxation in the wake of Duvalier's exit on the assumption that little had really changed in Haiti: supporters of Duvalier still held state power, class relations were largely unchanged, and the transition in Haiti was being managed by the United States State Department, precisely to forestall revolutionary change.

When the populist priest, Jean-Bertrand Aristide, ran for president in 1990, Manno sang at political rallies to support his candidacy and pledged the participation of his own political party. Manno's popularity was such that his appearance at a major rally could draw many thousands. Aristide's *Lavalas* [deluge] movement won an impressive majority, but only five months after his inauguration, the army and élite, feeling that they were losing control, were circulating rumors of an impending coup. Manno Charlemagne composed a song that threatened the élite with mass violence if the coup should come about, and he sang nightly vigils outside the jail cell of one of the most prominent supporters of the Duvalier regime to try to forestall a jailbreak. Nonetheless, the army soon took action and toppled Aristide, arresting Charlemagne twice without arrest warrants. Manno and his family sought asylum at the Argentine embassy, and he became the focus of an international campaign for his freedom and safety.

In exile, Manno campaigned to rebuild the movement to evict the military junta and restore democracy. In one song, he compared the oppressors to smoke that needed to be dissipated, and he clarified this image in the following statement:

> I am saying, these oppressors are smoke. The people, you are the masters of the land. They [the military and the élite] have to go. Don't be desperate. They have to go. I say *la pèsonn kanzo plisyè fwa*, meaning "the people do *kanzo* many times." *Kanzo* is a word referring to a Vodou initiation ceremony [employing fire]. So I'm saying, this is not the first time that we have survived a *coup d'état*. We've done it many times, and we will do it again. And the people know that those who die to give life, *pa ka pèdi*— they can't lose. (Averill 1994)

After the United Nations and the Organization of American States negotiated the end of the military régime and the return of Aristide, Manno came back to Haiti and ran for (and won) mayor of Port-au-Prince, considered the second most important political position in the country. In this role, he has come into repeated conflict with some of his former allies in the movement, and he has been criticized for, among other things, arming his own small military force. As is typical in Haitian politics, supporters are awarded with jobs and resources and opponents are dealt with harshly. Some of Manno's former musician allies began to assemble for a while outside the mayor's offices to sing his own songs at him as a form of protest. Yet many still argue that Manno Charlemagne's actions as mayor have been undertaken to further the cause of the poorest sectors in Haiti, the same groups that have always been fiercely loyal to him as a musician and now as a politician. Whatever the outcome of his political ambitions, it is safe to say that no artist in Haiti has had the impact on national consciousness that he has had, particularly among the urban poor and disenfranchised, and that few have produced songs of such biting political satire or have been able to galvanize the political consciousness of an audience or crowd through music, as has Manno Charlemagne.

Manno's history as a radical movement troubadour contrasts with the kind of political commentary sometimes found in Trinidadian calypso. In the latter case, the calypsonian operates within a broad social consensus about a role for calypsonians (at Carnival time) to skewer public figures and social morales. Seldom expressing revolutionary sentiments, calypsonians nonetheless have been associated with the labor movement and the subsequent independence movement in Trinidad and Tobago. Their annual corpus of topical calypsos, performed in the calypso tents in the months before Carnival, can still spark heated debate and even outrage.

TRINIDADIAN CALYPSO

Carnival 1994

The time is Carnival 1994 and the place is the Main Stand at the Queen's Park Savannah in downtown Port of Spain, Trinidad and Tobago. Throughout the crowded stands where thousands are on their feet dancing and *winin'* [rolling the hips], the loudspeakers are blaring a humorous calypso by the venerable calypsonian Lord Kitchener (Aldwin Roberts), called "Pan Earthquake." In the lyrics to the calypso, the singer is trying to convince a friend that the deep rumblings and shaking he's feeling aren't the result of an earthquake, but are only the famous steel bands The Desperadoes and The Renegades competing at the Savannah. People are singing along with the chorus:

Ex. 4–13.   Lyrics to "Pan Earthquake"

Earthquake! Mama woy woy
Earthquake, I tell dem
It ent no earthquake yuh hearing
Is Renegades and Despers jammin'
Earthquake! Oh Gorm!
Earthquake! Ah remind dem
Doh [don't] be misled by that tremor
Is pan jammin' in the Savannah
Earthquake! Still trembling
Earthquake! Ah say people
Can't you hear the steel band rhythm
Pum puh tum pum, pum puh tum tuh tuh tum . . .[25]

In the meantime the steel band Amoco Renegades are rolling their racks full of pans on to the stage and readying themselves for a steel-band performance of the same song, an arrangement nearly fifteen minutes long, crafted by their arranger Jit Samaroo. Dressed in orange jumpsuits with Amoco construction helmets on their heads, the band has flag-wavers dancing in front as they launch into the introduction to the song in a shockingly fast tempo. This is the Carnival Panorama, the finals of the steel-band competitions in Trinidad and Tobago, and one of the most important moments in the nation's artistic life.

The following sections of this chapter will introduce a genre of music (calypso), an instrument (pan), and an ensemble (steel band) that have their origins in Trinidad and Tobago, and that are some of the most important elements of the annual Carnival celebration on the island, the single most impressive festival in the Caribbean.

Cariso *to* Calypso

Calypso is a Creolized genre, drawing on early French musical forms and on African stick-fight drumming and singing, among other sources, and blending them into a peculiarly New-World expression. Nineteenth-century songs were generally in Creole, as in "L'année pasé mwen te yon fi" (Example 4–14), a *romance*-style song representative of a French poetic song tradition in four-line stanzas. The *romance* tradition in Trinidad was one key influence on the development of the *cariso* (an old term for calypso). Donald Hill sets the origin of the song in Martinique before the expression migrated to Trinidad—eventually it

Ex. 4–14.   Lyrics to "L'annêe pasé mwen te yon fi"

Lane pase mwen te yon fi	Last year I was a young girl
Mwen te you fi lan kay manman mwen	I was a young girl in my mother's house
Lane cela mwen se yon fanm	This year I am a woman
Mwen se yon fanm a sur lari	I am a woman out on the street

served as a melodic inspiration for "Rum and Coca Cola," the protest calypso by Lord Invader that was made into an international hit by the Andrews Sisters.[26]

The old Creole term for a singer in Trinidad was *chantwell*. The *chantwell* would lead work songs, songs for dancing with drum accompaniment (called *bel airs*), and stick-fight songs called *kalendas*. There are also stories about nine-teenth-century plantation owners who kept African-style *maît kaiso* [singers of praise and derision] as "court" singers. By the twentieth century, these two roles (*chantwell* and *maît kaiso*) melded into that of the *calypsonian,* who was to become a central figure in Trinidadian Carnival.

Carnival dates to the plantation era in Trinidad. Following the emancipation of slaves in Trinidad in 1838, blacks took part in Carnival celebrations in such numbers as to radically alter the look and feel of the event. Life for poor blacks—most of whom lived in tenement settlements called "barracks yards"—was often degrading, with little work or opportunity available. At Carnival, stick fighters went out in search of opponents while accompanied by *chantwells* and drummers. Stick fighting was called *kalenda,* and *kalenda* songs—short and tuneful—evolved over the next five decades into the Carnival *lavway* or road march (the songs that accompany the *mas'* or masquerade band in the streets). Carnival masqueraders dramatized the brutality of slavery with the costume called *nègre jardin* [field slave dressed in burlap, with chained legs] and with the torchlight parade called *canboulay* [burning cane, from the French *cannes brulées*], a re-enactment of the feverish efforts on the sugar plantations to rescue burning cane fields. The *canboulay* became the standard opening to Carnival, starting on *Dimanche Gras,* the Sunday night before *Mardi Gras* [Fat Tuesday, the last day of Carnival) and lasting until dawn, later superseded by the old-time *mas'* called *jouvay* [opening of the day, from French *jour ouvert*].

Impoverished black urbanites also parodied white society in a Carnival-time show called Dame Lorraine, featuring obscene skits and humor. They sometimes engaged in an outrageous masquerade called *pisenlit* [piss in the bed], in which masqueraders exposed themselves while dressed as women, mimicked menstruation, and threw powder and foul substances on bystanders. Terming these activities *jamèt* [existing below the horizon or diameter of good society—i.e., marginal or underworld], the colonial government and local élites derided the African and lower-class influence in Carnival and actively campaigned against it, citing public security and good public morals as justification for the repression of Carnival. They banned masking in 1858. In 1868 they banned Obeah (African magical prac-

Ex. 4–15.   Lyrics to "Iron Duke in the Land"

Iron Duke in the land, Fire Brigade
Iron Duke in the land, Fire Brigade
Bring the locomotive just because it's a fire federation
Bring the locomotive just because it's a fire federation
Sans humanité [without pity]

tices), playing drums, *chak-chaks* [rattles], and *banjars* [banjos] at night; they also banned obscene songs and carrying lighted torches. Between 1877 and 1880, the police cracked down on stick fighting. In 1881, however, revelers fought back and a notorious riot ensued. The Peace Preservation Ordinance of 1884 again banned carrying torches, playing drums, dances, processions, and the carrying of sticks. All of this regulatory activity reveals the degree of class struggle over Carnival culture.[27]

Beginning in the late 1890s, the business élite and the colonial government became more active in promoting certain forms at Carnival. *Mas'* [masquerade] bands received commercial sponsorship, calypso tents were started to serve as sites for the competitive singing of calypsonians, and a series of competitions, meant to domesticate and "improve" Carnival activities, was launched. Fancy *mas'* bands, including sailors, devils, dragons, robbers, bats, Pierrots/clowns, wild Indians, and other characters competed for prizes. Calypsonians Norman Le Blanc, Julian Whiterose, and Lord Executor opened commercial tents and hired other calypsonians to sing in them. The tents allowed new forms of calypso to flourish. The calypsos were sung more often in English than in Creole, and a new "oratorical" style of calypso—characterized by an impressive vocabulary and flowery oratory—took hold.[28] In addition, the accompanying ensemble changed from drums and *chak-chaks* to string bands based on Venezuelan ensembles. The simple *lavways* and *kalendas,* usually containing no more than four lines of text, were now dubbed single-tone calypsos, in contrast to the new style of calypso with eight lines to the verse, called double-tone calypsos. The tone here refers to a four-line block of melody and text. A well-known example of the single-tone calypso was recorded in 1914 by Julian Whiterose (born Henry Julian), a calypsonian who went by the sobriquet "Iron Duke."

The chorus to this self-aggrandizing calypso is shown in Example 4–15. The last line in the chorus ("*Sans humanité*" [without pity]) is a tag line in Creole sung in many calypsos of the day. It reflects the competitive spirit of the *kalendas* and *lavways,* in which one contestant attempted to best another without mercy or pity.

Musical Structure

"Iron Duke in the Land" was sung in a tonality called "mi minor," and indeed nearly all of the early calypsos were in one or another of the so-called "minor modes." Perhaps the most popular of these modes was the one constructed on the sixth note of the scale ("la"). Each of these minor modes had relatively conven-

Ex. 4–16. Lyrics and chord progression to "Money Is King," by Neville Marcano, a.k.a. Growling Tiger[29]

First tone

(1)	Am	—	E$_7$	Am
[If a]	man has	money	today,	People do not
(2)	Am	—	E$_7$	Am
	care if he	has	cocobe,	If a
(3)	Am	—	E$_7$	Am
	man has	money	today,	People do not
(4)	Am	—	E$_7$	Am
	care if he	has	cocobe,	He can commit

Second Tone

(5)	Am	—	Dm	—
	murder and	get off	free,	And live
(6)	G$_7$	G$_7$	C	C
	in the Governor's		company,	But if you are
(7)	Am	—	Dm	—
	poor, people	will tell you	"Shoo,"	And a
(8)	E$_7$	—	Am	—
	dog is	better than	you.	

tional chord progressions and melodies. Let's take a look at how a "la minor" chord progression fits a double-tone calypso. Example 4–16 is the first verse to a topical calypso called "Money Is King," by Neville Marcano, a.k.a. Growling Tiger, with the chord changes over the corresponding words. The comma represents the natural end of a text line, even though there may be some text sung to pick up notes for the next line. Line numbers appear on the left. *Cocobe* is a disease variously described as yaws (a syphilitic disease of open sores) or Hansen's disease (leprosy). In the first few decades of the century, the minor calypsos gave way increasingly to the major-mode calypsos, which tended to follow the thirty-two-measure chord progression I–I–V7–I (×4), I–I–IV–IV–V7–V7–I–I–(×2).

The calypso tents became, for a few decades at least, the sites for extemporaneous song duels called *picong* [piquant, spicy]. While most of these were not recorded for posterity, one of them spilled over into a series of recordings (presumably scripted, not extemporized on stage); this was the exchange between Trinidadian-based calypsonians and Wilmouth Houdini, an upper-class Trinidadian who took up singing calypso while abroad and who developed a successful recording and screen career in Hollywood. In "War Declaration" Houdini challenged calypsonians Lion and Lord Executor. In response, Lord Executor sang (in true oratorical calypso style) "My Reply to Houdini" (1937) (Example 4–17).

Ex. 4–17. Lyrics to "My Reply to Houdini," by Lord Executor[30]

So they had a proclamation going aroun' the town
That Houdini would sing the song
The motor lorry had it recognized
That the hero would be eulogized
He had recently arrived from America
And would sing at the London Theatre
Look here, me lad, that ballad
No good in Trinidad.

Changes in Carnival

At least until the 1970s, it can be said that calypso evolved rather slowly, keeping most of its stylistic features intact. Carnival, however, underwent great upheavals. The Carnival competition system was routinized, especially after independence (1962). The Carnival-governing bodies developed awards for Calypso Monarch, Best *Mas'* Band, King and Queen of the *Mas'* Bands (Best Costume), Best Steel Band (Panorama Competition), as well as parallel awards for school-age children, Best Pan-Around-the-Neck Band (traditional marching steel band), Best Old-Time *Mas'*, and so forth (see Illustration 4–12). Prizes are given for other calypso categories, such as for the most popular road march, the most popular calypso for steel band arrangements, etc. Many of these contests are held over Carnival weekend before the *mas'* starts on Monday morning. For example, the Panorama Competition (finals) for conventional steel bands is Saturday night, and the *Dimanche Gras* show (with the Calypso Monarch and King and Queen contests) occurs on Sunday night.

Carnival became much bigger business in this period. It is the country's most significant tourist draw, and Trinidad is not typically a popular tourist destination. The larger *mas'* bands now attract many thousands of participants, most of whom simply pay for a costume in order to participate in one section or another. The designers work year-round on the costume designs and may also design for expatriate Carnivals in the United States, Canada, or England.

In the late 1970s, however, the sound of calypso began to metamorphose rapidly. A calypsonian by the name of Lord Shorty helped to popularize a new kind of "party" calypso called *soca,* characterized by a heavy downbeat on the drum-set bass drum, by full dance band arrangements with horn "punches," and by an emphasis on shorter, singable texts and party lyrics. Hybrids of *soca* and Jamaican dancehall styles (i.e., *ragga binghi*), as well as Indo-Trinidadian dance musics (i.e., *chutney-soca*), have been common in recent years. And a *soca* feel tends to dominate the road-march calypsos, especially those derisively dubbed *jam 'n' wine* calypsos designed to get a crowd throwing their arms in the air and *winin'* their waists. All of the changes in calypso tend to generate similar kinds of heated discussions over whether these innovations represent the degradation of calypso or its survival. In the midst of these controversies, calypsonians like Black

Ill. 4–12. School (children's) *mas'*. Photo by Gage Averill, Port of Spain, Trinidad, 1994.

So if Ramsingh house up in the air because he start a business there
Don't hate, congratulate
If when he profits start to soar [and] he buy the property next door
Don't hate, emulate
And if he want to chop he big daughter because she love a nigger
Don't hate, educate . . .

Stalin, David Rudder, and others continue to generate text-centered topical calypsos, as in Colin Lucas's 1995 calypso "Don't Hate" (Example 4–18).

TRINIDADIAN PAN AND STEEL BAND

Tamboo-Bamboo *to Steel Band*

The decision by the colonial government to ban drumming (on membranophones) from Carnival in 1884 had far-reaching consequences, setting in motion a series of innovations in instrument design and use. In Port of Spain barracks yards (tenement neighborhoods), drummers responded by adopting lengths of bamboo as percussion and concussion instruments, striking, stamping, and scraping them for sound. This was the *tamboo-bamboo* (bamboo drum) band, the most popular Carnival ensemble of the early twentieth century.[31] Typically, a long bamboo pipe called a boom (perhaps five feet in length) would be stamped for bass tones; two short lengths *(foulés)* would be concussed for a higher pitch; and a length laid across the shoulder (called a cutter, related to the term *kata* discussed in the sections on Cuba and Haiti, above) would provide the highest-pitched pattern. These functions were derived from the roles of the drums in Shango drumming. *Tamboo-bamboo* bands incorporated bottles, spoons, and other household implements into the ensemble, along with a variety of metal implements (pot lids, biscuit drums, dust bins, pitch oil pans, salt boxes, etc.) for a loud and impressive clatter.

Somewhere around 1937 to 1939, a band led by Lord Humbugger (Carleton Forde) called the New Town Cavalry Tamboo-Bamboo changed its name to Alexander's Ragtime Band (after an American movie) and played entirely on metal instruments—and they became the sensation of Carnival. The year after, most other Carnival bands followed suit, and the idea of the steel band was born. By the outbreak of World War II, most observers of Carnival remarked how the metal instruments had largely replaced *tamboo-bamboo*. Like the *tamboo-bamboo* bands, these bands came out from the barracks yards and aggressively represented their neighborhoods. Players had a reputation for being *badjohns*—dangerous, lower-class thugs involved in illicit activities and in constant conflict with the authorities.

Of the contenders for the inventor of the pan, probably the most likely is a man named Winston "Spree" Simon, a member of a group called Newtown. During the latter years of World War II, he was attempting to hammer out a dent in a caustic soda drum when he discovered that the hammer changed the pitch of the dent, and that each dent he created had its own pitch. Reputedly, the first full tune played was "Mary Had a Little Lamb," and a couple of bands took this tune on the road after the war. Soon a range of metal instruments had been added, led by the *ping-pong* (soprano lead) made from a small oil barrel. This innovation was credited variously to Ellie Manette, Spree Simon, and Neville Jules, although it was Manette, a machinist by trade, who introduced the fifty-five-gallon oil drum as the standard for *ping-pong* construction, and who first conceived of making a concave surface to increase tensile strength and area. A postwar surplus of oil barrels helped in making fifty-five-gallon steel drums the raw material of choice for constructing pans. A number of steel-band pioneers contributed to the proliferation of instruments all based on the oil drum. Early instruments included the "quatro pan" for strumming chords (intervals, really) and a "tune boom" for playing bass notes. Tuners began to fire the metal to improve its acoustic properties, and they elaborated a number of different sizes and ranges of steel drum to form entire orchestras of pans (Recorded Selection 21, "Pan," played by Hummingbird Pan Groove).

Increasing Respectability and "Panorama"

In 1950, Trinidad organized a national steel band to represent the country at the Festival of Britain in 1951 (The Trinidad All-Steel Percussion Orchestra, TASPO). By 1959, the Invaders had a recording contract with Columbia Records. Over the first two decades of the steel band's history, social attitudes about the instrument and ensemble changed remarkably. The movement for independence claimed pan as an example of local cultural creativity, and the steel band was elevated to a national symbol. The rough-hewn "panmen" found themselves with champions among the media and the new governing élite, and they were soon competing with middle-class steel bands full of school boys or "jacketmen." Steel bands began to attract corporate sponsors, and pan music increasingly found its way into school curricula.

The heady period in the 1950s and early 1960s when the instrument took shape, the ensembles grew, and the steel bands earned a permanent place in Carnival, is considered by many to be a golden era for pan. The Invaders, Casablanca, Tokyo, The Desperadoes, and many of the other early bands borrowed the titles of Hollywood war movies and westerns for their names. Pannists carrying pans around their necks joined in with Carnival parades and accompanied sailor *mas'* bands. Steel bands prepared calypsos for the Carnival season and added surprise tunes, usually calypso arrangements of classical and Latin popular tunes that they practiced in secret in the early hours of the morning and launched on Carnival Monday; these were called "bombs."

Starting in 1963, the government and the steel band organization put together a national competition at Carnival called the Panorama, which remains the principal venue for steel band performance in Trinidad. Conventional steel bands of up to 120 people practice in panyards all over Trinidad in the months preceding Carnival, learning newly created ten- to fifteen-minute Panorama arrangements by ear. A band's arranger, often in consultation with core members, chooses a calypso from among those written that year for Carnival as the piece the band will present in competition. Some calypsonians write more than one calypso for each Carnival, one of which may be specially tailored for steel band performance (sometimes with a theme specific to pan and the steel band movement). The arranger takes a risk with the choice of calypso. If the calypso never becomes popular on its own, the audience at the competitions will not know it well and the arranger's creative variations on the tune will fail to impress the audience and judges. If the song is too popular, too many arrangers might choose the same tune, and the individual arrangements may become lost in the crowd.

Panorama arrangements are extremely fast, usually between 120 and 144 beats (half notes) per minute. The arrangements typically take shape over a period of many weeks, as the arranger teaches the piece to the pannists section by section. As they have developed over the years, arrangements include an introductory section, a song section that parallels the calypso with its verse and chorus, a variation section usually containing one or more modulations (changes) to new keys, and finally a repeat of the verse and chorus material in the original key attached to some kind of coda (tail) or final cadence. Arrangers can use interesting sound effects on the pans, rhythm breakdown sections, contrasting rhythms, and other techniques to enliven the performance. The performance is judged on the quality of the arrangement, the quality of play, and the tuning of the pans. Many arrangers will often keep some of their best material out of the performance until the finals in order to impress the judges with the progress of the piece between the semifinals and the finals. Others, sensing that the judges aren't appreciating something in the arrangement or that the pannists are unable to play an arrangement properly, will tinker with the arrangements up to the final hours before performance.

To perform, bands mount their pans on wheeled racks for rolling onto the stage for competition (see Illustration 4–13).

Panorama is held on a stage between the Main and North Stands, in the middle of a large park in downtown Port of Spain called Queen's Park Savannah. Flag and banner carriers dance and move across the stage, and the fringe on the racks sways with the rhythms of the steel band. The sound is amplified a bit for the Savannah stands, and before each presentation, the calypso chosen by the band is played in its recorded version to remind the audience of the tune. In Illustration 4–14 we see a photograph of a famous steel orchestra, The Desperadoes (from the hill community named Laventille), on their triumphant parade through Queen's Park Savannah, the day after winning Panorama with their original composition by Robbie Greenidge called "Fire Comin' Down." We can see one of the band's racks to the left; to the right is the Main Stand of the Savannah. Thousands of fans have managed to join the band and to walk along with it through the stands.

The purse from a successful competition (along with funds from a band's corporate sponsor) keeps many of the biggest steel bands in business. After Carnival, the bands that maintain a year-round schedule revert to smaller "stageside" bands to play parties, concerts, and festivals such as the Steel Band Music Festival,

Ill. 4–13. A steel band in racks on stage for the Panorama competition in Brooklyn, New York, modeled on the Port of Spain version. Photo by Gage Averill, 1994.

swelling to full size only in December or January in preparation for Carnival competitions. Some conventional steel bands still accompany the *jouvay* parade, playing on flatbed trucks and in racks rolled through the streets. Many bands will play on Tuesday night of *Mardi Gras* for a wrap-up celebration called *las' lap*.[32]

Steel Band Instruments

A conventional steel band consists of a variety of pans as well as a percussion section called the *engine room*. In the engine room one finds a rack of *irons* (brake drums from automobiles), a set of two *conga* drums played with sticks, a drum set, scrapers, a *shak-shak, claves,* cowbells, triangles, and other hand-held percussion instruments. These provide the driving pulse of the band and a layered composite rhythm pattern that gives steel band calypso and *soca* their signature rhythms. For pans, most contemporary steel bands use around ten different sets of different ranges and configurations. These include the following:

1. *Tenor or lead pan.* This took the place of the old *ping-pong*. It typically plays the lead melody and has the highest range. It is made from a single barrel with a

Ill. 4–14. The Desperadoes (from Laventille) are rolled through the Savannah reviewing stands. Photo by Gage Averill, Port of Spain, Trinidad, 1994.

thin skirt (approximately four inches) and a deep bowl containing thirty-two or more noteheads. The *skirt* (side of the drum) is whatever remains of the curved side of the barrel. The design of the tenor is relatively standardized, with the notes arranged counterclockwise in fifths (C, G, D, etc.). Its lowest note is the D above middle C, though there is also a low tenor with a middle C.

2. *Double tenor.* Two drums with thin skirts (five inches) and deep bowls are used primarily to play countermelody lines.

3. *Double second.* Two drums with somewhat longer skirts and a range slightly lower than that of the double tenors are used as strum pans, playing "chords" (see *guitar pan,* below).

4. *Guitar pan.* Two pans with half-length skirts are used to strum intervals; a single player activates only two notes at a time, so more than one strum instrument is needed to fill in chords. The function of strum instruments is equivalent to that of a strummed guitar accompaniment to a song.

5. *Quad (quadrophonic pan).* With two pans suspended horizontally and two vertically, the quadrophonics cover thirty-six notes and are perhaps the most versatile pans in the ensemble. They are often used to double the melody lines at an octave below the melody, or they may strum chords.

6. *Triple cello pan.* Three drums with half-length skirts are used to augment bass lines and fill in chords. (See the photograph in Illustration 4–15.)

Ill. 4–15. Cello pans, with note surfaces visible as convex shapes on the concave bowl. Photo by Gage Averill, Middletown, Conn., 1996.

7. *Four pans.* Four pans with half-length skirts that are hung horizontally are used to strum chords, as with a *guitar pan*.

8. *Tenor bass.* A set of four barrels with either full- or two-thirds-length skirts is used for bass lines or sometimes to harmonize with bass lines.

9. *Six or nine bass.* These are sets of six or nine barrels with full skirts that provide the bass lines in a composition. They usually have no more than three noteheads on a given drum. With the nine bass, three of the drums have to be suspended in front of the player for easy access. A few bands use bass sets with even more drums (ten or twelve).

Clearly, not all bands have to use all of these types of pans, as many of them overlap. The choice of pans, the number of each in a band, and the style of tuning them help to create an identifiable sound for each major conventional steel band.

Building and Tuning a Pan[33]

Building, tuning, and blending a pan are extremely demanding jobs in terms of skill, knowledge, time, strength, and energy. It takes many years of apprenticeship to achieve a knowledge of metal dynamics sufficient to create a well-tuned pan from an oil barrel. The following discussion is not meant to get students ready to build their own pans, but rather to help them to understand the care and study that go into building them.

To build a pan, a tuner first must pick out an appropriate fifty-five-gallon oil drum of about eighteen-gauge thickness. The bottom surface of the drum (the one without the plug) must be "sunk" to provide a concave playing surface. The center of the pan and two concentric circles are marked with a pencil, and then the surface is pounded down with a shotput or with a rounded sledgehammer, starting at the edge and working toward the center. When the desired depth and general shape are nearly achieved, a smaller sledgehammer is used to shape and smooth the bowl.

The outer notes on a drumhead are marked radially with a flexible ruler and the inner noteheads are marked with elliptical templates. A pan tuner keeps measurements and templates on file for all of the different types of pan. The areas around the notes (which have been measured and traced) are lowered still further with a hammer so that the note surfaces themselves begin to take on a convex shape (bubbled up). A metal punch with a flat, circular punching surface is struck with a hammer repeatedly to produce a groove around each of the notes. The groove helps to isolate the individual notes acoustically, so that playing one note doesn't activate all the notes on a pan. After grooving is completed, the tuner uses a sledgehammer or a ball-peen hammer to flatten parts of the bowl's surface not covered with notes (Illustration 4–16).

The *skirt* (side) of the drum is then marked and cut at the length appropriate for the range of the pan (wider for lower ranges, thinner for higher ranges). The pan must then be suspended upside down over a fire or burning tire in order to temper the steel. This produces a more consistent tension in the metal skin of the bowl, strengthens and stiffens the metal, and generally makes for a better sound.

Using a variety of hammers and specialized tools, the tuner must soften the metal by hammering the note in and out between five and twenty times. Doing this affects the tuning of all the other notes on the pan, so one has to work around from smallest to the largest notes and then repeat the process. After that, the tuner hits the surface around each note to shape the raised area and flatten its edge. The fundamental pitch of the note can be affected in different ways by hitting the middle of the note surface, hitting around its edge, or by tapping on the groove to stretch the metal. It is important to raise and lower the pitch of each note above and below the desired pitch, as the tuner gets the note closer to the desired fundamental. Once this has been done to all of the notes on a pan, the pan has been *rough-tuned* (or *coarse-tuned*).

Each note surface will vibrate in a number of "modes," or patterns, to produce not only the fundamental (strongest) pitch, but also many overtones, or partials, above this fundamental. These are not typically as loud as the fundamental, but they will certainly affect the timbre of the note and the degree to which it sounds in tune. The tuner needs to make each of the partials consonant with the fundamental pitch by tinkering long and hard with each notehead and by adjusting the shape of the note (the partials are understood to be responsive to different axes in the note surfaces). Tuners typically make use of electronic tuning instruments to adjust the partials.

Next, holes are cut in the rim for hanging the pans on their stands, and they are fine-tuned further while on their stands. Most drums these days have all of

Ill. 4–16. Pan tuner Cliff Alexis flattens the region between the three note surfaces on a bass pan with a ball-peen hammer. Photo by Gage Averill, Oshkosh, Wisconsin, 1991.

their paint stripped and are dipped in a chromium solution containing anodes that plate the chromium on the drum and give its surface more resistance to rust and deterioration (just as with an automobile bumper). Finally, all of the drums in an ensemble should be "blended" together to make sure that the volumes, partials, and timbres of all the instruments are consistent and sweet.

Pan Prospects and Perils

Building and tuning pans is extremely labor-intensive and very much an old-fashioned handcraft. It is therefore costly, despite the low cost of the raw materials. For decades, builders have discussed and sought ways to mass-produce drums by molding them, but the drums made in this fashion so far have all lacked the fine response and shimmering timbre of those tooled by hand. Although the design of the tenor pan has been largely standardized, the designs of the other pan types have not. This is in part because many of the first and second generation of pan tuners are still building pans, and they are reluctant to adopt a standard design, having worked for so many years with pans of their own design. There are, however, ongoing and vigorous efforts to improve the acoustics of the pan, to standardize the designs, to increase dynamic ranges, and to design more portable instruments.

The pan has been called the only completely new acoustic instrument invented in the twentieth century. Whether or not this is true, pans certainly represent one of the century's most original and creative efforts at instrument design and craftsmanship. Enormous strides in design, construction, tuning, and acoustics have been made in the scant fifty years since pans were first invented, and it is reasonable to expect this progress to continue and to produce startlingly new achievements.

In its fifty-year history, pan has become a potent symbol for Trinidad—a symbol of its blend of African and European cultural backgrounds, of the upward mobility of Trinidad's poor (who were pan's original exponents), and of the technological and aesthetic accomplishments of the small, formerly-colonized country. The worldwide popularity of pans and steel bands generates pride, but it also raises concerns that the global emergence of the genre will sever the origins of the pan and the special cultural links that it has to Trinidad. It is here that we see the degree to which musical instruments become much more than media for the production of sound: they can become repositories of cultural meaning and collective identity, as well.

CONCLUSION

At the dawn of the nineteenth century, both Haiti (Saint Domingue) and Trinidad were French Creole–speaking colonies with a majority population of African descendants. In both colonies one could encounter popular African spiritual practices and a common pool of African and creolized music-dance genres (*kalendas, bel airs,* quadrilles, etc.). In the intervening years, their different political and economic trajectories have resulted in startling contrasts in expressive culture. Calypso and pan in Trinidad and Tobago have been shaped by a long history of British colonialism and by the nation's relatively recent independence from Britain (1962). Haiti's enforced isolation and its early break with European colonialism resulted in vibrant neo-African practices in the countryside, represented in this chapter in the sections on Vodou and *rara*. Yet the music cultures in both countries represent a working-through of the legacies of colonialism, an unfolding of the cultural interplay between Europe and Africa, a confrontation with class and racial oppression, and a search for Creole identity in postcolonial societies. In both island nations, music, dance, and celebration have helped to shape these emergent identities and have given voice to both the contradictions and aspirations of their peoples.

References

Abrahams, Roger D. 1983. *The man-of-words in the West Indies: Performance and the emergence of Creole culture.* Baltimore and London: Johns Hopkins.

Aïbobo. 1995. Cave Wall Records 101932–5 (CD). (First edition Ciné Records, 1993.) Ensemble, Ram.

Angels in the mirror: Vodou music of Haiti. 1997. CD produced by Holly Nicolas, Y. M. David Yih, and Elizabeth McAlister. Ellipsis Arts CD 4120.

Averill, Gage. 1991. The whip and the whistle: Rara in Haiti. *The Beat* 10(3).

———. 1994. Konpa demokrasi-a: The rhythm of democracy (Demaske malpwote: Unmasking the opportunists). *The Beat* 13(5). Interview with Manno Charlemagne conducted by Mark Dow, August 29.

———. 1997. "Pan is we ting": West Indian steelbands in Brooklyn. In *Musics of multicultural America: A study of twelve musical communities,* ed. Kip Lornell and Anne K. Rasmussen, pp. 101–130. New York: Schirmer Books.

Béhague, Gerard. 1979. *Music in Latin America: An introduction.* Englewood Cliffs, N.J.: Prentice-Hall.

———. 1984. Patterns of *candomblé* music performance: An Afro-Brazilian religious setting. In *Performance practice: Ethnomusicological perspectives,* ed. Gerard Béhague, pp. 222–254. Westport, Conn.: Greenwood Press.

Brown, Karen McCarthy. 1991. *Mama lolo: A Vodou priestess in Brooklyn.* Berkeley and Los Angeles: Univ. of California Press.

Calypso lore and legend: An afternoon with Patrick Jones. 1956. Cook Laboratories LP 5016.

Chalmay (Charlemagne), Manno. 1989. *Le poukwa, le kòman?* Vol. 1. Port-au-Prince, Haiti: Organization Culturelle Konbit Kalfou.

Cosentino, Donald, ed. 1995. *Sacred arts of Vodou.* Los Angeles: Univ. of California at Los Angeles Fowler Museum of Cultural History.

Courlander, Harold. 1960. *The drum and the hoe: Life and lore of the Haitian people.* Berkeley and Los Angeles: Univ. of California Press.

Deren, Maya. 1970. *Divine horsemen: The living gods of Haiti.* London: McPherson & Co. (Originally published 1955.)

Dibb, Michael, dir. 1985. *¿Qué se toca en Cuba?* [What's Cuba playing at?], video produced by BBC Television in association with Cuban Television. 72 min. Center for Cuban Studies, 124 West 23d Street, New York, NY 10011.

Fleurant, Gerdès. 1996. *Dancing spirits: Rhythms and rituals of Haitian Vodun, the Rada rite.* Westport, Conn.: Greenwood Press.

Gillis, Verna and Gage Averill. 1991. Notes to CD, *Caribbean revels: Haitian rara and Dominican gaga.* Smithsonian Folkways CD SF40402.

Hill, Donald. 1993. *Calypso calalloo: Early Carnival music in Trinidad.* Gainesville: Univ. Presses of Florida. (Includes CD.)

Koetting, James T. 1992. Africa/Ghana. Chap. 3 in *Worlds of music: An introduction to the music of the world's peoples,* 2d ed., edited by Jeff Todd Titon, pp. 67–105. New York: Schirmer Books.

Konbit: Burning rhythms of Haiti. 1989. CD produced by Jonathan Demme, Gage Averill, and Fred Paul. A&M Records CD 5281.

Kronman, Ulf. 1991. *Steel pan tuning: A handbook for steel pan making and tuning.* Stockholm, Sweden: Musikmuseet.

Laveaud, Wilfrid. n.d. Tido. Unpublished manuscript.

Liverpool, Hollis. 1993. Rituals of power and rebellion: The Carnival tradition in Trinidad and Tobago. Ph.D. diss., Univ. of Michigan.

Locke, David. 1996. Africa/Ewe, Mande, Dagbamba, Shona, BaAka. Chap. 3 in *Worlds of music: An introduction to the music of the world's peoples,* 3d ed., edited by Jeff Todd Titon, pp. 71–143. New York: Schirmer Books.

McAlister, Elizabeth. 1995. "Men moun yo"; "Here are the people": Rara festivals and transnational popular culture in Haiti and New York City. Ph.D. diss., Yale Univ.

McDaniel, Lorna. 1986. Memory songs: Community, flight, and conflict in the big drum of Carriacou. Ph.D. diss., Univ. of Maryland.

Métraux, Alfred. 1972. *Voodoo in Haiti.* New York: Schocken Books. (Originally published 1959.)

Moore, Robin D. 1997. *Nationalizing blackness: Afrocubanismo and artistic revolution in Havana, 1920–1940.* Pitt Latin America series, ed. Billie R. DeWalt. Pittsburgh: Univ. of Pittsburgh Press.

Morisette, Maurice. 1991. Interview by Gage Averill and Elizabeth McAlister. Léogane, Haiti, March.

Nunley, John W., and Judith Bettelheim, eds. 1988. *Caribbean festival arts: Each and every bit of difference.* Seattle: Univ. of Washington Press.

Roberts, John Storm. 1999 [1978]. *The Latin tinge: The impact of Latin American music on the United States,* rev. ed. Oxford and New York: Oxford Univ. Press.

Spencer, Jon Michael. 1993. *Blues and evil.* Knoxville: Univ. of Tennessee Press.

Stuempfle, Stephen. 1995. *The steelband movement: The forging of a national art in Trinidad and Tobago.* Philadelphia: Univ. of Pennsylvania Press.

Super jazz de jeunes. n.d. LP, Ibo Records ILP 113.

Turino, Thomas. 1993. *Moving away from silence: Music of the Peruvian Altiplano and the experience of urban migration.* Chicago and London: Univ. of Chicago Press.

Vodou adjae. 1990. CD, with translations and liner notes by Gage Averill. Ensemble, Boukman Eksperyans. Mango 16253 9899–2.

Where was Butler? 1987. LP, Folklyric 9048, Arhoolie Records.

Wilcken, Lois, with Frizner Augustin. 1992. *The drums of Vodou.* Tempe, Ariz.: White Cliffs Media Co.

Yih, Yuen-Ming David. 1995. *Music and dance of Haitian Vodou: Diversity and unity in regional repertoires.* 2 vols. Ph.D. diss., Wesleyan Univ.

ADDITIONAL READING

Aho, William R. 1987. Steel band music in Trinidad and Tobago: The creation of a people's music. *Latin American Music Review* 8(1):26–55.

Austerlitz, Paul. 1992. Dominican merengue in regional, national, and international perspectives. Ph.D. diss., Wesleyan Univ.

———. 1997. *Merengue: Dominican music and Dominican identity.* Philadelphia: Temple Univ. Press.

Averill, Gage. 1997. *A day for the hunter, a day for the prey: Popular music and power in Haiti.* Chicago: Univ. of Chicago Press.

Béhague, Gerard H., ed. 1994. *Music and black ethnicity: The Caribbean and South America.* Miami: North-South Center, Univ. of Miami.

Cornelius, Steven. 1989. The convergence of power: An investigation into the music liturgy of Santería in New York City. Ph.D. diss., Univ. of California, Los Angeles.

———. 1995. Personalizing public symbols through music ritual: Santería's presentation to Aña. *Latin American Music Review* 16(1):42–57.

Crook, Larry. 1982. A musical analysis of the Cuban rumba. *Latin American Music Review* 3(1):92–121.

Daniel, Yvonne. 1995. *Rumba: Dance and social change in contemporary Cuba.* Blacks in the diaspora (series). Bloomington and Indianapolis: Indiana Univ. Press.

Davis, Martha E. 1972. The social organization of a musical event: The Fiesta de Cruz in San Juan, Puerto Rico. *Ethnomusicology* 16(1):38–62.

———. 1987. Native bi-musicality: Case studies from the Caribbean. *Pacific Review of Ethnomusicology* 4:39–55.

Duany, Jorge. 1994. Ethnicity, identity, and music: An anthropological analysis of the Dominican merengue. In *Music and black ethnicity: The Caribbean and South America*, ed. Gerard Béhague, pp. 65–90. Miami: North-South Center, Univ. of Miami.

Glasser, Ruth. 1995. *My music is my flag: Puerto Rican musicians and their New York communities, 1917–1940.* Berkeley: Univ. of California Press.

Guilbault, Jocelyne. 1985. A St. Lucian Kwadril evening. *Latin American Music Review* 6(1):31–57.

Guilbault, Jocelyne with Gage Averill, Edouard Benoit, and Gregory Rabess. 1993. *Zouk: World music in the West Indies.* Chicago: Univ. of Chicago Press.

Hagedorn, Katherine J. 1993. The "folkloricization" of Afro-Cuban religious traditions in Cuba. Ph.D. diss., Brown Univ.

Hernández, Prisco. 1993. *Décima, seis,* and the art of the Puertorican *trovador* within the modern social context. *Latin American Music Review* 14(1):20–51.

Hill, Errol. 1972. *The Trinidad Carnival: Mandate for a national theatre.* Austin: Univ. of Texas Press.

Holloway, Joseph E. 1990. The origins of African-American culture. In *Africanisms in American culture,* ed. Joseph E. Holloway, pp. ix–xxi. Bloomington: Indiana Univ. Press.

Largey, Michael D. 1991. Musical ethnography in Haiti: A study of elite hegemony and musical composition. Ph.D. diss., Indiana Univ.

Manuel, Peter, ed. 1991. *Essays on Cuban music: North American and Cuban perspectives.* Lanham, N.Y. and London: University Presses of America.

Manuel, Peter, with Kenneth Bilby and Michael Largey. 1995. *Caribbean currents: Caribbean music from rumba to reggae.* Philadelphia: Temple Univ. Press.

Martin, Denis-Constant. 1996. Popular culture, identity and politics in the context of the Trinidad Carnival: "I is another, all of we is one." *Studies in History* 12(2), Sage Press, London.

McDaniel, Lorna. *The big drum ritual of Carriacou: Praisesongs in rememory of flight.* Gainesville: University Press of Florida, 1998.

Pacini Hernández, Deborah. 1995. *Bachata: A social history of a Dominican popular music.* Philadelphia: Temple Univ. Press.

Robbins, James. 1990. Making popular music in Cuba: A Study of the Cuban institutions of musical production and the musical life of Santiago de Cuba. Ph.D. diss., Univ. of Illinois.

Vélez, María Teresa. 1996. The trade of an Afro-Cuban religious drummer: Felipe García Villamil. Ph.D. diss., Wesleyan Univ.

Warner, Keith Q. 1985. *Kaiso! The Trinidad calypso: A study of the calypso as oral literature.* Washington, D.C.: Three Continents Press.

Wilcken, Lois. 1991. Music folklore and Haitians in New York: Staged representations and the negotiation of identity. Ph.D. diss., Columbia Univ.

ADDITIONAL LISTENING

There are literally tens of thousands of recordings to choose from, so the list that follows focuses on compilations (which present a number of artists) that deal with the focal and subsidiary music areas of this chapter. These recordings should be available through national music catalogues and websites.

General

Black music of two worlds. Smithsonian Folkways F–4602.

Caribbean dances. Smithsonian Folkways F–6840, 1953.

Caribbean folk music, vol. 1. Smithsonian Folkways F–4533, 1960.

Caribbean island music: Songs and dances of Haiti, the Dominican Republic, and Jamaica. Recording and notes by John Storm Roberts. Nonesuch Explorer Series H–72047.

Caribbean rhythms. Smithsonian Folkways F–8811, 1957.

An island Carnival: Music of the West Indies. Recordings and notes by Krister Malm. Nonesuch Explorer Series 72091–1B, 1983.

Haiti

Angels in the mirror: Vodou music of Haiti. Produced by Holly Nicolas, Y. M. David Yih, and Elizabeth McAlister. Ellipsis Arts CD4120, 1997.

Bouyon rasin: First international Haitian roots music festival. Notes by Claus Schreiner and Gage Averill. Tropical Music.

Caribbean revels: Haitian rara & Dominican gaga. Notes by Verna Gillis and Gage Averill. Smithsonian Folkways CD SF 40402, 1991.

Meringue, buckle-rubbing street music from Haiti. Corason COCD107.

Rhythms of rapture: Sacred musics of Haitian Vodou. Compiled by Elizabeth McAlister. Notes by Elizabeth McAlister, Gage Averill, Gerdès Fleurant, and others. Smithsonian Folkways SF CD 40464, 1995.

Music of Haiti, vols. 1–3: Folk music of Haiti (Folkways Records, F–4407, 1951), *Drums of Haiti* (F–4403, 1950), *Songs and dances of Haiti* (F–4432, 1952).

Cuba

Afro-Cuba: A musical anthology. Produced by Morton Marks. Rounder Records CD 1088, 1994.

Cuban and Puerto Rican music from the African and Hispanic traditions. World Music Institute T–111.

Cuba: I am time. Blue Jackal BJAC5010–2, 1997.

Caliente=hot. New World Records. Notes by Roberta Singer and Robert Friedman.

Carnaval en Santiago. Egrem.

Cuban big bands (1940–42). Notes by Cristóval Diaz Ayala. Harlequin HQ CD 63, 1995.

Cuban counterpoint: History of the son montuno. Compilation and notes by Morton Marks. Rounder Records 1078, 1992.

The Cuban danzón: Its ancestors and descendants. Folkways FE 4066.

Cuban trios, 1940–1941. Notes by Cristóval Diaz Ayala. Harlequin HQ CD 62, 1995.

Hot dance music from Cuba, 1907–1936. Notes by Cristóval Diaz Ayala and Richard K. Spottswood. Harlequin HQ CD 23, 1993.

La música del pueblo de Cuba. EGREM LD 3440.

Oru de igbodu. Egren/Areito.

Sacred rhythms of Cuban santería. Smithsonian Folkways SF 40419.

Sextetos cubanos, vols. 1 and 2. Notes by Michael I. Avalos. Arhoolie Records ARH CD/C 7003 and 7006, 1995.

Trinidad and Tobago

A taste of soca. Ice Records 941302, 1994.

Calypso lore and legend: An afternoon with Patrick Jones. Cook Records 5016.

Calypso pioneers 1912–1937. Produced by Richard K. Spottswood and Donald R. Hill. Rounder Records 1039, 1989.

Calypso season. Mango 539 861–2.

Cult music of Trinidad. Recordings and notes by George Eaton Simpson. Smithsonian Folkways 4478, 1961.

When the time comes: Rebel soca. Shanachie 64010, 1988.

Wind your waist. Shanachie 64034, 1991.

Calypso calalloo: Early carnival music in Trinidad. Rounder Records 1993.

Pan all night: Steelbands of Trinidad and Tobago. Delos DE 4022, 1993.

Where was Butler? A calypso documentary from Trinidad. Notes by Richard K. Spottswood. Folklyric 9048.

The real calypso vols. 1–2: 1927–1946. (The Caresser, The Lion, Atilla the Hun, Lord Invader, others.) F–RBF13, 1966.

Send your children to the orphan home—Songs of social commentary and love troubles, 1930s–40s. (The Lion, Lord Executor, The Tiger, Atilla the Hun, others.) F–RF4, 1981.

ADDITIONAL VIEWING

Celebration! 1988. Produced and directed by Karen Kramer. Dr. Morton Marks and Dr. Donald Hill, consultants. 30 min. Ho-ho-kus, N.J.: Film Library.

Divine horsemen. 1951. Maya Deren. 60 min. Mystic Fire Video.

Dreams of democracy. 1988. Jonathan Demme. 52 min. Includes footage of Manno Charlemagne.

Haitian song. 1982. Karen Kramer. Ho-ho-kus, N.J.: Film Library.

Legacy of the spirits. 1985. Karen Kramer. Ho-ho-kus, N.J.: Film Library.

Machito: Latin jazz legacy. 1987. Produced and directed by Carlos Ortiz. Presented by Nubia Music Society. 58 min. New York: First Run/Icarus Films.

Mas fever: Inside Trinidad Carnival. 1987. Produced and directed by Glenn Micalleff. Photographed and edited by Larry Johnson. 55 min. Portland, Ore.: Filmsound.

Moko jumbie. 1990. Directed by Karen Kramer. Produced by Karen Kramer and James Callahan. 15 min. Ho-ho-kus, N.J.: Film Library.

One hand don't clap. 1988. Produced and directed by Kavery Dutta. 92 min. New York: Rhapsody Films.

Plena is work, Plena is song. 1989. Directed by Pedro A. Rivera and Susan Zeig. 37 min. Distributed by Cinema Guild.

Rara, a Haitian festival. 1985. Gail Pellet, research by Verna Gillis.

Routes of rhythm, vols. 1–3. 1989. With Harry Belafonte. 3 videos, 176 mins. Santa Monica, Calif.: Cultural Research and Communications. (In 1990 a three-CD set called *Routes of Rhythm* was released in conjunction with these videos. It is available from Rounder Records.

Steelband music in Trinidad and Tobago: The creation of a people's music. 1994. Produced by William R. Aho. 32 min. Akron, Ohio: Panyard, Inc.

Steelbands of Trinidad (Pan in a-minor). 1987. Daniel Verba and Jean-Jacques Mrejean. 49 min. Hurleyville, N.Y.: Villon Films.

To serve the gods. 1982. Karen Kramer and Ira Lowenthal. 30 min.

ENDNOTES

1. A wonderful recording of a *jumbie* dance reel can be found on *An Island Carnival: Music of the West Indies* (recordings and notes by Krister Malm; Nonesuch Explorer Series 72091–1B, 1983). This album contains some of the most interesting "small island" music commercially available.

2. For a wide-ranging comparison of Caribbean festive forms, see John W. Nunley and Judith Bettelheim, eds., *Caribbean Festival Arts: Each and Every Bit of Difference* (Seattle: Univ. of Washington Press, 1988).

3. Robin D. Moore, *Nationalizing Blackness: Afrocubanismo and Artistic Revolution in Havana, 1920–1940,* Pitt Latin America Series, ed. Billie R. DeWalt (Pittsburgh: Univ. of Pittsburgh Press, 1997).

4. John Storm Roberts, *The Latin Tinge: The Impact of Latin American Music on the United States* (Oxford and New York: Oxford Univ. Press, 1978), pp. 76–79.

5. There are many general works on Haitian *Vodou*. Harold Courlander's pioneering work on Haitian folklore resulted in *The Drum and the Hoe: Life and Lore of the Haitian People* (Berkeley and Los Angeles: Univ. of California Press, 1960), a book that still serves well as an introductory text in Haitian traditional culture. Maya Deren's fascinating *Divine Horsemen: The Living Gods of Haiti* (London: McPherson & Co., 1955, 1970) has held up over time and continues to provide insight into the experience of *Vodou* for its practitioners (especially when used in conjunction with her film of the same name). Alfred Métraux's *Voodoo in Haiti* (New York: Schocken Books, 1959, 1972) was for a long time the standard ethnographic work on *Vodou*. *Mama Lolo: A Vodou Priestess in Brooklyn,* by Karen McCarthy Brown (Berkeley and Los Angeles: Univ. of California Press, 1991) is easily the best-written and most accessible treatment of *Vodou*. For a look at the visual media of *Vodou*, however, there is nothing that compares with the splendid volume *Sacred Arts of Vodou,* edited by Donald Cosentino (Los Angeles: Univ. of California at Los Angeles Fowler Museum of Cultural History, 1995), which serves as the catalogue for the touring art exhibit of the same name.

6. For a parallel practice, see Larry Crook's and John Schechter's discussions of African-Brazilian *candomblé,* in chapters 1 and 5.

7. I worked on this project with Michael Largey, and we shared recordings, photographs, and other documentary work. I also consulted the writings of two other scholars, Wilfrid "Tido" Laveaud (unpublished manuscript) and Y. M. David Yih, "Music and Dance of Haitian Vodou: Diversity and Unity in Regional Repertoires" (Ph.D. diss., Wesleyan Univ., 1995).

8. Sub-Saharan African music cultures, along with African-American music cultures in Brazil and the Caribbean, frequently use a metal or wooden *idiophone,* such as a gong or iron bell, to enunciate the underlying rhythmic-structural unit (time-line) of an ensemble piece. See, for example, James Koetting's discussion of the role of the *dawuro* gong in a Ghanaian *Asante kete* ensemble (1992:89–90) and David Locke's discussion of the role of the *gankogui* iron bell in a Ghanaian *Ewe Agbekor* ensemble (1996:86–93).

9. Lois Wilcken's *The Drums of Vodou* (Tempe, Ariz: White Cliffs Media Co., 1992) and Gerdès Fleurant's *Dancing Spirits: Rhythms and Rituals of Haitian Vodun, the Rada Rite* (Westport, Conn.: Greenwood Press, 1996) are the best treatments available of the music of *Vodou*. Wilcken's book, written with master drummer Frizner Augustin, provides instruction in Haitian drumming. Drummers can certainly derive a lot of material for perfor-

mance from Fleurant's book as well, but its focus is on the meaning of one of the major rites of Haitian *Vodou* (the *Rada* rite) and the role of music and dance in Haitian religious ritual.

10. Liner notes to *Angels in the Mirror: Vodou Music of Haiti,* produced by Holly Nicolas, Y. M. David Yih, and Elizabeth McAlister, Ellipsis Arts CD4120, 1997.

11. Legba (or Exu among Gêge-Nagô cult groups of Bahia, Brazil), divine trickster and master of the crossroads, is sent away (*despacho de Exu*) at the outset of an African-Bahian *xirê* or *candomblé* ceremony. In this opening ritual, songs are sung and offerings are made to the trickster-deity (Béhague 1984:238). In his discussion of mythologies of the blues, Jon Michael Spencer discusses Legba's symbolic personification of the blues musician; Spencer cites Herskovits's argument that missionaries confounded Legba with Satan, and he offers lore as to the devil's (i.e., Legba's) alleged abilities to impart musical skills to blues musicians at crossroads (1993:11, 28–30, 32–33).

12. My accounts of San André and Briyant Solèy, among others, were first carried in somewhat different form in an article I wrote for *The Beat* called "The Whip and the Whistle: Rara in Haiti," *The Beat* 10(3), 1991. I worked on this preliminary research project with Elizabeth McAlister. This section also draws on my jacket notes to the Japanese version of the Smithsonian/Folkways compact disk *Caribbean Revels: Haitian Rara & Dominican Gaga,* notes by Verna Gillis and Gage Averill, Smithsonian Folkways CD SF 40402, 1991.

13. For an extended analysis of the relationship of sacred to secular elements in *rara,* see Elizabeth McAlister, "'Men Moun Yo'; 'Here Are the People': Rara Festivals and Transnational Popular Culture in Haiti and New York City" (Ph.D. diss., Yale University, 1995).

14. The strength of oral tradition in Haiti is nowhere more evident than in the common recourse in informal discourse to proverbs, or *pawol granmoun* [elders' talk]. Familiarity with, and deployment of, a large stock of proverbs demonstrates a special kind of speech and cultural competency. Many proverbs make sly reference to class relations and politics.

15. Interview with Maurice Morissette, March 1991 (with Elizabeth McAlister).

16. See Lorna McDaniel, "Memory Songs: Community, Flight and Conflict in the Big Drum of Carriacou" (Ph.D. diss., Univ. of Maryland, 1986) for the many uses and variations of the term *kata* in the Caribbean.

17. The recording is of the band Rara Delin, a group associated with a Sanpwèl secret society. It was recorded by Elizabeth McAlister in April 1993, near Tommasin, Haiti.

18. A sampling of *rara* recordings can be heard on *Caribbean Revels: Haitian Rara & Dominican Gaga,* recordings by Verna Gillis, notes by Verna Gillis and Gage Averill, Smithsonian Folkways CD SF 40402, 1991.

19. The first half of this century (especially 1919–1930) saw an *indigenismo* movement among intellectuals and middle- and upper-class artists in Peru, with an increased attention to Peruvian indigenous culture being reflected in new studies of highland Quechua folklore, in publications of Quechua poetry, in the establishment of neotraditional folkloric ensembles, and in regional composers' creations of stylized versions of traditional Andean musical genres and melodies, in works for piano, voice, chorus, orchestra, and ballet (Turino 1993:122, 125–126; Béhague 1979:166–176). This was likewise the period (1920–1934) of the Aztec Renaissance movement in Mexico, in which composers sought to recapture a sense of Mexico's remote cultural past, in Indianist works such as Carlos Chávez's *Sinfonía India* (1935–1936) (Béhague 1979:129–138).

20. *Super Jazz des Jeunes,* Ibo Records ILP 113.

21. "Vaksine" was compiled on *Konbit: Burning Rhythms of Haiti,* produced by Jonathan Demme, Gage Averill and Fred Paul, A&M Records CD 5281, 1989. "Kè-M Pa Sote" appeared on *Vodou Adjae,* translations and liner notes by Gage Averill, Mango 16253 9899–2, 1990. Ram's song is titled "Anbago" on *Aibobo,* Cave Wall Records 101932–5, 1993, 1995.

22. This interview was conducted by Mark Dow on August 29, 1994 and appeared in a fuller version in my column in *The Beat* magazine under the title "Konpa Demokrasi-a: The Rhythm of Democracy," *The Beat* 13(5) (1994), subtitled "Demaske Malpwote: Unmasking the Opportunists." Used with permission.

23. The song lyrics quoted in this section can be found in a book by Manno Chalmay, *Le poukwa, le kòman?*[Why and How?], vol. 1 (Port-au-Prince, Haiti: Organization Culturelle Konbit Kalfou, 1989).

24. "Ayiti pa fore" appeared on the album *Konbit: Burning Rhythms of Haiti,* A&M Records CD 5281, 1989.

25. "Pan Earthquake" by Aldwin "Kitchener" Roberts, copyright © 1993.

26. Donald Hill, *Calypso Calalloo: Early Carnival Music in Trinidad* (Gainesville: Univ. Presses of Florida, 1993), pp. 234–235. "L'annêe pasé" can be heard sung by calypsonian Patrick Jones on *Calypso Lore and Legend: An Afternoon with Patrick Jones,* Cook Records 5016 (distributed by Smithsonian Folkways). Lord Invader's "Rum and Coca Cola" complained of the influence of American sailors and their "Yankee dollars" on Trinidadian women; see Chapter 1.

27. Hollis Liverpool, a scholar and calypsonian who goes by the sobriquet "The Mighty Chalkdust," places the nineteenth-century controversies over Carnival's expressive culture in the context of class and racial struggle, in "Rituals of Power and Rebellion: The Carnival Tradition in Trinidad and Tobago" (Ph.D. diss., Univ. of Michigan, 1993).

28. For a cross-cultural analysis of "traditions of eloquence" in the Caribbean, see Roger D. Abrahams, *The Man-of-Words in the West Indies: Performance and the Emergence of Creole Culture* (Baltimore and London: Johns Hopkins, 1983).

29. Originally released on Decca 17254, 1935, this song can now be found on *Where Was Butler?* Folklyric 9048. This compilation provides vivid examples of the politically engaged calypsos in the years before World War II. Half the songs are devoted to general complaints about poverty and living conditions, and half to calypsos about the 1937 strike by oilfield workers led by labor activist Uriah Butler. Calypsonians appearing on this compilation include Lord Executor, The Lion, Attila the Hun, and The Tiger.

30. This calypso (as well as Houdini's "War Declaration") appears on the compilation *Calypso Pioneers 1912–1937* (Rounder Records 1939).

31. By far the most comprehensive account of the origins of the steel band and its social context is in Stephen Stuempfle, *The Steelband Movement: The Forging of a National Art in Trinidad and Tobago* (Philadelphia: Univ. of Pennsylvania Press, 1995).

32. Steel bands have spread rapidly abroad, first throughout the Eastern Caribbean, then among Caribbean migrants in the United States, Canada, and Europe, and finally among foreigners, who have helped to create an active steel band movement abroad. For a look at the performance of steel band music in diasporic carnivals, see Gage Averill, "'Pan Is We Ting': West Indian Steelbands in Brooklyn," in *Musics of Multicultural America: A Study*

of Twelve Musical Communities, ed. Kip Lornell and Anne K. Rasmussen (New York: Schirmer Books, 1997), pp. 101–130.

33. In steel band terminology, "tuning" is equivalent to "building" and the early stages of tuning. Using the fine manipulation of pitch, overtone, and loudness to balance the ensemble's instruments is called "blending." The best source on steel band construction and tuning is Ulf Kronman, *Steel Pan Tuning: A Handbook for Steel Pan Making and Tuning* (Stockholm, Sweden: Musikmuseet, 1991). I rely heavily on Kronman in this section, also drawing on workshops I took with master tuner Cliff Alexis and on conversations with and observations of pan tuner Carl Chase.

CHAPTER FIVE

Northeastern Brazil

LARRY CROOK

When you contemplate Brazil, you might imagine an elaborate urban *samba* parade full of glittery costumed dancers and musicians performing on the streets of Rio de Janeiro during Carnival time. Or you might picture an Amazonian jungle full of exotic wildlife and tropical plants. When I was a teenager, a popular image of Brazil—enhanced by *bossa nova* songs like "The Girl from Ipanema"—was of a sun-soaked beach full of beautifully tanned bodies and lined by palm trees. These popular images provide only the "chamber of commerce" postcard picture of Brazil. In order to appreciate Brazil at a deeper level, you need to understand some the diverse history of the largest and most populous country in Latin America.

Brazil is vast and complex. Its territory covers roughly half of the South American continent and is inhabited by some 165 million people. Although primarily populated by the descendants of Europeans (Portuguese), Africans (West and Central), and native Amerindians, today's Brazil is a multiracial and pluri-ethnic society with substantial Italian, German, Japanese, Slavic, Jewish, and Arabic communities.

Racial and ethnic mixing was profound from the beginning of colonization (early 1500s) as Portuguese men—only a few European women were brought— had sexual relations (often through violence and coercion) with Amerindian and African women. From such interactions originated much of Brazil's population, as well as classifications for multiraced progeny—*mulatto* (mixture of European and African), *caboclo* or *mameluco* (European and Amerindian), and *cafuzo* (African and Amerindian). These as well as dozens of other terms describing the wide spectrum of skin pigmentation, hair type, and other physical attributes, attest to the common belief that Brazil is the most miscegenated country on earth. Yet racial classifications are fluid in contemporary Brazil, and are not based on ancestry alone but on a combination of social, cultural, and economic markers in conjunction with physical attributes.

The Portuguese settlement of Brazil involved a combination of economic, political, and religious objectives and the combined efforts of the Roman Catholic

BRAZIL

Fig. 5–1. Map of Brazil

Church and the Portuguese Crown. The earliest area of contact and development was the northeastern coast, exploited first for its brazilwood and developed later as a major producer of sugar cane, tobacco, and other agricultural products. Pernambuco was a prosperous center of early activity, and Bahia became the first administrative center of Brazil. After Amerindians proved to be an unreliable labor force, Brazil became the largest consumer in the transatlantic slave trade.

European-based music and dance were important tools used by Jesuit priests and lay brotherhoods (*irmandades*) to convert and acculturate the Amerindian and African populations. At the same time, African and indigenous musical practices were maintained, reinterpreted, and mixed with each other. They were also mixed with European practices. While state, church, and private patronage of certain European musical styles (such as military bands and concert music) have been important aspects of the Brazilian national enterprise, Brazil's vastness also produced many regional differences in its vernacular musical culture. Mass-mediated popular culture in the twentieth century has drawn from this rich diversity in establishing several national mainstream popular musics as well as a variety of regionally associated styles of music. This chapter will focus on the folk and popular musical traditions of northeastern Brazil (hereafter, the Northeast), a large and highly diverse region of the country with a strong regional character. We will cover two important music cultures from this vast area: (1) the music of the interior regions associated with the *mestizo* populations known as *caboclo,* and (2) music of the African-Brazilian population located in the large urban centers, especially Salvador da Bahia.

CABOCLO TRADITIONS: MUSIC OF THE NORTHEAST INTERIOR

The music of the rural areas, towns, and small cities of the interior regions of the Northeast is a national treasure of the country. As a region, the Northeast interior is inhabited primarily by the *caboclo mestizo* population, a combination of Portuguese and Amerindian heritage mixed with varying degrees of African bloodlines. *Caboclo* musical traditions include secular song repertoires, songs associated with folk Catholicism, social dance music, and music to accompany dramatic dances. Secular songs sung by singer-bards derive primarily from the *romance* (an Iberian ballad tradition—see Chapters 1 and 6) and are generically called *cantoria* in the Northeast. *Cantoria* utilizes Iberian poetic forms (*quadras, sextilhas, décimas*) and musical characteristics (modal melodies, tertian harmony, stringed instrument accompaniment). In addition to precomposed sung poetry, *cantoria* also involves the *desafio* (song duel—see Chapter 6), in which two singers alternate improvised verses following a set sequence of fixed poetic forms. In its most common variety, the *desafio de viola,* the dueling singers accompany themselves on ten-stringed double-coursed guitars known as *violas* (see Waddey 1980). In another form (the *embolada*) singers use the *pandeiro* [Brazilian tambourine] as they sing comical tongue-twisters. *Cantoria* is performed in homes, at small bars, on street corners, at local markets, in public parks and other settings.

ZABUMBAS: NORTHEASTERN FIFE AND DRUM BANDS

Anyone who visits the famous street market in Caruaru (Feira de Caruaru) or the trinket shops found in airports throughout Brazil, will encounter miniature ceramic statues of six men standing in a line wearing leather hats with upturned brims, playing flutes and drums (see Illustration 5–1). These statues depict one of the most widespread musical traditions of the Northeast. The fife and drum ensemble known as the *Zabumba* (also generically referred to as *banda de pífanos* [band of fifes]) is the preferred musical accompaniment for a range of social festivities and religious rituals of the *caboclo,* and has become a symbol of the rural folkways of the backlands.[1] Although identified closely with the rural life of the

Ill. 5–1. Miniature ceramic statue of a *Zabumba* ensemble.

Northeast, most *Zabumbas* maintain close links to nearby urban centers, and many groups have relocated to cities in search of economic opportunities. In the cities they give staged performances as "folkloric" bands, make appearances on live radio programs, and play for commercial store promotions; some have produced commercial recordings. The city *Zabumbas* also continue to perform for traditional occasions associated with their rural origins.

Zabumba ensembles typically comprise four core instruments: two transverse cane fifes *(pífanos),* a double-headed bass drum *(zabumba)*,[2] and a thin snare drum *(tarol)*. In addition, a medium-sized tenor drum *(surdo)* and a pair of hand cymbals *(pratos)* are commonly added. With these instruments the groups are able to perform a wide range of music. They specialize in two distinct repertoires: (1) religious music associated with folk Catholicism, and (2) secular dance music known as *forró* (see Illustration 5–2).

Historical documentation is sketchy and inconclusive regarding the origins of the fife bands in Brazil. Similar groupings are found in Portugal and may have been brought by Portuguese settlers to Brazil's northeast coast during colonial times, and then spread throughout the backlands as the region was developed. Comparable ensembles are also found in West Africa and some Brazilian scholars believe that *Zabumbas* were first brought to the Northeast from the island of São Tomé (colonized by the Portuguese), off the West African Coast, in the late sixteenth century.[3] A common belief among contemporary *Zabumba* musicians holds that the *pífano* and the *Zabumba* ensemble originated among the native

Ill. 5–2. *Zabumba* **group from Caruaru, Pernambuco.**

tribes of Brazil. (See also Chapter 7 for an analogous belief regarding the origins of the Colombian Andean *rajaleña* ensemble.) As one musician told me:

> The *banda de pífanos* came from the Indians. For the *zabumba* drum, they took . . . round trunks of wood from the forest, killed animals, skinned and fastened the skin with a vine. They played and made some whistles out of cane and fire. . . . It began with the breath of the Indians. (interview with João Alfredo dos Santos, May 13, 1988)

Musicians also link *Zabumba* music to the class and ethnic distinctions that developed in Brazil, where Indian, black, *mestizo,* and *mulatto* populations were economically and culturally set apart from the upper-class Portuguese whites.

> The *banda de pífanos* was never anything among other types of people; it was born among the Indians of the forest . . . taken up by the *mulatto,* the black, and the *mestizo.* . . . It's not something the whites do. (ibid.)

The association of the *Zabumba* with the peasant and lower-class populations of the Northeast extends to the historically prominent role that domestic-centered folk Catholicism has played throughout the region. The decentralized nature of colonial society in Brazil, together with the vast geographical expanse of the land, restricted the Church's direct involvement in the daily life of rural inhabitants. After the expulsion of the Jesuits from Brazil in 1759, the Church maintained little direct contact with the Northeastern backlands and most religious functions were taken over by local lay leaders. This situation reinforced the region's already thriving folk Catholicism derived largely from European religious practices of the Middle Ages, mixed with Amerindian and African beliefs. In this context, saints and local religious figures assumed paramount importance, and a "cult of saints" evolved, featuring a variety of popular practices and rituals not sanctioned by the Roman Catholic Church. An important ritual was the *novena de casa* [house *novena*], a local adaptation of the nine-day *novena* first established in Spain and France in the Middle Ages.[4] According to popular legend, the Virgin Mary chose a *zabumba* to lead the very first *novena* procession. Musicians and hosts often cite this legend when asked why the *zabumba* is required for a first-rate *novena de casa*.

Novena de Casa

The *novena de casa* [house *novena*] is given by individuals in honor of Catholic saints or popular religious figures of the Northeast. In contrast to the official nine-day *novena*, which is organized and sanctioned by Church authorities, the *novena de casa* is typically a one-day (and all-night) celebration given by and for rural peasants and the working-class poor of the cities. This type of *novena* is frequently denounced by local Church officials because a priest is not present, and because the occasion usually includes a nondevotional celebration *(festa)* that lasts all night.

The hosting of a *novena de casa* constitutes an important act of religious devotion and a public demonstration of one's faith. It is typically given in order to "repay" a promise made to a specific saint in order to gain the intercessory powers of that saint in matters of health and prosperity. (Compare with T. M. Scruggs's discussion of the *promesa* in Nicaraguan saint's day celebrations, in Chapter 3.) The giving of a *novena* to the saint may then become a yearly event in the life of an individual. Referring to the yearly *novenas* that his father hosted when he was growing up, one participant at a *novena* I attended in 1988 told me:

> [Father] had a devotion with Saint Sebastian. He promised Saint Sebastian that if the year's planting and harvesting were prosperous, if he earned well, then at the end of the year he would give a *novena* to Saint Sebastian. . . . Every year he would give a *novena* for the same reasons. He made that promise, and obtained that grace. Every year that he was prosperous, presto, the *novena*.

As its name implies, a *novena de casa* takes place in a home, not a church. The religious ceremony is led by a lay specialist known as a *rezadeira* (female) or *rezador* (male). In the house, an altar is set up with a small statue of the saint of honor (see Illustration 5–3).

This is where the *rezadeira* leads the praying of the *terço* (one third of the Catholic rosary). This is also where most of the singing of praise songs (led by an informal group of women singers known as a *turma de mulheres,* see below), and the playing of instrumental devotional music by the *Zabumba* occurs. For large *novenas*, the altar may be erected directly in front of the house to accommodate more participants. The largest *novenas* I attended included more than 250 people. The *novena de casa* is also the occasion for a large party that features drinking, dance music, and other activities. Outside the house, multicolored paper flags are strung across the street and electric lights or kerosene lanterns are set up to

Ill. 5–3. Altar at a *novena de casa.*

give a festive atmosphere to the entire area. In this area games of luck, food stalls, and temporary cash bars may also be erected and run by local small-scale merchants—often by neighbors themselves who take advantage of the situation to earn some money.

About six weeks before the event, the one offering the *novena* makes arrangements with the *Zabumba*, the *turma,* and the *rezadeira.* The *Zabumba* is contracted to perform music for both the religious and secular activities while the *rezadeira* and *turma* take part only in the religious activities.[5] The *turma* is usually an informally structured group of women who love to sing and pray at *novenas,* and who go on pilgrimages to holy sites in the Northeast. Let's see how a typical *novena* unfolds.

Early in the afternoon, the *Zabumba* arrives and announces itself by marching into the house playing a special repertoire of *novena* music devoted to the saint. Their first obligation is to greet the saint by performing the *vênia do santo*—a short musical offering in front of the altar. The musicians of the *Zabumba* divide into two lines facing the saint. The front musicians switch places several times before kneeling and kissing the base of the saint's statue. They then turn and proceed to the back of the lines, allowing the next pair of musicians to come forward. Each pair has its turn and then the entire *Zabumba* forms a circle around the saint before returning to their original positions.[6] Several pieces of music may be performed with the same choreography repeated. The *vênia do santo* is completed with shouts of "viva!" to the saint and to the giver of the *novena.* Only now do the musicians exchange greetings and introductions with those present.

The music performed during the *vênia* consists of instrumental versions of hymns and praise songs as well as instrumental marches, waltzes, *dobrados,* and other genres idiomatic to the *Zabumba.* This religious repertoire is called the "music of the saints." *Zabumba* musicians say that when they perform music to the saint they try to imitate the way the *turma de mulheres* sounds when they sing praise songs. To achieve this, the *pífanos* play the melody in a legato fashion (connecting the notes of the melody) and keep the percussion parts simple. Recorded Selection 22 was taped in 1987 in the small rural hamlet of Lagoa de Jurema, Pernambuco, during a *novena de casa* to Saint Sebastian. The example fades in as the Zabumba Dois Irmãos marches into the house playing a *novena* march and performs a *vênia* in front of the altar. Immediately after the choreography is complete, they play a short instrumental version of the praise song to Saint Sebastian. The distinctive fife-and-drum sound features two *pífanos* playing the melody (usually in a seven-pitch scale) in parallel harmony at the interval of a third. The percussion parts are performed without much elaboration, the players preferring to maintain a solid and uncluttered accompaniment to the melody.

After the *vênia* is performed, the musicians of the *Zabumba* are usually fed—typical fare is rice and beans, chicken in blood gravy, and tomatoes and onion in vinegar—and then spend most of the afternoon relaxing, socializing, and entertaining the family with music. Meanwhile, family members and close friends make final preparations for the *novena*—food must be cooked, decorations set in place, firecrackers and candles gathered. At large *novenas,* local concessionaires

Ex. 5–1. *Pífano* **parts in parallel thirds to "Bendito São Sebastião"**

arrive and set up their stalls for the party that will follow the *novena*. Late in the afternoon the *rezadeira* and a *turma de mulheres* arrive. Many neighbors and townspeople also begin showing up. Just before dusk the *turma* helps organize and then lead a religious procession. Candles with paper or plastic wind-breakers are passed out and two lines are formed. In the middle of the procession are the *Zabumba*, the *rezadeira, turma de mulheres,* and most importantly, the statue of the saint, carried on a platform. Rockets are lit and the *Zabumba* begins playing a procession march as everyone slowly proceeds forward. The *Zabumba* alternates its musical pieces with the singing of hymns and praise songs led by the *turma de mulheres.* The procession serves to announce to the entire community that the *novena* has begun. As it winds through the community more rockets are lit, and neighbors join the procession and follow it back to the *novena* house. When the procession arrives at the house, the saint is placed on the altar and everyone gathers for the religious centerpiece of the *novena:* the praying of the *terço*.

The *terço* at a *novena de casa* is a ceremony of about thirty minutes to an hour in length, based on a fixed sequence of prayers drawn from the rosary, with devotional singing and *Zabumba* music inserted at specific points. The *terço* is led by a *rezadeira*[7] or *rezador*. It features collective praying and singing and the instrumental playing of the *Zabumba*. The singing is led by the *turma de mulheres* and is performed with the intent of encouraging group participation. While all of those present, male and female, are expected to join in, it is the women who dominate. At *novenas,* the singing and praying of the women is referred to with a single term: *rezando* [literally, praying]. This highlights the conceptual association of singing to praying.

This linkage is also found in the aesthetics of performance where women utilize many of the same style elements—fluid phrasing, elastic tempo, glides and slurs between pitches, collective coordination—in both praying and singing. It is this basic socioartistic style that the men of the *Zabumba* ensembles emulate when performing music of the saint. Listen to Recorded Selection 23, which was taped during the praying of the *terço* at a *novena de casa* in the town of Bezerra, Pernambuco. The song is a devotional praise song entitled "Bendita e louvada Seja" [Blessed and praised may You be].

Pay close attention to the way in which the participants sing and coordinate their voices. Most sing in simple unison or in octaves but there is an occasional harmony added in a parallel relationship to the main melody, at the interval of a third. Like the legato connection of pitches, the words of the text slur into one another. Directly after this song, the *Zabumba* performs the same melody with percussion accompaniment added. The two flutes articulate their notes in a legato manner similar to the singing. It is the overall sound of the singing and the devotion mood that they say they are trying to imitate.

When the *terço* is completed, the *Zabumba* performs another *vênia do santo* and then asks the host if their obligations to the saint have been fulfilled. The host may request the *Zabumba* to perform one or more additional pieces before indicating that the promise to the saint has been fulfilled and that the *festa* [party] may begin. One of the principal reasons *Zabumbas* are hired for *novenas de casa* is to animate the *festa* and keep it going all night. While fulfilling religious obligations is paramount, *Zabumbas* that cannot entertain the community are not in high demand. Referring to his displeasure with the *Zabumba* hired for the previous year's *novena,* one host told me:

[The *Zabumba* should] play all night long, till five in the morning, then it's over. . . . But when it was eleven o'clock at night they [the musicians] left . . . and the party was over. This party has never been over at eleven o'clock at night before! So I didn't want them this year. (interview with João Venácio, Jan. 14, 1988)

Ex. 5–2.   Lyrics (translated) to "Bendita e louvada Seja"

Blessed and praised may You be
In heaven the divine light
And on earth we also
Praise the Holy Cross

The *Zabumba* is expected to animate the *festa* with rhythmically aggressive music. At this time, quite a few women (especially the women prayers and singers), small children, and some of the more pious men return to their homes. Female family members and close women friends of the family remain to help prepare more food, clean the house, and converse. These women spend most of the rest of the evening in the house, where they talk and occasionally pray in front of the saint. Meanwhile, the men congregate outside the house, around the small bars. It is here that the *Zabumba* goes to carry the party into the night. And it is in this context that the lively *forró* style is performed.

In contrast to the *música de santo*, which is associated with religious values and is intended to inspire respect for and submission to the saint, *forró* (pronounced "faw-hoe") music has become synonymous with promiscuous behavior, foul language, excessive drinking, and fights between men over women. These associations are derived from activities that are common at secular *forró* dances. *Forró* dances in their purely secular context—that is, those not associated with *novenas*—are occasions for sexual encounters (often between married men and young unmarried women). The holding of an actual *forró* dance party at a *novena* is rare. However, the performance of *forró* music after the *terço* at a *novena* functions to encourage male bonding and to reinforce and reproduce a macho view of women as sexual partners. The association of *forró* with male virility and sexual prowess is highlighted through the metaphors used to describe the rhythm and through the song texts. For instance, a core metaphor used to describe the rhythmic intensity of well-played *forró* is *quente* [hot]. This term, and its related verb form *esquentar* [to heat up] are also used to describe the physical and sexual effect that the music has on women— *"esquenta mulher"* [it heats women up]. The phrase *ele é fogo* [he is fire] is used to describe a musician who is able to heat up a party through his intense performance abilities.

Forró song texts use many such metaphors and commonly deal with sexual themes. In the *forró* song "Nega boa" (Recorded Selection 24), the image of the swinging hips of a black woman is juxtaposed to the burning of a fire.

In this song, images of a woman's hip swing, *zabumba* drum beating, and a burning fire are linked together and connected to sexual arousal. The second line of the refrain, "Start swinging and heating things up," serves to connect the woman's hip swing to the semantic domain of heat. The first verse then links the woman's hip motion to the beating of the *zabumba* drum. After a repetition of the refrain, the second verse emphasizes the reciprocal interplay of the hip movement and drumming through repetition and inversion. Finally, the image of the burning fire gives substance to the centrality of the heat metaphor before the last two lines suggest that the black woman desires sexual arousal ("wants to get hot") with the man. When men of the *Zabumba* sing a song like "Nega boa" at a *novena,* they are not only asserting male privilege, they are also articulating longstanding aspects of gender relations in Northeastern society and their views on female as well as male identity.

Musical style (defined as a coherent set of structured sounds and social interaction) is also a resource used by the men of the *Zabumba* to construct and assert

Ex. 5–3.   Lyrics to "Nega boa" [Good black woman], a *Zabumba forró* by the Bandinha Cultural de Caruaru (in Portuguese with English translation)

Vem cá nega,	(Refrain) Come here black woman,
Balança pra esquentar.	Start swinging and heating things up.
Vem cá nega,	Come here black woman,
Até o dia clarear.	Till the break of day.
A nega é boa balançando pra valer,	(Verse 1) The black woman is good at swinging to keep
A pancada do zabumba até o dia amanhecer.	The *zabumba* beating till the break of day.
A nega é boa caprichando o rebolado	The black woman is good perfecting her hip-swing
Forró de Zé do Estado,	[At the] *forró* of Joe Civil Servant
Você não pode perder.	You just can't lose.
Vem cá nega,	(Refrain) Come here black woman,
Balança pra esquentar.	Start swinging and heating things up.
Vem cá nega,	Come here black woman,
Até o dia clarear.	Till the break of day.
O zabumba 'ta tocando	(Verse 2) The *zabumba* is playing
E a nega 'ta balançando	And the black woman is swinging
A nega 'ta balançando	The black woman is swinging
E o zabumba 'ta tocando.	And the *zabumba* is playing.
A fogueira 'ta queimando	The fire is burning
E a nega quer esquentar.	And the black woman wants to get hot.
Chega nega pra a gente balançar.	Come on over here black woman so we can swing.

their views of gender relations. During the secular *festa* at a *novena*, the style of social engagement and musical participation that occurs among men at the bars is prompted through the playing of the *forró* musical style. When a male participant at a *novena* says to the *Zabumba* "toca forró, bem quente" [play some *forró*, really hot], he is requesting not only an intense syncopated rhythmic style of music, but also his desire for a mode of social participation through which he can display his male virility. Similarly, when a *Zabumba* musician plays *forró* music at a *novena* he is demonstrating his musical competence and his own maleness.

The *forró* style used in "Nega boa" employs sociomusical processes that emphasize individual assertion, virtuosity, and the celebration of physical pleasure. It features a staccato *pífano* playing technique called "beating the lip" and a rhythmic scheme of interlocked percussion parts. Musicians are expected to heat things up by improvising in a highly rhythmic and aggressive style, asserting their command over the structure rather than submitting to it.

Ex. 5–4.   Rhythmic accompaniment to "Nega boa"

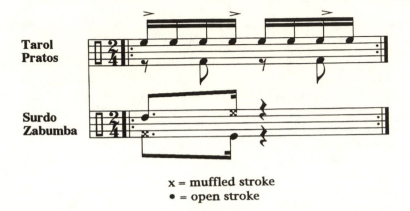

x = muffled stroke
• = open stroke

Listen again to "Nega boa" (Recorded Selection 24) as performed by the Band-inha Cultural de Caruaru. Sudden bursts of sound and punctuations of the beat add to the intensity of the performance. The basic rhythmic structure is highly syncopated. Notice how the surdo and *zabumba* drums interlock their parts with alternating muffled and open strokes. The lead *pífano*, played by Biu do Pife, is virtuosic. Short improvised sections called *passagenizinhas* [little passages] serve as vehicles for Biu to vary the melody, improvise new ones, and intensify the rhythm. Syncopation at the sixteenth-note level dominates the improvised varia-tions.

Ex. 5–5.   Lead *pífano* improvisation from "Nega boa"

While the *Zabumba* is performing a piece like "Nega boa," men are engaging in a kind of male clubhouse activity—drinking excessive amounts of *cachaça* [cane alcohol], singing along with the songs, and commenting on the sexuality of women, on extramarital affairs, and on their sexual prowess. The atmosphere here contrasts markedly with the tone that had prevailed earlier in front of the saint. While women are not prohibited from drinking with the men, they usually do not do so in public. In general, most women at *novenas* are focused on religious devotion to the saint, and they tend to congregate inside the house. Even late at night, when the *festa* is in full swing, the *Zabumba* may be called upon to play pieces for the saint. When this occurs, musicians are asked (usually by women) to come into the house and play *novena* music in front of the altar.

Novenas typically end at daybreak, with the musicians receiving breakfast before they perform their final piece in honor of the saint and the host of the *novena*. By this time only the family and the most die-hard drinkers are left. The leader of the musicians asks the host if their obligations to the saint have been fulfilled. When the host replies that they have, they are free to go. Though some of the musicians of the *Zabumbas* complain that these all-night affairs are too long and do not pay enough, the *novena de casa* continues to be the most important performance occasion for the *Zabumba*.

PROFILE OF JOÃO ALFREDO DOS SANTOS[8]

While I was living in Brazil during the late 1980s, one of my closest friends was João Alfredo dos Santos, a *Zabumba* musician and *pífano* maker from Caruaru,

Ill. 5–4. João Alfredo dos Santos playing a *pífano* at his home in Caruaru, Pernambuco.

Pernambuco. This section provides a sketch of his life as a *Zabumba* musician. All quotations are from conversations and interviews I had with dos Santos during 1987 and 1988.

In 1988 João Alfredo dos Santos revived his family's *Zabumba*. During the 1980s he had become increasingly conscious of himself as both a professional musician and commercial marketer of *pífanos,* and as a bearer of the tradition of his ancestors. This realization took shape during his ten years of performing with some of the most commercially successful *Zabumbas* from the Caruaru area. He also had experienced major fallings-out with his financial patron, Alfredo Francisco da Silva, and with his long time friend and musical soul mate, Biu do Pife. In a conversation with João in June of that year he told me:

> I like my profession. I do it because I like it. Now if you were to ask me, "João, does it allow you to live comfortably?" No. It doesn't. But I like it. And whether it does or not, I pursue my profession with vigor, with force. And I survive by my profession. I don't always live well, but I do survive. And with God's power and with those people who enjoy it, who come to me and buy *pífanos,* well, I'm able to buy a kilo of sugar and other things. That's how I get by. No, I don't have anyone's assistance. . . . There hasn't been any governmental assistance for me, nothing like that. Nobody has helped me. I live by my own means. I live alone in this rat race. And I pray to God that I won't quit till I'm dead. When I'm dead—old, broken and can't play any more—that's when I'll quit. I love this profession. I'll play for money. I'll play for free. I'll play for a party. I've even played for nothing and then returned home very satisfied. This [holds up a *pífano*] is a talent that God gave me. This is the music of the Indians who come from way over there. It was created in the forest.

João Alfredo dos Santos was born in 1942 in the hamlet of Sítio Chambá, about forty miles outside of Caruaru. His father, Alfredo Marcos dos Santos, was an agricultural worker who also played the *pífano* and led Zabumba Três Marcos. João and his older brother Severino grew up listening to *Zabumba* music, and often accompanied their father to all-night *novenas*—in 1954 they performed their first one:

> We weren't really part of the band. We were only learning and beginning, and the musicians of father's band were all there. All of the same family, all brothers. And father was the leader.
>
> Well, the biggest hit of the day was the song that goes like this [sings]: "Olê mulher rendeira, olê mulher renda." And this "Mulher rendeira" was all they wanted to hear at the festival. So they told father to play it. But his musicians didn't know it. They hadn't learned it. No, they hadn't rehearsed, weren't up on the latest hits; they only could play their own music, that old kind of music. They weren't hip to the new song of Luiz Gonzaga.[9] . . . So they [the musicians] asked me, "Can you play 'Mulher rendeira'? Everyone here at the festival is asking for it." So [we asked], "Will you give us the instruments? Then we'll play." . . .
>
> So anyway, we played . . . and when we finished playing . . . our pockets were full of money! They gave us money and other people gave us money too. The people said, "Play it again!" When we finished the music, when we finished that festival, our pockets were full of money. . . . And from that moment on we were part of the band.

During the next few years João and Severino played at many *novenas* with the family *Zabumba*. Then during the late 1950s and early 1960s, the nearby city of Caruaru grew as a regional urban center and as a center of folk arts. It was during this period that a local artisan named Vitalino, who also played *pífano* and led a *Zabumba* of his own, was "discovered" by Brazil's folklorists. Vitalino's ceramic figurines depicting daily activities of the Northeastern rural inhabitants drew national attention and put Caruaru on the map as a center of folklore, and it became a popular tourist destination. Caruaru also became famous for its *Zabumba* music.

In this context, the *Zabumba* itself became an important national symbol of rural Northeastern folk traditions, and notions of authenticity and cultural purity (not always authentic themselves) were applied to *Zabumba* performances. Like their father, João and Severino preferred the industrialized wooden flutes with five keys, instruments they considered advanced and sophisticated.[10] But as João would soon learn, the wooden flute was not considered an authentic folk instrument. In 1962 he met Benedito Biano, *pífano* player from the group Zabumba Caruaru, who suggested that he should switch to *pífanos* made from *taquara* [a type of cane].[11] Not only were they easier to play—the audiences in Caruaru preferred them. João eventually decided that the *pífano* was indeed better:

> It [the wooden flute] became unpopular, fell out of style. What survived was the *pífano* . . . the *pífano* of *taboca*. What I mean is that people didn't like the flute any longer; [they said,] "Ah, it's no good, a *pífano* is good." So we switched to the *pífano*.

On weekends João continued to perform *Zabumba* music at *novenas*. At one of the *novenas* he met a young girl of fourteen years named Nilsa, and soon they were married (1967). Life was hard in the Northeast, and no one could support a family as a *Zabumba* musician. Like the majority of other men in the rural areas, João worked primarily as an agricultural hand at large farms and rented a small plot of land on the side on which to grow his own food.

The Northeastern economy worsened and many men went south in search of jobs, becoming migrant laborers while their families stayed behind. João went to São Paulo, the most industrialized area of Brazil, and spent ten months of each year for the next eight years working as a bricklayer's assistant. In São Paulo there were no *Zabumbas* that he knew of, but he did continue to play the *pífano*:

> There in São Paulo it's like this: I used to work all week, hard labor. . . . And when the end of the week came, on Saturday, the other guys used to invite me to have drinks with them. They would say, "João, bring your *pífano*." I would arrive at the bar and they would order [me] a drink . . . and then say, "Play the *pífano* at the table." . . . So it happened that people liked it, . . . me playing alone on the *pífano*. They said it reminded them of Pernambuco.

After eight years of working in São Paulo (for two months of each year he returned to live in Pernambuco) João resolved to make music a full-time career and returned to the Northeast for good. He moved back to Sítio Chambá and began performing with the family *Zabumba* again. But João didn't want to stay in Sítio

Chambá—he was interested in breaking into the larger musical market of Caruaru which, by the mid-1970s, had become a thriving center for *Zabumba* music. João took his *Zabumba* to Caruaru to play for a weekly radio program that featured local musicians. There he met a *pífano* virtuoso named Biu do Pife who led a *Zabumba* called Bandinha Cultural de Caruaru. This was a new kind of *Zabumba*, an all-star grouping of some of the best players from the area. Biu was impressed with João's musicianship, and after approval from the band's financial backer—a well-to-do patron named Alfredo Francisco da Silva—invited João to join the band.

Alfredo Francisco paid to relocate João and his family to Caruaru and arranged a house for him to rent at a reduced rate. The relationship between Alfredo Francisco and João followed the well-established system of patron-client. Within this system, peasants link themselves to upper-class patrons who provide access to strategic resources (credit, capital, medical aid, general information, housing, land) and give them security and protection. Small loans for life's hardships and basic welfare are provided by the patron in return for menial work, social loyalty, and general cultural deference from the client. Since the inception of Bandinha Cultural, Alfredo Francisco has served as patron to each member of the group. The Bandinha is Alfredo Francisco's band—he owns the instruments and the uniforms, provides transportation and rehearsal space, and takes twenty percent of all group earnings to pay for overhead. As patron, he commands respect and demands loyalty from the musicians in his group. His authority over them extends to such matters as religious orientation and political affiliations. In short, a set of submissions, dependencies, and reciprocal obligations has been established through the social contract between Alfredo Francisco and his musicians. While playing in Alfredo Francisco's band kept João fairly busy, it often couldn't provide him with enough money to support his family. During these times he went to Alfredo Francisco for help, but the small loans for medicine and food never seemed to be enough. According to João, the assistance he received was minimal.

At the time that João joined the band, Biu do Pife already had an established part-time business selling *pífanos* and other items of local folk art at the artisan's market in Caruaru. João began to help in making and selling the *pífanos*. In 1984 João took over the *pífano* business when Biu obtained a full-time day job (arranged by Alfredo Francisco).

With the Bandinha Cultural, João learned and perfected an urbanized presentation format that stressed technical proficiency, stage presence, set planning, and costuming—and that demanded regular rehearsals. His eldest son Manuel also joined the group to play *zabumba* drum. The Bandinha traveled all over Brazil, recorded two albums, and performed on radio and television. João also learned the processes of contracting for jobs and dealing with upper-class promoters, businessmen, and governmental bureaucrats. During the next few years, João devoted most of his time to performance and *pífano* manufacture. In the mid-1980s he quit the band for a short time to lead another group, Zabumba de Mestre Vitalino, sponsored by Vitalino's son.

Then in 1988, João quit the Bandinha Cultural for good. João wanted to revive his own family's *Zabumba* and had nearly come to the end of his relationship with Alfredo Francisco. He was also going through a separation from his wife Nilsa. Reflecting on his past career and his future artistic direction he told me:

I would like to say . . . that my career began at a *novena,* and that's why I like *novenas.* I adore them. We play presentations, all kinds of presentations in Recife, São Paulo, Bahia, in all of the states we perform, and it's true—I like to do this, it's my profession, I make a living this way, from my profession. I make a *pífano* to sell and I survive . . . thanks to God. . . .

But if I left my profession and went to struggle in another line of work, it would be even worse. Earning a menial salary is not for me. If I were to earn a menial salary, I wouldn't be able to live. So I have my profession and I earn more. It's a hard life. . . .

I'm very passionate when . . . an old friend, any man or woman, comes to contract a [*novena*] festival, like the festival that just happened; I get excited. I spend the entire month getting prepared. I arrange everything. But the old guy says, "No, it's too expensive, I can't pay that kind of money." So I say, "No, I can't do it for this much [less]." But I'll play it because I love it. . . .

How many festivals have we played for free? People say, "Ah, I can't pay . . . to have my *novena terço.*" [So] we go without earning anything. . . . We arrive and play and I'm satisfied. We've done this. We don't only play for money. We play free of charge too, that's no problem. This is a tradition, created by our father when we were born. We created it in our house. . . . I'll only stop playing *novenas* when I can't physically do it any more.

By 1988 João was increasingly torn between the sense of obligation to carry on the tradition of playing for *novenas*—for friends, neighbors, and other peasants, a tradition that his father had taught him—and expanding his opportunities as a professional musician in the urban environment. João had quit the Bandinha Cultural and had re-formed his family band. The newly named Zabumba Dois Irmãos [two brothers *Zabumba*] featured João, two of his sons, and his brother Severino as musicians. João dreamed of moving to the city of Recife, the state capital, where he felt his *Zabumba* would be kept busy performing all the time:

I left Riacho [the town closest to his natal hamlet] and came here [Caruaru]. I think that the larger the place, the better. Now I'm thinking that Caruaru is very small. . . . I hope to form a band in Recife. When I get an idea in my head, I don't stop until I do it. I'll start a band in Recife yet. I've already had some opportunities.

They don't have these kinds of *novenas* inside the capital [Recife]. But those places more remote, there they pray the *terço* [the essential prayer in a *novena*] and other things. But it's not so much for a *novena,* no! Ha-ha-ha. If the opportunity comes up— "Ah let's play a *novena* for those older people"—then we'll do it. You know that a little band there [in Recife] wouldn't be able to stop. It would work a lot. Giving presentations paid for by the mayor, drinking and eating like that. Dealing with those kinds of people. Getting known. They would enjoy the band. . . . Presentations to honor those kinds of people, lots of things.

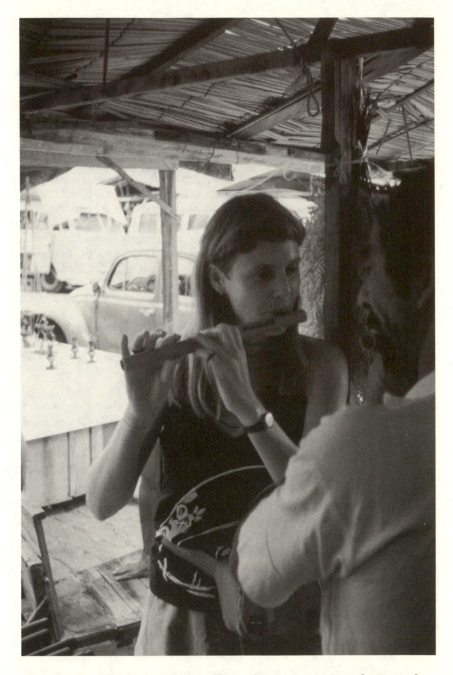

Ill. 5–5. João Alfredo dos Santos selling *pífanos* to tourists at the Feira de Caruaru artisan's market.

Because if . . . we lived there we could charge a little less. You would work more because, let's say from here [Caruaru] to there we have asked for ten thousand . . . apart from anything else, without transportation. And us being there, we could do it for five [thousand].

When I returned to Brazil in 1994 I visited João. He and his *Zabumba* were still performing widely in and around Caruaru, and he was still selling *pífanos* at the market. And he was still dreaming of opportunities in Recife.

MAKING A CANE *PÍFANO*

João learned the art of making fifes from his father, and the skill of marketing them at the Fiera de Caruaru from fellow fifer Biu do Pife. After João moved to Caruaru in the early 1970s, Biu invited him to help make *pífanos* and sell them at the market. With Biu, João perfected the construction and marketing of *pífanos*. In 1985, Biu obtained full-time employment with benefits and left the *pífano* business to João.

Pífanos are traditionally made from a cane called *taquara* or *taboca* that is abundant in southern Pernambuco and in other states of the Northeast. In the 1960s, some instrument builders began using plastic plumbing pipe (PVC) or metal tubing. The advantage of these industrialized materials was their strength and easy availability. However, many musicians maintain that the sound is inferior and that the smell is bad.

There are three sizes of *pífanos: meia-régua* (40 to 45 cm), *três-quartos* (48 to 50 cm), and *régua-inteira* (50 to 60 cm). Instruments are made in pairs of equal length and tuning because they are always played in pairs. Whatever the size, each *pífano* has six finger holes and one blow hole.

The first step in making a pair of *pífanos* is choosing the cane. It should be straight, long between the joints, and approximately two centimeters in diameter. After being harvested, the cane is dried for two months. When it is ready, João cuts just below the nodes so that each *pífano* will have one open end and one closed end. With a large knife he then scrapes a straight line down the length of the cane. Guided by the scraped line, João next measures and marks the proper location of the holes using his fingers. Starting at the open end he marks the width of three fingers. From this mark he measures the distance from his thumb to his index finger when stretched to its farthest position and makes a second mark. From this mark he repeats this step and makes a third mark. The third mark will locate the blowhole. Returning to the first mark, João then uses the width of his thumb to measure out the six finger holes (the final mark should be very close to the second mark he made earlier). He uses this *pífano* carefully to mark the holes for the second *pífano*.

The seven holes are burned out with a red-hot iron poker with a tapered end—drilling the holes would split the cane. João prepares a fire of coal and puts the end of the poker directly into it. When it is red-hot, he burns a hole at each mark, being careful to hold the poker at a ninety-degree angle to the cane. The aroma of burning cane fills the room. After all seven holes are burned, he slides the poker

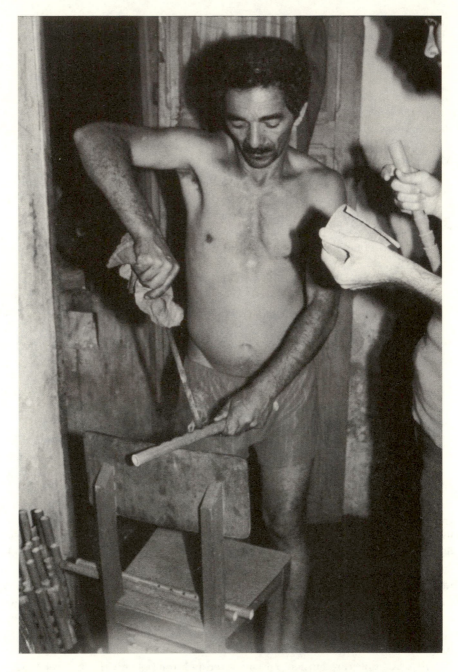

Ill. 5–6. João Alfredo dos Santos burning the finger holes into a *pífano*.

inside the cane to burn away any splinters, and to temper the interior with heat and smoke.

Now João takes a short cylindrical cork slightly larger in diameter than the interior of the cane and, applying pressure with the palm of his hand, compresses it by rolling it on a hard wooden surface. He then inserts the cork into the open end of the cane and knocks it down the length of the cane with a wooden dowel until it is positioned approximately one centimeter past the blowhole. The *pífano* must now be tested by playing it. Final tuning is accomplished by knocking the cork slightly more or by cutting off a little of the open end of the cane.

FORRÓ

Secular Dance Music of the Caboclo

The social dance music of the interior region is dominated by accordion-based groups featuring a core trio of accordion, triangle, and *zabumba* [bass drum]. Most of the music known as *forró* derives from nineteenth-century country dances. The accordion was first brought to southern Brazil by Italian immigrants in the mid-nineteenth century and then taken to the Northeast in the 1860s by returning veterans of the Brazil-Paraguay war. Today this historical linkage is maintained through the *bacamarteiros,* honorary associations of Northeastern men whose forefathers fought in the war. Dressed in military outfits complete with old-time rifles loaded with gunpowder and blank cartridges, *bacamarteiro* units parade on special holidays to honor their veteran ancestors. During parades each group (numbering up to a hundred men) is led by an accordion, triangle, and *zabumba* drum trio.

During the same time period that the accordion was introduced to Brazil, European (polka, quadrille, waltz, mazurka, and schottische) and Hispanic (*tango, habanera*) social dances of the day were also imported and influenced the evolution of both regional and national forms of music in Brazil. In the Northeast, the accordion became the preferred instrument among the *caboclo* peasants to accompany country dances that featured their own versions of these imported dances, as well as several indigenous forms.

Two basic types of accordions are used in the Northeast: (1) *sanfona*, a full-sized instrument with melody keys arranged like a piano and multiple rows of bass buttons, and (2) *oito baixos*, a smaller instrument with button melody keys in two rows and eight bass notes, from which it derives its name. The *zabumba* drum used with the accordion is a thin bass drum of approximately twenty-four inches in diameter, with two heads. The drum is strapped in front of the drummer's stomach and played tilted at about a forty-five-degree angle. The primary pattern of the rhythm is played on the top head with a short padded mallet; counter rhythms are played on the bottom head with a very thin stick, while the palm of the hand controls the amount of open ringing and dampening desired.

The month of June (wintertime south of the equator) is an active period for *caboclo* expressive culture, and a time of winter festivals celebrating the harvesting of corn and three of the most popular Catholic Saints—Anthony, John, and

Ill. 5–7. An accordion trio leads a *bacamarteiro* unit during the festival of São João in Caruaru. Photo by Larry Crook, 1987.

Joseph. During the June festivals, accordion groups provide musical accompaniment for satirical folk plays, *quadrilhas* [square-dancing competitions], and *forró* [social dancing for couples]. The *forró* dancing takes place in temporary huts with thatched roofs and dirt floors in an atmosphere similar to a North American country hoedown. The dances are the *xote*, a Northeastern version of the schottische; *arrasta-pé,* a fast foot-dragging dance; *baião*, a syncopated two-step; and the *forró* itself, a modern hybrid of the *baião.* This is good-time music for dancing, drinking, and general merriment. The accordionist makes the squeezebox roar and the *zabumba* drummer heats up the rhythm to a fevered pitch—a successful *forró* party is likely to last from midnight until daybreak.

Listen to Recorded Selection 25, accordion music that I recorded at a live radio program in Caruaru on April 4, 1987, featuring Toninho do Calderão. Tonhinho is accompanied by triangle, *zabumba,* and *tarol* as he plays a lively piece set to the *forró* rhythm.

Luiz Gonzaga, Baião, *and* Forró *as a Brazilian Popular Music*

Forró music has also been popularized nationally and extended beyond its seasonal association with June-fests via recording and broadcast media and the establishment of commercial *forró* clubs in major cities throughout Brazil.

By the turn of the twentieth century Rio de Janeiro had established itself as the capital of Brazil's music and entertainment industry, like New York City did in the

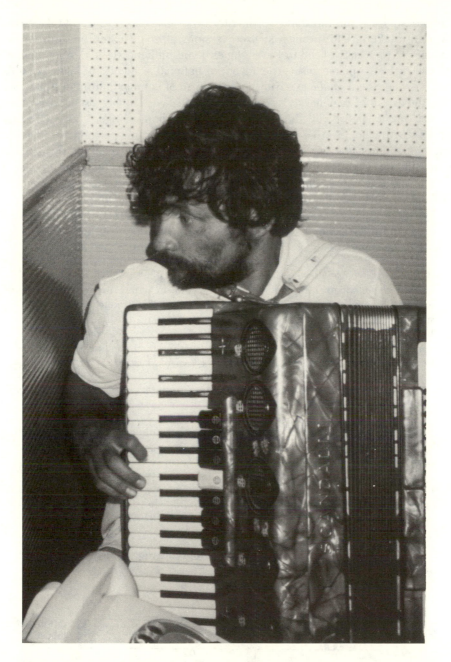

Ill. 5–8. Toninho do Calderão plays a *sanfona* during a live radio program in Caruaru. Photo by Larry Crook.

United States. From the start, Northeastern musicians such as Catulo da Paixão Cearense (1866–1946) brought stylized versions of guitar-based music from the interior of their native land to Rio de Janeiro and influenced the development of Brazil's urban popular music. The advent of national radio (1936) made possible not only the rise of *samba* as a truly national form of popular culture in Brazil, but also the ascent of regional styles on the national stage. The biggest success of regional music began in the 1940s with accordionist-singer Luiz Gonzaga (1912–1989) who, together with a succession of songwriting partners, molded the traditional musics of the Northeastern interior into a popular format for national consumption. Gonzaga is widely regarded as creator of the commercial *baião,* a dance and song genre which became synonymous with Northeastern folk music. Indeed, his nickname became "Rei do Baião" [king of the *baião*].

When Gonzaga was interviewed, he always stressed that the term *baião* existed throughout the Northeast before he developed the popular musical form for which he became famous.

> Before me, the *baião* already existed, but in a very indistinct and loose form. It was known as *baiano* in many parts of the Northeast. I mean, in its primitive form the *baião* was not a musical genre. It existed as a characteristic, as an introduction [played] by singers on their *violas* [ten-stringed double-coursed guitars]. It was a rhythm, a dance. Before tuning the *viola,* the singer plays an introduction. . . . When the singer . . . feels that the *viola* is tuned properly, he beats [out a rhythm] on the sound board, like this: t-chum, t-chum. I took the *baião* from this beat. (Angelo 1990:53)

Gonzaga also mentioned the influence of the *Zabumba* ensembles on the development of the *baião:*

> When I was a kid, I used to play in those little *pífano* bands, and my instrument was the *zabumba* drum. When I decided to create the *baião,* I remembered the *Zabumba.* (unsigned article, "O eterno rei do baião," 1972).

Combining the rhythmic pattern of the *viola* players with the syncopated patterns of the *zabumba* drum, the essence of the new *baião* rhythm was created.

Ex. 5–6.   The basic *baião* rhythm on the *zabumba* drum, as developed by Luiz Gonzaga

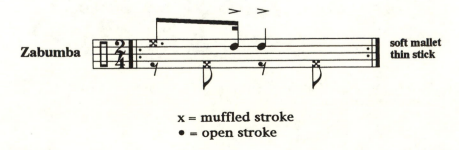

x = muffled stroke
• = open stroke

Ex. 5–7.   Some lyrics from "Baião," by Luiz Gonzaga and Humberto Texeira

Eu vou mostrar pra' vocês	I'm going to show all of you
Como se dança um baião	How to dance a *baião*
E quem quiser aprender	And whoever wants to learn
É favor prestar atenção	Please pay attention

Gonzaga also standardized the core trio format of accordion, *zabumba* drum, and triangle. As Chris McGowan and Ricardo Pessanha have stated, "Gonzaga had created a vivid new dance music, whose accordion/bass drum/triangle instrumentation gave it a rocking, earthy sound, akin to American *zydeco* (1991:136). In 1946 Gonzaga recorded the song "Baião"—thus began the vogue of a musical movement of the same name, which for a while rivaled the *samba* in national popularity. The song, coauthored with Humberto Texeira, invited the public to learn the *baião* (Example 5–7).

Through his popularity, Gonzaga became the primary spokesman for the culture and history of the Northeast at a time in which thousands of migrant workers were leaving the region to work in the industrialized cities of the south. In one of his most popular recordings, "Asa branca" (1947), Gonzaga articulated the migrants' experience and the bittersweet relationship of the *caboclo* population to their beloved Northeast.

The lyrics of "Asa branca" describe the effects of drought on the rugged and arid *sertão* backlands (a major drought besets the area about every ten years). During these periods, thousands of people starve and mass migrations occur. In the song, even the white-winged dove—reputedly the last bird to leave the *sertão* during droughts—abandons the land. But as in the song, a *caboclo* never abandons the Northeast for good, and always dreams of the rains that will allow him to return to his land once again.

"Asa branca" became the de facto hymn of the Northeast, and one of the most popular songs of all time in Brazil. Between 1946 and 1956, Northeastern music was a national fad, led by Gonzaga's string of hits based on the *baião* and other genres.[12]

By the early 1960s a more syncopated rhythm was being developed by *zabumba* drummers, which came to define a new genre called *forró*. The *forró* structure involved a strong dampened stroke just before the second beat of a two-four measure, as well as a variety of offbeat counter-rhythms performed with a thin stick on the underside of the drum. Listen to Recorded Selection 25 again, and you can hear the *forró* pattern.

While the national popularity of Northeastern music—now generically dubbed *forró*—waned in the 1960s, hundreds of *forró* musicians began releasing records on migrant labels that catered to the millions of Northeastern migrants who frequented the commercial *forró* dance clubs of Rio de Janeiro and São Paulo. In the Northeast itself, the June festivals became commercial tourist events rivaling

Ex. 5–8. **Lyrics to "Asa branca" [White wing], by Luiz Gonzaga and Humberto Texeira**

Quando olhei a terra ardendo	When I saw the land burning
Qual fogueira de São João	Like a bonfire on St. John's Day
E perguntei ao Deus do céu ai	And asked God in the heavens above
Por que tamanha judiação?	Oh, why such a cruel torment?
Que braseiro! que fornalha!	What hell-fire, what a furnace!
Nem um pé de plantação	Not even a single planted tree
Por falta dágua perdi meu gado	I lost my cattle for lack of water
Morreu de sede meu alazão	My horse died of thirst
Inté mesmo a asa-branca	Even the white-winged dove
Bateu asas do sertão	Flew away from this backland
Entonces eu disse adeus Rosinha	So I said, farewell Rosy
Guarda contigo meu coração	Keep my heart with you
Hoje longe muitas léguas	Today a long way away
Numa triste solidão	In a sad solitude
Espero a chuva cair de novo	I wait for rain to fall again
Para mim voltar pro meu sertão	So I can go back to my land
Quando o verde dos teus olhos	When the green of your eyes
Se espalhar na plantação	Spreads over this land again
Eu te asseguro, não chora não viu?	I assure you, don't cry, hear?
Que eu voltarei, viu, meu coração	That I will return, my dear

Ex. 5–9. **The *forró* pattern on the *zabumba* and triangle**

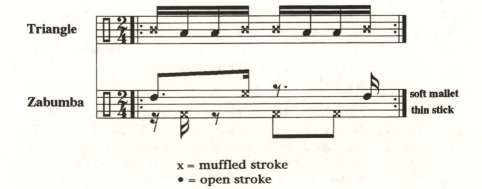

x = muffled stroke
• = open stroke

Carnival and providing substantial employment for professional and semiprofessional *forró* groups.

This brief discussion of the music of the interior region of the Northeast has only scratched the surface of the diversity and richness of the area. We will now turn our attention to the Northeastern coast, where African traditions and influence are the strongest.

BLACK MUSICAL TRADITIONS FROM BAHIA

Brazilians of African descent constitute roughly half the country's population, and African influence is embedded into virtually all aspects of Brazilian society and culture. This influence is particularly pronounced in music, dance, cuisine, and religion. Brazil was the single largest destination of black African slaves in the Americas, and Brazil's slave trade continued well into the nineteenth century. This trade in human lives brought people from highly diverse African groups to Brazil, including Sudanese (Yoruba, Ewe, Fon, Fanti-Ashante), Bantu (Abunda, Cabinda, Benguela), and Islamic (Hausa, Mandinka, Nupe). In 1888 slavery was abolished in Brazil.

While Brazilians of African descent are found throughout the country, the coastal state of Bahia—especially the area in and around the city of Salvador da Bahia—is generally acknowledged as the most "African" part of the country. Salvador da Bahia was the principal port of entry for African slaves into the country, and it is here that the most orthodox varieties of the African-based *candomblé* religion were first practiced (compare with Chapter 1). Throughout its history, Bahia has been at the forefront of social movements centering on issues of black consciousness, civil rights, and racial equality. Our investigation of music from Bahia will focus on two traditions: (1) music of the *candomblé* religion, and (2) music of contemporary Bahian Carnival groups known as *blocos afros* [Afro blocs].

CANDOMBLÉ[13]

Candomblé refers to a wide array of religious groups in Bahia that maintain African beliefs and practices. Likely derived from the Yoruba terms *candombe* and *ile* [house of the dance], *candomblé* also refers to the religion and to the locale where ceremonies take place in which West African deities (*orixás* and *vodouns*) are personified and brought to life through spirit possession of the initiates.

Candomblé is a religion of diverse groups classified according to tribal nations. The most orthodox groups are the Ketu and Ijexá (Yoruba), the Gêge (Fon/Ewe), and the Congo-Angola. More acculturated groups are called *candomblé de caboclo* (referring to mixture with Brazilian Indian practices) and *umbanda* (a highly syncretic, spiritist religion extremely popular throughout Brazil). There are hundreds of *candomblé* houses in Bahia today. How did the more orthodox *candomblé* centers, which maintain primarily the religious belief systems and practices of the Yoruba and Fon peoples of West Africa, get established and then flourish in Bahia?

The dominant role of the West African Yoruba traditions in *candomblé* is often attributed to the historical fact that from about 1700–1850 (the latter half of the slave period in Brazil), most of the slaves came from the Yoruba and Fon areas (Southwest Nigeria and Benin). During slavery, the practice of African religions in Brazil was tolerated to varying degrees as long as it was confined to the slave quarters *(senzalas)* and not practiced in public temples. In Bahia, the earliest *candomblé* center of known origin dates to the 1830s and was founded by three African priestesses. According to Gerard Béhague, "This center was known as Ilê Iyá Nassô [house of the priestess Nassô], the African title of one of them. From this center, of Ketu affiliation, originated the largest and best-known *candomblé* houses in Salvador [da Bahia] during the twentieth century. . . ." (1984:223).

Candomblé was considered offensive to public morality by the civil authorities and condemned as "witchcraft" by the Church. After the abolition of slavery in 1888, the *candomblé* religious community suffered police repression of their houses and brutality towards themselves. Police raids and other forms of social discrimination peaked during the 1920s and 1930s. Nevertheless, *candomblé* persisted and even flourished, as a point of struggle for black cultural identity rooted in African values. During the 1950s, overt repression was replaced by a more subtle form of control in which *candomblé* centers were required to register and obtain permits with the police to perform religious ceremonies. Though *candomblé* centers have attained status as respected institutions in recent times, the legacy of an intolerant past is still quite strong.

Music and dance are essential elements of the ritual practices of the *candomblés*. Indeed, as *candomblé* scholar Gerard Béhague has written, in *candomblé* "music and dance become the main vehicle of religious fulfillment." (1984:223). Adherence to "correct" performance practice and knowledge of important songs are ways that cult leaders establish their authority. Likewise, the lead drummer *(alabê)* must have an extensive knowledge of song repertoires, sequences, and correct drum patterns *(toques)* in order to fulfill the main function of the music—bringing about spirit possession among the initiates during special ceremonies. Let's take a closer look at the drum ensemble used in *candomblé*.

Like most West African–derived drum groups, the *candomblé* ensemble involves a family of drums of different sizes. In the Ketu and Gêge cult houses, three single-headed wooden drums are used—*lê* [small], *rumpi* [medium], and *rum* [large]. Collectively called *atabaque* or *ilu*, these *conga*-like drums are constructed with barrel-coopering techniques using wooden staves. Traditionally, animal skins were tensioned by means of pegs angled into the wooden shells of the drums. Today, metal bolts and lugs are used to pull the skin tightly across the drum.

Musicians play highly repetitive patterns on the small and medium drums while the lead drummer, on the large drum, plays set variations and improvisations. A fourth musician plays fixed *ostinato* (or time-line) patterns on an iron double bell *(agogô)*.[14] Example 5–10 presents typical patterns played on the supporting drums and *agogô* bells.

Ill. 5–9. *Atabaque* **drums—from left to right,** *lê, rumpi, rum.* ***Agogô*** **bells are in front of the middle drum.**

Listen to Recorded Selection 26 on the CD accompanying this book. This piece to the *orixá* Ogum was recorded by Gerard Béhague during a *candomblé* ritual, explained in Chapter 1 and below. For now, focus on the *agogô* bell pattern, a twelve-beat time-line, to keep your place, and then try to hear the other parts of the music as they relate to the bell. Notice that the accompanying drums (*lê* and *rumpi*) synchronize their repetitive *ostinato* pattern together, while the lower-pitched *rum,* played by the *alabê,* performs constantly evolving variations, adding a great deal of rhythmic excitement to this music. Variations on the *rum* become shorter as the piece unfolds. While dancing, the cult initiates pay close attention to the *rum,* as it is this part that controls their choreography and that calls Ogum, the god of iron and a fierce warrior.

The *alabê* is typically the oldest and most knowledgeable initiate among the drummers. Drumming and dancing—and frequently singing as well—are controlled by the *alabê* through the *rum* drum, and dances are organized by various rhythmic sequences led by the *alabê.* The religious significance of the drums is further revealed in the fact that the instruments must undergo an initiation ritual of "baptism" and annual "feeding" rituals to insure the strength of their spiritual force *(axé).* In addition, the drums themselves are thought to possess individual "voices" irresistible to the *orixás* [gods].

Ex. 5–10.   (a) Rhythmic scheme for Ogum drum pattern, used in *candomblé*, (b) Rhythmic scheme for *ijexá* drum pattern, used in *candomblé*

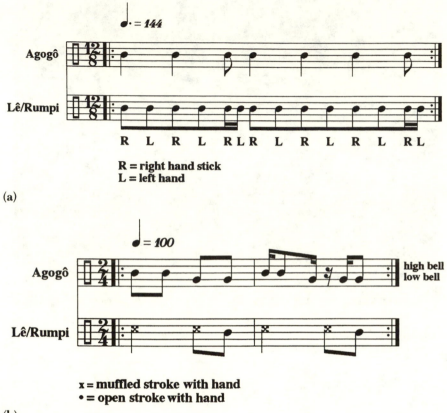

Candomblé drumming is present during both private and public ceremonies. All members of the cult are required to fulfill their obligations to the *orixás* during such ceremonies, but initiates who have undergone extensive training and have had a specific *orixá* "placed in their head" must fulfill weekly, monthly, and yearly obligations to their individual *orixá*. Private ceremonies are limited to the principal members of the cult, while public ceremonies are open to members of other *candomblé* houses, friends, and the general public, including tourists. During the public ceremonies, the initiates dress in their finest attire, representing individual *orixás*. The most common public ceremony is known as a *xiré*, which serves to conclude a series of festive events.

The *xiré*[15] ceremony takes place at night in the main room of the *candomblé* center with the drums placed in a prominent location and decorated with cloth. The priest of the *candomblé* is seated in a large armchair with dignitaries of the cult seated at both sides. Guests and other outsiders are seated on benches around the edges of the room. The ceremony starts with the entrance of the initiates to a special drum rhythm known as *avaninha,* followed by a sequence of three to seven songs to the *orixá* Exú (god of the crossroads), performed to ensure an uninterrupted ceremony.[16] After this, the *xiré* is divided into two parts: the first is a "call to the gods" and the second is the "presence of the gods." The purpose of the first part is to call the *orixás* down to the ceremony to possess the initiates. Three to seven songs accompanied by appropriate drumming patterns are typically performed for each *orixá.* Initiates dance and sing all of the songs and become possessed by their individual *orixá.* This portion of the ceremony lasts from two to three hours. If initiates have difficulty attaining a state of possession, a special drum rhythm known as *adarrum* may be performed, which calls all of the *orixás* down at once.

Before the beginning of the second part of the ceremony, each of the possessed initiates backs out of the large area and goes to a special room in the cult center to be dressed in the ritual attire of his or her *orixá.* The second part of the *xiré* begins with the song "Agolonã," accompanied by a drum rhythm known as *batá.* This song signals the solemn entrance of the *orixás* into the dance area, symbolized by the possessed initiates' new garb. Specific rhythms and three to seven songs are performed for each *orixá* as they dance, stressing individual choreography. Each one of the gods is allowed to dance and display his or her skill, and may go around the room and single out individuals, via embrace, for special honor. After this is completed, the *orixás* are led out of the room to the same *avaninha* rhythm that began the ceremony.

The music of the *candomblé,* especially the drumming, serves not only as a crucial element of the *candomblé* rituals themselves, but is also important symbolically as a cultural focus of African values. In the past, police restrictions on holding *candomblé* ceremonies were often justified through citing the loud "noise" that the drums made. Júlio Braga has noted that in the 1950s a license to *bater candomblé* [to beat *candomblé,* to beat a drum] was required in order for a *candomblé* house to perform its religious ceremonies. From within the religious community and within the Afro-Bahian community in general, *candomblé* drumming was a powerful expression of African heritage and values. The drumming also influenced the development of secular forms of music-making in Bahia.

RACE RELATIONS AND CONTEMPORARY AFRO-BAHIAN MUSIC

The officially projected national image of Brazil as a multicultural paradise and a racially nonconflictual society has been challenged on numerous fronts during the last few decades. In response to the dire social, economic, political, and cultural situation of Brazil's black population, a black consciousness movement of unprecedented proportions began to form in the early 1970s. As part of this process, musical activities of black youth have become directly linked to the questions of race, racial identity, and racial politics in Brazil.

Within Brazil's black movement, a dispute developed between activists engaged in explicitly political activity and others, often labeled "culturalists," who focused on redefining black identity through the valorization of selected cultural practices linked to Brazil's African heritage. Activists in the movement, as well as many foreign social analysts, believe that the excessive valorization of African-Brazilian cultural practices will impede the formation of an effective black national political organization (Hanchart 1994). They stress that Brazil's African-related cultural traditions have been overly romanticized and "folklorized" by the dominant white society, and have been used to construct an image of a "frozen" Africa safely distanced in time and space from the contemporary realities of blacks in Brazil.

This reasoning is not without merit. However, it represents only a partial truth of a much more complex and nuanced situation. In fact, many of the same cultural practices that were "folklorized" also served as mechanisms of resistance and potent resources with which blacks could construct their own identities within Brazil (e.g., *candomblé*). African-Brazilian cultural practices have persisted and evolved in spite of—perhaps in many cases because of—the long history of political and social repression to which they were subjected. These cultural practices are inseparable from broader political and social processes, and have been important components in the development of black consciousness and political organization in Brazil (Crook and Johnson, forthcoming 1999). Music has played an extremely important role in this process.

In contemporary Brazil, many black youth engage in leisure activities that seem to fly in the face of Brazil's media-supported image of a harmonious multicultural paradise. In the slums of Rio de Janeiro and São Paulo, black youth have largely rejected traditional African-Brazilian forms such as *samba*, which they perceive as having been corrupted by white cultural dominance, and have turned to the musical practices of their North American counterparts for inspiration. The Black Soul and Funk phenomenon centered in Rio de Janeiro, as well as the emergence of Brazilian rap in São Paulo and Brasília, are—to paraphrase an article from *Veja e Leia,* Brazil's leading national news magazine—mobilizing the hearts and minds of youth from the slums. These "angry" cultural expressions, as they have been called in Brazil, are easy targets of the Brazilian media, who attack them in a knee-jerk fashion as products of United States cultural imperialism and as components of the culture of urban violence. Meanwhile in Bahia, twenty-five years of sustained activity among the city's black Carnival groups have created new eclectic Afrocentric musical performance styles and have spawned a new style of nationally and internationally marketed popular music known as *axé,* which is closely linked with Bahia's African roots.[17] Although it is an eclectic style drawing freely on foreign sources (mainly African and African-Caribbean), it lays claim to a Brazilian pedigree in a way that Brazilian rap and funk do not. The black Carnival groups known as *blocos afros* have aesthetically underlined the importance of race through the revitalization and transformation of African-Bahian musical forms and the selective adoption of foreign sources. It is to this music that we now turn our attention.

The Bahian Carnival

For over one hundred years Bahia's Carnival, a yearly celebration occurring just prior to Lent in the Roman Catholic calendar, has been a public stage for both the expression and repression of the region's rich African heritage. (See also Gage Averill's discussion of Trinidadian Carnival in Chapter 4.) Soon after the abolition of slavery in 1888, Bahia's Carnival celebration witnessed the flourishing of black cultural associations known as *afoxés*, which took to the streets singing, dancing, and drumming. The *afoxés* or African Nations, as they were known, were closely tied to the *candomblé* houses of the city. During the early part of the twentieth century, *candomblé* houses were periodically invaded by the police; sacred musical instruments were gathered and taken to police headquarters, where they were impounded alongside guns and knives that had been used to commit crimes. The *afoxés* were also subject to various forms of discrimination, but persisted as an African-Bahian component to Bahia's Carnival.

By the 1960s, the streets of Salvador da Bahia during Carnival were ruled by electric guitar trios playing atop high-tech sound trucks. These *trios elétricos* catered primarily to the Carnival groups of middle-class youth, and many of these associations denied participation to blacks. Bahia's majority black population, especially its youth, needed contemporary expressions of their black identity during Carnival.

In the 1970s and 1980s, the formative period for Brazil's black movement, Bahia's Carnival celebrations underwent a process of Africanization (Risério 1981). The long-standing *afoxé* was revitalized, as popular musicians like Gilberto Gil actively participated and dozens of new *afoxés* were formed. The *ijexá* rhythm, derived from *candomblé* repertoire, was played by the *afoxé* groups as they marched in the streets. This rhythm was quickly adapted by middle-class-oriented *trios elétricos* and other popular music groups in Bahia.

In addition to the revitalization of the *afoxé* tradition and the incorporation of the *ijexá* rhythm into Bahia's popular music, Bahia's Carnival also witnessed the creation of a completely new type of black Carnival association known as *bloco afro* [Afro bloc] during the 1970s. African heritage and contemporary black identity were publicly celebrated by these large Carnival organizations from Salvador's predominantly poor black neighborhoods. At first, the *blocos afros* modeled their music on Rio-style *samba* drumming and vocals, and their songs reinforced a separatist ideology of black pride and a Yoruba-based Nagô-centrism.

Ilê Aiyê was the first *bloco afro,* emerging from the largest black section of the city, Liberdade. The name *Ilê Aiyê* is derived from Yoruba and means "house of life." The group was formed with an exclusively black membership and had the purpose of glorifying the values of the black race. Ilê Aiyê is credited by many black activists throughout Brazil as being the initial expression of a new black consciousness movement in Brazil.

Ilê Aiyê's songs spoke of black pride and focused on their members' identity as blacks, not as Brazilians. The lyrics of the song Ilê Aiyê sang in the Carnival of 1975, "O que bloco é esse" [What group is that?], are indicative of their black pride message.

Ex. 5–11.   Some of the lyrics to "O que bloco é esse," by Paulinho Camafeu

We're crazy blacks
We're really all right
We have kinky hair
We are black power.

White man, if you only knew
The value that the black man has
You would take a bath of tar
So black you would be too.

Ilê Aiyê quickly became an important vehicle for expressing black pride during Bahian Carnival. The public displays of black pride and the exclusive membership policy were attacked through the media as racist (Crook 1993). Denying racist intent, the leaders of Ilê Aiyê maintain that they were only trying to demonstrate that African-Brazilian heritage was beautiful, and that African values were important.[18]

Ill. 5–10. Front cover of Ilê Aiyê's album *Canto Negro*. Cover art by J. Cunha.

Expressing the "art and beauty" of blacks during Carnival time involved the creation of an Afrocentric aesthetic movement involving dance, music, poetry, visual designs, costuming, and poetics, around a variety of African and African-diasporic themes. Ilê Aiyê's music was influenced by the Rio-style Carnival *samba* school and featured drums, percussion, and vocals. By the early 1980s a more distinctive *bloco afro samba* was emerging in Bahia, featuring a slowed-down tempo, an emphasis on the low drums of the groups, call-and-response vocal organization, and lyrics dealing with African and African-Brazilian subject matter. The basic texture of drums and vocals, without any supporting harmonic or melodic instruments, distinguished the *bloco afro* sound from the sound of *trios elétricos* and other commercialized popular music genres of the time. Additionally, the greater emphasis given to the low drums of the group (typically, half of the drums were *surdos*) related directly to West African drum ensemble principles, where low drums are used to lead. Another important component of the *bloco afro* sound emerged when Jamaican *reggae* and its pan-African message were absorbed into the context of Bahian life by young blacks in Salvador da Bahia.

In addition to Ilê Aiyê, by 1983 there were fifteen other *blocos afros* parading officially in the Bahian Carnival. Ilê Aiyê was the first *bloco afro,* but it was a new group, named Olodum, that internationalized the music.

Olodum was founded in 1979 by ex-members of Ilê Aiyê. They took the name Olodum from the Yoruba deity Olodumaré, and they first marched in the 1980 Carnival. From the outset, a sociopolitical agenda of black consciousness, antiracism, and economic enfranchisement was embedded in Olodum's music. The band formed only one part of an elaborate organizational structure devoted to fighting racism and to promoting social and economic justice in Brazil and throughout the world. According to João Jorge Santos Rodriguez, former president of the Olodum Cultural Association, they followed an ideological path that had two primary influences: (1) the American black movement—the Black Panthers, the nonviolence of Martin Luther King, Jr., and the verbal violence of Malcolm X; and (2) an extremely diversified African heritage (Santos Rodriguez, personal communication with author). Through their songs they told of the history and contemporary situation of blacks in Brazil, in Africa, and in the diaspora. As an organization, they worked at the community level to educate and empower the black community. In the mid-1980s they began publishing a biweekly journal that grew to a circulation of five thousand, and they sponsored seminars, lectures, and numerous public events in Salvador.

But it was a new musical style that first catapulted them to prominence. The new style developed by Olodum's musicians involved interlocking rhythms played on large bass drums, while high-pitched *repique* drums articulated additive rhythms. This served as the basic foundation over which vocal parts in call-and-response texture and melodies featuring syncopated offbeat phrasing were added.

The head of Olodum's percussion, Neguinho do Samba, began mixing the *bloco afro samba* beat with *salsa, merengue, reggae,* and other rhythms. Olodum first brought out the results of these experiments during rehearsals for the 1986 Carnival.

Ill. 5–11. Olodum's first head of percussion, Neguinho do Samba.

Two new drumming patterns emerged from this experimentation, which eventually came to be called *samba reggae.* Both patterns involved the division of the low *surdo* drums into four distinct and interlocking parts, while the high-pitched *repiques* and snare drums filled out the rhythm. The first rhythm was patterned on the loose feel of *reggae* and performed primarily at a slow tempo.

The second rhythm, known as *merengue,* was built around an additive pattern of 3 + 3 + 4 + 3 + 3 played on the *repiques,* a pattern reminiscent of the *clave* and other rhythms found in a variety of African-Caribbean musics.

Olodum's drummers made other innovations as well—they replaced the thick wooden sticks traditionally used on the high-pitched *repiques* with thin flexible switches, giving the drums a sharper attack. Additionally, a set of three *timbales*

Ex. 5–12.   Bahian *bloco afro reggae* rhythm

(drawn from *salsa*) was added to elaborate the basic pattern and to give cues to the other drummers. These innovations further distinguished Olodum's sound from that of the other *blocos afros*. By drawing on African-Caribbean and African-Brazilian styles, the new drumming patterns made aesthetic links between Bahian and other black diasporic communities of the Caribbean.

The *samba-reggae* style of Olodum became a major force in Bahia's Carnival during the late 1980s and propelled Bahia's dynamic participatory Carnaval cele-

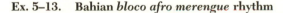

Ex. 5–13.   Bahian *bloco afro merengue* rhythm

Ex. 5–14.   Some of the lyrics to "Faraó, divinidade do Egito"

Tutancâmon, Akahenaton . . .	Tutankhamen, Akahenaton . . .
Pelourinho, uma pequena comunidade	Pelourinho, a small community
Que porém, Olodum unira	Which Olodum unites
Em laços de confraternidade	In the bonds of fraternity
Despertai-vos para a cultura egíptico no Brasil	Awaken us to Egyptian culture in Brazil
Em vez de cabelos trançados	Instead of braided hair
Veremos turbantes de Tutancamon	We'll see the turbans of Tutankhamen
E, nas cabeças, enchem-se de liberdade	And our heads will be filled with freedom
O povo negro pede igualdade	The black community asks for equality
Deixando de lado as separações	Leaving behind the separations

bration to new heights, as national media coverage, both print and broadcast, increased dramatically. While Rio's Carnival dominates national media coverage, Bahia's celebration has gained increasing attention since the late 1980s. What the country witnessed on TV were thousands of people moving to the heavy beat of the *samba reggae.*

In 1987, Olodum's new style of *samba reggae* drumming and the year's controversial Carnival thematic rubric, "Egypt of the Pharaohs," were the undisputed successes of the Bahian Carnival. One of the major songs of the 1987 Carnival was Olodum's "Faraó, divinidade do Egito" [Pharaoh, divinity of Egypt], written by Luciano Gomes dos Santos. This song asks for the empowering of Bahian blacks through an Egyptian-like awakening in Pelourinho, the historic center of Salvador da Bahia, and the home of Olodum.

In the early 1990s, Olodum gained international exposure via their work with Paul Simon (*Rhythm of the Saints*) and soon linked the new Bahian sound to the "world beat" music scene. They toured Europe and the United States and were later featured on the CD *Bahia black: Ritual beating system.* When Michael Jackson and Spike Lee came to Brazil in 1996 to record the video "They Don't Really Care About Us," they came to Bahia and used the drummers from Olodum, led by Neguinho do Samba.

The impacts of Olodum's success and of the *bloco afro* movement are now seen throughout Brazil. Dozens of *blocos afros* have formed in the poor neighborhoods of cities like Recife, São Paulo, and Rio de Janeiro as alternatives to gang life and other marginal activities so chronic among Brazil's street youth. Olodum and other *bloco afro* organizations have also helped spawn the new Bahian music known as *axé.* Within Brazil's national music industry, *axé* music represents black Bahia, that most African of Brazilian cities. On the international scene, it is Brazil's entrée into World Music.

With its elaborate organizational structure, Olodum has been successful not only in controlling its own interests in the marketplace, but also in continually reinforcing the link of this music to the politics of black identity in Brazil and in the diaspora. The Olodum organization produces Olodum's musical shows at home and abroad as well as its records and CDs. Olodum also operates its own boutique, with products such as hats, T-shirts, and key chains, as well as a music bar, a factory where drums and Carnival costumes are produced, and a graphics department. The organization has more than 350 employees. According to João Jorge Santos Rodriguez, Olodum's former president, these activities relate to the group's belief that the "struggle for culture must bring wealth to the community" (Santos Rodriguez, personal communication with author). Because they have extended their organization beyond purely educational and cultural activities to include business activities as well, they yield considerable power in Salvador da Bahia today.

Olodum's seventh album, titled *Olodum o Movimento* [Olodum the movement], was launched at an extremely well-orchestrated and media-savvy "release party." The event took place on November 20, 1993, three months before Carnival. November is the month chosen by Brazil's black movement as Black Consciousness Month. November 20 marks the day in which Zumbi, the legendary black resistance leader of a seventeenth-century fugitive slave society, was killed by a colonial military unit. At the release party, black political leaders, activists, and entertainment luminaries lauded Olodum for its music and for its commitment to social issues. The event was staged as a free concert in the Praça Castro Alves in downtown Salvador da Bahia, and some fifteen thousand people attended. The event was covered on the national television news hour, and newspapers from all over Brazil printed stories the next day. On the inside cover of Olodum's recording *A Música do Olodum,* the following dedication appears:

> In the name of God the merciful we dedicate this record to the people of Maciel-Pelourinho, to the fight against racism, to the fight for world peace, to the maestro Neguinho do Samba, to the performers, composers, and counselors of Olodum, to the directors and members of Olodum, and to the fantastic musicians of the Olodum Band. Long life to the positive ideas of social justice and equality contained in the dreams of Malcolm X for the black people of the Americas and of the world . . . (Santos Rodriguez)

Here, the local realities of Salvador's black community are linked to a diasporic and global black consciousness. The music contained on the grooves of the record also makes these links in an aesthetic way by fusing African-Brazilian, Caribbean, North American, and African sources. Precisely because *samba reggae* and *axé* music are strongly linked to local African-Bahian traditions, but also to the larger world of the diaspora, they have been extremely efficient in articulating a transcultural, pan-African perspective relevant to Brazil's black population.

In this chapter we have touched on just a few of the musics that make up one region of Brazil. Brazil's musical landscape, like the country itself, is vast and complex. As Brazil finds its way into the twenty-first century, its music will undoubtedly be a major way in which its various peoples convey themselves to each other and to the world.

REFERENCES

Angelo, Assis. 1990. *Eu vou contar pra vocês*. São Paulo, Brazil: Icone.

Bahia black: Ritual beating system. 1992. Audio CD. Axiom/Island Records (U.S.) 314–510856–2.

Béhague, Gerard. 1977. *Afro-Brazilian religious songs. Cantigas de candomblé/candomblé songs*. Lyrichord Discs LLST 7315.

———. 1984. Patterns of *candomblé* music performance: An Afro-Brazilian religious setting. In *Performance practice: ethnomusicological perspectives*, ed. G. Béhague, pp. 222–254. Westport, Conn.: Greenwood Press.

Braga, Júlio. Forthcoming, 1999. Candomblê in Bahia: repression and resistance. In *Black Brazil: Culture, identity, and social mobilization*, ed. Larry Crook and Randall Johnson. Los Angeles: Univ. of California at Los Angeles Center for Latin American Studies.

Crook, Larry. 1991. *Zabumba* music from Caruaru, Pernambuco: Musical style, gender, and the interpenetration of rural and urban worlds. Ph.D. diss., Univ. of Texas.

———. 1993. "Black Consciousness, *samba reggae*, and the re-Africanization of Bahian Carnival music in Brazil." *The World of Music* 35(2):90–108.

Crook, Larry, and Randall Johnson. Forthcoming, 1999. Introduction to *Black Brazil: Culture, identity, and social mobilization*, ed. Larry Crook and Randall Johnson. Los Angeles: Univ. of California at Los Angeles Center for Latin American Studies.

Crook, Larry and Charles A. Perrone. 1997. *Folk and popular music of Brazil*. Series II of The Brazilian curriculum guide specialized bibliography. Albuquerque: Latin American Institute/Univ. of New Mexico.

Duarte, Abelardo. 1974. *Folclore negro das Alagoas: Pesquisa e interpretação*. Maceió, Brazil: Departamento de Assuntos Culturais/SENEC.

Gonzaga, Luiz. 1989. *O melhor de Luiz Gonzaga*. Audio CD. RCA CDM 1003.

Hanchart, Michael George. 1994. *Orpheus and power: The movimento negro of Rio de Janeiro and São Paulo, Brazil, 1945–1988*. Princeton: Princeton Univ. Press.

Locke, David. 1996. Africa/Ewe, Mande, Dagbamba, Shona, BaAka. In *Worlds of music: An introduction to the music of the world's peoples*, 3d ed., edited by Jeff Todd Titon, pp. 71–143. New York: Schirmer Books.

McGowan, Chris and Ricardo Pessanha. 1991. *The Brazilian sound: samba, bossa nova and the popular music of Brazil*. New York: Billboard Books.

Meagher, Paul Kevin. 1967. Novena. In *New Catholic Encyclopedia*, edited by the editorial staff at Catholic Univ. of America, vol. 10, pp. 543–544. New York: McGraw Hill.

O eterno rei do baião (unsigned article). 1972. *Veja e Leia* 184 (March 15):80–82.

Risério, Antônio. 1981. *Carnival Ijexá: Notas sobre afoxés e blocos do novo carnaval afrobaiano*. Salvador da Bahia, Brazil: Corrupio.

Santos, João Alfredo dos. 1988. Interview by author. Caruaru, Pernambuco, Brazil, May 13.

Santos Rodriguez, João Jorge. Personal communications with author, n.d.

Santos Rodriguez, João Jorge. Liner notes to the recording *A Música do Olodum,* by Banda Reggae Olodum, Continental/Warner Music (Brazil) 1–07.800.515, n.d.

Tinhorão, José Ramos. 1986. *Pequena história da música popular: Da modinha ao tropicalismo.* 5th ed., revised and enlarged. São Paulo, Brazil: Art Editora.

Venácio, João. 1988. Interview by author. Caruaru, Pernambuco, Brazil, Jan. 14.

Waddey, Ralph C. 1980. Viola de Samba and Samba de Viola in the Recôncavo of Bahia (Brazil). [Part 1]. *Latin American Music Review* 1(2): 196–212.

ADDITIONAL READING

Browning, Barbara. 1995. *Samba: Resistance in motion.* Bloomington: Indiana Univ. Press.

Carvalho, José Jorge de. 1984. Music of African origin in Brazil. In *Africa in Latin America,* ed. Manuel Moreno Fraginals, pp. 227–248.

———. 1994. Black music of all colors: The construction of black ethnicity in ritual and popular genres of Afro-Brazilian music. In *Music and black ethnicity: The Caribbean and South America,* ed. Gerard Béhague, pp. 187–206. New Brunswick, N.J.: Transaction Publishers.

Carvalho, José Jorge de, and Rita Segato. 1992. *Shango cult in Recife, Brazil.* Caracas, Venezuela: Fundación de Etnomusicología y Folklore.

Lewis, Lowell J. 1992. *Ring of liberation: Deceptive discourse in Brazilian capoeira.* Chicago: Univ. of Chicago Press.

Murphy, John. 1997. The rabeca and its music, old and new, in Pernambuco, Brazil. *Latin American Music Review* 18(2):147–172.

Olsen, Dale A. and Daniel E. Sheehy, eds. 1998. *South America, Mexico, Central America, and the Caribbean.* Vol. 2 of *The Garland encyclopedia of world music.* New York: Garland Reference Library of the Humanities, vol. 1193.

Perrone, Charles A. 1985. *Masters of contemporary Brazilian song: MPB 1965–1985.* Austin: Univ. of Texas Press.

Reily, Suzel Ana. 1992. *Música Sertaneja* and migrant identity: The stylistic development of a Brazilian genre. *Popular Music* 11(3):337–358.

———. 1996. Tom Jobim and the Bossa Nova Era. *Popular Music* 15(1):1–17.

ADDITIONAL LISTENING

Banda de Pífanos de Caruaru. *A Bandinha Vai Tocar.* Discos Marcos Pereira 10097, n.d.

Brazil Classics CD series, edited by David Byrne published by Luaka Bop/Warner: *Beleza Tropical,* 1988, 9 25805–2; *Samba,* 1989, 9 26019; and *Forró Etc.,* 1991, 9 26323–2.

Ilê Aiyê. 1992. *Canto negro.* Eldorado 167890577.

Olodum. 1990. *The best of Olodum.* Continental 1–07–800–499.

Timbalada. 1993. *Timbalada.* Polygram 518 068–2.

Pé de Serra Forró Band. 1992. *Dance music from the countryside.* Germany: Haus der Kulturen der Welt SM 1509–2.

Brazil forró music for maids and taxi drivers. 1989. Rounder Records 5044.

The discoteca collection: Missão de pesquisas folclóricas. 1997. Library of Congress Endangered Music Project, Ryko 10403.

ADDITIONAL VIEWING

Forró no original. 1991. Produced by Igor Paulista. Recife, Brazil.

Bahía: Africa in the Americas. 1988. Directed by Geovanni and Michale Brewer. 58 min. Univ. of California Extension Media Center, 2176 Shattuck Ave., Berkeley, Calif. 94704.

The spirit of samba: Black music of Brazil, 1981. Directed by Jeremy Marre. Beats of the Heart series, part 7.

ENDNOTES

1. Other common names used to designate the fife-and-drum ensemble grouping include *banda cabaçal, terno de Zabumba,* and *esquenta mulher.*

2. The term *zabumba* designates both the bass drum and the entire fife-and-drum ensemble. In Portuguese, when referring to the drum itself, the term takes the masculine article "o" (*o zabumba*); the feminine "a" is used to refer to the ensemble (*a zabumba*). For clarity in this chapter, when the term is capitalized (*Zabumba*) it will refer to the ensemble and when in lower case (*zabumba*) it will refer to the drum. The *zambomba* is a friction-drum used in Spain, Ecuador, and Guatemala. The *zambumba* is a snare drum used in El Salvador. The *zambumbia* is a Guatemalan/Honduran musical bow.

3. Abelardo Duarte (1974:122) asserts that when the sugar cane industry controlled by the Portuguese was abandoned on the island of São Tomé in the late sixteenth century, many white and black colonists came to Northeast Brazil and probably brought the *Zabumba* with them.

4. According to Meagher (1967), the nine-day devotional *novena* was originally associated with the period leading up to the feast of Christmas. It later came to precede the feasts of numerous popular saints and especially the feast of the Virgin Mary. While there was nothing specifically objectionable about *novenas* in official Roman Catholic doctrine, they have long been attacked by Church leaders because of the many miracles and superstitions attributed to them. It was not until the nineteenth century that the Church legitimized official *novenas* by the granting of indulgences.

5. I was told that a *rezadeira* may also receive monetary compensation, but I never witnessed this firsthand. The *rezadeira* and *turma* are generally provided transportation, fed, and treated as special participants at the *novena.*

6. I witnessed many variations on this basic choreography.

7. Quite often it is the leader of the *turma de mulheres* who takes these responsibilities.

8. This material is drawn largely from Crook 1991.

9. Luiz Gonzaga was a popular music luminary from Pernambuco who popularized Northeastern music throughout Brazil in the 1940s and 1950s. However, the song "Mulher rendeira" was not popularized by Gonzaga, but by another musician, Zé do Norte, in the 1953 film *O cangaceiro* (Tinhorão 1986:226).

10. According to João's father Alfredo, during the 1930s he and his neighbor used wooden flutes manufactured in France.

11. *Taquara* and *taboca* are alternative names for a type of cane preferred for the manufacture of *pífanos.*

12. This and other Gonzaga songs have been reissued on the CD *O melhor de Luiz Gonzaga,* 1989.

13. Information for the section on *candomblé* relies substantially on the published research of Gerard Béhague, as well as on my own personal work with *candomblé* drummers in Bahia.

14. Many of the patterns are quite similar to some of the patterns played on the Ewe drums from Southeast Ghana. See, for instance, Locke 1996:89.

15. For a more detailed account of a *xiré* ceremony see Béhague 1984, from which the information presented here is taken. For a recording of the musical accompaniment of a *xiré* see Béhague 1977.

16. See Chapter 4, n. 11 on Legba, Exu's counterpart in Haitian Vodoun.

17. *Axé* is a Yoruba term and complex concept for essence of spiritual power and life force. Its use references a host of African aesthetics that permeate Bahia's daily life.

18. In 1995, when I interviewed Antônio Carlos dos Santos Vovô, the leader and original founder of Ilê Aiyê, this point was emphasized.

CHAPTER SIX

Music in the Southern Cone

Chile, Argentina, and Uruguay

ERCILIA MORENO CHÁ

SOCIAL, CULTURAL, AND HISTORICAL BACKGROUND

This chapter addresses selected musics of the *cono sur* [southern cone] of South America, comprising Chile, Argentina, and Uruguay. Together, these countries occupy the bottom of this roughly cone-shaped continent.

CHILE

Of a vast variety of indigenous peoples who populated the Chilean territory prior to the arrival of the Spanish, many are now extinct. Only the Mapuche have maintained a distinct cultural presence within the society at large (see Chapter 1). The Spanish conquest of the Chilean region began in 1537; it was confirmed with the founding of the first city, Santiago, in 1541 (the capital today), and it concluded with Chile's independence in 1818. During the colonial period, Chile belonged to the Viceroyalty of Peru. This extensive political-administrative unit, seated in Lima, was practically Chile's only contact with the outside world, given its situation of geographic isolation by land and sea.

Between 1830 and 1861, Chile acquired political organization, great economic prosperity, and a high level of intellectual activity.

In the first years of the twentieth century, the bourgeois and proletarian sectors began to appear in the political panorama, emerging from mining activity, large public works projects, industry, and commerce.

From the sixteenth to the eighteenth century the population flow proceeded from Spain, such that Chile now has a *mestizo* population of such ethnic homogeneity that it accounts for almost ninety percent of the total. Germans began arriving in the middle of the nineteenth century, and during the twentieth century there have been minor immigrations from other European countries and the Near East. Since the colonial period, the Roman Catholic Church has remained firmly rooted at all sociocultural levels. Within the rural population today, notable demonstrations of popular religion appear throughout Chile.

ARGENTINA

Indigenous peoples were numerous when the Spaniards arrived in Argentina, but today they compose only about one and a half percent of the country's population. Although the territory was sighted by the *conquistadores* when they discovered the Río [river] de la Plata in 1516, only in 1553 could the first stable settlement be established with the founding of Santiago del Estero, the current capital of the province bearing the same name.

During the colonial period and until the end of the eighteenth century, all of the territory that is currently Argentina pertained to the Viceroyalty of Peru until, in 1776, the Viceroyalty of the Río de la Plata was founded. Its capital was Buenos Aires, and it also included what is now the Argentinian territory of Cuyo, Uruguay, southern Bolivia, and Paraguay. Independence from Spain came in 1810.

Lengthy internal struggles provoked by the supremacy claimed by Buenos Aires over the rest of the territory, and the efforts of the separatists in some regions, led to the emergence of three nations—Paraguay (1814), Bolivia (1825), and Uruguay (1828). By 1820, the economy had developed considerably, based principally on cattle-raising and mining. In 1880, major developments in agriculture would begin and persist to the present day.

An unpopulated territory and a growing need for manual labor provoked a vigorous programmed immigration toward Argentina that began in the mid-nineteenth century and continued with intensity until 1939. The greatest percentages derived from Italy and Spain, with a notably smaller proportion of immigrants from France, Poland, Russia, Germany, and Lebanon. Thus, the population is eighty-five percent European and approximately thirteen and a half percent *mestizo.*

At the beginning of the twentieth century, an urban and rural middle class emerged in the national political panorama, and significant industrial development changed the appearance of the social and cultural panorama.

Recently, numerous workers have been incorporated into the population from neighboring countries and from South Korea.

URUGUAY

The territory that is now Uruguay was first sighted by the Spanish when the Río de la Plata was explored in 1516. Nothing has remained of its indigenous population, which was considered extinct by the first decades of the nineteenth century. These lands were coveted by both the Portuguese, who were installed in Brazil, and the Spanish, who occupied the west banks of the Río Uruguay and the Río de la Plata, in what is now Argentina. The latter displaced the former with the establishment of Montevideo in 1726, and later the systematic populating of the so-called República Oriental [eastern republic] del Uruguay began, famous at the time for its numerous wild cattle.

The transportation of African slaves to the port of Montevideo was significant from the middle of the eighteenth century until 1810. The abolition of slavery was a slow process lasting from 1825 until 1851. Currently, the *mulatto* and black population of Uruguay is estimated at six percent of the total. In 1816, the first efforts at gaining autonomy began, and in 1828 the "Orientals" were recognized as independent by both Brazil and Argentina. Immediately thereafter, intense immigration from Italy and France greatly stimulated agricultural and ranching activity along the coasts of Uruguay's most important rivers. Today, the European population accounts for eighty-six percent of the total, while the *mestizo* population is approximately eight percent of the total.

During the three first decades of the twentieth century, administrative, political, and cultural bases were established in a country whose economy is based predominantly on cattle-raising and agriculture.

In contrast to Chile and Argentina, the Catholic presence on the popular level is quite weak in Uruguay. However, since 1950 an increasing penetration by African-Brazilian religions, mixed with Catholicism and Spiritualism, has been apparent, particularly along the border with Brazil and in Montevideo.

SUMMARY OF MUSICAL TRADITIONS

While the musical traditions in the Southern Cone present notable differences according to the various subregions, there are two repertoires that extend over the entire region, with great homogeneity in terms of their tonal and rhythmic system as well as the structure of their unaccompanied vocals. These are (1) the world of children's music, and (2) the various demonstrations of popular Catholicism. The latter is almost extinct in Uruguay. Outside of these two repertoires, we will consider a variety of musical traditions that are prevalent today, treating them in accordance with studies of areas already in existence in each country. In the case of Argentina and Chile, we have included references to musical phenomena that seem most outstanding in each area.

For Chile, Manuel Dannemann (1969) has proposed the demarcation of nine music-cultural areas:

I. The Andean area, and II. The Atacameña-Hispanic area. These pertain to a broader cultural zone, shared with contiguous regions of Argentina, Bolivia, and Peru. Vocal as well as instrumental tritonic and pentatonic expressions subsist to accompany pre-Columbian agrarian rituals. The presence of Catholic religious sanctuaries, such as La Tirana (Tarapacá), promotes the existence of numerous brotherhoods, with ritual collective dances expressing devotion to the Virgin Mary (Moreno Chá 1992).

III. The Diaguita-Picunche-Hispanic area. Music of a religious nature has its greatest expression in relation to the sanctuary of the Virgin of Andacollo (Coquimbo). Music of a recreational nature is associated with national and family

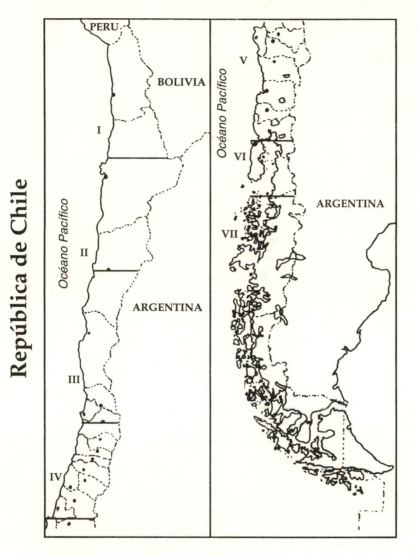

REFERENCIAS
I- Area Andina: Tarapacá - Antofagasta.
II- Area Atacameña-Hispana: Antofagasta - Atacama
III- Area Diaguita-Picunche-Hispana: Atacama - Coquimbo - Aconcagua -
Valparaíso - Santiago.
IV- Area Picunche-Hispana: Santiago - O'Higgins - Colchagua - Curicó -
Talca - Maule Linares - Ñuble - Concepción.
V- Area Mapuche-Huilliche-Hispana: Arauco - Biobio - Malleco - Cautín -
Valdivia - Osorno Llanquihue.
VI- Area Chilota: Chiloé.

Fig. 6–1. Chile's music-cultural areas

celebrations, with songs such as the *tonada,* and picaresque dances for noninterlocking couples, such as the *cueca.*

IV. The Picunche-Hispanic area. Commonly denominated the Central Region, this is the area of greatest agricultural and cattle-raising activity and with the highest demographic density. It is from this environment that the *huaso* has emerged—the rural worker and horseback rider whose image defines a virtual human type that has become a national symbol. Recreational music is especially relevant in the celebration of equestrian skills and the competition called *rodeo,* which is the most typical of the region.

V. The Mapuche-Huilliche-Hispanic area. This is the area in which the Mapuche population has managed to maintain its community and to continue numerous traditional musical manifestations. The *mestizo* population has retained dances for noninterlocking couples, such as the *sajuriana,* the *refalosa* (both of decreasing frequency), the *cueca,* and the more modern dances for interlocking couples, such as the waltz and the *corrido.*

VI. The Chilota area. This region covers the province of Chiloé which, having been the last Hispanic bastion on the continent, and due to its insular character, has remained a redoubt of both *huilliche* and Hispanic traditions. Relative to the latter, there persist popular Renaissance dances originating from central Spain, such as the *seguidilla,* and ancient Catholic religious canticles and *romances,* indicating a context of firm traditions, contrasting with the more modern adoption of dances for interlocking couples—such as the waltz, Mexican *corridos,* and Argentine *rancheras* (the Creole version of the European mazurka).

VII. Fuegino-Hispanic area. This scarcely populated area presents an Argentine influence distinguished by songs that are sung with guitar accompaniment, such as the *milonga* or the *cifra,* and by contemporary dances of interlocking couples such as the *ranchera* and the *chamamé,* originating in the coastal zone. The area has also adopted the Mexican *corrido* and *ranchera.*

VIII. The Antarctic area. This area consists of the Antarctic territory, which does not have a stable population.

IX. The Pascuense area. This area consists of Easter Island, where there are remnants of Polynesian music rapidly being displaced by music with folk roots originating in the Picunche-Hispanic area, a region that has achieved a character emblematic of Chilean identity during the twentieth century.

For Argentina we will adhere to the proposal of Augusto Raúl Cortazar (1965), who established a division of seven geographical-folkloric areas. In general terms, Argentina presents a greater variety of traditional dances and songs, but they are not being as intensely conserved as in the case of Chile.

1. In the **Central area** there are two opposing poles. In the province of Córdoba, which has a high urban demographic concentration and level of industrialization, there is a strong current of local dance music, expanding into other areas with increasing success. In contrast, the province of Santiago del Estero appears

República Argentina

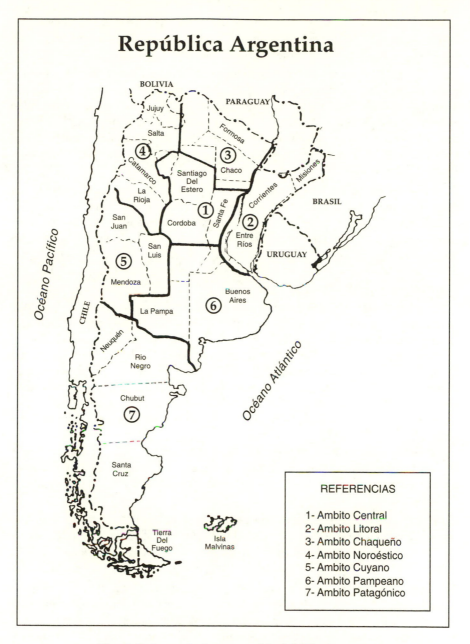

BOLIVIA

PARAGUAY

Jujuy

Salta

Formosa

④

Catamarco

Santiago Del Estero

Chaco

③

Misiones

La Rioja

Santa Fe

Corrientes

BRASIL

San Juan

Cordoba

①

②

Entre Ríos

URUGUAY

San Luis

Océano Pacífico

⑤

Mendoza

Buenos Aires

CHILE

La Pampa

⑥

Neuquén

Río Negro

Océano Atlántico

Chubut

⑦

Santa Cruz

Tierra Del Fuego

Isla Malvinas

REFERENCIAS

1- Ambito Central
2- Ambito Litoral
3- Ambito Chaqueño
4- Ambito Noroéstico
5- Ambito Cuyano
6- Ambito Pampeano
7- Ambito Patagónico

Fig. 6–2. Argentina's geographical-folkloric areas

to be a bastion of tradition where, in addition to the Quechua language, older dances have been conserved for noninterlocking partners, dances such as the *escondido*, the *gato*, the *chacarera*, and songs such as the *vidala*.

2. In the **Littoral area** are found such currently popular dances for interlocking pairs as the polka, the *rasguido doble*, and the *chamamé*. While the polka denotes a strong influence from the Paraguayan repertoire, the *chamamé* is a dance that evolved in the province of Corrientes, from which a unique process of diffusion has taken place over the last twenty years that has transcended Argentine borders. Other dances, such as the *chamarrita*, are common in the bordering countries of Uruguay and Brazil.

3. The **Chaqueña area,** with a strong indigenous presence, has belatedly entered into the process of intermixing cultures, which only began on a massive scale at the beginning of the twentieth century with migrations from neighboring provinces. The Creole population dances *chamamés* and polkas, and the songs tend to be *bagualas* and *vidalas* with accompaniments of various types of drums. There are important festive celebrations, such as carnival and other celebrations tied to cycles of agriculture.

4. The **Northwest area** is the zone that has remained the most firmly rooted in its traditional culture, with a great affinity for the cultural practices of the neighboring areas of Bolivia and Chile. A strong indigenous substratum and a history of cultural hegemony from Lima have been juxtaposed, with both currents being quite clearly delineated geographically—the first in the Andean altiplano, and the second in the valleys and mountain passes. As in areas I and II of Chile, described above, there is an important presence of the tritonic and pentatonic systems that are manifested in vocal and instrumental expressions possessing analogous functions.

Collective dances (without the concept of the couple) such as the *wayno*, and dances for noninterlocking couples such as the *gato*, the *chacarera*, or the *zamba*, are currently popular and denote an influence from ancient Alto Peru throughout the area.

5. The **Cuyana area** provides a repertoire that is linked to that of the neighboring Chilean area, to which it was related until the end of the eighteenth century. There, the *tonada* is the quintessential song, and the *cueca* and the *gato* are the dances, both for independent noninterlocking couples.

6. The **Pampeana area** is the area with the highest concentration of European immigration, and the one that has best adopted dances of European origin such as the waltz, the mazurka (currently called the *ranchera*), and the polka, all for interlocking couples. Songs such as the *estilo* and the *milonga* constitute the best expression of the *gaucho*, the prototypical rural worker of this region, the horseman of innumerable virtues who was immortalized in the literature and who became a national symbol both in Argentina and Uruguay.

7. The **Patagonian area** has remained vastly unpopulated and has sustained the descendants of the Mapuche Indians on the slopes of the Andean mountains. An

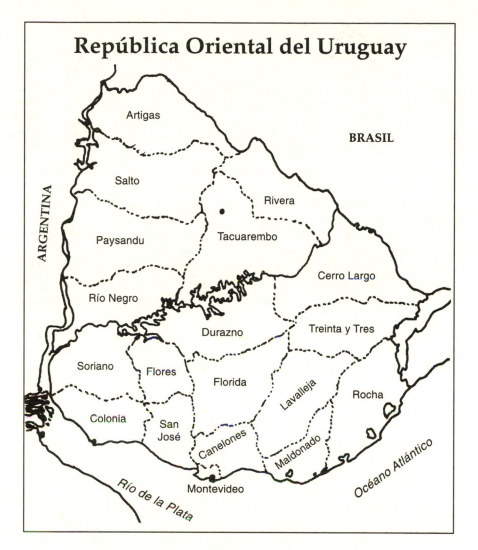

Fig. 6–3. Map of Uruguay

incipient Creole population, arriving from other regions of the country, and a numerous Chilean population of temporary immigrants, as yet have not produced a repertoire typical of the region.

In contrast, the situation in Uruguay is very different, inasmuch as elements can be detected of African cultures, which arrived due to the slave system, and of a population of Brazilian origin who populated a large part of the territory until the last century. Lauro Ayestarán (1967) classified the traditional music of Uruguay into four large groups:

1. Afro-Uruguayan music has its principal center in Montevideo and is inscribed in the occasion of Carnival, at which time a variety of groupings appear. One type—that of the Negros Lubolos—has maintained the *candombe* tradition active into the present time. Since the middle of the eighteenth century, this name has been used to designate a dance representing the coronation of the African Congo kings. Nowadays, from that complex choreographic pantomime, there are remnants of certain of its typical characters as well as the typical instrument, called the African-Uruguayan *tamboril* (Ayestarán 1990), which has been converted into the emblematic instrument of national identity.

2. Along the entire Uruguay-Brazilian border lies what Ayestarán called the Cancionero Norteño [northern song-region]. Marita Fornaro (1994) updated and broadened the studies of Ayestarán along this border, drawing the conclusion that there are two Cancioneros, which she called Luso-Brasileño and Afro-Brasileño. The first of these includes dances for interlocking partners such as the *maxixa, fado, marcha, samba, baión, ranchera,* polka, and *chamamé,* all of recreational and festive character. The Afro-Brasileño Cancionero entails expressions related to the cults of this origin, expressed in private and public rituals, with songs for soloists as well as choruses, and with the accompaniment of drums, rattles, and bells of ritual character.

3. Another group identified by Ayestarán consists of the rural dances and songs spread over the entire country, coinciding with those of the Pampeana area of Argentina and extending into the extreme south of Brazil, in the state of Rio Grande do Sul.

4. Finally, and also dispersed throughout Uruguay, there is the so-called Ancient European Cancionero, which includes the repertoire of children's songs, rounds, and dramatic games.

URBANIZATION OF REGIONAL RURAL MUSICS

In the Southern Cone, the traditional rural repertoires slowly spread into the urban spheres during the twentieth century. This process is directly related to the increasing prominence of the proletariat sectors of rural origins in the economic and political life of their respective countries. Such developments ran more or less parallel courses in Chile (Advis 1998, González 1998) and Argentina (Moreno Chá 1987) beginning in the decade of the 1920s, and in Uruguay (Martins 1986) beginning in the 1950s, attaining wide recognition in Europe in the 1970s. Although this phenomenon assumed diverse forms and names in these countries, we can say that its emergence peaked by the early 1960s and entered a decline toward the end of that same decade.

This current of urbanization of traditional repertoires generated the birth of a type of professional artist that unleashed upon an urban public traditional repertoires as well as those of contemporary authors and composers. A notable influence was exercised inside and outside of the Latin American Southern Cone by the most prominent figures of these countries. Among them, we should recall, at the very least, the Chilean soloists Violeta, Isabel, and Angel Parra (Chapter 9 discusses a Violeta Parra song), Rolando Alarcón, Patricio Manns, Víctor Jara, and such groups as Quilapayún, Aparcoa, and Inti-Illimani; the Argentine soloists Atahualpa Yupanqui, Eduardo Falú, pianist Ariel Ramírez, singer Mercedes Sosa, and groups such as Los Chalchaleros and Los Fronterizos; and the Uruguayan soloists Daniel Vigleti, Alfredo Zitarrosa, and the duo Los Olimareños.

Although the sung poetry initially concerned the rural landscape, it soon took on urban themes as well and later became a song of social commitment, such that powerful political ideas were ascribed to it, with a tendency toward protecting Latin American identity and ideals. Chile and Uruguay are most illustrative of this aspect.

In the three countries this current received vigorous support in the mass media and conquered a vast public that crossed the entire sociocultural spectrum, filling the theaters, clubs, and traditional centers (peñas) and giving rise to the most typical of the arenas for performances—the open-air festivals, with massive audiences, such as that of Cosquín in Argentina (since 1961) and San Bernardo in Chile (since 1970).

In general, this movement retained traditional musical forms and rhythms, while intensely modifying the harmonic and timbric aspects of the respective traditional repertoires with the introduction of a traditional Latin American, as well as academic-European, instrumentation. An effort was made to emulate compositional forms typical of academic music, resulting in various works that acquired emblematic qualities and international diffusion—in Argentina, "La misa criolla" by Ariel Ramírez (1964), and in Chile the cantata "Santa María de Iquique" by Luis Advis (1970) (the latter of which is discussed in Chapter 9).

The song for soloist, or for duet, with guitar accompaniment—notably developed in the Southern Cone—maintained its poetic structure, enriched the basic melody, and acquired a new form of voicing through the appearance of quartets, quintets, and sextets with instrumental accompaniment, generally called "groups" or "folkloric groups."

In short, this phenomenon produced—upon the foundations of traditional bodies of music—new repertoires and forms of expression that constituted a representative language of the era, a language which nowadays is undergoing a process of fusion or extinction. It is noteworthy that only in Chile was there, and has there been, a true concern on the part of some professional groups and dance groups for developing a staging of the rural ceremonies and festivities with fidelity to the traditional musical phenomenon. In this respect, the groups Cuncumén (1955) and Millaray (1958) were outstanding for their performances.

From the Southern Cone came a dance that is known throughout the world and that is currently experiencing a moment of resurgence—the tango. Although it was not essentially a rural dance, its nomadic situation and deterritorialization qualify it as a unique phenomenon among the Latin American dances of this century (Pelinski 1995). This dance, which originated toward the end of the last century on both banks of the Río de la Plata, is claimed by Argentines and Uruguayans alike. It is very popular in Japan today; it has passed through various periods of resurgence in numerous cities of the Americas and Europe; and it is currently being danced by young people in major cities throughout the Southern Cone, who learn the complicated choreography from specialized masters of the dance. As a dance, it has had scant acceptance in the rural areas of the region. The true cultivators of the *tango*—and those who have continued dancing it uninterruptedly, ignoring the comings and goings of international fashion—are small groups in urban and suburban areas for whom the *tango* has always been a tradition, conserved by families and in small neighborhood clubs (Moreno Chá 1995).

We will now examine two characteristic forms of the region—the *tonada* and the *milonga*. If we recall, as indicated above, the dependency of the Cuyana area of Argentina relative to the General Captaincy of Chile, until the Viceroyalty of the Río de la Plata was established in Buenos Aires (1776), it can be inferred that this political link also gave rise to other links of a cultural and economic nature, ties that persisted far beyond the eighteenth century. Thus, until well into the nineteenth century, all of Cuyo (as the region is also known) remained more united with the Picunche-Hispanic area of Chile than with the rest of Argentina, from which it was separated by poor roads and indigenous incursions. Here lies what we shall call the "Andes axis," which had at its two poles the cities of Santiago, Chile and Mendoza, Argentina, on either side of the highest mountain chain in the Americas. From this axis we will focus on the *tonada*.

In contrast, upon the estuary of the Río de la Plata that empties into the Atlantic Ocean, we have the other axis, that which unites two of the most important city-ports on the American Atlantic coast at the end of the eighteenth century—Buenos Aires and Montevideo. Both cities were constituted as extensions of European and African culture through commercial exchange, smuggling, and the slave trade. During the following century, already consecrated as political and cultural centers, the two cities disseminated certain American dances that traveled from port to port, and a European repertoire as well, which, now Creolized, is currently danced in most parts of both countries. From this Río de la Plata axis, we will focus on the *milonga*.

THE ANDES AXIS—SANTIAGO, CHILE TO MENDOZA, ARGENTINA

THE CHILEAN *TONADA*

The *tonada* is the quintessential song of Chile. Its origins can be traced to the first periods of Spanish domination during which time the songs arriving with the first *conquistadores* began to be adopted and adapted. Travelers of different periods mention *canciones, tonadas*, and *tonadillas* with local characteristics, but without offering the detailed descriptions that might permit an evolutionary study of this musical form, particularly when these three terms were used as synonyms for *canción* [song].

The poetic texts of the *tonadas* of today reveal a medieval and Renaissance Hispanic influence with respect to the strophic forms, the themes, and the poetic devices employed. Nowadays, the *tonada* is found in Chilean areas with slight indigenous presence, and its radius mostly includes areas III and IV in Figure 6–1.

Traditionally, it is a form for a solo, feminine voice—it is only during the second half of the twentieth century that the male figure has gradually been added. Currently, the *tonada* is also performed in duets, preferably feminine, though there are also mixed duets and groups of three or four musician-singers who generally belong to a family group.

There are two criteria employed in the determination of different types of *tonadas:* (1) the poetic form used, and (2) the function that emerges from the text and the occasion. Thus, for example, many (but not all) of the *tonadas* whose poetic text is a *romance* are classified as *romance*. The *romance* is a story with a dramatic design, narrated by a supposed witness of the events or by the protagonists, which may include direct dialogues between the characters. In addition to forming part of the repertoire for adults, it is also part of numerous children's games and rounds. In the remaining cases, the function is what determines the specific type and name of the *tonada.* Thus, a *tonada* that is sung during a marriage celebration for a wedded couple is called a *parabién* [well-wishing] in order to wish them happiness; a *tonada* that is sung for someone in honor of his/her birthday or saint's day is called an *esquinazo;* and a *tonada* sung at Christmas time is called a *villancico,* this latter form being a song of praise, in the vernacular, often on a Christmas theme.

"Religious *tonada*" is the generic term applied to *tonadas* that accompany the numerous expressions of popular Catholicism dispersed throughout Chile for paying tribute to saints, the dead, the Cross, etc. In turn, the term *tonada* without any other ulterior specification is used most commonly for the recreational type of *tonada* that accompanies family events, chores, or rural festivities such as the wine harvest.

What determines the function of the *tonada* is its allusive text, such that each singer may choose from his/her repertoire the *tonadas* that are most appropriate for the moment and circumstance. In turn, the function does not delimit specific structural characteristics with respect to the poetry and music, but does define the musical character and style. This style may be distinguished by the type of vocal production, by the tempo, or by the presence or absence of the *rebec*—a violin of three strings that descends from the European Celtic *crouth*—which is used in religious *tonadas* and which may be heard in Recorded Selection 28 on the CD accompanying this book ("San Miguel abrió sus puertas").

The sung poetry of the *tonada* is marked by a predominance of octosyllabic meter, whereas verses of five, six, or seven syllables are rare. The most common poetic forms are the *romance,* the *décima,* and quatrains of different rhyme and meter.

The *romance* may be composed of an indefinite number of octosyllabic verses arranged in a continuous form, with rhyming paired verses (Example 6–2) or they may also (with the same rhyme scheme) adopt the form of the quatrain, which is common for the *romances* that remain linked to children's music. The *décima* is comprised of ten octosyllabic verses that rhyme the first line with the fourth and fifth lines, the second with the third, the sixth with the seventh and tenth, and the eighth with the ninth (Example 6–7). Finally, the quatrain consists of a series of four octosyllabic verses which, in the most common form, rhymes the second line with the fourth (Example 6–3).

In the Chilean tradition, Hispanic *romances* are as common as locally composed *romances* sung as *tonadas*. The ancient epic-narrative form—which arranged the verses in equal measures without strophes, respecting the rhyme scheme of paired verses—was maintained in Chile, with a narrative character and with a structure based upon the action of the characters (Barros and Dannemann 1970).

One of the *romances* of Hispanic origin that enjoys the greatest popularity today is that of "Blanca Flor y Filomena." The song refers back to the Greek legend in which Filomena (Philomela), the daughter of the King of Athens, is the victim of the incestuous passion of her brother-in-law Tereo (Tereus), King of Thrace, husband to Blanca Flor (Procne). The following version is presented as a *tonada* and was taken from the fourth volume of the *Antología del folklore musical chileno* [Anthology of Chilean folk music], covering the province of Maule (1965:17–18). The musical phrases possess a descending character, moving in stepwise motion, each phrase corresponding to two verses of the *romance*.

This version continues with other verses that we will exclude here. It contains a number of colloquialisms and contractions that are characteristic of rural speech: *pos = pues* [then], *'ta = está* [she is], *'e = de* [of], *pa' = para* [for]. In addition, the rural pronunciation has transformed the word *Filomena* into *Felumena*.

Ex. 6–1.   Musical Transcription of "Blanca Flor y Filomena"

Ex. 6–2.   Text of "Blanca Flor y Filomena"

Estando tan bien sentada	Being so daintily seated
A la luz de una candela	By the light of a candle
Donde estaba Blancaflor	There was Blancaflor
Blancaflor con Felumena.	Blancaflor with Felumena.
Y pasó el galán Turquía	When along came the gallant Turk
Se enamoró de una de ellas	In love with one of the ladies
Se casó con Blancaflor	He did marry Blancaflor
Y pena por Felumena.	And sorrow for Felumena.
De que se vido casado	Seeing himself now married
Se retiró a lejas tierras.	He withdrew to a distant land.
Los nueves meses cumplidos	The nine months once completed
Volvió a casa de la suegra.	He returned to his in-laws'.
—Y, buenos días, pos, suegra	—And, good day, then, mother-in-law
—Y, buenos días, pos, yerno	—And, good day, then, son-in-law
¿Cómo ha quedado Blancaflor?	How are things with Blancaflor?
—Blancaflor 'tá muy enferma	—Blancaflor is very ill
Y le mandó suplicar	And has sent me to request
Que le mande a Felumena.	That you send her Felumena.
—Cómo yo mandaré a esta hija	—How can I send this daughter there
por ahí	
Cuando esa hija está doncella.	When that daughter is a virgin!
—Mándela, no más, señora,	—Send her quick along, *señora*
Sin ni un cuidado por ella.	Without fears on her behalf.
—Felumena, anda a tu pieza	—Felumena, go to your room
A ponerte el traje de seda	To put on your suit of silk
Toma las ancas 'e tu cuñado	Sit behind your brother-in-law
Él sabrá pa' donde te lleva.	He'll know whereabouts to take you.
A tanto que había andado,	Hardly had they been riding
Y de su cuerpo la usó	Before her body he did use
Y pa' no salir pillado	And to keep from getting nabbed
La lengua le rebanó.	He sliced her tongue right through.
Y ella, la pobrecita	And she, the poor little thing
Con la sangre de su lengua	With the blood of her own tongue
Una carta es que escribió.	She managed to write a letter.
Luego pasó un pastorcito,	Later there passed a shepherd,
Con la mano lo llamó.	To whom, with her hand, she called.
—Toma, toma, buen pastor	—Take this, take this, good shepherd
Y llévale esta cartita	Take to her this short letter
(A mi hermana Blancaflor)	(To my dear sister, Blancaflor)
Y dile que su marido	And tell her that her husband
Su marido es un traidor	That her husband is a traitor.
Blancaflor oyendo esto	Blancaflor, upon hearing this
Y ahí casi abortó	At once she almost aborted
Se atracó por un peñasco	She flung herself upon the rocks
Y ahí casi se murió.	And there she almost perished.

Exceptionally, in the Chilean tradition, there will sometimes appear the gruesome epilogue in which the two sisters exact revenge by killing the son of Blancaflor and Tereo and serving the entrails to Tereo during a banquet without revealing to him the true ingredients.

Another common poetic form of the Chilean *tonada* is the octosyllabic quatrain, with assonant rhyme in the second and fourth lines, as illustrated in Recorded Selection 27, "Tonada al niño Dios" [*Tonada* to the baby Jesus]. It is composed of three quatrains between which a refrain is inserted. This is a frequent poetic device, consisting of a set of two or more verses of meter that is either equal or unequal to that of the sung *tonada,* which do not necessarily have any relation to the poetic subject that is being developed. In the present case, the refrain is of four pentasyllabic verses and is poetically related to the lyrics of the *tonada* to which it pertains.

In our selection, while the refrain is always sung the same way and with the same melody except for the last note, the quatrains are sung split in halves. The first and the second verse-lines are repeated with the same melody (A), and the third and fourth lines are also repeated, but with a different system, which gives the entire strophe a tremendous melodic unity. The second couplet initially presents a different musical idea (B), but upon its repetition it repeats the melody of the first couplet (A). The musical structure of the quatrain is thus AABA.

Musically, the refrain is distinguished from the rest of the *tonada* by presenting a differentiated melody (C) and guitar-accompanimental style. The strum here is commonly called *chicoteado* in an analogy to the snapping sound made by the *chicote* [whip]. The *chicoteado* here is the dry snapping sound produced upon the guitar strings that delays the two strong beats of each measure of the refrain, without altering the course of the sung melody, which maintains its own beat.

This *tonada* was collected in 1968 by Margot Loyola in the province of Maule (area IV in Figure 6–1). It is a typical example of the *tonadas* sung at Christmas, before the crèche, in homage to the newborn Christ.

Devotion, rather than celebration, is the character of religious *tonadas* that are sung principally in honor of Roman Catholic saints. "San Miguel abrió sus puertas" [Saint Michael opened his doors], Recorded Selection 28, illustrates this context, and at the same time verifies the presence of two very old poetic devices that are still found today in the Chilean *tonada.*

The *cogollo* or *despedida* [farewell] is a verse that may be included in the poetry of the *tonada,* or it may be coincidental and added on the spur of the moment by the singer. Generally, it maintains the same metric form as the *tonada* and is invariably located at the end. In the case of the *cogollo*—which in very old songs was used twice, once at the beginning of the song and once at the end—its function is to pay homage to the person or circumstance to whom the song is directed. In contrast, this verse is called the *despedida* when it announces the end of the text and the singer bids farewell with a moral or final comment, as in "San Miguel abrió sus puertas" (Example 6–4). (Note that this *despedida* is not included in Recorded Selection 28.)

Ex. 6–3.   Text of "Tonada al niño Dios"

Señora Doña María	*Señora Doña* María
Yo vengo de allá muy lejos	I come from far away
Y a su niñito le traigo	And to your little son I bring
Un parcito de conejos.	A little pair of rabbits.
Estribillo	*Refrain*
Ya viene el día	Here comes the day
Ya amaneció	It has already dawned
Los gallos cantan:	The cocks are crowing:
Cristo nació.	Christ is born.
Señora Doña María	*Señora Doña* María
Memorias al 'ño José	Regards to the massa' [?] José
Si pregunta por la huasa°	If he asks for the *huasa*°
Dígale que ya se fue.	Tell him she is gone.
(Estribillo)	(Refrain)
Señora Doña María	*Señora Doña* María
El canto aquí se acabó	The song here must close
El canto se acabará	The song will have to end
Pero mi cariño nó.	But my fondness no.
(Estribillo)	(Refrain)

°The feminine form of *huaso*, a term given to the peasant of the central region of Chile.

These *cogollos* and *despedidas* [farewells] are remnants of a practice that was very common during the fifteenth century in Spain, where they were called *finidas, cabos,* or *fines* [endings] and were inserted at the end of long *cantares* [poetic songs]. This practice has remained firmly rooted in the *tonada* of both South American countries (Chile and Argentina), as well as in the Mexican *corrido*.

The other poetic device contained in this *tonada* pertains to the ancient system of linked strophes, also common during the Spanish Renaissance and of which three different types remain in Chile. In the case of our *tonada*, the type em-

Ex. 6–4.   *Despedida* of "San Miguel abrió sus puertas"

Para todos los que escuchan	For all those who are listening
Rezarán esta oración	Who will recite this devotion
Tendrá descanso el pecado	The sin will be put to rest
Y Dios le dará el perdón.	And God will grant His pardon.

ployed has the last verse of one strophe repeated in its entirety at the beginning of the following strophe. The *tonada* employing this device is called *tonada de coleo* [*tonada* with tails] because the *cola* [tail] or last verse of the previous strophe is used to begin the next. The first three strophes are presented in Example 6–5. This is a fragment of an ancient prayer that forms part of the rich cultural heritage left by Catholicism in Chile.

Gabriela Pizarro, a notable scholar of the *romance* and of the religious *tonada*, conducted a study of this piece and its instrumentation in the peasant style. She selected it for inclusion in her work *Veinte Tonadas Religiosas* [Twenty religious *tonadas*], which includes a cassette from which this example was taken.

This *tonada* begins with an introductory strophe mentioning the saint to whom the prayer is directed, and it ends with the farewell presented above, in which the virtues of the prayer are emphasized (Pizarro S. and Chandía T. 1993:97–98). Especially noteworthy here is the presence of the *rebec (rabel)*, an early violin of three strings that is laid upon the thighs of the musician in the ancient European manner (see Illustration 6–1)—it is still used among indigenous populations in Argentina, Brazil, Guatemala, Mexico, Panama, and Paraguay. With its timbre, the instrument instills this *tonada* with a special character of devotion and retreat. The *rebec* plays an *ostinato* on the fifth scale-degree in a rhythmic formula that is identical to that of the guitar, which together with the guitar's steel strings, produces a very special sonorous quality, rich in trebles.

The melody, with a very restricted range, maintains a prominent presence of the fifth scale-degree, the absence of the first (tonic), and conclusion on the third. This last feature is frequent in *tonadas*, but essential for the conclusion of *cuecas*.

In the central area of Chile, these religious *tonadas* are most common in the context of *novenas*, celebrations of the Cross, and children's wakes. The *novena* consists of a nine-night celebration with canticles and prayers, in a private home with family and friends. The *novena* may celebrate the fulfillment of a vow, a

Ex. 6–5. Text of "San Miguel abrió sus puertas"

San Miguel abrió sus puertas	San Miguel opened the doors
De sus cubiertos cupillos	Of his small compartments
Para darle la oración	To deliver the prayer
Pidiendo perdón al Niño.	Asking forgiveness of the Baby Jesus.
Pidiendo perdón al Niño	Asking forgiveness of the Baby Jesus
Lamentaba su destino	Mourning his destiny
Le rezaba la oración	He recited the prayer
La Oración del Peregrino.	The Pilgrim's litany.
La Oración del Peregrino	The Pilgrim's litany
Que son de tan grandes penas	Which are of such great pains
Dando voces y llorando	With voices of grieving
San Juan y la Magdalena.	Saint John and Mary Magdalene.

Ill. 6–1. Gabriela Pizarro playing guitar and José Cabello Parada playing
rebec/rabel. **Studio photograph.**

miraculous event, the birthday or saint's day of a person, or it may pay homage to
a saint or to the baby Jesus (see the discussion of *novena de casa* in Chapter 5).
The celebrations of the Cross take place in processions and on two fixed dates:
May 3, in honor of the *cruz de mayo* [May cross], and October 4, in honor of the
cruz del trigo [wheat cross]. In the latter case, the *tonada* together with *cuecas*
and other dances accompanies the fertility ritual that is celebrated in the recently
germinated wheat fields.

In the Southern Cone, the child's wake is the funeral ritual held when a child
less than seven years old (an *angelito*) dies. This phenomenon, dispersed throughout Hispanic America (see Schechter 1983 and 1994) and to which John
Schechter refers in Chapter 1, survives in some regions of Chile with the participation of male singers who perform religious *décimas,* and female singers who
perform three types of *tonadas* over the course of the all-night wake. The first set
of *tonadas* refers to the child, the family, and the godparents; the intermediate set
consists of religious *tonadas* addressing various subjects; and finally the *tonadas* of
despedida [farewell] are sung, through which the dead child supposedly bids
farewell to her/his loved ones and to this world (Pizarro S. and Chandía T.
1993:51; also Chapter 1 of this book).

The Chilean *tonada* possesses much less freedom in its musical character than
in its poetic aspect, which allows for remarkable compositional devices and great
thematic and metric variation. Generally, the *tonada* possesses two clearly distinguishable sections (AB) and, in exceptional cases, one or three sections. The latter

Ex. 6–6.   Rhythmic figures for the Chilean *tonada*

case occurs if and only if there is a refrain (ABC). Each of these sections varies in length and always consists of even numbers of measures and verses, inasmuch as in octosyllabic verse each line of verse corresponds to two measures. The poetic text adopts diverse forms of repetition which may be independent of the music. Thus, for example, in Recorded Selection 27 there are quatrains of two sections (AB) which are repeated (AABA), the music in conjunction with the poetry. Section C appears only in the refrain. In contrast, in Recorded Selection 28, in which only the third and fourth lines of each strophe are repeated, the repetition occurs accompanied by a different musical section, hence ABA.

The melody of the Chilean *tonada,* which is simple and of small intervals, is generally accompanied by guitars, harp and guitar, or *rebec* and guitar, in its most common rural forms. The presence of the refrain may introduce a change in tempo or rhythm, and often borrows typical strumming styles from the *cueca.* When the refrain introduces a rhythmic change and a greater harmonic variety that may come to modulate to the relative major tonality, it is normally considered a *tonada-canción.*

The true rhythmic splendor of the *tonada* resides in the alternation of binary and ternary rhythms in the sung melody (horizontal *hemiola*—3/4 and 6/8 meters juxtaposed), which at times produces vertical *hemiola* with the harmonic-rhythmic support of the accompaniment, which also alternates its rhythm. In Recorded Selection 27, the vertical *hemiola* in the refrain can be appreciated.

The most common rhythmic figures for the accompaniment to the Chilean *tonada* are shown in Example 6–6. The harmony generally develops over a European major scale, basically over the tonic and the dominant, which may use chords of the seventh or the ninth degrees. There are also some bimodal *tonadas* whose section A is in a minor key, while section B modulates to the relative major key.

THE FEMININE PRESENCE

Since the birth of the colony, the distinctive feminine presence in the music of Chile has attracted the attention of chroniclers and travelers alike, and this tradition has remained deeply entrenched in rural areas up to the present time, to such an extent that it is common to hear men singing in feminine ranges. It is in these areas that the *cantora* [female singer] has taken on a number of traits that have no direct relation to the musical phenomenon that she perpetuates, but rather relate to the prestige that she has acquired as such. Her figure is projected beyond the music itself, and it acquires powers that permit her to foretell the future, to forewarn of death, and to manage the regional pharmacopoeia in order to apply and perform cures. On the other hand, she will know the Catholic prayers that accompany illness and dying, such that her assistance is necessary at the moment of death. The profile that the popular *cantora* acquires in her community is undeniably analogous to that of the Mapuche woman, who occupies a central role in her community. This position derives from the power which, through a form of chanting called *tayil,* she possesses for controlling access to supernatural phenomena (Robertson 1987), and which attains its maximum expression in the shamanic role that the woman embodies within this culture in the figure of the *machi* (see Chapter 1).

The training of the *cantora* is always carried out from an early age in the bosom of the family, or with close neighbors, through listening and imitation. She comes to possess a vast repertoire that she administers according to the particular requirements of her performance at weddings, celebrations of saints, wakes for children, baptisms, etc. for which she may be invited or hired. Her activity as *cantora* is legitimized and respected by her community, at whose service she places her art. This awesome female presence, as repository for the traditional Chilean repertoire, is verified in greater measure in the sphere of the *tonada* than in that of the dances.

Given this strong feminine presence, it is not coincidental that the great compilers and masters of Chilean musical folklore in this century have been women: Violeta Parra (1917–1967), Margot Loyola (b. 1918), and Gabriela Pizarro (b. 1932) are the three most distinguished figures. All these women carried out extensive labors of recovering the traditional music of their country, though each took a different professional path. Violeta Parra (see Chapter 9) accomplished a great feat in the diffusion and composition of much of her own music, with deep political commitment and intense artistic activity communicated through recordings and live performances. Early on, Margot Loyola dedicated herself to artistic pursuits, and later she turned to research and teaching, attaining unique national recognition. Gabriela Pizarro fundamentally oriented herself toward research, teaching, and promotion, directing the work of groups such as Millaray, which represented an entire era in the dissemination of traditional music, through performances and recordings that were a faithful reflection of the traditional music phenomenon.

PROFILE OF MARGOT LOYOLA

Margot Loyola was born in 1918 in the province of Linares (in Chile's Picunche-Hispanic area), where the *tonada* is most deeply rooted (Illustration 6–2). When she learned that I was dedicating myself to the study of the *tonada,* she summarized her views for me in this way, with the poetic force that characterizes her: "In Chile, the *tonada* is the unifying and most representative form in the feminine folk repertoire. *Tonada*-woman-guitar: the inseparable trilogy, symbol of femininity and nationality." She has also said:

In my life, it [the *tonada*] has been the umbilical cord that has maintained me firmly connected to the earth. If it were taken from me I would find myself isolated and drifting through space. In its rhythms and cadences I live roadways and green fields, I relive the joy and suffering of the people, I escape from the hustle and bustle of life, I return to the peacefulness of the past, and I feel proud to be Chilean. (Loyola 1997)

Born in Linares, I lived a large part of my childhood in the country. I was brought up by my *nana* Melania, a noble country woman who taught me as a small child to knead bread, to wash clothing in the river, to serve *mate* [tea], to cook *tortilla de rescoldo* [a type of griddle-cake], to prepare the *pebre* [dressing for salads and meats], and to use and prepare home remedies. Together we participated in *trillas a yegua* [threshing performed by horses] and attended children's wakes. I listened to my mother singing *tonadas,* and it was she who taught me my first *finares y toquíos* [tunings and melodies] on the guitar. From my father, I inherited legends and superstitions. All of these things marked my beginnings. (Quoted by Sepúlveda Llanos 1983).

At the age of eight Loyola began to travel to the capital city for piano lessons, and it was to play this instrument that she first went on-stage. Some time later she would go on-stage again to dance with her sister, Estela, and eventually to sing. Thus was born the duo of Las Hermanas Loyola [the Loyola sisters], two adolescents with a long road ahead of them:

When we began, the first piece we learned was "El imposible," a *tonada.* My mother had taught me that song; we would sing it together. She would sing the second voice for me. With my sister it was the other way around: it was extremely hard for me. (Quoted by Andreu Ricart 1993)

Ill. 6–2. Margot Loyola. Photo by Osvaldo Cádiz Valenzuela.

At a friend's request, they sang on Radio del Pacífico, in Santiago:

> We sang the three *tonadas* our mother had taught us. We didn't know any other songs.
> My sister had a very beautiful voice and we were so little! . . . The result: we won the
> contest. . . . Our artistic beginnings were full of joy. It was the relief we needed after so
> much suffering. We had nothing, not even guitars. The ones we had were borrowed.
> (ibid.)

Those first years with her sister, living in a rooming house in Santiago, were
very hard, and in order to continue her piano studies, Margot had to sell coffee
door-to-door and to accompany gym classes on the piano.

They continued performing on Radio del Pacífico, presented some modest
shows, and began to meet some of the important *cantoras* of the day who performed in Santiago and Valparaíso, performers who would pass along their traditional repertoires to the girls.

In 1943, the Instituto de Investigaciones Musicales organized a concert in the
Teatro Municipal and invited the young duo to participate. A year later they participated in a memorable and pioneering project, the anthology *Aires tradicionales y folklóricos de Chile* [Traditional and folkloric songs of Chile], for which
they were recorded for the first time, together with the most consecrated exponents of traditional Chilean folk music:

> Our country innocence was taken by surprise when in 1950 the Asociación de Cronistas
> de Teatro, Cine, y Radio, gave us the "Caupolicán" award for the best folk music group.
> We had been singing on the radio for ten years, and on large stages, such as the *rodeos*
> at Rancagua . . . San Fernando. So, that was a miracle. The Loyola sisters, two
> inexperienced young girls, with a limited repertoire . . . and just look, we could do both
> things: sing in *rodeos* as well as in events at the Instituto de Investigaciones Musicales.
> Don Eugenio Pereira Salas [a Chilean musicologist] enjoyed inviting us to perform on
> his radio program. (Quoted by Andreu Ricart 1993).

In 1950, Margot's sister decided to stop singing and Margot began her career
as a soloist. "People had grown accustomed to the sound of the Hermanas Loyola.
Nobody in Chile wanted to listen to just me. So, I decided to go to Buenos Aires
and knock on the door of the big names, to see what they would have to say about
me. I had to get ready for my trip" (quoted by Andreu Ricart 1993).

As her financial situation was becoming increasingly difficult, Margot took advantage of a surprising invitation from the rector of the Universidad de Chile to
give classes on how to dance the *cueca*—the national dance—in the summer
schools that the university was just then initiating. This gave her the opportunity
to gain in-depth knowledge of her country, and for three months of every year
over the next fourteen years she traveled all over. These tours provided her with
beautiful memories: "Hundreds of students were spread all over the country,
helping to keep our national dance alive and giving birth to the first folkloric
groups . . . Finally! Thanks to these schools I was able to save the money necessary for my long-awaited trip to Buenos Aires. It happened in 1951: my first voyage outside of the country" (quoted by Andreu Ricart 1993).

On her first trip to Buenos Aires, Margot made contact with Carlos Vega, Isabel Aretz, and Augusto Raúl Cortazar, among others, and in Montevideo with Lauro Ayestarán. All of these scholars, in one way or another, would value the work of this artist who, based on her own extensive personal knowledge, demonstrated a calling for the artistic expression of the traditional repertoire.

Margot was the first scholar to approach the ritual dances in the extreme north of Chile. This took place in 1952, but her real interest in studying them took hold much later:

> It would be 25 or 30 years before I began to take research work seriously. . . . For me, research is not work properly speaking, but simply an approach to someone else. And this is what is important, because one learns through living with the popular artist. . . . When I go to the country, two things happen to me: first, I live, I don't think. I live the landscape, I am moved. I discover the man and I learn from him all that he wants to, and can, teach me. I enjoy watching a woman walk. I like to listen to them, to look at them, to touch them; I like to discover the human dimension. In this way I learn things that I have never thought to ask. Direct observation and personal contact are the first things that I experience. Later, I record and then I study. I investigate, I see musical parameters, stylistic features, etc. Then, I think. . . . Later I apply what I have learned to my own interpretation. Now . . . how does the interpretation turn out? This, for me, is a big problem. Whether it is a question of a dance or a song, there has to have been some previous understanding for me, only then can I project it. But this is a long process. It took me five years to be able to dance the *cachimbo.* To enact a *machi,* it took me seven years. (Quoted by Ruiz Zamora 1995)

She felt an equal attraction to both the dances and the songs of her country. In the decade of the 1950s she founded the first folkloric group in Chile, The Conjunto de Alumnos de Margot Loyola [Student Group of Margot Loyola], and she had a strong influence on the emergence of the first folkloric dance troupe in her country, The Loncurahue. From this dance company would later arise the Aucamán group, which after 1968 became the Ballet Folklórico Nacional (BAFONA), pertaining to the Ministry of Education.

Tracking the origins and relations of Chilean dances, Margot traveled numerous times to Peru and Mexico. Some of her projects materialized in two books, published by the Universidad Católica de Valparaíso, *Bailes de tierra en Chile* [Earth dances in Chile] (1980) and *El Cachimbo* (1994), and in numerous articles, video recordings, and theater, radio, and television productions. These latter productions gave her work massive exposure, even reaching into the remotest regions of her country.

Among the song types, her favorite has always been the *tonada,* and it is fitting to note the splendid work she did in tracing the folk processes involved in the evolution of the Spanish *couplé* in Chile during the twentieth century. The vast majority of this repertoire was compiled by Margot as pertaining to the *tonada* genre in diverse rural areas. Part of this magnificent work is presented on her cassette *El couplé,* in which she sings the Spanish versions as well as the corresponding Chilean Creole versions, each one with its own particular form of expression. Margot does not consider herself a researcher, but rather a scholar, a connoisseur of the traditional music and dance of her people.

Since the first recordings she made at the request of Chilean musicologists of the past until the present, the catalogue of her recordings has increased significantly and includes sixteen different recording labels from Chile, France, Spain, Romania, and Russia. A total of thirty-two records at 78 rpm, thirty-one long-playing records recorded at 33 rpm, thirteen cassette tapes, and five compact disks attests to her intensive labor as a performer. Painstaking voice training has been necessary to acquire and produce the different sounds of the various cultural regions of her country, as well as training in the use of numerous traditional instruments, all of which she has managed to do together with the fieldwork she continues to the present day.

In 1972, she was invited by the Universidad Católica de Valparaíso to teach and carry out research at the School of Music and in the Department of Aesthetics, where she remains active and enjoys wide recognition.

In 1994, Margot was awarded the Premio Nacional de Arte en Música, which has been awarded annually to performers and composers of art music in Chile since 1944. This award is an important landmark for two reasons: for the first time, the award was given to an artist dedicated to traditional music and, in addition, to a woman.

The significance of this award for Margot Loyola acquires many dimensions. On the one hand, what was awarded was the labor and commitment of an entire lifetime dedicated to the compilation, dissemination, and teaching of Chilean folk music and dance, with magnificent results both on the national and international levels. On the other hand, it represented the official validation of an important area of traditional culture through the recognition of a person who, in spite of her professional success, never ceased to be a *cantora*. As such, she represents her people and shares this award with them, participating in all the tributes given in her honor in the many different communities throughout Chile (Moreno Chá 1995).

THE *TONADA CUYANA*

The Argentine *tonada* is called *cuyana* because Cuyo has been the focal point for its dissemination. This area includes the provinces of San Juan, Mendoza, and San Luis, as well as adjacent areas.

Although the *tonada* in Cuyo, as in Chile, is the quintessential song, it has not attained the same varied degree of insertion into the daily lives of those who recognize it as part of their habitual repertoire. Its context is restricted almost exclusively to recreational festivities; it is a compulsory feature of family and neighborhood gatherings. It is also still used for the nightly *serenata,* the well-rooted custom of celebrating birthdays by singing at the doorway of the celebrator's home. This custom extends throughout Latin America (see Chapter 7), where it adopts various musical characteristics and diverse functions, such as to pay tribute to someone on their saint's day, to serenade a beloved woman, to raise funds, etc.

Although historical, humorous, religious, and news-oriented themes were not alien to the *tonada,* nowadays it is dedicated almost exclusively to themes dealing with love. It is on this subject that it incorporates poetry of the greatest conceptual refinement in Argentina, sharing with another genre, called the *estilo,* the virtue of having preserved age-old poetic subjects and devices, very much as in Chile.

Carlos Vega (1965) supports the hypothesis that the *tonada* probably arrived in Cuyo from Chile, initially flourishing during the first half of the nineteenth century. From then on, it would have developed along independent lines on either side of the Andes—on the Chilean side influenced by the *cueca,* and on the Argentine side influenced by the *estilo* and the *zamba.* The Cuyan *tonada* is generally sung by male duos, in parallel thirds, exclusively with guitar accompaniment. Its lyrics—always octosyllabic—are generally arranged in ten-line verse forms (*décimas*) and quatrains, and less commonly in eight-, six-, and five-line strophes; occasionally the lyrics can be in *romance* form.

One distinctive characteristic of the *tonada* of this region is the system of verse repetition, used as a compositional artifice. In contrast to what evolved in Chile, where the repetition of verse pairs is frequent in quatrains, in Cuyo the repetition of verses occurs in all types of strophes: they may be of one or two verses, within the same musical section in which they first appeared (A) or within the second section (B).

Example 6–7 is an example of an old *tonada* from Mendoza, "Dichoso de aquel que vive" [Fortunate is he who lives]. The second and fourth lines are repeated, such that the original ten-line form is prolonged over twelve lines rather than ten. (The repeated lines are marked accordingly in Example 6–7.) Other common repetitions are those of the first, fourth, and eighth lines.

This *tonada* is a magnificent illustration of the exquisite treatment given to the theme of love in this genre. As is frequent in the *tonada,* the singer assumes the role of the unrequited lover, who describes the various nuances of his suffering.

We can take advantage of these lyrics briefly to consider the structure of the strophes. The ten octosyllabic lines are tightly interwoven to form the following rhyme scheme: ABBAACCDDC. That is to say, the first line rhymes with the fourth and fifth, the second with the third, the sixth and seventh with the tenth, and the eighth with the ninth. This type of *décima* is known as *décima espinela,* as its creation is attributed to Vicente Espinel Gómez Adorno, Spanish poet, novelist, and musician (1550–1624). Although it is not the only type of *décima* used in the Spanish Renaissance, this is the most widely accepted form in the Americas.

The *espinela* establishes a strong point of union in the *fifth* line: through *rhyme,* it is connected to the first and fourth lines, while through *poetic content* it is connected to the remaining lines. A detailed observation of all the *décimas* presented in this chapter—in the *tonadas* as well as the *milongas*—reveals that the tendency is to establish an idea in the first four lines and to develop the idea in the remaining six lines.[1]

Ex. 6–7. Text of the *tonada cuyana* "Dichoso de aquel que vive"

Dichoso de aquel que vive	Fortunate is he who lives
Día y noche en tu presencia [repetido]	Day and night in your presence [repeated]
Gozando la complacencia	Enjoying the complacence
Que por tu vista recibe.[repetido]	That through your glance he receives. [repeated]
Dichoso del que consigue	Fortunate is he who achieves
Mejoría así en su suerte	Improvements in his fortune
Y que sus penas divierte	And that his pains are amused
Viendo a la prenda que adora	Seeing the loved one he hallows
¡Triste de mí que a toda hora	At all hours I have such sorrows
Vivo con la sed de verte!	Living with this thirst to see you!
Viene el día y me entristece	Comes the day and with it sorrow
Ver el sol y no mirarte [repetido]	To see the sun but not see you [repeated]
Porque quisiera adorarte	Because I long to adore you
Desde que el alba amanece [repetido];	From the dawning of the morrow [repeated];
Mas, como el deseo crece	Yet, as my desire does grow
Me parece te estoy viendo	It seems to be you I'm seeing
Y como voy conociendo	And as I am discovering
Que es engaño y fantasía	What is deceit and fantasy
Estoy de noche y de día	By night and by day it is me
A todas horas muriendo.	Who is at all hours dying.
Qué pena, qué confusión	What sorrow, what confusion
Cuando no te puedo hablar [repetido]	When with you I cannot converse [repeated]
Porque te quiero entregar	Because to you I would disburse
Alma, vida y corazón.[repetido]	My soul, my heart, and my person. [repeated]
Esta pena, esta pasión	My sorrow and all my passion
Me atormenta a cada instante	Torments me in every instant
Y el dolor más incesante	And the pain is more incessant
Es ver que de mí te alejas	To see that you are retreating
Cuando te envío mis quejas	Even as I am entreating
Y te busco más amante.	Seeking you, your lover most ardent.
Qué pena podrá igualar	What sorrow could be equated
A la que yo estoy pasando [repetido]	To that which I'm enduring [repeated]
Cuando me llevo adorando	As I go on adoring

Ex. 6–7.   Text of the *tonada cuyana* "Dichoso de aquel que vive" (continued)

Lo que nunca he de gozar.[repetido]	That which will never be tasted. [repeated]
Mi corazón de pesar	My heart is so very weighted
Quiere morir aquí dentro	It desires inside to die
Saliéndose de su centro	Away from its center to fly
Entre mis penalidades:	Among my tribulations:
Yo busco facilidades	I search for consolations
Sólo imposibles encuentro.	Just impossibilities I find.

Another interesting textual characteristic of the Cuyan *tonada* is the insertion of certain words as fillers *(ripios)* in order to conform to the length of the musical phrase. Example 6–8 is an example in which the words *sí* and *ay* are inserted before the repetition of the last line of the quatrain. Musically, just as in the case of the Chilean *tonada,* there is an absolute preponderance of the European major mode here, and the formal structure chiefly responds to the presence of two sections. The repetition of the first section is much more frequent than in Chile, and the formula ABA, or ABA', is predominant, except in Mendoza, where the formula AB also appears in equal proportion. While in Chile, the B section may appear with the same accompaniment in terms of rhythm and tempo, the *tonada cuyana* invariably differentiates with respect to these devices. Nonetheless, the refrain, which is much less frequent than in Chile, does not always change in tempo and rhythmic accompaniment, such that the two sections only differ in terms of melody.

The melody of the *tonada cuyana* uses a vast variety of devices in the constitution of its phrases, which may incorporate duplets and triplets and also, with great frequency, binary and ternary rhythms, which produces both vertical and horizontal *hemiola*. The *tonada cuyana* shares one of its principal melodic characteristics with the Chilean *tonada:* conclusion on the third scale-degree, and an upbeat beginning *(anacrusis)*—that is, beginning the melody on a weak beat of the measure. This may be observed in Example 6–1 and heard on Recorded Selections 27 and 28, while on Recorded Selection 29 we can hear the contrary effect as the melody begins on a strong beat.

Ex. 6–8.   An example of insertion, recorded in 1967 by the author in Mendoza, Argentina

Los tiempos nunca han podido	The times have never succeeded
Borrarte de mi memoria	In erasing you from my memory
Y viviendo dolorido	And living so aggrieved
Penas se han vuelto mis glorias	My pains have become my glory
Sí, ay ay ay	Yes, ay ay ay
Penas se han vuelto mis glorias.	My pains have become my glory.

A real difference between the two types of *tonadas* may be observed with respect to modulation, inasmuch as the *cuyana* is very modulatory, to such a point that, within the panorama of Argentine folk music, it is the genre that most exemplifies this characteristic. The most common formulas are such that both sections A and B begin and end in the same key, or it may be that the second section B begins in another key but later ends in the same key as that in which A began.

These and other features may be heard on Recorded Selection 29, which we collected in San Juan province. This *tonada* is known as "No sé qué tiene esta calle" [I don't know what it is about this street] (Example 6–9), as determined by the first line of the lyrics. Following an old *cuyana* tradition, this *tonada* is sung by two male voices in parallel thirds, with guitar accompaniment. The text uses the metaphor of rain on a wet street for the lament of a forlorn lover. In the *tonada* he sings his farewell, cherishing the affection he will always carry with him. (It is worth recalling here that we already heard this same musical structure, AABA, for each strophe on Recorded Selection 27.)

The guitar accompaniment for this genre reveals a profound difference between the two countries. While in Chile the guitar accompaniment generally marks the strong beats, in the *tonada cuyana*, in contrast, an older and more generalized accompaniment is used, with a strum that is always syncopated and maintained constant throughout the piece (Example 6–10a).

A distinctive characteristic of the *tonada cuyana* is the marked presence of plucked interludes inserted before each strophe, and sometimes inserted incompletely after the second line. In Chile, the interludes are rare and of greater sim-

Ex. 6–9.   Text of "No sé qué tiene esta calle"

No sé qué tiene esta calle	I don't know what it is about this street
Que parece que ha llovido [A, bis A]	It seems to have rained [A, repeat A]
Habrá llorado un amante	A lover must have been weeping
Que lo han hechado al olvido. [B, bis A]	Cast into oblivion. [B, repeat A]
Adiós, que de tí me alejo	Farewell, I am leaving you
Dueña querida de mi alma [A, bis A]	Dear mistress of my soul [A, repeat A]
Ya se va mi amor en calma	Here goes my love calmly
Queda en tí mi pensamiento. [B, bis A]	My thoughts stay with you. [B, repeat A]
Si me voy con el tormento	If I go away with the storm
Del cariño que perdí [A, bis A]	From the darling I have lost [A, repeat A]
Lo he de conservar aquí,	I have preserved it here
Dentro de mi pensamiento. [B, bis A]	Within my thoughts. [B, repeat A]

Ex. 6–10.   **(a) Basic rhythmic formula of the *tonada***
(b) Basic rhythmic formula of the *estilo*

plicity in rural areas, while in the cities they have gradually been adopting this nontraditional feature.

Let's examine the interlude that we heard on Recorded Selection 29, "No sé qué tiene esta calle" (Example 6–11). This interlude presents an aggressive nature with sustained movement. It begins with a progression that then searches for the tonic, discovering it first through a descending movement and then by another ascending movement. The interlude should probably have as its time signature 3/4 and 6/8—suggesting *sesquiáltera* or horizontal *hemiola,* because its first section is felt perhaps more clearly in 6/8 time—with movement in sixteenth notes, its second section in 3/4 meter. The metrical ambiguity continues with the entry of the A-section vocal melody: here, the first bar seems to be in 6/8 time, and the following three bars in 3/4 time. To this effect, there is usually added another that is also of a rhythmic nature and that is clearly present in this example—a vocalization with great rhythmic freedom (*rubato*), which does not always respect the marking of the beats by the guitar.

The *cogollo* in the *tonada cuyana* is much more prevalent than in the Chilean *tonada.* Example 6–12 shows two different *cogollos* that we collected in the province of San Juan in 1969. In these *cogollos,* arranged in quatrains, the singer maintains the rhyme between the second and fourth verses—a characteristic of this strophic form. In the first verse he names the person he is addressing, which is a purely *cuyana* custom.

Ex. 6–11.   **"No sé qué tiene esta calle," musical transcription of the interlude**

No sé qué tie-ne-es-ta   cal - le que pa - re-ceque ha llo - vi   -   do,

Ex. 6–12. *Cogollos*

Cogollo Jocoso

Amigo Lucho, ¡que viva!
No le pase lo que a mí
Aquella que tanto me quiso
Ni el nombre me quiere oir.

Humorous Cogollo

Friend Lucho, that you may live!
Suffer not what happened to me
She who loved me so
Not even my name does she wish to hear.

Cogollo Amoroso

Señora Estela, ¡que viva!
Del cielo caiga una nuez
Con letras de oro que digan
"Rendido estoy a sus pies."

Amorous Cogollo

Señora Estela, that you may live!
From the sky let fall a seed
With words of gold that say
"Prostrate am I at your feet."

THE RIO DE LA PLATA AXIS—BUENOS AIRES, ARGENTINA TO MONTEVIDEO, URUGUAY

THE *MILONGA*

In contrast to the situation of the *tonada* in Chile and Argentina, the *milonga*—also shared by two countries—does not display differences from one side of the Río de la Plata to the other.

The studies carried out by Argentine Carlos Vega (1965) and Uruguayan Lauro Ayestarán (1972) coincide in pointing out that toward 1870, in both their respective countries, a musical type called the *milonga* had been very much alive and developing over the years in rural areas. This genre had settled into a long-established musical substratum that, from the early colonial period, ran along the entire east coast of South America and part of Central America and the Caribbean. From the end of the eighteenth century until about 1850, this zone was rich in dances of great continental resonance, such as the *lundú,* which radiated from Rio de Janeiro, Brazil, and the *danza,* which issued from Havana, Cuba, and was later known as the *habanera* (Vega 1944). This substratum has a basic rhythmic formula that is still active throughout the region (Example 6–13).

Toward the end of the nineteenth century there were different types of *milongas* that have survived to the present day with distinctive characteristics and various degrees of prevalence and areas of dispersion. One form is purely instrumental and played on the guitar. Another has functions for singing, distinguishing between those with composed poetry (sung by one singer) and those with improvised poetry (sung by two singers). Still another accompanies a dance

Ex. 6–13.   Basic rhythmic formula of this broad musical substratum

for interlocking couples. The first three of these four forms have survived to the present and are associated exclusively with the guitar—they have been taken up by professional artists during this century and have been projected throughout Argentina and Uruguay, as well as abroad. The dance form was born in the suburbs of the great port cities of the Río de la Plata—Buenos Aires, Argentina and Montevideo, Uruguay—toward the end of the last century, and it has remained popular in some urban areas of both countries, in the hands of professional musicians and associated with the repertoires and instruments of the *tango*.

The Milonga *as a Rural Tradition*

The purely instrumental *milonga* is played exclusively by men and has remained very active in the Pampeana area of Argentina, and throughout Uruguay. In this form, the guitar player demonstrates the full extent of his technical capabilities, above the basic accompanimental formula for this genre, without adhering to any set melody or formal structure, preferring the harmonic minor mode to the major mode. Thus, it is a purely technical display, a "plucking pastime," in the words of Carlos Vega—one that many travelers of the last century found to be "interminable and boring."

Nonetheless, this *milonga* is very attractive to small groups for listening and appreciation, as the player has the opportunity to dazzle with all of his technical ability, combating the monotony of the tonic and dominant chords, which he sporadically enriches with chromatic progressions and with modulations to neighboring keys. Examples of true virtuosity emerge, in the development of the basic and potential formula, with occasional, more or less brief, plucked phrases. This is the case in the *milonga* heard in Recorded Selection 30, which we collected from a musician in Argentina's La Pampa province.

Going back to the last century, however, the form that is most commonly given the name *milonga* refers to a song accompanied by guitar, and this is the name's most common use today also, sometimes appearing as *milonga pampeana*. In this way, the instrumental accompaniment has lost the leading role that it had in the former type, and is only present to back up the sung lyrics, gaining relevance only in the introduction and in the interludes between strophes.

Ex. 6–14.   Rhythmic formulas of the *milonga* strums

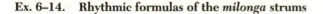

The accompaniment to the sung *milonga* is the result of a very personal search on the part of the guitarist, as he seeks to vary the basic formula. Thus, it is an open-ended accompaniment with repetitive rhythmic formulas that alternate tonic and dominant chords every two measures.

Melodically, the oldest *milonga* was structured on a single section of two phrases in four measures; it was documented by Lauro Ayestarán in Montevideo. It was sung in quatrains, each of which required the repetition of the single musical section, for each phrase corresponded to a line of octosyllabic verse. Later, this form developed into a longer structure of four phrases in eight measures, leading to the development of other strophe-forms, such as the *sextina* (six verses) and the *octavilla* (eight verses). The older and newer structures can be observed in Example 6–15.

Finally, the more current *milonga* acquired another formal structure, one which is generally sung in *décimas espinelas,* the same strophic form that we saw in the *tonada.* Melodically, these *milongas* are structured in five sections of two musical phrases each, which in turn correspond to two lines of text in the *décima.*

The rhythm of the melody, like its accompaniment, is invariably binary, within a 4/8 measure. Its most outstanding melodic characteristics are the *anacrustic* beginning, the distinct presence of syncopation, or the dotted first beat, of each measure, and the final descending cadences, preferably ending on the tonic. Often, there are duplets and triplets.

The *milonga* in *décimas* generally features an introduction and interludes that are plucked on the guitar and, depending on the skill of the performer, may be more or less elaborate. The introduction tends to be longer than the interludes—which sometimes reproduce only a portion of the introduction—as may be heard on Recorded Selection 31, the *milonga* titled "A Juan Bautista Bairoleto."

Ex. 6–15. (a) Transcription of an earlier form of the *milonga*, recorded by Lauro Ayestarán, Montevideo (Ayestarán 1972:72) (b) Transcription of a later form of the *milonga*, recorded by Carlos Vega, Buenos Aires province (Vega 1965:319)

We were able to record this *milonga* as performed by Hugo Gómez Porcel, a horse trainer who lives in an isolated area of La Pampa province, Argentina. This *milonga* (Example 6–16) is one of many sung in the area that recall Juan Bautista Bairoleto, a romantic outlaw who stole from the wealthy to help the poor. This subject is also prevalent in the Mexican *corrido,* among the so-called *corridos de bandoleros* [bandit *corridos*] as classified by Vicente T. Mendoza (1954), inasmuch as they describe the feats of armed men and rebels against their governments. One of these *corridos,* that of Joaquín Murieta, is discussed by John Schechter in Chapter 1.

Bairoleto was killed by the police in 1941 and his memory—suffused with legend—remains alive in rural areas of La Pampa and neighboring provinces where he was also active.

The first two *décimas* describe the *pampa* landscape where the protagonist of the poem spent his life. The poem mentions the trees of the region in their plural forms (*caldenes, sauzales*), the wild horses (*baguales*), and the typical powerful winds of the region (*pampero*) that lift the dry branches of the spiny shrubs called *cardos*—specifically, *cardales* [thistles]—into the air. With great economy of words, the warm-air calm-before-the-storm is described to prepare for the presentation of Bairoleto, the regional hero.

The third strophe refers to the undying memory of this romantic bandit and recalls his figure with a white scarf around his neck, which is a typical feature of the *gaucho pampeano* costume. The last *décima* contains two representative words of *gaucho* speech in which the ending "do" is replaced by "u." Thus, *mentado* [famous] becomes *mentau* (plural *mentaus*), and *necesitado* [needy] becomes *necesitau.* This strophe recalls frequent events in the life of Bairoleto—his assistance to the poor and help for the sick. He would visit the sick to comfort them, and sometimes he would bring them a doctor who rode double with him on the haunches of his own horse. The poem ends by expressing the desire that the province in which Bairoleto was born and lived should recognize his heroism by erecting a monument for him.

There are many *milongas* written for this figure, but almost all of them narrate his adventures and lament his sad fate. This example, however, praises his activities and expresses the desire that Bairoleto be legitimized as a folk hero, in the same way as the founding fathers and national heroes.

In traditional circles, the *milonga* has been and continues to be a song for men—whoever sings always does so while plucking the guitar. In general, the singing always maintains great rhythmic independence relative to the beat sustained by the instrument.

The singer adopts a variety of expressive devices for use in accordance with the text or the circumstances. Some of these devices can be seen in this example. After the first and eighth lines, the guitar accompaniment is interrupted, creating a sense of tension and allowing Bairoleto's name to be mentioned in three of the four strophes. The last two verses of each strophe are accompanied by strong chords, signaling the poetic and musical conclusion. This entire *milonga* has a declamatory (*recitativo*) character that reaches its climax with the sudden change

Ex. 6–16.   Text of "A Juan Bautista Bairoleto"

Se estremecen los caldenes	The *calden* trees tremble
Y sopla fuerte el pampero	And the *pampa* winds blow strong
Hay que apretarse el sombrero	One holds one's hat
La vincha el pelo sostiene.	A band retains one's hair.
Porque la tormenta viene	Because the storm is coming
Como azote al vendaval	The whip-like gale
Y entra a volar el cardal	And the thistles begin to fly
Mientras, los baguales quietos:	Meanwhile, the wild horses are still:
Juan Bautista Bairoleto	Juan Bautista Bairoleto
Hoy te quiero recordar.	I remember you today.
Se despeinan los sauzales	The willow groves are all disheveled
Los caldenes te dan sombra	The calden trees give you shade
Si hasta el pampero te nombra	Even the *pampa* winds call your name
Y te relinchan los baguales.	And the wild horses whinny for you.
Y gimen los pastizales	And the pastures moan
Luego se acallan un tanto	Later they will calm down
Y vuelve a tirarle un manto	And, returning to toss over you an evening cloak
La noche con sus afectos.	The night shows its affection.
Juan Bautista Bairoleto	Juan Bautista Bairoleto
Para el pobre ha sido un santo.	For the poor you've been a saint.
Muchos años ya pasaron	Many years have passed
Que te fuiste para el cielo	Since you rose to the heavens
Con ese blanco pañuelo	With that white scarf
Que muchas te codiciaron.	That so many envied.
Si hasta hoy muchos lloraron	Even today many still cry
Y lo ven por el camino	And see him on the road
Al hombre noble y genuino	The noble and genuine man
Siguiendo su trayectoria	Continuing along his way
Y perdura en la memoria	He persists in the memory
De todos los argentinos.	Of all the Argentines.
Allá por tus correrías	There in your incursions
En tus años más mentaus	In your most famous years
Le diste al necesitau	You gave to the needy
Sacaste al que más tenía.	And took from those who had the most.
Y con esa gran hombría	And with that great manliness
Al pobre diste sustento	You gave the poor sustenance
Al enfermo el sentimiento	Caring for the ill
Y un doctor llevaste en ancas.	And a doctor rode behind you.
A vos te debe La Pampa,	La Pampa owes you,
Juan Bautista, un monumento.	Juan Bautista, a monument.

of tempo that presents the last strophe. Its first four lines are quite literally re-cited, and the *milonga* only resumes its original tempo in the fifth line. In some cases, the device of recitation is applied to an entire strophe, most often the first one. The melody emphasizes the presence of the fifth scale-degree and offers a very characteristic feature of this form—conclusion on the third scale-degree, after a descending cadence.

Since the nineteenth century, the lyrics of the *milonga* have tended to deal with political, historical, humorous, provocative, and patriotic subjects. Its most generalized form was narrative, and thus it has arrived in the present. The *mi-longa*'s primary function is recreational but, according to the texts selected, it has been transformed into an effective tool in the struggles for reorganization in both countries, with respect to political positions and social demands, to the oral chronicling of real historical or current events, to tributes to local heroes, or to the description of rural customs and tasks. One event, absolutely linked to the politi-cal and cultural histories of both Argentina and Uruguay at critical moments in the consolidation of their respective nationalities, situates the *milonga* in a privi-leged position. We will see why, but not before examining certain situations that were critical in making this possible.

The propagation of new European social ideologies in the Río de la Plata in the middle of the nineteenth century, the great economic reforms suffered locally after the incorporation of new technology and after the fencing of pastures, and the great European immigration experienced by these two countries between 1850 and 1914 led to a nationalistic reaction of immense proportions. Buenos Aires and Montevideo entered a period of accelerated urbanization that was ac-companied by a process of change and upheaval. On the one hand, there was the arrival of immigrants who did not always continue their journeys to the least pop-ulated areas of the countryside, but rather accumulated on the outskirts of the port cities. On the other hand, there was the movement of the rural population from the provinces toward the cities as a result of unemployment caused by the fencing off of pasture-lands that had previously known no limits. Furthermore, added to this panorama of mass movement, the dissolution of the armies that had operated until the middle of the last century in struggles over political organiza-tion, gave rise to massive unemployment.

For both countries, the decade of the 1880's marked a critical moment of tur-moil in their nationalist movements. The great thinkers of the period, on both sides of the Río de la Plata, led the reaction on the intellectual level—such names as Argentine Ricardo Rojas and Uruguayan Elías Regules emerged, among oth-ers. Rojas was a prominent figure in the Argentine literature of the period, and in his 1909 work *La restauración nacionalista* . . . [The nationalist restoration] he summarized his warning of the dangers of cosmopolitization that would oblige Ar-gentina to forget its traditions. Doctor Elías Regules, in turn, emerged as a leader of the movement in Uruguay and succeeded in founding the Sociedad Criolla [Creole society] in Montevideo, which to this day is a mainstay for the promotion and development of events evoking *gaucho* traditions. These Creole or traditionalist centers sprang up everywhere in both countries. Their mission was to defend the memory of the *gaucho,* who was already being lost from the national panorama as a real figure, and who had been chosen as an archetype of the Creole tradition.

The literature on the *gaucho*—called *literatura gauchesca*—had given birth to its masterpiece in 1872—*El gaucho Martín Fierro,* by José Hernández. This poem provoked—in the midst of this unique period and climate—an endless series of consequences in the fields of literature, art, theater, music, politics, etc., leading to the idealization of the *gaucho* as the national archetype. It was at this time that the figure of the *gaucho* was recovered from certain urban circles and, with it, his music—the *gato,* the *cifra,* the *estilo,* and the *milonga.*

This subject matter of the reappearance of a lost tradition is still one of the preferred subjects for the *milonga* today. Over the long history of the *gaucho,* two important periods must be recognized—the first is that of the *gaucho* as horseman, circulating freely upon the unclaimed land, hunting wild cattle, and the second, which begins at the end of the nineteenth century, is that of private property, fenced pasture-lands, and the increased use of technology.

Appropriately, the *milonga* "La tradición" (Example 6–17), recorded in La Pampa in 1973, is situated at the beginning of this second stage. The singer begins by pointing out that the traditions have died from the period of Martín Fierro—symbol of the free *gaucho* who resisted change—and, with an old refrain ("tagging along like a dog lost in a procession"), he alludes to his alienation with respect to the world around him. This situation is emphasized by his circumstances of vagrancy and unemployment.

Let us examine the verses. The campfires are a meeting place for the *gauchos,* around which they usually sit in circular fashion. There the presence of foreigners (*gringada*) becomes more visible. They appear mixed (*mesturada*) with the peons (*piones*) or rural workers. The most recent arrivals wear pants rather than *bombachas,* which are the traditional broad, loose-fitting legwear. The few Creoles who remain are described as soft and humble, and are compared to the *guachos,* a word used for animals that have been orphaned.

The last strophe summarizes the most prized belongings of the Creole (the *paisano*), which were his small herd of cattle, his wife, and his house (*rancho*). Today, none of this remains—he has no place of residence and he wanders aimlessly, "going round and round" (*dando güeltas [vueltas]*) like a vulture (*carancho*); certain birds appreciated for their song (the lark) have departed, and other undesirables have arrived, such as the sparrows. The memory has also been eclipsed of a mythological *gaucho* like Santos Vega—a singer of improvised verse (*payador*) to whom many works of *gaucho* literature from the last century, in prose and verse, were dedicated—and, in the face of the poverty in which the *gaucho* lives, even the possibility of owning a horse has been lost. As this is one of the most prized possessions of the *gaucho,* traveling "on foot" signifies not only the loss of his condition as a horseman, but also—even more serious—his condition as a free man.

Ex. 6–17.   Text of the *milonga* "La tradición"

Ha muerto la tradición	Dead is the tradition
Del tiempo de Martín Fierro	Of the time of Martín Fierro
Y anda el gaucho como perro	The *gaucho* tags along like a dog
Perdido en la procesión.	Lost in a procession.
Es una decoración	He is a decoration
Que tiene picos de plomo	That has studs of lead
No es criollo, ni por asomo	He isn't Creole, not by a long shot
Tristes van los argentinos	Sad are the Argentines
Paseando por los caminos	Traveling the roads
Con la linyera en el hombro.	With rags on their backs.
Es basta ver los fogones	It's enough to see the campfires
Pa' darse cuenta es la cosa	To realize the situation
Una gringada asombrosa	An amazing gathering of foreigners
Mesturada con los piones	Mixed with the peons
Todos van de pantalones	All wearing pants
Luciendo su triste facha,	Sad pouting faces
Ya se ha muerto la bombacha	The bombacha is dead
Y si hay un criollo en la rueda	And if there's a Creole in the circle
Tiene blanduras de seda	He has soft spots of silk
Y es humilde como guacho.	And he's humble as a stray.
Los paisanos han tenido	The peasants have all had
Tropilla, mujer, y rancho	A herd, woman, and shack
Y hoy andan como el carancho	And today they go along like the vulture
Dando güeltas afligidos	Going round and round aggrieved
Los gorriones han venido	The sparrows have arrived
Y la calandria se fue	And the *calandria* lark has gone
Ni una payada se vé	Not even a *payada* to be seen
Que recuerde a Santos Vega:	To remind of Santos Vega:
El gringo a caballo llega	The *gringo* on horseback arrives
Y el pobre criollo de a pié.	And the poor Creole on foot.

This process of increasing nationalism in Argentina and Uruguay, to which we referred earlier, has a bearing on the symbolic value of *gaucho* music at that time, as represented in the repertoire of the Pampeana area. Here is why we previously said that the *milonga* had had a privileged position, due to this process. Of the entire *gaucho* repertoire, the *milonga* runs a special course, as it is the preferred form of the singers of improvised verse (the *payadores*) who, though born as a rural phenomenon in both countries, were increasingly approaching the new forms of public performance emerging in the cities at the beginning of the twentieth century. It is this fact that assured the survival of the *milonga*.

The Urban Milonga

There were various and diverse settings in which the countryside and the city came together—for example, the carriage markets, the grocery markets with fruits and vegetables from all regions, the slaughterhouses, the suburban saloons and bars, the confectioneries, and many others. Among the shows for entertainment, the one that served as the greatest nexus between the two worlds, at an early stage, was the circus. The traveling circus took in the *payador* as a folk artist with great drawing power in both countries. The *payador*'s participation in this setting is registered in Argentina between the years 1888 and 1916 (Di Santo 1987).

The *payador* developed his art as a spontaneous poet in two ways—singing as a soloist, improvising upon a subject that the public would request in the very moment, or performing a form of song-duel *(payada)* with a colleague, debating subjects proposed by the public or that arose naturally from the event itself. From the beginning of this century, the preferred form for performing the *payada* has been the *milonga,* and from this early period of the professional *payador* there have remained some texts that permit our appreciating the classic forms of the *payada,* which were performed as questions and answers, in quatrains (Moya 1959:214) (Example 6–18).

This question-and-answer form fell into disuse, whereas the form used for discussion of the most varied of subjects was maintained—at the turn of the century, for open competition and direct challenge, and by mid-century, in a friendly manner. The *payada* expounds upon subjects that are historical, political, philosophical, or related to local customs or current events, and it often involves differences of opinion.

The *payada* of the Río de la Plata axis involves two singers improvising lyrics, and is nothing other than the regional manifestation of a phenomenon of broad diffusion in Latin America, inherited from medieval minstrelsy.[2] These duel songs are performed using different types of strophes and with unique musical characteristics according to region—nonetheless, there is a notable preference for *décimas,* with instrumental accompaniment (usually some type of guitar). This is the case in countries such as Argentina, Brazil, Chile, Colombia, Cuba, Ecuador, Mexico, Panama, Peru, Puerto Rico, the Dominican Republic, Uruguay, and Venezuela. One distinctive characteristic that the *payada* of the Río de la Plata has among the improvised songs in *décimas* of the subcontinent is that the singer must improvise his *décima* without pauses, and very quickly. In other countries, during the course of the *décima,* interludes are permitted in order to give the singer time to think.

The contemporary *payador* in the Río de la Plata region generally continues to be largely of rural origins, and likewise to perform in rural areas, but his professionalism increasingly leads him to seek urban audiences and the mass media. This was achieved progressively in the 1950s, the period of greatest broadcast exposure in both countries (Moreno Chá 1997).

In performances—which take place during rural festivals as well as in theaters and specially organized competitions—the *milonga* sung in *décimas* is the pre-

Ex. 6–18.   *Payada* **in questions and answers**

Question

Venite p'acá muchacho	Come here my lad
Ahurita has de responder	Now answer me
¿Cuántos pelos tiene el gato	How many hairs has a cat
Al momento de nacer?	At the moment it is born?

Answer

La pregunta que me ha hecho	The question you have just asked
Se la quiero responder.	I wish to answer.
Si no se le cayó ni uno	If not one fell off
Toditos ha de tener.	He should have all of them.

Question

Y ya que a cantar vinimos,	Since we came here to sing
Dígame a ver si acabamos	Tell me so we can be going
Lo que persiguiendo vamos	What we are pursuing
Sin pensar que perseguimos . . .	Not reflecting that we are pursuing . . .

Answer

Los guascazos de la suerte	The strokes of chance
Nos llevan casi corriendo	Have us almost racing
Lo que vamos persiguiendo	After that which we are chasing
Y sin pensarlo, es la muerte.	Not supposing it's our last dance.

ferred form, whereas other strophic types and musical forms are used mostly for didactic purposes or to lend variety to shows. In the *payada*, each *payador* sings his *décimas* in alternation with those of his companion. Only at the end is the custom altered as they sing the closing strophe between the two of them. They do this by alternating every two verses, always giving their names at the end. The strophe in Example 6–19 was sung at the end of a *payada* between Nilo Caballero (Uruguay) and Víctor Di Santo (Argentina), in this order: Verses 1–2, 5–6, and 9–10 were sung by Caballero, and verses 3–4 and 7–8 were sung by Di Santo.

The melodies used in the *payadas* always have a more restricted range than that of the sung *milongas*, rarely exceeding that of a sixth. With respect to the melody, there are two ways of performing a *payada*—the singers may use the same melody line, or each may sing a different melody line that is maintained until the final strophe, as may be heard on Recorded Selection 32 ("El payador de ayer, el payador de hoy" [yesterday's *payador*, today's *payador*]). In both cases, the melody line is taken as a basic contour upon which variations are constantly created, in accordance with the needs of the text and expressions.

The following transcribed example illustrates the way in which a veteran and prestigious Uruguayan *payador* varies the same melody over the course of two

Ex. 6–19.   Text of the final *décima* of a *payada* sung by Caballero and Di Santo

—Bueno, acollare argentino,
   acompañe al oriental.

—Como nó, en forma cordial
   yo lo sigo en el camino.
—Por Hidalgo, por Gabino,°
   por toda la patria entera.
—En una forma certera
   aquí termina este canto:
—Son Caballero y Di Santo
   hermanando las banderas.

—Well, let's end this, Argentine,
   accompany the Easterner [the
   Uruguayan].
—Of course, with jubilation
   I'll follow along behind.
—For Hidalgo, for Gabino,°
   for the entire nation.
—In a form of condensation
   here ends our song:
—We are Caballero and Di Santo
   with our flags in fraternization.

°Bartolomé Hidalgo (1788–1822) was an outstanding Uruguayan poet, and Gabino Ezeiza (1858–1916) a renowned Argentine *payador*.

strophes. We can observe how subtly the artist varies the melody through rhythmic changes. Except for the last measure, which ends on the tonic, over the course of nineteen measures only five coincide rhythmically—measures 1, 2, 6, 7, and 13. The first strophe has greater tension, thanks to the use of syncopation and dotted figures, devices which are used to a lesser extent in the second strophe.

Examples 6–20 and 6–21 set forth the first and second strophes sung by Héctor Umpiérrez in a *payada* celebrated with Abel Soria. The first *décima* begins this *payada* with sarcastic poetry. Umpiérrez is being ironic in announcing to his less experienced and less prestigious companion that he will gain the victory in this encounter (very improbable). The second *décima* maintains the sarcastic tone, mentioning Abel Soria's personal history as a rural worker and indicating that his current success as a singer has not quite succeeded in erasing the features of his past, such as his stride and manner of moving about on the stage.

The singing of the *milonga* during a *payada* does not have dynamic variation. It is always performed at full voice and at maximum volume. The tempo is faster than for the sung *milonga* and accelerates to the extent that the improvised poetry excites the *payadores* and the audience. Of the expressive devices mentioned previously relative to the sung *milonga*, the pause at the end of the first and eighth verse is also used in the *payada*. The voice has great rhythmic independence from the guitar accompaniment, moving via *rubato* that is regulated by each singer in his own way.

The guitar sustains a monotonous accompaniment, alternating between the tonic and dominant chords every two measures. The two *payadores* play their guitars together in the same key, usually E minor, during the entire *payada*, each maintaining his own personal formula.

During this type of performance, in which the *payador* places his prestige at risk, all of his energies are dedicated to his poetic improvisation, inasmuch as this is the essence of his art and will lead to either victory or defeat, as determined by the public or a jury.

Ex. 6–20.   Melody of *payada* sung by Héctor Umpiérrez

The skill of producing improvised lyrics is cultivated through reading, study, and observation. This art is governed by strict rules of oral transmission that regulate what is permitted and what is not accepted with reference to the verbal and corporal expression of the participants, but also with respect to their ethical behavior. In addition to literary devices, there are others that are used in the relation between the *payador* and his occasional opponent, as well as in relation to his public (Moreno Chá 1997).

Taking into account, then, that in a *payada* the *payadores* put to the test their knowledge, shrewdness, depth of thought, verbal ingenuity, poetic inspiration, mental agility, memory, and rhetorical skills, let's now listen to Recorded Selection 32.

This is a fragment of a *payada* that was held in the Teatro Presidente Alvear in Buenos Aires in 1995 to celebrate *Payador* Day. This event was organized by the Museo de Motivos Argentinos José Hernández, and has been held annually for the last eleven years under the title *Encuentro de Payadores Rioplatenses* [Río de la Plata *payadores* encounter], as it brings together singers from Argentina and Uruguay. In this case, the singers are Roberto Ayrala and José Curbelo, two of the most prestigious *payadores* in the region, both of whom have been invited to sing in other countries, such as Spain, Brazil, Cuba, and Puerto Rico (Illustration 6–3).

Ex. 6–21.   Text of *payada* sung by Héctor Umpiérrez

Payador don Abel Soria	*Payador don* Abel Soria
Cantar hoy al lado suyo	To sing today at your side
Será para mí un orgullo	Will give me great pride
Y para usted la victoria.	And for you a victory.
Yo aplaudo su trayectoria	I applaud your history
De legítimo cantor	As a legitimate song-man
Que pese a ser un señor	That despite being a gentleman
De encumbrados escenarios	Of eminent stages
No perdió el tranco canario	You keep your *tranco canario*
[paso campesino]	[peasant's stride] through the ages
De su tiempo de arador.	From your time as a plowman.
Hoy que usted conoce el brillo	Today you discover the luminosity
Del éxito y de la fama	Of success and fame
Con un pueblo que lo aclama	From a people who do you acclaim
Por triunfador y sencillo.	As a winner, and modest.
Antes plantaba en Cerrillos	In Cerrillos you planted with industry
Batata, papa, y acelga	Yams, potatoes, and chard
Y eso es tan obvio que huelga	And it's so obvious it's not hard
Develar cuál fue su cuna	To perceive where you come from
Porque sube a la tribuna	As you rise to the rostrum
Como quien corta una melga	Like one who plows a sward [furrow].
[huella que deja el arado].	

From a *payada* of sixteen strophes, we have selected four, as shown in Example 6–22. The subjects upon which they must improvise are usually chosen by the public or are allotted by a drawing from a pool of proposed topics. In this case, the artists are improvising (performing the *payada*) on the subject of the *payador* of yesterday and the *payador* of today. Uruguayan José Curbelo (whose lines are marked II) sings of the *payador* of today, and Argentine Roberto Ayrala (with lines marked I) sings of the *payador* of the past. Each sung strophe is awarded by the listening public with applause, graduated according to the skill that the *payador* has demonstrated in his improvisation and to the impact that is thereby provoked.

The first strophe recalls the Argentine General San Martín's epic campaign crossing the Andes from Cuyo to liberate Chile from the Spanish. The first battle in Chilean territory was in Chacabuco (1817), at which the Spanish were defeated. The second strophe refers to the economic insecurity of the *payador* today—he is the purveyor of an art form that joins hands with the unemployed. The third strophe recalls García (1897–1935), an Argentine *payador* whose singing was clearly oriented toward the working class. The fourth strophe sketches with delicate irony the critical situation of today's *payador*, whose playing can now be recorded so that the errors he commits during his improvisation

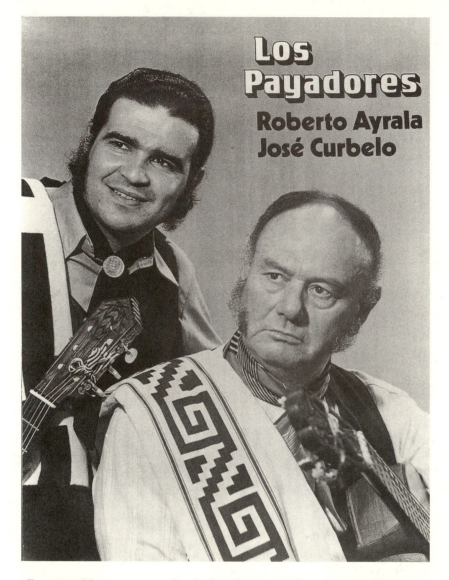

Ill. 6–3. Publicity poster with which Roberto Ayrala and José Curbelo announce their performances. Studio photo.

are easily discovered. Here, there is a clear reference to the rules mentioned earlier. Of the numerous infractions possible, he mentions an error that is so gross that no good *payador* would ever commit it: the repetition of a verse.

The reference to, or memory of, national heroes is very frequent, as well as of prestigious *payadores,* writers, and thinkers, as we see here in the case of General San Martín, who played a major part in expelling the Spanish from Chile (1818) and later from Peru (1821).

Ex. 6–22. Text of a *payada* between Roberto Ayrala and José Curbelo (fragment)

(I)

Cuando San Martín cruzó
A la fría cordillera
Y junto con la bandera
Al payador lo llevó.
Y estaba pensando yo
Mirando esa inmensidad
En honor a la verdad
Que peleó y le dio un retruco
  [respuesta final y contundente]
Y le cantó en Chacabuco
Loas por la libertad.

(II)

Canta el payador ahora
Sumamente preocupado
Nombra a los desocupados
Que esperan nuevas auroras.
Y en su guitarra sonora
Marcha por estos senderos
Y dando el canto sincero
Puede sufrir una herida:
El de ayer jugó su vida
El de hoy se juega el puchero
  [comida típica].

(I)

Pero hubo quien defendía
Eso con todita el alma
Y le tributo una palma
Don Luis Acosta García.
Su guitarra, su armonía,
A veces era salobre
Aunque le faltaba un cobre [dinero]
Pero cumplió con su credo,
Porque nunca tuvo miedo
Pa' defender a los pobres.

(II)

El payador—el que vale—
Pienso yo en el del pasado
Dejó su verso grabado
A oyentes circunstanciales.

(I)

When San Martín made his way
Across the cold Andes chain
Together with the flag in train
The *payador* he did convey.
And thinking there was I
Looking at that immensity
In honor of the veracity
That he'd fought a *retruco* [final and
  clever reply]
And in Chacabuco he vocalized
Praises for liberty.

(II)

Now the *payador* sings on
So very worried
He names the unemployed
Who await a hopeful dawn.
And in his guitar's mellow song
He walks those winding ways
A sincere song he says
He could suffer pain:
His life yesterday he played
Today with a *puchero* [typical dish] he
  pays.

(I)

But there was one who defended
That with all his soul
And he I do extoll
Don Luis Acosta García.
His guitar, his harmony,
At times a little fickle
Though he didn't have a nickel
But he fulfilled his creed,
Because he never went weak-kneed
At defending the poor and sick.

(II)

The *payador*—the actual—
I'm thinking of the past
Left verse that would last
For his listeners so casual.

Ex. 6–22.   Text of a *payada* between Roberto Ayrala and José Curbelo (fragment) *(continued)*

Con valores naturales	With values that are natural
Hoy también tiene un valor:	Today they're still precious:
Tiene que ser creador	You have to be ingenious
Y ser contínuo en su esfuerzo	Your efforts you must nurse
Donde repitas un verso	If you repeat a verse
Te descubre el grabador.	The tape recorder gets you.

If we analyze the four *décimas* presented here, we will see that each expresses one idea in the first four lines. This idea is developed in the following four lines, leading up to the "climax" or *remate,* in which the principal idea is rounded off in the last two lines—ideally of synthesis, beauty, and solid reasoning. This ending may provide a foothold for the companion *payador* to re-create or debate the same idea, or not to follow the sequence at all.

Finally, we will briefly mention the fourth *milonga* form that was commonly found in Argentina and Uruguay at the end of the nineteenth century—the *milonga bailada* [danced *milonga*]. This form reached its greatest popularity in the suburbs of the two port cities of Buenos Aires and Montevideo, and enjoyed a golden era during the 1890s, being presented in the theaters of Buenos Aires as part of revues, comedies, and *zarzuelas* [operettas on Spanish subjects].

The *milonga bailada* consolidated its presence in the public dance halls, brothels, and gambling halls, which went by a variety of names and different characteristics in the two cities. In Montevideo, it should be noted that the evolution of *milonga* choreography was strongly influenced by the presence of an African-Uruguayan public in these establishments.

It was in this context that the *milonga* came into contact with other dances, such as the European mazurka and polka, and the Cuban dance called the *habanera.* These dances for couples were already being danced in the halls with the choreographic elements that later characterized the *milonga* and its successor, the *tango—cortes* and *quebradas.*

While the old *tango,* during a period ranging from 1890 to 1910, enjoyed a certain degree of popularity in rural areas, accompanied by the accordion, the danced *milonga* always remained part of an urban and suburban repertoire. *Habanera,* danced *milonga,* and *tango* coexisted in this context as purely instrumental forms during a period of great confusion and mixing of names and analogous choreographic movements. The *tango* was established as an independent and popular genre toward 1900, emerging as a new product of a variety of common elements with respect to rhythm, structure, and melody. In rising above the other two dances, the *tango* drew upon a depth of creativity in terms of the choreography that developed over the years, and that evolved into a new form of dancing in couples—the embrace. Around 1910, after it was accepted by and also disseminated from Paris, it became the first dance for embracing couples in the West and embarked upon a long international voyage that has continued into the present (Pelinski 1995).

In Uruguay during the 1930s, the *milonga* experienced a renaissance as a dance for couples, with rhythmic accompaniment by African-Uruguayan drums *(tamboriles).* Thus, the *candombe* emerged in Montevideo and rapidly spread throughout all of Uruguay (Ayestarán 1990:11). By the 1960s it had become one of the rhythms that was most emblematic of the African-Uruguayan population, and of Uruguay in general.

In summary, we can say that of these four forms of the *milonga,* the first three have followed diverse routes and are now found both in rural contexts, among more traditional cultures, and in urban contexts among more global cultures. The instrumental *milonga* that is played on solo guitar has remained primarily in rural contexts, being projected outside of this environment by professional artists dedicated to folk music, as well as by composers with academic training involved in the movement of musical nationalism. This movement took place approximately between 1850 and 1950 and drew upon the *milonga* for symphonic and chamber works.

The *milonga pampeana,* sung with guitar, remains a folk song with widespread popularity in the Argentine Pampeana area and in all of Uruguay. Projected beyond these areas, its enormous success is owed to Atahualpa Yupanqui in Argentina (see Chapter 9) and to Alfredo Zitarrosa in Uruguay.

The *milonga* of the *payada de contrapunto* [song duel] survives rather weakly among aficionados in rural areas as a spontaneous phenomenon. In the cities, it is performed almost exclusively among professionals.

THE GUITAR

CONSTRUCTION PROCESS

The guitar (Illustration 6–4) is the most common instrument in Hispanic America. It is used more intensely than any other instrument, and it has generated the greatest number of variants. Just as in Europe, in America the guitar developed numerous variants of *guitarra, guitarrón,* and *guitarrilla.* The guitar has assumed various and diverse forms, with new technologies and materials of construction as well as new tunings and playing techniques, the latter being its most relevant feature (Moreno Chá 1993).

In the three countries of the Southern Cone, the guitar is the quintessential folk instrument. In Uruguay the guitar is found throughout the country, but in Chile and Argentina it has just barely penetrated the high-altitude Andean areas in the provinces of the extreme north, where there is a strong indigenous substratum. In Argentina and Uruguay, the instrument is played almost exclusively by men because the playing of traditional instrumental music by women is very limited.

As an instrument for solo instrumentals, the guitar was developed extensively in the most European urban areas of the region, where the plucking technique originating with the Spanish *vihuela* was maintained. This technique has undergone nearly virtuosic developments in the rural areas of the Pampeana area of Argentina and in Uruguay, which is evident to this day. However, what accounts for its widespread diffusion is its double function of providing accompaniment to songs and its capacity to accompany other instruments, earning its keep by maintaining both rhythm and harmony. This latter aspect earned the guitar a wide diversity of instrumental associations that vary according to region.

It has been more than forty years since the manufacture of guitars in the Southern Cone was taken over by small factories specializing in techniques of mass production. There are few luthiers who still persist in their handicraft, but José Jacoppi is one of the exceptions. The son of an Italian luthier, Jacoppi learned his craft from his father. He lived with his father in Spain, where he was born, and in France. He has now lived in San Fernando, in the suburbs of Buenos Aires, for fifty years and is considered the most prestigious guitar maker in Argentina. Over the last twenty years, his guitars have been commercialized outside of Argentina by the Japanese firm of Yamaha.

A visit to Jacoppi's workshop offers a guided tour through the steps of the craft, explained by the owner of the house and demonstrated by his disciple, Pedro Caccefo. The guitar consists of three different sections—the head, the neck, and the body, the last being composed of the back, the soundboard, and the ribs (Illustration 6–4). The Jacoppi guitars—one meter in length—are made of five different woods. The head and the neck are constructed of Argentine or Paraguayan cedar. The fingerboard, which is placed over the neck, is made of African or Indian ebony. The back and ribs of the body are made of Argentine or Paraguayan carob, African mahogany, or African or Indian *jacaranda,* and the soundboard is made of imported Scandinavian silver fir. The proportions and construction techniques are those established by Spaniard Antonio de Torres Jurado (1817–1892), of the Andalusian School of guitars. Having been the quintessential guitar maker of his era, his designs continue to serve as models for luthiers all over the world.

In the workshop we visited in October 1997, the wood that was used was acquired in strips and stored in the open air. Using chalk, the forms of the back, the top, and the sides are sketched directly onto the strips of wood (Illustration 6–5). These sketches are drawn from preexisting templates that represent halves of the corresponding sections, and will later be joined together. Each of the pieces is carefully polished.

Once cut to size, the ribs acquire their arched forms through a gentle warming process that permits the craftsman to achieve the desired curvature. The two halves of the back are joined and reinforced by two or three transverse bars, and later the form is placed in a mold in the form of the guitar, where it will remain for several days until each of the glued parts is perfectly dry (Illustration 6–6). Later, the back is joined to the two ribs. The soundboard is assembled by joining the halves together, and then the *rosette* that borders the mouth of the body is set in place (Illustration 6–7). On the backside, which will be on the inside of the guitar, the top receives a rib reinforcement that is in the form of a fan located at the

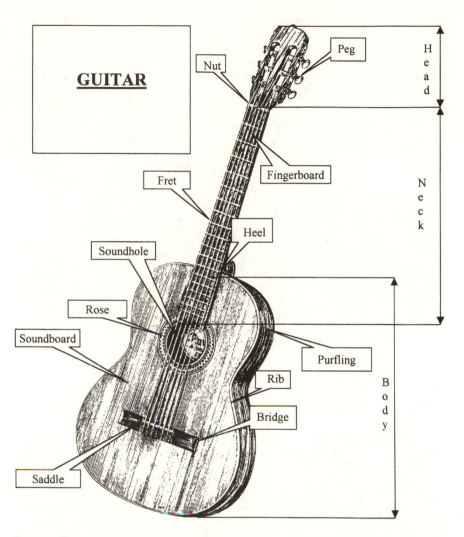

Ill. 6–4. The guitar

inferior lobe. Once this is done, the soundboard is joined to the ribs while still in the press.

The next stage entails gluing the neck and the heel to the body. Finally, the guitar is removed from the press, carefully polished and adorned with purfling along the edges of the soundboard. This finishing process, which formerly involved adorning the mouth and the edges of the soundboard with ivory and mother-of-pearl, is now done with different types of wood while maintaining the design of the ancient technique called *taraceada* [inlaying], which the Spanish attributed to their Arabian heritage.

Ill. 6–5. Pedro Caccefo begins the process of marking the wood, following the shape of the templates. Photo by Ercilia Moreno Chá.

Ill. 6–6. Press used for joining the various parts of the guitar. Photo by Ercilia Moreno Chá.

Once the inlaying of the edges is complete, the fingerboard is attached to the neck and then fitted with frets of nickel silver. The head of the guitar is perforated in order to be fitted with a machine head, responsible for tightening the six strings (Illustration 6–8). The strings vibrate between the nut, made of calf's bone and located at the union of the machine head and the fingerboard, and the nut located on the bridge, once the latter has been attached to the soundboard after lacquering (Illustration 6–9). The lacquering of the guitar is done manually, with several layers of a preparation called *goma laca* [lacquer gum].

The entire construction of the guitar is based on gluing together the wooden sections and interior reinforcements, which are located at the most critical points of union. Only the machine head is fitted with metal screws to the head of the guitar. The sonority of the guitar depends on the type and condition of the wood used, the design of the construction, and the type of lacquer used to finish the instrument.

TUNING SYSTEMS

It is generally accepted that the guitar in Latin America followed the same evolution as in Spain. There the guitar was used with four groups of strings until the middle of the sixteenth century, at which time the first guitars with five pairs of strings were documented. Toward the end of the eighteenth century, the double strings were replaced by single strings, and in 1800 guitars of six strings began to appear in Spain. This version completely replaced the previous version of five strings, but in Chile and Argentina there are some vestiges of its former presence,

Ill. 6–7. Placement of the *rosette* on the upper surface. Photo by Ercilia
Moreno Chá.

Ill. 6–8. Creating the perforations of the head with a lathe, in which, subsequently, the six pegs will be seated. Photo by Ercilia Moreno Chá.

Ill. 6–9. Guitar with small press situated at the bridge, once it has been glued to the surface, to await drying. Photo by Ercilia Moreno Chá.

as some such instruments remain, or some playing techniques deliberately avoid the sixth string, or certain tunings only involve the first five strings though the instrument itself may have six strings.

The possibility that the guitar has always offered of varying the tuning led to the development in these countries of a very particular feature. Rural tunings developed so as to allow for a number of new timbric possibilities and hand positions on the fingerboard. The advantages of these tunings lie in the sonority of the instrument and in simplifications for the left hand. The sonority of the guitar increases because more open strings are played, and because the strings that are pressed are done so with greater precision. The action of the left hand is facilitated because its position on the fingerboard is more comfortable, fewer strings are pressed (in some cases, none), and the entire barre finger can be positioned above the neck, a possibility that is seen only in Chile.

Finares campesinos [Peasant tunings], a study carried out in Chile on rural tunings used traditionally, discovered fifty-seven tunings different from the common or universal tuning (Díaz Acevedo 1994). Only three of those that appear in this study had been previously recorded by María Ester Grebe (1967). The research work of Díaz Acevedo extended from the Diaguita-Picunche-Hispanic area to the Chilota area; this was the broad zone with the most intensive guitar use in his country. There, the universal tuning is recognized by its normative or institutionalized character and is termed *por común* [in common], *por correcta* [in correct], *por derecho* [in straight], *por escuela* [in school], *por música* [in music], *por normal* [in normal], or *por solfeo* [in sol-fa]. The remaining rural tunings possess a nomenclature that obeys different criteria and that varies regionally and locally.

Throughout Chile, there is a rural tradition that speaks to the existence of forty traditional tunings. Knowledge of one more would imply a pact with the devil, and there exist various versions of the consequences that such a pact would entail. But in practice, a good guitar player has at his disposal four to seven basic tunings. To those he adds the corresponding variations.

The work of Díaz Acevedo detected twelve mother tunings, from which derived many variations, and four independent tunings. Of the fifty-seven traditional tunings that were recorded in Chile in this study, anywhere from one to all six strings may be modified, and there has been a preference for modifying four strings.

Although the common, or universal, tuning is the most widespread in Chile, the rural guitar player has generally preferred two other tunings that have been specifically maintained—*por transporte* [in transport] and *por tercera alta* [in high third]. The *por transporte* tuning is preferred for plucking techniques and *trinado* (discussed below) because the open stringing affords an unblemished major chord with the duplication of all its sounds. Nine variations of this tuning have been collected.

Por tercera alta is the most commonly used tuning for strumming, and it is the preferred tuning for learning the guitar because of the ease it affords for left-hand fingering. In effect, the tonic and dominant chords of the most commonly used

Ex. 6–23. *Por tercera alta* **tuning**

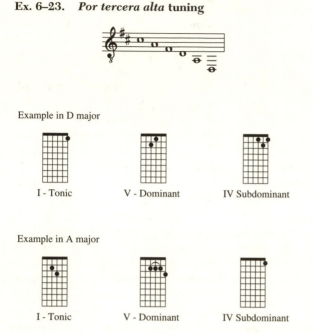

Example in D major

I - Tonic   V - Dominant   IV Subdominant

Example in A major

I - Tonic   V - Dominant   IV Subdominant

keys in this tuning only require the use of one or two fingers, respectively. The dominant chord is played with a barre finger on the second fret, using the index finger on the first, second, third, and fourth strings. We will show the tuning first and then some chords in the most common keys (Example 6–23), so that the student who so wishes may try to discover these possibilities for him/herself.

Example 6–24 provides a table with the tuning for the ten variations offered by the *por tercera alta* tuning. The respective names are (a) *por banda* [in band], (b) *tercera baja* [in low third], (c) *huemulina*, (d) *tercera falseada* [in false third], (e) *doble común* [in common double], (f) *por rabel* [in rebec], (g) *tercera alta* [in high third], (h) *baja sencilla* [in simple low], (i) *común por tres* [in common for three], and (j) *tercera menor* [in minor three].

Díaz Acevedo's *Finares campesinos* revealed the specificity of certain tunings—some are reserved for reinforcing the bass notes among groups of various guitars, others are preferred only for plucking, or remain exclusively in use for one particular kind of music, or are valued because they facilitate the minor key, so rare in Chilean folk music.

There is another very peculiar practice in Chilean guitar playing, which is the simultaneous use of two guitars in different tunings. *Tonadas* have been documented in which one guitar was tuned in C major while the other was tuned in D major (Chavarría 1995), as well as guitar strumming in *por tercera alta* accompanying the plucking of a guitar in *por común* (Díaz Acevedo 1994:142).

For guitar tunings collected in Argentina, we are indebted to Carlos Vega and Isabel Aretz. In *Los instrumentos musicales aborígenes y criollos de la Argentina*

Ex. 6–24. **Variations of** *por tercera alta*

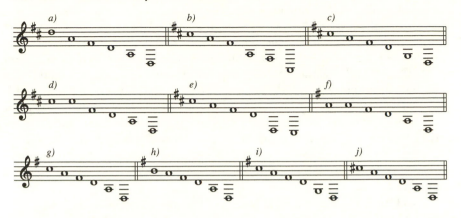

[The aboriginal and creole musical instruments of Argentina] (1946), Vega registered twenty-five tunings differing from the common tuning, some of which coincide with the Chilean tunings.

In turn, Isabel Aretz added twenty-eight different rural tunings to this panorama in *El folklore musical argentino* [Argentine folk music] (1952) and in *Música tradicional de La Rioja* [Traditional music of La Rioja] (1978). In total, these two musicologists collected fifty-three different tunings which, compared with the studies carried out in Chile, reveal a preference for extending the tunings toward the higher registers, tuning up with respect to the natural tuning, whereas in Chile the tendency is toward the lower registers. In both countries, the strings whose tunings are most commonly altered are the fifth and sixth strings.

Comparing all the tunings presented by these studies, we conclude that the tunings related to the old double-course strings are more common in Chile. In Uruguay, Lauro Ayestarán collected five tunings that differ from the common tuning, but he published only their names (1968:61–62), so we do not include Uruguay in our survey here.

Guitar Performance Traditions in the *Tonada* and the *Milonga*

The guitar performance practices of the two genres we have considered here in depth—the *tonada* and the *milonga*—provide examples of some very distinctive Latin American playing techniques. In Europe, the early guitar inherited the plucking technique from the *vihuela* and the lute, such that the strings are played one, two, or three at time. The right hand utilizes the fingernails, the fingertips, or the pick. In the mid-sixteenth century, a new strumming technique (*música golpeada*) was thought to have begun in Spain, though it is believed that this technique had been in use since long before then (Bermudo 1555). From the end of the sixteenth century until the mid-seventeenth century, the Spanish guitar vigorously developed this technique under the new name of *rasgueado* [strumming], and it was quickly dispersed throughout the folk population, arriving finally at the courts. From the beginning of the seventeenth century on, many ways were tried of transcribing this new technique, which involved playing all the strings simultaneously. Beginning with Italian Giovanni Paolo Foscarini (1630), who introduced the blending of both techniques—plucking and strumming—guitar method books indicated the importance of this new technique. Books were published with scores that were exclusively for guitar plucking, for guitar strumming, or for a mixed style (Bordas and Arriaga 1991:72). The strum became one of the most sophisticated performance aspects of the guitar in the seventeenth and eighteenth centuries until, in the nineteenth century, it became completely obsolete as a performance practice for classical guitar music, where even today it is used only in isolated cases and in search of special effects.

In contrast, and as demonstrated by the playing of the *flamenco* guitar, the strum has endured in Spanish folk guitar practice up to the present day, and it is with this practice that the guitar arrived in America at the beginning of the colonial period. In these Latin American countries, highly characteristic strums emblematic of distinct geographic locations were developed which, together with various tunings, gave the guitar its true Creole character.

The Chilean *tonada* offers a whole range of different strums, which is not the case with the *tonada cuyana*. The strums may be played with a downward or an upward motion, over all or part of the strings. According to the technique of the guitar player, different fingers of the right hand are used. One of the most notable devices of the Chilean strum is the *chicoteado*, which was demonstrated on Recorded Selection 27 ("Tonada al niño Dios"). This type of strum—almost inevitable in the refrain of the *tonadas* that are sung in relation to Christmas—is a distinctive feature of every singer, or *cantora*, and is apparent in the rhythmic aspect. Among the most characteristic features is the accentuation of the weak beats of each measure (through which a syncopated effect is attained), and that of producing delayed effects on certain beats (which is heard on the example).

The strum is usually combined with a muting effect on the strings, which may be attained with the palm of the hand or with the knuckles of the right hand. This effect is called *quedo* in Argentina, *chasquido* in Chile. The strums for the *tonada* are shown in Example 6–25 as provided by Margot Loyola, with the *chasquidos* indicated by the symbol ° over the corresponding note.

In addition to the strumming technique, there are two other very common forms of playing the Chilean *tonada*. The *punteo* involves picking the strings one, two, or three at a time, and may appear in the introduction and the interludes—the first three high strings are usually played, in chords in thirds, with the fingertips or with the nails of the index, middle, and ring fingers. The plucking may also accompany parts of the singing, in which case the picking is usually a third below the melody line. The *trinado* is the technique that the guitar player uses to combine simultaneously the plucking and the strumming accompaniment. The first three strings are played in the plucking, and the thumb plays the remaining bass strings. This technique is used only with those transposed tunings in which the

Ex. 6–25.   **Strums for the *tonada* with *chasquido***

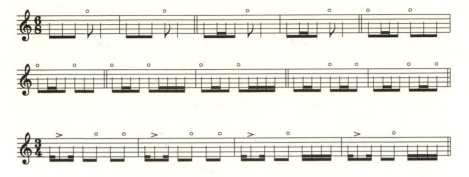

three bass strings occur in the tonic or dominant chords of the key being played, such that they are always in harmony with the melody that is being plucked.

The *tonada cuyana* employs only strumming and plucking. The frequent use of two guitars assures the separation of the two techniques—the introductions and the interludes are plucked by the more skillful of the two guitarists, while the other guitarist maintains the strumming.

In contrast, the *milonga* is plucked (Example 6–26). In the case of a *milonga* that is played in a purely instrumental fashion, the strum appears only briefly and for effect, as heard on Recorded Selection 30. Both the introductions and the interludes may entail melodic plucking, which can be appreciated on Recorded Selection 31 ("A Juan Bautista Bairoleto"). Another type of interlude does not have a melodic design but rather plays on rhythmically varying the basic strumming formula (later maintained during the singing section), which in this case is of four sixteenth-notes per measure.

When the *milonga* is sung, a varied plucking accompaniment is employed, which is used by each singer to differentiate himself from the others. Example 6–27 shows six selections. The plucking of the *milonga* when sung in *contrapunto* or as a song-duel is a constant bass line that alternates between the tonic and dominant chords, in general with two measures for each. Both are open chords; the tonic is always in root position, and the dominant appears generally as a dominant seventh, and in first inversion. Some of the accompaniments for these *milongas* are presented in Example 6–28.

Ex. 6–26.   ***Milonga* interlude**

Ex. 6–27.   **Accompaniment for the sung *milonga***

There are no apparent differences between the *rasgueos* [strumming] for the *milonga* in Argentina and Uruguay, except the peculiar omission of the sixth string, something that appears in some traditional *rasgueos* of the Uruguayan *milonga*.

Ex. 6–28.   **Accompaniment for *milonga de contrapunto***

CONCLUSION

It is in the Southern Cone of South America that distinct routes of penetration of different cultural streams arriving in South America since the beginning of the colonial period may best be observed. One such current, extending to the first half of the eighteenth century, arrived from Spain, through the Pacific to Lima, the great viceroyal capital and the most important center for the dissemination of European culture via that Iberian country. Its penetration extended strongly to the central area of Chile and throughout the Creole-populated areas of Argentina.

The other current arrived via the Atlantic and became most significant after the second half of the eighteenth century. The ports of Buenos Aires, Argentina, and Rio de Janeiro, Brazil, played major roles as centers for the diffusion of Latin American, European, and African cultural features.

What we have called the Andes axis has its base in the Pacific current, exemplified here by the *tonada*. We have detected in the *tonada* numerous elements of great antiquity, as well as local and regional characteristics. We may recall the use of early tunings; the preference for strumming over plucking; the preference for beats of ternary divisions; the use of parallel thirds in the melody as well as in some instrumental accompaniments; the antiquated poetic devices (linked verses, the presence of refrains and *ripios*); the elegant character of lyrics; the various functions served by the *tonada;* and the use of the *rebec.* In accordance with the tradition of a strong feminine presence in the Chilean musical world, the *tonada* has been the most representative Creole genre of this tradition. In the Argentine area of Cuyo, this custom was lost in the first half of this century due to a notable masculine dominance in the traditional music of Argentina, increasingly consolidated by the mass media. In both countries, the *tonada* is considered a disappearing form by the exponents of the music themselves.

What we have called the Río de la Plata axis has its base at the Atlantic current, exemplified here by the *milonga.* We may recall the basic rhythmic formula, one that is common to various Atlantic coastal countries; the exclusive presence of beats with binary divisions; a guitar more plucked than strummed; the development of refined plucking techniques of great technical difficulty, indicating the influence of the classical guitar; and the exclusive presence of the masculine singing voice.

The *milonga* has penetrated into the urban areas, and it has fused with contemporary repertoires in Uruguay. Both in these repertoires and in the special case of the *payada,* the lyrics seem to be suffused with the surrounding reality. Through the *payada,* the *milonga* has maintained, in the Río de la Plata region, the long-established custom of sung poetic improvisation disseminated throughout Latin America. The *milonga,* which appears as a purely masculine genre, has embarked upon new avenues during the twentieth century; while its rural manifestations seem to be wavering, it has found in the *tango* a unique way to survive. Together with the Cuban *habanera,* the Brazilian *maxixe* and *lundú,* the Río de la Plata *tango,* and the North American foxtrot, the *milonga* belongs to the group of American dances that have achieved the greatest diffusion worldwide.

In this scheme, the *tonada* represents a Creole nexus of Andean characteristics that is moving towards extinction. The *milonga,* in contrast—nourished by American and African elements—represents a nucleus that has taken shape and grown into dances of great extracontinental significance.

REFERENCES

Advis, Luis. 1998. Historia y características de la Nueva Canción Chilena. In *Clásicos de la música popular chilena, 1960–1973, Raíz folklórica,* vol. 2, ed. Luis Advis, Eduardo Cáceres, Fernando García and Juan Pablo González, pp. 29–41. Santiago, Chile: Sociedad Chilena del Derecho de Autor, Ediciones Universidad Católica de Chile.

Antología del Folklore Musical Chileno. 1965. Vol. 4, *Maule.* Santiago, Chile: Instituto de Investigaciones Musicales.

Andreu Ricart, Ramón. 1993. *Cantando cuento mi vida: Cantares y contares de Margot Loyola.* Unpublished manuscript.

Aretz, Isabel. 1952. *El folklore musical argentino.* Buenos Aires, Argentina: Ricordi.

———. 1978. *Música tradicional de La Rioja.* Caracas, Venezuela: Instituto Internacional de Etnomusicología y Folklore (INIDEF).

Ayestarán, Lauro. 1967. *El folklore musical uruguayo.* Montevideo, Uruguay: Arca.

———. 1968. *Teoría y práctica del folklore.* Montevideo, Uruguay: Arca.

———. 1972. *La música en el Uruguay.* Vol. 1. Montevideo, Uruguay: Servicio Oficial de Difusión Radioeléctrica.

———. 1990. El tamboril afro-montevideano. In *El tamboril y la comparsa,* pp. 7–48. Montevideo, Uruguay: ARCA.

Barros, Raquel and Manuel Dannemann. 1970. *El romancero chileno.* Santiago, Chile: Ediciones de la Universidad de Chile.

Bermudo, Juan. 1957. *Declaración de instrumentos musicales.* Kassel, Germany: Bärenreiter. (Originally published 1555.)

Bordas, Cristina and Gerardo Arriaga. 1991. La guitarra desde el barroco hasta ca. 1950 [The guitar from the Baroque period to the 1950s]. In *La Guitarra Española* [The Spanish guitar], pp. 69–94. Madrid, Spain: Sociedad Estatal Quinto Centenario.

Cortazar, Augusto Raúl. 1965. *Selecciones folklóricas.* Buenos Aires, Argentina: Códex.

Dannemann, Manuel. 1969. Estudio preliminar para el atlas folklórico musical de Chile. *Revista Musical Chilena,* año XXIII, 106:7–34.

Díaz Acevedo, Raúl. 1994. *Finares campesinos.* Temuco, Chile (published by author).

Di Santo, Víctor. 1987. *El canto del payador en el circo criollo.* 25 de Mayo, Buenos Aires, Argentina (published by author).

Fornaro, Marita. 1994. *El "cancionero norteño": Música tradicional y popular de influencia brasileña en el Uruguay.* Montevideo, Uruguay: Ediciones de la Banda Oriental.

González, Juan Pablo. 1998. Música popular chilena de raíz folclórica. In *Clásicos de la música popular chilena, 1960–1973, Raíz folclórica,* vol. 2, ed. Luis Advis, Eduardo Cáceres, Fernando García and Juan Pablo González, pp. 9–27. Santiago, Chile: Sociedad Chilena del Derecho de Autor-Ediciones, Ediciones Universidad Católica de Chile.

Grebe, María Ester. 1967. *The Chilean verso: A study in musical archaism.* Translated by Bette Jo Hileman. Los Angeles: Univ. of California Latin American Center.

Grupo Palomar. *Cantos tradicionales de cielo y tierra.* Raíces RAC 027–9, Santiago, Chile. Audiocassette.

Guitarra campesina: Testimonio de tradición. 1995. Directed by Patricia Chavarría. 60 min. Fondo de Desarrollo de la Cultura y las Artes, Santiago, Chile. VHS videocassette.

Hernández, José. 1872. *El gaucho Martín Fierro.* Buenos Aires, Argentina: Imprenta de La Pampa.

Loyola, Margot. 1980. *Bailes de tierra en Chile.* Valparaíso, Chile: Ediciones Universitarias de Valparaíso.

———. 1986. *El couplé.* Star Sounds STS-299, Santiago, Chile. Audiocassette.

———. 1994. *El Cachimbo: Danza tarapaqueña de pueblos y quebradas.* Valparaíso, Chile: Ediciones Universitarias de Valparaíso.

———. 1997. Conversation with author, February.

Martins, Carlos A. 1986. *Música popular uruguaya 1973–1982: Un fenómeno de comunicación alternativa.* Montevideo, Uruguay: Ediciones de la Banda Oriental.

Mendoza, Vicente T. 1984. *El corrido mexicano.* Mexico City: Fondo de Cultura Económica. (Originally published 1954.)

Moreno Chá, Ercilia. 1970. *La forma de la tonada cuyana.* Buenos Aires, Argentina: Instituto Nacional de Musicología Carlos Vega. Unpublished manuscript.

———. 1987. Alternativas del proceso de cambio de un repertorio tradicional argentino. *Latin American Music Review* 8(1):94–111.

———. 1992. Encounters and identities in Andean brotherhoods. In *Musical repercussions of 1942: Encounters in text and performance,* ed. Carol E. Robertson, pp. 413–427. Washington, D.C. and London: Smithsonian Institution Press.

———. 1993. New research generated by the UMH project: Chordophones of traditional use in continental Latin America. *Revista de Musicología* 16/2. *Actas del XVC Congreso de la Sociedad Internacional de Musicología,* pp. 1095–1101.

———. 1995. La significación del Premio Nacional de Arte 1994 otorgado en Chile a Margot Loyola. In *Segundas jornadas nacionales de folklore: Ponencias presentadas* (unpublished manuscript).

———. 1997. Acerca de las normas y recursos de la payada urbana contemporánea. In *Actas de las IV Jornadas de estudio de la narrativa folklórica,* pp. 190–197. Santa Rosa, La Pampa, Argentina: Subsecretaría de Cultura de La Pampa.

———. 1997. Por los caminos del payador profesional actual. *Revista de Investigaciones Folklóricas* 13, 103–111.

Moya, Ismael. 1959. *El arte de los payadores.* Buenos Aires, Argentina: Editorial P. Berruti.

Pelinski, Ramón, ed. 1995. *Tango nomade. Etudes sur le tango transculturel.* Montréal, Canada: Triptyque.

Pizarro, Gabriela. *Veinte tonadas religiosas.* Stereo cassette 001–11–92, Ediciones Gabriela Pizarro S., Santiago, Chile.

Pizarro S., Gabriela and Chandía T., Romilio. 1993. *Veinte tonadas religiosas.* Santiago, Chile: Ediciones Gabriela Pizarro S.

Robertson, Carol E. 1987. Power and gender in the musical experiences of women. In *Women and music in cross-cultural perspectives,* ed. Ellen Koskoff, pp. 225–244. Westport, Conn.: Greenwood Press.

Rojas, Ricardo. 1909. *La restauración nacionalista: Crítica de la educación argentina y bases para una reforma en el estudio de las humanidades modernas.* Buenos Aires, Argentina: Imprenta de la Penitenciaría Nacional.

Ruiz Zamora, Agustín. 1995. Conversando con Margot Loyola. *Revista Musical Chilena,* Año XLIX, 183:11–70.

Schechter, John Mendell. 1983. *Corona y baile:* Music in the child's wake of Ecuador and Hispanic South America, past and present. *Latin American Music Review* 4(1):1–80.

———. 1994. Divergent perspectives on the *velorio del angelito:* Ritual imagery, artistic condemnation, and ethnographic value. *Journal of Ritual Studies* 8(2):43–84.

———. 1996. Latin America/Ecuador. In *Worlds of music: An introduction to the music of the world's peoples,* 3d ed., edited by Jeff Todd Titon, pp. 428–494. New York: Schirmer Books.

Sepúlveda Llanos, Fidel. 1983. Entrevista a Margot Loyola. *Aisthesis* 15:83–85. Santiago, Chile: Universidad Católica de Chile.

Solomon, Thomas. 1994. *Coplas de todos santos* in Cochabamba: Language, music, and performance in Bolivian Quechua song dueling. *Journal of American Folklore* 107(425):378–414.

Vega, Carlos. 1944. *Panorama de la música popular argentina, con un ensayo sobre la ciencia del folklore.* Buenos Aires, Argentina: Losada.

———. 1946. *Los instrumentos musicales aborígenes y criollos de la Argentina.* Buenos Aires, Argentina: Centurión.

———. 1965. *Las canciones folklóricas argentinas.* Buenos Aires, Argentina: Instituto de Musicología.

ADDITIONAL READING

Argentina

Antología del Tango Rioplatense. 1980. Vol. 1, *Desde sus comienzos hasta 1920.* Buenos Aires, Argentina: Instituto Nacional de Musicología Carlos Vega. (Contains a book and 3 LP records.)

Gravano, Ariel. 1983. La música de proyección folklórica argentina. In *Folklore Americano* No. 35:5–71.

Moreno Chá, Ercilia. 1995. *Tango tuyo, mío, y nuestro.* Buenos Aires, Argentina: Instituto Nacional de Antropología.

Pérez Bugallo, Rubén. 1993. *Catálogo ilustrado de instrumentos musicales argentinos.* Buenos Aires, Argentina: Ediciones del Sol.

Portorrico, Emilio Pedro. 1997. *Diccionario biográfico de la música argentina de raíz folklórica.* Buenos Aires, Argentina: Banco de la Provincia de Buenos Aires.

Rodríguez, Alberto. 1938. *Cancionero cuyano: Canciones y danzas tradicionales.* Buenos Aires, Argentina: Númen.

Rodríguez, Alberto and Elena Moreno de Macía. 1991. *Manual del folklore cuyano.* Mendoza, Argentina: Ediciones Culturales de Mendoza.

Seibel, Beatriz. 1991. *El cantar del payador: Antología.* Buenos Aires, Argentina: Ediciones del Sol.

Chile

Advis, Luis and Juan Pablo González. 1994. *Clásicos de la música popular chilena, 1900–1960,* ed. Luis Advis and Juan Pablo González, pp. 11–49. Santiago, Chile: Universidad Católica de Chile.

Kurapel, Alberto. 1998. *Margot Loyola: La escena infinita del folklore.* Santiago, Chile: Centro Latinoamericano de Teatro-Performance.

Lavín, Carlos. 1955. *El rabel y los instrumentos chilenos:* Colección de ensayos, no. 10. Santiago, Chile: Instituto de Investigaciones Musicales.

Henríquez, Alejandro. 1973. *Organología del Folklore Chileno.* Santiago, Chile: Ediciones Universitarias de Valparaíso.

Pereira Salas, Eugenio. 1941. *Los orígenes del arte musical en Chile.* Santiago, Chile: Imprenta Universitaria.

Pizarro Soto, Gabriela. 1986. *Cuaderno de terreno: Apuntes sobre el romance en Chile.* Santiago, Chile (published by author).

Uruguay

AssunVao, Fernando. 1984. *El tango y sus circunstancias (1880–1920).* Buenos Aires, Argentina: El Ateneo.

Carvalho Neto, Paulo de. 1967. *El carnaval de Montevideo: Folklore, historia, sociología.* Sevilla, Spain: Facultad de Filosofía y Letras, Universidad de Sevilla.

Fornaro, Marita. 1989. *Organología tradicional uruguaya; panorama general y caracterización; cuartas jornadas argentinas de musicología.* Buenos Aires, Argentina. Unpublished manuscript.

———. Forthcoming, 1999. La música tradicional del Uruguay. In *Latin American music: An encyclopedic history of musics from South America, Central America, Mexico, and the Caribbean,* ed. Malena Kuss. New York: International Council of Music/Schirmer Books.

Guitar

Bacon, Tony, Harvey Turnbull, and James Tyler. 1984. Guitar. In *The New Grove Dictionary of Musical Instruments,* ed. Stanley Sadie, vol. 2, pp. 87–109. London, U.K.: Macmillan.

Pinnell, Richard T., with Ricardo Zavadivker. 1991. *The early guitar and its context in Argentina and Uruguay.* Vol. 1 of *The Rioplatense guitar.* The bold strummer guitar study series, no. 3. Westport, Conn.: Bold Strummer.

ADDITIONAL LISTENING
Argentina

Cantoras del Neuquén. Vol. 1. Recorded by Centro de Estudios Folklóricos. Subsecretaría de Estado de Cultura, AN 3005 C, Neuquén, Argentina, 1987. Audiocassette.

Documental folklórico de la provincia de La Pampa. Recorded by Ercilia Moreno Chá. Qualiton QF–3015/16, Buenos Aires, Argentina, 1975. (Contains a 16-page booklet and 2 LPs.)

Documental folklórico de cuyo (tonadas, cuecas, estilos). Serie Mapa musical de la Argentina, vol. 5. Recorded by Leda Valladares. Gala OTF 15.003 LP, Buenos Aires, Argentina [1970].

Guitarra: Folklore Musical y Música Folklórica Argentina. Vol. 4. Fondo Nacional de las Artes, Qualiton QF 3003 LP, Buenos Aires, Argentina, 1968. (Contains a 19-page booklet and an LP.)

Las canciones folkóricas de la Argentina (antología). Instituto Nacional de Musicología, Buenos Aires, Argentina, 1969. (Contains a 31-page booklet and 2 LPs.)

Los payadores. Published by author, Buenos Aires, Argentina, 1997. (Contains a 34-page booklet by Héctor Lorenzo Lucci, and a cassette with early recordings of *payadores* from 1904 to 1913.)

Chile

Antología del folklore musical chileno. Vols. 1–4. Instituto de Investigaciones Musicales de la Universidad de Chile, 1960, 1961, 1963, 1965. (Each volume contains a booklet and an LP.)

Nuestra navidad: Navidad campesina. Recorded by Gabriela Pizarro. Odeón 780781–2 CD, Santiago, Chile, 1997.

Voces del Maule. Margot Loyola Palacios, Alerce CD CADE–0266, Santiago, Chile, 1995.

Uruguay

Ayestarán y su verdad folklórica. [Recorded by Lauro Ayestarán and Flor de María Rodríguez de Ayestarán]. Consejo de Educación Básica y Superior, CONAC–002 LP [Montevideo, Uruguay, 1974?].

Contrapunto 3. Sondor 84.291, Montevideo, Uruguay. (Audiocassette containing three *payadas.*)

El arte del payador. Ayui A/37 LP, Montevideo, Uruguay, 1982. (Notes by Coriún Aharonián.)

ADDITIONAL VIEWING
Argentina

Cochengo Miranda. 1974. Directed by Jorge Prelorán, produced by Dirección de Cultura de la Provincia de La Pampa—Fondo Nacional de las Artes. 60 min. 16 mm. (Shot in La Pampa; shows the costumes of the region.)

Duodécimo encuentro de payadores rioplatenses. 1996. Produced by Museo de Motivos Argentinos José Hernández. 60 min. VHS videocassette.

Séptimo encuentro de payadores rioplatenses. 1991. Produced by Museo de Motivos Argentinos José Hernández. 60 min. VHS videocassette.

Undécimo encuentro de payadores rioplatenses. 1995. Produced by Museo de Motivos Argentinos José Hernández. 60 min. VHS videocassette.

Valle fértil. 1972. Directed by Jorge Prelorán, produced by Fondo Nacional de las Artes. 60 min. 16 mm. (Shot in Valle Fértil, a village in San Juan province. Shows the costumes of Ambito Cuyano.)

Chile

A lo humano. 1998. Directed by Alberto Kurapel, produced by Centro Latinoamericano de Teatro-Performance. 60 min. VHS videocassette.

Músicos campesinos de Chiloé. 1994. Directed by Catherine Hall, produced by Linterna Mágica, Puerto Montt, Chile. 32 min. VHS videocassette.

ENDNOTES

1. *Décimas* were a principal song form in the American Southwest in the eighteenth and nineteenth centuries, and the *décima* has still served in the twentieth century as the framework for songs and *corridos* in New Mexico and in the narrative *corridos* of the Mexico–United States border region. The *décima* form is an important part of Mexican *son jarocho* tradition (see Chapter 2). *Décimas* are fundamental as well in the tradition of Chilean *verso,* Mexican *valona,* Panamanian *mejorana,* Colombian and Venezuelan *corrido,* and the Cuban and Puerto Rican *punto,* among other genres.

2. The song-duel still appears in different parts of Spain and Portugal. In Latin America, some of the most prominent song-duel types include the Mexican *topadas,* the Cuban *controversias,* the Caribbean and Venezuelan *porfías,* the Peruvian *contrapunto,* the Chilean *paya,* the Argentine and Uruguayan *payada,* and the Brazilian *cantoria* or *desafío.* For a concise summary of several different Latin American song-duel genres and their respective verse structures, see Solomon 1994:388.

CHAPTER SEVEN

Andean Colombia

William J. Gradante

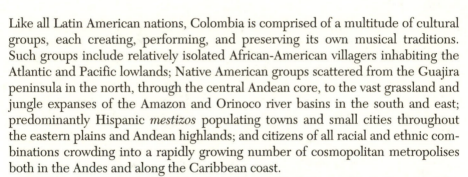

Like all Latin American nations, Colombia is comprised of a multitude of cultural groups, each creating, performing, and preserving its own musical traditions. Such groups include relatively isolated African-American villagers inhabiting the Atlantic and Pacific lowlands; Native American groups scattered from the Guajira peninsula in the north, through the central Andean core, to the vast grassland and jungle expanses of the Amazon and Orinoco river basins in the south and east; predominantly Hispanic *mestizos* populating towns and small cities throughout the eastern plains and Andean highlands; and citizens of all racial and ethnic combinations crowding into a rapidly growing number of cosmopolitan metropolises both in the Andes and along the Caribbean coast.

While in one sense it would be desirable to afford the reader a glimpse of the music culture of the entire region, the enormous variety of music cultures inhabiting this area makes this difficult in the present context. Moreover, it is the nature of ethnomusicological field research to focus investigation upon more clearly defined, sometimes musically homogeneous groups within a particular culture or locale, in order to gain deeper insights into the workings of that particular society, rather than to study a national music culture in a wide-ranging, necessarily generalistic fashion. The former has been my approach in exploring Colombian folk music.

This chapter will focus on the folk music of the Colombian Andes, with particular emphasis on that of the *mestizos* inhabiting the small towns of the southern ranges, zones where I have conducted music-cultural research—specifically Silvia, in Cauca province, and La Plata in the province of Huila. My intention is not to deprive the reader of the opportunity to explore any of the enormous number of other music cultures extant in Colombia, but rather to present a more intimate understanding of a single—though multifaceted and relatively widespread—music culture. Although many Colombians share the traditions examined in these pages, these cultural expressions are in no way to be considered more valid or important than any of those not addressed.[1]

While the *mestizos* of Andean Colombia are certainly aware of and frequently enjoy the musics of other regions of Colombia, the Caribbean, South America,

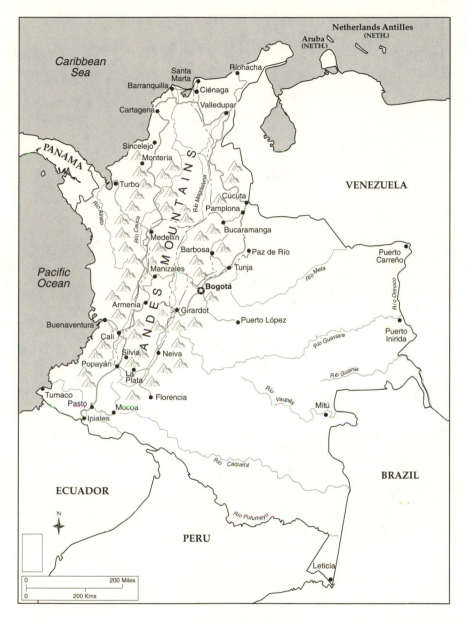

Fig. 7–1. Map of Colombia

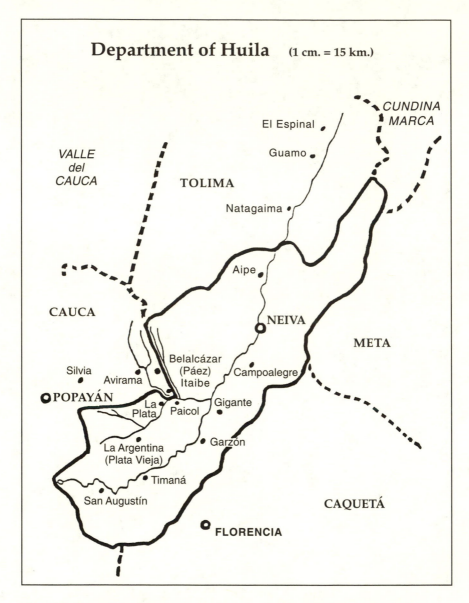

Department of Huila   (1 cm. = 15 km.)

CUNDINA
MARCA

El Espinal

Guamo

VALLE
del
CAUCA

TOLIMA

Natagaima

Aipe

CAUCA

NEIVA

META

Silvia

Avirama

Belalcázar
(Páez)
Itaibe

Campoalegre

POPAYÁN

La
Plata

Paicol

Gigante

La Argentina
(Plata Vieja)

Garzón

Timaná

San Augustín

CAQUETÁ

FLORENCIA

Fig. 7–2. Map of the Department of Huila, showing the locations of Silvia
(Cauca) and La Plata

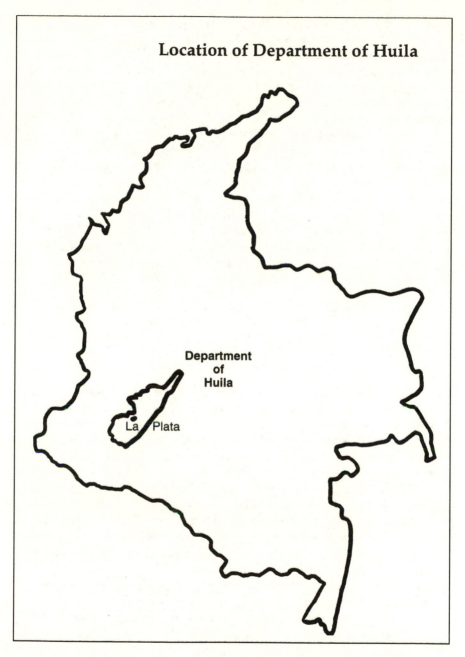

Location of Department of Huila

Department
of
Huila

La Plata

Fig. 7–3. Relative location of the Department of Huila, Colombia

and increasingly the rest of the world, our focus is on the music that they claim as their own cultural heritage. The inhabitants of this region use the term *lo colombiano* [that which is Colombian] as a marker of a cultural boundary, meaning that which reflects the *mestizo* culture of the highlands. Virtually anything reflecting cultural influences external to this is considered *costeño* [reflective of African-Colombian culture from the Caribbean coast] or *ajeno* [foreign, not ours], and thus not truly *"colombiano."*

After centuries of relative isolation, the town of La Plata has only recently been thrust into the role of an emerging city with socioeconomic, political, and communicational links to the rest of the province of Huila and to the nation as a whole, encouraging a stronger sense of self, of peoplehood, of local identity. The most concrete manifestation of this phenomenon is El Reinado del Bambuco [The pageant of Bambuco music and dance], which may be considered a living monument to and celebration of local pride, history, and folk culture. But the very fabric of this festival has, in fact, been woven of the variegated strands of something Eric Hobsbawm has called "invented traditions" rather than from a compilation of empirically verifiable ethnographic facts:

> "Invented tradition" is taken to mean a set of practices, normally governed by overtly or tacitly accepted rules and of a ritual or symbolic nature, which seek to inculcate certain values and norms of behavior by repetition, which automatically implies continuity with the past. In fact, where possible, they normally attempt to establish continuity with a suitable historic past. (Hobsbawm 1983:1)

Thus, ironically, our approach will not deprive the reader of the opportunity to become acquainted with certain aspects of the music cultures of the African-Colombian and indigenous populations. In fact, in our examination of the musical instruments employed in El Reinado del Bambuco, the "most traditional" of the southern Colombian *mestizo* music festivals, we find that nearly all of the instruments revered as locally unique have in fact been permanently "borrowed" from either African or indigenous sources and "folklorized"—incorporated into the local *mestizo* culture. A similar process of adoption and adaptation is evident in the predominant musical style of the festival. But then, isn't that precisely what *mestizo* means—a mixture of people, cultures, and traditions? Bombarded by a rapidly growing number of musical styles encroaching upon his ancestral "territory" from all angles, the southern Colombian *mestizo* has concocted a mixture according to his own tastes. Certain desirable ingredients have been decided upon and deemed *lo nuestro* [ours]. All else is considered "outsider." The recipe for the invention of a local tradition appears to have been followed in textbook fashion.

Such behavior may be interpreted as an intentional, generally rebellious response to the encroachment of modernization and the disruption of traditional community life by the changes concomitant with late twentieth-century industrialization and urbanization. This is clearly the case in Silvia, as residents desperately defend their traditional Semana Santa [Easter Holy Week] celebration from the encroaching big-city tourists from Cali. As in La Plata's celebration, the inculcation of cultural values during Semana Santa is facilitated by a ubiquitous emphasis on the strictly "traditional" and "authentically folkloric," the idea that "the old ways were best," repeatedly invoking what Hobsbawm has labeled the "sanction of perpetuity." While some elements may in fact have historical roots within the culture, other, often quite prominent aspects may be borrowed or actually "invented" for the purpose of displaying the local culture in the most favorable light.

In this chapter, then, we examine the musical life of these two small towns perched on either side of the Cordillera Central, the central range of the southern Colombian Andes. After looking at the role of music in daily life in Silvia, the reader will be invited to share the experience of Semana Santa, the Easter Holy Week observances, which in Silvia is the most important social, religious, and musical event of the year. We will then turn our attention to the role and nature of the folk music tradition known as *la vieja guardia* [the old guard], as observed both in Silvia and in the slightly larger town of La Plata, but shared by *mestizos* throughout the Colombian Andes. After describing the experience of a traditional serenade, the most common context for the performance of *vieja guardia* music, we turn our attention to the multifaceted celebration of regional folklore officially referred to as El Reinado del Bambuco, the most important social and cultural event of La Plata.

Popularly known in La Plata as the *Fiesta de San Pedro* [Feast of Saint Peter], or often simply *el sampedro,* this Roman Catholic holiday season is widely observed throughout Spain and Latin America. Its celebration in southern Colombia, however, retains little of its former religious significance and bears a wide variety of names, focusing alternatively upon the individual feast days of either Saint John (June 24), Saint Peter (June 29), or Saint Paul (June 30), depending upon the custom of the locale. The reader is introduced to Don Augusto Cuéllar, expert musician and master improviser-singer of *coplas del rajaleña plateño,* a regional folk-music genre featuring performance of humorous, satirical, and often pornographic verses delivered for the purpose of heightening the festive experience for everyone in attendance. After describing the music and musical instruments integral to this unique musical context, the chapter closes with a discussion of the role of the *coplero* [*copla* creator and singer] as festival clown, social critic, and mediator of cultural values, as he imaginatively manipulates both the audience and the *copla* itself, during this festive event.

MUSIC IN DAILY LIFE

The focus of my initial exploration of southern Colombian folk-music culture was the role of music in everyday life. My first impression was that daily life was absolutely full of music. Engaged in the daily round of cooking, washing, ironing, and cleaning chores, women sing folk songs in the home, in the company of other women—female family members, *comadres* [close female friends], or neighbors. As in earlier times, men still perform folk music after working hours in a *cantina* context, in the company of other men, or most often within the home, for gatherings of mixed ages and genders. In addition, every household has at least one radio tuned to any one of several stations featuring folk and popular music—nonstop, day and night.

There was little observable generational bias regarding musical styles, especially when compared to the United States. Young children were often cared for by members of the extended family, but there was very little "babysitter" activity when it came to the frequent social gatherings attended by the parents. Children of all ages accompanied adults to parties and other outings, in all of which music played a central role. When there was singing, the tradition of the *vieja guardia* (discussed below) provided the repertoire. When there was dancing, however, it was to recordings of *música bailable,* commercially produced dance music recorded in the larger cities by professional musicians recognized both nationally and throughout the Caribbean region.

Salsa from Panamá, Cuba, Puerto Rico, Miami, and New York; *cumbias, porros,* and *música vallenata* from the Colombian coast; and *merengue* music from the Dominican Republic all enjoyed widespread popularity, as did romantic ballads recorded by singers generally from Mexico, Argentina, Brazil, and Spain. Significantly, the musical traditions were not mutually exclusive—adults were not shy about dancing to the *música bailable* currently in vogue, and their children knew and enjoyed the folksongs of the *vieja guardia.* Friday nights, Saturday nights, and Sunday afternoons at the local dance halls, however, were the province of the teenagers and unmarried young adults. *Música bailable* and alcoholic beverages such as *aguardiente* [literally, firewater, a highly intoxicating beverage made of distilled sugar cane juice with anise flavoring] and rum mixes were standard fare, with young women only recently beginning to partake openly of beverages stronger than cola and the wide array of carbonated drinks flavored with mango, apple, tamarind, pineapple, grape, lemon, and other tropical fruits.

SEMANA SANTA

In both Silvia and La Plata, such gatherings occur throughout the year, both in private homes and in the dance halls. The single exception in Silvia occurs during the observance of Semana Santa, when the dance halls are closed and public sale of alcoholic beverages is prohibited. The purpose of Semana Santa is to commemorate the salient events marking the final week of the life of Jesus Christ, leading up to the celebration of his resurrection on Easter Sunday. Unlike locales in which townspeople physically reenact the often bloody scenes from the Passion and Crucifixion, the drama of these events centers in Silvia around daily processions featuring a total of nineteen large allegory floats called *imágenes* [images]. These include figures of Saint John, Saint Peter, Saint Veronica, the Virgin Mary, and Mary Magdalene, along with depictions of scenes such as: the flagellation and crowning with thorns; carrying, and later stumbling beneath, the weight of the cross; the Crucifixion; the entombment; and finally, the Resurrection.

The entire production and presentation of each procession was the responsibility of a specific *barrio* [neighborhood] citizens committee. Each committee designated teams of young women to canvass their *barrio* for donations to pay for the participation of the municipal band and to create the garments worn by the carved figures on the *imágenes* to be featured in their procession. Each of the sacred images was mounted on an ornate litter carried upon the proud shoulders of eight upstanding men of their *barrio.* Furthermore, the route of each procession traced the boundaries of the sponsoring *barrio.* By the end of the Semana Santa's nine processions, the totality of Silvia's geographical and cultural self would be re-peatedly demarcated, unified, and reconsecrated.

The processions promote community cohesiveness, celebrating the time-tested bonds of love, friendship, and stability binding Silvia's citizenry in a fellowship of the faithful. This, in turn, gives rise to a feeling of social leveling, an equality of all men before God. Aided by the musical ambience provided by the municipal band, the populace as a whole shares an extended, sacred moment outside the bounds of ordinary, secular time, entering what Victor Turner has termed the realm of "communitas" (1974:24). The individual melts away, as all the socioeco-nomic, political, and cultural structures compartmentalizing everyday life—which tend to categorize and separate individuals and groups—are temporarily aban-doned in favor of group values.

Significantly, Semana Santa is the single occasion in which the parish priest has the undivided attention of the entire populace—male and female. All good *sil-vianos* [people from Silvia]—not just the devout attendees of daily mass—are ex-pected to turn out for the processions, to contribute time and money to the dressing of the allegory floats, and to refrain from fighting and general hell-raising for an entire week. Thus, *silvianos* from every *barrio*—male and female, young and old, outcasts and upstanding, powerful and subservient—join in the antistruc-tural state of total religious devotion, praying and rendering scripture readings re-sponsorially and, moving as one through the communally shared space recognized as Silvia, demonstrating to the world the value of being *silviano*. Furthermore, all have agreed to refrain from indulging in an array of proscribed behaviors, includ-ing work, dance, sale or consumption of alcoholic beverages, the wearing of bright colors, consumption of meat, or use of any implement (including scissors or table knives and forks) that might metaphorically associate to the spear that pierced Christ's side. Together, these behaviors serve not only to bind *silvianos*—they also allow them to see themselves as distinct from their neighbors, the *guam-bianos*, who inhabit reservation lands beyond the hills surrounding the town, and distinct also from the many unwelcome, pleasure-seeking *caleño* tourists from the lowland metropolis of Cali.

If Silvia's *barrio* asssociations charged with organizing and sponsoring the nightly processions are the right hand of the parish priest, then the municipal band is certainly his left. The *banda municipal* or *banda del pueblo* is ubiquitous in Latin America, usually consisting of amateur or semiprofessional musicians, and it performs an essential role in small-town life. La Banda de Silvia was com-prised of sixteen men from a variety of vocations and socioeconomic stations. Band director Adolfo Vidal was a tailor and the high-school music teacher—he had been retained by the town to lend them instruments and teach them to play. The only "semiprofessional" musicians in Silvia, band members received small stipends to attend weekly rehearsals and perform public concerts in front of the church on Thursday evenings and after High Mass on Sunday afternoon.

Semana Santa, however, was a bonus. The band members understood that their music played an indispensable role in each of the processions. Performing selections classified generically as *alegre* [festive, danceable], *religiosa* [religious], or *fúnebre* [funereal, dirge-like], the band was charged with the task of "giving the procession and the participants the proper tone of somber respectfulness and solemnity," according to the priest. Thus, the music played in each procession was carefully selected in accordance with the prevailing spiritual mood of the day.

The choice of up-tempo, lively music for performance on Palm Sunday, Holy Tuesday (afternoon), and Easter Sunday ensured that the pace of these joyful processions would be spirited, inviting active participation of the entire populace—a few *caleños* [people from Cali] even joined in the merriment. On Palm Sunday, a figure of Jesus Christ was led on his burro from the outskirts of town into the village church, where he was greeted with palm branches and was welcomed as the Savior. Likewise, on Tuesday afternoon the procession of townspeople followed the band's lively *marchas* [marches] and *paso dobles* [Spanish two-step genre] to the jailhouse, where the prisoners were given a banquet and reminded that they were still considered members of the community of faith. This was symbolically represented by freeing a selected prisoner and inviting him to reassume his former place in society. Finally, on Easter Sunday, the band's joyous offerings of popular tunes greeted the spirit of Christ, returning from the realm of the dead to invite Silvia's faithful to join him in the Kingdom of Heaven.

The more somber mood of the processions of Tuesday and Wednesday evenings was reflected in the band's choice of music characterized as *música religiosa*. From Thursday through Saturday, the period corresponding to Christ's imprisonment, scourging, crucifixion, and death, the church bells were silenced, replaced by the unsettling clatter of the *matracas* [wooden rackets]. In addition, the robes worn by the image of the Virgin Mary on the allegory float known as La Mater Dolorosa [The mother of sorrows], previously bright red, were now exchanged for black vestments. The most prominent factor in the creation of the desired mood of somber reflection upon the tragic events being commemorated, however, was the music. The band's offerings now consisted exclusively of dirges, music which otherwise would be performed only within the context of a funeral. While the discriminating listener may question the musical skills exhibited by the members of the municipal band, the success with which they performed the function for which they were contracted—"giving the procession and the participants the proper tone of somber respectfulness and solemnity"—remains indisputable. As I recount my experience of a typical evening procession in Silvia, the reader is invited to listen to Recorded Selection 33, entitled "Pésame" [sympathy], as performed on Good Friday.

VIGNETTE: SEMANA SANTA

"¡Se fue la luz! ¡Se fue la luz!" [The lights have gone out!] More than any other statement I heard during my several months living in Silvia, this was probably the most annoying. I would always ask myself why it was necessary to announce to an individual sitting in a suddenly pitch-dark room that the lights have gone out. Reassured, then, that I had not been struck blind, I would do my best either to carry on my studies by flashlight or to call it quits for the evening. Lying at the end of a very treacherous mountain road, Silvia is very susceptible to power failures, especially during the rainy season (December to May) when mudslides routinely take power lines to the bottoms of gorges. But this time the darkness was welcome, albeit not entirely unexpected. It was Semana Santa, and tonight there would be another candlelight procession. This Easter season had already been the most deeply moving and meaningful of my life, the processions of sacred Biblical images through the village streets bringing to life that which had previously been little more than a dry Sunday School lesson.

But even more impressive was a candlelight procession in pitch darkness, the only illumination being that provided by the moon, the Milky Way, and the flickering of the candles carried by my fellow processioners. I recalled a tale about a sixteenth-century Spanish explorer who had been intrigued by his first view of Popayán. (Today the provincial capital of Popayán, Cauca province, is renowned for the solemn splendor of its Semana Santa observances, known to have been reenacted since at least 1558 [Arboleda Llorente 1957:7]). From a ridge above the settlement he saw what appeared to be a long, fiery snake slowly winding its way across the valley below. Like the one viewed from above by the *conquistador,* our own procession would inch its way through the dark streets toward the village church just as that earlier procession had done centuries ago. (Evidence that similar processions took place in Jerusalem as early as 380 A.D. is presented by Collins [1993:18].) I have since witnessed analogous processions in larger cities, such as Guadalajara, Mexico, but none was as meaningful to me as these.

I had been hoping that it would be another such night, as I strapped on my tape recorder and extra battery packs underneath my *ruana* (Quechua for *poncho*—in this region, a heavy, calf-length, woolen garment) and prepared to join the congregation already gathering in the church. Under the spreading *ceiba* [silk-cotton] trees in the plaza I joined several members of the Municipal Band, who began to ask about my recordings of the afternoon's Via Crucis [The stations of the Cross] procession. Don Guillermo was anxious to know if I would consider erasing the segment where he had dropped his snare drum and had had to chase it a block and a half down the hill in the middle of the priest's sermon. I was in the process of reassuring him when the first allegorical float, that of the black-robed Mater Dolorosa, emerged from the church. At the urging of Don Adolfo, the band now lurched into action, beginning the first of several pieces of funeral music.

In all, thirteen members of the band participated, although two did not join ranks until well after the procession had begun. Instrumentation included a *bombo* [bass drum], *redoblante* [snare drum], two trombones, a baritone horn, *saxhón* [small baritone horn], *bombardino* [still smaller horn], piccolo, *contrabajo* [tuba], alto saxophone, clarinet, and two trumpets. The selections performed included titles such as "El Gólgota" [Golgotha], "La María" [Mary], "Plegaria" [Prayer], "El Señor de la expiración," [The dying Lord], "Tú reinarás" [You shall Reign], "El descendimiento" [The descent from the Cross], "En el huerto" [In the garden], "Meditación" [Meditation], "Pésame" [Sympathy], "La Mater Dolorosa" [Our Lady of Sorrows], and "Las últimas lágrimas" [The final tears]. Extensive repetition of certain sections of each piece was common, ensuring that the musical repertoire would not be exhausted before the last of the allegory floats had been returned to its place in the church.

The musicians were aided in their efforts to create the desired mood of pious mourning by the solitude of the overwhelming darkness, pierced only by the dim flickering of the candles borne along by the columns of parishioners on either sidewalk. Shuffling slowly along on the right (the men's) side of the street, I did my best to stay under the overhanging eaves to avoid a slow soaking by the steady drizzle. While the women and young girls huddled similarly along the opposite curb, the shivering band members found no shelter in the middle of the gradually puddling street. By the time the procession disbanded in front of the church nearly three hours later, the warm, dry shelter of the band's tiny rehearsal hall must have seemed almost heavenly to the musicians, who quickly traded dripping band jackets for warm *ruanas* and scurried home.

VIEJA GUARDIA MUSIC

Meanwhile, a group of folk musicians began a *serenata* [serenade] to the Virgin Mary, just inside the narthex of the church. The four selections they performed belonged to the tradition of the *vieja guardia* [old guard]. The theme of martyrdom is not uncommon in Colombian folk songs, but, as expressed in the *pasillo* entitled "Hacia el Calvario" [Toward Calvary] (Recorded Selection 34), it was especially appropriate in the context of this Easter season serenade. The text and music are presented in Examples 7–1 and 7–2.

Ex. 7–1. Text of "Hacia el Calvario," by Carlos Vieco

Señor, mientras tus plantas nazarenas	Lord, while your Nazarene feet
Suben hacia la cumbre del Calvario	Climb to the summit of Calvary
Yo también, cabizbajo y solitario	I also, dejected and alone
Voy subiendo hacia la cumbre de mis penas.	Climb to the summit of my suffering.
Tú para redimir los pecadores	You, in order to redeem the sinners
Cargado con la cruz, Mártir Divino,	Burdened with the cross, Divine Martyr,
Y yo, por un capricho del destino,	And I, through a twist of fate,
Cargado con la cruz de mis dolores.	Burdened with the cross of my sorrows.
Siquiera en tu agonía silenciosa	Even in your silent agony
Tienes, oh sin igual crucificado,	You have, oh incomparable crucified one,
Una dulce mujer, cerca a tu lado—	A sweet woman, close by your side—
La inmaculada Madre Dolorosa.	The Immaculate Lady of Sorrows.
Yo, que perdí, desde que estaba niño	I, who since childhood have been without
Mi santa madre, que tan buena era . . .	My saintly mother, who was so good . . .
Contéstame, Maestro, cuando muera—	Tell me, Master, when I die—
¿Quién cerrará mis ojos con cariño . . .?	Who will close my eyes with such tenderness . . .?

A stylistic trait observed in this and many other *vieja guardia* compositions is the use of dramatic pauses—referred to locally as *pausas* [pauses] or *cortes* [cuts]—in the delivery of a particularly emotional vocal line. Such pauses are spontaneously used by musicians, who are not only very familiar with the musical material but also aware of the manner in which their singing partners customarily interpret a particular passage.

The structure of this folk song is also quite typical of the *vieja guardia* tradition. It is comprised of two vocal sections, the first (B1) beginning in the minor mode (A minor), with a brief excursion through the relative major key (C major).

Ex. 7–2. Musical transcription of "Hacia el Calvario"

Hacia el Calvario

pasillo lento

(Capo II, rendered in A Minor)

Ex. 7–2. Musical transcription of "Hacia el Calvario" (continued)

yo tam - bién, ca - biz - ba - jo y so - li ta - rio,

Am F G⁷ C

voy su - bien - do ha - cia la cum - bre de mis pe - nas.

C E⁷ E⁷ E⁷ Am

Ex. 7–2. Musical transcription of "Hacia el Calvario" (continued)

Ex. 7–2. Musical transcription of "Hacia el Calvario" (continued)

Ex. 7–2. Musical transcription of "Hacia el Calvario" (continued)

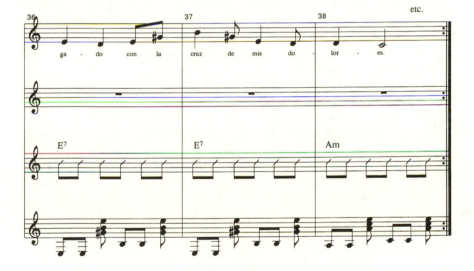

The second (C1) opens in the parallel A-major key before quickly returning to the A-minor mode. This format is repeated for the rendering of the third (B2) and fourth (C2) stanzas of text, which utilize the melodic lines of the first and second stanzas, respectively. All singing is preceded by an instrumental introduction (A1, A2, A3, A4), rendered in the minor mode, typically by the guitar or *bandola* [fourteen- to sixteen-string mandolin], to *tiple* [small twelve-string guitar] accompaniment, as indicated in Example 7–3.

Harmonies used in the performance of *vieja guardia* music are usually limited to primary chords, sprinkled with brief excursions to related keys through the use of secondary dominants, as seen in "Hacia el Calvario." Furthermore, choice of keys is directly related to the physical nature of the guitar and the *tiple*. That is, the key in which a given song may be performed is often chosen for the ease with which the musicians may render it. The keys of E minor and A minor are very common, not only because the primary chords in these keys are easy to render on the instruments basic to the ensemble, but because both their parallel and relative major keys are easily performed by the amateur musician as well. Due to the relatively limited number of keys commonly used, then, it is easy for ensembles to assemble casually and render successful harmonies to pieces of music in impromptu fashion. Use of *capos* is widespread and further facilitates selection of keys amenable to vocalists, while limiting the number of barred chords required of the accompanists.

Characteristic guitar and *tiple* accompaniment patterns used in the most prominent genres of Colombian Andean folk music are presented in Examples 7–4 through 7–8, and a chart of relative tuning patterns is provided in Example 7–9. Both here and in the transcribed examples, these should be taken as generalized guides to performance—suggested strummed accompaniment patterns—rather than as either obligatory patterns to which one must adhere, or precise, note-for-note quotations from a single performance.

An open invitation to improvise and embellish lies at the heart of this tradition, both in the vocal or instrumental rendition of the melodies and with the strumming patterns of the accompanists. This freedom to improvise even extends to the overall structure of a given piece of music. That is, neither the sequence nor the precise number of repetitions of each instrumental or vocal section is predeter-

Ex. 7–3. Formal structure of the *pasillo* "Hacia el Calvario"

A1   instrumental passage
B1   vocal (stanza 1)
A2   instrumental passage
C1   vocal (stanza 2)
A3   instrumental passage
B2   vocal (stanza 3)
A4   instrumental passage
C2   vocal (stanza 4)

Ex. 7–4. *Bambuco* **accompaniment pattern**

Or:

Ex. 7–5. *Pasillo* **accompaniment pattern**

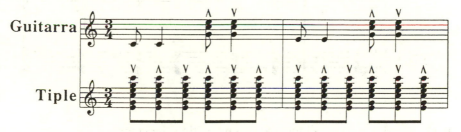

Or:

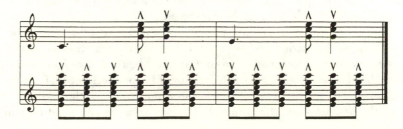

Ex. 7–6. *Pasillo lento* accompaniment pattern

Ex. 7–7. *Vals* accompaniment pattern

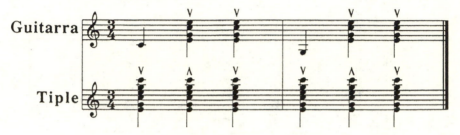

Ex. 7–8. *Danza* accompaniment pattern

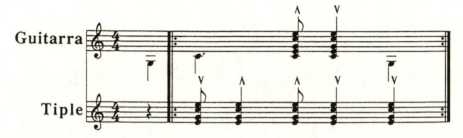

mined, allowing the overall form to emerge within the course of a given performance. Thus, the actual structure of the piece is highly dependent upon the ambience of the specific performance context and the number and mood of the musicians and audience members involved.

As we look at the characteristic accompaniment patterns, two important observations may be made. First, we note that within the tradition of the *vieja guardia,* only the *danza,* descended from the Caribbean *danza habanera,* displays a quadruple meter (4/4). Secondly, it should be pointed out that, although all the other types are written in 3/4 meter, this is done only for the sake of convenience, for the *bambuco* and the *pasillo.* In the performance of the latter genres, liberal

Ex. 7–9. Characteristic tunings of cordophones of the Colombian Andes—
bandola, tiple, and guitarra

alternation between 3/4 and 6/8 meters *(sesquiáltera)* is characteristic, and in fact indispensable. (See Daniel Sheehy's discussion of *sesquiáltera* in Mexican musics [Chapter 2], and Ercilia Moreno Chá's discussion of *sesquiáltera* in the Argentine *tonada cuyana* [Chapter 6].) Accompanying *pasillos* or *bambucos* with six eighth notes per measure, the *tiplero* often uses accented strokes on every third eighth note to emphasize a compound duple feeling. This alternation of accented strums between down- and upstrokes is referred to by *tipleros* as *machetazo* [blow by a *machete*]. It should be noted in passing that the choreography of the traditional *bambuco,* and of its derivative the *sanjuanero,* also emphasizes this metric ambivalence of the *sesquiáltera.*

Our examination of the *vieja guardia* tradition continues as the reader is invited to accompany a group of folk musicians on a moonlight *serenata* in the southern Colombian Andes.

VIGNETTE: THE *SERENATA*

Kerplunk-itty-clang! "¡Les dije!" [I told you so!] The four *trovadores* [serenaders] peered down through the darkness in embarrassment and disbelief. There was Don Andrés, head slumped over his knees, and the new *bandola* [sixteen-string mandolin] lying face-down in the dirt. "¡Les dije!" Don Augusto Cuéllar angrily repeated in as loud a whisper as he could muster. It had all started several hours earlier, after dinner at the Cuéllars' place. Don Augusto's wife and their eight youngest children were gathered around the dinner table, exuberantly engaged in their nightly potpourri of word games, stories, songs, jokes, and anecdotes. Meanwhile, according to their own nightly custom, Don Augusto and eldest son Fernando sat off to one side in the patio, softly fiddling around on the *tiple* and guitar, respectively.

The merriment only increased when family friend Miyo Fajardo walked in, reminding the amateur musicians that at midnight it would be his wife Luz María's birthday. They'd be delighted to help him out with a romantic *serenata*, wouldn't they? He produced the usual "fee"—a liter of *aguardiente*—from beneath his poncho, wordlessly sending the youngest daughter to the kitchen for a tray and glasses. The focus of the evening magically turned musical.

The task of the next several hours was a familiar one. Specific songs, the keys in which each would be rendered, and the order in which they would be performed all had to be painstakingly discussed and decided upon in advance. No talking would be allowed once outside Luz María's window. The musicians would suggest a number of songs for Miyo's approval, singing portions with the most poignant lines, in the effort to settle on precisely four titles for the serenade.

Everyone familiar with local custom knew that a *serenata* should include four musical selections, and that they shouldn't all be of the same genre. A *pasillo/bambuco/pasillo lento/guabina* serenade was always nice, but there were some very romantic *valses*—or even *danzas*—that Luz María might prefer. All agreed that one selection ought to be of the purely instrumental variety and performed before the others. It was with this last requirement in mind that Miyo had made a fateful decision. Earlier that afternoon he had called on Don Andrés, the schoolteacher, inviting him to join the *serenata* entourage. While Don Andrés was a marvelous *bandola* player, the tradition of drinking a number of rounds of *aguardiente* while rehearsing to *coger el tono* [acquire the appropriately romantic mood and musical intonation, of course] was his well-known undoing.

That is why Don Augusto let out a soft groan as Don Andrés appeared in the doorway a half hour later, beaming. His shiny new *bandola* instantly became the talk of the gathering, especially after he showed off the label inside, which read, "Tomás Norato, Chiquinquirá." Instruments crafted in this town in the northeastern province of Boyacá enjoy a special prestige throughout Colombia, comparable to the renown accorded instruments made in Paracho (Michoacán), Mexico. While Don Augusto was clearly delighted at Don Andrés's new acquisition, his occasional sidelong glances at his son betrayed his doubts that its notes would ever be heard by Miyo's wife. As it turned out, Don Augusto's apprehensions were only partially justified.

About fifteen minutes before midnight, after several hours of rehearsing, and discussing—and several more bottles of *aguardiente*—the *trovadores* quietly took to the streets. Silence was strictly enforced as we slowly made our way to the outlying *barrio* were Miyo lived, stopping twice along the way for sips of *aguardiente* to ensure that we would remain "in tune." We arrived a few minutes early, but as beginning a *serenata* before midnight was simply not right, we sat, instruments on our knees, on the gravel outside the darkened window and waited. Don Augusto made a few last-minute adjustments to the tuning of his *requintillas* [the thinnest, highest-pitched strings of the *tiple*] and then suddenly, as the town church bells began to ring out midnight, motioned for us to rise. It was after about the fourth chime that Don Andrés suddenly slumped clumsily forward, totally inebriated, the shiny new *bandola* rolling noisily onto the pebble-strewn roadbed. Kerplunk-itty-clang!

Before the twelfth chime, Don Fernando, taking advantage of the opportunity to try out the new instrument for himself, calmly took up the *bandola,* handing me his guitar with a confident nod. He then eased Miyo's anxiety by effortlessly executing the electrifying instrumental *pasillo* entitled "Vino tinto" [Red wine] (Recorded Selection 35) as his father and I accompanied. The three romantic vocal duets were performed—as Don Augusto had suspected all along—by the fa-ther/son team, and I returned to my tape recording, silent *bandola* in hand. We decided it was best not to wake Don Andrés until it was time to leave.

The entire performance—excluding the nearly five hours of "rehearsing"—lasted about fifteen minutes. At no time did a light appear in any of the windows, nor was any acknowledgment of our presence detectable or expected. In some parts of Colombia, the simple turning on of a light is the anticipated reward of the *trovador.* But in southern Colombia, tradition dictates that a woman who in any way acknowledges the efforts of a *trovador* is forward or "easy," even if, as in this case, the man responsible is her husband.

Serenading is commonly practiced throughout the Hispanic world, and local traditions vary widely. *Serenatas* may be performed to celebrate a variety of occa-sions, including birthdays, anniversaries, Mother's Day, or, for example, to raise funds for children's Christmas gifts or sports uniforms. An unmarried man may perform or arrange for a *serenata* to inform a young lady of his amorous inten-tions or to "make up" with her after a disagreement. *Serenatas* are frequently per-formed for no other reason than to show a wife, mother, or girlfriend how much the man cares for her.

THE TRADITION OF THE *VIEJA GUARDIA*

It is the music of the *vieja guardia* [old guard] that provides the repertoire for An-dean Colombian *serenatas* and other more informal performance contexts. It is alternatively referred to as *música folclórica* [folk music], *música típica* [typical music], or simply *música colombiana* [Colombian music], all of which serve to dis-tinguish it from non-Andean Colombian or urban popular music. It arose amid a kind of Colombian cultural renaissance which began to flower at the close of the nineteenth century in Bogotá. The setting was after-hours in the *piqueteaderos* [combination general stores/cantinas/coffee houses], which had become centers for informal congregation and cultivation of a bohemian nightlife. The nucleus of the society of folk and popular musicians was comprised of young men, frequently with conservatory training, who earned a living teaching, singing, or playing reli-gious music in church ensembles, or performing in the chorus for visiting opera or *zarzuela* companies.

Musicians such as Pedro Morales Pino and his protegés Emilio Murillo, Ale-jandro Wills, Luís A. Calvo, Fulgencio García, and Carlos Escamilla began to as-sociate with the great Colombian poets Julio Flórez, Clímaco Soto Borda,

Eduardo López, Carlos Villafañe, José Velásquez García (Julio Vives Guerra), Rafael Pombo, and others. Playing, singing, improvising (music, *coplas*, and sonnets), and drinking together, these artists collaborated in the creation of the rich repertoire of *bambucos, pasillos, valses, danzas,* and *guabinas* that serves as the foundation of the folk and popular music tradition performed today. Together, they inspired the flowering of a new cultural milieu which has been called *"la edad de oro de la canción colombiana"* [the golden age of Colombian popular song], which reached its zenith in the first few decades of the twentieth century (see Añez 1951:47). It was during this period that two of the most important types of Colombian folk musical ensemble emerged—the *dueto bambuquero* and the *estudiantina*. The third (and by far the least formal) ensemble is the *murga,* which will be discussed at the end of this chapter, as it is found almost exclusively in the context of festivals.

Dueto Bambuquero

In the professional context the music of the *vieja guardia* is typically performed by the *dúo* or *dueto bambuquero,* which consists of two vocalists accompanying themselves on *guitarra* and *tiple* (Illustration 7–1). Melodic instrumental introductions and interludes are generally performed on the *guitarra* with a strummed chordal *tiple* accompaniment, though these roles are occasionally reversed. When not rendering instrumental interludes, the guitarist performs a combination of bass notes (played by the thumb on the fourth, fifth, and sixth strings) and full chords (strummed with the fingers on the first, second, and third strings). Originally a serenading song for the solo voice, the modern *bambuco* is sung in duet in parallel thirds and sixths. It is not typically sung in unison or in more than two-part harmony, though brief responsorial or solo passages are not uncommon. Some of the more prominent *duetos bambuqueros* to record professionally either in Colombia or internationally include Garzón y Collazos, Los Tolimenses (Emeterio y Felipe), and more recently Silva y Villalba.

In the folk context, either the guitar or the *tiple* may be doubled. In the event that one or more *bandolas* are added, they will perform the instrumental interludes and vocal adornments, while all others accompany. Rather than strumming full chords, a *bandola* player uses a flat-picked tremolo style to harmonize or play in unison with a vocal melody, or to improvise embellishments between individual lines of sung poetry. Occasionally a *bandola* player will also participate vocally, but this is unusual, due to the complex task of providing melodic ornamentation that he must perform. Alternatively, in some regions, the role of melodic embellisher may be assumed by an accordion player, though this is not considered strictly traditional practice.

Estudiantina

While the music of the *vieja guardia* is most commonly performed by the *dueto bambuquero*, it also provides a large percentage of the repertoire of the *estudiantina*. Also known as the *lira, rondalla,* or *tuna,* such ensembles specialize in the performance of instrumental music, often of the classical variety, as well as instru-

Ill. 7–1. Don Augusto *(tiple)* **and his son Don Fernando** *(guitarra)*
comprise the Dueto Los Cuéllar.

mental *pasillos* and other genres of Colombian folk and popular music. The *estudiantina* is a large ensemble, adding any number of *bandolas* to a core group of *tiples* and guitars. In 1898, composer and arranger Pedro Morales Pino (1863–1926) formed La Lira Colombiana, Colombia's first *estudiantina,* with three *bandolas,* two *tiples,* and a guitar, with which he toured the Andean region of Colombia, Central America, and the United States. Morales Pino's second Lira Colombiana (1912) was an expanded version, featuring five *bandolas,* four *tiples,* one guitar, and a cello. Reaching the zenith of their popularity (on the professional level) during the first few decades of the twentieth century, *estudiantinas* today exist in schools, businesses, churches, and other social organizations where the ensemble's size (some including as many as twenty or thirty musicians) and flexibility of instrumentation allow for maximum participation among the membership. Many *estudiantinas* also work in association with choral groups or, as in the case of La Lira Colombiana, rely on their own instrumentalists to perform vocal parts.

It was at this time, near the beginning of the twentieth century, that Colombian folk and popular music first came to be performed by musicians with conservatory training. Performances moved from the countryside and the city's back streets into the theaters and salons. Musicians discarded the peasants' *ruana* in favor of the tuxedo and performed *música brillante,* an international menu of waltzes, *gavottes,* and minuets—including pieces by Mozart, Beethoven, and Brahms, as well as by Colombian composers—alongside *danzas, tangos, boleros,* and ultimately native Colombian folkloric genres. Later, in order to effect the "true" folk image of the musical tradition to which they hoped to draw international attention, these same performers returned to performing in "typical folk dress" and set off to tour the world.

Whereas in the nineteenth century Europe had been the ideal destination for all aspiring Colombian musicians, it was the recording studios of neighboring North America that now began to claim their attentions. In the decade of the 1910s the first recordings of Colombian music were made in New York and Mexico City. It is ironic that because of the artists who immortalized Colombian folk and popular music—by putting it on records, on the radio, and thus into the very homes of the Colombian music consumer—the *piqueteaderos,* the Golden Age, and the associated lifestyle no longer had a reason for being. Amateur musicians began to learn the music that grew out of the tradition of the *vieja guardia* by listening to recordings and to the radio at home, and the domain of the music began to spread from the artistic élite to the general public.

Morales Pino is still considered the greatest *bandola* player in Colombian history, and he is remembered for both the addition of a sixth course of strings to that instrument and for his authorship of a *bandola* method book. Fulgencio García (1880–1945), a leading disciple of Morales Pino and another extraordinary *bandola* player, is the author of several pieces still popular within the instrumental *pasillo* repertoire. Most notable are three 1912 compositions entitled "Coqueteos" [Flirtations], "La gata golosa" [literally, The sweet-toothed cat, but actually named for a popular *piqueteadero*], and "Vino tinto" [Red wine], which is presented in Example 7–10.

Clearly, the instrumental *pasillo* is quite different from the sung *pasillo lento* [slow *pasillo*], and should probably be considered a genre unto itself. While the latter is performed slowly and deliberately for optimum expression of its emotional texts, the former is traditionally performed as fast as the musicians can render it. As a result, the characteristic guitar accompaniment is altered to facilitate its performance at accelerated tempos. The intricate melodies are most often rendered on a *bandola,* but the role of soloist may also be performed by a guitarist. Instrumental *pasillos* are sectional, comprised of from two to four sections, almost always in contrasting keys, but usually cadencing in the original key, facilitating, for example, an ABACA structure. As is the case with the vocal genres of *vieja guardia* music, the overall form a piece ultimately takes is usually determined by the interaction between musicians and audience within a given performance context.

Ex. 7–10. Fulgencio García's *pasillo,* "Vino tinto"

Vino Tinto

pasillo (instrumental)

Ex. 7–10. Fulgencio García's *pasillo,* **"Vino tinto" (continued)**

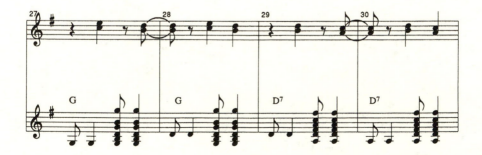

Ex. 7–10. Fulgencio García's *pasillo*, "Vino tinto" (continued)

Ex. 7–10. Fulgencio García's *pasillo*, **"Vino tinto" (continued)**

Ex. 7–10. Fulgencio García's *pasillo*, "Vino tinto" (continued)

TEXTUAL THEMES OF *VIEJA GUARDIA* MUSIC

As sonneting was a popular activity among the artists contributing to the rise of the *vieja guardia* tradition in turn-of-the-century Bogotá, it is not surprising that examples of this poetic structure may still be found among the texts of the contemporary musical repertoire. Sonnets composed in Shakespearian times commonly dealt with themes such as nostalgia, loneliness, longings for love, and extolling the natural beauty of a particular region or one's homeland (see Chapter 1). José A. Morales has had enormous success in the past several decades by using these same themes in *bambucos* such as "María Antonia" (see the text excerpt of this *bambuco* in Chapter 1), "Yo también tuve veinte años" [I too was once twenty years old], and in his revered *vals* [waltz] "Pueblito viejo" [Beloved old village]. Currently still more popular are the works of medical doctor and enormously prolific composer, Jorge Villamil Cordovez, who has endeared himself to the Andean Colombian by virtue of his *vals* "Oropel" [Fool's gold], his *guabina* "Los guaduales" [The bamboo plants], his *vals* "Llamarada" [Blazing inferno], and many other songs, several of which have been recorded in various styles throughout Latin America. The text of the best-known of his *pasillos*, the beloved "Espumas" [Frothy bubbles] (Recorded Selection 36) is presented in Example 7–11; it combines several of these themes, and like "Pueblito viejo" it has become almost an anthem for the Andean Colombian, both at home and among nostalgic expatriots abroad.

Ex. 7–11. Text of "Espumas," a *pasillo* by Jorge Villamil Cordovez

Amores que se fueron,	Loves of times past,
Amores peregrinos,	Wandering loves,
Amores que se fueron	Loves which have gone
Dejando en el alma	Leaving in one's soul
Negros torbellinos. . . .	Dark whirlwinds. . . .
Igual que las espumas	Like the frothy bubbles
Que lleva el ancho río,	That the wide river carries away,
Se van sus ilusiones	One's hopes and dreams
Siendo destrozados	Are carried off and
Por el remolino.	Shattered in the whirlpool.
Espumas que se van,	Frothy bubbles that are carried off,
Bellas rosas viajeras	Like beautiful wandering roses
Se alejan en danzantes	Move dancing away
En pequeños copos	In tiny tufts
Ornando el paisaje.	Adorning the countryside.
Ya nunca volverán	They will never return
Las espumas viajeras,	These traveling frothy bubbles,

Ex. 7–11. Text of "Espumas," a *pasillo* by Jorge Villamil Cordovez (continued)

Como las ilusiones	Just as the hopes and dreams
Que se depararon	That have given us
Dichas pasajeras.	Fleeting moments of happiness.
Espejos tembladores	Trembling mirrors
De aguas fugitivas	Of fleeing waters
Van retratando amores	Leave portraits of loves
Y bellos recuerdos	And beautiful memories
que deja la vida.	That life leaves us.
Se trenza una corona	A crown is woven
De blancos azahares	Of white orange blossoms
Cual rosadas diademas	Like rosy gems
Cuando llevan flores	When they bear flowers
De la siempre vida.	Of eternal life.

But not all is blissful in the poetry associated with the music of the *vieja guardia*. A wave of new compositions, collectively referred to as *bambucos de protesta*—but not restricted to that single genre—has come to comprise a new category of Andean Colombian popular song. With their roots in the intense disillusionment with current national political trends, these songs provide a medium for the expression of a sociopolitical consciousness previously absent from this repertoire. In Arnulfo Briceño's *bambuco* entitled "¿A quién engañas? abuelo" [Who are you fooling, grandfather?] (Recorded Selection 37), we note the same kind of major key/relative minor key modulation typical of the more sentimental *vieja guardia* songs (Example 7–12). The abruptness of such changes, however, creates a feeling of tonal instability enhancing in turn the feeling of emotional instability expressed in the poetic text (Example 7–13). Though needing little explanation, the text, a conversation between a little orphan and his grandfather, is an attempt to deal with the still lingering feelings of confusion, desperation, and horror of the Colombian peasant trying to come to grips with the sweeping violence which has become almost routine in Colombia since the late 1950s. (Phrases in italics represent local dialect.)

Like "¿A quién engañas? abuelo," another *bambuco*, "'Ora sí, entiendo por qué," [Now I understand why] by Pedro J. Ramos uses the traditional melodic, harmonic, and poetic patterns of the *vieja guardia* to tackle a notably nontraditional theme, one never even imagined in the *piqueteaderos* of turn-of-the-century Bogotá—the image of the Colombian peasant, frustrated, without hope for the future, and victimized by a social, political, and economic power structure far beyond his control.

Ex. 7–12. Arnulfo Briceño's *bambuco,* **"¿A quién engañas? abuelo"**

¿A Quién Engañas?, Abuelo
bambuco de protesta
(Tiple and Guitarra accompaniment patterns are standardized, subject to variation according to the desires of the performer.)

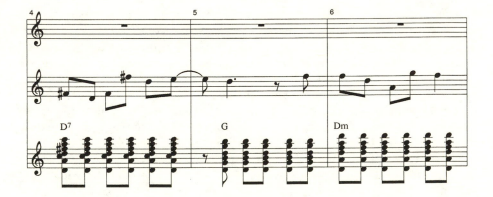

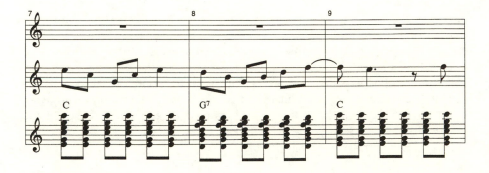

Ex. 7–12. Arnulfo Briceño's *bambuco*, "¿A quién engañas? abuelo" (continued)

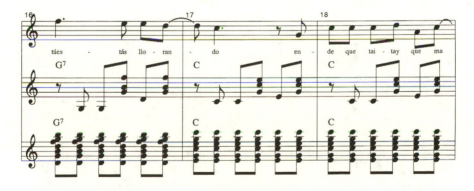

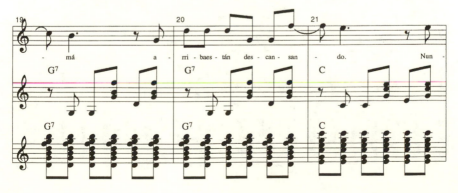

Ex. 7–12. Arnulfo Briceño's *bambuco*, "¿A quién engañas? abuelo" (continued)

ca me di - jis - te có - mo. Tam - po - co me has di - cho cuán

- do, pe - ro en el cer - ro hay dos cru - ces que te lo es -

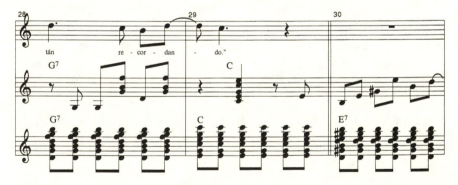

tán re - cor - dan - do."

Ex. 7–12. Arnulfo Briceño's *bambuco*, "¿A quién engañas? abuelo" (continued)

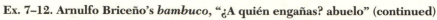

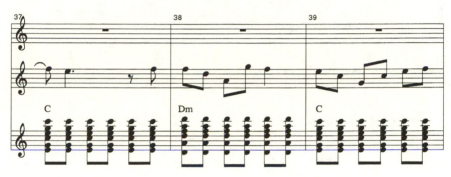

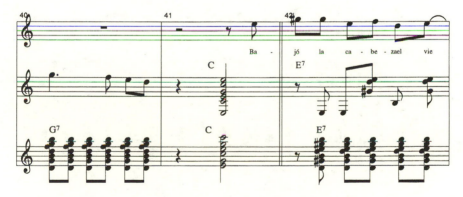

Ex. 7–12. Arnulfo Briceño's *bambuco*, **"¿A quién engañas? abuelo" (continued)**

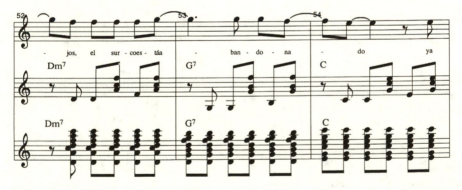

Ex. 7–12. Arnulfo Briceño's *bambuco*, "¿A quién engañas? abuelo" (continued)

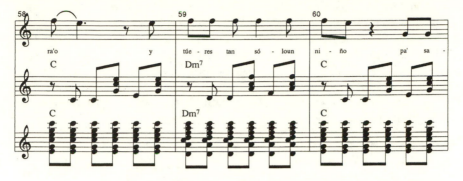

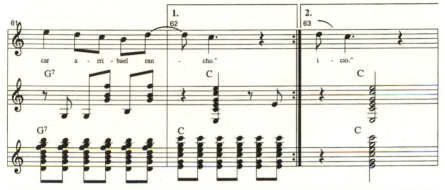

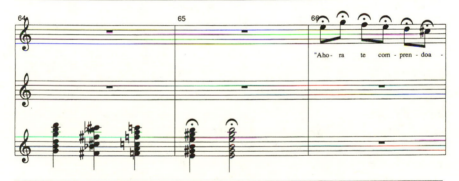

Ex. 7–13. Text of Arnulfo Briceño's "¿A quién engañas? abuelo"

"¿A quién engañas? abuelo
Yo sé que tú estás llorando—
Ende que *taita*° y que mamá
Arriba están descansando.
Nunca me dijiste cómo
Tampoco me has dicho cuándo
Pero en el cerro hay dos cruces
Que te lo están recordando."

"Who are you fooling, Grandfather?
I know that you're crying—
Since Dad and Mom
Are resting up in heaven.
You never told me how
Nor ever told me when, but
Up on the mountain are two crosses
That keep reminding you of it."

Bajó la cabeza el viejo
Y, acariciando al muchacho
Dice: "Tienes razón, hijo.
El odio todo ha cambiado.
Los *piones* se fueron lejos
Y el surco está abandonado
Y a mí ya me faltan fuerzas . . .
Me pesa tanto el arado
Y tú eres tan sólo un niño
Para sacar arriba el rancho."

The old man lowered his head
And caressing the boy
Says: "You're right, son.
Hatred has changed everything.
The farmhands have run off
And the furrowed land lies abandoned
And I just haven't the strength . . .
The plowing is too much for me
And you're still too young to get
The ranch back on its feet again."

"Me dice Chucho, el arriero,
Él que vive en los cañales
Que a unos los matan por *godos*
Y a otros por liberales.
Pero eso, ¿qué importa? abuelo
Entonces ¿qu' es lo que vale?
Mis *taitas* eran tan *güenos*
Y a *naide* le hicieron males.
Sólo una cosa comprendo:
Que antes Dios, somos iguales.

"Chucho, the muleteer who lives in
The canebrake, says that some folk
Get killed for being conservatives
And others for being liberals.
But what does that matter, grandfather?
What is really important?
My parents were so good
And they did nobody any harm.
All I really understand is:
Before God, we are all equal.

"Aparecen en elecciones
Unos que llaman *caudillos*
Que andan prometiendo escuelas
Y puentes donde no hay ríos
Y al alma del campesino
Llega el color partidizo
Y entonces aprende a odiar
Hasta quien fue su buen vecino—
Todo por esos malditos
Politiqueros de oficio."

"At election time there appear
Those men called *caudillos*
Who go around promising new schools
And even bridges where there are no rivers
And the peasant's heart turns
The color of his political party.
Then he learns to hate even him
Who used to be his good neighbor—
All because of those damned
Professional politicians . . ."

"Ahora te comprendo, abuelo . . .
Por Dios no sigas llorando. . . .

"I understand now, Grandfather . . .
For God's sake, please stop crying. . . ."

°*Taita* is the Quechua word for "father." It has entered the local Spanish dialect in this region, where it means both "father/parent" and "ancestor."

We close this section with the presentation of a more lighthearted selection from the repertoire of virtually every *vieja guardia* musician, the *bambuco fiestero* [festive *bambuco*] entitled "El guaro" [Homemade sugar-cane liquor] (Recorded Selection 38). The ubiquitous presence of alcoholic beverages in both festival and private music performance contexts has already been illustrated; in "El guaro," it is celebrated (Example 7–15). The terms *guaro* and *guarapo* refer to the sugary juice squeezed from sugar cane—in this case in its fermented, highly intoxicating, homemade form. In La Plata the more common term is *guarapo,* which due to its delightfully sweet taste, is deceptively potent.

Ex. 7–14. The *bambuco fiestero* "El guaro"

El Guaro

bambuco fiestero

Ex. 7–14. The *bambuco fiestero* "El guaro" (continued)

Ex. 7–14. The *bambuco fiestero* "El guaro" (continued)

Ex. 7–14. The *bambuco fiestero* "El guaro" (continued)

cha - ca que ca -ram -bay   el gua -ro tam -bién se   chu - pa,   y   e - ra   la que me de

cí - a   que   nun - ca meol -vi -dar -   í   a

Ex. 7–14. The *bambuco fiestero* "El guaro" (continued)

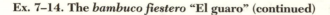

Ex. 7–14. The *bambuco fiestero* "El guaro" (continued)

This enjoyable song is customarily sung as fast as the increasingly intoxicated musicians can perform it (Example 7–14) and usually elicits enthusiastic audience participation. Often the awareness of one's own state of drunkenness becomes hilariously obvious as one encounters increasing difficulty in achieving proper rhythmic pronunciation of each succeeding stanza.

With this background of Colombian traditional musics in mind, we now turn to the life and art of La Plata's master musician and *coplero,* Don Augusto Cuéllar.

Ex. 7–15. Text of "El guaro"

De la caña sale el guaro—	*Guaro* comes from sugar cane—
¡Qué caramba!—	Whew!—
Sí la caña es buena fruta.	Sugar cane sure is great.
Si la caña se machaca—	If the cane is squeezed—
¡Qué caramba!—	Whew!
El guaro también se chupa . . .	Then you can even drink it . . .
Y era la que me decía	And it was she who told me
Que nunca me olvidaría.	That she'd never forget me.
Vámonos emborrachando	Let's go get drunk—
¡Qué caramba!—	Whew!—
Hasta que amanezca el día.	Until the sun comes up.
¡Ay! Dulce trigueña	Oh! Sweetheart with skin
De mi corazón	The color of golden wheat
Tú eres la causa de mi perdición.	I'm lost because of you.
Vino que del cielo vino	Wine that came from heaven—
¡Qué caramba!—	Whew!—
Tú me tumbas, tú me matas	You knock me over, you kill me
Tú me haces voltear las patas	You send me head over heels—
¡Qué caramba!—	Whew!—
Pero yo siempre te pido.	But I always ask for more of you.
Para él que toma aguardiente	For he who drinks *aguardiente*—
¡Qué caramba!—	Whew!—
Sí, el tomar no es cosa mala	Drinking sure isn't a bad thing
Y no hay cosa más galana	And there's nothing more exciting—
¡Qué caramba!—	Whew!—
Que una *juma* de aguardiente.	Than getting drunk on *aguardiente*.

DON AUGUSTO CUÉLLAR AND THE *SAMPEDRO*

Don Augusto Cuéllar is a very special man. He is both mechanically and musically gifted, deeply in love with his wife and nine children, perpetually involved in church and civic projects, and above all a natural showman. He spends most of his free time performing music of the *vieja guardia* with his son Fernando and other friends, and he is always ready with a serenade for whoever asks. Adopting the stage name of King Karló, he presents magic shows at schools and private homes. He drives weekly to Bogotá in his 1950 Ford truck, hauling cargoes of fruits, vegetables, beans, rice, cacao, or coffee, and returning with industrial products unavailable locally. Recognizing my shared love for the traditions of his beloved La

Plata, he insisted that I live in his home, and he invited me to accompany him on many of his overnight journeys to the capital. It was during these agonizingly slow (thirteen hours at twenty-five miles an hour) but incredibly beautiful rides on the precariously narrow roads through the moonlit Andes, that he shared his wealth of knowledge of the region's folklore.

Above all, Don Augusto was born for the *Fiesta de San Pedro* [Feast of Saint Peter]. In Andean Colombia, the *fiestas juninas* [June festivals] hold a special place in the calendar.[2] While other towns may focus their celebrations on the Feasts of Saint John (June 24) or Saint Paul (June 30), the most important day of the year in La Plata is, without question, the Feast of Saint Peter (June 29). While the festival enacts several age-old sociocultural functions—such as the provision of a sacred time in which the established social order can be temporarily inverted, allowing the release of social tensions and promoting citywide spiritual renewal— the principal reason to look forward to the festival is its opportunity to let loose and have fun. This is Don Augusto's specialty—having fun, and making sure that everyone else does, too.

The festival itself officially spans three or four days, and the key events feature the antics of La Banda de Los Borrachos [Band of the drunkards]. Performances of Los Borrachos function both to open and close the frame of festival for the general populace by welcoming and dispatching an effigy representing the festival spirit, named Pericles Carnaval. Like European mummers, Los Borrachos stage house-to-house performances beginning before dawn on June 29 in order to awaken the populace and to invite them to join the celebration. They also take this opportunity to request a contribution of alcoholic beverages to La Doña Anastacia [Lady Anastasia], the "girlfriend" of King Pericles—an effigy built around an enormous bottle whose highly intoxicating contents will be shared by the entire citizenry at the festival's closing ceremonies. Throughout the festival, Los Borrachos provide the populace with the opportunity to dance and sing to the music of the *rajaleña plateño* (discussed below).

But who or what is La Banda de Los Borrachos? In 1979, as the musical director of the ensemble, Don Augusto described the situation in a formal statement:

> Twenty-one years ago [1958], for the Feast of Saint Peter, a group of gentlemen led by Carlos Ibatá and Augusto Cuéllar organized a typical *murga* with the aim of entertaining the people of La Plata. They used copies of the instruments used by a concert band, but in this case, all constructed from gourds. The group took the name "Band of the Drunkards." In this way, by means of this public criticism, they sought to inspire a reorganization of the municipal band which was, in those days, a disgrace.
>
> But what they never dreamed was that this ensemble, a pack of wandering rogues, would ultimately become something like this, a virtual "institution" of local tradition. On the nineteenth of June, 1979, the band departed for the nation's capital to record on the [television] program called *Musical Galaxy*. Today, Saturday, the twenty-third of June, the eve of the Feast of Saint John, we have gathered to view this program—and we now present the recording of that memory, which is so very gratifying for all of us. (Cuéllar 1979)

In 1958, the members of the seminal group enlisted the support of Augusto Cuéllar, a talented young musician who had been raised in the mountains among the Páez people, but who had recently moved to La Plata, where he earned his living as a bus driver. He was known as a versatile singer and player of the *tiple,* as well as the Páez *flauta de carrizo* [transverse reed flute] and the *tambora* [drum]. While all the founders had some knowledge of the traditional *murga* [informal folk musical ensemble], none was a musician, so they agreed to follow their young mentor's advice, as far as its organization was concerned.

In La Plata the *murgas* are often called *rajaleñas.* Similar informal ensembles encountered in other locales—and featuring flutes, clarinets, drums, rattles, scrapers, jawbones, tambourines, *tiples,* spoons, accordions, or guitars—may be referred to as *cucamba, chirimía, música de las siete cosas* [music of the seven instruments], or *banda mocha.* We now see how musical instruments carry symbolic weight in La Plata's revered *murga,* La Banda de Los Borrachos.

MUSICAL INSTRUMENTS AS LOCAL MARKERS

Ya está listo el alfandoque	The *alfandoque* has been made ready
Las flautas con los tambores	The flutes, the drums
El carángano y el tiple	The *carángano* and the *tiple*
Pa' que toquen los señores.	So that the musicians can perform.

The musical instruments integral to La Plata's traditional *rajaleña* ensemble are locally perceived to be not only authentic replicas of pre-Columbian indigenous musical instruments, but unique to *plateño* folk-musical culture. A common theme—echoed in newspapers, local festival advertising, and the semischolarly, often tourist-oriented literature that appears in mass quantities during festival season—is the presumed authentic Indian origins of most if not all traditions. Eloquently romanticized references to the roles played by the *carángano, carrasca, puerca, flautas,* and *tamboras* in the idyllic daily life of the revered indigenous ancestors are commonly heard, reflecting nostalgic regional pride. Only the *tiple* is deemed Spanish in origin, and then only partially so, as it is hailed as the "most Colombian" of musical instruments, a product of the process of New World creolization, not unlike the Colombian peasant himself. It is with nothing less than a fierce and stubborn local pride that the typical *colombiano* proclaims himself, his music, his culture, his festival, and all its component parts to be a cherished patrimony born of half a millennium of Indian-Spanish cultural intermingling.

It is with much irony, then, that we learn that only the most insignificant of the musical instruments of the traditional *murga* may be considered truly indigenous to the Western Hemisphere. When the sixteenth-century *conquistadores* under Sebastián de Belalcázar first penetrated the southern Colombian Andes, the native peoples he found were probably only familiar with instruments such as vertical flutes (of bone, reed, or bamboo), drums (of wood, hollow trunks, or inflated skins—occasionally of the human variety), gourd or shell trumpets, and rudimentary idiophones such as rattles or rhythm sticks. Thus, the only instruments integral to the contemporary Banda de Los Borrachos that may possibly have roots in the native tradition are the *chucho* or *alfandoque* [shaken bamboo rattle] and the *instrumentos de calabazo* [gourd trumpets]. The *quijada* [struck jawbone], found also in Peru back to the eighteenth century, and strung rattles such as the *jala jala* are encountered almost universally, and thus may also have figured in the inventory of pre-Columbian musical instruments.

According to the musicians themselves, the four musical instruments essential to the typical folkloric *murga* of southern Colombia are, in order of importance, the *tambora,* the *flauta,* the *carángano,* and the *tiple.* None of these is indigenous to the Western Hemisphere, at least not in the form commonly employed today. The *tambora* is clearly derived from the European military drum and is played in a manner reflecting either European or West African practices. Contemporary *flautas* are exclusively of the transverse variety and imitate European folk flutes in construction, number of finger holes and scales, and performance practices. West African and African-Caribbean correlates of the *carángano* are still extant (but distinct from the ground-harp *carángano* described by List [1983:80–83, 568]). Ancestors of the *tiple* may have arrived in the Western Hemisphere as early as the first or second voyage of Columbus. More nonessential instruments, such as the *puerca* [gourd friction drum], are easily traceable to the folk music traditions of western Europe. Most scholars agree that the scraped idiophone known in La Plata as the *carrasca* arrived in South America as a result of diffusion from centers of African-European culture in the Caribbean.

How then may we account for the widespread and tenaciously defended belief among the people of La Plata that La Banda de Los Borrachos epitomizes and perpetuates the revered musical traditions of the indigenous ancestors?[3] The modern Colombian often tends to "ennoble" the vanquished and downtrodden Native American of Colombia, wrongly deprived of his ancestral lands, riches, and natural innocence by the imperialist intruders from Europe. In the process, the Native Colombian has become a powerful folk symbol of "the good old days." Uniquely Colombian, uncompromising, uncomplicated, and culturally uncontaminated by the "outside world," he is the perfect centerpiece around which this glorious—but clearly "invented"—tradition that is proudly displayed during festival season has been elaborated. All that is associated with him—lack of ethnographic or historical accuracy notwithstanding—becomes thus imbued with his symbolic power.

In the five centuries since the conquest, musical instruments, together with musical styles, tastes, and traditions, have undergone a process of "creolization," gradually being absorbed into the continuously evolving folk culture of southern Colombia. In the case of the musical instruments of La Banda de Los Borrachos, this has been true to the extent that they are today considered to be indigenous to the region, whereas they are most likely local adaptations or outright adoptions of instruments encountered over the course of nearly half a millennium of cross-cultural contact between Hispanic, African-Colombian, and indigenous inhabitants of the region. The instruments of La Banda de Los Borrachos project an image of ethno-historical and sociocultural continuity, linking the lore of tradition and local history with the contemporary cultural validation and self-expression made possible only within the context of festival performance. This image is further enhanced by Los Borrachos' incorporation of traditional costuming and masking behaviors into their annual activities (see also Gradante 1986:172–186, 1991:469–555).[4]

Let us now examine each of the musical instruments integral to the traditional southern Colombian *rajaleña* ensemble.

Tambora Sanjuanera

Un rajaleña se canta	A *rajaleña* is sung
Con la flauta y la *tambora*	With a flute and a drum
La puerca y el carángano	A *puerca* and a *carángano*
Y todo lo que ven ahora.	And everything else you see here.

Don Augusto Cuéllar set out in 1958 to fulfill his mission as musical director of La Banda de Los Borrachos by attempting to acquire the kinds of musical instruments that were traditional to the typical regional *murga:*

> Each member had to get his own musical instrument. So, since I'm from way up in the mountains, born in Tierradentro—and the *tambora* is a very popular instrument up there—well I, of course, had known how to play it well since I was small. So I drove back up there one Saturday. I left the truck at Belalcázar, walked over that hanging rope bridge that lets you cross to the other side of the abyss, and continued on as far as Avirama.
>
> Then I walked all around that area . . . searching. And finally, far away, I bought a *tambora* from some Indians from Avirama. That was the first *tambora* we ever had here. And that drum—well, I was going to play it myself, because that's why I'd bought it! But, as it turned out, since there was no one else to play the melody, and since I, of course, could also play the *flauta,* well, they got a *flauta* for me to play. So then we began to give the *tambora* to one guy, then another, and the next, and the next—and no one could play the rhythm correctly. But when Chucho Castañeda grabbed it—and he played that rhythm just perfectly—I said: "This is my drummer!" So we handed him the *tambora* right then and there, because he was the only one who could play it well.

The *tambora sanjuanera* [Saint John drum], played in the Festival of Saint John, is a double-headed cylindrical drum played with two sticks and is clearly European in construction. The manner in which it is played, on the other hand, suggests West African influences. It is probable that the ancestors of the drums brought by the Spanish to the New World were those that led the Moorish armies in their conquest of medieval Christian Spain. Following a path of adoption and adaptation, the north African military drum made its way into Spanish popular culture and then with the *conquistadores* to this hemisphere. From the early accounts it is known that the Indians regarded the playing of drums by the Spaniards as a threat of hostility. It has also been established that, together with flutes and trumpets, the drums of the Indians performed a similar military function. Indian drums—*atambores, atabales, cajas,* and *bombos*—are mentioned extensively by the chroniclers, but none have survived in the archaeology of Colombia.

While both the Africans and the Spaniards brought their native drums to the Americas, the Native Americans generally adopted those of the Europeans. Although the *tambora sanjuanera* is virtually identical to the drums used by both the Guambiano and Páez Indians who have inhabited the region at least since the colonial era, it is almost certainly an adaptation of a Spanish ancestor. In La Plata, however, it is considered to be of unquestionable local indigenous origin, a belief from which many *plateños* derive intense pleasure and local cultural pride.

The *tambora sanjuanera* used by La Banda de Los Borrachos is cylindrical and measures sixty centimeters in height and thirty-five centimeters in diameter. It is made of plywood, though the more traditional and painstaking way of the Páez Indians, which involves the fire-hollowing of a *cabuya* stump, is still occasionally practiced locally. Drum heads are attached by means of indirect bracing, with the bracing cords running through equidistantly spaced holes in the outer (or counter) hoops and laced in alternation from head to head in the form of the letter V or N. It is tuned by adjusting two additional cords wrapped around the drum and running parallel to the outer hoops and perpendicular to the bracing cords. Sometimes, however, exposing the drum head to the sun is the preferred manner of tuning a drumhead which has become slack since its last performance.

The drummer *(tamborero)* holds the instrument by slinging its coarse *cabuya* fiber strap over his right shoulder, across his back, and under his left arm. The drum hangs diagonally—almost horizontally—across the front and left side of his body, leaning upon his left hip. The left hand lies directly upon the upper side of the drum, while the right hand is left free to strike the upper drumhead.

The key to the performance of any composition of the *sanjuanero* or *rajaleña* genres is the relatively simple but musically effective rhythmic pattern established by the *tamborero*. This pattern is rendered in 3/4 meter, supported by the steady beat of the *puerca* and the *instrumentos de calabazo* (see below). The great rhythmic appeal of the *rajaleña* is created by combining this with the pulsating duple meter of the *carángano, tiple, carrasca, chucho,* and *jala-jala* patterns, along with the melody of the pair of *flautas*. Ironically, it is the relatively infrequent sounding of the *quijada* that brings the contrasting patterns together on the initial beat of each measure.

The manner in which the fundamental *tambora* pattern is executed is referred to as *mazo y palito* [big stick and little stick]. The right hand strikes the center of the goatskin drumhead with a large, heavy stick with a padded head—the *mazo*. The left hand strikes the wooden upper side of the drum with the side of a thinner, headless stick—the *palito*. The left-lower head, however, may occasionally be struck with the *palito* as part of improvised flourishes at the ends of phrases. Analogous styles of performance are reported among African-Hispanic peoples of Venezuela, Colombia, and northwestern Ecuador, and among Indian and *mestizo* cultures in Colombia and elsewhere in South America, as well as in West Africa.

Drums similar to the *tambora* (often called *bombos*) are used throughout the Andean region of South America by indigenous, African-Hispanic, and *mestizo* musical groups. It may also be noted that professional, more commercially or politically oriented (and internationally recognized) *Nueva Canción* ensembles feature similar drums. In southern Colombia, the *tambora* is highly romanticized as a symbol of the idealized indigenous past, despite the fact that the instrument is most probably the descendant of a European military drum played in a West African performance style.

Flauta

Y la *flauta* coquetona	And the flirtatious *flauta*
Enamora el carángano.	Seduces the *carángano*.
La tambora está celosa	The *tambora* is jealous
De ver semejante zángano.	To observe such a fool.

In various parts of Colombia, the term *flauta* [flute] may refer to both pan-pipes and either vertical or horizontal flutes. In southern Colombia, however, the term refers specifically to the transverse reed flute played by members of the informal ensembles known as *murgas*. Since the Middle Ages such flutes have customarily been played in tandem with cylindrical drums in military ensembles. Thus, it is quite probable that the transverse flute accompanied the fifteenth- and sixteenth-century *conquistadores* on any number of missions of conquest and colonization in the New World, probably together with the military drum.

From the early years of the colonial era, Roman Catholic priests coupled the teaching of reading, writing, and Church doctrine with singing and with the playing of flutes (as well as other instruments such as the harp and violin), finding in European musical pedagogy a very effective method of religious instruction and conversion. The seemingly innate affinity of the Native American peoples for the European flute was likely the result of their previous experience with indigenous flutes, but whether these were of the horizontal or vertical variety remains unknown. Among contemporary indigenous groups in the southern Colombian Andes, the characteristic native musical ensemble consists of two or three six-holed cross flutes accompanied by the *tambora*. It is not clear whether the existence of such ensembles may be attributed to a process of adoption and adaptation of European musical instruments by the Native Americans, but it seems probable that the indigenous peoples were familiar with somewhat similar instruments in pre-Columbian times.

Don Augusto Cuéllar was invited to join the original Banda de Los Borrachos specifically because of his mastery of the traditional *flauta*. He had learned to play it as a young boy, having been raised among the Páez inhabitants of the isolated mountain village of Santa Rosa, in the province of Cauca. The *flautas* upon which he and his son Fernando perform in parallel-third harmony are slightly smaller than those of the Páez of Santa Rosa, but they are identical in all other respects (see Illustration 7–2 and listen to Recorded Selection 39, an example of Santa Rosa Páez flute music). *Flautas* are fashioned in pairs with reference to an existing instrument. The six finger-holes are nonequidistant, the holes being opened with a hot nail and spaced in accordance with a predetermined diatonic scale of pitches. (Compare with Larry Crook's description of the manufacture of cane *pífanos* used by the *Zabumba* ensembles of northeastern Brazil, Chapter 5.)

Ill. 7–2. The *flauta* and *tambora* as played by the Páez Native Americans in the isolated village of Santa Rosa, Cauca province.

Performance in semitones is achieved primarily through the utilization of half-hole fingerings.

The aperture into which air is introduced is located at the upper or proximal end of the reed, which has been previously plugged with a piece of wood or cork, or a plastic bottle top, and sealed with hot wax. Wax may be applied anywhere on the instrument, both inside and outside, to seal fissures caused by the drying of the reed material and to prevent new cracks from developing. As a rule, *aguardiente* is poured over and inside a flute any time it is to be played, in order to facilitate performance and to improve its tone quality by swelling the fiber of the flute's interior and, thus, filling the natural pores of the *carrizo*.

When asked why he did not exchange his *flauta de carrizo* for the much more easily attainable plastic recorders used by some of the younger flautists, Don Augusto explained that the *flauta de rajaleña* simply had to be a *flauta de carrizo* like the *indígenas* used, a *flauta de indios*. Tradition demanded it. It was supposed to be raucous in timbre. Just as the voice of the *coplero* was not supposed to caress the ear, but rather accost it, exhibiting the essence of the *voz del arrabalero* [informally trained voice of the lower-class street singer], impudently demanding the listener's full attention, the shrill tone quality of the *flauta de carrizo* should help to *rajar la leña* [split wood, demand attention loudly and irritatingly]. It should be kept in mind that the two *flautas* are the only melodic instruments featured in the *murga* and their melodic lines must be clearly discerned over the din of both the crowd noise and the several accompanying rhythm instruments.

Whether the transverse flute is indigenous to the South American continent or was appropriated from the European or African newcomers at some point during the past five centuries of conquest and colonization cannot be definitively determined, given the current state of archaeological research, at least in the specific case of southern Colombia. Certainly, reed/bamboo flutes and drum types are indigenous to multifarious cultures worldwide. What is of real importance, however, is that to the *mestizo* the *flauta de carrizo,* more than any other local musical instrument, functions as a highly potent symbol of the romantic notion of their "pure" and "uncontaminated" native, "indigenous" past. To the festival participant, the *flauta de carrizo* is a Páez, Guambiano, or Pijao musical instrument. As the contemporary Páez people play a transverse *flauta*, it doesn't matter that the ethnographically "true" or "pure" Indian flute may in reality have been quite different. We recall that Don Augusto's membership in the original Banda de Los Borrachos was not valuable for the social, political, economic, or even personal connections it implied, but rather for the cultural connections that his *flauta*-playing would establish and represent. Don Augusto and his *flauta de carrizo* were essential components of La Banda de Los Borrachos because they, in effect, gave the band and the town as a whole a cultural legitimacy by giving them tangible roots in the local folk cosmology.

Vignette: *Carángano*

The roar of Don Augusto's 1950 Ford was always pretty frightening, but it never seemed quite so outrageous as during that predawn "mission" to the *guadual* [bamboo grove]. Wrapped in our ponchos against the early morning chill, we had huddled sleepily together on the dusty planks that served as the floor of the flatbed trailer and had rumbled noisily down the dusty streets to Don Carlos's place. Rail-thin Carlos and his muscular *compadre,* the jolly Don Campo Elías, were already waiting for us in front of the bamboo-and-adobe house, *machetes* dangling menacingly from their loose hempen belts. Both wore baggy work clothes, woven palm-leaf hats, and *alpargatas,* the traditional rope-soled sandals worn by both farmers and more urban laborers throughout the Hispanic world. Don Campo carried a flashlight and Don Carlos a curiously bulging *mochila de cabuya* [traditional loosely-woven hemp shoulder bag]. Neither shared our sleepy countenances, radiating instead the determined look of men "on a mission," earnestly attempting meticulously to follow the dictates of tradition. Everyone understood that the bamboo must be cut during the waning phase of the lunar cycle, and now, precisely at dawn, so the *compadres* quickly ambled onto the trailer and we were on our way out of town.

In southern Colombia, the word *monte* doesn't literally mean "mountain" as often as it refers to "wild country," "uncultivated lands," or in this case "jungle." Don Carlos directed us to just such a spot a short distance from town and, leaving the truck on the side of the road, we immediately plunged into an emerald morass of palms, vines, chest-high grasses, enormous ferns, and a cacophony of tropical birds. We dutifully followed the *compadres,* a few cautious paces behind their flashing *machetes,* as they blazed a trail ever deeper into the increasingly dense and dark forest, in search of our goal. After about ten minutes, an excited shout from Don Campo announced that we had found what we had come for—we were entering the *guadual.*

Don Augusto, Don Campo, and Don Carlos immediately launched into a frenzy of trunk-tapping, *canuto* [jointed segment] counting, and circumference-measuring, as they examined one enormous bamboo trunk after another. After about half an hour they finally agreed on the one that would have the honor of becoming that year's *carángano.* The bright green trunk had all the traits of a perfect specimen—it was tall and straight, with an unblemished surface for the required eight *canutos,* not too thick or too thin, and possessed of a fine resonance. Equally important, we had arrived early enough to cut it down before the day's water supply had been drawn up into the upper branches and absorbed. So although the trunk was extremely cumbersome and heavy with moisture, it would make an ideal musical instrument because it would produce a dull, muffled, *sordo* [literally, deaf] sonority. Old, dry, "aged" *caránganos* are given to youngsters forming new *murgas* or are recut and used as building materials, because after the *guadua* has been allowed to dry, its inherent sound qualities are irretrievably lost. It is for this reason that the same *chucho, puerca, jala jala, carrasca, esterilla* [a rubbed, reed idiophone], and *instrumentos de calabazo* are taken out of storage for festival use year after year, but a fresh, new, moist *guadua* trunk must be cut each year for the *carángano.*

Don Carlos now set down his *mochila* and, removing its strange bulge, produced a liter of *aguardiente,* Colombia's revered alcoholic beverage. Passing the bottle among ourselves, we drank a toast to the plant and its incipient role as a central part of the musical ensemble. Then, in a flash, Don Carlos scurried up the giant stalk. At a height of about ten meters he swung out from the trunk, allowing his body weight to bend it earthward. At this point Don Campo began furiously hacking at the trunk until the specimen—and his *compadre*—came crashing to the jungle floor. Now, the trophy had to be formally "baptized." Don Augusto chanted a few *coplas* befitting the occasion, including the following *copla:*

Un rajaleña se canta	A *rajaleña* is sung
Con la flauta y la tambora	With a flute and a drum
La puerca y el *carángano*	A *puerca* and a *carángano*
Y todo lo que ven ahora.	And everything else you see here.

The entire plant would be used—if not for the *carángano* or other musical instruments, such as the *chucho* [shaken idiophone], then for various household repairs. First, a section including the eight most perfect segments was selected and cut to the rough size of the *carángano*. Then the remainder of the trunk was subdivided into more manageable pieces, which were carried back to the truck by the younger members of the party. Finally, more *aguardiente* was splashed on the chosen portion, and with a shout of "¡Viva San Pedro!" we disposed of the remainder of the bottle.

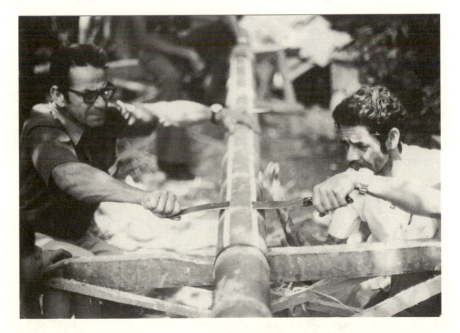

Ill. 7–3. Don Carlos and Don Campo Elías separate the vibrating strip from the center segments of the *guadua*.

After being allowed to dry for several days, the bamboo is cut into a segment consisting of precisely eight internodes, giving it finished dimensions of from two-and-a-half to three meters in length and from fifteen to twenty centimeters in diameter. A strip of the cortex six internodes in length is then removed by *machete* from the middle of the tube, great care being taken neither to detach it at either end nor to inadvertently puncture the hollow inner tube, itself. A length of wire wrapped tightly around each of the two remaining intact end internodes prevents further splitting of the cortex strip during performance. Next, a small piece of wood is inserted as a "bridge" at each extremity, raising the strip of cortex to a height of six or eight centimeters. Alternate internodes of the main tube may now be punctured with small rectangular sound holes, allowing the tube to more effectively serve as a resonating chamber. Production of the *carángano*'s characteristic sound is the result of violent pounding upon this strip which, in turn, strikes the resonating chamber, the main body of the tube. Striking portions of this strip of cortex above perforated internodes may produce a somewhat fuller, deeper sound, but the overall goal is the production of great volume—like the chopping down of a hollow tree—not exploiting subtleties of sonority.

In the context of performance, the *carángano* is held at waist level by a pair of young men who consider it an honor to be accorded the privilege. The primary player of the *carángano* alternately strikes the raised strip of cortex with two large sticks, approximately thirty centimeters in length and three or four centimeters in diameter, causing it to vibrate noisily. A pair of *vejigas* [dried, inflated cow bladders containing dried corn kernels] are pressed against the vibrating "string" of the cortex by an additional musician on either side, making the *carángano* an idiophone and a cordophone, simultaneously. Idiochordic tube zithers, as the *carángano* may be classified, are found primarily in Asia, West Africa, and Madagascar, though similar instruments have been found throughout the Colombia/Venezuela region in both predominantly African and relatively unacculturated indigenous groups. The people of La Plata prefer to believe that the *carángano* originated among the Timaná Indians who inhabited the region at the time of the Spanish conquest. It is said that these "noble indigenous ancestors" triumphantly performed upon *caránganos* in the course of battle, and both before and after the actual fighting, in preparatory and celebratory war rituals.

In fact, the *carángano* and its role in local folk tradition had been largely forgotten by the 1950s. When Don Augusto Cuéllar was asked to organize a regionally "typical" folk music ensemble for the 1958 San Pedro festival, he found himself relying heavily upon the elders of the community to learn just what it was that could be considered "typical," explaining:

> The *carángano* is a really ancient instrument. Some of us had heard talk of *caránganos*, but no one knew what it was like. Then a man who worked with Don Aniceto Amaya at the beer company came along and showed him how a *carángano* was built. I don't know where that man was from, though. . . . But we were most concerned with having an instrument that was really big, one that would attract a lot of attention. They call the *carángano* the "Hundred Feet," because it takes two men just to carry it—they have

Ill. 7–4. Don Alfonso pounds out the rhythm on the *carángano*, while Don Libardo allows the *vejigas* to buzz on the vibrating strip.

four feet—and it's usually played with two other men rubbing *vejigas* against it. So there are two, four, six—that's eight feet, no? Plus the guy who's pounding it with those sticks—so there are ten feet altogether.

There always seem to be a number of young supporters closely following the *murga* who help to carry the heavy and awkward *carángano,* join in the singing of the *copla* chorus, and keep a steady supply of *aguardiente* close at hand. Their behavior is closely monitored by Los Borrachos, as it is from among these supporters that new Borrachos are pulled aside and selected for integration into the ensemble. The *carángano* continues to serve as the centerpiece of the band, for its visual impact, for its symbolic import, and for its preeminent role in providing the characteristic rhythmic flavor. While its original provenience and evolutionary history many never be categorically ascertained, the *carángano* of La Plata enjoys a revered status as a symbol of the region's proud pre-Conquest history and of its tenacious desire to reenact that history through its celebration.

The Tiple

Las guitarras piden chicha	The guitars ask for *chicha*
Y los *tiples* aguardiente	And the *tiples* [ask for] *aguardiente*
Y ¿los señores cantores . . .?	And the gentlemen singing . . .?
¡Muchachas de quince a veinte!	Young girls from fifteen to twenty!
El *tiple* que me acompaña	The *tiple* accompanying me
Tiene boca y sabe hablar.	Has a mouth [sound hole] and knows how to speak.
Sólo le faltan los ojos	Only its lack of eyes
Pa' ayudarme a llorar.	Keeps it from weeping with me.

The *tiple* is considered the most "Colombian" of musical instruments by both the people and the students of the musical folklore of the Andean region of Colombia. The literature devoted to the study of the history of the *tiple,* however, is characterized by controversy and confusion. The cause of this uncertainty appears to revolve around the identity of the *tiple*'s most direct ancestor. Some scholars view the *tiple* as a simple "degeneration" of the guitar—a modern guitar missing the fifth and sixth courses of strings. The validity of this line of thinking, however, rests entirely upon the unproven supposition that the *tiple* did not evolve until sometime after the middle of the eighteenth century, for it wasn't until that time that the six-string Spanish guitar came into existence.

On the other hand, the instrument of choice in the era in which the Spanish first arrived in the Western Hemisphere was probably the four-stringed *gittern,* a flat-backed cordophone closely related to and probably descended from the lute of medieval Europe. It is believed that such instruments may have arrived as early as Columbus's second voyage. By the middle of the sixteenth century, when the *conquistadores* first ascended the Colombian Andes, the *gittern* featured three pairs of strings plus a single *chanterelle* [highest-pitched string], all made of gut, with the second string of each pair doubling at the octave. This configuration closely resembles that of the modern *tiple*. Little more than a modest leap of the imagination would seem necessary to inspire the subsequent expansion of these four double courses to the modern *tiple*'s triple courses of strings, at some point in its 450 years in Colombia. There is evidence that *tiples* and *guitarras* coexisted in the Colombian-Venezuelan plains region as distinct musical instruments as early as the late seventeenth century (Perdomo Escobar 1963:26, Abadía Morales 1973:146).

The five-course *vihuela* first appeared in the third quarter of the sixteenth century, spreading by the seventeenth century from Spain to Italy and from there throughout Europe, where it became known as the Spanish guitar. Pairing of strings, including doubling at the octave in the lowest (or lowest two) courses of strings, occurred during the seventeenth century, and by 1677 the tuning of such instruments was raised two semitones to its modern level. It was not until the era of Colombian independence from Spain that the modern guitar emerged. During the course of the eighteenth and nineteenth centuries the instrument was enlarged and strengthened, strings were thickened and standardized, a sixth (bass) string was added, and the pairs of strings were reduced to single strings, thus facilitating playing technique for the amateur musician.

The modern *tiple* features twelve steel strings grouped in four courses of three strings each. The *primas*, the first or highest-pitched strings, are tuned in unison to e^1. The middle strings of each of the three remaining courses are tuned in intervals equivalent to those of the guitar, to b^0, g^0, and d^0, for the *segundas, terceras*, and *cuartas*, respectively. The two companions of each of these are tuned an octave higher, to b^1, g^1, and d^1, respectively (see Example 7–9). The term *requintilla* is used to designate these higher-pitched strings, which contribute greatly to the unique tone quality of the *tiple*.

The inhabitants of the Colombian Andes are tenacious in their romanticization of the *tiple*—not as a "degeneration," or even a copy of a European bequeathal of the *conquistadores*, but as a revered product of the process of creolization, a unique historico-cultural treasure symbolic of the Colombian *mestizo* himself. In this case, it seems that the wisdom of the peasant may be closest to the truth.

As part of a performing ensemble, the role of the *tiple* is to render its characteristic, percussive, chordal accompaniment, whether as a component of a *murga* or serving as an accompanist for vocal, *bandola*, and *guitarra* melodies in a string ensemble. The *tiple*'s functional equivalent in the *guabina* ensembles of northeastern Colombia is called the *requinto* or *tiple requinto*, and is a slightly smaller version, also made preferably of pine, cedar, or walnut, but with each course tuned in unison. Unlike the *tiple*, some *requintos* have a total of ten strings, with only the first and second, or first and fourth string courses tripled. It may occasionally be plucked with a plectrum, as well. The *guitarra* is the standard classical guitar, larger than the *tiple*, and featuring six single strings, tuned e^1, b^0, g^0, d^0, A^0, and E^0. The traditional nylon strings are occasionally replaced by steel strings. In tandem with the *tiple*, the *guitarra* is an essential part of the *dueto bambuquero*, the *estudiantina*, and most other Colombian *mestizo* folk music ensembles.

Ill. 7–5. Don Augusto performing on the *tiple*.

The Tiple *in Regional Folklore*

The striking sonority of the *tiple* is a source of great regional pride among Colombians, particularly within the Andean region, where it enjoys its most widespread popularity. It is generally believed by *colombianos* that the strumming of *tiples* accompanied Simón Bolívar's troops in the wars of independence against the Spanish in the early nineteenth century. Beginning in August of 1852, American botanist and explorer Isaac F. Holton spent twenty months traveling in the Colombian Andes, collecting both botanical specimens and what has since become invaluable information concerning contemporary lifestyles. The amusing account presented below is his description of an informal musical performance at an evening rest stop, apparently some sixty kilometers west-northwest of Bogotá:

> There was music too, vocal and instrumental, and, I believe, dancing. The principal musical instrument was the *tiple*, a diminutive of the *bandola*, which is itself a reduction of the common guitar. The length of this implement of torment is a little more than a foot, and I do not think the strings are ever shortened by stopping them, as in the guitar and violin. This banjo, jr. is easily played, when once in tune, by drawing your fingers across it in any manner, only keeping time. It costs only two or three dimes, and the number that infest the land, not only in the *tiendas*, but by the roadside, is dreadful. (Holton 1857:62–63)

Clearly, the object of Holton's contemptuous recollection was a smaller relative of the modern *tiple*, which measures almost a full meter in length, making it appreciably larger than the closely related *bandola*. These larger *tiples*—and their proud and often highly talented owners—still "infest" the region.

The instrument plays a significant role in regional popular culture. The *tiple* is known as the favorite plaything of El Duende, an impish, elf-like creature identified by his oversize *sombrero* and the cloven-hoofed footprints left by his tiny, backward-pointing feet. It is said that any *tiple* left hanging on its peg in an untuned state runs the risk of being smashed to splinters by El Duende, who lacks the patience required to tune all twelve strings—particularly the dangerously thin *requintillas*.[5]

While one could cite numerous examples of wordplay born of this preoccupation with and deep affection for the beloved *tiple*—many deriving from the similarity between its curvaceous form and that of the equally beloved *colombianas*—only two will be presented here. The first utilizes the term *rascado*—literally, "scraped" or "torn up," but used in the local vernacular to mean "drunk" "worn out," or "spent." *Rascado*, or the more colloquial *rasca'o* (and the near homonyms *rasgado* and *rasga'o*) are also commonly used to describe the scratching and scraping of the fingers in the act of strumming a *tiple*. From this springs the common saying, "Estoy más rasca'o qu' el tiple" [I'm more drunk/worn out/strummed than my *tiple*]. The second example is a commonly heard popular expression that refers with double meaning to the traditional role of the *tiple* in the courtship of a young lady: "El tiple es el camino más corto a la India (india)" meaning "The *tiple* is the shortest route to India," or "The *tiple* is the quickest way to an Indian girl's heart." In both cases we find evidence of the *tiple* as an integral part of everyday life among the people of the working class.

Considerations of space preclude extensive discussion of other, less prominent instruments of the *rajaleña* ensemble; we mention them here briefly. The Atlantic coastal *carrasca* is a scraped idiophone, known throughout Colombia and Venezuela by a variety of names (*güiro, guacharaca, charrasca, carrasca,* or *carraca*); transverse grooves are etched across the surface of a gourd or bamboo, a stick being used to scrape across these grooves. The *quijada,* a scraped or struck idiophone, is the jaw of a horse, mule, or donkey, with the teeth left in; either the teeth are scraped with a stick, or the jawbone itself is struck with the fist.[6] The *puerca* [pig] or *zambomba* is a friction drum consisting of a wax-covered friction stick inserted and tied into a treated cow's bladder which is, in turn, stretched over the open end of a dried, hollow gourd. Used in Christmas activities in Spain, and in Ecuador and Guatemala as well, the *zambomba* is also used in the *guabinero* ensemble of northeastern Colombia, as well as on Colombia's Atlantic coast. The *jala-jala* (or *quiribillo*) is a strung rattle, a shaken idiophone, consisting of reed segments strung along multiple lengths of twine, which are looped over head and shoulder and then shaken. The *alfandoque* (or *chucho*) is a different type of "dropped-then-caught" idiophone, consisting of a bamboo internode closed at both ends and containing small rattling objects.

Instrumentos de Calabazo

Horns and trumpets of various kinds have figured in the arsenal of musical instruments of the indigenous peoples of South America since pre-Columbian times. These instruments vary widely in terms of their size, shape, provenience, sociocultural function, and materials of construction. Called *bocinas* by the *conquistadores* (*bocina* is still the term for a trumpet of multiple cowhorn segments among the highland Ecuadorian Quechua), trumpets of various kinds were termed *botutos* or *fotutos* among the *indigenes* of Colombian territory, as they are today. (*Pututu* is the Quechua term for a trumpet of Bolivia and neighboring countries, formerly made from conch shell, today made from a reed with attached animal horn.) While it is clear that, for sixteenth-century Native Colombians, the large conch enjoyed the highest stature among the various kinds of indigenous trumpets, it is probable that the hollow gourd variety predated it. Gourd trumpets have been reported throughout the extent of the Andean territory and as far north as the Yucatán peninsula and the Antilles, from pre-Columbian times to the present. Examples in our time include the *chile frito* ensemble of gourd band instruments of Guerrero, Mexico, and the *banda mocha* ensemble of gourd band instruments of African-Ecuadorians of the Chota River Valley, highland Ecuador—not a great distance from the southern Colombian Andes.

When instrument maker Carlos Ceballos of La Banda de Los Borrachos sits down to work on his gourd-and-wax creations in preparation for the Fiesta de San Pedro, it is with confidence that he is reenacting the traditions of his ancestors, the indigenous people of the valley of the La Plata River. While both Don Carlos and his mentor on matters folkloric, the venerable Don Carlos Ibatá, sometimes overindulge in somewhat fancifully romanticized versions of the folk cultural history of southern Colombia, their views seem to be empirically substantiated here. The town of La Plata was founded in the fertile Valley of the Cambis, the Cambis Indians having taken their name from the Páez word *cambich* [calabash, gourd]. Although Don Carlos sometimes complains that the gourds currently cultivated just aren't as big, plentiful, or easily obtainable as they used to be, he always seems to be able to rustle up enough to keep his fellow *plateños* delighted with his latest creations.

Don Carlos strictly adheres to what he understands to be traditional procedures in the construction process. The gourds must be picked, hollowed, and dried during the waning phase of the moon in order that they last longer, better resisting damage due to insects or natural decomposition. It should be noted that this is also true of the bamboo and reeds used in the production of the other instruments of La Banda de Los Borrachos. With the notable exception of the *guadua* for the *carángano,* all instrument-making materials are cut in the late afternoon, when they are inherently driest, so that their resultant sonority will be clear, raucous, and resonant.

After allowing the hollowed gourd shell to dry and harden, it is cut so as to fit comfortably alongside the adjacent *totumas* [gourds]. Small perforations are made around the interfacing surfaces in order to allow Don Carlos to literally "sew" the *totumas* together with wire. Then a mixture of beeswax and black vegetable carbon is applied to the juncture, rendering the seam airtight. In honor of the twentieth anniversary celebration of La Banda de Los Borrachos in 1978, Don Carlos painted this wax sealer silver and wrote "20 Años" [Twenty Years] across the largest segments of the Band's largest gourd trumpets. Musically the role of the gourd horns is to reinforce the repetitious rhythm patterns and tone quality of the *puerca* friction drum. This generally consists of alternation between sounding on all three quarter notes in 3/4 meter and playing on only the last two beats. None of the players of the gourd instruments of La Banda de Los Borrachos considers himself a musician at any other time of the year, and performance practice is only very vaguely prescribed.

In summary, we may view the role of the *instrumentos de calabazo* from a couple of perspectives. Symbolically, Don Carlos Ceballos's creations serve to reinforce the theme of fidelity to the honored traditions of the indigenous ancestors. On a more concrete level, they serve as comic reminders of one of the principal reasons for originally organizing La Banda de Los Borrachos—the enactment of a public satire on the behavior of the members of the municipal band during traditional *fiestas.* The irritating cacophony of grotesque, homemade musical instruments, played by an unruly gang of masked fools clad in ragged burlap motley, loudly proclaimed such behavior unworthy of La Plata's cherished *fiesta* tradition. Thus, by providing a ludicrous model of how music, musicians, musical instruments, and the *fiesta* itself should *not* be, La Banda de Los Borrachos—albeit not entirely intentionally—took the first major step toward redefining the way in which the Fiesta de San Pedro in La Plata should and would be celebrated from 1958 forward.

COPLAS AND COPLEROS

One summer evening I was startled by the sudden, silent appearance of Don Augusto Cuéllar peering inquisitively over my right shoulder at the index cards scattered across my writing table. As I proudly explained that each precious card bore the text of a single *copla,* he closed his eyes and shook his head. He considered my prized stack of a couple hundred cards not only unimpressive and inconsequential, but, incredibly, an exercise in futility. But he reassured me, quietly warning: "Te va a costar mucho trabajo, Guillermo—esto, ¡esto es infinito!" [You've got quite a job on your hands, Bill—the number of *coplas* is infinite!]

The improvisation and performance of *coplas* in the festival context is probably the most exciting aspect of Colombian folk music today. But just what are *coplas?* The term *copla* [couplet] was originally used to refer to the rhyming pairs of sixteen-syllable lines which comprised the *romance* of the Spanish ballad tradition during the period known as the Reconquista (A.D. 718–1492), the liberation of Spain from Moorish domination (see also Ercilia Moreno Chá's discussion of *romance* and *tonada* in Chapter 6). However, the existence of alternatives to the ABCB rhyme scheme, such as ABAB, AABB, and ABBA, seems to indicate that the *copleros* [*copla* singers and composers] in Colombia have come to conceptualize the *copla* primarily in its four-line form. All four lines of the *copla del rajaleña plateño*—La Plata's variety of *copla*—are typically octosyllabic and exhibit an ABCB rhyme scheme.

Unlike the multiple *coplas* comprising the *romance* or, for example, the Mexican *corrido,* the *copla* of which we speak stands alone—it is not a *copla corrida.* That is, in spite of its brevity, it makes a complete statement within its allotted four lines, whether it be a flirtatious remark:

El bejuco, cuando nace,	When the bejuco vine sprouts,
Nace hoja por hojita.	It grows leaf by tiny leaflet.
Así nació nuestro amor—	Our love was born in the same way—
Palabra por palabrita.	Word by sweet little word.

a pornographic joke using double-entendre:

Todas las mujeres tienen	All the women have
Un trapiche qu' es muy guapo.	A beautiful sugar-cane press.
Por dura que sea la caña	No matter how hard the cane may be
Siempre saca todo el guarapo.	It always gets all the juice out.

or bitter social commentary:

Que nos gobiernen los godos	Let the Conservatives govern
O mande el liberalismo—	Or let Liberalism rule—
Para tirarse a los pobres	When it comes to screwing the poor people
Todos resultan lo mismo.	They're both the same anyway.

At its worst, the context of *rajaleña* performance becomes an open-air arena for vulgar jesting and sexual boasting, especially when performed by less "artistically motivated" singers. At its best, the *rajaleña* serves as a musical medium for the expression of witty folk poetry and the transmission of sly, humorous, and often pornographic bits of folk wisdom, featuring ingenious manipulation of local vernacular, double-entendre, and audience expectations. Ultimately, it provides a forum for the public projection of *plateño* local identity, class consciousness, and sociocultural commentary.

Copla singing in southern Colombia is essentially a revival of what was once a common regional practice but appears to have fallen into a period of decline by the middle of the twentieth century. Don Augusto Cuéllar is the principal flautist, musical director, and lead *coplero* of La Banda de Los Borrachos. Surprisingly, he first learned of the *copla* tradition only in his twenties, when, on inquiring about past customs, he was told that the most important facet of the "old celebrations" was to sing *rajaleña*.

Performance of *rajaleña plateño* is tied exclusively to the Fiesta de San Pedro. Folk musical performance during the remainder of the year consists of the playing and singing of what we have called music of the *vieja guardia*. Thus, learning to create and deliver *coplas* is a trial-and-error sort of business, with rarely more than a single pre-festival rehearsal. Actual performance in the context of the festival is the only real "school" for aspiring *copleros*.

There are two principal types of *copla* in Colombia, at least in terms of their ostensible origins and provenience. These include *coplas* adopted directly or adapted from Spanish tradition, and those created by local *copleros* themselves, thus expressing a uniquely Colombian perspective. The *copleros* of La Plata are generally unaware—but probably would not be too surprised to learn—that some of the *coplas* they sing are also known and performed elsewhere in the Hispanic world, and thus likely belong to the former category.

They themselves recognize three categories of *copla*. The first may be designated *coplas conocidas* [familiar, known *coplas*] and includes the enormous number of verses heard from various sources, memorized, and reinterpreted by the *coplero* during the course of his life. The *coplero* finds it useful to have a number of humorous *coplas conocidas* in mind in order to get the audience initially involved in the event. While not requiring the poetic genius needed to create verses of the second or third categories, a sharp memory and a high level of verbal dexterity are continuously and assiduously cultivated over many years in order spontaneously to perform *coplas* from the large corpus of preexisting verses of this first category.

The second category is referred to as *coplas pensadas,* those prepared prior to the festival and usually crafted for the purpose of making public criticism of specific current social, cultural, or political situations. Such *coplas* also comprise the lengthy "Testamento de Pericles," a comical list of bequeathals from the effigy representing the Carnival King Pericles to various townspeople, and publicly read—not sung—at the offical festival closing ceremony. Finally, a smaller number of *coplas pensadas* may also be created by participants in big-city *copla* singing contests, where inspiration arises not from social consciousness but from cash incentives offered by the organizers.

The third category includes those verses improvised in the context of an actual street duel, and *surgen del momento* [emerge at the moment of their performance]. While there are far more examples of the second and especially the first category—from which the experienced *coplero* may recall and reinterpret a large number of examples—it is the performance of *coplas* of the third category which is most exciting and which sheds most light upon the actual creative process of the *copleros*.

Although they may not be consciously considered a class of *coplas* themselves, there are also *coplas* that perform a specific function within the context of any given performance event. In a practice reminiscent of Mexico-Texas border *corrido* singers, the La Plata *copleros* adhere to mandatory formulas for beginning and ending any *copla* performance, starting with a rendition of the widely recognized flute melody. This sets the emotional tone for *rajaleña* behavior, transforming the setting from one of what we might call "frivolous" play to a more "serious" or "deep" play (see Geertz 1971). The first *copla* performed to initiate any performance event must function as a public request for permission and with apologies in advance, such as:

Permiso pido, señores,	I ask permission, gentlemen,
Para ponerme a cantar.	That I may begin singing.
Si alguna falta cometo	Should I become at all offensive
Me tendrán que perdonar.	You'll just have to excuse me.

Then, finishing up, one may sing:

Ahora sí no canto más	Now I'll stop singing
Y de todos me despido.	And I bid everyone goodbye.
Sólo ruego perdonar	I only beg forgiveness
Por si alguno se ha ofendido.	In case anyone has been offended.

Such *coplas* perform the function of *desculpa* [apology] and *despedida* [farewell], closing the metaphorical parentheses that circumscribe the play event. Keeping in mind that *coplas* are performed throughout Spain and Latin America in many different ways, let us now examine more closely the actual procedure by means of which they are performed by La Banda de Los Borrachos, suggesting that such performance might possibly be replicated in the classroom.

COPLA PERFORMANCE FORMAT

The following is one of the most common performance-opening *coplas* in La Plata:

Permiso pido, señores,	I ask permission, gentlemen,
Pa' cantar mi rajaleña	To sing my *rajaleña*
Con La Banda 'e Los Borrachos,	With La Banda de Los Borrachos,
La vieja murga plateña.	The old *murga* from La Plata.

The highly repetitive performance format, however, transforms the four-line *copla* into an ostensibly twelve-line entity, inasmuch as it is characteristically rendered in the manner illustrated below:

Order	*Text*	*Performers*
1	Permiso pido, señores,	*coplero* alone
2	Permiso pido, señores,	two *copleros* in thirds
3	Pa' cantar mi rajaleña	*coplero* alone
4	Pa' cantar mi rajaleña	two *copleros* in thirds
5	¡Lai, lai, lai, lai, morena!	*copleros* and chorus
6	Pa' cantar mi rajaleña	*copleros* and chorus

If a *copla* is spontaneously improvised in the context of the performance, there may be a slightly elongated, very "pregnant," pause at this juncture, as the *coplero* makes final adjustments to the last two lines:

7	Con La Banda 'e Los Borrachos,	*coplero* alone
8	Con La Banda 'e Los Borrachos,	two *copleros* in thirds
9	La vieja murga plateña.	*coplero* alone
10	La vieja murga plateña.	two *copleros* in thirds
11	¡Lai, lai, lai, lai, morena!	*copleros* and chorus
12	La vieja murga plateña.	*copleros* and chorus

In successful performances, the refrains—lines 5–6 and 11–12—are performed by all present, including spectators. When the *copla* is well known, the chorus and spectators may even join in singing lines 2, 4, 8, and 10. Similar performance formats are found throughout the region, though variant forms of lines 5 and 11 are common.

Between renditions of *coplas,* the two flautists perform, freely, the instrumental interlude presented in Example 7–16. On occasion, one of the flautists may drop out momentarily in order to greet a friend or to take a drink of *aguardiente,* perhaps. The basic melody is eighteen measures in length and requires about seventeen seconds to perform. But if the *coplero* requires additional time to organize his thoughts and make final adjustments in his improvisation, the interlude may be expanded to twenty-four measures (approximately twenty-three seconds) or even thirty measures (twenty-eight seconds) through the repetition of measures 9 through 14. The performance of all twelve lines of the *copla* itself usually lasts only twenty to twenty-five seconds, meaning that the entire vocal/instrumental cycle typically lasts about three-quarters of a minute.

The melody traditionally used for the singing of *coplas* during the Fiesta de San Pedro in La Plata is presented in Example 7–17. The melody of the first line, from which each of the subsequent three is clearly derived, is quite simple. All note values are the same, and repeated notes abound, there being a total of only three different pitches used. The pattern of sung accents coincides with the first beat of each measure. At the same time, the *tiple*'s percussive accompaniment consists of strict alternation between tonic minor and dominant seventh chords

Ex. 7–16. Flute instrumental interlude, between *coplas*

Coplas de Rajaleña:
Flauta Interlude
(typical performance, but open to artist's interpretation)

with each measure. This combination of factors further strengthens the emphasis on the third and seventh pulses of each line in the mind of the performer. Meanwhile, all other instrumentalists—they themselves hesitate to call themselves musicians—provide background accompaniment, as illustrated in Example 7–18.

COPLAS DEL RAJALEÑA PLATEÑO

The term *rajaleña* literally means "to split wood," invoking a violent image of the act of striking repeatedly, when one's efforts produce sparks and splinters. The

Ex. 7–17. Melody used for singing *coplas* during the Fiesta de San Pedro in La Plata, Colombia

Coplas de Rajaleña:

Vocal Melody

Per - mi - so pi - do, se - ñor - es, per - mi -
so pi - do, se - ñor - es, pa' can - tar mi ra - ja -
le - ña, pa' can - tar mi ra - ja - le - ña...
Ay, lai, lai, lai, mo - re - na, pa' can -
tar mi ra - ja - le - ña con La Ban - da'e Los Bor -
ra - chos, con La Ban - da'e Los Bor - ra - chos, la gran
or - ques - ta pla - te - ña, la gran or - ques - ta pla -
te - ña... Ay, lai, lai, lai, mo - re - na, la gran
or - ques - ta pla - te - ña.

better the performer of the *rajaleña,* Don Augusto explained, the greater the profusion of "sparks and splinters" he produces—that is, the more poignant the public reaction he is capable of provoking:

> *Rajaleña* is essentially "impact," you know? Because in order to cut wood, one must strike it. And one "strikes" with *coplas.* The ax hits the log in order to split it. It strikes it, you see? And the log, if it had feelings—would hurt, because chips and splinters

Ex. 7–18. Instrumental accompaniment to *copla* singing

Coplas de Rajaleña:

Instrumental Interlude
(measures 9-14 are played 3 times)

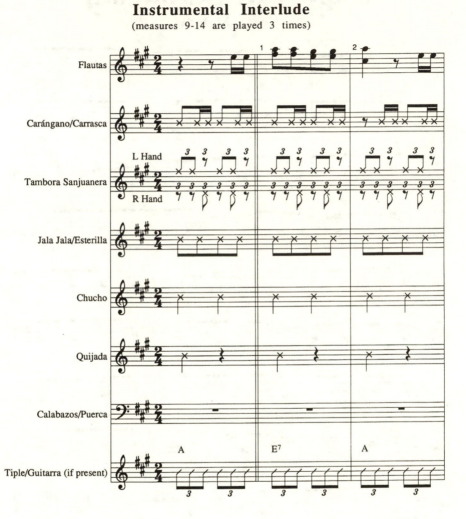

Ex. 7–18. Instrumental accompaniment to *copla* singing (continued)

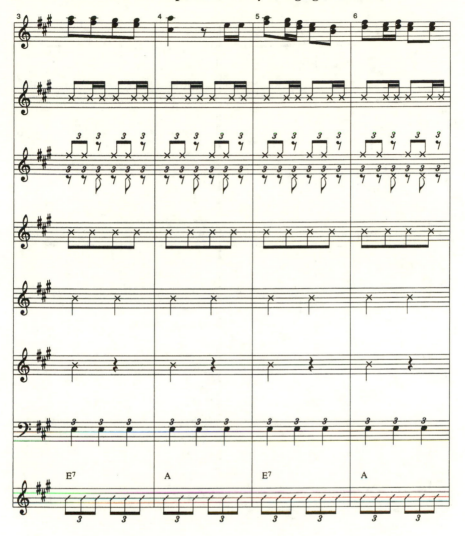

Ex. 7–18. Instrumental accompaniment to *copla* singing (continued)

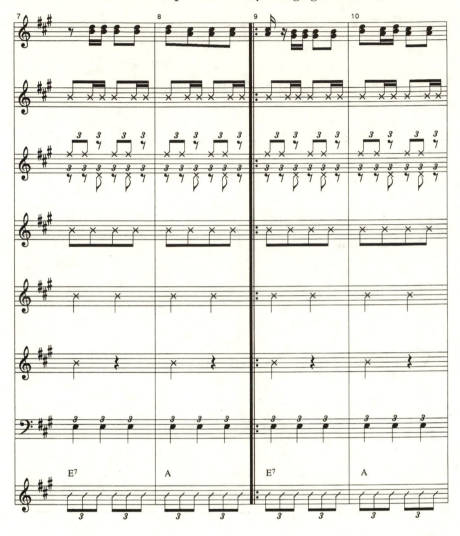

Ex. 7–18. Instrumental accompaniment to *copla* singing (continued)

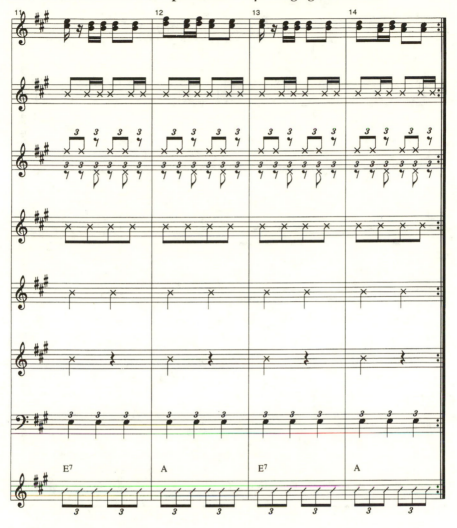

Ex. 7–18. Instrumental accompaniment to *copla* singing (continued)

have been knocked out of it. And that is just what we do with our *coplas*—grab some poor devil and knock splinters out of him [laughs]. That is, more or less, the meaning of *rajaleña*. (Cuéllar interview)

But the verbal ax wielded by the *coplero* is of the double-edged variety, and blows are rarely struck with blunt brutality. The best *coplas* craftily merge humor and carefully selected wordings, seasoned with just enough double meaning, misdirection, and obfuscation that only those listeners truly "in the know" will get the full punch line (Recorded Selection 40). For example, in poking fun at a local doctor who was having a not-so-clandestine nocturnal affair with a young woman named Flores [literally, flowers], the *coplero* turned the good doctor into a horticulturalist:

El Doctor Llanos Arana	Dr. Llanos Arana
Que trabaja con esmero	Who works so conscientiously and elegantly
En el día en su consultorio—	In his office during the day—
Por la noche es "jardinero."	Becomes a "gardener" at night.

The difference between *coplas* that "sting" and those whose "bite" is less painful, due to the poetic genius of the *coplero,* is clearly illustrated in the following *copla,* which playfully comments upon the plight of a good friend of the *coplero,* known both as an avid fisherman and as a long-married but still childless husband:

Pesca y pesca con frecuencia	Always fishing and fishing
Mi amigo Aniceto Amaya	Is my friend Aniceto Amaya
Y a pesar de su insistencia	But in spite of his persistence
Nada cae en su atarraya.	Nothing ever falls into his net.

Surfacing here is a recurrent theme in Colombian verbal art, put succinctly by Don Augusto as follows: "No es lo que dijiste, sino cómo lo has dicho." [It's not what you've said, but rather how you've said it.]

Defense of traditional local culture is a prevalent theme during the festival. Resentment toward radio programs originating in the provincial capital of Neiva was aroused by the decreasing airtime allotted to regional traditional music:

Neiva, "Sede del Bambuco,"	They call Neiva "Home of the *Bambuco*"
Y "Tierra de La Gaitana"—	And "Land of the Gaitana"—[7]
Sus emisoras no tocan	But her radio stations still don't broadcast
La música colombiana.	Colombian [Andean] music.

This defensiveness regarding local music culture surfaced in a *copla* performance recorded back in the days when North American "disco" and African-Colombian (accordion-based) music from the coast began to invade southern Colombia, and thus became a target of the *coplero's* verbal art:

Nosotros ya de los viejos	We older folks
Nos hemos puesto arrugados,	Have grown old and wrinkled,
Pero eso del acordeón—	But this business of the accordion music—
Lo pueden dejar a un lado.	They should cast it aside.

El rescate del folclor	The recovery of our folklore
Es lo que más nos importa—	Is the most important thing to us—
Que no bailen en las fiestas	During the *fiestas* no one should dance
Eso que llaman "Travolta."	To that so-called "Travolta" music.

It must be kept in mind that once an individual has decided to enter the arena of the *desafío* [*copla* jousting or dueling], he must be prepared to deal competently with the responses of his adversaries or risk loss of artistic respect.[8] For example, the following poetic thrust simultaneously evoked laughter and struck a sensitive spot in the proud flautist's ego:

El señor Fernando Cuéllar	Mr. Fernando Cuéllar
Es buen músico de cuerdas	Is a good guitarist
Pero esa maldita flauta	But that damned flute
¡Ya con nadie se concuerda!	Is not in tune with anyone!

The flautist responded almost immediately:

Esa copla me gustó	I liked that *copla*
Pero ésta, no se la pierda:	But don't you forget this:
Si yo no sé tocar flauta	If I can't play the flute well
¡Váyanse a comer mierda!	You can go eat shit!

Aficionados of the *desafío* particularly appreciated Don Fernando's impromptu response because, in the heat of the moment, he was able not only to respond within the accepted parameters of both rhyme and meter, but actually to manipulate his adversary's own choice of rhyming vowel to his own advantage. Don Fernando thus simultaneously "excused" his own use of profanity and earned the respect and the appreciative laughter of both his rival and the larger audience. The *coplero*'s personal repertoire and rendering must satisfy the audience's desire to hear *coplas picantes* [spicy *coplas*], which will both make them laugh and poke fun at popular targets in a good-natured manner. *Coplas* alluding to sexual situations are mandatory. Once the continued attention and appreciation of the audience is secured through the performance of a series of known *coplas*, the *coplero* may perform one or more *coplas pensadas*, carefully prepared to make a specific point, or he may even dare to improvise new ones.

The distinction between the mere *cantante* [singer] of *rajaleña* and the true *coplero* is clear. Whenever a performer decides to *echar una copla* [toss out a *copla*] containing controversial ideas, he knows he had better be prepared to accept and react to the responses of any other *copleros* present, or else lose his credibility as a performing artist. Thus, only an experienced, knowledgeable *coplero* will dare allow himself to be drawn into a dueling situation.

For the capable verbal artist like Don Augusto, however, the reward for such "daring" is the knowledge that the optimal context for exciting improvisational behavior can only be achieved in the event that one *coplero* is able to elicit an effective impromptu response from another—repeatedly. When the creativity and verbal skills of the involved *copleros* are sufficiently matched to permit them consistently and imaginatively to respond to each other's offerings, simultaneously abiding by the prescribed standards of rhyme and meter and maintaining a mutually inoffensive emotional "tone," an audience may be held spellbound for the duration of the resultant encounter. Such events ostensibly take place in La Plata on only very rare occasions, probably due to the relatively small number of expert *copleros* actively participating in *murgas* and the fact that such activity takes place only during the Fiesta de San Pedro. Further, as mentioned above, *desafíos* constitute what scholars have called "deep play," entailing all of the potential risk to social status inherent in such activity, and thus are not entered into lightly.

CONCLUSION

Don Augusto Cuéllar and many of his southern Colombian Andean *compadres* are multitalented musicians and creative verbal artists. Their verse types and musical instrument types are grounded in strongly established Spanish and Native Colombian practices, yet reinvigorated with a special burst of contemporary pride and invention. What is in the air and in the mind, in La Plata and Silvia? *Vieja guardia* (*bambuco* and *pasillo*); Semana Santa; *serenata* and *aguardiente*; *carángano* and *copla* and *Sampedro*. These ways of life begin to create the local music-cultural "DNA" of Silvia and La Plata, in the southern Colombian Andes, much as other analogous configurations have comprised the vital structures of the other music-cultural regions examined in this book.

REFERENCES

Abadía Morales, Guillermo. 1973. *La música folklórica colombiana.* Bogotá, Colombia: Universidad Nacional de Colombia.

Añez, Jorge. 1951. *Canciones y recuerdos.* Bogotá, Colombia: Ediciones Mundial.

Arboleda Llorente, José María. 1957. *Popayán en el cuarto centenario de sus procesiones de Semana Santa, 1558–1958.* Popayán, Colombia: El Carmen.

Collins, Patricia Lacy. 1993. *Holy Week in San Miguel: A story of faithfulness.* Houston: San Rafael.

Cuéllar, Augusto. 1979. Interview by author. La Plata, Colombia.

Friedmann, Susana. 1982. *Las fiestas de junio en el Nuevo Reino.* Bogotá, Colombia: Editorial Kelly.

Geertz, Clifford. 1971. Deep play: Notes on the Balinese cockfight. In *Myth, symbol, and culture,* ed. Clifford Geertz. New York: W. W. Norton & Co.

Gradante, William J. 1986. The Message in the mask: Costuming in the festival context. In *The many faces of play,* ed. Kendall Blanchard, pp. 172–186. Champaign, Ill.: Human Kinetics Publishers.

———. 1991. "¡Viva el San Pedro en La Plata!": Tradition, creativity, and folk musical performance in a Southern Colombian festival. Ph.D. diss., Univ. of Texas at Austin.

Hobsbawm, Eric and Terence Ranger, eds. 1983. *The invention of tradition.* New York: Cambridge Univ. Press.

Holton, Isaac F. [1857] 1967. *New Granada: Twenty months in the Andes.* Edited by C. Harvey Gardiner. Carbondale, Ill.: Southern Illinois Univ. Press.

Koorn, Dirk. 1977. Folk music of the Colombian Andes. Ph.D. diss., Univ. of Washington.

List, George. 1983. *Music and poetry in a Colombian village: A tricultural heritage.* Bloomington, Ind.: Indiana Univ. Press.

Perdomo Escobar, José Ignacio. 1963. *La historia de la música en Colombia.* Bogotá, Colombia: Editorial ABC.

Solomon, Thomas. 1994. Coplas de todos santos in Cochabamba: Language, music, and performance in Bolivian Quechua song dueling. *Journal of American Folklore* 107(425):378–414.

Turino, Thomas. 1983. The *charango* and the *sirena:* Music, magic, and the power of love. *Latin American Music Review* 4(1)(spring/summer):81–119.

Turner, Victor. 1974. *Dramas, fields, and metaphors: Symbolic action in human society.* Ithaca, N.Y.: Cornell Univ. Press.

ADDITIONAL READING

Araújo de Molina, Consuelo. 1973. *Vallenatología: Orígenes y fundamentos de la música vallenata.* Bogotá, Colombia: Ediciones Tercer Mundo.

Arbena, Joseph, Henry Schmidt, and David Vassberg. 1980. Colombia. In *Regionalism and the musical heritage of Latin America,* pp. 53–65. Austin: Institute of Latin American Studies, Univ. of Texas at Austin.

Bermúdez, Egberto. 1994. Syncretism, identity, and creativity in Afro-Colombian musical traditions. In *Music and black ethnicity: The Caribbean and South America,* ed. Gerard H. Béhague, pp. 225–238. Coral Gables, Fla.: Univ. of Miami North-South Center.

Bermúdez Silva, Jesús and Guillermo Abadía M. 1970. *Aires musicales de los indios guambianos del Cauca (Colombia).* Bogotá, Colombia: Imprenta Nacional.

Davidson, Harry C. 1970. *Diccionario folklórico de Colombia: Música, instrumentos y danzas.* 3 vols. Bogotá, Colombia: Banco de la República.

Friedmann, Susana. 1996. Gender, religion and music in an Afro-Colombian community. Paper presented at Gender and the Musics of Death, a study group of the International Council for Traditional Music: Music and Gender Study Group, November 8, at Univ. of Maryland, College Park.

Gradante, William J. 1980. *"Somos todos silvianos":* Semana Santa and *communitas* in Silvia. Folklore papers of the University Folklore Association, No. 9, pp. 27–55.

———. 1998. Colombia. In *The Garland encyclopedia of world music,* vol. 2, *South America, Mexico, Central America, and the Caribbean,* eds. Dale A. Olsen and Daniel E. Sheehy, pp. 376–399. New York and London: Garland Publishing, Inc.

List, George. 1966. The musical bow at Palenque. *Journal of the International Folk Music Council* 18:(36–49).

———. 1968. The Mbira in Cartagena. *Journal of the International Folk Music Council* 20:(54–59).

———. 1973. El Conjunto de Gaitas de Colombia: La herencia de tres culturas. *Revista Musical Chilena* 27(123–124):43–54.

———. 1980. Colombia II: Folk music. In *The new Grove dictionary of music and musicians,* ed. Stanley Sadie, vol. 4, pp. 570–581. Washington, D.C.: Grove's Dictionaries of Music.

Marulanda, Octavio. 1973. *Folklore y cultura general.* Cali, Colombia: Ediciones Instituto Popular de Cultura de Cali.

Ortega Ricaurte, Carmen. 1973. Contribución a la bibliografía de la música en Colombia. *Revista de la Divulgación Cultural* 12:(83–255).

Pardo Tovar, Andrés. 1965. Traditional songs in Chocó, Colombia. *Inter-American Music Bulletin* 46/47:(1–28).

——— and Jesús Bermúdez Silva. 1963. *La guitarrería popular de Chiquinquirá.* Bogotá, Colombia: Universidad Nacional de Colombia.

——— and Jesús Pinzón Urrea. 1961. *Rítmica y melódica del folclor chocoano.* Bogotá, Colombia: Universidad Nacional de Colombia.

Restrepo Duque, Hernán. 1971. *Lo que cuentan las canciones: Cronicón musical.* Bogotá, Colombia: Editorial Tercer Mundo.

Sabio, Ricardo. 1963. *Corridos y coplas: Canto a los llanos orientales de Colombia.* Cali, Colombia: Editorial Salesiana.

Stoddart, D. R. 1972. Myth and ceremonial among the Tunebo Indians of eastern Colombia. *Journal of American Folklore* 75(296):147–152.

Velázquez, Rogerio. 1961. Instrumentos musicales del alto y bajo Chocó. *Revista Colombiana de Folclor* 2(6)(segunda época):77–113.

Wade, Peter. 1998. Music, blackness, and national identity: Three moments in Colombian history. *Popular Music* 17(1):1–19.

Waxer, Lise. 1996. Salsa in Cali [Colombia]: Popular identity and local style in a hemispheric music culture. Paper presented at the Forty-First Annual Meeting of the Society for Ethnomusicology, November 1, in Toronto, Canada.

———. 1997. Salsa and black identity in Colombia. Paper presented at the Inter-American Conference on Black Music Research, Chicago, July 19.

Whitten, Norman E., Jr. 1974. *Black frontiersmen: A South American case.* Cambridge, Mass.: Schenkman Publishing Company.

Zapata Olivella, Delia. 1962. La cumbia: Síntesis musical de la nación colombiana: Reseña histórica y coreográfica. *Revista Colombiana de Folclor* 3(7):187–204.

Zapata Olivella, Manuel. 1961. Caña de Millo: Variedades y ejecución. *Revista Colombiana de Folclor* 2(6):153–157.

———. 1962. El acordeón en el Magdalena. *Boletín Cultural y Bibliográfico* 5(1):81–82.

ENDNOTES

1. Various aspects of the musical life of the African-American and Native American peoples of Colombia have been analyzed in studies by George List, Norman Whitten, Rogerio Velázquez, Andrés Pardo Tovar, Consuelo Araújo de Molina, Egberto Bermúdez, Jesús Bermúdez Silva, Peter Wade, Delia and Manuel Zapata Olivella, Susana Friedmann, and Lise Waxer. The citations to works by these and other scholars are presented at the close of this chapter to provide direction for further readings in the broad field of Colombian ethnomusicology. On the other hand, beyond doctoral dissertations by Dirk Koorn (1977) and William Gradante (1991), the musical tradition discussed in the present chapter remains almost completely unrepresented in the current ethnomusicological literature, certainly if one considers English-language publications exclusively. To that end, it is hoped that the present offering may help at least partially to fill this void.

2. See Susana Friedmann, *Las Fiestas de Junio en el Nuevo Reino* (Bogotá, Colombia: Editorial Kelly, 1982) for detailed discussions of historical and contemporary celebrations of the June festivals of Corpus Christi and San Juan [Saint John] in Colombia.

3. Along the same lines, many Guatemalans believe that their revered *marimba* is a survival of their own indigenous past, rather than the descendant of an instrument originally imported from Africa. See T. M. Scruggs's discussion of the Guatemalan *marimba* in Chapter 3.

4. For traditional costuming and masking behaviors in contemporary Peru, see Raúl Romero, ed., *Música, Danzas y Máscaras en los Andes* (Lima: Pontificia Universidad Católica del Perú, Instituto Riva-Agüero, 1993). Romero is also the author of Chapter 8, below.

5. For a discussion of the relationship between another relatively small, Andean guitar type, the south Andean *charango,* and another supernatural figure, the *sirena*—including folkloric beliefs pertaining to the *sirena*'s alleged ability to tune the instrument—see Thomas Turino, "The Charango and the Sirena: Music, Magic, and the Power of Love," *Latin American Music Review* 4(1) (spring/summer 1983):96–101. Additionally, both *tiple* and *charango* are instruments used in courting.

6. The *quijada* has some historical depth in Peru. Today, it is a part of ensembles performing African-Peruvian musics.

7. La Gaitana was the legendary war chief of the local Native Americans who valiantly defended the region against the invasion of the *conquistadores.*

8. See Ercilia Moreno Chá's discussion (Chapter 6) of the Argentine *payada* song-duels, in *décimas,* for a comparison with these Colombian song-duels, in *coplas.* See also Thomas Solomon's study (1994) of his 1990 recording of the improvising of *coplas* among the Bolivian Quechua, also in a song-duel *(takipayanaku)* context.

CHAPTER EIGHT

Andean Peru

RAÚL R. ROMERO

∿

THE HISTORICAL SETTING AND PERUVIAN MUSIC CULTURES

When Francisco Pizarro and his Spanish troops arrived in Peru in 1532, they put an abrupt end to the autonomous development that Native Americans in South America had enjoyed until then. The encounter between European and Native American culture was a violent one, beginning with the abduction and execution of Inca Atahualpa in Cajamarca. Land usurpation and forced labor soon followed; colonial administrative practices assured that the riches of this hemisphere would pass quickly into the hands of the conquerors. But the conquest also meant a confrontation of cultures and races. The first Europeans who arrived in Peru sought Native American women, giving rise to a new racial and social group called *mestizos*. The Europeans also brought with them black African slaves, who maintained an important presence during the colonial years. Later on, the offspring of the Europeans in the Western Hemisphere, called *criollos* [creoles], began to acquire increasing prominence, despite the subordinate position they had in relation to the *chapetón*, as the European who had been born in the old continent was known.

When Peru became independent from Spain in 1821, the social hierarchy of the new republic changed little, though the *criollos* succeeded the Europeans at the top of the social scale. The Native Americans still remained at the bottom of that scale and remained marginal to the political and economic decisions that affected the young nation. Following a trend established in colonial times, they took refuge in the rural areas of the Andean mountains, leaving the coastal valleys to the dominion of the *criollos* and their black slaves. This geographical and cultural division of the country has remained much the same until today. On the other hand, the Amazonian region of Peru continued to be a secluded area, relatively isolated from the national dynamics and inhabited by diverse and scattered seminomadic peoples.

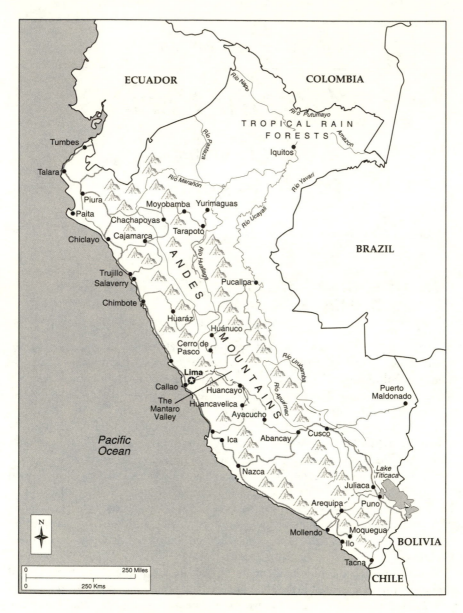

Fig. 8–1. Map of Peru

Until well into the twentieth century, Peruvian civil society had shown little interest in social change, and its peasantry and urban working classes had been unable to create the conditions for a social and economic revolution. It was only in 1969 that a major agrarian reform was instituted, uprooting the feudal system of large landholders. Until that time the ethnic panorama in the rural Andes had consisted of (1) native Quechua- or Aymara-speaking peasants, (2) *mestizos,* who despite their indigenous heritage were equally fluent in Spanish and had strong ties with the major urban centers through trade and commerce, and (3) a small European élite of professionals—lawyers, landholders, businessmen, and doctors.

With time, the ethnic terminology used in the Andes came to reflect cultural trends rather than racial attributes. The term *mestizo,* for example, came to denote the Andean middlemen who stood between European and Native American cultures. The term *criollo* also lost its original racial and geographical connotations and came to denote loosely a group who remained culturally and romantically attached to a Spanish heritage in Peru.

Modern Peru still expresses this mixture of cultures, races, and identities, but with increasingly blurred boundaries. Lima, the capital city, is a cosmopolitan center of eight million inhabitants, and its highly differentiated population is a reflection of the diversity of the nation's people. While the Andean élites had regularly migrated to the coastal urban centers, in the 1950s Andean peasants began to migrate massively to the coastal cities, changing urban demographics. The majority went to live in *barriadas* [squatter settlements] on the periphery of the city. But their imposing presence, and the re-creation of their culture, festivals, and customs changed forever the traditionally European colonial flavor of the coastal cities, especially Lima. This phenomenon was referred to by many observers in the 1960s as the "ruralization" of the capital.

These processes gave birth to new ethnic terms, such as *cholo,* which was used to describe a Native American peasant who had learned urban ways in order to survive in a new environment. A *cholo* was credited with a superior status to that of the peasant who had never departed from his rural village. The *cholo,* however, was denigrated for quite some time by members of the wealthier classes. Until the 1960s, the higher Peruvian social classes were composed largely of whites who were descendants of Spanish or other European families. Until then it was common to find in the literature associations between the "whites" and the dominant wealthier sectors—but that was about to change. Juan Velasco's revolutionary government (1968–1975), the Peruvian Agrarian Reform, and massive migration changed the ethnic and racial configuration of the nation. The replacement of the term *indio* [Indian]—used often as an insult by wealthier whites—by the neutral term *campesino* [peasant] is an example of the political trend in this period. The importance of other economic reforms, the redistribution of wealth, and the further democratization of national institutions during this period prompted the emergent social sectors to play a more significant role in the national arena.

This geographical and ethnic diversity of Peru is expressed in the various music cultures that exist today in the country. Although Andean music is generally acknowledged as the representative music of Peru on the global scene, in the coastal area of the country creole music evolved since the mid-nineteenth century into a large and very popular repertoire of songs. Creole music consists mainly of European song genres, like the waltz and the polka, which went through a process of local adaptation. Creole music enjoyed great popularity, especially among the urban lower and middle classes of Lima and other coastal urban centers. After the 1950s, however, its acceptance and presence began to decay. It was around this time that the repertoire of "black music" disengaged itself from the creole genre, changed its designation to "African-Peruvian music," and began a process of reconstruction and repopularization. Today, African-Peruvian music has an important presence. On the other hand, the music from the tropical forest of Peru displays a rich variety of sounds and genres, but it has remained circumscribed within the perimeters of each of the nearly sixty ethnolinguistic groups that inhabit the Peruvian Amazonian region.

Andean music, by contrast, is the most widespread music culture in Peru because of the sheer numbers of its audience. In a country of 24 million inhabitants, roughly half are of Andean origin or heritage. The diversity and richness of Andean musical genres and styles is such that a complete list of its musical genres and musical instruments is seldom available. Many musical genres adopt local styles and even take on different designations in different geographical settings. Musical instruments too have different names and an assortment of different shapes and configurations. The Andean region is not a homogenous whole, and in fact distinct cultural areas can be observed within its boundaries. In Peru, for example, different varieties of the Quechua language are spoken in the Andes—someone from one region may be unable to understand the Quechua of someone from another zone. Many authors have distinguished at least eight large cultural regional areas in Andean Peru, and within them a considerable range of local variation. It is not rare to run into two neighboring Andean communities that maintain different musical or choreographic traditions.

The musical contexts in which Andean music develops are also diverse. The rural areas are still the setting where ritual and ceremonial music endure, associated with a strictly peasant patronage. In the past this music was named Indian or indigenous, because of its strong and conspicuous heritage of pre-Hispanic musical archetypes. In the larger Andean villages, musical manifestations display mixtures with European models and are labeled as *mestizo* music. The music in these places consists, in large proportion, of dance music at public festivals.

Migration has taken Andean peoples and music into new geographical spaces (the cities of the coast) and has given rise to new styles created under urban influences. *Chicha* music, for instance—a blend of *cumbia* from Colombia and Andean *wayno* from Peru—developed initially in the larger cities of the Andes but primarily in Lima, from the late 1960s onward. But before that, in the early 1950s, when the concentration of Andean migrants in cities was sufficiently large to constitute a market, commercial records of Andean music were massively produced by the record companies in the capital. This cultural dynamic gave birth to a new urban musical Andean style and to the appearance of Andean recording stars. Beginning in the 1970s, the cassette industry made more accessible than ever the consumption of this music, and production of local music became widespread. In this chapter I will concentrate on Andean music and I will explain in detail its rural, urban, and modern manifestations.

FIXED MUSICAL GENRES

Andean musical genres come from different sources—from a pre-Hispanic heritage, from colonial derivations, and from recent modern developments. Among the pre-Hispanic song genres cited by early chroniclers is one that still endures in the southern Andes: the *harawi*. It is a monophonic (with one musical line) song genre comprising one musical phrase repeated several times, with extensive melismatic passages and long glissandos. The *harawi* is associated with specific ceremonies and rituals like farewells and marriages, as well as with agricultural labor (sowing and harvest). It is generally sung in a high-pitched nasal voice by a group of elder women called *harawiq* (Cavero 1985:237). In other regions, such as Cuzco, this genre is known as *wanka* and is associated with the same ritual contexts (Arguedas, cited in Pinilla 1980:390). Recorded Selection 41 (Example 8–1) is an example of this genre.

The *kashwa* is another genre of pre-Columbian origins. It is a song, but it is also a collective circle dance performed by young and single men and women; it is usually associated with daylight and evening courting rites (Turino 1983) and with nocturnal harvest rituals (Roel 1959). The *haylli* is a call-and-response genre performed during communal agricultural work in the fields.

Among other Andean song genres that display strong colonial influences is the *carnaval* [carnival], a type of song and dance for the festivity of the same name. *Carnaval* has several regional variants and designations, such as the *wifala* and the *puqllay* (in Ayacucho, Puno, and Cuzco), the *araskaska,* the recently introduced *pumpin* (Ayacucho), and the more disseminated *pasacalle* (in Ancash and in the southern Andes).

The *yaraví* is a slow and lyrical *mestizo* song genre in triple meter and binary form. Mostly sung in the southern Andes but also in Ecuador, it is generally associated with troubled love affairs and nostalgic moods. José María Arguedas has suggested that in Cuzco the *mestizo yaraví* evolved from the indigenous *harawi*, from which it took its main sentimental theme—frustrated love (cited in Pinilla 1980:390). Its melody, built on a minor tonality, is generally sung in parallel thirds and in a flexible tempo (Carpio Muñoz 1976, Pagaza Galdo 1961). Of analogous musical characteristics is the *triste*, which is pervasive in northern Peru. The *muliza* has taken the nostalgic function of the *yaraví* in the central Andes, but it is distinctive in style and form.

Ex. 8–1.   Transcription of the *harawi* in Recorded Selection 41

THE *WAYNO*

The *wayno* is the most popular song and dance genre in the South Andes. You can hear *waynos* sung by Native American peasants in the rural areas, but also in the larger *mestizo* villages in the Andes. You can also hear them on the commercial records produced since the 1950s in the coastal cities. You may already have heard the *wayno* because it is the most frequently played song genre of Andean ensembles that perform widely throughout the streets and subways of the world, from Boston to Paris. One reason is that the *wayno* can be played, sung, or danced in a variety of contexts. Not being a ritual genre, it is not circumscribed to specific ceremonies or a special period of the year. The *wayno* can also be performed by a variety of ensembles and in a variety of styles. It can be sung a cappella or accompanied by a single musical instrument. It can be performed instrumentally as well as by a large ensemble. The highly adaptable quality of the *wayno* is one of the reasons for its widespread acceptance.

Despite the popularity of the *wayno*, there is scant evidence of its existence in pre-Hispanic times. No colonial chronicler or traveler mentioned a song or a dance by that name, though they did describe many other genres and dances. Only Diego Gonçales Holguín, who wrote a Quechua dictionary in 1608, incorporates the term, referring to the act of dancing while holding hands—implying that it was a couple dance. Judging from the written sources, therefore, we may conclude that the *wayno* did not enjoy in pre-Hispanic times the huge popularity it gained during the colonial and republican periods.

As to the origins of the *wayno*, the Peruvian ethnomusicologist Josafat Roel asserts that the *wayno* developed into its modern form during the colonial era. This development was favored by the Spanish policy of *reducciones* [colonial settlements], by which natives were forced to settle in towns and villages built around a central square, where a church and a municipality were erected. Roel alleges that the *wayno* became the most suitable dance in such a setting, since it was of a social and recreational nature. It was performed by independent couples who could dance it in closed and small spaces, generally inside homes. In contrast, other pre-Hispanic dances of ritual character, like the *kashwa*, had a different evolution in the colonial period. Since the *kashwa* was a circle dance requiring large and open spaces, it did not find in the colonial towns and villages an adequate setting for its development. The *kashwa* was then confined to the outskirts of the villages and enacted only in selected places and periods of the year.

The music of the *wayno* is generally in duple meter and its inner pulse is highly syncopated. The redundant rhythmic figure of the *wayno* consists of an eighth and two sixteenth notes, or a sixteenth-eighth-sixteenth note figure. Most *waynos* use the pentatonic scale (A–C–D–E–G), but the hexatonic scale (A–C–D–E–F$\sharp$–G) and the European diatonic scale are also widely used. It may occur in one single section or part (A) or it may have two related, noncontrasting sections (AB). In any case, the strophe is repeated several times, each time with a different verse. The *wayno* performed by *mestizo* groups often concludes with a section called *fuga* [escape], which is generally set in a faster tempo and sung to a different strophe. The *fuga* section is generally repeated at will, until the song finally ends. The *wayno* is known by different names in different localities. It is called *chuscada* in Ancash, *pampeña* in Arequipa, *cachua* in Cajamarca, *chymay-cha* in Amazonas and Huánuco, and *huaylacha* in the Colca Valley of Arequipa. The style of the *wayno* changes according to the locality, the region, and the social group that performs it. Listening to a rendition of a *wayno,* someone familiar with this music can discern to which region it corresponds. Within a regional style, a peasant "Indian" *wayno* will probably sound more straightforward compared to the *wayno* of the *mestizos,* which will favor sounds and ranges more akin to urban aesthetics. The former may sound something like Recorded Selection 42, a vocal version of a *wayno* recorded in the rural areas of Cajamarca, in northern Peru.

A *mestizo wayno* from the Mantaro Valley in Central Peru, conversely, is a two-part song accompanied by an ensemble of various instruments, as in Recorded Selection 43. A *wayno* performed on the guitar by a member of the professional élite from Ayacucho will sound very smooth and almost "classical." Listen to Recorded Selection 44, a *wayno* for the Spanish guitar.

The *wayno* is not only song and dance, but also a form of popular poetry. Its lyrics are sentimental, with a strong use of metaphor. *Waynos* speak of passionate love, of family, of nostalgia for the homeland (see Chapter 1), of humorous themes, and of political issues. Most *waynos,* however, are of an amorous nature. Despite the immense variety of *waynos,* many depict nostalgia for a lost love. In this case, the poem generally uses recurrent allegories of the beloved with birds, flowers, and elements of nature. The theme alludes to a relationship that has been interrupted or terminated by undisclosed forces. The three strophes in Example 8–2 correspond to three different *waynos.*

FLEXIBLE MUSICAL GENRES

Contrasting with the above-mentioned fixed genres—those having a concrete musical form—there are several more flexible types. These are organically linked to specific ritual contexts such as fertility rituals, agricultural communal work, the cleaning of irrigation canals, the building of communal or private edifices, and specific ceremonial phases of the life cycle (baptism, courting, marriage, funerals). In many of these cases the music accompanying these ceremonies carries the name of the ritual involved, and only in exceptional cases may a fixed musical form be associated with the ritual.

In the Mantaro Valley in the department of Junín, the nocturnal harrowing of grains was until recently carried out by young single men and women who sang a cappella, or with guitar accompaniment, and who danced on top of a mound of cereals while separating the seeds from the husks (Romero 1990:17). In the same region, music for *pincullo* [vertical duct flute] and *tinya* [small drum], played by one performer in a pipe-and-tabor fashion, is reserved for times when the peasants gather to work in the fields at specific junctures of the agricultural calendar—turning of the soil, the first tillage of the land, and harvest (ibid., 14). Both musical repertoires pertain solely to their corresponding performance contexts,

**Ex. 8–2.   Three different strophes corresponding to three different *waynos*
(Roel 1959)**

(1)

Amores tengo de sobra	I have plenty of loves
Como las flores del campo.	Like flowers in the fields.
Lloraré porque te quiero	I will cry because I love you
No será porque me falta.	Not because I am lacking [love].

(2)

Yo no soy venado	I am not a deer
Para cargar cuernos	To have horns
Yo soy vicuñita	I am a vicuña [Andean camel]
De amor conocido.	Of one known love.
Si porque te quiero	Because I love you
Y porque te adoro	And because I adore you
Quieres que yo cargue	You want me to carry
Cuernos como el otro.	Horns, like the other one.

(3)

Solo, he salido	I have left, alone
Solo de mi tierra	Alone, from my homeland
Con el destino	With my destiny
No sé para dónde	Going to the unknown
Con el destino	With my destiny
No sé para dónde.	Going to the unknown.

and while each tune is given a descriptive name, the whole repertoire lacks any concrete denomination other than the occasion for which it is intended. In the northern Peruvian Andes, in Cajamarca, the *clarín* [long transverse trumpet] is played during the *minka* [traditional communal work], especially during the harvest of grains (Jiménez Borja 1951:75, Cánepa-Koch 1993:150). A photograph is shown in Illustration 8–1.

The cleaning of irrigation canals, called the *fiesta del agua* [water festival], is a ceremonial task performed by all the members of the peasant community. It is an especially strong tradition in Puquío, Ayacucho, and San Pedro de Casta, Lima. Here, the *walina* is a fixed song genre exclusively associated with this ritual. The long repertoire of *walinas* is sung only by the men who perform the ceremonial cleaning, and it is accompanied by the *chirimía* [type of oboe], which plays a relatively independent countermelody to the song of the lead singer.

The communal construction of buildings is one event in which communal labor fulfills an indispensable function and in which music is vital to its ceremonial aspect. In the Mantaro Valley the *pirkansa* (from the word *pirqay* [Quechua, to build a wall]) takes place when the walls of an edifice are being built, during which a performer of *pincullo*-and-*tinya* music (as in agricultural music) partici-

Ill. 8–1. *Clarín* [long, straight trumpet] player during the harvest of cereals in Cajamarca. Photo: Raúl R. Romero. Courtesy of the Center for Andean Ethnomusicology, Catholic University of Peru.

pates as another worker in the event (Romero 1990:17). A similar instrumental combination is used in Ancash in the same setting (den Otter 1985:113).

Ceremonial phases of the life cycle (baptism, courting, marriage, and funerals) are also contexts of major musical repertoires. The role of music in courting rituals is solidly established in the Cuzco region. In Canas, Cuzco, young single men court their chosen women playing the *tuta kashwa* on their *charangos* [small Andean guitars] in the *fiestas* of San Andrés (December 3) and Santa Cruz (May 2) (Turino 1983). Specialists sing funeral music at wakes, burials, and during the festivities of the Day of the Dead (November 2). In the Mantaro Valley the repertoire of the *responseros* [singers of funeral songs] has Quechua texts with strong European musical liturgical influence. In other areas the relatives of the deceased themselves may weep and grieve, combining spoken passages with musical cadences. In Puno, when an infant dies, a lively *wayno* is sung with *charango* accompaniment because it is believed that when an infant dies he/she goes to Heaven in a state of grace—thus, it is an occasion to celebrate and not to languish (see John Schechter's discussion of *velorio del angelito* in Chapter 1).

The branding of animals is one of the most ubiquitous fertility rituals in the central and southern Andes of Peru. It is a ritual associated with the Andean mountain deities (the *wamani*, the *apu*, or the *achachila*, depending on the region), and it is usually enacted in specific seasons of the year. In the highland areas of the Colca Valley in Arequipa, the music of a large *pincullo* and a *tinya* is played in the *tinka*, which is celebrated during the season of Carnival in which a *llama* is sacrificed and ritual offerings are buried for the deities (Raez 1993:281). The music accompanies the various steps of the ritual, and during the rest periods in which the participants dance and enjoy a period of relaxation after the lengthy ritual events. In Puno, an ensemble of eighteen *kenas* [notched flutes], also called *chaqallos,* accompanied by two *bombos* [double-headed drums] and a snare drum, fulfills the same function during a similar ritual called *wylancha* (Cánepa-Koch 1991).

THE BRANDING OF ANIMALS IN THE MANTARO VALLEY

We have seen that the *wayno* is music for social or individual recreation that can be performed at any time and any place. For that reason it is a very popular musical genre in the Andes. Let us explain a very different musical manifestation now. The music for the branding of the animals, called *herranza* in the Central Andes of Peru, is ritual music, performed only once a year in a sacred context. In the Mantaro Valley of the central Peruvian Andes (one of the largest intermontane valleys of the entire Andes), it is invariably rendered by a female singer accompanied by a *wakrapuku* [spiral-shaped horn trumpet] (Illustration 8–2), a European violin, and a *tinya.*

The *herranza* is often described as a fertility ritual because its main purpose is to seek the protection of livestock and lands. It is a complex ceremony comprised of several phases that involve marking animals, presenting material offerings and gifts, engaging in collective play and prediction rites, and performing music and dance, all in a general state of jubilation. In most cases, only the nuclear and extended family of the animal owners participate. But when the entire community is the owner, it becomes a communal event. In both cases it maintains its private and secluded character. However, it does not go unnoticed in the Mantaro Valley, since around these days the local markets stock themselves with plenty of goods for the ritual, and there is considerable commercial activity around the purchasing of gifts and materials to be used in the *herranza.* Among these are fabric for the ritual table, liquor, mountain flowers, cigarettes, various gifts such as candy and pastries, *cuyes* [a type of rodent, a traditional Andean meal], *cancha* [toasted corn], and cheese for the generous feast to be offered during the ritual. In the blooming commercial city of Huancayo (the main economic center of the Valley), hundreds of *herranza* musicians come from the higher communities with their *wakrapukus,* violins, and *tinyas,* and gather in the vicinity of Plaza La Inmaculada, waiting to be hired by the heads of family households.

The central day of the *herranza* is July 25, which coincides with the Catholic celebration of the apostle Santiago, but contrary to the public festival—in which the mass, the Virgin, or the saint are guiding events and images—no Catholic elements are present in this ritual. The *herranza* is also called "Santiago" in many villages because of the association made between the European imagery of the apostle Santiago and the Andean deities called *wamani,* who are believed to in-

Ill. 8–2. The *wakrapuku* is played during the *herranza* ritual, usually in pairs, at a distance of a third. The group is often expanded by a violin player and a woman singer who also plays *tinya*. Courtesy of the Center for Andean Ethnomusicology, Catholic University of Peru.

habit the mountains. In fact, the *herranza* ritual is celebrated as an offering to these deities, who are believed to own the crops and cattle, and who are both revered and feared. Santiago was for the colonizers a symbol of conquest, nicknamed Son of Thunder, a killer of Moors, who in the war against them was considered an inspiration for the victorious Spanish soldiers. The Andeans associated Santiago with Illapa, the god of thunder and lightning, and in time the two became consolidated into a single supreme being, *wamani* or Santiago.

The phases of the *herranza* are many, and they proceed over a span of two days. On the evening of the first day the initial arrangements are made, and the ritual *mesa* [table] is put in place (Illustration 8–3). The table consists of a fabric placed on the ground around which the participants gather, and upon which the meal and drinks are served, and the gifts and ritual utensils displayed. There are periodic rest periods called *chaupi mesas,* during which the participants eat and drink wine and *chicha* [fermented corn]. There are several *chaupi mesas* during the entire ritual, separating the different steps of the *herranza.*

Around midnight, participants join in a general dance called *chaupi tuta* [Quechua, middle of the night] in which everyone, without distinctions, takes part with more intensity than ever. While there is dancing during all of the ritual, this phase is the more intensive and the longer in duration. The dancing is so intense at this juncture of the ritual that the entire group dances through the streets of the village, stopping to visit the houses of relatives along the way. Meanwhile the

Ill. 8–3. The ritual table *(mesa)* of the *herranza* and peasants from the
Andean town of Masmachicche gathered around it, in the Mantaro Valley.
Photo: Manuel Ráez. Courtesy of the Center for Andean
Ethnomusicology, Catholic University of Peru.

musicians play tunes called *zapateo* [shoe tapping], *pasacalle, paseo,* or
visitacha—all terms alluding to the act of strolling through the streets or visiting.
This part of the ritual sometimes continues until dawn. *Chaupi mesas* are also
performed during this phase, since rest periods are always necessary. The musical
transcription in Example 8–3 and Recorded Selection 45, taken from the *herranza* in Pariahuanca (as are all of the subsequent transcriptions), feature a song
performed during this phase, with a tritonic scale built on an A-major triad. The
second musical phrase (B) is reiterated at will.

One of the most ubiquitous prediction rites in the South Andes, the *koka
kintu,* is performed during one of the *herranza* rest periods or *chaupi mesas.* It
consists of the reading or interpreting of *coca* leaves (Romero 1990:9). A specific

Ex. 8–3. Transcription of an *herranza* song, recorded in Pariahuanca

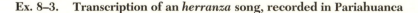

quantity of leaves is given to all the participants, who have to choose the healthy ones—that is, those that are intact or not broken. Each *coca* leaf represents a previously designated amount of cattle—ten, a hundred, or a thousand animals, depending on the size of the leaf. Meanwhile, the participants chew *coca* leaves, drink, and perhaps indulge in conversation while a competent reader *(caporal)* interprets the signs of the selected leaves and predicts a good or bad year for the owner of the cattle. The *koka kintu* has many variants in its interpretative phase. One is that the participants who fail to collect the adequate quantity of healthy leaves are punished, or rewarded if they succeed. The tune for this phase is built fundamentally upon an anhemitonic (without semitones) pentatonic scale and, as in all the *herranza* tunes, part (B) is persistently reiterated, as shown in Example 8–4.

At dawn everyone is expected to participate in the *luci-luci,* a ritual chase of animals in a corral, leading them out into the place where they will be marked. This involves play with fire, since the participants use torches to chase the animals, and even simulate that they frighten each other, as well. The *luci-luci* marks the end of the first day, after which everyone goes to sleep for a few hours—the next day the animals will be branded. Example 8–5 shows the tritonic melody, with subsidiary notes E and G, sung in this *luci-luci* episode.

On the following day the *señalacuy* takes place. It consists of the actual branding of the animals, variously involving cattle, *llamas,* horses, and even donkeys. Those animals not marked the previous year are marked first. They are branded by inserting ribbons in their ears with a needle. These are not merely ornamental. In the district of Masmachicche, for example, yellow ribbons are for the males, orange for the females, green for the "native" stallions, red for purchased stallions, and blue for the female mothers. Everyone collaborates in the marking, since the animals do resist and substantial effort is required to keep them still. During the process, the animals are given *coca* leaves to chew, and in certain districts the blood of the animals is mixed with *chicha* and drunk by the participants, and some may also paint their faces with the same blood. After the branding, the

Ex. 8–4. Transcription of an *herranza koka kintu* song

KOKA-KINTU

Ex. 8–5.   Transcription of an *herranza luci-luci* **song**

animals are separated according to their own species, and they are sent back to their original locations. Special food is showered upon them—a mixture of flour, candy, and cookies in animal shapes.

As a conclusive act, the *señal pampay* [bury the marking], a ceremonial offering of gifts, takes place in a special location (called sacred by some) where pieces of the ears of the animals, unused ribbons, *coca* leaves, and liquor are buried. In some districts this burial is carried out in secrecy by a designated community member. This act suggests certain similarities with the offering to the *wamani* as described earlier, but in the Valley the ritual is not explicitly described as such, nor is the term *wamani* used. The ritual burial of ceremonial paraphernalia is, however, a pan-Andean custom related to supernatural deities—burials that take place in the context of similar rituals.

There are a few variants to the general description of the *herranza* presented here. The branding of sheep (not other animals) is usually enacted by some communities during Carnival, rather than on July 25. Also, when the animals are the property of a peasant community instead of a nuclear family, the *herranza* is performed collectively, but following the same phases. In the district of San Jerónimo, for example, there is a distinction between the *patrones* [patrons] and the *pastores* [shepherds]—the *patrón* is the community, which appears in the ritual personified as an individual patron, and the shepherds are the members of the community who are in charge of the animals during the year. Instead of the head of the nuclear family, the treasurer of the community is in charge of preparing the *mesa* and organizing the ritual. The *herranza* takes place in the communal corral, which can be located far from the town. The patrons and the shepherds act as if they were in an unequal relationship, engaging in a ritualized play in which the former may reprimand the shepherds for a supposed mishandling of the animals, and the shepherds may in turn complain and challenge the patrons for being abusive and for their hard working conditions. These complaints are usually sung rather than verbalized and have a satirical character, many times in the form of an improvised musical contest between both parties.

The *herranza* or Santiago tunes open with an introduction of the violins and *wakrapukus* (playing in thirds), and the tune itself begins when the *cantora* sings it, while the violin doubles the melody in heterophony (slightly different version of same melody), filling the pauses with riffs. The *wakrapukus* play only during the interludes, when the *cantora* rests after a series of stanzas; they do not play while the *cantora* is singing. The music of the *herranza* is generally based on a tritonic scale built on the major triad, and only in very rare cases are other scales found, such as the pentatonic (Romero 1990:10). My analysis of *herranza* melodies from four different districts reveals that all of them were in two parts (AB), part A repeated once and part B repeated at will, numerous times. The musical ensembles for the *herranza* come generally from the higher communities of the Valley. There are *herranza* musical groups in the Valley but they are few and cannot meet the demands for the entire area. The idea of an *"herranza* musical ensemble," however, could be misleading. *Herranza* music is only performed once a year, and during two days, so that the musicians who do play this music integrate themselves into a group only a few days before the ritual, at Carnival or at the end of July.

Herranza musicians are not professionals, in spite of the fact that they are paid for their services. They are highly specialized musicians, since *herranza* is their main performance context, and since none of its members perform in other professional ensembles of the Valley. Many of the *herranza* musicians who come to the Valley from the higher-elevation villages are generally peasants of scant financial resources. Their economic and social status differs greatly from that of the professional ensembles who are considered to be well-paid professionals all year round. The *herranza* musician is a seasonal performer, and his status as musician is not even clear, since there is an association in the Valley between music and "professionalization." There are two factors to be considered here. First, as happens in other realms where music does not stand apart from ritual or labor, *herranza* music is so remarkably fused with the ritual as a whole that its musicians tend to be regarded like any other participants. Second, the character of this ritual is private and secluded, a condition that favors the amalgamation of the musicians into the general group of participants.

DANCE-DRAMAS: CHOREOGRAPHY AND MUSIC

The annual festival calendar is the natural context for the numerous dance-dramas that exist in the Peruvian Andes. The *fiesta* calendar is prolific throughout the Andean region, the result of the blending of the pre-Hispanic agricultural calendar with the Christian annual calendar imposed by the Spanish conquest. Different types of festivals are celebrated according to each region and locality, with greater or lesser intensity. There are some *fiestas* that have achieved pan-Andean relevance, such as the Virgen de la Candelaria (February 2), the Fiesta de la Cruz (May 3), San Juan (June 24), San Pedro y San Pablo (June 29, see also Chapter 7), Santiago Apostol (July 25), Santa Rosa (August 30), the Nativity of the Virgin (September 8), and Christian liturgical festivities such as Christmas, Epiphany, Holy Week (especially Palm Sunday), and Corpus Christi. Carnival is also celebrated in the entire Andes region, many times closely linked with the festivity of the Virgen de la Candelaria on February 2.

There are numerous dance groups and choreographic representations in the Andes. Classification of Andean dances has been based on either thematic or chronological criteria. The following thematic types have been distinguished in Andean dances: religious, totemic, martial, associational (guilds), satirical, regional, pantomime, entertainment, agricultural, and strolling (Valcárcel 1951:11–13). Others have preferred a chronological model, classifying dances as pre-Hispanic, conquest, colonial, independence, and republican (Merino de Zela 1977:70). More recent perspectives on dance, however, have called attention to the fact that ethnic or historic representation, if in fact the most notorious external trait that these classification systems emphasize, is not necessarily the most important factor involved in Andean dance. The significance of local concepts of time, space, and hierarchy in representing the "other" goes beyond the mere illustration of a personage (see Poole 1990:101).

Music and dance are integral parts of the Andean *fiesta*. The music for dance-dramas follows the structure of the dance-dramas themselves—typically multisectional forms consisting of from two to six sections, each with different tempos and styles. The music of the dance-dramas is unique and closely linked with the choreography of the dance whence it takes its name. Besides the dances in the *fiestas*, other festive music applies to fireworks, bullfighting, horse races, processions, special offerings, and orchestral salutes (welcomes and farewells). Music for dance-dramas can be performed either by a single musician or by a large ensemble. The performers may be members of the community or hired musicians who may perform professionally in regional markets. In many regions *mestizo* sponsors of *fiestas* can hire native Andean performers, to stay closer to the tradition. In this sense, performers of music for dance-dramas may have a less conspicuous profile than the dancers themselves. In some contexts, the dancers generally dance because of a religious promise to the Virgin, while musicians are generally hired to play the music for the dancers (Cánepa-Koch 1998:126). Instrumental ensembles can range from more traditional and austere instrumentation (one flute and one drum) to larger regional orchestras. The brass band consisting of trumpets, trombones, tubas, drums, and cymbals became widely popularized in the Andes at the outset of the twentieth century due to mandatory military service, which few young Andean males could avoid (Romero 1985:250). Today this type of ensemble is one of the most popular vehicles for dance-dramas in the Peruvian Andes.

THE *CH'UNCHU* DANCE

(This section relies substantially on Cánepa-Koch 1993:139–178.) The *ch'unchu* is an all-male dance from the northern region of Cajamarca that represents the inhabitant of the Amazonian jungles of Peru. Throughout the Peruvian Andes dance-dramas depicting this character are widespread, taking on different names depending on the locality. They concur, however, in depicting the *ch'unchu* as an uncivilized and untamed being. Notwithstanding, in many festivals the *ch'unchus* are considered to be favorites of the Virgin, to whom homage is being made. They dress elegantly with feathers and arrows, and follow an elaborate choreography, commonly martial in character.

The dance of the *ch'unchu* is widespread in the northern Cajamarca region, and it is performed during select festivals of the Roman Catholic liturgical cycle. The members of the *ch'unchu* dance constitute well-organized groups that perform in these festivals when invited by festival sponsors. The *ch'unchus* are provided with shelter, meals, and other facilities during the festival. They dance in devotion to the virgin or to a saint, never in exchange for compensation. In Cajamarca the *ch'unchus* perform during the months of June to December, coinciding with the time of preparation of the fields for a new harvest.

Four characters are depicted in the *ch'unchu* performance: (1) the *ch'unchu* themselves; (2) the *capitán* [captain] or chief of the *ch'unchus*, who directs the choreography; (3) the character of the *negro(s)* [black(s)], who fulfills a comic role but who is at the same time a figure of authority in charge of discipline within the dance group—he wears a black mask and uses a whip to impose authority and supervise the appropriate movements of the dancers; and (4) the *cachacos*, who wear military uniforms and are supposedly former army conscripts. These characters carry the *chicha* that the dancers drink during the dance. All of these characters are dressed in different costumes and take different roles in the choreography (Illustration 8–4).

The Cajamarca *ch'unchus* themselves wear white pants, white shirts, and sandals. Attached to their feet are the *maichiles*, dried fruits that rattle when they dance. On top of their heads the *ch'unchus* wear a feather crown called an *amazona*. They also wear on their chests a band of several colors ornamented with small mirrors. The dancers use a whip as an element in the choreography. Recorded Selection 46 is music of the *ch'unchu* dance. The sound resembling a rattle is made by the *maichiles*.

The dance of the *ch'unchu* is divided into several sections. It begins at dawn on the *fiesta's* central day with music called *llamada*, and continues with the *adoración* in front of the church (Cánepa-Koch 1993:152). At this stage the dancers come to a halt and enter the church to pay homage to the saint. Before entering, the dancers sing the *adoración* in front of the main door. Simultaneously, a *clarín* also plays an *alabado* [song of praise] in homage to the saint. The lyrics of a typical *adoración* are set forth in Example 8–6.

The section of the *paseo* [stroll] is performed while the dancers walk along the streets of the town. Other sections of the dance known as the *kishke*, the *ronda*, and the *pacchilla* (all local names) are parts of the dance in which more complex choreographic movements are performed (Cánepa-Koch 1993:153). In the *alabado* and the *paseo*, for example, the dancers perform with intensive use of foot stomping, but without a fixed choreography. When they walk along the streets the dancers form two parallel lines, a figure that constitutes the basic characteristic of the dance. The younger dancers stand in front of both lines. The *negros*, dancing around and in front of the lines, make space for the dancers to move along, while

Ill. 8–4. *Ch'unchu* dancers performing in the main plaza of Llacanora, Cajamarca province. Photo: Raúl R. Romero. Courtesy of the Center for Andean Ethnomusicology, Catholic University of Peru.

the *cachacos* encircle the group realizing physical exercises (bouncing and doing push-ups). Once in a while the dancers clap their hands to emphasize the musical rhythms. The basic step throughout the performance comprises marking the basic pulse of the music with each foot stomping the ground in alternation. Other movements involve zig-zag and circle dancing, which is alternated with parallel lines. The whip is used in the choreography to help the dancers to accomplish specific patterns.

The musical accompaniment of the *ch'unchus* consists of performers of *caja-y-flauta* [flute-and-drum, played in pipe-and-tabor fashion] and of one or several *clarines* [long, straight, transverse trumpets]. The *caja* [drum] is a small wooden membranophone with animal skin, generally of sheep. The three-hole flute is made of a curved piece of wood. There are two types of flutes in Cajamarca—the *silbadora* [whistling flute], which produces a smooth sound, and the *roncadora* [raucous flute], which has a harsher tone. A single musician plays both instruments. The *clarín* is, as has been mentioned, a transverse trumpet made of cane, and is three meters in length. This instrument is widely used during communal work in the fields as well. The playing of the *clarín* is an arduous task, since physical strength is required both to wield the instrument and to blow into it (Cánepa-Koch 1993:149–151).

Ex. 8–6.   Lyrics of the *adoración* (Cánepa-Koch 1993:152)

Buenos días mi padre	Good morning my father
Hijo de tu santo padre	Son of your holy Father
Yo buscando el regocijo	I seeking the joy
[De que des] a Dios por hijo	Of seeing you have God as your son
Y alabado sea tu hijo	And holy be thy son
Sacramento de verdad	Truly sacred
Y en la virgen concebida	Conceived in the immaculate Virgin
Sin pecado original	Without original sin
Y con otro sacramento	With another sacrament
En la gloria, donde estés	In glory, wherever you are
Unos rezos y alabados,	Prayers and praises
En los cielos y en la tierra	In heaven and earth
Y alabado sea el santísimo	And praised be the Lord
Sacramento de verdad	Truly holy
Y en la virgen concebida	And in the immaculate Virgin
Sin pecado original.	Without original sin.

MUSICAL INSTRUMENTS

Many of the musical instruments in use today in Andean Peru are of pre-Hispanic origin. Thanks to the early colonial chroniclers who wrote extensively about Inca culture, we know of the importance of many types of drums (*huancar*), flutes (*pincullu, quenaquena,* and *antara* [panpipes]), trumpets (*qquepa*), and idiophones used in the Inca empire. We also know that no multiple-stringed instruments existed in the Andes prior to the arrival of the Europeans. One chronicler, Garcilaso de la Vega, described panpipe ensembles briefly but concisely. He alluded to its interlocking performance technique (see Schechter 1996:440–443) and suggested the foremost intervallic relationship of the fifth in these ensembles. These traits continue to exist today in the Aymara panpipe ensembles of southern Peru. Another chronicler, Guaman Poma de Ayala, wrote about the musical accompaniment of the *pingollos* and *quenaquena* in several dances and songs. Both terms, for two types of vertical flutes, are still the most commonly used in the Peruvian Andes.

During the colonial period other instruments, which are still very popular today, evolved as the result of the cultural encounter between European and indigenous cultures. The *charango* [small twelve-string guitar], for example, was a local adaptation of the Spanish guitar. The *wakrapuku* [spiral horn trumpet] was conceived and built from cattle horns brought to the Americas by the Spaniards. Various instruments were directly imported to the South American Andes and were adopted by Native Americans and *mestizos* alike. Among these, the guitar, the accordion, the harp, and the violin are the most prominent. In the twentieth century, instruments like the saxophone, the clarinet, and those pertaining to the brass band have gained rapid acceptance, sometimes taking on the character of "traditional" instruments.

In modern Peru different types of flutes—vertical end-notched (i.e., *kenas*), vertical-duct (i.e., *pincullos, tarkas*), and transverse (i.e., *pitos*)—are widely disseminated throughout the Andes. The *kena,* also known by a variety of local names like *lawata, chaqallo,* and *quenacho,* is made generally from cane, but also from wood and in recent times plastic. It can have diverse lengths but most of them fluctuate from 25 to 120 centimeters and may have from three to eight finger-holes. One of the most ubiquitous types has six holes in front and one in back, and measures 30 to 40 centimeters in length. The *kena* can be played as a solo instrument in private and contemplative situations, but in public performances it is usually played in ensembles combined with other instruments.

Duct flutes are generally considered to have arisen in the colonial period, since no archaeological evidence has yet been discovered for determining their origins. The term *pingollo,* nonetheless, was usually used by the early chroniclers to refer to pre-Hispanic flutes. It is most frequently made of wood or cane and may be of different sizes (from 30 to 120 centimeters long) and may have a variable number of finger holes. One of the most common types of duct flutes in the Peruvian Andes is the *pincullu (pinkuyllo, pincullo, pinkillo),* but it is also called *flauta* in Cajamarca; *roncadora* in Ancash, Cajamarca, and Huánuco; and *chiska* or *rayán* in Ancash (den Otter 1985:93). One of the most widely disseminated types is the three-hole duct flute, which is played in a pipe-and-tabor mode. Duct flutes can also be played in ensembles of instruments of the same type—an example is the five- and six-hole *pinkillo* ensembles in Conima, Puno, which are played in unison, accompanied by drums in groups that range from eight to fifteen performers (Turino 1993:48, 50).

Another popular duct flute called *tarka* is geographically restricted to the southern department of Puno. Its foremost feature is its hexagonal shape. It generally has six finger holes, and is played in public festivals in large ensembles called *tarkeadas,* though it has also been reported as a solo instrument among shepherds in the mountains (Bellenger 1981:24).

Transverse flutes are known by diverse local names in the Andes like *flauta, pito, phalahuita,* or even *kena.* In Puno, where it is called *pitu,* it is made of cane, has six finger holes in the upper side, and is played in large ensembles in community festivals (Turino 1993:47–48). In Cuzco, two six-hole *pitus* are accompanied by drums in the *banda de guerra* [war band], an ensemble appearing in public festivals throughout the region (Cánepa-Koch 1998).

Panpipe musical traditions such as the *sikuri,* the *ayarachi,* and the *chiriguano* in Puno are always performed collectively (Valencia 1983, 1989). These panpipes are usually named after the ensemble of which they are a part, and they are tuned to the diatonic scale. The panpipe is designed to be performed in pairs, each component having complementary pitches. One of them is designated as *arca* [that

Ill. 8–5. Performer on a large *pinkuyllo* in the highlands of the Colca Valley, Arequipa region, playing at a *tinka* ritual, during which an *alpaca* is sacrificed. Photo: Gisela Cánepa-Koch. Courtesy of the Center for Andean Ethnomusicology, Catholic University of Peru.

Ill. 8–6. Performer on a small *pincullo* in Paccha, Mantaro Valley, playing at the harvest of cereals. Photo: Raúl R. Romero. Courtesy of the Center for Andean Ethnomusicology, Catholic University of Peru.

which leads] and the other as *ira* [that which follows]. The performance technique of these groups is also complex. The *sikuri* ensembles consist of different sizes of panpipes or *sikus*, some of which are tuned in octaves while others *(contras)* are tuned to the fifth. An ideal ensemble configuration would include nine different groups of instruments, but all the ensembles do not always present all the possible combinations (Valencia 1989:46–53). Other panpipe traditions like the *chiriguano* and the *ayarachi* are subdivided into three different groups, each of which is tuned to the octave (Turino 1993:45). *Sikuris* and other panpipe ensembles perform intensively throughout the annual calendar of *fiestas* but also in weddings and other life-cycle events, like the *corte de pelo* [child's first haircut] (Turino 1993:46). In other regions the panpipe is played as a solo instrument, like the *andara* in Cajamarca (Instituto Nacional de Cultura 1978:209–210).

Different types of locally constructed trumpets are widely used in Peru; examples include the *wakrapuku* in the central Andes, the *clarín* in the northern Andes, and the *pampa corneta* in Huancavelica. The *wakrapuku* is made of cattle horns in spiral shape and is usually played in pairs called *primera* and *segunda* in intervals of thirds (Romero 1990:31). The *wakrapuku* is played only once a year during the fertility rituals of branding the animals (see the discussion of *herranza*, above). Its origins are colonial, inasmuch as cattle were introduced by the Europeans. The *clarín* is very popular in Cajamarca—to review, it is a long cane transverse trumpet, three meters in length, and as we have seen, is used in festivals and in agricultural music (Cánepa-Koch 1993:150). The *pampa corneta* is a vertical type of trumpet three to four meters in length and made of wood. It is restricted to Ayacucho and Huancavelica and is performed mainly in the ritual of branding the animals (Instituto Nacional de Cultura 1978:261). The *pututu* [conch-shell trumpet] is still used in the southern Andes for signaling and for opening special communal ceremonies. It is also called *churu* in Amazonas and in Ecuador, and *quipa* in San Martín (Instituto Nacional de Cultura 1978:259). In Cuzco it is used in the *faenas comunales* [communal work] in Pisac and Paucartambo (Jiménez Borja 1951).

The Spaniards introduced reed instruments like the *chirimía* [a type of wooden oboe], which was frequently used during colonial times for official ceremonies related to municipal affairs in the urban centers (Jiménez Borja 1951:78). The *chirimía* is still played in the northern coastal and Andean areas in public festivals (Casas Roque 1993:324–326) and in highland Lima, Huancavelica, and Ayacucho, where it is known by the name *chirisuya* (Jiménez Borja 1951:79).

Drums receive different names according to their different sizes and localities, such as *caja, wankara, tinya,* or the Spanish denominations of *bombo* or *tambor,* depending on local usage. There are drums of different sizes, ranging from a small *tinya* of approximately twenty centimeters in diameter to a large *caja* of seventy centimeters in diameter (Instituto Nacional de Cultura 1978:91–108). Most of them are double-headed drums, of cylindrical shape. Contrasting with the aerophones which are played only by men, small drums like the *tinya* are, as in pre-Hispanic times, mostly played by women. They are used on several occasions, as in the animal-branding music of the central Andes (Instituto Nacional de Cul-

Ill. 8–7. *Andara* [pentatonic panpipe] player in the highlands of Cajamarca. Raúl R. Romero. Courtesy of the Center for Andean Ethnomusicology, Catholic University of Peru.

Ill. 8–8. Women usually play the small Andean drum called a *tinya*, like this woman in the Colca Valley, Arequipa region, playing at a *tinka* ritual. Photo: Gisela Cánepa-Koch. Courtesy of the Center for Andean Ethnomusicology, Catholic University of Peru.

tura 1978:108). Bigger drums are played by men mostly as accompaniment to wind instruments in small or large ensembles.

Since no multiple-string cordophones were used by ancient Peruvians, many of those currently in use—the guitar, the mandolin, the *bandurria*, the harp, and the violin—were introduced by the Spaniards during the colonial period. The *charango*, termed in certain localities *quirquincho* or *chillador*, is a small guitar twenty-three to forty-five centimeters in length, made with wood or *armadillo* shell, and used in southern Peru. This instrument has diverse tunings and numbers of strings according to the region. The most common tuning is the Santo Domingo (A minor) in the five-string *charango* (E–A–E–C–G). (Instituto Nacional de Cultura 1978:136). In Cuzco, the *charango* is played by Andean peasants, with a predominant strumming style while a single string carries the melody, whereas *mestizo* performers play it in a plucked melodic mode interspersed with strumming sections (Turino 1984:259).

The European guitar has not suffered any drastic morphological change in its adaptation to Andean musical practices, but its tuning varies according to the region. Besides the standard system there are a variety of tunings depending on the locality, each of which receives a specific name. (See also the discussion of multiple Chilean and Argentine guitar tunings in Chapter 6.) In Ayacucho the most common tuning pattern is called *comuncha* (E–B–G–D–B–G), which predominates in the rural areas. This tuning is used primarily to play peasant *waynos* in the E-minor tonality (Pinto 1987:85). Other tunings, like the *temple arpa* (E–B–F♯–D–A–F♯) used to play *waynos* and *carnavales* in B minor, or the *temple diablo* (E–C–G–D–B♭–G) used to play *yaravíes* in G minor, are also widely used (Pinto 1987:84–86). In Jesús, Huánuco, Villareal Vara has found six different tunings in carnival guitar music, one of them referred to as *llano* [plain], which corresponds to the standard European tuning E–A–D–G–B–E (Villareal Vara 1958:35).

The European harp and the violin were musical instruments actively propagated by Spanish missionaries throughout the Andean area. Today, both instruments are widely dispersed in the communities of the Peruvian Andes, being generally played in combination or individually as part of larger ensembles. The harp, contrasting with the guitar and the violin, has experienced considerable morphological adaptation, ranging from the triangular-shaped *arpa indígena* to the smaller *domingacha* type, in which the sound box is shaped like a longitudinally sliced pear (Schechter 1992, Olsen 1986–1987). The Peruvian harp is diatonic, usually tuned to the scale of C major; it uses from twenty-six to thirty-six metal or nylon strings. It has no pedals and it is designed to be easily transported by the performer—it is played over his shoulders while processioning (Instituto Nacional de Cultura 1978:149). Harp performance styles vary according to region. Dale Olsen has distinguished six principal regional styles: (1) Callejón de Huaylas-Huánuco, northern Andes, (2) *mantaro*, central Andes, (3) *ayacucho*, south-central Andes, (4) *urubamba-abancay*, southern Andes, (5) *chancay*, central-coastal Andes, and (6) urbanized Lima (Olsen 1986:48–50). The harp can be played as a solo instrument and in large ensembles, where it provides a bass line and a harmonic function (Olsen 1986:56). In some regions of the country the harp is also played as a percussion instrument (Instituto Nacional de Cultura 1978:149).

In more recent times, Andean music has also adopted the European accordion, widely used throughout the region but especially in ensembles like the *conjuntos* in Cuzco (Cánepa-Koch 1998), in the string ensembles in the Callejón de Huaylas, Ancash (den Otter 1985:91), and in the *estudiantina* group in Puno. Andean Peru also sees wind instruments of the European brass band, such as the trumpet, the trombone, the tuba, the saxophone, and the clarinet; these form the basis of the most popular ensemble in the central Andes, the *orquesta típica*.

There are regional instrumental ensembles that are widely used in a variety of contexts. Throughout the Andes ensembles combining the harp and the violin are pervasive, as well as the combination of flute-and-drum played by a single performer or by several performers, such as in the *banda de guerra* ensemble of Cuzco. The *orquesta típica* [typical orchestra] of the central *sierra* (the department of Junín and neighboring areas) consists of saxophones (alto, tenor, and baritone), clarinets, violins, and a harp. In Cuzco, the *conjunto* or *orquesta* combines *kenas*, accordion, mandolin, harp, and violin. The *banda típica* in northern Cajamarca mixes *kenas* and percussion instruments (*caja*, snare drum, and cymbals). Large ensembles of one instrumental type, such as aerophones like *pitus*, *pinkillus*, and *tarkas*, are common. The *estudiantina* ensemble of Puno includes guitars, *charangos*, *mandolinas*, and an accordion. As already discussed, the *herranza* group that accompanies the herding rituals in the Central Andes merges the violin with *wakrapukus* and *tinya*. The *conjunto de cuerdas* [string orchestra] in Ancash combines a violin, mandolin, and sometimes a harp or a *kena*, and an accordion. (See Illustration 8–9.)

PROFILE OF MÁXIMO DAMIÁN AND THE SCISSORS DANCE

The scissors dance is performed exclusively in the regions of Ayacucho, Huancavelica, and Apurímac, during the festival cycle. D'Harcourt (1925) (plate XXXVIII) depicts musicians and multiple harpists in an Ayacucho scissors dance. The scissors dance may also be performed today in Lima by highland migrants (see John Cohen's film *Mountain Music of Peru*). It is a syncretic dance blending European and Andean elements; it most likely took shape during the colonial period, and assumed its current form in the nineteenth century. Study of the scissors dance demonstrates how the European violin has become a "traditional" instrument in Andean Peru.

Unlike most of the Andean dance-dramas, the scissors dance is a dance of ritual competition. The dancers compete against each other in a demonstration of their choreographic abilities and boldness. The dance consists of several phases that develop in increasing degrees of difficulty. Each phase has a specific name and is accompanied by a specific melody, played by an ensemble of violin and

Ill. 8–9. A string ensemble of *mandolinas*, guitar, and *charango* playing during a public fiesta. Courtesy of the Center for Andean Ethnomusicology, Catholic University of Peru.

harp (Bigenho 1993:236). The dancers perform while plucking two separated pieces of metal ("scissors"), and in so doing they follow the rhythmic patterns of the main melody. The dancers are dressed in elaborate and colorful costumes.

It is believed that the dancers have made a deal with the devil, because of the difficult trials that they have to endure. They are thought to have received magical powers from the devil and the strength of the *wamanis,* the Andean deities of the mountains. Consequently, the dancer is seen with both admiration and fear by the villagers.

There can be almost eighteen different steps in the dance. The first ones consist of rapid foot movements alternating the use of the toes and the heel, footstomping, and jumps. A second phase involves acrobatic and gymnastic figures, with the dancers moving flat on the ground or on their knees. The third phase is the more strenuous one, since they attempt "magical" steps and *fakir*-like demonstrations. They eat small live animals (frogs and lizards) and stick needles in their flesh.

The music of the scissors dance is unlike any other Andean musical style, especially in the rhythmic patterns used. The melodies are fundamentally pentatonic, but include changes in the tonal center, which is a procedure not common in other Andean genres. The violin is the lead instrument in this dance of competition, since it is the loudest sound in the ensemble. Recorded Selection 47 is a sample of music for the scissors dance.

Ill. 8–10. Violinist Máximo Damián. Photo: Jean-Paul Dumontier. Courtesy Máximo Damián.

Máximo Damián, a Quechua violinist, is among the most celebrated living musicians of the scissors dance (Illustration 8–10). He was born on December 20, 1936 in the small village of San Diego de Ishua in Lucanas, Ayacucho, in the southern Andes. He now lives in Lima, where he has become a major proponent of the scissors-dance tradition. In his village, Máximo's parents were always telling him how prosperous life in Lima was. Moreover, he saw that his fellow villagers returned from Lima elegantly dressed, speaking Spanish, and with enough resources to help their families. Máximo was the older brother, so he was expected to help his younger ones, but he did not want to leave the village. He owned cattle and a small farm on which he cultivated corn, beans, and potatoes. But one day his uncle spoke to his parents and convinced them that Máximo should go to Lima with him.

Máximo's father had been a reputable violinist in his village and in neighboring areas. People came from many villages to hire Máximo's father, Justiniano, to play in the scissors dance. But he did not want Máximo to play the violin. He said to Máximo, "You should be a lawyer or a doctor." Violinists had to work in festivals where people got drunk, and he thought it was a rough existence (for a comparison, see the discussion of the career of Ecuadorian harpist Don César Muquinche in Schechter 1996:475–481). But Máximo, still young, learned the violin on his own and one day surprised his father, who was so impressed that he began to send Máximo to play in festivals for money, and Máximo enjoyed the assignments. In his first gig, Máximo played with an old, seasoned harpist accompanying the dance of the Machoj, and he did it very well. After that occasion he played for the Christmas festival, for the adoration of infant Jesus. It was at this time that his uncle came and took him to Lima.

The day of his departure was a sad one. His mother cried while making *cancha* [toasted corn], a staple of the Andean kitchen. His father was waiting for him at the entrance of the village, crying and playing the violin. He gave Máximo some money for the trip. Máximo and his uncle had to walk for two days to arrive at the nearest town. When they arrived in Puquío, Máximo thought it was Lima. But the trip was longer than that. From Puquío they took a car to Nazca, the next big town on the coast. Then they took a bus to Ica, a bigger coastal city, and from there they traveled to Lima.

Máximo had many relatives in the nation's capital. In the house of his uncle and cousins he learned the ways of the city. Máximo found employment as a domestic worker with a middle-class family in Lima. He cooked, washed clothes, and cleaned house, working sixteen hours a day. He received a minimal salary, but he managed to send money to his village for a violin, an instrument which he had learned to play when he was twelve years old.

Soon Máximo began to play again. He went to Radio El Sol (a radio station) with a friend who played the guitar. In the early 1960s, Radio El Sol broadcast a program of live Andean music in the early morning. A prominent intellectual and music devotee, José María Arguedas, heard Máximo there and started to promote him around Andean music circles in Lima. Máximo became increasingly popular and played in the renowned Festival of Amancaes at the municipal theatre of downtown Lima, and in migrants' gatherings and festivals. Soon he quit his job as a domestic worker and began performing every morning at Radio El Sol. On Sundays he attended and performed in migrant festivals and gatherings. On the radio he played without charge, but for the Sunday festivals he was hired and paid. He was also hired eventually for marriages, birthdays, and baptisms.

But working as a musician at that time was not enough, and during the day he sold vegetables in the market of Pueblo Libre to supplement his income. Afterward he landed a job in a textile factory. Soon, however, Máximo's excellence with the violin allowed him to resume his musical activities. He was invited to play in folklore festivals in other countries such as Chile and Venezuela, and in Peru contracts began pouring in from different regions. He also played in *coliseos* [open-air theaters] with a scissors-dance group—first at the Coliseo Nacional, then at Coliseo Lima. On other occasions, he accompanied *waynos* with his violin as part of large ensembles. Soon Máximo became one of the most celebrated violinists in Lima.

His income as an Andean musician was, however, still insufficient to maintain a family in the big city. After years of struggle in Lima, Máximo had married and was raising three children. He began to work as a porter in a bank, assigned primarily to cleaning duties. Máximo says that at first he was afraid to apply for the job, since he had not continued in school past the fourth grade, and since he did not speak good Spanish. He was also afraid of *mestizos*. He preferred a job in a factory. But his friends insisted, and he took the job. He worked in the bank until his retirement. He was eventually given greater responsibilities, finally being commissioned to the bank's archives, a post in which he felt very comfortable.

In his free time, Máximo continued to perform the violin, but mostly during the weekends and especially on Sundays, when the migrants organized their activities in Lima. When the Peruvian government founded the National School of Folklore, they called Máximo to be a violin teacher. He worked in the late afternoon three days a week and taught many students the musical techniques of the scissors dance. Today, Máximo performs frequently in theaters, at public events, and for television specials. He has recorded a compact disc and lives comfortably in a two-story house in San Miguel, a middle-class district in Lima.

ANDEAN MUSIC IN THE CITIES

As we mentioned in the introduction, migration from the Andes to Lima and other coastal cities became intensified during the 1950s. The migrants settled on the outskirts of the city capital, where they gathered and bonded on the basis of common regional origin. Soon they were so many that they constituted a large market for urban products—among them, commercial records of Andean music. In 1949 the first 78-rpm records of Andean music were recorded as a commercial experiment, and their success was such that many other recordings followed. The new media gave birth to a new urban, modern Andean style associated with the new technology of electronic sound reproduction. One of the novel stylistic developments of this time was the appearance of a solo singer backed up by a large orchestra. Such a format was rare in Andean rural sites, since in the open air a solo singer would not be heard under the weight of a large instrumental group. With amplified sound, however, solo singers gained popular acceptance, not only in the record studio but also in live presentations, where amplified sound was also made available.

The solo singer became a pivotal figure in the dissemination of Andean music from Lima throughout the nation. The new urban popular style, with roots in regional musical traditions, was characterized by the theater-staged performance context, the leading figure of the solo vocalist, the use of audio amplification, and orchestral accompaniment. This type of performance became the most widespread, but it was not the only one, since instrumental soloists, duos, trios and orchestras also achieved popularity in their own right. However, the solo singer versus orchestra format became by far the most admired, and also the more dependent on electronic amplification for live performances. The singing style derived from Andean *mestizo* patterns, favoring the middle vocal range rather than the high vocal registers preferred in rural Andean contexts.

The solo singer, as we have seen, had developed from the *compañías folklóricas*, in which they had attained wide popular endorsement in the presentation of regional dances, as popular comedians of Andean heritage (who entertained the public between acts), and within strictly instrumental ensembles. By the time of the golden age of the *coliseos* the solo singers were on their way to becoming stars, and commercial records simply sustained this dominant role and furthered the fame of these artists. There were hundreds of solo singers performing in the *coliseos* of Lima, Huancayo, and other cities of Peru, but only a few of them became prominent celebrities and best-selling record stars. Each followed his or her own regional style, and the core of their supporters were migrants and residents of their own regions; nevertheless, due to the intense media exposure (mainly radio and commercial records) and the originality of the format, they acquired recognition beyond their own regional publics. For example, La Pastorita Huaracina (María Alvarado Trujillo, The Shepherdess from Huaraz) and El Jilguero del Huascarán (Ernesto Sánchez Fajardo, The Goldfinch of the Huascarán) were linked to the regional styles of the northern department of Ancash, and El Picaflor de los Andes (Víctor Alberto Gil Malma, The Hummingbird of the Andes) and La Flor Pucarina (Leonor Chávez, The Flower from Pucará) to folklore of the central Andes. There were many other record stars, but by popular perception and by the testimonies of their own record executives, these four were among the ones who sold more records and whose names have remained strongest in the memory of the people. Ima Sumac, who acquired international fame, displayed a musical style that differed from the styles of these regional artists. She also developed her musical career outside of Peru, mainly in the United States, where she made many recordings.

The main song genre disseminated in this new Andean urban popular format, and in Andean commercial records, was definitely the *mestizo wayno*. The supremacy of the *wayno*, however, was attained only in the 1960s, since the first recordings of the 1950s also featured music from dance-dramas. At some moments during the 1960s, at the height of the golden age of Andean commercial recordings, the records of Andean orchestras matched or even surpassed those of Andean soloists, in numbers of releases. But in the popular mind the solo singers were imbued with unusual magnetism.

PROFILE OF VÍCTOR ALBERTO GIL MALMA, "THE HUMMINGBIRD OF THE ANDES"

One of the most famous Andean singers was El Picaflor de los Andes ("The Hummingbird of the Andes," Víctor Alberto Gil Malma) (Illustration 8–11). When he died in 1975, thousands of followers mourned and attended his funeral. Picaflor died while touring in La Oroya, the mining center near Huancayo in the central Peruvian Andes, and the vehicle bringing his remains to Lima had to stop at every town along the way. Everyone living near the central highway to Lima wanted to see him and pay their respects. His body was displayed at the Coliseo Nacional [national coliseum] in Lima, which had been one of his frequent stages.

Picaflor had been a hardworking man. Born in the Andean city of Huancayo, the busy commercial center of the Mantaro Valley in central Peru, he had left his

Ill. 8–11. A reproduction of the cover of a commercial LP by "El Picaflor de los Andes."

home town as a teenager to work in the nearby mining centers; he thus followed seasonal migration patterns that have been a source of additional income in the Valley since the development of the mining industries. In 1959, at age thirty, he went to Lima to participate in a contest promoted by Radio Excelsior. It took him only a few years to record his first hit song in 1963, "Aguas del río Rímac" [Waters of the Rimac river], which sold thousands of copies then and is still included in every anthology of his music.

Picaflor became one of the greatest singers of the golden age of Andean commercial music (1950 to 1980). His recordings are still widely sold, now in cassette and CD formats; he is so popular that twenty-seven years after his death a CD was released by El Virrey, one of the two major record companies in Peru (*Bodas de Plata* [Silver anniversary], CD VIR 00001403), with a selection of twenty-four of his best-selling songs.

Picaflor had a relatively brief career as a recording artist; only twelve years separated his first hit song, released in 1963, from his death of a heart attack in 1975, at the peak of his popularity. During that time, he recorded fourteen LPs and numerous 45-rpm discs. His repertoire was overwhelmingly comprised of *waynos*. In this respect they followed the trend of most regional commercial musics. The commercial *wayno* was not very different in musical form from the regional one. Naturally, performers now had to adapt their renditions to the two- or three-minute duration of the phonograph record. The traditional long introduction by harp and violin became much shorter on records, as did the concluding bars.

Picaflor's vocal style was tense and edgy, stressing his middle range, with no attempt to explore lower or higher vocal confines. Traits such as the use of a strong vibrato, predominant staccato singing, the intensive use of slight ascending and descending glissandos to attack a note, and the use of nonstandard Spanish, contributed to his style. The nonstandard Spanish involves the noncorrespondence between the syllabic spoken accent with the musical and rhythmic accent of the piece. As a result Spanish words appear accented in the wrong places, an effect perceived by most non-Andean *limeños* as a sign of "bad" Spanish, of definite rural origins. The unity of the overall performance style is furthermore emphasized by certain common features shared with the ensemble that accompanied Picaflor, the *orquesta típica* [typical orchestra] from the central Peruvian Andes, formed by saxophones, clarinets, harp, and violin. The clarinets and the saxophones also played using vibrato and staccato, alternatively, and used the same type of swift glissandos to attack a note.

The *waynos* of El Picaflor de los Andes are similar in form to the noncommercial regional ones, but have some flexibility in terms of their rendition. The *wayno* consists primarily of a musical phrase exposed in a periodic form, with a clear, if not necessarily symmetrical, antecedent and consequent. A *wayno* can consist of one of these periodic phrases, which in this case is repeated likewise as antecedent-consequent—for example, A, A1, A, A1. But other *waynos* may consist of two periodic phrases, the second being a contrasting unit. In this case, there are two possibilities: the first phrase A can be repeated and then the piece may proceed to the second phrase B (A, A, B, B) or the second phrase B may be rendered directly after the first phrase (A, B, A, B).

Ex. 8–7.   Transcription of "Aguas del río Rimac," by El Picaflor de los Andes

These patterns are repeated at will, but in commercial records repetitions are usually determined by the constraint of time (two to three minutes). (See Recorded Selection 48.) Picaflor's rendition of "Aguas del río Rímac" has the A phrase, with its antecedent—consequent subsections, repeated several times (Example 8–7).

The lyrics of most *waynos* sung by the Picaflor are related to romantic love—highly nostalgic, even tragic, most of the time referring to a lost relationship, rejection, or abandonment. Some of them are harsher than others. In "For you, ungrateful," he sang:

Habrías sabido de mi vida, ingrata,	You might have heard of my life, ungrateful,
Que ando sufriendo tu falso cariño,	That I am suffering because of your false love
Seguramente tú ríes y cantas	For surely you are laughing and singing
Pero no sabes el dolor que causas.	But you do not know the pain that you cause

Of the few *waynos* that do not correspond to this theme, some foster regional identities, with lyrics speaking of the Picaflor's native land—the town or the region, such as "I Am from Huancayo" or "Huancayo Feeling." The *mulizas* tend to be less ruthless when singing about lost loves, as in "I will always remember you":

Quiero recorrer el camino	I want to follow your path
Que dejaste tú para mi feliz consuelo,	That you left for my comfort,
Quiero recorrer tu sonrisa	I want to travel through your smile
Que iluminó como tú quisiste siempre.	That lighted like you always wanted.
Fuiste para mí, mi cielo	You were for me, my Heaven
Estrella fugaz que se pasa	Shooting star that goes away
Nunca olvidaré tu acento	I will never forget your accent
Ni el mirar de aquellos ojos. . . .	Nor the look of those eyes. . . .

Notwithstanding the presence of the singer, all the musicians of the *orquesta típica* play the same melody (some instruments doubling in parallel thirds), following the customary performance practice. Understandably, while the song is being rendered by the singer, the orchestra plays more softly, allowing him or her to reaffirm the leading role and to convey the lyrics accordingly. This is not so much a technical requirement, since the singer uses a microphone and loudspeakers, but more a stylistic gesture, a matter of musical courtesy. But when the singer finishes a stanza, the orchestra plays by itself the song theme with renewed intensity, if excluding the time-consuming repetitions.

The soloist is not, therefore, such an independent performer after all. She or he does not symbolize opposition to the notion of "group integration," which for many analysts (e.g., Turino 1993) represents a peasant egalitarian music-cultural trait. The *orquesta típica* has not abandoned its routine performance practice when accompanying soloists, and everyone—soloists and instrumentalists alike—plays the same melodic theme—facts that continue to emphasize collective performance, as well as providing a distinguishable urban-Andean pattern.

A MODERN URBAN ENSEMBLE: A *CHICHA* GROUP

In the late 1960s, at the height of the popularity of Andean commercial records, a new Andean urban style appearing as a result of migration slowly began to evolve—*chicha* music. The main difference between the first period, illustrated by the figure of El Picaflor de los Andes, and that of *chicha* music was that the latter was the expression of second-generation migrants—children of the first migrants who had arrived in the city around the 1950s, and who had prepared the way for them in the urban environment. The young Andean migrants who arrived in the city joined this large group to form a huge market for *chicha* music, which developed through the 1970s into the biggest popular musical style in the 1980s. But *chicha* music was primarily for the younger generations—unmarried men and women in their teens or early twenties.

Chicha music was played with electric guitars and bass, an electric organ, and Latin percussion (Illustration 8–12). The influence of global currents such as rock 'n' roll and Latin Caribbean popular music was obvious. The main beat, the rhythmic patterns, and the dance of *chicha* music corresponded to the *cumbia,* the popular rhythm from Colombia, which has gained ample popularity throughout Latin America. The songs, however, were melodically and stylistically Andean *waynos;* the first *chicha* hits consisted of *waynos* adapted to the style of *chicha* music. The vocal style was also reminiscent of the *wayno.*

While Lima became the most important center for the production and dissemination of *chicha* music, many of the first groups originated in the vicinity of Huancayo in the Mantaro Valley. The Shapis, to become the most celebrated *chicha* group of all, originated in Huancayo and took their name from a local dance-drama very popular in the town of Chupaca, the hometown of Chapulín, its lead singer. The group's director, Jaime Moreyra, recalls how their first hit record consisted of the adaptation of the popular *wayno* "El Alizal" into a *chicha* song renamed "El Aguajal" (Recorded Selection 49):

> We began playing in Huancayo in front of 200, 250, 300 people. In the region of Mantaro there existed great support for this music. We began in 1981, and in 1982 Radio Moderna awarded us a special prize for the song "El Aguajal." This song was recorded on the suggestion of the producer, and because it was a blend of the *chicha*

Ill. 8–12. The Shapis, probably the most famous *chicha* group, in a live performance. Courtesy newspaper, *La República*.

and the *wayno*. We recorded it to go beyond the realm of "El Alizal," which was popular folklore but not fashionable among the children of migrants" (Hurtado Suárez 1995:20).

In the 1980s *chicha* music attained remarkable popularity. In the majority of the popular districts of Lima, specific locales for *chicha* events called *chichódromos* appeared. Especially during the weekends, thousands of Andean second-generation migrants (young and unmarried) got together. The rise of *chicha* music was so sudden, and the proliferation of its performance locales so rampant, that it became news for tabloids and a novel sociological topic for many writers. *Chicha* music was often seen by Peruvians as a sign of the new times, in which the Andean migrants had taken over the nation's capital—even in the musical arena. The popularity of *chicha* music, however, went far beyond Lima. In all the central Andes, *chicha* music was heard on the radio and in dances organized in small or large towns. It was the music of the young, associated with modernity, cosmopolitanism, and courting.

In the 1990s the popularity of *chicha* music has decreased slightly, and other Andean genres now share the migrant market. It is also true that today Andean youngsters have expanded their musical tastes considerably beyond a single musical style. Also, many *chichódromos* were outlawed in downtown Lima and other districts because they were considered sources of violence and drunkenness. But *chicha*, also known as *cumbia andina* [Andean *cumbia*], continues to be popular.

CONCLUSION

Peru is a country divided by immense geographical distances and cultural boundaries. Since the arrival of the colonizers the coast became the natural setting for European, and later creole, sensibilities. Meanwhile, the Andean mountains became the refuge of precolonial regional cultures. The tropical forests of Peru continued throughout these ages in relative isolation. In this chapter we have touched only on Andean musical manifestations, because in terms of demographics it is the most significant cultural heritage and influence in modern Peru. These expressions, however, have developed continuously with pre- and postcolonial musical traditions. We have seen that in modern Peru ancient rural musical expressions still endure simultaneously with innovative expressions created in the Andes, or in the urban centers where migrants from the Andes have settled during the twentieth century.

In this sense, it should not surprise the reader that a ritual of marking of animals may occur in the same chronological moment in which urban *chicha* music with electric guitars is intensively popularized. The dissemination of Andean music uses aural tradition, but also commercial records and stage performances, in order to re-create itself. The *wayno* as the central musical and cultural genre in the Peruvian Andes is more alive than ever, from the most secluded mountain villages to the more cosmopolitan urban settings. In the context of an expanding globalization process, Andean cultures and musics continue to endure, develop, and become transformed. In Andean countries like Peru, music reminds us that in spite of the forces of political and economic modernization, indigenous cultures constantly reinvent themselves rather than tending to disappear—and they stand today as strong as ever.

REFERENCES

Bellenger, Xavier. 1981. Les instruments de musique dans les pays andins: Deuxième partie. *Bulletin de L'Institut d'Etudes Andines* 10(1–2):23–50.

Bigenho, Michelle. 1993. El baile de los negritos y la danza de las tijeras: Un manejo de contradicciones. In *Música, danzas, y máscaras en los Andes,* ed. Raúl R. Romero, pp. 219–251. Lima, Peru: Pontificia Universidad Católica del Peru.

Cánepa-Koch, Gisela. 1991. *Wylancha.* 28 min. Produced by Pontificia Universidad Católica del Perú—Archivo de Música Tradicional Andina, Lima, Peru. VHS videocassette.

———. 1993. Los ch'unchu y las palla de Cajamarca en el ciclo de la representación de la muerte del Inca. In *Música, danzas, y máscaras en los Andes,* ed. Raúl R. Romero, pp. 139–178. Lima, Peru: Pontificia Universidad Católica del Peru.

———. 1998. *Máscara, transformación e identidad en los Andes.* Lima, Peru: Pontificia Universidad Católica del Peru.

Casas Roque, Leonidas. 1993. Fiestas, danzas y música de la costa de Lambayeque. In *Música, danzas, y máscaras en los Andes,* ed. Raúl R. Romero, pp. 299–337. Lima, Peru: Pontificia Universidad Católica del Peru.

Carpio Muñoz, Juan. 1976. *El yaraví arequipeño*. Arequipa, Peru: La Colmena.

Cavero, Jesus A. 1985. El qarawi y su función social. *Allpanchis* 25:233–270.

Cohen, John. 1984. *Mountain music of Peru*. Produced by Cinema Guild, New York. 16 mm film and videocassette.

den Otter, Elisabeth. 1985. *Music and dance of Indians and mestizos in an Andean valley of Peru*. Delft, Netherlands: Eburon.

d'Harcourt, Raoul et Marguerite. 1925. *La musique des Incas et ses survivances*. Paris, France: Librairie Orientaliste Paul Geuthner.

Hurtado Suárez, Wilfredo. *Chicha peruana: música de los nuevos migrantes*. [No city], Peru: ECO, 1995.

Instituto Nacional de Cultura. 1978. *Mapa de los instrumentos de uso popular en el Perú*. Lima, Peru: Instituto Nacional de Cultura.

Jiménez Borja, Arturo. 1951. Instrumentos musicales peruanos. *Revista del Museo Nacional* 19–20:37–190.

Merino de Zela, Mildred. 1977. Folklore coreográfico e historia. *Folklore Americano* 24:67–94.

Olsen, Dale A. 1986–1987. The Peruvian folk harp tradition: Determinants of style. *Folk Harp Journal* 53:48–54, 54:41–48, 55:55–59, 56:57–60, 57:38–42, 58:47–48, 59:60–62.

―――. 1986. Towards a musical atlas of Peru. *Ethnomusicology* 30(3):394–412.

Pagaza Galdo, Consuelo. 1961. El yaraví. *Folklore Americano* 8–9(8–9):75–141.

Pinilla, Enrique. 1980. Informe sobre la música en el Perú. In *Historia del Perú*, vol. 9, ed. Juan Mejia Baca, pp. 363–677.

Pinto, Arturo. 1987. Afinaciones de la guitarra en Ayacucho. *Boletín de Lima* 9(49):83–87.

Poole, Deborah. 1990. Accommodation and resistance in Andean ritual dance. *The Drama Review* 34(2):98–126.

Raez Retamozo, Manuel. 1993. Los ciclos ceremoniales y la percepción del tiempo festivo en el Valle del Colca. In *Música, danzas y máscaras en los Andes*, ed. Raúl R. Romero, pp. 253–297. Lima, Peru: Pontificia Universidad Católica del Peru.

Roel, Josafat. 1959. El wayno del Cusco. *Folklore Americano* 6–7(6–7):129–245.

Romero, Raúl R. 1985. La música tradicional y popular. In *La Música en el Perú*. Lima, Peru: Patronato Popular y Porvenir Pro Música Clásica.

―――. 1990. Musical change and cultural resistance in the central Andes of Peru. *Latin American Music Review* 11(1):1–35.

―――. 1992. Preservation, the mass media and dissemination of traditional music: The case of the Peruvian Andes. In *World music, musics of the world: Aspects of documentation, mass media and acculturation*, ed. Max Peter Baumann. Wilhelmshaven, Germany: Florian Noetzel Verlag.

Schechter, John M. 1992. *The indispensable harp: Historical development, modern roles, configurations, and performance practices in Ecuador and Latin America*. Kent, Ohio and London: Kent State Univ. Press.

―――. 1996. Latin America/Ecuador. In *Worlds of music: An introduction to the music of the world's peoples*, 3d ed., edited by Jeff Todd Titon, pp. 428–494. New York: Schirmer Books.

Turino, Thomas. 1983. The charango and the sirena: Music, magic, and the power of love. *Latin American Music Review* 4(1):81–119.

―――. 1984. The urban mestizo charango tradition in southern Peru: A statement of shifting identity. *Ethnomusicology* 28(2):253–270.

―――. 1993. *Moving away from silence: Music of the Peruvian Altiplano and the experience of urban migration.* Chicago: The Univ. of Chicago Press.

Valcárcel, Luis E. 1951. Introduction to Pierre Verger, *Fiestas y danzas en el Cuzco y en los Andes.* Buenos Aires, Argentina: Editorial Sudamericana.

Valencia, Américo. 1983. *¿El siku bipolar altiplánico?* Lima, Peru: Artex Editores.

―――. 1989. *The Altiplano bipolar siku: Study and projection of Peruvian panpipe orchestra.* Lima, Peru: Artex Editores.

Villareal Vara, Félix. 1958. Las afinaciones de la guitarra en Huánuco, Peru. *Revista Musical Chilena* 12(62):33–36.

ADDITIONAL READING

Baumann, Max Peter. 1981. Music, dance and song of the Chipayas (Bolivia). *Latin American Music Review* 2(2):171–222.

―――. 1982. Music of the indios in Bolivia's Andean highlands. *The World of Music* 25(2):80–98.

―――. 1985. The Kantu ensemble of the Kallawaya at Charazani (Bolivia). *Yearbook for Traditional Music* 17:146–166

―――. 1996. Andean music, symbolic dualism and cosmology. In *Cosmología y Música en los Andes,* ed. Max Peter Baumann. Frankfurt, Germany: Vervuert Verlag.

Bellenger, Xavier. 1980. Les instruments de musique dans les pays andins: Les instruments dans leur contexte historico-geografique. *Bulletin de L'Institut d'Études Andines* 9(3–4):108–149.

Mendoza-Walker, Zoila. 1994. Contesting identitites through dance: Mestizo performances in the southern Andes of Peru. *Repercussions* 3(2):50–80.

Olsen, Dale A. 1980. Folk music of South America. In *Musics of many cultures,* ed. Elizabeth May. Berkeley: Univ. of California Press.

―――. 1992. Implications of music technologies in the pre-Columbian Andes. In *Musical repercussions of 1492: Encounters in text and performance,* ed. Carol E. Robertson. Washington, D.C.: Smithsonian Institution.

Poole, Deborah. 1991. Rituals of movement, rites of transformation: Pilgrimage and dance in the highlands of Cuzco, Peru. In *Pilgrimage in Latin America,* ed. Ross Crumrine and Alan Morinis. New York: Greenwood Press.

Romero, Raúl R., ed. 1993. *Música, danzas y máscaras en los Andes.* Lima, Peru: Pontificia Universidad Católica del Peru.

―――. 1994. Black music and identity in Peru: Reconstruction and revival of Afro-Peruvian musical traditions. In *Music and black ethnicity: The Caribbean and South America,* ed. Gerard Béhague, pp. 307–330. New Brunswick, N.J.: Transaction Publishers.

―――. 1998. Peru. In *The Garland encyclopedia of world music,* vol. 2, *South America, Mexico, Central America, and the Caribbean,* pp. 466–490, eds. Dale A. Olsen and Daniel E. Sheehy. New York and London: Garland Publishing, Inc.

Schechter, John M. 1979. The Inca cantar histórico: A lexico-historical elaboration on two cultural themes. *Ethnomusicology* 23(2):191–204.

Stevenson, Robert. 1960. *The music of Peru.* Washington, D.C.: Organization of American States.

———. 1968. *Music in Inca and Aztec territory.* Berkeley: Univ. of California Press.

Tompkins, William D. 1981. The musical traditions of the blacks of coastal Peru. Ph.D. diss., Univ. of California at Berkeley.

Turino, Thomas. 1988. The music of Andean migrants in Lima, Peru: Demographics, social power, and style. *Latin American Music Review* 9(2):127–150.

———. 1990. Somos el Perú: Cumbia andina and the children of Andean migrants in Lima, Peru. *Studies in Latin American Popular Culture* 9:15–37.

———. 1993. The history of a Peruvian panpipe style and the politics of interpretation. In *Ethnomusicology and modern music history,* ed. Stephen Blum, Philip V. Bohlman, and Daniel Neuman. Urbana: Univ. of Illinois Press.

———. 1998. Quechua and Aymara. In *The Garland encyclopedia of world music,* vol. 2, *South America, Mexico, Central America, and the Caribbean,* pp. 205–224, eds. Dale A. Olsen and Daniel E. Sheehy. New York and London: Garland Publishing, Inc.

ADDITIONAL LISTENING

Arequipa: Música y pueblo. Recordings and notes by Juan G. Carpio Muñoz. Instituto Nacional de Cultura and Corporación Departamental de Desarrollo, Arequipa, Peru, 1984.

Bolivia: Larecaja and Omasuyos. Field recordings and notes by Xavier Bellenger. GREM G–8901, France, 1989.

El charango cusqueño: Julio Benavente Díaz. Recordings by Xavier Bellenger. Notes by Thomas Turino. UNESCO, Lima, Peru, 1981.

Chicha Belén [musical group]: *The drink, the culture, the music.* TUMI CD045, Bath, U.K., 1994.

Fiestas of Peru: Music of the high Andes. Recordings by David Lewiston. Notes by Josafat Roel Pineda and David Lewiston. Nonesuch H–72045, New York, 1972.

Flutes and strings of the Andes. Recordings by Bob Haddad, Julio Cutipa, and Elayne Zorn. Notes by Bob Haddad. Music of the World T–106, New York, 1988.

Huaynos and huaylas: The real music of Peru. Studio recordings by various artists. Notes by Lucy Duran. Globe Style Records CDORBD–064, U.K., 1991.

Huayno music of Peru. Vol. 1, *1949–1989.* Compilation and notes by John Cohen. Arhoolie Productions and Discos IEMPSA, El Cerrito, Calif., 1989. (Reissue of master commercial recordings from IEMPSA.)

Huayno music of Peru. Vol. 2, *1960–1975.* Compilation and notes by John Cohen. Arhoolie Productions, El Cerrito, Calif., 1991. (Reissue of master commercial recordings from Discos Smith.)

The Inca harp: Laments and dances of the Tawantinsuyu, the Inca empire. Recordings and notes by Ronald Wright. Lyrichord LLST 1359, Canada, 1980.

Indian music of the upper Amazon. Recordings by Harry Tschopik. Notes by Harry Tschopik and Willard Rhodes, Jr. Folkways FE 4458, New York, 1964.

Kingdom of the sun: Peru's Inca heritage. Recordings and notes by David Lewiston. None-such H–72029, New York.

Mountain music of Peru. Vol. 1. Recordings and notes by John Cohen. Smithsonian Folk-ways CD SF 40020, Washington, D.C., 1991.

Mountain music of Peru. Vol. 2. Recordings and notes by John Cohen and Thomas Turino. Smithsonian Folkways CD SF 40406, Washington, D.C., 1994.

Music of Peru. Edited by Harry Tschopik. Folkways FE 4415, New York, 1959. (Record-ings by several collectors.)

Música andina del Perú. Edited by Raúl R. Romero. Pontificia Universidad Católica del Perú—Archivo de Música Tradicional Andina, Lima, Peru, 1986. (Recordings by several collectors.)

Musiques du Perou: Paucartambo, indiens q'eros. Recordings and notes by Pierre Allard. Disques Ocora OCR 30, Paris, France, 1966.

Paucartambo: La mamacha Carmen. Recordings and notes by Bob Haddad. Music of the World T–109, New York, 1987.

Perou: Taquile, ile du ciel. Recordings and Notes by Xavier Bellenger. Paris: Ocora 558651, 1984.

Peru: Ayarachi and chiriguano. Recordings and notes by Xavier Bellenger. UNESCO Col-lection DCP 1, Paris, France, 1983.

Peru: Guitar, Raúl García Zárate [performer]. ASPIC X55506, Paris, France, 1988.

Peru: Máximo Damián [performer], *el violín de Ishua.* ASPIC X55514, Paris, France, 1992.

Peru: Music of the indigenous communities of Cuzco. Field recordings and notes by Raphael Parejo. AUDIVIS/UNESCO D–8268 (UNESCO Collection), Paris, France, 1997.

Peru: Music from the land of Macchu Picchu. Recordings by Verna Gillis and David Moisés Martínez. Notes by Verna Gillis. Lyrichord LLST 7294, New York, 1975.

Peru and Bolivia: The sounds of evolving traditions, central Andean music and festivals. Music of the Earth MCM 3009, Barre, Vt., 1997.

Peruvian harp and mandolin: The blind street musicians of Cusco. Recordings and notes by Bob Haddad. Music of the World CDT 105, Chapel Hill, N.C., 1995.

Sierra central I. Recordings by Nueva Fusa, S.A. Notes by Josafat Roel Pienda. Instituto Nacional de Cultura, Lima, Peru, 1982.

Sound of the Andes: The blind street musicians of Cusco. Recordings and Notes by Bob Haddad. Lyrichord LLST 7393, New York, 1985.

Traditional music of Peru. Recordings by Babs Brown and Samuel Martí. Notes by Samuel Martí. Folkways FE 4456, New York, 1959.

Traditional music of Peru: Cajamarca and the Colca Valley. Recordings, compilation, and notes by Raúl R. Romero, Gisela Cánepa-Koch, and Manuel Raez. Smithsonian/Folkways SF CD 40468 Washington, D.C., 1996.

Traditional music of Peru: Festivals of Cusco. Recordings by Gisela Cánepa-Koch, Leonidas Casas Roque and Manuel Raez Retamozo. Notes by Gisela Cánepa-Koch. Smith-sonian/Folkways SF CD 40466, Washington. D.C., 1995.

Traditional music of Peru: Lambayeque. Produced by Raúl R. Romero. Notes by Leonidas Casas Roque. Smithsonian/Folkways SF CD 40469. Washington, D.C., 1996.

Traditional music of Peru: The Mantaro Valley. Recordings and notes by Raúl R. Romero. Smithsonian/Folkways SF CD 40467, Washington, D.C., 1995.

Voces e instrumentos de la selva. Recordings by Alberto Chirif and Stefano Varese. Notes by Josafat Roel Pineda. Casa de la Cultura and Universidad Nacional Mayor de San Marcos, Lima, Peru, 1969.

ADDITIONAL VIEWING

Carnival in Queros. Directed by John Cohen. Univ. of California Extension Media Center, Berkeley, Calif., 1990. 16 mm film and videocassette.

Dancing with the Incas. Directed by John Cohen. Univ. of California Extension Media Center, Berkeley, Calif., 1992. 16 mm film and videocassette.

Fiesta de la mamacha Carmen. Directed by Gisela Cánepa-Koch. Pontificia Universidad Católica del Perú—Archivo de Música Tradicional Andina, Lima, Peru, 1989. Videocassette in Spanish and English.

Instrumentos y géneros musicales de Lambayeque. Directed by Gisela Cánepa-Koch. Pontificia Universidad Católica del Perú—Archivo de Música Tradicional Andina, Lima, Peru, 1990. Videocassette in Spanish and English.

Tinka de Alpaca. Directed by Gisela Cánepa-Koch. Pontificia Universidad Católica del Perú—Archivo de Música Tradicional Andina, Lima, Peru, 1988. Videocassette in Spanish and English.

Wylancha. Directed by Gisela Cánepa-Koch. Pontificia Universidad Católica del Perú—Archivo de Música Tradicional Andina, Lima, Perú, 1991. Videocassette in Spanish and English.

CHAPTER NINE

Beyond Region

Transnational and Transcultural Traditions

JOHN M. SCHECHTER

WITHIN AND BEYOND REGION

We have looked through a spectacular kaleidoscope of Latin American musics:

• *herranza* songs for the branding of Andean animals, interspersed with the predictive reading of *coca* leaves, accompanied by the colonial-era cowhorn *wakra-puku,* all part of a ritual offering to Andean deities, the *wamani;*

• the *son jalisciense* of the Mexican *mariachi,* with its unique, recognizable bass guitar, the *guitarrón,* and with the ensemble garbed in stylized *charro* dress, evocative of the deeply rooted *charro* tradition;

• the distinctive *rajaleña* ensemble of Colombia's southern Andes, with *carángano* and *tiple,* specially designated to accompany the spicy double entendre of the area *copla;*

• the mini-kaleidoscope of Central American *marimba* musics—Guatemalan *marimba de tecomates, marimba sencilla,* and *marimba doble,* and Nicaraguan *marimba de arco;*

• the brilliant hues of the Argentine *milonga en décima,* such as "A Juan Bautista Bairoleto," with its multicolored depiction of the plants, trees, animals, and winds of the Argentine *pampa,* and one of its major historical figures;

• the *seremoni* songs of Haitian Vodou, part of spirit-possession ritual practices with roots fixed deep in the belief system and rhythmic practices of the African homeland; and

• the *Zabumba* ensemble of northeastern Brazil, with its cane *pífano* and its central role in the *novena de casa.*

These and the other rich musical traditions you have studied here are redolent with the special texture and flavor of their home regions. Musical instruments and their materials, text form, text content, and ritual belief systems and practices all reflect the unique histories and expressive cultural evolution of particular regions. The principal purpose of this book is to bring to your nostrils many of these individual, distinctive aromas.

We can also approach music in Latin American culture in a different manner. After viewing and hearing these remarkable regional musics, we can try to look at Latin American music as a whole. There are at least three perspectives through which we can begin to appreciate broader issues, to perceive more complex patterns in Latin American musical expressions, patterns that ignore regional and national boundaries—each of them transregional, transnational, transcultural:

- the perspective of a contemporary song movement, *nueva canción*
- the perspective of diverse women's musics
- the perspective of the symbolic character of musical expression, and the search for continuity in music culture.

As we began this book examining four broad themes in Latin American music cultures, to open our minds to major cultural concerns in Latin America, so we conclude exploring each of these three perspectives, seeking to understand how they can further enrich our appreciation of the roles and uses of music in Latin America. The first perspective is the view through a lens with a political filter, the second through the lens of gender, and the third through a distinctly wide-angle, philosophical lens.

NUEVA CANCIÓN

CONTINUITY OF TRADITION

The *nueva canción* [new song] tradition in Latin America, appearing initially in the 1960s, was a song movement that, first and foremost, sought the renewal and reinvigoration of a long-standing *canción* tradition on the continent. *La nueva canción chilena* and its relatives, *nuevo cancionero argentino* and Cuban *nueva trova,* as well as parallel song movements throughout Latin America, sought to reinvoke, to revitalize popular national musics of earlier generations, in their respective countries. Thus, for example, in his song "El Lazo" (c. 1964), Víctor Jara used as the underlying rhythm a version of the Chilean *cueca*—the national dance of that country (see Schechter 1996:430). Patricio Mann's "El Sueño Americano" (1965) comprises several named subsections—among these are sections in the rhythms of *cueca, chacarera, zamba,* and *"canción"* (Rodríguez Musso 1988: 178–187).

Nueva canción was a continent-wide musical tradition, originating in the Southern Cone countries and having manifestations in many other Latin American nations. Eduardo Carrasco Pirard notes that the phrase *nueva canción* itself has been used for this popular music of renewal in Mexico, Nicaragua, Costa Rica, Puerto Rico, Venezuela, Peru, Colombia, and Ecuador (1982:600). Musical exchanges among *nueva canción* musicians of many Latin American countries have taken place in festivals in Cuba (1978), Mexico (1982), Nicaragua (1983), Ecuador (1984), and Argentina (1985) (Fairley 1985:308, Reyes Matta 1988).

In Argentina, the *nuevo cancionero argentino* developed from the musical legacy of one of the great pioneers of Latin American New Song, Atahualpa Yupanqui. Widely read in the literature of Cervantes, in anthropology, and in history, Yupanqui nevertheless absorbed the essence of the folklore of his native Argentina by travel on horseback. He made many journeys through the Calchaquí Valley, searching out gatherings where he and his companions would listen to dances, *vidalas* (an Argentine musical genre), folk poetry, tales, and discussions of historic events (Luna 1986:41–45). Yupanqui was gifted with both remarkable guitar technique and an eloquence of thought and spirit. Carrasco Pirard summarizes Atahualpa Yupanqui's contribution in these terms: "All his [Yupanqui's] research work into his country's folklore is reflected in his songs; they bring together the purity of ancient tradition and the poetic creativity of one of the most profound artists of his generation" (Carrasco Pirard 1982:605).

In the same strongly metaphoric character of many of the songs of Chile's *nueva canción* artists Violeta Parra and Víctor Jara, Atahualpa Yupanqui, in his "Camino del indio," offers a haunting nexus of poetry and music (Example 9–1), in which he presents a rural track as symbolic of the trials of the *campesino* of the countryside. There is much musical in this song about a rural footpath. Set in a halting tempo, in the minor, with hesitant, expressive guitar portamentos, the musical setting is befitting the grief expressed in the lyric. The poetry itself is music-referencing—the Argentine Andean dweller sings in the mountains; the all-knowing pathway is touched by the poet Yupanqui's song. The poet hears the Andean wanderer calling, through the song of his *kena* flute, to his beloved—a tradition hearkening back to Incaic times. One hears the mournful *baguala,* an Argentine song type, along the way. In all, this is a highly moving expression, a profoundly musical one.

It was again Atahualpa Yupanqui's musical bequest that fell into the hands of a grouping of artists that emerged toward the end of the 1950s: the *nuevo cancionero argentino.* Major figures included the poet Armando Tejada Gómez, who issued an important tract for the movement in 1958; composer Oscar Matus; the remarkable vocalist Mercedes Sosa; and singer-composers Horacio Guaraní, César Isella, and José Larralde. Important ensembles included Los Trovadores, Los Andariegos, Los Huanca-Hua, Los Nocheros de Anta, and Los Tucutucu (Carrasco Pirard 1982:605–606). The interpretations of Los Tucutucu, such as their versions of the *chacarera* "Añoranzas" and the *zambas* "La tucumanita" and "Viene clareando," are marked by a tremendous vitality, carefully executed close harmony, and great precision and expressiveness, overall.

Cuban *nueva trova,* a New Song movement existing not as a music of protest but as a government-supported art form, is rooted in the turn-of-the-century "old *trova*" in Cuba. A town's tailors, barbers, and tobacconists would gather at some-

Ex. 9–1.   Partial lyrics for Atahualpa Yupanqui song, "Camino del indio" (Luna 1986:99)

Camino del indio, sendero coya sembrao de piedras	Path of the Indian, Incaic path sown of stones
Caminito del indio que junta el valle con las estrellas . . .	Little path of the Indian, which links the valley with the stars . . .
Cantando en el cerro	Singing in the hills
Llorando en el río	Weeping at the river
Se agranda en la noche	At night the grief
La pena del indio.	Of the Indian broadens.
El sol y la luna	The sun and the moon
Y este canto mío	And this, my song
Besaron tus piedras	Kissed your stones
Camino del indio	Indian pathway
En la noche serrana llora la quena su honda nostalgia	In the mountain evening the *kena* mourns its deep longing
Y el caminito sabe quién es la chola que el indio llama.	And the small pathway understands who is the woman the Indian is calling to.
Se levanta en el cerro la voz doliente de la baguala	There arises in the hills the sorrowful voice of the *baguala*[1]
Y el camino lamenta ser el culpable de la distancia.	And the pathway laments being guilty of creating the distance [between them].
Cantando en el cerro . . .	Singing in the hills . . .

one's home on Sunday for an afternoon of *trova,* when they would sing in *boleros, guarachas,* and *guajiras* of the beauty of the Cuban landscape, and of the Cuban women (see the section on musical nostalgia in Chapter 1), of ideal love, of patriotic struggles. A new performance site was created in Santiago, Cuba, in 1966 called La Casa de la Trova, where *trovadores* of the older generation could gather. This center subsequently spawned similar *trova* locales in Havana, Camagüey, and elsewhere. In 1967, the Casa de las Americas sponsored El Primer Encuentro de la Canción Protesta [First meeting of the protest song], attended by many contemporary *nueva canción* composer-performers, among them Pablo Milanés, Silvio Rodríguez, and Noel Nicola. The *movimiento de la nueva trova* (MNT) began to take shape. By the time a second Casa de las Américas–sponsored meeting took place in 1972, the *nueva trova* movement was now more clearly defined and had begun to spread beyond the confines of the island nation (Díaz Ayala 1981:301–302).

The singers of *nueva trova,* through their choice of name, linked themselves with their parent *trova* tradition, while at the same time creating something quite new, with a declaration of new values (Benmayor 1981:11–12, 19–20). These young songwriters aided in developing literacy, cut cane, served in the army—thus, *nueva trova* "was a spontaneous, uncoordinated effort on the part of young people to speak about the experience of growing up in a revolution" (ibid., 13). Silvio Rodríguez played guitar in the army, performing in the barracks; Pablo Milanés had sung with pop groups and was familiar with black spirituals; Noel Nicola was from a musical family, though he did not study music formally; Sara González had been a teacher prior to embarking on her singing career; Vicente Feliú was the offspring of a composer of *boleros*. *Trovadores* were salaried cultural workers, with heavy performance schedules—at regular provincial and national meetings, they would investigate issues of revolutionary art and would evaluate each other's recent compositions.

Influenced notably by Bob Dylan, the Beatles, and the major figures of South American *nueva canción,* the *nueva trova* troubadours took their own Cuban musical forms and modernized them. Pablo Milanés turned frequently to the Cuban *son* and *guajira* forms; Sara González worked in a more up-tempo ensemble framework, sometimes with a Brazilian influence. As for textual themes, Peter Manuel remarks that "while many *nueva trova* songs do in fact protest against imperialism, sexism, and exploitation, underlying such themes is a more positive vision of mature, egalitarian emotional relationships and a just, humane society" (Manuel 1988:38). Silvio Rodríguez's "Rabo de nube" uses the central image of the tail of a tornado or hurricane to suggest both the upheaval of love and social torment, the violence of the vortex ultimately leading to the tranquility of restored hope. Sara González's "¿Qué dice usted?" juxtaposes, over a lively, syncopated *son* rhythm, past images of the Cuban woman with modern *trova* images (Benmayor 1981:30–32).

POLITICAL CONDITIONS

The 1950s to 1970s in Latin America was a period of violent upheaval, witnessing the Plaza de Mayo massacre in Buenos Aires, and subsequently the fall of Perón in Argentina (1955); the fall of Cuba's Batista government and the victorious Cuban Revolution (1959); the fall of the João Goulart government in Brazil (1964), beginning a fifteen-year hard-line era; the American intervention in Santo Domingo (1965); an increase in guerrilla activity in Peru, Colombia, and Bolivia; the death of Ernesto Che Guevara in Bolivia (1967); the subsequent spread of guerrilla fighting in Central America and Venezuela, and the Tlatelolco massacre in Mexico (1968); and the victory of the Unidad Popular in Chile (1970), initiating three years of government under Salvador Allende, followed by the 1973 military coup (Carrasco Pirard 1982:604).

This was the intensely violent era in which *nueva canción* came of age, and the movement's compositions reflect the political tensions of these years. Thus, as seen in Chapter 1, Víctor Jara's 1967 song, "El aparecido," dedicated "to E.(Ch).G." (Ernesto Che Guevara), made famous in an arrangement by Inti Illimani, depicts the flight of the revolutionary from his pursuers, climaxing in an emotional refrain: "Córrele, córrele, córrela; córrele, que te van a matar; córrele, córrele, córrela!" [Run, run, run; run, for they are going to kill you; run,

run, run!] The sensitivity to contemporary revolutionary currents was counter-balanced by a sensitivity to past and current atrocities. The "Cantata Popular Santa María de Iquique," written in 1969 and premiered in Santiago in 1970, with text and music by Luis Advís, was a central work of the *nueva canción chilena*. Its stirring music commemorates the 1907 massacre of workers, their wives, and their children, in the Santa María School of the port city of Iquique, Chile: "Murieron tres mil seiscientos, uno trás otro . . . tres mil seiscientos obreros asesinados" [Three thousand six hundred died, one after the other . . . three thousand six hundred workers, assassinated]. The extended text of this cantata concludes prophetically in *cueca* rhythm with a call to Chileans not to become complacent, but rather to become united, possibly to confront another such massacre in the future. (The full text appears in Rodríguez Musso 1988:207–218.)

Jara's song "Preguntas por Puerto Montt" was briefly mentioned in Chapter 1, under the heading "Commentary on Current Events, and Outrage at Injustice." Once again, on March 9, 1969—following orders from the Chilean Minister of the Interior, Edmundo Pérez Zúcovic, and under the command of Jorge Pérez, acting governor of Llanquihue province—250 police attacked ninety-one peasant squatter families on the outskirts of the Chilean port city of Puerto Montt. Eight were killed and some sixty wounded. This provoked an enormous demonstration four days later in Santiago, at which Víctor Jara premiered his musical response to the slaughter, "Preguntas por Puerto Montt." In this song, a straightforward stream-of-consciousness attack on the murderers (Example 9–2), Jara did what few Chilean troubadours had ever done in the past—he directly named the blameworthy party (Rodríguez Musso 1988:81). Example 9–2 begins with the last stanza cited in Chapter 1 and continues with the stanzas naming and condemning Pérez Zúcovic. During the final, bloody massacre in September 1973, some 2,800 Chileans, including President Allende, lost their lives in the military coup.

During the 1960s, Chilean *nueva canción* activities centered to a considerable extent on the *peñas* [coffeehouses with folkloric music] of Violeta Parra and her children, Isabel and Angel, in Santiago. Singer-composers collaborated at these sites, polishing their craft and creating songs in established musical forms but ex-pressive of their contemporary political concerns. Reflecting this intense activity was the 1969 *Primer Festival de la Nueva Canción Chilena*, under the auspices of the Catholic University in Santiago. Fernando Castillo, rector of the University, expressed the feelings of those in attendance when he declared that "our purpose here today is to search for an expression that describes our reality. . . . Isn't it true that our radio and television programs seldom encourage the creativity of our artists . . .? Let our fundamental concern be that our own art be deeply rooted in the *Chilean* [speaker's emphasis] spirit so that when we sing—be it badly or well—we express genuine happiness and pain, happiness and pain that are our own" (Morris 1986:120).

The festival intended to explore the state of Chilean popular music of the day and included a contest among twelve invited composers. Tied for the first prize was Víctor Jara's remarkable "La plegaria a un labrador" [Supplication to a

Ill. 9–1. Víctor Jara. Photo courtesy of Mrs. Joan Jara and the Fundación Víctor Jara, Santiago, Chile.

worker]. In the words of his wife Joan, this song "was a call to the peasants, to those who tilled the soil with their hands and produced the fruits of the earth, to join with their brothers to fight for a just society. Its form, reminiscent of the Lord's Prayer, was a reflection of Víctor's newly reawakened interest in the Bible for its poetry and humanist values, at a time when a deep understanding was

Ex. 9–2.   Partial lyrics for "Preguntas por Puerto Montt"

Hay, ¡qué ser más infeliz!
Él que mandó disparar
Sabiendo cómo evitar
Una matanza tan vil.
¡Puerto Montt, oh Puerto Montt!

Oh, what a "bastard" of a being
He who ordered to shoot
Knowing how to avoid
Such an evil massacre.
Puerto Montt, oh Puerto Montt!

Usted debe responder
Señor Pérez Zúcovich
Por qué al pueblo indefenso
Contestaron con fusil.

You must answer
Mr. Pérez Zúcovich
Why to unarmed people
They responded with guns.

Señor Pérez, su conciencia
La enterró en un ataúd
Y no limpiarán sus manos
Toda la lluvia del sur
Toda la lluvia del sur. . . .

Mr. Pérez, your conscience
Was buried in a coffin
And your hands will not be cleansed
By all of the rain of the South
By all of the rain of the South. . . .

growing between progressive Catholics and Marxists in Latin America" (Jara 1984:131).

In the 1970 presidential campaign of Salvador Allende, *nueva canción* musicians supporting his Unidad Popular performed on his behalf at political rallies. "Venceremos" [We will triumph], by Claudio Iturra and Sergio Ortega, became the campaign rallying cry for Allende. Some of the lyrics to the song appear in Example 9–3.

Following the election, *nueva canción* musicians sustained their sympathy for the Allende government, composing songs about major happenings during its three years, a period that produced likely the most famous song of the *nueva canción* movement, throughout the continent—"El pueblo unido jamás será vencido" [The people united will never be defeated].

The objective of the junta that staged the 1973 military coup was to eliminate Marxism in Chile. Political parties were prohibited from organizing. *Nueva canción* music was severely repressed by the new régime; Quilapayún and Inti Illimani performed abroad in exile. *Nueva canción* within Chile was transformed into *canto nuevo*. Canto nuevo musicians, within this difficult environment involving substantial restriction of opportunity for group meeting and group expression, found themselves forced to create songs in the spirit of *nueva canción* but without uninhibited political messages (Morris 1986:121–124). Continuing the tradition of metaphoric text, in the strong lineage of the poetry of Atahualpa Yupanqui, Violeta Parra, and Víctor Jara, *Canto Nuevo* composers now exaggerated the metaphoric expression, in order to express thoughts that likely would have been censored if stated more directly. Thus, for example, winter frequently came to signify the trials people faced in Chile, following upon the 1973 coup, as in Pato Valdivia's song "Cuando llega el invierno" (ibid., 127).

Ill. 9–2. Víctor Jara sings with Chilean children. Photo courtesy of Mrs. Joan Jara and the Fundación Víctor Jara, Santiago, Chile.

PHILOSOPHY

There is no question that *nueva canción* developed and evolved as a mirror of its own tumultuous political times. But *nueva canción* also arose in part as a cultural reaction against the waves of foreign popular music from the United States and Europe. Thus one finds, for example, the song "El drug store," by Angel Parra, son of Violeta Parra, which includes the verse "Vamos a bailar go-go en un drive-in especial. Tengo un poster de los Beatles y un long-play sensacional." The confrontation between the United States and Latin America is symbolized in the song

Ex. 9–3.   Partial lyrics for "Venceremos," by Iturra and Ortega (Morris 1986:121, Toqui Amaru 1978)

Desde el hondo crisol de la patria	From the depths of our country
Se levanta el clamor popular.	The cry of the people rises.
Ya se anuncia la nueva alborada.	Now the new dawn is announced.
Todo Chile comienza cantar.	All of Chile begins to sing.
. . .	
Venceremos, venceremos.	We will triumph, we will triumph.
Mil cadenas habrá que romper.	A thousand chains will have to be broken.
Venceremos, venceremos.	We will triumph, we will triumph.
Al facismo podemos vencer.	We can defeat Fascism.
. . .	
Venceremos, venceremos.	We will triumph, we will triumph.
La miseria sabremos vencer.	We will learn how to conquer misery.
Sembraremos las tierras de gloria.	We will sow the fields of glory.
Socialista será el porvenir.	The future will be Socialist.
Todos juntos seremos la historia.	Together we will make history.
A cumplir, a cumplir, a cumplir.	Carry on, carry on, carry on.

"Conversation Between the Eagle and the Condor" by the *nueva canción* ensemble Quilapayún.

Nueva canción composers and performers, then, presented music that addressed current social problems, expressing outrage at unprovoked violence and injustice, and seeking to promote change. Concordantly, *nueva canción*'s artists—composers and performers—attempted to speak for and about the common people of their countries. Composer-musicians such as Argentina's Atahualpa Yupanqui and Chile's Violeta Parra and Víctor Jara were able to accomplish this, in the first instance, by virtue of their substantial collecting of folk songs in the rural areas of their nations. Drawing on this accumulated knowledge of their countries' musical folklore, *nueva canción* composers and performers achieved this underlying goal in various ways—song subject matter, selection of song genre, specific musical features, selection of musical instruments, and even dress.

Víctor Jara's songs "Angelita Huenumán" and "El lazo" each sketched a musical biography of a different rural Chilean artisan, the first a blanket-weaver (recall our brief discussion of "Angelita Huenumán" in Chapter 1), the second a lasso-maker.[2] In his "La Plegaria a un labrador," as noted above, Jara essentially penned and sang an interpretation of the Lord's Prayer, now recast as a call for justice and worker solidarity.

Jara and the great pioneer of *nueva canción*, Violeta Parra, further revealed their esteem for the *mestizos* and for the native Mapuche of the Chilean countryside by creating musical-ethnographic reenactments of traditional rural celebrations and rituals. In "Despedimiento del angelito," Jara skillfully presented the atmosphere of a Chilean child's wake with the proper guitar rhythmic patterns and harmonies, melodic shapes, and actual words—all recapitulating the musical structures and text phrases of the *versos* sung at actual Chilean children's wakes. You can verify this by listening to Jara's song[3] and comparing it with the musical transcription of the Chilean *verso* "Por despedimiento" in Grebe 1967:93–97. Moreover, in "Despedimiento del angelito" Jara also echoes traditional rural Chilean folk song in his use of a modal scale, here the Mixolydian mode (flat seventh scale-degree). As María Ester Grebe points out (1967:59–61, 77), the use of Mixolydian flat VII harmonies (e.g., C major, in a song in the key of D major) in Chilean *versos* is an archaic "modal connection" that one can trace back to the *villancico* of sixteenth-century Spain. Finally, Jara is careful to have the words reflect local dialect; thus, he uses *maire* [mother] and *Alto Paire* [Great Father, God], instead of *madre* and *Alto Padre*.

And what is this song about? Why the references to "mother" and "Great Father"? As noted in the conclusion of Chapter 1, this type of song is sung by adults present at a Latin American child's wake. The adult poet-singers take the part of the deceased child and bid "farewell" *(despedimiento)* to its "mother," as "I" (i.e., the deceased child) am on "my" way to Heaven. Examples 9–4 and 9–5 compare the verses of Jara with words from an actual Chilean *verso* "Por despedimiento"— you will see that Jara faithfully uses the same turns of phrase that appear in *versos* performed in the natural setting of a Chilean child's wake.

Violeta Parra captured an analogous child's-wake *despedimiento*, with dialect, in her *décima* "Maire mía, no me llores" (Parra 1976:153–154). Excerpts of this *décima* appear (in English) at the conclusion of Chapter 1.[4] Parra musically en-

Ex. 9–4.   Partial lyrics for Víctor Jara's "Despedimiento del angelito"

Gloria dejo en memoria	Glory, I leave in memory
Y estas razones aquí	And these reasons here
De que no llore por mí	That you not weep for me
Porque me quita la gloria.	For that takes Glory away from me.
Ve, como maire y señora	Look, as mother and woman
Pídele a Dios que te güarde.	Ask God that he care for you.
Me voy con el Alto Paire	I am going to be with the Great Father
Y a los reinados de Dios	And to God's reign
Digo con el corazón	I speak with all my heart
Y adiós mi querida maire . . .	Farewell, my beloved mother . . .
Virgen de nos y pariente	Our Lady and Relative
Yo a todos les digo adiós	To all I say goodbye
Ya mi plazo se cumplió	Now my term is up
Y conmigo la muerte.	And with me, death.

Ex. 9–5.   Partial lyrics from an actual Chilean *verso*, "Por despedimiento"
(Grebe 1967:93–96)

Adiós, mis padres queridos	Farewell, my beloved parents
Póngamen [*sic*] la bendición	Put me in your blessings
Que con todo corazón	For with all my heart
Hoy de todos me despido	Today I bid farewell to all
Me llegó el plazo "cumplío"	My term is up
Que me voy a retirar . . .	I am going to withdraw . . .
Madre, te dejo en memoria	Mother, I leave for your memory
Estas palabras aquí	These words here
Pa' que no llores por mí	So that you not weep for me
Porque me quita la gloria . . .	For that takes Glory away from me . . .

acted other traditional ritual settings as well. In her 1964–1965 song "El nguillatún" (for text, see Rodríguez Musso 1988:155–156), she alludes to the traditional Chilean female shaman, the *machi*, and her self-accompanimental *kultrún*
drum. (The *machi* and her *kultrún* are briefly discussed in Chapter 1.) The *nguillatún* is fundamentally an agricultural fertility rite in which Mapuches gather to
state their needs to their ancestors and to their gods; the *machi* plays a critical
leadership role in this ceremony (Schechter 1976:7–8). In a rare opportunity for a
non-Mapuche visitor, Violeta Parra was permitted to attend a *nguillatún* in the
course of more than ten years of field collection of Chilean folk songs and stories.
In "El Nguillatún," Parra has the Mapuche people asking the *machi* to intervene
with the gods, seeking drier weather for the harvest, which she does successfully
(Juan Armando Eple, in Levy 1988).

By comparing the musical transcription in Example 9–6, below, with the transcription of a Mapuche *machi* song in Chapter 1, Example 1–20, we can tell that
Violeta Parra has taken musical as well as textual pains to capture this *nguillatún*.
Skillfully, Parra has honed in on both the Chilean *machi*'s characteristic musical
phrasing—continuous compound-metric groupings of three eighth notes, in short
phrases, often but not exclusively in 12/8 meter—and the *machi*'s characteristically strong rhythmic emphases, though Parra accompanies herself with her standard *charango*, not with a *kultrún*. She attends not only to phrasing and to the
rhythmic character, but also to the melodic (and here is where the depiction really shows some teeth): Parra's strophic setting, basically in three distinct musical
phrases (Example 9–6), is dominated by a pendular motion between musical
pitches a major-second apart (here, F♯-E and E-D), very much as the *machi* does
in the field-recorded *machi* chant transcribed in Example 1–20. Parra even preserves the 1-3-2 (scale-degree numbers) motion—which appears occasionally as a
motive in the *machi* chant—prior to her cadential 9/8 measure. In all, what appears to be an instance of remarkable musical attention to detail, to serve the
composer's purpose of creating a true-to-life musical glimpse of the *machi* and
her musical style.

Ex. 9–6. **Musical transcription of the melody line to Violeta Parra's "El nguillatún." Transcribed by John M. Schechter.**

Ca - mi - na   la   ma - chi   pa - rael   ngui - lla - tún, ____

cha - maly   re - bo - zo   trai - lin - co   y   cul - trún,

yhas - ta   los   en - fer - mos   de - su   ma - chi - tún ____

au - men - tan   las   fi - las   dee - se   ngui - lla - tún ____

dee - se ngui - lla - tún ___   de   e - se ngui - lla - tuú _____

PEOPLE

In *nueva canción,* students and intellectuals sought to join with workers and with the peasants of the countryside—resulting, for example, in Víctor Jara's "Angelita Huenumán" about a Mapuche blanket-weaver, his "El lazo" about a rural lasso-maker, and his eloquent lyric "La plegaria a un labrador." The attempt to conjoin these different cultures was symbolized not only by songs praising the skills of isolated rural craftspersons and by odes to worker solidarity, but also by the use in a single ensemble of musical instruments from divergent cultures—notably native Andean panpipes and *kenas* [notched flutes], hybrid Andean *charango* [small guitar] and *bombo* [Andean double-headed drum], and European guitar. Together with the decision of the performers to wear the *campesino's poncho* (the black *ponchos* of Quilapayún, the red of Inti Illimani), these hybrid instrument groupings formalized the symbolic alliance, student–worker/peasant (Fairley 1985: 308–309).

Nueva canción chilena was a middle-class movement, with strong support from university students. At the moment of the September 1973 military coup, which produced his own martyrdom, Víctor Jara was among students and teachers of the State Technical University in Santiago. (Joan Jara describes her husband's final days in stark detail in her biography of him, *An Unfinished Song* [Jara 1984:233–251].) Jan Fairley has commented that, though *la nueva canción lati-*

noamericana "is defined as much by who is singing it, to whom, where and when, [as well as] by important considerations of content and form, theme and language, poetry and symbol, instrumentation and arrangement, melody, rhythm, harmony, tempo, timbre, . . . [i.e.], a complex confluence of musical elements as well as aspects of performance practice and style[,] initially it is the music of a particular *young* (author's italics) generation . . . [notably] within the [Latin American] universities" (Fairley 1985:308).

The two major ensembles of Chilean *nueva canción* were Quilapayún [Three beards, Mapuche] and Inti Illimani [Sun, name of mountain, Quechua]. The two ensembles, comprised of middle-class university students, were born in the *peña* of the State Technical University in Santiago, Chile (Rodríguez Musso 1988:71–72). Violeta Parra's "Me gustan los estudiantes" (see Rodríguez Musso 1988:144–146 for the full text) praises students—the group always at the forefront of political battles in Latin America, and incidentally the group that could afford to travel to Parra's own cultural center, La Carpa de la Reina (established in 1964, after Parra's return from Europe), in the neighborhood of La Reina, on the outskirts of Santiago. (Many singers later famous in the *nueva canción* movement would perform at La Carpa de la Reina.) A ballad of eight-line octosyllabic stanzas, "Me gustan los estudiantes" expresses Parra's admiration for students' bravery, among other virtues. Humorously, she concludes each stanza with an expression of praise for a particular academic specialty. A transnational analogue for the central role of student ensembles in the development of Chilean *nueva canción* is Peru's Asociación Juvenil Puno [Puno Youth Association], a panpipe ensemble—originating in the early 1970s as a social club of middle-class Puno-area students in Lima—that played a central role in the dramatic rise in the numbers of urban panpipe ensembles in Lima and other Peruvian towns (Turino 1993).

Summary

The songs of *nueva canción* and of its parallel song movements elsewhere in Latin America achieved many goals. They declared intolerance for injustice; they demonstrated the concern of young musicians throughout the continent for their own cultural sovereignty; and they illustrated their composers' regard for their own rural peoples and workers. We are given to visualize ceremonies (e.g., child's wake, *nguillatún*); crafts; musical rhythms, styles, and genres; and suffering. These idealistic composer-musicians possessed firsthand knowledge of their people's musical folklore—and, in the case of Cuba, revolutionary experience. They were sensitive to past and current injustices, and they revealed ample poetic gifts and vision. What is not so often emphasized is that, in the final analysis, they were gifted musicians—voices with the profundity of Mercedes Sosa and Violeta Parra, guitarists with the skill of Atahualpa Yupanqui, and composers with the careful musical-ethnographic sensitivity and purposefulness of Violeta Parra and Víctor Jara. The *nueva canción* movement was a continent-wide musical upheaval of seismic proportions, leaving in its wake new mountains of rich musical poetry for the generations and eons to come.

THE SONGS OF WOMEN AND THE IMAGES OF WOMEN IN SONG

The contributions of Violeta Parra and Margot Loyola demonstrate that women have been recognized as musical leaders in Latin America. This realization begins to debunk the myth that music-making in Latin America is essentially a male activity. One can point to certain spheres of traditional music-making—the *mariachi* earlier in the twentieth century; the profusion of male vocal quartets in Argentina; the predominance in the twentieth century of males as harpists in much of Latin America; the flute among South Amerindians and Venezuelan shamans (Olsen 1996)—and find a predominance of males as performers/practitioners. Yet having said that, we can also identify realms in which women have taken leading musical roles—African-Brazilian cult leaders and assistant cult leaders (Béhague 1984:224, 226); harpists in eighteenth- and nineteenth-century Chile, Peru, and Ecuador (Schechter 1992, Chapters 1 and 2); "pullers" of *tayil* among the twentieth-century Argentine Mapuche (Carol Robertson's work, discussed in Chapter 1); and drummer-chanters in Incaic and modern Peruvian culture (Schechter 1979:194; Chapter 8 of this book).

As Ercilia Moreno Chá pointed out in Chapter 6, Chile in particular is one region in which women have been notably evident in traditional music-making. We have already discussed, in this chapter and in Chapter 1, the central role of the female shaman, the *machi,* in healing and fertility rituals within Chilean Mapuche culture. *Mestizo* women in twentieth-century Chile have sustained their earlier role as harpists, performing traditional *cueca* and *tonada* at festivities that would include the festive child's wake. Moreno Chá emphasized the *tonada* as being traditionally a women's genre. We recall Margot Loyola's dictum: "*Tonada*-Woman-Guitar—inseparable trilogy, symbol of femininity and nationality." Introducing her biographical sketch of Margot Loyola, Moreno Chá emphasized the central role of women as musicians in Chile, going back to colonial times. Given this sociocultural background, it is not surprising to discover, she continues, women as leading collectors, disseminators, and artists in their own right, within Chilean traditional and *nueva canción* musics.

In this section of the chapter, and in keeping with its transnational focus, we will now explore the perspective of various women's musics among different cultures outside of Chile. We will focus on the musical expressions of female Native Americans, but we will also look at the changing image of the woman in the Mexico-Texas border *corrido,* and at Nicaraguan women's liberation songs.

At the beginning of Chapter 1, we suggested that the lullaby was probably as close to a universal musical expression as one could identify. Although there may be certain societies in which lullabies have not been documented,[5] one can find lullabies in the great majority of cultures. David McAllester presented the music and text of the lullaby of a Zuni Pueblo grandmother of New Mexico;[6] this song, sung to her grandson and, like all lullabies, meant to soothe the infant, consisted of two musical pitches a fourth apart, and used as lyrics animals—in affectionate diminutive form—from the local desert environment: little cottontail, little

Ex. 9–7.   Musical transcription of a Shuar lullaby from eastern lowland Ecuador (Coba Andrade 1990)

All pitches are sung with trilled lips, except for the phrasing-ending notes, which are sung on the syllable, "chee."

(Coba Andrade 1990)

jackrabbit, little rat. Analogously, the *hoerekitane* [lullabies] of the Warao of the Venezuelan Orinoco River Delta speak of the birds, monkeys, and jaguars of the rain forest. Where the Zuni grandmother's lullaby contained two musical notes, the two *hoerekitane* transcribed by Dale Olsen confirm his statement that Warao *hoerekitane* follow a tonal system of three pitches: 4-3-1 (scale-degree numbers, in minor) (Olsen 1996:135–137, 139). This "lullaby" tonal system fits in very closely with the tonal system of Warao shamanic curing songs, notably their critical "naming" section (ibid., 174); thus, Warao lullabies go hand in hand, musically, with other important musical forms of that riverine culture. A lullaby recorded and transcribed by Natalie Curtis some one hundred years ago, among the Yuma, near the California/Arizona border not far from the Zuni and the Hopi (see below), uses four different notes, all within the range of a diminished fifth, and uses a small number of phrases that cycle through the song (Curtis 1907:571).

In addition to using a small number of different musical notes, some lullabies have what may seem distinctive types of sounds, to our ears. Lullabies of the Shuar (Jívaro) Native Americans of the eastern jungle region of Ecuador use a trilling of the lips, and may also employ notes of the major triad or chord as their principal pitches—a musical framework found frequently in other types of Shuar music.[7] Example 9–7 provides a transcription of one of these Shuar lullabies. From the other side of the Andes mountains of Ecuador, among the Chachi of Esmeraldas Province, we also find major-triadic lullaby singing, as shown in Example 9–8.

Studies of these and other lullabies of Native Americans of the South and North Americas have begun to suggest certain prominent features of the way a mother thinks about—and perhaps unconsciously organizes—her expressions to her infant. We have already noted the obvious: since the lullaby is designed to lull

Ex. 9–8.   Musical transcription of a Chachi lullaby from coastal Ecuador (Coba Andrade 1990)

no text was provided

(Coba Andrade 1990)

the baby to sleep, it is sung in what the baby will perceive as a soothing, relaxing tone; the lyrics will be affectionate, perhaps alluding to well-known local animals, and perhaps referring to them in a diminutive form. Musically, we find that lullabies are set in repeated melodic phrases, sometimes in cycles, with perhaps two to five different musical pitches (the Qawashqar lullaby mentioned below is a special case), based on either triadic outlines, as with the Shuar and Chachi lullabies transcribed above, or in a restricted melodic range; there is often a focus on the tonic, or home note.

Moreover, it seems that lullabies often share notable music-stylistic features with other musics of the same society. For example, Shuar lullabies may use the same major-triadic outlines found in so many other musics of that culture, as documented back to the 1930s (Moreno Andrade 1930, Karsten 1935); lullabies of the near-extinct (in 1972) Qawashqar culture of Chile's Tierra del Fuego region are monotonic—fundamentally composed of a single musical tone, in keeping with other musics of that culture.[8] And the Venezuelan Warao *hoerekitane* are close in pitch-content to the shamanic chants of that culture. As Sandra Smith McCosker has remarked, "lullabies illustrate the use of improvisational techniques within a framework of stylistic conventions." (McCosker 1974:4) As to the words of Amerindian lullabies, we see a limited number of different vocables—or meaningful words/syllables—repeated in cycles. Finally, the musical material seems to be sparser than the textual material.

On the issue of text organization in Native (South and North) American lullabies, we have some insightful material with regard to the Kuna Indians, who live off the coast of Panama. Sandra Smith McCosker studied the lullabies of Kuna women in 1970–1971. She decided to focus on lullabies because she had discovered that Kuna women were the main bearers of tradition in Kuna matriarchal society, and that Kuna women had fewer contacts with foreigners than did Kuna men (this is characteristic of many Native American peoples). As an ethnomusicologist, she found she had access to the lullaby repertoire, observing that Kuna lullabies were "not restricted by those performance situations which surround ritual chanting and instrumental music. The fieldworker, therefore, is not required to deal with the community in obtaining approval for making recordings. Such recordings are not community functions, but rather are private affairs between the fieldworker and the lullaby singer in her home" (McCosker 1974:4). Smith McCosker was particularly pleased to be able to study Kuna lullabies because she concluded that they showed very little Western influence. Her investigations revealed the fact that a major function of lullaby singing is to enculturate the infants into their particular society, teaching them—through many repetitions of the same text—of their future duties as women or men in Kuna society (ibid., 21, 26–27).

Smith McCosker's comparisons of text organization in Kuna lullabies published in 1951 with those she recorded in Kuna society twenty years later showed common principles of repetitive patterning, something one would expect in an oral tradition, but distinctive nonetheless: reduplication of particular words, direct repetition of word sequences, common words appearing in various phrases,

Ex. 9–9.   The first fifteen lines of a Kuna lullaby recorded by Sandra Smith McCosker in 1970

1   Pani kala pani poa nai tai ye
2   <u>Poe pii poe pii</u> pani tai *maloye*
3   ***Nana* peka u kachi pa kine**
4   *Nana* peka nai kucha pani nukku pa kine pani <u>poa tii</u> pa ye um
5   <u>Poe pii pii</u> na pipi pak
6   **Naa pe a tummuwali *malo***
7   Pani nukku kpa ki pani
8   Nukko we ye
9   ***Nana* peka**
10   **U kachi pa kina**
11   *Nana* peka nai kucha ye
12   Pani pii nana pani poe tii kpaa um
13   Puna tola pii pii *maloye*
14   Machi tola o kanapi
15   **Na pe o tumnotali *maloye***

and common initial and closing (cadential) words (ibid., 1974:28–30). Three of these four principles are illustrated in the first fifteen lines of a lullaby sung by a Kuna woman for Smith McCosker in 1970 (Example 9–9). Direct repetition of word sequences appears in **boldface type,** common words are <u>underscored</u>, and common initial or closing words are in *italic type*. The word sequence "naa pe a tummuwali malo" or "na pe o tumnotali maloye" is directly repeated in lines 6 and 15, and "nana peka u kachi pa kine" in lines 3, 9 and 10. In lines 2, 4, and 5, the common words "poe pii," "poa tii," or "poe pii pii" are found. The common initial word pattern of "nana" occurs in lines 3, 4, 9, and 11, and the cadence word "maloye" or "malo" appears in lines 2, 6, 13, and 15.

Thus, as one would expect, Kuna lullabies reveal text-repetitive patterns—but they are complex and subtle, revealed through careful study. These four principles of lullaby text organization, moreover, have been applied to other Amerindian lullabies, confirming their applicability. You might think of a lullaby or two you can remember from childhood (students in class can often recall these) and see if, in fact, one or more of these text principles is in operation.

Ex. 9–10.   Text of "P*u*w*u*ch tawi," a Hopi lullaby published in 1907 (Curtis 1907:480)

Puva, puva, puva.	*Puva, puva, puva.*
Hohoya*wu*	In the trail the beetles
Sh*u*hpö pave-e	On each other's backs are sleeping
Na-ikwiokiango	So on mine, my baby, thou
Puva, puva, puva!	*Puva, puva, puva!*

Ex. 9–11.   Musical transcription of "Puwuch tawi" (Curtis 1907:498–499)

We have seen the consistency, in text organization, of Kuna lullabies over a period of twenty years. In fact, lullabies appear to show remarkable continuity over time, as illustrated by a particular Hopi Pueblo lullaby. In 1907, Natalie Curtis published *The Indians' Book,* in which she transcribed 149 songs from eighteen different tribes; her transcriptions are thought to have been quite reliable. One lullaby, for which she provides both text (Example 9–10) and music (Example 9–11), is "Puwuch Tawi." Example 9–12 is a Hopi lullaby field-recorded in 1949 and published on a Library of Congress LP (AFS L43, side B, band 5).

Ex. 9–12.   **Musical transcription of a Hopi lullaby, field-recorded in 1949 (transcribed by John M. Schechter)**

In comparing the two lullabies, you will notice first that they have the same words (see Example 9–10), with the 1949 version adding the "zi-zi" vocables. What does the text refer to? Already "one of the oldest Hopi songs" by the turn of the century, according to Curtis, and sung widely in Hopi settlements (Curtis 1907:480), this lullaby is a metaphor of babies and beetles. The mother binds her baby on a board to sleep. Then she fastens board and baby on her back, and swaying to and fro, becomes herself a living cradle, gently rocking to sleep the little one. As she rocks, she sings this ancient crooning lullaby:

The song tells of the beetles asleep on the trail. In Hopi-land, the beetles carry one another on their backs in the hot sun. The Hopis say, "The beetles are blind; the beetles are sleeping." So the child upon its mother's back must close its eyes, and, like the beetle, see no more. (Curtis 1907:480)

Not only is the text identical (and thus the metaphor intact), but the music of 1949 is highly reminiscent of that published in 1907. The melodic shape, interval structure, and general rhythm of each musical phrase, from the earlier to the later version, all bear a remarkable resemblance—despite the passage of nearly fifty years. The suggestion of this comparison of two Hopi lullabies separated by generations, is that the lullaby as a musical genre may demonstrate notable continuity, over time, in both words and music. The fact that Amerindian lullabies, of both North America and Latin America, adhere to identifiable constraints of musical and textual usage, and the fact that lullabies may be unusually durable, suggest that the way women put infants to sleep may be more timeless than many other aspects of a culture.

Women in Latin American Amerindian cultures are, of course, occupied with other tasks besides singing lullabies. One of their major chores is maintaining the family gardens, to assure the necessary crops for the family's survival. In the Ecuadorian Andean lowlands and jungle regions, Native American women sing songs seeking the healthy growth of their food-producing plants. The Shuar (or Jívaro), whom we have already met through one of their lullabies, and the Canelos Quechua, who also reside in the tropical forest of eastern Ecuador but who speak a dialect of the Quechua language, both believe in an earth mother (Jívaro) or master-spirit of the garden-soil (Canelos Quechua) named Nunguí. The Shuar believe she makes the crops grow by pushing them up through the ground; her help is required in order to maintain a successful garden. Shuar women must weed their gardens carefully, or they believe Nunguí will plunge back into the ground and depart, for another woman's better-weeded plot. Therefore, while digging up her tubers in the morning, the Shuar woman sings, or "think-sings" (Nunguí can hear such expressions, as well) songs to placate Nunguí and to keep her from re-entering the ground (Harner 1973:70–72). Canelos Quechua women harvest *manioc (cassava)*, then cook, pound, and masticate it, to be stored as *chicha*, or fermented gruel, a staple in the diet (Whitten 1976:173). An example of a Jívaro woman's song seeking Nunguí's aid is set forth in Example 9–13.

Ex. 9–13.   Partial lyrics of a Jívaro (Shuar) song of propitiation to Nunguí (Harner 1973:72)

I am a woman of Nunguí
Therefore I sing
So that the *manioc* will grow well
For when I do not sing
There is not much production.
I am of Nunguí . . .

The important role of the woman in the Andean Native American household today echoes the high esteem in which women were held hundreds of years ago, in Andean civilization. Andean women in preconquest Inca culture were held in high regard in both religious and social realms. Inca queens, called *coyas*, were mentioned in mythical lore as being knowledgable cultivators. Inca noblewomen performed highly valued tasks in their society, such as spinning/weaving royal cloth, and as we have already observed, making beverages used in ritual. In preconquest Andean kinship, there were parallel lines of descent, with men believing themselves descended of a male line, women of a female line. Traditionally, in the Andes a woman keeps rights to all things—including land—that she might inherit; there was and is no concept of joint property (Harrison 1989:117–119).

Today in Peru, one can find a complementary division of labor between husband and wife, each respecting the other. Similarly, in the Ecuadorian Quechua women's songs Regina Harrison has examined, women's roles are defined specifically as being symmetrical to those of men. One song she collected (Example 9–14) implies a kind of "marriage contract," suggesting that both wife and husband must work to maintain the family.

By contrast, one also finds reflected in these Quechua women's song texts the lamentable fact of wife abuse in the Andes. The Quechua women use such verbs as *taksana* [to wash clothes]—that is, men beat their wives like one pounds clothes on a rock, in a river, while washing them: "Kusashitu imasna taksakpis pasangalla warmimi" [My dear little husband, no matter how often he washes clothes, I'm a pay-no-attention kind of woman] (Harrison 1989:132). These Quechua women seek protection against their husbands' abuse from their women friends and from their families.[9]

Closer to the realm of supernatural communication discussed in Chapter 1 is a category of Ecuadorian lowland Quechua women's songs called *llaquichina* songs, or songs to make one feel sadness (Seitz 1981, Harrison 1989:147). Performance of these songs involves a confluence of the woman singer; her personal spirit helper (who inspires the song and who, transformed typically into bird form,

Ex. 9–14.   Partial lyrics of an Ecuadorian Quechua woman's song (Harrison 1989:125)

Kanpish trabajangi	Both [of us], you work
Ñukapish trabajo	And I work.
Kawsashunmi kusa	We'll get by, husband
Kawsashunmi runa	We'll get by, my man
Ishki trabajashpa	Both [of us] working
Alli kawsashunmi . . .	We'll live well, for sure . . .
Ishki trabajashpa	When the two of us work
Kushi kawsashunmi	We'll live happy
Ishki trabajashpa	When the two of us work
Kushi purishunmi.	We'll get along fine.

transmits the song's message to its recipient); jungle imagery; and a usually distant "recipient," who often perceives the song's message in the form of a bird's cry. Women sing *llaquichina* songs to achieve a transformation in the listener's heart. The perception of such a song by the designated listener allegedly "cause[es] [the] person to feel overwhelming sorrow and, while in this extreme emotional state, to experience a change of heart. . . . [The] success or failure [of the songs] is said to depend upon the quality of the relationship between the singer and her personal spirit helper" (Seitz 1981:228). *Llaquichina* songs are learned from hearing older relatives' performances. Core plots only are transmitted via this oral tradition, melody and actual text being largely improvised. All *llaquichina* songs are designed to improve a social relationship. Motivated by the absence of a husband or lover, women will often sing *llaquichina* songs to them. The performance of these songs allegedly results in the man's returning to the singer's presence.

We have looked at a variety of Native American women's musics now, both in this chapter and in the book as a whole. Many of these categories of song—shamanic and patrilineage chant, lullaby, garden song, *llaquichina*—have revealed a decidedly functional nature, their performance designed to achieve a particular end—lull/enculturate an infant, heal, provoke a lover's return, encourage the fertility of the soil. There is a very different body of music—largely a man's domain, in *mestizo* culture: the Mexican and Mexico-Texas border *corrido*, in which women have nevertheless been regularly *depicted*.

Recall our discussions in Chapter 1 of the *corridos* of "Joaquín Murieta," "Gregorio Cortez," "Corrido pensilvanio," "El lavaplatos," and one of the "Kennedy" *corridos*. The protagonists of all of these *corridos*—a music traditionally played and sung by men—are male: a Robin Hood figure, a border hero, men migrating to steel mills in search of employment, a dreamer of a Hollywood career, and a United States president.

One can also, however, trace a body of Mexican and border *corridos* centering on the subject of women; in doing so, one can discover a particular evolution in the way women have been depicted in Mexican culture. María Herrera-Sobek has isolated a particular evolution of images, in one hundred years or more of *corrido* singing—a chronology that reflects the changes in a community's mores. In roughly chronological order of their development, the images are: "(1) the unfaithful wife, (2) women as soldiers, (3) women as mothers, (4) women as evil, (5) women as lovers, (6) women as sex objects, and (7) the image of the aggressive female of the 1970s" (Herrera-Sobek 1979:56).[10]

Men at war, absent from their homes, have historically been preoccupied with the faithfulness of their wives. The Spanish Reconquest (711–1492) and the Crusades (eleventh through thirteenth centuries) gave way in the Western Hemisphere to colonial-era battles against Native Americans, the Wars of Independence (1810–1821), and the Mexican-American War of 1848. During these conflicts, men were absent from their wives and came to express in song the tensions created by this absence. Thus, in the early "El corrido de Elena" and "El corrido de la esposa infiel" (or "El corrido de la Martina"), the man returns home to discover that his wife has not been faithful. The mores of these earlier times included a double standard: a husband was permitted to kill his unfaithful wife, but a wife could not kill her unfaithful husband. Both of these *corridos* picture women, then, as having no rights and as being doomed to death for their infidelity.

Things began to change for Mexican women under the régime of Porfirio Díaz (1880–1910). Under his campaign to strengthen foreign investment and bolster Mexican capitalism, women became a source of cheap labor for new industries. Abandoning their stay-at-home roles, women helped create unions, participated in organizations seeking Díaz's overthrow and, in the ensuing Mexican Revolution of 1910–1917, served as *soldaderas*. As always, reflecting its times, the *corrido* now showed women with new characteristics—loyalty to a cause, bravery, etc. A new image of women as aggressive began to appear (Herrera-Sobek 1979:56–61). Hence, in one version of the famous "La Adelita" of the Mexican Revolution, one heard a *corrido* containing the following verse (Herrera-Sobek 1990:107):

Popular entre la tropa era Adelita	Popular among the troops was Adelita
La mujer que el sargento idolatraba	The woman the sergeant adored
Porque además de ser valiente, era bonita	Because she was not only valiant but beautiful
Y hasta el mismo coronel la respetaba.	So that even the colonel respected her.

Together with the growing image of female aggressiveness, however, was a different image of woman as suffering mother. This image derived in part from the worship of the Virgin Mary—particularly as the bereaved mother of her dying son Jesus in the Roman Catholicism of medieval Europe, as well as from Mexico's own Virgen de Guadalupe, generally considered the Mexican Native American parallel to the Virgin Mary. One finds several *corridos* in which a mother weeps at the death of her son (Herrera-Sobek 1979:63–66). As we discovered in our "nostalgia" discussion of Chapter 1, the praising of the women of a region is a major subject of Latin American folk song. The border *corrido* is no exception. In some *corridos*, a man depicts the great beauty of his beloved, notably when he can no longer be by her side.

Going along with the fact of the *corrido* as a genre elaborated by men—typically revolving around male protagonists and directed to a male audience, and with the tradition of *machismo*—is the presence of boasting about sexual exploits. In Herrera-Sobek's words, "The image of the female in this context is that of a sex object used and abused by the male 'hero' with the approval of the male audience" (1979:69). Thus, the hero of "Bagino barrera" is portrayed as "leaving women left and right with children everywhere" (ibid., 70). Again by contrast, another image of the woman in the *corrido* refutes the helplessness of the woman in a *machismo*-dominated society and portrays the Mexican woman now as willful, even evil—a woman whose behavior leads either to her lover's death or to her own, at the hands of her lover. Thus, in "Jesús Cadena" (or "La güera Chavela"), the woman is shot by the man she "betrayed" by dancing with another man

Ex. 9–15.   Partial lyrics of the *corrido* "Jesús Cadena" ("La güera Chavela")
(Sonnichsen 1975:8)

Señores, voy a cantar	Gentlemen, I will sing for you
De versos una veintena	Twenty verses
Para recordar de un hombre	To recall a man
Llamado Jesús Cadena.	Called Jesús Cadena.
Jesús le dice a José,	Jesús says to José,
"Vamos al baile a La Parra	"Let's go to the dance at La Parra
A cantar una canción	To sing a song
A compás de una guitarra." . . .	Accompanied by a guitar." . . .
Llegaron a San Andrés	They got to San Andrés
Y se fueron acercando	And they got closer
A ese baile de La Parra	To that dance at La Parra
Que se estaba principiando . . .	Which was just beginning . . .
Decía doña Manuelita	Doña Manuelita said [to Chavela],
"Comadre, no andes bailando.	"Friend, don't run around dancing.
Por aquí pasó Jesús	Jesús is around
Dice que te anda tanteando."	And he says he's spying on you."
Y le contestó Chavela	Chavela answered
Con una fuerte risada	With a strong laugh
"No tengas miedo comadre	"Don't be afraid my friend
Que al cabo no me hace nada."	He won't harm me, anyway."
Un baile se celebraba	A dance was celebrated
De mucho pompa y corrido	With much pomp and festivity
Chavela andaba en los brazos	Chavela was in the arms
De un hombre desconocido . . .	Of a stranger . . .
Jesús le dice a Chavela	Jesús says to Chavela
"Tú no vayas a bailar.	"You'd better not dance.
Si sigues en tus caprichos	If you continue with your flirting
Te puedes perjudicar." . . .	You can get yourself in trouble." . . .
Jesús sacó su pistola	Jesús took out his pistol
Para darse de balazos.	For a shootout.
Chavela le respondió,	Chavela answered him,
"Véngase prieto a mis brazos."	"Come to my arms you swarthy one."
Y le contestó Jesús,	Jesús answered,
"Quítate de aquí Chavela.	"Get out of here, Chavela.
No creas que tú estás tratando	Don't think that you're dealing
Con un muchacho de escuela."	With a schoolboy."

Ex. 9–15.   Partial lyrics of the *corrido* "Jesús Cadena" ("La güera Chavela")
(Sonnichsen 1975:8) (continued)

Chavela lo agarró el brazo	Chavela grabbed his arm
Metiéndole para adentro,	And took him inside,
Brindándole una cerveza	Toasting him with a beer
Para borrarle el intento.	To erase his intentions.
Jesús sacó su pistola	Jesús took out his pistol
Tres tiros le disparó.	And fired three shots.
Dos se fueron por el viento	Two went into the air
Y uno fué él que le pegó.	And one hit her.
Decía la güera Chavela	Said the fair Chavela
Cuando estaba malherida,	When she was badly wounded,
"Esto de querer a dos	"This business of loving two
Comadre cuesta la vida." . . .	My friend, can cost your life." . . .

(Example 9–15). Though she pays with her life, Chavela emerges as something of a heroine—her own woman. In the final analysis, she submits to the reigning mores: the female must defer to the male, or pay dearly for her refusal to do so.

By the 1970s, society had changed to the degree that, where Chavela was killed for breaking the submissiveness standard of her day, "Pancha la contrabandista" [Pancha the smuggler] and "Camelia la Tejana" are hardened smugglers who themselves will not hesitate to execute those men who cross them.

On the whole, though these images of woman in the *corrido* vary, most—except those of the Revolutionary period, and the more recent ones dealing with smuggling activities—portray Mexican and border women in a passive way, a feature of expressive culture that has delayed the proper recognition of the woman in Mexican and Mexican-American society (Herrera-Sobek 1979:73–75).

A similar evolution in image, or self-image, appears in recent women's songs in Nicaragua. There, as in Mexico, the ethos of *machismo* is deeply rooted, and in Roman Catholic Nicaragua women, in keeping with *marianismo* [cult of the Virgin Mary], have traditionally identified with the madonna personage, the image of the virtuous, loyal mother. The song "Cómo te extraño, mi amor," sung to Barbara Seitz by a Nicaraguan *campesina* in 1990, offers an example of pure love, enduring loyalty (Seitz 1991:26–27). The vision of a woman's role began to change substantially with the revolution to overthrow the Somoza regime in Nicaragua. Women like Luisa Amanda Espinosa and Lidia Maradiaga were regarded as heroines in the Revolution; several women's organizations received sponsorship from the Sandinista National Liberation Front. Two of these were AMPROVAC, the Association of Nicaraguan Women to Confront the National Problem (begun in 1977) and AMNLAE, the Luisa Amanda Espinosa Nicaraguan Women's Association. The former group contributed to the raising of women's consciousness; the latter organization sought the emancipation of women to become free to realize their full potential, through education and legislation (Seitz 1991:32, 34).

The changing view of the woman in Nicaragua emerged in the later songs. The assertiveness we observed by women in the more recent "smuggler" *corridos* of Mexico is reflected in the songs of Nicaragua's Doña Orbelina Soza Mairena, director of a local AMNLAE chapter. In "Diciembre me gustó" [I liked December] and "La vida es la ruleta" [Life is a roulette wheel], she responds with considerable defiance to her husband's abandonment and contemplated return (Seitz 1991:35–38). Example 9–16 provides part of the latter song.

The women who sing these more recent songs are often the most politically active, thus "liberated," of their peers. These songs are championed by women who seek an equal portion of respect from their spouses, rather than passively permitting their husbands to mistreat them with impunity.

We have seen how today's women in Latin American culture are active music-makers, both in traditional settings and in more politically charged contexts. The outcries against injustice penned by Parra and Jara are now emerging in more personal expressions, by women, of intolerance for spousal mistreatment. There can be no question of the major role of women in Latin American music culture,

Ex. 9–16.   Partial lyrics of the Nicaraguan women's song, "La vida es la ruleta" (Seitz 1991:37–38)

Y tú que te creías	And you who believed yourself
El rey de todo el mundo	The king of everyone
Tú, que nunca fuiste	You, who never were
Capaz de perdonar . . .	Capable of forgiving . . .
¿Dónde está tu orgullo?	Where is your pride?
¿Dónde está el coraje?	Where is your fighting spirit?
Por hoy que estás vencido	Today you are losing
Mendigas caridad.	Begging charity.
Ya ves que no es lo mismo	You see now that it is not the same
Amar que ser amado	To love as to be loved
Hoy que estás acabado	Now that you are done for
¡Qué lástima me da!	What a pity I feel!
Maldito corazón	Cursed heart
Me alegro que ahora sufras	I am happy that you suffer now
Que llores, sí, tú	That, yes, you cry
Antes que sea el gran amor.	You who were the Great Lover.
La vida es la ruleta	Life is a [game of] roulette
En que apostamos todos	In which we all place our wagers,
Y a ti la vida que has tocado	And for you the life you have chosen
No más va a ganar . . .	You're not going to win at anymore . . .

across regional, national, and cultural (indigenous, *mestizo*) lines, as active practitioners of critical functional songs and chants, as collectors and champions of their nations' folk songs, as leaders in the *nueva canción* movement, and as singers of contemporary songs of personal independence. Furthermore, the woman has been present in dozens of Latin American song genres, in images ranging from ideal object of affection to devoted, suffering mother, to lover, to brave soldier, to aggressive criminal.

We have looked in this chapter at Latin American culture through the perspectives of *nueva canción* and women's musics. The former was a movement produced by international political and cultural forces, the latter a phenomenon fundamentally more traditional and timeless. Both broad outlooks have been manifest in different regions, in different nations, in different cultures. Their study reminds us that one can speak of "Latin American music" not only for its cultural themes, as we did in Chapter 1, but also for its unity perceived through the dispersion of musically expressed ideals and concerns and through the shared musical practices of its women.

THE SYMBOLIC CHARACTER OF MUSICAL EXPRESSION, AND THE SEARCH FOR CONTINUITY IN MUSIC CULTURE

Certainly, the universal presence of life-cycle rituals (those pertaining to an individual's life stages of birth, puberty, wedding, and death) and calendric rituals (those reflecting calendric cycles of agriculture, nation, or religion) would be another way to view Latin American music culture transnationally. We could speak, then, of the broad international dispersion, in Latin America, of the calendric rituals of Carnival (recall Gage Averill's discussion of Trinidadian Carnival and the mention of Carnival celebrations throughout the Caribbean in Chapter 4), Semana Santa (discussed by William Gradante in Chapter 7), and Corpus Christi (celebrated typically in June to honor the presence of the body of Jesus Christ in the Holy Eucharist).[11] For life-cycle rituals we could explore, as an example, the broad manifestations of the *velorio del angelito* throughout the continent. For healing rituals, sometimes referred to as rituals of affliction, we could examine in depth the variety of shamanic music rituals among Native Americans of Venezuela, Ecuador, Peru, Chile, and elsewhere. One might reasonably conclude that the proper study of music rituals of Latin America would require its own separate book—perhaps several, in a series.

Our conclusion will take a more philosophical tone—focusing on a people's attribution of symbolic character to musical instrument and to musical expression, and their search for continuity in music culture. Something that infuses all the music cultures of Latin America, regardless of region, nation, or culture-group, is the attribution of symbolic weight to musical instruments and musical genres. Consider again Margot Loyola's "*tonada*-woman-guitar: inseparable trilogy, symbol of femininity and nationality" (Chapter 6), constructing a symbolic nexus for

Chile around its leading song type, its principal practitioners, and its accompanimental musical instrument. Or consider the *tiple,* that most "Colombian" of Colombian musical instruments, as discussed by William Gradante in Chapter 7—an instrument whose sound is much loved in the Colombian Andean countryside, whose accompanimental presence is taken for granted for *rajaleñas* and *bambucos,* whose presence in Colombian folkloric expressions brings a twinkle to the Colombian eye.

For Central Americans, there is the *marimba,* which Guatemalans have long considered their national instrument, one with which they identify acutely (recall Chapter 3). Nicaraguans take the *marimba de arco* as a symbol of nicaraguanidad. Both of these are devout attributions of symbolic value to this instrument type, despite its confirmed historical roots on the African continent.

In Trinidad, we saw the panmen's determination to create and continuously to improve their new instrument, the steel pan, that instrument ultimately capturing the soul of Trinidadians. Its development paralleled their own, as a nation, and in Stephen Stuempfle's words, "The excellence of a [Trinidadian] steelband is perceived as symbolic of the excellence or potential of the people of its community" (Stuempfle 1995:190). Trinidadians listening to steel bands at Panorama and Carnival (see Chapter 4) are made to "appreciate qualities that are believed to be key aspects of their national experience: local creativity, struggle and achievement, and festivity" (ibid., 234). In Paraguay, colonial-era Jesuit missionaries, as part of their evangelization, taught their indigenous charges the harp. Today, the harp is officially Paraguay's national instrument; the country boasts an enormous number of harpists and harp ensembles, many of whom have traveled widely abroad (Ortiz 1992:5). Unquestionably, the Paraguayan harp "has evolved as a trademark of the nation. . . . The harp gives musical and emotional expression to its peoples' love and pain, hope and misery, pride and sorrow" (Robinson 1973:8). Musical instruments bearing a symbolic burden extend to Native American cultures, as well. Among Chile's Mapuche the *machi*'s *kultrún* drum, discussed in Chapter 1, belongs in this category. Its single head is painted with one of many abstract designs, all of which clearly divide the drumhead, pie-like, into four segments; these four sections are said by the Mapuche to symbolize their cosmic vision of a natural world seen oppositionally as a square with four corners, in which west (the sea) and north are associated with evil, east (the mountains) and south with good (Grebe 1973:24–28).

The emblematic role of Latin American musical instruments is counterbalanced by the power of representation with which selected musical genres are endowed. Whether actually termed "national dances" or merely serving as well-recognized hallmarks of particular regions, the following musics—and many others we do not mention here—occupy a special position in their respective cultural habitats:

- the different regional *sones* of Mexico
- the *corrido* of greater Mexico and of the Mexico-Texas border
- the *bambuco* of Colombia

- the *albazo* and *pasillo* of Ecuador, the *sanjuán* or *sanjuanito* within northern highland Ecuador, and the *bomba* among African-Ecuadorians of that same region
- the *wayno* of Peru
- the *cueca* of Bolivia and Chile
- the *joropo* of Venezuela
- the *zamba, tango,* and *chacarera* of Argentina

These are the musics that frame distinctive folk dances, the genres that serve as vessels for the poetic inspirations of a people.

Many of these forms demonstrate a substantial history, typically reaching back at least to the nineteenth century—in some cases, such as the *wayno,* considerably further, into the colonial era. We are led to contemplate the sense of continuity they represent. Certainly for Latin Americans as well as for all the world's citizens, important to our sense of feeling alive is to perceive our existence, our condition, as having continuity with what came before us, with the past—with our parents, our grandparents, our home village and region, and our religion. This is part of the explanation for family photographs on the wall, for popular "oldies" stations on the radio, for the lines of people awaiting entry to the Ellis Island Immigration Museum in New York harbor (legal and medical inspection site for some twelve million immigrants to the United States from 1892 to 1954).

The continuity through time of the musical genres mentioned above is complemented by other Latin American musical continuities, some explored in this book, others not. Thus our Hopi lullabies, with the two versions suggesting both substantial continuity for this song per se, and the hypothesis of substantial continuity for the genre as a whole. Today's Peruvian and Bolivian altiplano panpipes having sounded for at least four hundred years in the south Andes, with Peruvian coastal panpipes going back thousands of years. The Caribbean Carnival tradition, going back to the nineteenth century. The Andean Corpus Christi tradition, going back two hundred years in Ecuador and Peru (seven hundred years in Spain). Two hundred years' worth of festive child's wake observances throughout Latin America, dating back to the late eighteenth century, in Puerto Rico. *Nueva canción* musicians preserve continuity with an esteemed past, via their choices of genres and musical instruments. *Nueva trova* composers seek continuity of practice with "old *trova*" in Cuba. In-migrants to Lima establish, through their performance of panpipe music in regional clubs, cultural continuity with their highland regional roots (Turino 1993). There is evident continuity—in Caribbean and African-Brazilian *candomblé, Vodoun,* and other analogous spirit-possession rites—with the deities and belief system of African forebears. Chileans maintain, in their folk musics and in their contemporary, ethnographically based songs, the modal harmonies of their Chilean predecessors, ultimately reaching back to a Renaissance Iberian ancestry. South Andean *comparsas*—masked, processioning dancers often dressed in satirical costumes evocative of particular personages of the past—are a communal manifestation reinforcing a sense of local identity, sparking generational memory of figures such as 1920s muleteers and colonial lawyers (see several essays in Romero 1993).

Music in Latin American culture is, in the final analysis, both regional and supraregional. People sing, dance, and ritualize their own distinctly regional musics, while at the same time implicitly and explicitly elevating certain of these musics and musical instruments to a lofty, symbolic status. All the while, in their music-related endeavors, they are acting as all of us do: seeking—with unique, creative forms of poetry, musical genre and style, music instrument design, choreography, and musical-ritual practice—a decided, communally acknowledged connection with their own people of an earlier day. We noted at the outset that Latin Americans, and all of us, need to be making music as one of several vital endeavors of life. We hope this book has demonstrated that Latin Americans of every culture, region, and nation feel this need and channel it in ways that make them and their neighbors respectful of their own musics and musical practices, and that help them feel at one with their musical and cultural forebears.

REFERENCES

Amerindian music of Chile: Aymara, Qawashqar, Mapuche. Recorded and annotated by Christos Clair-Vasiliadis, Rodrigo Medina, Adalberto Salas, and Mirka Stratigopoulou. Ethnic Folkways FE 4054, 1975.

Béhague, Gerard. 1984. Patterns of candomblé music performance: An Afro-Brazilian religious setting. In *Performance practice: Ethnomusicological perspectives*, ed. Gerard Béhague, pp. 222–254. Westport, Conn.: Greenwood Press.

Benmayor, Rina. 1981. La "nueva trova": New Cuban song. *Latin American Music Review* 2(1)(spring):11–44.

Carrasco Pirard, Eduardo. 1982. The *nueva canción* in Latin America. *International Social Science Journal* 94 (vol. XXXIV, No. 4):599–623.

Coba Andrade, Carlos Alberto, coordinación general. 1990. *Música etnográfica y folklórica del Ecuador*. Instituto Otavaleño de Antropología, Otavalo, Ecuador. 2 LPs.

Curtis, Natalie. [1907] 1968. *The Indians' book*. New York: Dover Publications, Inc. (Second edition republished by Harper and Brother, 1923).

Díaz Ayala, Cristóbal. 1981. *Música Cubana del areyto a la nueva trova*. 2d ed., rev. San Juan, Puerto Rico: Editorial Cubanacan.

Fairley, Jan. 1985. Annotated bibliography of Latin-American popular music with particular reference to Chile and to nueva canción. In *Popular music 5: Continuity and change*, ed. Richard Middleton and David Horn (yearbook), pp. 305–356. Cambridge: Cambridge Univ. Press.

Folk music of the United States: Pueblo: Taos, San Ildefonso, Zuni, Hopi. Series *Archive of Folk Song*. Recorded and edited by Willard Rhodes. Library of Congress, Music Division, Recording Laboratory LP AAFS L43, 1954.

Grebe, María Ester. 1967. *The Chilean verso: A study in musical archaism*. Translated by Bette Jo Hileman. Los Angeles: Univ. of California Latin American Center.

———. 1973. El Kultrún mapuche: un microcosmo simbólico. *Revista Musical Chilena* 27(123–124):3–42.

Harner, Michael J., rec. and ed. 1972. *Music of the Jívaro of Ecuador.* Ethnic Folkways LP FE 4386.

―――. 1973. *The Jívaro: People of the sacred waterfalls.* Garden City, N.Y.: Anchor Press/Doubleday.

Harrison, Regina. 1989. *Signs, songs, and memory in the Andes: Translating Quechua language and culture.* Austin: Univ. of Texas Press.

Herrera-Sobek, María. 1979. Mothers, lovers, and soldiers: Images of woman in the Mexican corrido. *Keystone Folklore* 23(1–2):53–77.

―――. 1990. *The Mexican corrido: A feminist analysis.* Bloomington and Indianapolis: Indiana Univ. Press.

Jara, Joan. 1984. *An unfinished song: The life of Víctor Jara.* New York: Ticknor & Fields.

Karsten, Rafael. 1935. The head-hunters of Western Amazonas: The life and culture of the Jíbaro Indians of eastern Ecuador and Peru. *Societas Scientiarum Fennica, Commentationes Humanarum Litterarum* vol. XIX, no. 5. Helsingfors, Finland: Centraltryckeriet.

Levy, Lisa, prod. and narr. 1988. *Violeta madre.* 2 cassettes. KAOS-FM, Evergreen State College, Olympia, Washington. Four-part series on the life and work of Violeta Parra.

Luna, Félix. 1986. *Atahualpa Yupanqui.* 2d ed. Madrid, Spain: Ediciones Júcar.

Manuel, Peter. 1988. *Popular musics of the non-Western world: An introductory survey.* New York: Oxford Univ. Press.

Monitor presents Chile's great singer-poet, Víctor Jara. Vol. 4, *Desde Lonquén hasta siempre.* Monitor Music of the World, Monitor Records MFS 810.

Moreno Andrade, Segundo Luis. 1930. La música en el Ecuador. In *El Ecuador en cien años de independencia 1830–1930,* vol. 2, pp. 187–276. Quito, Ecuador: Imprenta de la Escuela de Artes y Oficios.

Morris, Nancy. 1986. Canto porque es necesario cantar: The new song movement in Chile, 1973–1983. *Latin American Research Review* XXI(2):117–136.

Olsen, Dale A. 1996. *Music of the Warao of Venezuela: Song people of the rain forest.* Gainesville: Univ. Press of Florida.

Ortiz, Alfredo Rolando. 1992. *Latin American harps: History, music, and techniques for pedal and non-pedal harpists.* 3d ed., rev. Corona, Calif.: Alfredo Rolando Ortiz.

Parra, Violeta. 1976. *Décimas: Autobiografía en versos.* Barcelona, Spain: Editorial Pomaire.

Reyes Matta, Fernando. 1988. The "New Song" and its Confrontation in Latin America. In *Marxism and the Interpretation of Culture,* pp. 447–460. Edited by Cary Nelson and Lawrence Grossberg. Urbana: Univ. of Illinois Press.

Robinson, Roland. 1973. The harps of Paraguay. *Folk Harp Journal* 1 (June):8–10.

Rodríguez Musso, Osvaldo. 1988. *La nueva canción chilena: Continuidad y reflejo.* Havana, Cuba: Casa de las Américas.

Romero, Raúl, ed. 1993. *Música, danzas, y máscaras en los Andes.* Lima, Peru: Pontificia Universidad Católica del Perú, Instituto Riva-Agüero.

Schechter, John M. 1976. Music of the Mapuche Trutruka and the Mapuche ngillatun ceremony. Unpublished manuscript.

————. 1979. The Inca cantar histórico: A lexico-historical elaboration on two cultural themes. *Ethnomusicology* XXIII(2)(May):191–204.

————. 1991. Afro-Ecuadorian and Quichua compositional processes in Imbabura: The inspirations and innovations of Fabián Congo and Segundo Galo Maigua. Paper presented at the Thirty-Sixth Annual Meeting of the Society for Ethnomusicology, Chicago, October 11.

————. 1994a. Divergent perspectives on the *velorio del angelito:* Ritual imagery, artistic condemnation, and ethnographic value. *Journal of Ritual Studies* 8(2):43–84.

————. 1994b. Corpus Christi and its octave in Andean Ecuador: Procession and music, "castles" and "bulls." In *Music-cultures in contact: Convergences and collisions,* eds. Margaret J. Kartomi and Stephen Blum, pp. 59–72. Sydney, Australia: Currency Press.

————. 1996. Latin America/Ecuador. Chap. 9 in *Worlds of music: An introduction to the music of the world's peoples,* 3d ed., edited by Jeff Todd Titon, pp. 428–494. New York: Schirmer Books.

Seeger, Anthony. 1987. *Why Suyá sing: A musical anthropology of an Amazonian people.* Cambridge: Cambridge Univ. Press.

Seitz, Barbara. 1981. Quichua songs to sadden the heart: Music in a communication event. *Latin American Music Review* 2(2)(fall/winter):223–251.

————. 1991. Songs, identity, and women's liberation in Nicaragua. *Latin American Music Review* 12(1)(spring/summer):21–41.

Smith McCosker, Sandra. 1974. *The lullabies of the San Blas Cuna Indians of Panama.* Etnologiska Studier, vol. 33. Göteborg, Sweden: Etnografiska Museet.

Sonnichsen, Philip. 1975. Texas-Mexican border music. Notes to the LP *Una historia de la música de la frontera: Texas-Mexican Border Music,* vol. 2, *Corridos,* part 1, *1930–1934.* Folklyric Records 9004.

Stuempfle, Stephen. 1995. *The steelband movement: The forging of a national art in Trinidad and Tobago.* Philadelphia: Univ. of Pennsylvania Press.

Toqui Amaru. 1978. Unpublished concert recording, Univ. of Texas at Austin, August 11.

Turino, Thomas. 1993. *Moving away from silence: Music of the Peruvian Altiplano and the experience of urban migration.* Chicago and London: The Univ. of Chicago Press.

Whitten, Norman E., Jr., with assistance of Marcelo F. Naranjo, Marcelo Santi Simbaña, and Dorothea S. Whitten. 1976. *Sacha Runa: Ethnicity and adaptation of Ecuadorian jungle Quichua.* Urbana: Univ. of Illinois Press.

ENDNOTES

1. The *baguala* is a traditional song type of northwestern Argentina. *Bagualas* are often tritonic, with notes of the major triad.

2. See Schechter 1996 for a close look at the music and text of "El lazo."

3. Víctor Jara, "Despedimiento del angelito," on the LP *Monitor Presents Chile's Great Singer-Poet, Víctor Jara: Desde Lonquén Hasta Siempre,"* vol. 4, side 1, band 4, Monitor Music of the World MFS 810.

4. Such "farewell" verses sung in Chilean, Venezuelan, and Ecuadorian child's-wake traditions have roots in the early Christian era. See Schechter 1994a:60.

5. Anthony Seeger notes, with regard to the Suyá Native Americans of the Brazilian Amazon region, that "the kinds of music found in lowland South American societies do not include many of those prominent elsewhere. The Suyá, for example, sing no . . . lullabies" (Seeger 1987:8).

6. In *Worlds of Music: An Introduction to the Music of the World's Peoples* (New York: Schirmer Books, 1984), pp. 17–20; preserved in the second (1992) and third (1996) editions.

7. You can hear a Shuar lullaby on *Music of the Jívaro of Ecuador*, ed. Michael J. Harner, Ethnic Folkways FE 4386, 1972, and another on *Música Etnográfica y Folklórica del Ecuador,* ed. Carlos Alberto Coba Andrade, Instituto Otavaleño de Antropología, 1990. The latter lullaby is the one transcribed in Example 9–7. The Jívaro lullaby recorded by Michael Harner is not major-triadic, but does use trilled lips and the *chee* vocable.

8. You can hear a Qawashqar lullaby, "Toyaqa" [Lullaby], on the LP *Amerindian Music of Chile: Aymara, Qawashqar, Mapuche,* Ethnic Folkways FE 4054, 1975, side A, band 7(d).

9. The theme of wife abuse appears in songs composed by Ecuadorian Quechua men as well as women. A well-known Quechua *sanjuanito,* "Antonio Mocho," composed by Segundo Maigua Pillajo of the village of Ilumán in northern highland Ecuador, attacks the protagonist for beating his wife. For further information, see Schechter 1991.

10. The second, third, and fifth of these images are expanded and developed as archetypes in Herrera-Sobek 1990.

11. For a discussion of the celebration of Corpus Christi in central highland Ecuador, see Schechter 1994b.

Glossary

afoxé A type of black cultural association that first flourished at Carnival in Bahia, Brazil, following the abolition of Brazilian slavery in 1888. **Afoxés,** or African Nations, are closely tied to the **candomblé** houses of the city and use musical elements derived from **candomblé.**

agogô Brazilian iron double-bell. This ubiquitous instrument is used in many African-Brazilian musical genres. Within the **atabaque** drum ensemble of **candomblé,** the *agogô* plays a time-line pattern. *See also* **ogan.**

al talón Literally, on foot (*talón* means heel). A type of performance context for the Mexican **mariachi** ensemble. Typically, it involves wandering from table to table, playing for customers who pay a stipulated amount for each piece performed.

alabê Lead drummer in African-Brazilian **candomblé.** Typically the *alabê* is the oldest and most knowledgeable initiate among the drummers.

albazo A traditional dance of the Ecuadorian highlands, in **sesquiáltera** meter and in a lively tempo, often with a nostalgic character.

alfandoque In Colombia, a "dropped-then-caught" bamboo rattle used by **La Banda de los Borrachos.** *See* **chucho.**

andara A type of panpipe played as a solo instrument in Cajamarca, Peru.

angaje songs Engaged, politically committed songs in Haiti—for example, those of Manno Charlemagne and fellow singer Marco Jeanty.

areíto Song-dances performed by Native Americans on the island of Hispaniola in the sixteenth century. These songs recounted past events, notably the lives of their leaders.

arpa The harp, in Latin America. It exists in many configurations, in many countries, though the instrument is especially prominent in particular traditional musics of Mexico, Venezuela, Colombia, Ecuador, Peru, Chile, and Paraguay. The harp is played solo or in ensemble, depending on the particular musical genre.

asotò Largest drum-type in Haiti. The term also refers to a ceremony for this drum, and for the spirit of the same name that is believed to reside in the drum.

atabaque A conical, single-headed drum used (in different, named sizes) in African-Brazilian **candomblé.** *See* **candomblé.**

axé music A contemporary, eclectic style of African-Brazilian popular music from Bahia, Brazil.

bacamarteiro Honorary association of northeastern Brazilian men whose forefathers fought in the Brazil-Paraguay war of the nineteenth century.

baguala In Argentina, a type of song for one or more voices, accompanied by a **caja.**

baião   Syncopated two-step dance of Brazil. Luiz Gonzaga is considered the creator of the commercial *baião*. Characteristic instrumentation for the *baião* is the trio of accordion, **zabumba** drum, and triangle. For a period of time, the *baião* rivaled the **samba** in popularity in Brazil.

baión   Uruguayan term for **baião.**

baile de la marimba   A series of folk dances in western Nicaragua, performed to the accompaniment of **marimba de arco** trios, usually a central feature of saint's day celebrations in the greater Masaya region.

bambuco   The national dance of Colombia, in **sesquiáltera** meter. A couple "pursuit" dance, with lyrics on themes of love, nostalgia, and more contemporary concerns. The *bambuco* was originally a serenading solo performed by solo voice; today it is sung in duet in parallel thirds and sixths. Today in Andean Colombia the music is played in small ensembles with guitar, **tiple,** and/or **bandola** (*see* **dueto bambuquero**). It can also be played in larger ensembles (*see* **estudiantina**).

bambuco de protesta   A more contemporary **bambuco.** Not restricted to **bambucos** per se, these more recent Colombian songs are rooted in disillusionment with current national politics, facilitating the expression of a sociopolitical consciousness previously absent in the repertoire of the **Vieja Guardia.**

banbou   *See* **vaksin.**

banda de chicheros   *See* **chicheros.**

La Banda de los Borrachos   Literally, The Band of the Drunkards. In La Plata, Andean Colombia, an ensemble of musical rogues who, with gourd and bamboo instruments, flutes, and drums, succeed both in mocking the local **banda municipal** and in establishing a unique local tradition. They are seen performing at La Plata's **Fiesta de San Pedro.** *See* **carángano.**

banda de pífano   Fife-and-drum ensemble of Northeast Brazil. Also called **Zabumba.**

banda municipal   Municipal band, ubiquitous in Latin America. It consists of largely amateur or semiprofessional musicians who perform on European-derived wind instruments and drums. The ensemble plays a central role in village life—an example is its typical participation in **Semana Santa** as in Silvia, Colombia. *See also* **chicheros.**

bandola   Fourteen- or sixteen-string mandolin of Andean Colombia. In small guitar ensembles, the Colombian bandola performs instrumental interludes and melodic ornamentation. The *bandola* also appears in Venezuela and Guatemala.

baqueta   Term for **marimba** mallet in Guatemala.

bèlè   A Creolized version of the *contredanse* in Trinidad, Martinique, and Grenada, often performed in fancy dress. (From the French *bel aire.*)

bloco afro   Afro-Bloc, a kind of black carnival group in contemporary Bahia, Brazil, that appeared in the 1970s. The blocos afros celebrated African heritage and contemporary black identity.

bocina   Multiple-cowhorn trumpet used by the Quechua people of the Ecuadorian highlands. *See* **wakrapuku.**

bolero   Slow-paced, romantic, sentimental song-type in Mexico. It occupies an important place in the repertoire of **mariachi** ensembles. The bolero was widely diffused throughout Latin America in the 1940s and 1950s, notably in connection with Mexican films.

bombo Double-headed frame drum of substantial size. Used in a variety of Andean and Argentine regional musical traditions, as well as in **Nueva Canción** ensembles. *See* **tambora.**

caboclo *Mestizo* of Brazil.

cachua Name for the **wayno** in Cajamarca, Peru. **Kashwa** is also the name for traditional day and evening courting rituals in southern Peru, in which the **charango** plays a central role.

caja Andean frame drum. Often played in a **banda municipal** (with snare), in tandem with some kind of flute or, as in Argentina, in pipe-and-tabor fashion by a single musician. It may also accompany voice, alone.

cajón Wooden box used as a percussion **idiophone** in African-Peruvian and African-Cuban musics.

calypso Type of song sung for about one hundred years in the vernacular of Trinidad and Tobago. A Creolized genre, with traces of early French musical forms and of African stick-fight drumming and singing, among other influences. The calypso is associated with Carnival time, and is sung in the streets or on stage. In the early days, calypso tents featured competitive singing by so-called calypsonians, many of whom became celebrated. The modern calypsonian evolved from the earlier **chantwell** and **maît kaiso.** This is a highly topical genre noted for its economy of words, its satire and wit, and its rhythmic syncopation. Early calypsos were usually written in "minor modes"; later calypsos are usually in "major modes."

canboulay Literally, burning cane (from the French *cannes brulées*). In Trinidad, a torchlight parade of Carnival, reenacting the efforts on the sugar plantations to rescue burning cane fields. The canboulay has become a standard opening for Trinidadian Carnival.

canción ranchera Type of sentimental song in Mexico. A centerpiece of the repertoire of many **mariachi** groups.

candombe Term with two meanings; in Uruguay, on the one hand, it refers to the dances performed by costumed dancers at Carnival. On the other hand, the term refers specifically to the music that they dance, with vocals and drum accompaniment.

candomblé An African-Brazilian religious practice, with West African polytheistic origins. The term, which means "house of dance," also refers to the locale of the cult center itself, in which one finds spirit possession of initiates who are induced into possession by dancing and highly rhythmic drumming on **atabaque** drums of different sizes, together with call-and-response chanting. The diverse *candomblé* groups are classified according to African "nations." *See* **orixá.**

candomblé de caboclo In Brazil, an acculturated form of **candomblé** involving a mixture with Brazilian Indian practices.

cantar histórico Historical chant, among the Inca of pre-Conquest and immediate post-Conquest Peru. Gifted bards would chant these songs, which highlighted Inca history, at the Incas' June solstitial festival of *Inti Raymi* [Feast of the sun] and at the death of an Inca.

cantora In Chile, a female singer of songs and dances accompanied by guitar.

cantoria Term used in Northeast Brazil to refer to **caboclo** secular songs sung by singer-bards. These songs use Iberian poetic forms and musical features.

capetillo   In Cuban **rumba,** a term for the third or final "groove" section of call-and-response between the lead singer and the rest of the group. Also called **montuno.**

carángano   In southern Colombia, an **idiochord** tube zither made of bamboo. The raised strip of bamboo cortex is struck with two sticks. Regional musicians consider it one of four requisite instruments of the typical folkloric **murga** of southern Colombia, along with **flauta, tambora,** and **tiple.** Carángano is also the name for a ground harp in Atlantic-coastal Colombia.

cariso   An earlier term for **calypso.**

Carnival   Pre-Lenten processional festival celebrated particularly in Trinidad and Tobago but also in Haiti; Cuba; Martinique; Guadeloupe; Antigua; Bahia, Brazil; Barranquilla, Colombia; and elsewhere. The festival dates back to the plantation era in Trinidad. *See also* **rara.**

chacarera   A picaresque folk dance of Argentina dating at least to c. 1850 and danced today in certain areas of northern Argentina. The *chacarera* is a loose-couple dance in lively character that features **zapateado** (foot-tapping), syncopated rhythm, and **sesquiáltera** meter, and often includes virtuosic playing on one or two **bombo** drums.

chamamé   Embracing-couple dance that arose in northeastern Argentina, then diffused to other regions of that country, to Uruguay, and to southern Chile, with its characteristic accordion-bandoneon-guitar ensemble.

chamarrita   Embracing-couple dance of northeastern Argentina, Uruguay, and southern Brazil.

chamba   A casual, informal engagement for a Mexican **mariachi** or **son jarocho** ensemble.

chan pwen   Literally, sung point. In Haiti, a song whose lyrics frequently target an unnamed person or institution. The *chan pwen* is a popular form of **rara** song. These topical songs feature double-entendre and metaphor.

chantwell   In Trinidad, the old Creole term for a singer. The chantwell would lead work songs, dance songs, and stick-fight songs. *See* **kalenda.**

charango   Small Andean guitar used in courting rituals in Canas, Cuzco, Peru, and in Andean ensembles found throughout Andean South America, and increasingly throughout the world. The *charango* typically has five single, double, or triple courses of strings. Cultural associations exist between the charango and the *sirena* [mermaid], such that the *sirena*'s power to attract with music may, through a variety of means, be conveyed to the charango player, thereby assisting him in successful courting endeavors.

charleo   Buzzing sound of **marimbas** found in **marimbas** both in Africa and in Latin America. The sound is created by making a small hole near the bottom of each resonator and covering the hole with some type of membrane, such as the sac of a spider egg, a plant leaf, or more commonly, pig intestine.

charro   Mexican horseman distinguished by his unique dress, skills, and implements. Mexican **mariachi** ensembles characteristically don the suit and hat of the *charro.*

chasè   One of two cycles of **seremoni** songs at the **Fèt Daome,** Souvenance, Haiti, devoted to two camps (or battalions) of deities. The *chasè* is named after the colonial military's light infantry divisions and has its own songs and rhythms. *See also* **grennadyè.**

chasquido   In Chile, a synonym of **quedo.**

chicha music In Peru, a hybrid of Colombian **cumbia** and Peruvian Andean **wayno.** Chicha developed in the larger Andean cities but especially in Lima, beginning in the late 1960s, and it broadened in popularity in the 1970s and 1980s. It is played with electric guitars, electric bass, electric organ, and Latin percussion.

chicheros (Abbreviated form of **banda de chicheros.**) A Nicaraguan semiprofessional brass band that, like other Latin American **bandas municipales,** performs primarily for church functions and in local saint's day processions.

chicoteado In Chile, the timbral and rhythmic effect created by a **chasquido** percussing upon the strings of the guitar.

chirimía Type of oboe in Peru, used to accompany **walina** songs. The *chirimía* is also found in many other Latin American countries. In Colombia, the *chirimía* is a type of ensemble.

chucho In Colombia, a "dropped-then-caught" bamboo rattle used by **La Banda de los Borrachos.** See **alfandoque.**

ch'unchu An all-male dance of Cajamarca, Peru, that represents inhabitants of the Amazon jungle region. The dance is performed at designated festivals of the Roman Catholic liturgical cycle. It typically incorporates four personages—the *ch'unchu* themselves; their *capitán;* the *negro,* an authority figure; and the *cachacos,* supposedly former army conscripts. The *ch'unchu* is accompanied by flute and drum, played in pipe-and-tabor fashion, and by one or more **clarín** trumpets.

churu Conch-shell trumpet in Ecuador. Used among northern Ecuadorian Quechua to call community members for **minka.** *See* **pututu.**

chuscada Name for the **wayno** in Ancash, Peru.

chymaycha Name for the **wayno** in Amazonas, and in Huánuco, Peru.

cifra Men's song, performed to guitar accompaniment; a preference among Argentine and Uruguayan **payadores** of the nineteenth century.

clarín In the Andes, a long transverse trumpet. In Cajamarca, Peru, it is played during the **minka,** a traditional Andean community workfest, especially during the harvest of grains.

clave In Cuban **rumba,** a well-known rhythmic pattern, which is asymmetric within its two-measure cycle—one half is syncopated, the other not.

cogollo In Argentina and Chile, a stanza concluding the singing of a **tonada** that typically mentions either the person or the circumstance being honored.

colombia One of three types of traditional Cuban **rumbas.** Linked to the city of Matanzas, this is a male exhibition **rumba** in quick tempo.

compás A short, repeated section of rhythm and harmony, as for example in Mexican **son jarocho.**

copla One of a number of different Spanish-language verse forms, or a four-line Spanish-language stanza. See, for example, **copla de rajaleña.**

copla de rajaleña In Southern Colombia (specifically in La Plata, for example), a sung tradition involving the improvisation of four-line **coplas.** Unlike the multiple story-line **coplas** of the Mexican **corrido,** the Colombian *copla de rajaleña* stands alone as a four-line unit. *Coplas de rajaleña,* which are improvised and performed in festival context, make statements that may be flirtatious, pornographic, or sociopolitical. The "splitting wood" aspect (see **rajaleña**) derives from the "sparks and splinters" (audience reaction) produced by creatively improvised **coplas.**

corrido   Derived from the Spanish **romance,** a narrative ballad genre of Mexico and the Mexico-Texas border region, in strophic form and with characteristic formulaic features. The *corrido* is traditionally a male genre, performed by male musicians on male themes. However, many corridos over a 130-year period also depict an evolving image of the woman in Mexican and Mexican-American society. Corridos of the border region highlight the historically rooted cultural conflict of this area, with Robin-Hood figures, celebrated local and regional heroes, references to the Mexican Revolution, and sagas of migration. Also refers to a narrative song form of Venezuela.

cueca   Loose-couple dance of great consequence, in **sesquiáltera** meter, danced today in Chile, Bolivia, and Argentina. *See also* **zamba.**

cumbia   African-Colombian/African-Panamanian genre of dance and song, in moderate tempo. It is often performed at night, with lyrics highlighting coastal ways of life. The characteristic rhythmic figure is an eighth rest, then two sixteenth notes. Its beat and rhythmic patterns have combined with features of the Andean **wayno** to create **chicha music.** *Cumbia* has achieved great popularity in the countries of the Southern Cone, beginning in the 1960s.

cumbia andina   *See* **chicha music.**

danza   Type of Colombian *mestizo* folksong, in slow to moderate tempo.

décima   Ten-line stanza. *Décimas* were a principal song form in the American Southwest in the eighteenth and nineteenth centuries, and the *décima* has still served in the twentieth century as the framework for songs and **corridos** in New Mexico and in narrative **corridos** of the Mexico–United States border region. The *décima* form is an important part of the Mexican **son jarocho** tradition. *Décimas* are fundamental as well in the traditions of Chilean *verso,* Mexican *valona,* Panamanian *mejorana,* Colombian and Venezuelan **corrido,** Cuban and Puerto Rican *punto,* and Argentine and Uruguayan **milonga,** among other genres.

décima espinela   Octosyllabic stanza form comprising ten lines with the assonant rhyme scheme ABBAACCDDC.

desafio   Song duel of Brazil.

desafio de viola   Brazil song duel in which the dueling singers accompany themselves on **violas.**

dueto bambuquero   In Colombia, two vocalists accompanying themselves on guitar and **tiple,** typically performing the music associated with the **Vieja Guardia—bambucos, pasillos,** and other regional genres. *See* **Vieja Guardia.**

engine room   The percussion section of a conventional Trinidadian steel-band ensemble.

escondido   Picaresque loose-couple dance performed today in certain areas of northern Argentina.

estilo   Argentinian and Uruguayan song with one or two voices, performed to guitar accompaniment.

estribillo   Refrain.

estudiantina   Instrumental ensemble of Colombia and Peru. In Colombia, it is a large ensemble, also known as **lira, rondalla,** or **tuna.** It consists of a core group of **tiples** and guitars, with additional **bandolas.** Many *estudiantinas* work in connection with choral groups. The Colombian *estudiantina* has as the bulk of its repertoire the musics of the **Vieja Guardia.** In Puno, Peru, the *estudiantina* includes guitars, **charangos,** mandolins, and accordion.

fado   Dance of Brazilian origin, performed in loose couples during the nineteenth century. It was subsequently transported to Portugal, where it was transformed into a widely accepted song type.

Fèt Daome   Ceremony for Dahomey. In the village of Souvenance, Haiti, a week-long ritual that attracts servants of the **lwa** [African deities] from all over the region, coinciding with Easter. The music begins with **seremoni** songs performed in **chasè** and **grennadyè** cycles.

Fiesta de San Pedro   Feast of Saint Peter. In Colombia and elsewhere in Latin America, a June festival, part of the complex of Feasts of Saint John (June 24), Saint Peter (June 29), and Saint Paul (June 30). In La Plata, Andean Colombia, the Feast of Saint Peter takes center stage, providing a forum for the musical antics of **La Banda de los Borrachos.**

flauta   In southern Colombia, a transverse reed flute. Regional musicians consider it one of four requisite instruments of the typical folkloric **murga** of southern Colombia, along with **tambora, carángano,** and **tiple.**

flauta de carrizo   *See* **flauta.**

forró   In northeast Brazil, a social dance music of the **caboclo.** Accordion-based groups featuring accordion, triangle, and **zabumba** drum typically perform *forró* music. Commercial *forró* clubs exist in the major cities of Brazil. *Forró* is also performed by **Zabumba** ensemble during the *festa* following the devotional segment of a **novena de casa.**

gato   Picaresque loose-couple dance performed today in Argentina and Uruguay.

gaucho   Term with various meanings in Argentina and Uruguay—most commonly, a man of the countryside who performs agricultural/ranching tasks, and who possesses a characteristic traditional culture.

grennadyè   One of two cycles of **seremoni** songs at the **Fèt Daome,** Souvenance, Haiti, devoted to two camps (or battalions) of deities. The *grennadyè* is named after the colonial military's artillery divisions and has its own songs and rhythms. *See also* **chasè.**

grito   A type of shout. Particular *gritos* are characteristic of particular genres of Iberian-American folk music throughout Latin America, and the sounding of these *gritos* creates the appropriate atmosphere for the performance of the particular dance music.

guaguancó   One of three types of traditional Cuban **rumbas,** characterized by an intricate percussive texture and a lively character. It is a nontouching couple dance of flirtatious character.

guaya   In Nicaragua, a shaker percussion instrument comprising a hollow metal container containing seeds or pebbles. The *guaya* is added to the **marimba de arco** trio for the recreational repertoire (but usually not for accompanying the **baile de la marimba**).

guayo   In Cuba and the Dominican Republic, a metal, gourd, or cowhorn scraper.

guitarilla   In Nicaragua, a small, four-stringed guitar that, along with standard guitar, accompanies the **marimba de arco.**

guitarrón   A type of bass guitar used by the **mariachi** of the Jalisco area of Mexico.

gwonde   Smallest and highest-pitched drum of the Haitian **Vodou** percussion battery at Souvenance. *See also* **ountò.**

harawi   An Andean song genre that existed in the sixteenth century and still endures. It is a monophonic genre that has a single musical phrase repeated several times, with melismatic passages and glissandos. Today, the *harawi* is associated with rituals like marriages and farewells, as well as with agricultural labor—sowing and harvest. Among the Inca, the *araui* or *arawi* was a love song or festival song.

haylli   An Andean call-and-response genre performed during communal agricultural work.

herranza   In Central-Andean Peru, a ritual branding of animals, performed once a year in a sacred context. In the Mantaro Valley, it incorporates singing by a female musician, accompanied by violins, **tinya,** and **wakrapuku.** The music of the *herranza* is generally based on a tritonic scale, major-triadic in character. The *herranza* is seen as a fertility ritual aimed at protecting livestock and lands. The rite has associations with the **wamani,** feared mountain deities who are believed to own the crops and the cattle.

huapango   *See* **son huasteco.**

huaylacha   Name for the **wayno** in the Colca Valley, Arequipa, Peru.

huéhuetl   Large single-headed drum of the Aztecs, cylindrical in shape, three-footed, and often inscribed with carving. It is considered a sacred instrument.

idiochord   Instrument in which a string (strip of cortex) is raised from the body of the instrument itself—often bamboo cane. The raised string may be struck or plucked. *See* **carángano.**

idiophone   Instrument in which sound is created from the material, or body, of the instrument itself.

indigènisme   In Haiti, an ideology emanating during the period of the American occupation of Haiti (1915 to 1934) among black middle-class artists and intellectuals. *Indigènisme* advanced the notion that Haiti's culture was primarily African, not European, and that peasant culture should be examined and integrated to produce a truly national art.

inspiración   Term for the improvised lead lines by the lead singer in the final call-and-response section of a Cuban **rumba.** *See also* **capetillo** and **montuno.**

instrumentos de calabazo   Gourd instruments, used in La Plata, Colombia, by **La Banda de los Borrachos.** Gourd-instrument ensembles also appear under different names in Chota, Ecuador *(banda mocha)* and Guerrero, Mexico *(chile frito).*

irmandade   In Brazil, a lay brotherhood.

jala jala   In Colombia, a strung rattle.

jarana   A type of guitar used in **música jarocha.** It comes in several named sizes and plays principally rhythm and chords.

jarocho   Rural inhabitant of the region of Veracruz, Mexico.

Jazz des Jeunes   In Haiti, a pioneering ensemble of the **Vodou-jazz** genre.

John Canoe   *See* **jonkonnu.**

jonkonnu   **John Canoe.** Caribbean festival tradition celebrated in the Bahamas, in Jamaica, and among the Garifuna of Belize and Honduras.

jumbie   In Tobago, a spirit dance (reel) in an ancestor possession ceremony.

kalenda   Trinidadian stick-fight, and stick-fight song. *See* **chantwell.**

kashwa   In Andean Peru, a song genre of pre-Columbian origin. More than a song type, it is also a collective circle-dance performed by young and single men and women, associated with daylight and evening courting rites and with nocturnal harvest rituals.

kata   In the music of Haitian **rara,** a time-line pattern played on a piece of iron within an ensemble of **vaksins.**

katabou   Lowest-pitched drum of the Haitian **Vodou** percussion battery at Souvenance. *See also* **ountò.**

kena   Andean notched flute with a variety of local names. It is now a principal instrument (sometimes in pairs) in Andean ensembles throughout the world.

Kennedy corridos   A special series of Mexican and Mexican-American border **corridos** written in 1963 and 1964, spurred by the assassination of United States President John F. Kennedy. These corridos emphasized certain aspects of Kennedy's life and character, themes with which Mexican Americans particularly empathized.

kilti libète   In the Haitian diaspora, a freedom culture movement among Haitian expatriates, featuring political theater, song, and poetry performance troupes who employed **rara** to symbolize socialist models of collectivization and organization.

kimpeñ   A patrilineally shared soul among the Argentine Mapuche people. A *kimpeñ* serves as the text of a sung **tayil**.

kitar   In eastern Nicaragua, a modified type of guitar among the Miskitu people. *See* **tiun.**

koka kintu   Within the Peruvian **herranza** ritual, a prediction rite involving the reading of coca leaves, with associated songs.

kòlonèl   Personage who is responsible for security and control of the processional route of a Haitian **rara** band.

kònè   In the Haitian **rara** ensemble, a flared trumpet made of hammered tin, which may complement the *ostinato* parts of the **vaksins.**

konpa   A Haitian dance and music modeled on the *merengue* style of the Cibao region of the Dominican Republic.

kontradans   In Haiti, a figure dance *(contredanse)* done to calls of a dance master, and to the sound of flute and percussion ensemble.

koudyay   In Haiti, a street party sponsored by a political leader. These parties typically employ **rara** bands.

kultrún   Small kettledrum of the Mapuche people of Chile and Neuquén, Argentina; principal instrument of the **machi.**

la diana   The first formal section in a Cuban **rumba.** Also known as **lalaleo** or **nana.**

lakou   Literally, courtyard. In Haiti, a large, extended-family habitation that may house **Vodou** ceremonies. *See also* **peristil** and **ounfò.**

lalaleo   *See* **la diana.**

lavway   In Trinidad, a road march of Carnival that accompanies the **mas'** (masquerade) band in the streets.

lira   *See* **estudiantina.**

luci-luci   In the Peruvian **herranza** ritual, a ritual chase of animals in a corral out to the place where they are to be marked, with associated songs.

lundú   Brazilian dance probably of African origin, also adopted in Portugal, where it was transformed into a type of song during the nineteenth century. It was a very sensual dance, with a single couple performing in the middle of a circle of onlookers.

lwa   African-Haitian **Vodou** spirits. In the **Vodou** belief system, the *lwa* may enter a ceremony by "riding the horse" of one of the **ounsis** (initiates), thus displacing a part of the soul of the "horse." Thus, Haitian **ounsis** sustain direct contact with their deities.

machetazo   Literally, blow by a machete. Among Colombian players of the **tiple,** the alternation of accented strums, on every third eighth-note beat, between downstroke and upstroke.

machi   Female **shaman** of the Chilean and Argentinian Mapuche or Araucanian people. The *machi* is self-accompanied on the **kultrún** drum.

maît kaiso   African-style praise singer kept by nineteenth-century Trinidadian plantation owners as "court" singers. Together with the **chantwell,** the **maît kaiso** evolved into the modern calypsonian.

majo jòn   (From French *majeur jongleur.*) In Haitian **rara** processions, a baton twirler with the rank of major. He wears an elaborate costume, modeled on reconstruction of European court dress and on imagined garb of the preconquest indigen of the region. The *majo jòns* are spiritual symbols of the **rara** bands.

manje lwa   Food for the spirits. A ceremonial meal during the **Fèt Daome** at Souvenance, Haiti.

manman tanbou   Single-headed, hand-beaten drum of Haitian **rara** drummers. These drums are identical to those employed in **Vodou Petwo** ceremonies.

marcha   Characteristic dance of Brazilian carnival arising in Rio de Janeiro toward the end of the nineteenth century. It manifested a very free choreography, being danced as much in collective fashion as by loose couples.

mariachi   A traditional music of western Mexico, localized by the early 1900s to the Jalisco region. *Mariachi* attained national prominence in the twentieth century. Traditional instrumentation had melody in violins and/or harp (later, trumpet was added), chordal accompaniment with guitar-types, and bass in the **guitarrón.**

marimba   Struck **idiophone.** A xylophone with wooden keys, typically with resonance chambers of gourd, wood, or bamboo under each key, placed onto a wooden frame, and struck with rubber-tipped mallets. *Marimbas* are found particularly in Mexico, Central America, and the Ecuadorian-Colombian Pacific littoral region. The instrument has taken on regional and national symbolic value in Guatemala and Nicaragua.

marimba de arco   Nicaraguan diatonic **marimba** with a range of three octaves, constructed with an arc or hoop. It is the principal type of **marimba** in Nicaragua, centered in the Masaya region. The instrument is always accompanied by guitar and **guitarilla,** and it is associated with a group of folk dances collectively known as the **baile de la marimba.** *See also* **marimba de tecomates.**

marimba de doble teclado   *See* **marimba doble.**

marimba de tecomates   Guatemalan diatonic **marimba** with approximately twenty-eight keys aligned in a single row. The instrument is named for the *tecomates* [gourds] that hang beneath each key. It may have a wooden hoop or arc attached to the ends of the frame, with the single musician sitting inside the hoop to play it (similar to the Nicaraguan **marimba de arco**).

marimba doble Named for its double row of keys, a type of chromatic **marimba** originally developed at the end of the nineteenth century in Guatemala and southern Mexico, to emulate the full chromatic possibilities of the piano. The instrument can be elaborately adorned with wood carvings, and is found in the larger cities of Central America. The *marimba doble* ensemble features marimbas in pairs—the larger instrument is called **marimba grande,** and the second instrument is the **marimba cuache or marimba tenor.**

marimba cromática *See* **marimba doble.**

marimba cuache *See* **marimba doble.**

marimba grande *See* **marimba doble.**

marimba pura In Guatemala, the term used to describe a "classic" ensemble of **marimba grande, marimba cuache,** stand-up bass, and drum set.

marimba sencilla In Guatemala, a type of diatonic **marimba** played by several musicians at once. The instrument is distinguished from the **marimba de tecomates** by its larger range, four to five octaves (thirty-three to forty keys), legs to support its weight, and rectangular wooden resonance chambers in place of the gourd resonators of the **marimba de tecomates.** It may be played in ensembles with other instrument types.

marimba tenor *See* **marimba doble.**

marinera In Peru, a traditional dance, in **sesquiáltera** meter, with a lively character. It is related historically to the **cueca** and the **zamba.**

mas' In Trinidadian Carnival, a band that masquerades through the streets.

matraca A type of clapper or rattle on a handle—often a cog rattle. In Silvia, Colombia, the *matraca* is played from Thursday through Saturday of **Semana Santa**—the period of Christ's imprisonment, scourging, crucifixion, and death.

maxixa Term commonly used in Uruguay to refer to **maxixe.**

maxixe Couple dance of complicated choreography, diffused from the salons of Rio de Janeiro during the second half of the nineteenth century.

mento In Nicaragua, the most common musical form among Atlantic-coastal Creoles, who have their cultural roots in the West Indies. Many aspects of Nicaraguan-coastal *mento* resemble features of the Jamaican music of the same name. In Nicaraguan *mento* one finds 4/4 meter, moderate tempo, major tonality, and instruments including donkey jawbone, banjo, and washtub bass.

mesa In the Andes of Peru and Ecuador, a "table" consisting of foodstuffs laid upon cloths set on the ground, within a larger ritual context such as the Peruvian **herranza** ritual, or the Ecuadorian Quechua child's wake ritual.

milonga Term with two modern meanings—first, it is a solo song sung with guitar in the rural regions of Argentina and Uruguay. Second, it refers to a couple dance closely related to the **tango,** appearing in both these countries in urban and suburban zones.

milonga pampeana Solo song sung with guitar, typical of the Argentine *pampa* region.

mini-djaz A small commercial dance band in Haiti, dedicated to performing Haitian **konpa.**

minka In the Andes, a traditional community work gang or work festival, held either weekly or sporadically to repair damage resulting from natural calamities. In rural Ecuador, one may be called to *minka* by the sounding of the **churu.**

mizik rasin   Literally, roots music. In Haiti, an urban, middle-class, countercultural music movement dedicated to Haitian **Vodou** and **rara** which developed during the 1980s. It was partly inspired by Jamaican Rastafarianism and became commercially successful both in Haiti and abroad.

montuno   In Cuban **rumba,** a term for the third or final "groove" section of call-and-response between the lead singer and the rest of the group. Also called **capetillo.**

murga   In Colombia, an informal folk-music ensemble. In La Plata, Andean Colombia, the revered *murga* is **La Banda de los Borrachos.**

música de mariachi   *See* **mariachi.**

música jarocha   Music of the **jarochos** of Veracruz, Mexico. At the turn of the twentieth century, typical ensemble instruments included the **jarana** guitar-type, the **requinto jarocho** guitar-type, and the **arpa.** The **jarana** appears in several different named sizes.

nana   *See* **la diana.**

novena   Devotional rite of the Roman Catholic religion, celebrated to honor a saint, over the course of nine consecutive nights, in a private home or in a church.

novena de casa   House **novena.** A festive celebration given by northeastern Brazilians in honor of Roman Catholic saints or popular religious figures of the region, with music played by a **Zabumba** ensemble. *Novena de casa* is a celebration lasting one day and one night, in contrast to the nine-day **novena** sanctioned by church authorities. The occasion incorporates a nondevotional *festa* [celebration] that lasts throughout the night, during which **forró**-style music is performed. A *novena de casa* is given to "repay" a promise made to a specific saint.

Nueva Canción   An international song movement, beginning in the Southern Cone countries (Chile, Argentina, and Uruguay) in the 1960s, in which one's own culture and people are defended in song against totalitarian oppression or foreign cultural intrusions.

ochan   In the tradition of Haitian **rara** and **Vodou,** a type of musical salute. The *ochan* is an honorific song performed for a local dignitary, for an allied band, for an ancestor, or for a **lwa.**

ogan   An iron bell used to keep time in the Haitian **Vodou** battery of percussion. The *ogan* plays a time-line pattern. *See also* **agogô.**

oito baixos   Button accordion with eight bass notes used in northeast Brazil for older-style **forró** music. *See* **sanfona.**

orixá   The generic name for the multiple deities in the Yoruba-related African-Brazilian **candomblé** religion. Each *orixá* has characteristic sets of attributes, and each initiate in the religion is spiritually related to a specific deity and represents that deity through possession and **candomblé** dancing during ceremonies. *See* **xiré.**

ounfò   Spirit house. In Haiti, a small room with an altar for worship, within the larger **lakou** complex. *See also* **peristil.**

oungan   In Haiti, a **Vodou** priest.

ounsi   In Haitian **Vodou,** an initiate. An *ounsi* serves as the "horse" for a **lwa,** who "rides the horse" during a **Vodou** ceremony, temporarily displacing a portion of the initiate's soul. *See also* **lwa.**

ountò   Spirit invocation (from the Fon language). The large "mother drum" of the Haitian **Vodou** percussion battery at Souvenance. The drum is held at an angle by a seated assistant, while the master drummer stands and plays it with a single stick.

palo de mayo   In Nicaragua, an electrified version of the Nicaraguan **mento** of the Atlantic-coastal Creoles, developed in the 1970s. This form was the dance music of choice for many Nicaraguans on both Atlantic and Pacific coasts during the 1980s, increasing awareness among western Nicaraguans of the culture of eastern Nicaragua.

pampa corneta   A long, vertical, wooden trumpet in Huancavelica, Peru.

pampeña   Name for the **wayno** in Arequipa, Peru.

pan   In Trinidad and elsewhere, a single instrument in a steel-band ensemble. Great skill is required to build, tune, and blend a *pan*.

pandeiro   Tambourine of Brazil.

Panorama   National competition in steel-band performance at the annual Trinidadian Carnival.

pasillo   Type of waltz (3/4 meter) in Colombia and Ecuador, appearing in both Iberian-American and African-American music cultures. In Colombia, the instrumental *pasillo* is played rapidly, while the sung *pasillo* is performed slowly, bringing out the emotion of its texts.

payada   In Argentina and Uruguay, a sung contest of improvised poetry between two participants, accompanied by guitars.

payada de contrapunto   In Argentina and Uruguay, a synonym for **payada** when strong differences of opinion are in evidence.

payador   In Argentina and Uruguay, a term referring to the singer of improvised poetry.

peristil   In Haiti, a covered area for **Vodou** rituals and dances. *See also* **lakou** and **ounfò.**

Petwo   One of two branches of Haitian **Vodou.** *See also* **Rada.**

picong   Piquant, spicy. In Trinidad, an extemporaneous song duel held for several decades in the calypso tents.

pífano   Transverse cane fife of the northeastern Brazilian **Zabumba** ensemble.

pincullo   Andean end-blown duct flute dating back to the Incaic period. Sometimes the *pincullo* is played in pipe-and-tabor fashion with some type of drum. It exists in different sizes, under a variety of labels.

planta   Regular daily or weekly performance by a Mexican **mariachi** ensemble, at a restaurant or nightclub.

ponche   In African-Cuban musics, the punch beat, the last beat of every four-beat measure; an open, resonant hit.

por común   In Chile, a term for the universal guitar tuning.

por derecho   In Chile, a term for the universal guitar tuning.

por tercera alta   In Chile, the term for a specific guitar tuning.

por transporte   In Chile, the term for a specific guitar tuning.

pratos   Pair of hand cymbals used in the northeastern Brazilian **Zabumba** ensemble.

pregonero   Caller or lead singer, as for example in the Mexican **son jarocho.**

prèt savann   Bush priest. One who officiates in certain Haitian **Vodou** ceremonies. The *prèt savann* often leads in the singing of Roman Catholic hymns and in the recitation of Catholic prayers.

puerca   Gourd friction drum of Andean Colombia, as used, for example, by **La Banda de los Borrachos** of the town of La Plata.

punteo   A guitar technique involving the sounding of one, two, or three strings simultaneously.

pututu   Conch-shell trumpet of the southern Andes used for signaling and for opening special communal ceremonies. Called **churu** in Ecuador.

quedo   In Argentina, a guitar effect in which the strumming hand stops the sound from resonating by means of a blow upon the strings.

quijada   In Colombia and Peru, a shaken or struck donkey jawbone. The quijada dates at least to the eighteenth century in Peru. In La Plata, Colombia, it is used by **La Banda de los Borrachos.**

quince años   Literally, fifteen years. "Debutante" celebration in Mexico for fifteen-year-old girls.

Rada   One of two branches of Haitian **Vodou.** *See also* **Petwo.**

rajaleña   Literally, to split wood (from Spanish *rajar leña*). In Colombia, the local name (as for example in the town of La Plata) for an informal folk music ensemble or **murga,** or for the music that ensemble plays. Among the instruments one might find in such an ensemble would be flute, clarinet, drum, rattle, scraper, donkey jawbone, tambourine, **tiple,** spoon, accordion, and guitar. The instruments of La Plata's *rajaleña* are perceived locally to be replicas of indigenous instruments. *See also* **copla de rajaleña.**

rara   A multifaceted phenomenon in Haiti—a genre of music, a season, an event, and a procession. The *rara* season commences at the end of **Carnival. Rara** bands are competitive with one another, seeking to project their power into the streets. The *rara* tradition possibly derives from an early French "second Carnival" rite, held to commemorate the conclusion of Lent.

rasgueado (rasgueo)   Strumming. A guitar technique involving the simultaneous playing of the body of strings with all or some of the fingers of the right hand.

rasguido doble   Embracing-couple dance performed in northeastern Argentina.

rebec   In Chile, a *rabel* or country violin of three strings held in place by means of lateral friction pegs.

reducción   Colonial settlement. In the colonial period, Native Americans of Latin America were forced by the Spaniards to settle in these villages built around a central square, where a church and a municipal center were located.

refalosa   Traditional loose-couple dance performed today in Chile and Peru.

remate   Among the **payadores** of Argentina and Uruguay, this term refers to the two final verses of each **décima.**

requinto   Type of small guitar.

rezadeira   In the **novena de casa** of northeastern Brazil, a female lay specialist who leads the praying of the **terço** (one third of the Roman Catholic rosary). *See also* **rezador.**

rezador Male specialist in Brazilian **novena de casa.** *See* **rezadeira.**

romance Ballad/narrative form dating back to the fourteenth century in Spain. It was brought to this hemisphere during the Conquest. Early Iberian versions of this genre can be heard today in Colombia and Chile. The *romance* was the ancestral form for the modern Colombian **copla.**

rondador Single-rank panpipe of Ecuador often played by blind mendicants. Tubes are arranged not by order of length, as in south Andean double-rank panpipes, but in a kind of zigzag fashion. Traditional performance practice calls for frequent blowing of two adjacent tubes, sounding either thirds or fourths simultaneously.

rondalla *See* **estudiantina.**

rumba Literally, party. In Cuba, a form of African-Cuban drumming-dance-song, with several named traditional varieties—**guaguancó, yambú,** and **colombia. Rumba** is now a national symbol of Cuba. Rumba songs explore a variety of themes.

sajuriana Traditional loose-couple dance of Argentina, Chile, and Peru, now extinct.

samba Generic term for diverse Brazilian dance-types. Among the most well-known sambas are those danced as collective dances by **Carnival** groups called "Samba Schools," and those danced in cities as loose-couple or embracing dances.

samba reggae Brazilian musical style developed by drummers of **blocos afros** (especially from the group called Olodum) in the 1980s in Bahia. This genre included a mixture of contemporary Caribbean and African-Bahian rhythms.

Sampedro The Festival of San Pedro. *See* **Fiesta de San Pedro.**

sanba In Haiti, a **rara** song leader.

sanfona Full-sized accordion of northeastern Brazil. *See* **oito baixos.**

sanjuán Song-dance genre of the Quechua people of highland Ecuador. The *sanju*án is rhythmically related to the **wayno** of Peru, but the two are not identical. The characteristic rhythmic figure is sixteenth-eighth-sixteenth, possibly preceded by and/or followed by two eighth notes. Phrase structure is isorhythmic; the rhythm of the first half of the typical eight-beat phrase is identical to the rhythm of the second half. Tonal gamut is pentatonic or hexatonic. Lyrics, often those of a highly distilled ballad, are in repeated couplets, each of which often displays semantic and syntactic parallelism, as well as locally rooted metaphor. Published examples of this loose couple dance date back to the 1860s.

sanjuanito More contemporary version of the **sanjuán,** performed by *mestizos* as well as Quechua. Phrase structure is often in two parts, each repeated (AABB).

scissors dance Dance performed in Ayacucho, Huancavelica, and Apurímac, Peru, as well as by Andean migrants in Lima. It is a dance of ritual competition, in which the dancers compete against each other in demonstrating choreographic boldness. The accompanying ensemble is violin and harp. This dance has associations with the **wamani.**

Semana Santa Easter Holy Week, widely observed in Latin America, as for example in Silvia, Colombia. The multiday processions through the streets—often with allegory floats—and the chanting of the Passions and other liturgical music commemorate the principal events marking the final week in the life of Jesus Christ, leading up to the celebration of the Resurrection on Easter Sunday. Often the processions highlight different neighborhoods or local areas, while at the same time promoting the cohesiveness of the larger community.

señalacuy   Within the Peruvian **herranza** ritual, the actual branding of the animals; the marking of cattle, *llamas,* horses, and donkeys with ribbons inserted in the ears by means of a needle.

seremoni   In the **Fèt Daome** of Souvenance, Haiti, a song cycle representing the first part of the week's musical segments. The *seremoni* songs are performed in call-and-response fashion between the songleader and the congregation (**ounsis**).

serenata   Serenade. Performance of a small selection of songs by a small ensemble in Mexico, Colombia, or elsewhere, sometimes linked to a special occasion such as a birthday, or for a spouse or girlfriend, or perhaps to raise funds for a particular community need. Particular local traditions may stipulate a fixed number of pieces and/or a particular sequence or grouping of genres.

sesquiáltera   A meter prominent in the traditional and composed musics of Spain and Hispanic Latin America. *Sesquiáltera* features the thoroughgoing juxtaposition (vertically and/or horizontally) of compound duple (6/8) and simple triple (3/4) meters over the span of six eighth-note beats. Among the many Iberian-American traditional genres featuring *sesquiáltera* are the Mexican **son jarocho,** the Colombian **bambuco** and instrumental **pasillo,** the Ecuadorian **albazo,** the Bolivian-Chilean **cueca,** the Peruvian **marinera,** and the Argentine **zamba** and **chacarera.**

shaman   Indigenous healer, and musicant (music-maker) for her or his own trance-state. To cure ills, shamans rely on ethnomedical more than biomedical tradition. A musical implement, such as a rattle, shaker, leaf-bundle, or drum, is shaken or beaten in a highly rhythmical fashion in order to assist in attaining a state of trance, in which the shaman communicates with a world of spirits who aid in diagnosing and curing a patient. This book discusses shamans of the Venezuelan Warao and of the Chilean Mapuche peoples. *See* **machi.**

sikuri   In the south Andes, a hocketing (dialoguing) panpipe musical tradition.

soca   A new kind of "party" calypso that developed in Trinidad during the late 1970s, noted by a heavy downbeat, full dance-band arrangements, and an emphasis on shorter, singable texts. *Soca* was popularized by the calypsonian Lord Shorty.

son   Name given to one of many possible types of traditional music for the dance in Latin America. Examples are the Mexican **son huasteco** and **son jarocho.** Many Mexican *son* varieties exhibit **sesquiáltera** meter and a foot-tapping dance. One can also find varieties of *son* in the musics of Mexican and Guatemalan indigenous cultures.

son huasteco   A traditional music/dance of the Huastec region of Mexico, often with two singers alternating text, and with violin. Also called **huapango.**

son jalisciense   Son of the Jalisco region of Mexico, in strophic form, played by **mariachi** ensembles.

son jarocho   Son of the Veracruz-area **jarocho.** The *son jarocho* is characteristically in **sesquiáltera** meter, with instrumentation of harp, **jarana,** and guitar, in strophic song form. Greater emphasis is placed on improvisation than in **son jalisciense.**

son nica   In Nicaragua, a type of popular song promulgated by Camilo Zapata. The *son nica* was derived from the repertoire of **marimba de arco** trios used to accompany the **baile de la marimba.** *Son nica* is characterized by rapid repetition of words in sections of notably compressed rhythm, together with references to Nicaraguan situations and characters.

spirit possession In African-Haitian and African-Brazilian religious practices (**Vodou** and **candomblé,** respectively), the manifestation of deities to properly initiated, dancing members of a cult house, the possessed state being musicated by a drum ensemble. The spirit possession is a high point of the ceremony.

steel band A type of ensemble that developed during the 1940s in Trinidad, subsequent to the **tamboo-bamboo** ensembles. Steel bands emerged from the barracks yards and aggressively represented individual neighborhoods. The instruments are metal, notably shallower or deeper segments of oil barrels, and each size has a name. The steel band is a permanent fixture of Trinidadian Carnival. During the Trinidadian independence struggle, it was elevated to the level of national symbol, and it now has a broad international diffusion.

surdo A generic term for double-headed tenor and bass drums used throughout Brazil. In the **Zabumba** ensembles of northeast Brazil, the *surdo* used is a medium-sized tenor drum.

tamboo-bamboo Bamboo "drum" band popular in Trinidadian Carnival ensembles of the late nineteenth and early twentieth centuries. Its development was prompted by the colonial government's decision, in the late nineteenth century, to ban drumming (on membranophones). Lengths of bamboo were used as percussion and concussion instruments. Bottles, spoons, and other household implements were also used.

tambora Double-headed, cylindrical drum of Andean Colombia, played with two sticks. The *tambora* is similar to the **bombo.** Regional musicians consider it one of four requisite instruments of the typical folkloric **murga** of southern Colombia, along with **flauta, carángano,** and **tiple.**

tambora sanjuanera St. John drum. *See* **tambora.**

tango Embracing-couple dance of sophisticated choreography that emerged in Argentina and Uruguay at the end of the nineteenth century, which is danced today throughout the world.

taraceado Decorative element applied to the edges of the soundboxes of some cordophones. The design is achieved by combining distinct types of wood and mother-of-pearl.

tarima In the Mexican **son jarocho,** a traditional dance platform raised above the ground so that the sound of the dancing feet might be amplified.

tarka Hexagonal wooden duct flute of Puno, Peru, and of Bolivia. The *tarka* is played at public festivals in large ensembles called *tarkeadas.*

tarol Thin snare drum of the northeastern Brazilian **Zabumba** ensemble.

tayil Patrilineage chant of the Argentine Mapuche people. The *tayil* is sung by Mapuche women through clenched teeth. The chant traces a map of visual imagery in which a patrilineally shared soul is delivered to ancestral, as well as living, members of the particular named lineage. *See* **kimpeñ.**

tchatcha Type of rattle in the Haitian **Vodou** battery of percussion at Souvenance. *See* **Fèt Daome.**

teponaztle   or **teponaztli**   Aztec slit-drum. A hollowed-out log with H-shaped slits, creating two tongues struck with sticks. This was considered a sacred instrument, and is still used in several regions of Mexico.

terço   One third of the Roman Catholic rosary, recited in the northeast Brazilian **novena de casa.**

tinya   Small drum of the Andes, sometimes played in conjunction with the **pincullo** in pipe-and-tabor fashion.

tiple   Colombian Andean guitar-type, with four courses of triple strings. The *tiple* characteristically serves a percussive chordal accompanimental function. It is often felt to be the most "Colombian" of Andean Colombian musical instruments. It is essential to the **dueto bambuquero.** Regional musicians consider it one of four requisite instruments of the typical folkloric **murga** of southern Colombia, along with **flauta, carángano,** and **tambora.** The instrument appears in regional folklore.

tiun   In Nicaragua, a mainly secular type of music of the Miskitu people, using basically European tonal harmony and modified guitar (**kitar**).

tonada   In Chile, a term that encompasses a broad grouping of song types for one or more voices, accompanied typically by cordophones. In Argentina, the term refers to a specific type of song for one or two voices, accompanied by guitar.

tonada canción   In Chile, the form of **tonada** with **estribillo,** in which the **estribillo** is sung to a more rapid rhythm than the rest of the poetic text.

tonada cuyana   In Argentina, the type of **tonada** sung in the Cuyo region.

tonada de coleo   In Chile, the type of **tonada** in which the last verse of each strophe is repeated as the first verse of the following strophe.

tonada esquinazo   In Chile, the form of **tonada** that is sung in order to flatter or honor a person or saint.

tonada parabién   In Chile, the form of **tonada** that is sung in honor of newlyweds, wishing them blessings and happiness in their new life.

tonada romance   In Chile, a **romance** sung with the **tonada** musical genre.

tonada villancico   In Chile, a **tonada** sung at Christmas in honor of the baby Jesus.

trinado   In Chile, a guitar technique involving the simultaneous combination of **punteo** and **rasgueo.**

trios elétricos   Electric guitar trios playing atop high-tech sound trucks in Bahia, Brazil, during the 1960s. They catered to Carnival groups of middle-class youth.

tumba francesa   Literally, French drum. In Cuba, a ceremony of Haitian descendants that preserves early *contredanses.*

tumbadora   In Cuba, a *conga* drum covered with cowhide.

tumbao   In Cuban **rumba,** a basic percussion pattern or *ostinato.*

tuna   *See* **estudiantina.**

turma de mulheres   In the northeastern Brazilian **novena de casa,** an informal group of women singers.

umbanda   In Brazil, an acculturated form of **candomblé**; a highly syncretic, spiritist religion popular throughout Brazil.

vaksin   In the music of Haitian **rara,** a single-note bamboo trumpet of varying length. The three or more *vaksin* trumpets in a **rara** ensemble play hocketed (dialoguing) melodic-rhythmic patterns.

velorio del angelito   In Latin America and Spain, going back several hundred years, a festive musical ritual for a deceased, baptized infant or small child. The ritual features prominent display of the corpse amid dancing to regional musical genres performed on regional musical instruments of the period. *Despedida* [farewell] verses may, in some traditions, be sung by adults who take the role of the departing infant bidding farewell to mother and father, as she or he prepares to enter Heaven. In rural Latin America, the rite goes back to the late eighteenth century and has been practiced by Native American, African-American, and Iberian-American cultures.

vênia do santo   In northeastern Brazilian **novena de casa,** a short musical offering made by the **Zabumba** ensemble in front of the altar of the saint.

via crucis   Stations-of-the-Cross procession and meditative devotion, on Good Friday.

viceroyalty   Political-administrative entity with which the Spanish kingdom divided up its colonies in America.

vidala   Song for one or more voices, sung to the accompaniment of guitar or of membranophones in Argentina.

Vieja Guardia   Literally, Old Guard. A tradition in Colombian *mestizo* folk music that arose in a cultural renaissance beginning at the end of the nineteenth century in Bogotá. Young musicians congregated in coffeehouses and taverns and, improvising music and verse, created a repertoire of **bambucos, pasillos,** and other genres. Subsequently, there emerged both the **dueto bambuquero** and the **estudiantina.** Many *Vieja Guardia* compositions use dramatic pause in the delivery of particularly emotional lines. Songs of the *Vieja Guardia* highlight textual themes of nostalgia, longings for love, and regional beauty.

vihuela   Five-stringed guitar type. The back of the *vihuela's* soundbox is curved outward. Mexican varieties today have strings of nylon and feature a form of re-entrant tuning.

villancico   Religious song of praise in the vernacular, with lyrics often but not always referring to the Christmas season. The refrain (**estribillo**) alternates with strophes (**coplas**). The **sesquiáltera** found in many genres of Iberian-American music can be traced back at least to *villancicos* composed during the colonial period.

viola   Ten-stringed double-coursed guitar of Brazil. The *viola* accompanies the **samba** and the **desafio de viola.**

Vodou   African-Haitian religion, referred to by Haitians as "serving the **lwa** [spirits]." *Vodou* encourages reverence for ancestral spirits and for a variety of African deities. The religion involves **spirit possession** of devotees. In addition to African features, *Vodou* has incorporated Christian, European spiritist, Masonic, and Islamic elements.

Vodou-jazz   In Haiti, post–World War II fusion of Cuban dance band orchestrations with local rhythms and songs, notably those related to **Vodou.** The pioneering ensemble of this genre was **Jazz des Jeunes.**

voz de gallo   Rooster voice. In Cuba, a prized vocal quality of the lead singer of **rumba.**

wakrapuku   In the Peruvian Andes, a spiral-shaped cowhorn trumpet played during the **herranza** ritual. *See* **bocina.**

walina In Peru, a fixed song genre associated with the cleaning of irrigation canals. The *walina* is sung by the men doing the cleaning, and the singing is "accompanied" by a countermelody played by a **chirimía.**

wamani Andean mountain deities. The Peruvian ritual branding of animals (**herranza**), a fertility rite, is associated with the *wamani,* as is the south-Andean **scissors dance.**

wanáragua Another term for **jonkonnu.**

wanka Name for the **harawi** in certain regions of Peru, such as Cuzco.

wayno or **wayñu** Traditional, lively folk dance of Peru and Bolivia, among the most widely popular song and dance genres of the south Andes and likely dating back to the sixteenth century. The *wayno* is not circumscribed to a particular ritual or time period in the year. It exists under a variety of regional labels, varying in style according to the particular locality and social group performing it. Meter is either simple duple (2/4) or a combination of simple duple and simple triple (3/4). The characteristic rhythmic pattern is eighth-sixteenth-sixteenth (or triplet eighth notes). *Wayno* texts often reflect, with substantial metaphor, nostalgia for a lost love. *Waynos* are now performed on the streets of cities throughout the world by itinerant Andean ensembles.

wayñu *See* **wayno.**

xiré The most common, public ceremony of African-Brazilian **candomblé.** The *xiré* takes place at night in the main room of the **candomblé** center. The first of its two parts is a "call to the gods," and the second is the "presence of the gods." The goal of the first part is to call the **orixás** down to possess the dancing initiates who, in a transformed state, then enter in the second part as **orixás.**

yambú One of three types of traditional Cuban **rumba.** The yambú is a slower-paced courtship dance.

yaraví In the Andes, a slow, lyrical *mestizo* song genre largely in triple meter and in binary form. It is associated with troubled love affairs and nostalgic moods.

yuka Predecessor dance form of the Cuban **rumba.**

Zabumba Fife-and-drum ensemble of northeast Brazil, also called **banda de pífano.** The term also refers to the double-headed bass drum used by such ensembles. The *Zabumba* ensemble has come to symbolize the rural folkways of the **caboclo.** The four main instruments are two **pífanos** [transverse cane fifes], one *zabumba* drum, and one **tarol** [thin snare drum]. A **surdo** [medium-sized tenor drum] and **pratos** [a pair of hand cymbals] are frequently used also.

zamba A traditional loose-couple dance of amorous character, danced in northern Argentina. It is a musical cousin to the **cueca,** sharing that dance's **sesquiáltera** meter, though now typically in a distinctly slower tempo.

zambomba In Colombia, a gourd friction drum. *See* **puerca.**

zapateado Dance with often complex, rhythmic footwork, as for example in *flamenco*, in the Mexican **son jarocho,** in the Nicaraguan **baile de la marimba,** or in the Argentine **chacarera.**

Contributors

Gage Averill (Ph.D. University of Washington, 1989) is an Associate Professor at New York University where he heads the ethnomusicology program in the Department of Music and is affiliated with the Center for Latin American and Caribbean Studies. His publications include *A Day for the Hunter, a Day for the Prey: Popular Music and Power in Haiti* (University of Chicago Press, 1997), the co-edited *Making and Selling Culture* (Richard Ohmann, first editor, Wesleyan University Press, 1996), and articles in journals such as *Ethnomusicology* and *Latin American Music Review.* He serves as Book Review Editor for the *Yearbook for Traditional Music* and has been a contributor or consultant for recordings, films, festivals, and organizations such as The Ford Foundation and the National Endowment for the Arts (Heritage Arts). He was the Haitian music columnist for eight years in the magazine *The Beat,* and he performed in or directed musical ensembles playing pan (steelband), Afro-pop, Irish, Brazilian, and Afro-Cuban musics. He is married to Giovanna Maria Perot-Averill and lives in Port Chester, New York.

Larry Crook is Associate Professor of Music and co-director of the Center for World Arts at the University of Florida. An ethnomusicologist and a performing musician, he has carried out field research projects in Bahia and Pernambuco, Brazil, and in Nigeria. He has received grant awards from the NEA, Southern Arts Federation, and Florida State Division of Cultural Affairs, to create and produce artistic collaborations with musicians and dancers from Brazil, Ghana, Guinea, India, and the United States. He specializes in a wide variety of Brazilian and African percussion instruments and he directs two performing groups: Jacar Brazil, and Agbedidi Africa. His research into musical traditions from Brazil and the Caribbean has been published in books, journals, and encyclopedias. He is co-editor of the forthcoming book, *Black Brazil: Culture Identity and Social Mobilization.* He is currently researching the history and contemporary manifestations of the Maracatu de Baque Virado carnival tradition from Recife, Pernambuco.

William J. Gradante received a B.A. in Music from Middlebury College, where Ronald Smith ignited his interest in Hispanic folk music. His master's and doctoral degrees were earned at The University of Texas at Austin, under the guidance of Américo Paredes, Richard Bauman, Steven Feld, and Gerard Béhague. His master's thesis treats the construction of the Colombian *tiple, guitarra,* and *bandola.* His doctoral dissertation explores the multi-faceted celebration of the feast of San Pedro in southern Colombia. After helping to organize the *mari-*

479

achi ensemble at The University of Texas, he served as Artist-in-Residence in the Mexican barrio of Fort Worth, Texas, establishing award-winning *mariachi* programs at the middle school, high school, and college levels. His students have performed in festivals from California to Florida, as well as internationally. A professional singer and guitarist for over 25 years, he has performed Hispanic folk music throughout North Texas, as well as in Japan and Hungary. He is currently developing a textbook for the study of *mariachi* music. Other interests include the folk-cultural aspects of lowriding, *El Día de los Muertos,* and the Mardi Gras celebrations of rural Louisiana.

Ercilia Moreno Chá completed her studies at the Universidad Católica Argentina (Buenos Aires), where she was a student of Alberto Ginastera, Carlos Vega, and Lauro Ayestarán. From 1967 to the present, she has pursued field work in Argentina, Chile, and Uruguay. She undertook research in Chile for the Instituto de Investigaciones Musicales of the Universidad de Chile (1967–1970), and in Argentina for the Instituto Nacional de Antropología (1971–1979). In her native Argentina she was Director of the Instituto Nacional de Musicología "Carlos Vega" from 1979 to 1990. Currently, she is a researcher at the Instituto Nacional de Antropología. Her articles on Latin American music have appeared in several periodical journals, anthologies, and encyclopedias. She is the editor of *Tango tuyo, mo y nuestro,* she has produced several ethnomusicological LP recordings, and has worked as advisor on ethnographic films at the Fondo Nacional de las Artes of Argentina.

Raul R. Romero is a Peruvian ethnomusicologist. After graduating from the Catholic University of Peru, he obtained his M.A. degree from Columbia University and his Ph.D. degree from Harvard University. He has published various articles on Peruvian music in academic journals and books worldwide. He edited *Música, danzas y máscaras en los Andes* (1993), and he is the editor of the ongoing record series, *Traditional Music of Peru,* being released on the Smithsonian-Folkways label. In an Andean music-culture preservation project since 1985, he and his research team have traveled extensively throughout the Andes region, recording in audio and video the musical, choreographic, and ritual expressions of diverse regional cultures. His own theoretical research has focused on the Mantaro Valley in the Central Peruvian Andes, where he has studied the impact of modernization and the discourses on cultural authenticity in the Valley. His research also highlights the complexities of cultural *mestizaje* in the Andes, within the process of defining regional identities, as against national homogenizing paradigms. He is currently the director of the Archives of Traditional Andean Music at the Catholic University in Lima, Peru.

John M. Schechter holds a Ph.D. in ethnomusicology from the University of Texas at Austin. He has taught ethnomusicology and music theory for thirteen years at the University of California, Santa Cruz. His recent research activities have been in the areas of Andean Ecuadorian Quichua rhetoric and verbal style; formulaic expression and ritual-induced improvisation in Andean Quichua *sanjun;*

and, the ethnography, semiotics, and history of the Latin American festive child's wake music-ritual. He is the author of *The Indispensable Harp: Historical Development, Modern Roles, Configurations, and Performance Practice in Ecuador and Latin America*. In September 1997, together with his colleague, Guillermo Delgado-P., he organized at UC Santa Cruz the international and interdisciplinary symposium, "The Quechua Expressive Art: Creativity, Analysis, and Performance." In the conference, twenty-five invited native Andean and non-Andean scholars and performers from nine countries held discourse in panel sessions, round tables, and performances on the nature of music, narrative, poetry, folktale, myth, and riddle, among the Quechua of Andean South America. Based on the papers of this assembly, Schechter and Delgado are now preparing the volume, *Documenting Andean Voices: Interdisciplinary Discourse on Historical and Contemporary Quechua Verbal Artistry*.

T.M. Scruggs did his graduate work in ethnomusicology with Gerard Béhague and Steven Feld, and in anthropology with Richard N. Adams and José Limón, at the University of Texas at Austin. For his master's thesis on Texas-Mexican *conjunto* and in his dissertation on music and dance in western Nicaragua, he explored the use of music in constructing social identity. He has pursued research in various parts of Latin America and the Caribbean, and he has conducted extensive fieldwork in Central America. He has published on *conjunto*, jazz, steel pan in Trinidad and Tobago, and music and dance in Central America, including audio and video recordings. He has also been the major contributor and consultant on Central American music for major reference works. Before pursuing his graduate degree, he organized and recorded cultural events and concerts in Chicago, and he played piano in several salsa and Haitian *konpas* bands there. He has taught at the Universidad Centroamericana in Managua, Nicaragua, and at Florida International University in Miami. He is currently at the University of Iowa, where he directs a steel pan ensemble.

Daniel Sheehy is an ethnomusicologist, a federal government arts administrator, and a musician. He carried out fieldwork in Veracruz under a Fulbright-Hays scholarship in 1977–78 for his doctoral dissertation, "The *Son Jarocho*: History, Style, and Repertoire of a Changing Mexican Musical Tradition," supervised by UCLA-based Latin American music scholar Robert M. Stevenson. Based on his fieldwork with Mexican musicians in southern California, he assisted in curating the regional California section of the Smithsonian's Bicentennial Festival of American Folklife. He has produced several recordings of Latin American traditional music and has numerous articles on Mexican *mestizo* music to his credit. He served as co-editor of the recently released volume of the Garland Encyclopedia of World Music covering the Caribbean, Mexico, Central America, and South America. In 1978, he joined the National Endowment for the Arts, where he has remained to the present, overseeing the funding of projects in the folk and traditional arts. He has performed Mexican *mariachi* music professionally for the past thirty years.

List of Recordings

Digital editing and mastering by Richard Karst at Prema Music Studio, Santa Cruz, California

One compact disc
Actual total time of CD: 73'48"

CHAPTER 2—Popular Mexican Musical Traditions: The Mariachi of West Mexico and the Conjunto Jarocho of Veracruz.
Daniel Sheehy

Recorded Selection 1: (0'22") Simple *vihuela* rhythm pattern (*mánico*) for the first portion of the *son jalisciense*, "Las abajeñas." Performed by Daniel Sheehy.

Recorded Selection 2: (0'20") Same rhythm pattern with flourishes (*redobles*) added. Performed by Daniel Sheehy.

Recorded Selection 3: (1'45") Margarito Gutiérrez and his two sons at home, improvising a version of "Las abajeñas," with a false start. Home of Margarito Gutiérrez, Guadalajara, Jalisco, Mexico. December 1, 1997. Field recording by Daniel Sheehy.

Recorded Selection 4: (1'12") The *son jalisciense* "El pasajero" (The Passerby), performed by Mariachi San Matías in Philadelphia, Pennsylvania, a group organized by Margarito Gutiérrez for a tour of the eastern United States in 1988. This selection was recorded by Peter Reineger on October 22, 1988, for the National Council for the Traditional Arts (NCTA), during the national tour of Mexican regional music, "Raíces Musicales," sponsored by the NCTA. It is provided courtesy of the National Council for the Traditional Arts. Used by permission of Lorenzo Martínez.

Recorded Selection 5: (0'16") Simple *jarana jarocha* rhythmic pattern to the *son jarocho* "Siquisirí." Performed by Daniel Sheehy.

Recorded Selection 6: (0'28") Same pattern with variations. Performed by Marcos Ochoa Reyes. Home of the mother of José Gutiérrez, Veracruz, Veracruz, Mexico. July 17, 1998. Field recording by Daniel Sheehy.

Recorded Selection 7: (3'29") "Siquisirí" performed by Trío Jarocho Chalchihuecán (Felipe Ochoa Reyes, Marcos Ochoa Reyes, and José Gutiérrez). Home of the mother of José Gutiérrez, Veracruz, Veracruz, Mexico. July 17, 1998. Field recording by Daniel Sheehy. Used by permission.

CHAPTER 3—Central America: Marimba and Other Musics of Guatemala and Nicaragua.
T.M. Scruggs

Recorded Selection 8: (1'12") Guatemalan *marimba de tecomates*. Sebastián Carlel Mejía, Guatemala, 1990. Field recording by T.M. Scruggs.

Recorded Selection 9: (0'43") Guatemalan *marimba sencilla maya*. Piece: "T'xeˈxpele.n (Año Nuevo)." *Marimba Indígena Flor Bataneca*, Guatemala.

Recorded Selection 10: (1'14") Guatemalan *marimba grande*. Piece: "Atitlán." Marimba de Concierto, Guatemala, 1990. Field recording by T.M. Scruggs.

Recorded Selection 11: (1'31") Nicaraguan *marimba de arco* trio. Piece: "Aquella." ("That Woman"). Martínes brothers, Nicaragua, 1990. Field recording by T.M. Scruggs.

Recorded Selection 12: (0'20") Sample of guitar part in a *marimba de arco* trio, Nicaragua. Carlos Palacios, 1988. Field recording by T.M. Scruggs.

Recorded Selection 13: (0'55") Nicaraguan *son nica*. Piece: "Posol con leche," Nicaragua, c. early 1970s. (Discos Andino 003).

Recorded Selection 14: (1'08") Nicaraguan *Miskitu tiun*. Piece: "Syrpiki Mayram." Nicaragua. Lyrichord Records 7364: "Patria," recorded by D. Blair Stiffler. Courtesy of Lyrichord Discs, Inc. Copyright © 1976. Used by permission.

Recorded Selection 15: (1'02") Nicaraguan *Palo de Mayo*, acoustic style. Piece: "Anancy Oh." Zinica, Nicaragua, 1983 (ENIGRAC MC-022).

Recorded Selection 16: (0'55") Nicaraguan *Palo de Mayo*, electric style. Piece: "Syrpiki Mayram." Grupo Gamma, Nicaragua, 1986 (ENIGRAC CE-6003).

CHAPTER 4—Caribbean Musics: Haiti and Trinidad and Tobago.
Gage Averill

Recorded Selection 17: (1'47") "Congo Yambumba" ["Congo King"] (*rumba yambú*). Composed by Jesús Alfonso. Performed by Los Muñequitos de Matanzas. From the album, *Live in New York City*. Qbadisc, Inc., QB 9026. © 1998 Qbadisc, Inc. (p) 1992 World Music Productions. Used by permission.

Recorded Selection 18: (1'30") "Danbala Wèdo Nou Solid O. . ." Liner notes: "A song for the *lwa*, Danbala Wèdo, discussed on p.149 of this text, sung in *seremoni* style by the *larenn* (song leader) and chorus at Lakou Souvenans in Gonaïves, Haiti. It features the *tchatcha* rattle and voices but without drum accompaniment and is typical of the songs that are sung in the *sogbadji* (inner temple with altar space) before the congregation files out into the *peristil*." Recorded April 1998 at Souvenans, Gonaïves, Haiti. Copyright © Lakou Souvenans. (p) Product rights: Crowing Rooster Arts, Inc. Executive producer: Katharine Kean (KeKe). Music producer: Ronald Derenoncourt (Aboudja). Sound recording: Felix Andrew. Studio sound engineer: Chen Harpaz. Studio: Post Production Playground (P.P.P.). Mastering: Paul Goodrich at Merlin Studios, Inc. Production: Crowing Rooster Arts, Inc. Used by permission.

Recorded Selection 19: (1'30") "Kebyesou, Badji-M Anwo, Badji-M Anba." Another song from Lakou Souvenans, this one dedicated to the *lwa* Kebyesou, discussed on p.149 of this text. This recording features the full drum battery, song leader, and the congregation serving as chorus in the *peristil* of the temple. Field recording by Katharine Kean and Aboudja. Recorded April 1998 at Souvenans, Gonaïves, Haiti. Copyright © Lakou Souvenans. (p) Product rights: Crowing Rooster Arts, Inc. Executive producer: Katharine Kean (KeKe). Music producer: Ronald Derenoncourt (Aboudja). Sound recording: Felix Andrew. Studio sound engineer: Chen Harpaz. Studio: Post Production Playground (P.P.P.). Mastering: Paul Goodrich at Merlin Studios, Inc. Production: Crowing Rooster Arts, Inc. Used by permission.

Recorded Selection 20: (1'30") "Bann Sanpwèl la nan Lari-O" (*rara* music), performed by Rara Delin, a Sanpwel (secret society) *rara* band. Recorded by Elizabeth McAlister on the road from Tommasin to Kenskoff, Haiti, April 1993. Used by permission.

Recorded Selection 21: (1'30") "Pan." Liner notes: "This composition by leading composer and arranger Ray Holman was the Panorama competition entry of the conventional steel band, Hummingbird Pan Groove, in 1993." Performance by the ensemble, Hummingbird Pan Groove. Composed and arranged by Ray Holman. Field recording by Shannon Dudley in their panyard, 1993 Port-of-Spain, Trinidad and Tobago. Used by permission of Ray Holman.

CHAPTER 5—Northeastern Brazil.
Larry Crook

Recorded Selection 22: (2'00") *Zabumba* (ensemble) music for a *novena de casa*. Lagoa de Jurema, Pernambuco, Brazil. Zabumba Dois Irmãos. October 31, 1987. Field recording by Larry Crook.

Recorded Selection 23: (1'32") Song of devotional praise, sung during the praying of the *terço*, at a *novena de casa* in Bezerra, Pernambuco, Brazil. Piece: "Bendita e louvada Seja." March 21, 1987. Field recording by Larry Crook.

Recorded Selection 24: (3'28")The *Zabumba forró* song, "Nega boa." Bandinha de Pífanos Cultural de Caruaru, during a live radio program on May 23, 1987, in Caruaru, Pernambuco, Brazil. Field recording by Larry Crook.

Recorded Selection 25: (1'00") Accordion music recorded at a live radio program in Caruaru, Brazil, April 4, 1987. Features accordionist Toninho do Calderão, accompanied by triangle, *zabumba*, and *tarol*. Piece set to *forró* rhythm. Field recording by Larry Crook.

Recorded Selection 26: (1'00") African-Brazilian *candomblé*. Piece to the *orixá* Ogum, recorded by Gerard Béhague during a *candomblé* ritual. [from:] *Afro-Brazilian Religious Songs*, Lyrichord Discs LLST 7315: Side A, Band 4. Used by permission.

CHAPTER 6—Music in the Southern Cone: Chile, Argentina, and Uruguay.
Ercilia Moreno Chá

Recorded Selection 27: (1'25") Piece: "Tonada al Niño Dios." Chile. Raíces cassette, RAC 027-9. Grupo Palomar, Side A, Example 7. Voice and guitar, Gladys Ferrada. Used by permission.

Recorded Selection 28: (1'47") *Tonada religiosa*. Chile. Piece: "San Miguel abrió sus puertas." Source: *Tonadas Religiosas*. 1993. Ediciones Gabriela Pizarro S. Cassette 001-11-92. Side A, Example 1. Voice and guitar, Gabriela Pizarro; rebec, José Cabello Parada. Used by permission.

Recorded Selection 29: (1'20") San Juan Province, Argentina. *Tonada cuyana*. Field recording by Ercilia Moreno Chá, 1968. Piece: "No sé qué tiene esta calle." Voices: César Oro and Raúl Quiroga; guitar, Raúl Quiroga.

Recorded Selection 30: (0'40") Victorica, La Pampa, Argentina. Field recording by Ercilia Moreno Chá, 1983. "Milonga." Solo guitar: Félix "Quelo" Priani.

Recorded Selection 31: (3'02") Caleufú, La Pampa, Argentina. Milonga. Field recording by Ercilia Moreno Chá, 1974. Piece: "A Juan Bautista Bairoleto." Voice and guitar: Hugo Gómez Porcel.

Recorded Selection 32: (2'14") Buenos Aires, Argentina. *Payada de contrapunto*, between Roberto Ayrala and José Curbelo. Field recording by Ercilia Moreno Chá, 1995.

CHAPTER 7—Andean Colombia.
William J. Gradante

Recorded Selection 33: (0'44") *Música fúnebre*, Good Friday. Silvia, Cauca, Colombia. Piece: "Pésame." Banda Municipal de Silvia. With intermittent bell-ringing from the priest's assistants. April 1974. Field recording by William J. Gradante.

Recorded Selection 34: (1'07") *Pasillo lento*. La Plata, Huila, Colombia. Piece: "Hacia el Calvario," by Carlos Vieco. Los Sucesores de Antaño: Antonio Obando (vocal; lead guitar); Augusto Cuéllar (vocal; *tiple*); Carlos Serrato (vocal; second guitar); Luís Alvino Muñoz Silva (guitar). March 1974. Field recording by William J. Gradante.

Recorded Selection 35: (0'50") *Instrumental pasillo*. La Plata, Huila, Colombia. Piece: "Vino tinto," by Fulgencio García. Antonio Obando, lead guitar; Carlos Serrato, second guitar. March 1974. Field recording by William J. Gradante.

Recorded Selection 36: (1'00") *Pasillo lento*. La Plata, Huila, Colombia. Piece: "Espumas," by Jorge Villamil. Los Sucesores de Antaño: Antonio Obando (*bandola*); Augusto Cuéllar (vocal; *tiple*); Carlos Serrato (vocal; guitar); Luís Alvino Muñoz Silva (vocal; guitar). March 1974. Field recording by William J. Gradante.

Recorded Selection 37: (1'34") *Bambuco de protesta*. La Plata, Huila, Colombia. Piece: "¿A quién engañas?, abuelo," by Arnulfo Briceño. Dueto los Cuéllar: Augusto Cuéllar (lead vocal; *tiple*) and Fernando Cuéllar (guitar; vocal). August 1979. Field recording by William J. Gradante.

Recorded Selection 38: (1'10") *Bambuco fiestero*. Piece: "El Guaro." "Cantan Garzón y Collazos." Industria Electro-Sonora Ltda. Medellín, Colombia. SONOLUX. LP 12-104 / IES-1. Side 2, Band 3.

Recorded Selection 39: (1'00") Páez Native American flute and drum music, for the Fiesta de Santa Rosa de Lima. Santa Rosa, Cauca, Colombia. (sound of rocket going off toward end of recording). August 1978. Field recording by William J. Gradante.

Recorded Selection 40: (1'16") *Rajaleña: Coplas del Rajaleña Plateño*. La Plata, Huila, Colombia. Fiesta de San Pedro. "Banda de los Borrachos." Fernando Cuéllar (lead *coplero*; second *flauta*); Augusto Cuéllar (second voice; lead *flauta*). June 1978. Field recording by William J. Gradante.

CHAPTER 8—Andean Peru.
Raúl R. Romero

Recorded Selection 41: (0'45") *Harawi*. Vocal rendition by peasant women during a marriage ceremony in the town of Huaylaucucho, province of Tayacaja, Huancavelica.

Field recording by Hebner Cuadros on April 8, 1987. Courtesy of the Center for Andean Ethnomusicology, Catholic University of Peru.

Recorded Selection 42: (0'45") Peasant *wayno*. Vocal version of a peasant *wayno* by a woman in the town of Tuco, province of Angaraes, Huancavelica. Field recording by Alex Huerta-Mercado on February 24, 1998. Courtesy of the Center for Andean Ethnomusicology, Catholic University of Peru.

Recorded Selection 43: (0'45") *Mestizo wayno* performed by an accordion, harp, violin, and *batería* (jazz band) in the district of Quiquijana, province of Quispicanchis, Cuzco. Field recording by Manuel Raez on July 19, 1989. Courtesy of the Center for Andean Ethnomusicology, Catholic University of Peru.

Recorded Selection 44: (0'50") "Adiós Pueblo de Ayacucho." A *wayno* performed on the guitar by the well-known performer Raúl García Zárate. From CD *Raúl García Zárate: Guitarra del Perú*, Lima 1997 (Raúl García Zárate Productions, Telefax 51-1-449 7200).

Recorded Selection 45: (1'29") *Herranza* ritual ensemble from the town of Pariahuanca in the Mantaro Valley in Junin, central Peru. Field recording by Raúl R. Romero and Manuel Raez on July 1, 1985. Courtesy of the Center for Andean Ethnomusicology, Catholic University of Peru.

Recorded Selection 46: (0'50") Music of the *Ch'unchu*, during the Festival of Saint John the Baptist on June 23, 1987. Field recording by Raúl R. Romero, Gisela Cánepa Koch, and Leo Casas Roque in the town of Llacanora, Cajamarca, Peru. Courtesy of the Center for Andean Ethnomusicology, Catholic University of Peru.

Recorded Selection 47: (1'20") Musical ensemble of the Scissors Dance, featuring Máximo Damián (violin), Florentino Basilio (harp), and Mario Salcedo (scissors). They are performing the music played during the section called "Atipanakuy" (competition). Field recording by Raúl Romero in Lima, Peru, at the home of Mr. Damián, March 17, 1984.

Recorded Selection 48: (1'14") Rendition by Víctor Alberto Gil Malma, best known as "El Picaflor de los Andes" [The Hummingbird of the Andes"]. The song is "Aguas del Río Rímac." In CD *Bodas de Plata: Picaflor de los Andes*, Lima: El Virrey Industrias Musicales, CD-VIR 1403.

Recorded Selection 49: (1'00") *Chicha* music [*chicha* song]. Piece: "El Aguajal." Los Shapis. In CD *Los Shapis y su Historia Musical*, Lima: El Virrey. CD-COL-1362).

Index